THE USE
OF FORCE

Written under the Auspices of
The Center for International Affairs
Harvard University

THE USE OF FORCE

International Politics and Foreign Policy

Edited by

Robert J. Art and
Kenneth N. Waltz
Brandeis University

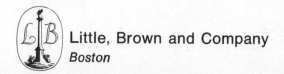 Little, Brown and Company
Boston

Preface

The subject of this book, the use of military power in twentieth-century international politics, is by no means new. In putting the book together, however, we have adopted a strangely neglected perspective by emphasizing the relation of technology to military strategy and foreign policy. In making the selections, we have kept these questions in mind: (1) What role has the threatened or actual use of military force played in international politics? (2) How has military power changed in the last seventy years? (3) How have changes in the instruments of force affected the use of force by statesmen? (4) What materials will help most to answer the first three questions?

Two types of selections are included: those which treat general problems or principles directly and those which deal with applications of force and, in doing so, illustrate general principles. An introduction by the editors is included to enable the student to follow the intricacies of the subject, to understand the dilemmas faced by statesmen, and to identify recurrent patterns in military strategy and foreign policy.

Robert J. Art
Kenneth N. Waltz

Contents

vii

THE USE
OF FORCE

*Technology, Strategy, and
the Uses of Force*

ROBERT J. ART
KENNETH N. WALTZ

The dropping of an atomic bomb on Hiroshima in August of 1945 was heralded at the time as inaugurating a new era in the relations of states. The awesome power of the atom made disarmament necessary according to some, world government imperative according to others, and war impossible according to many. Twenty-five years after the event we can no longer be so sure. Wars have been fought; disarmament and world government have been as difficult as ever to achieve. Indeed, the accumulation of nuclear weapons in the arsenals of America and Russia, and the spread of nuclear weapons to today's total of five states, have not produced any widespread agreement that disarmament and world government are desirable as ends in themselves.

No one would deny that nuclear power in the hands of separate states has made the world different. But just what differences can be attributed to nuclear weaponry is not clear enough to permit their identification with certainty and the specification of their causes with precision. Is it, for example, because of the beneficent presence of nuclear weapons that the world has enjoyed a longer period of peace since 1945 than had been known in this century — if peace is defined as the absence of general war among the major states of the world? The second world war followed upon the first one within twenty-one years. As of 1970, twenty-five years had elapsed since the Allies' victory over the Axis powers. Conflict marks all human affairs. In the past quarter of a century, conflict has generated hostility among states and has at times issued in violence among the weaker and the smaller ones. Even though the more powerful states of the world have occasionally been direct participants (most noticeably the United States and China), war has been confined geographically and limited in the number of states engaged in the fighting. Remarkably, general war has been avoided in a period of rapid and far-reaching changes — decolonization; the rapid economic growth of some states; the formation, the tightening, and the loosening of blocs; the emergence of new technologies and strategies

1

of nuclear and guerrilla warfare. The prevalence of peace, together with the fighting of circumscribed wars, indicates a high ability of the international system to absorb changes and to contain conflict and hostility.

One may be inclined to say simply that the destructive power of nuclear weapons has dissuaded their possessors from using them, that local wars did not become global wars for fear of the world's destruction. But such a dampening effect can never be reliably assumed, nor did it emerge spontaneously. Intricate decisions in foreign and in military policy have constantly been required.

They are decisions made within a wide range of choice. In recent years, American defense spending has run to less than 10 per cent of gross national product (GNP). To suggest a range of feasible variation, one may notice that in 1944 American military expenditure exceeded 40 per cent of GNP and that in 1947 and again in 1948 it fell below 5 per cent of GNP. In the first two years of President Eisenhower's administration, the amount of federal spending for national defense fell by 27 per cent, and in the first year of President Kennedy's administration, it rose by 10.3 per cent.[1] Clearly, American defense expenditures could be increased or decreased by 25 per cent over a few years without profoundly disturbing the American economy. Countries with capacious economies and fertile technologies have a wide range of choice in military policy. Such choice is heavily affected by the strategic ideas that come to prevail.

One of the most striking effects of the fission and fusion of atoms is found in the burgeoning of strategic studies. "At least until World War I," Bernard Brodie wrote, the study of military strategy "could proceed profitably from the study of campaigns going back to antiquity."[2] Because the instruments of warfare changed little and slowly, the principles of warfare endured. Nelson's flagship at the battle of Trafalgar was forty years old and none the worse for its age. The sailing ships of 1850 were little different from those in use two centuries earlier, and naval guns had, if anything, changed even more slowly.[3] In a book completed in 1960 one can read, however, of a revolution in weapons taking place every five years since the end of World War II.[4]

[1] Malcolm W. Hoag, "What New Look in Defense?" *World Politics*, XXII (October, 1969), 1, 3.

[2] Bernard Brodie, *Some Strategic Implications of the Nuclear Revolution* (University of Utah: Institute of International Studies, no date), p. 3.

[3] See the selection by Samuel P. Huntington in Part IV.

[4] Herman Kahn, *On Thermonuclear War*, 2nd ed. (Princeton: Princeton University Press, 1961), pp. 311–315.

"War stimulates invention, but the army resists it!"[5] If prior to this century technological change was slow, military adaptation was still slower. The interests of military men vested in their regiments and fleets, with traditions, customary ways of recruitment, and established systems of weaponry acting as impediments to change. Strategic studies were written largely by peripheral military figures — more men of the pen than men of the sword — who challenged professional orthodoxy but whose influence was weakened by the positions they occupied on the fringes of the military establishment. With the dominance of science and technology, civilians have now come to enjoy almost a monopoly in the field of strategic studies. They are not confined to the fringes of the policy-making establishment; they have instead invaded its heartland. The change that has been worked is striking. The vested interest of civilian strategists has not been in helping to preserve traditional military arrangements by providing suitable rationales for them. They have instead established a vested interest in innovation. Their reputations have been made by working changes in our perspectives, by challenging and reversing old maxims, and by showing that unthinkable weapons can usefully be thought about. Thus, the two great revolutions in the military thought of our time have been produced, in nuclear warfare, largely by intellectuals, and in guerrilla warfare, largely by political revolutionaries.[6]

Even the production of nuclear weapons of a form and quantity that give to men the power to destroy man has not meant that military strategy would be written on a clean slate. Slow annihilation has always been possible. In razing Carthage and sowing the site with salt so that new life could not emerge, Rome showed a capability for extirpation and a capacity for ruthlessness usually, but wrongly, identified with modern totalitarianism. The Thirty Years' War, ending in 1648, inflicted death upon perhaps a third of the people who lived in the area of Germany. In the same area, the extent of death and destruction during World War II approached the havoc that would have been wreaked by model-T atomic bombs. It is not that in the nuclear age near annihilation has suddenly become possible. It always had been. What is new is that *sudden* annihilation has become possible.[7]

[5] Lewis Mumford, *Technics and Civilization* (London: George Routledge, 1934), p. 95. And see the selection by Edward L. Katzenbach, Jr., in Part III.

[6] The considerable literature on guerrilla warfare is not represented in this volume, partly because of the limits of space and partly because good readers on the subject are available. See especially Franklin Mark Osanka, ed., *Modern Guerrilla Warfare* (New York: Free Press, 1962).

[7] See the selection by Thomas C. Schelling in Part I.

The web of social and political life is spun out of inclinations and incentives, deterrent threats and punishments. Eliminate the latter two, and the ordering of society will depend entirely upon the former — an anarchic ideal that is unworkable this side of the Garden of Eden. Depend entirely upon threat and punishment, and the ordering of society will be based on pure coercion. International politics tends toward the latter condition. The daily presence of force and recurrent reliance upon it mark the affairs of nations. Since Thucydides in Greece and Kautilya in India, the use of force and the possibility of controlling it have been the preoccupations of international political studies. They still preoccupy the men who are responsible for the military and foreign policies of their nations. Atomic and hydrogen bombs are new things under the sun, but the military and political strategies that have accompanied them are not wholly so. Revolutions in weapons systems have not destroyed the continuity of strategy partly because the range of national objectives has not changed much. States still seek to preserve themselves; some states continue to entertain ends that can be gained only at the expense of others. Partly, also, continuity remains because nuclear power, though revolutionary in the magnitude of its destructive force and in the speed of its deliverability, is nevertheless still only an instrument of force — usable to threaten and deter, to punish and destroy. And these are the ways in which force in the hands of rulers has always been used. The continuity of strategy means that much that is useful in the present can be learned from contemplating the strategies and the practices of the past. We should not slip into thinking that because some things are new nothing has endured.

We should also guard against the opposite error of believing that because some principles remain valid nothing has changed. What then is new in the strategies of the nuclear age? The most general and fundamental answer is this: the immense and sudden destructive power of nuclear-tipped missiles has shifted the emphasis of strategic planners from victory and defense to deterrence.[8] Concern over the use of force to strike for victory or to hold off an attacker is not absent in present-day strategic discourse, nor was concern over deterring an enemy's attack so that a defense would not have to be mounted absent in the old days. But the distinction between victory and defense, on the one hand, and deterrence, on the other, has been sharpened; and the emphasis has shifted from the first to the second.

---

[8] See the selection by Robert E. Osgood in Part I.

DEFENSE AND DETERRENCE

In the 1930s, Stanley Baldwin had stressed that the bomber would always get through, a dictum that helped to demoralize England.[9] Despite such seeming or momentary advantages for the offense, prior to the age of nuclear-tipped missiles, advances in offensive arms had always been countered by improved defenses. The possibility of successful defense made a world of independent states tolerable. By the mid-1950s, however, the approximate equality of offensive forces at an awesomely potent level seemed to produce a world of states comparable to Hobbes's state of nature among men. The misery of that world, as Hobbes imagined it, rested on everyone's ability to do harm to anyone else. The weakest man could kill the strongest man by striking at him while he slumbered.[10] The metaphors that appeared early in the atomic age reflected the vision of Hobbes. Two scorpions in a bottle: each can kill the other but in doing so the killer authors his own death. Two cowboys armed with six-guns on the western frontier with neither being sure of the other's intention: each must try to shoot first, not in anger, but out of fear that if he does not the other fellow will. In the strategic trade, this is known as "preemption."

The equality of offensive forces and the absence of effective defenses, however, have not presented to states the impossible alternatives of unavoidable death or unattainable world government, but have instead permitted the contriving of a third way.[11] The logic of Hobbes does not apply to a state among states as it does to a man among men. States can devise strategies and produce the means for

[9] Both Britain and Germany believed that no defense against the other country's bomber force could be effectively mounted. Each of them initially accepted the doctrine that only a preemptive blow against the other country's bomber force could save the homeland from devastation. And yet, when World War II came, neither launched a preemptive strike. For the restraints at work between Britain and Germany in the initial phase of World War II, see the selection by George H. Quester in Part II. For an assessment of the effects that beliefs about bomber destruction had on foreign policy in the 1930s, see Herbert S. Dinerstein, "The Impact of Airpower on the International Scene, 1933–1940," *Military Affairs*, XXIX (Summer, 1965), 65–71.

[10] Thomas Hobbes, *Leviathan* (Oxford: Blackwell, no date), p. 80.

[11] As examples of those who, in effect, have accepted the logic of Hobbes and followed it to the world-government conclusion, see Robert Maynard Hutchins, "The Constitutional Foundations for World Order," in *Foundations for World Order* (Denver: University of Denver Press, 1949), pp. 99–105; Bertrand Russell, *New Hopes for a Changing World* (New York: Simon and Schuster, 1951), pp. 92–93; Kahn, *On Thermonuclear War*, pp. 6–7.

their implementation as men acting alone cannot possibly do. One way to counter an intended offense is to build fortifications and to muster forces that look forbiddingly strong. The other way to inhibit a country's intended aggressive moves is to scare that country out of making them by threatening to visit unacceptable punishment upon it. "To deter" literally means to stop someone from doing something by frightening him. In contrast to dissuasion by defense, dissuasion by deterrence operates by frightening a state out of attacking, not because of the difficulty of launching an attack and carrying it home, but because the expected reaction of the opponent will result in one's own severe punishment.[12]

In a simple two-party situation, state A's deterrent force accomplishes its purpose by frightening state B out of making the military strike that it would have made had the deterrent threat been ineffective. What B would actually have done had A's force been absent or weaker can only be surmised. Claims for the success of deterrence must rest on assertions about why something did *not* happen. Neither logically nor empirically, however, can one conclusively demonstrate why something did not happen. The abstract and rationalist quality of recent military analysis has often been criticized. But this quality is inescapable because of the emphasis put on deterrence and because nuclear weapons have never been used in a world in which two or more countries possessed them. When there is no opportunity to learn from direct experience, and hopefully will be none, military analysis can only proceed by reasoned abstractions and on the basis of appropriate analogies. The criticism is often turned in another direction. The conclusions of the strategists, it is said, rest on the assumption that in the heat of a crisis the rulers of states will decide with cool rationality whether to press their nuclear buttons. This criticism, too, is wide of the mark. A strategist's assumption that rulers will behave rationally cannot directly affect their behavior. That much is obvious. In a nuclear world, however, the incentives to cautious and reasoned behavior are strong. It is important to make them still stronger by devising strategies and by deploying forces in ways that will reduce the chances of reckless behavior and of desperate decisions by military commanders and statesmen.

VICTORY AND DEFENSE

The distinctions between defense and deterrence, the conditions conducive to preemptive and offensive uses of military power, the effects that military technology can have on strategic planning, and

---

[12] Definitions of "defense" and "deterrence," of course, vary from one author to another.

the constraints that foreign policy goals can create for military planners — all these points can best be made clear by examples. Two good ones are French and German strategic planning prior to World War I and American strategic planning after World War II. The comparisons and contrasts between these two periods will also bring out the qualitative differences in strategic planning in the nuclear and pre-nuclear ages.

At approximately the same time but for different reasons, France and Germany adopted offensive strategies that committed each of them to strike with full force at the other. A country may adopt an offensive strategy simply because it wants to conquer its opponent in order to gain some tangible advantage. Even without such an ambition, a country may adopt an offensive strategy out of its concern for security and its conviction that a good offense is the best defense, or even that it is the only defense possible. France fits well into the first category; Germany into the second.

Germany was wedged in between two great powers, France and Russia, who were diplomatically united by the alliance they had formed in 1894.[13] Germany had to expect that if she went to war against either France or Russia, the other would come in against her. Under these trying circumstances, Alfred von Schlieffen, Chief of the Great German General Staff from 1891 to 1905, developed and refined a daring strategy.[14] Schlieffen predicated his plan upon a belief that was widespread throughout military and civilian circles in the several decades prior to 1914: modern warfare, were it to be drawn out, would wreck the highly complex and delicately balanced industrial economies of all the participants, Germany included. Confronting the prospect of a protracted two-front war, German officials could see no way to avoid their country's being ground to pieces between her two antagonists other than by concentrating her armies in the west and striking to defeat France before wheeling eastward to meet the slower-moving armies of Russia. To defeat two enemies without fighting a sustained two-front war required that one of them be eliminated before the forces of the other could become fully effective.

The Schlieffen Plan was a bold one and entailed many risks. Execution of the Plan rested on Germany's physical ability to move more rapidly than her adversaries and on her psychological ability to take the risk of leaving the eastern front open in the first weeks of

[13] Among other provisions, the Franco-Russian Alliance of 1894 committed Russia to deploy one-third of her army against Germany in the east if France and Germany should go to war.

[14] The Schlieffen Plan was formally adopted in 1906. The following discussion relies heavily on Gerhard Ritter's *The Schlieffen Plan* (London: Oswald Wolff, 1958), especially pp. 17–69.

the war. If her army did not move rapidly enough, the French army would gain the time to redeploy forces to counter the advance through northern France. Quick victory in the west would be possible only if the German army could outflank the French fortresses facing the Rhine by skirting them and going through Belgium. The Schlieffen Plan thus required Germany to violate Belgian neutrality and run the grave risk of bringing Britain into the war. The prospect of British entry intensified the need for speed: France would have to be beaten before either Russian or British armies could roll into action with full force. If her military and political leaders did not have the nerve to leave the eastern front lightly defended at the outset of the war, then her army would be too weak in the west to overwhelm the French. The success of the strategy thus depended upon surprise, rapid advance through Belgium and northern France, and great nerve on the part of commanders and statesmen.

The geographic situation of Germany, along with diplomatic developments, strongly affected the military policy she adopted. Shortly before World War I, France too adopted an offensive strategy, but not for reasons of geography or diplomacy. For France, national ambitions and military beliefs reinforced each other. Only by taking the offensive in any future European war could France hope to regain Alsace and Lorraine. To adopt a defensive strategy, moreover, would have implied France's acquiescence in her defeat at the hands of Prussia in 1870 and the acceptance of a permanent position of inferiority to Germany. At the same time, French military leaders were imbued with an almost mystical faith in the efficacy of élan — human will, drive, energy, spirit. The most famous and influential exponent of this line of thinking among the French military before World War I was General Ferdinand Foch, director of L' École Supérieure de la Guerre, or War College, where the French Army's intellectual elite studied. Long before Mao Tse-tung, Foch preached the doctrine of men over weapons, or what Bernard Brodie has called "the subordination of the material to the moral."[15] The following excerpts from his *Principles of War* capture the essence of his doctrine:

> In order that our army be victorious, it must have a moral superiority to that which the enemy possesses or receives from his commander. To organize battle consists in enhancing our own spirit to the highest degree in order to break that of the enemy.
>
> A battle won, is a battle in which one will not confess oneself beaten.

---

[15] For a comprehensive discussion of Foch's doctrines, see chapter 2 of Brodie's *Strategy in the Missile Age* (Princeton: Princeton University Press, 1959).

> The will to conquer: such is victory's first condition.
> Therefore: War = the domain of moral force. Victory = moral superiority in the victors; moral depression in the vanquished. Battle = a struggle between two wills.[16]

Foch, in short, put his faith in the all-conquering human spirit.

The belief that the spirit could triumph over the material firmly wedded French strategists to the offense. Commitment to the offense led the French in May of 1913 to adopt something called "Plan 17." This provided for a massive thrust by the entire French army eastward into Germany, and left the Belgian frontier to the north unprotected. Thus, while the Germans were planning to move most of their army around the French defenses on the Franco-German border by marching through Belgium, the French were preparing to move their forces out from these defenses headlong into Germany. The French and German commitment to the offense led both to opt literally for carrying the battle to the enemy.

Not only did the commitment to the offense cause the French to neglect their defenses on the Belgian frontier before the war. It also led them during the war to a tragically costly use of their infantry. Perhaps the greatest irony for France in World War I was that the faith in élan both saved her from defeat and bled her white. The emphasis on will led General Joffre, Chief of the General Staff, to refuse to admit defeat in August and September of 1914. Joffre's sheer stubbornness was one of the ingredients in the French army's successful stand at the Battle of the Marne. Success there spelled doom for the Schlieffen Plan. And yet, at the same time, the faith that the French military had in élan caused France to lose more men on the western front than either Britain or Germany. Believing in élan, the French generals hurtled masses of men against the withering fire of opposing forces that were dug in and well armed with machine guns and artillery. This strategy gained little and lost much. After the first few months of the war, battle lines did not change significantly, but millions of lives were sacrificed. Events proved the futility of this tactic, and yet military leaders on both sides continued to believe in its efficacy, repeated it over and over, and achieved the same result — or lack of result. Clearly, military doctrine about how the infantry could best be used did not lead to its best use in World War I. Men may die easily, but beliefs do not.

Two sides, quite evenly balanced and both driving for victory, may well land themselves in a stalemate. That this happened in World War I should not have been very surprising. But notice that

---

[16] Marshal Foch, *The Principles of War*, translated by Hilaire Belloc (London: Chapman and Hall, 1918), pp. 286–287.

this result was not inevitable. Instead the outcome, wanted by no one, was a product of technology, capability, military strategy, and political policy. The message conveyed by the two opposed alliances of European states, and by the military arrangements they had made, was this: if a major state on either side should mobilize, all the great powers would do so, and mobilization would mean war. As the Chief of the Great German General Staff wrote to his Austrian counterpart in January of 1909, "two mobilized armies such as the German and French will not be able to stand face to face without a passage at arms." Writing with remarkable prescience, he nevertheless drew a falsely optimistic conclusion. That mobilization means war is, he reasoned, "familiar enough to the whole European diplomacy, and in that fact lies the guarantee that none of the Great Powers will light the torch of war on account of Serbian ambitions, which would put the fire to the roof of all Europe."[17]

Unfortunately, contemplating a future situation that would pit the armies of the opposed sides against each other deterred neither of them. To understand why will make clear the difference between conditions that emphasize victory and defense and those that lead to the possibility of deterrence. Whether offensive strategies convey threats that deter depends partly on the design of forces and the strategy for their use and partly on physical capabilities and technology. Both France and Germany planned to take the offensive at the outset of a war. Both aimed for victory. Both believed that the key to victory lay in an offensive first strike against the other's forces. Each knew that to be the first to strike required that it be the first to complete full mobilization. German leaders realized that the success of the Schlieffen Plan depended upon Germany's greater speed of mobilization and movement. The mere increased likelihood of French mobilization would therefore strongly pressure Germany to order the actual mobilization of her forces. Under these circumstances, a threat of preparation or action by one state does not deter another from taking action, but instead creates a strong incentive for counteraction. Military technology was such that the steps that reduced a nation's vulnerability to attack also increased its readiness to launch a war.[18] In a climate of fear, the fact that defensive preparations could be viewed as offensive preparations meant that they would in fact be viewed as such. One who believes in the maxim that "a good offense is the best defense" scares the hell out

[17] From the correspondence between Helmuth von Moltke and Conrad von Hötzendorf, as quoted in Alfred Vagts, *Defense and Diplomacy* (New York: King's Crown Press, 1956), p. 97.
[18] Cf. Thomas C. Schelling, *Arms and Influence* (New Haven: Yale University Press, 1966), pp. 221–227.

of his opponent each time he makes efforts merely intended to improve his defensive position! If two or more states believe in the maxim, the situation becomes highly unstable.

At first glance, French and German plans look like deterrent strategies whereby neither side plans to defend itself but instead, if struck, plans to strike back at the other. The effectiveness of a deterrent threat rests on the ability of the threatener to punish his would-be attacker with reasonable certainty and speed. If A's striking first to hurt B does not eliminate, or reduce to limits that A finds tolerable, B's ability to hurt A by mounting a retaliatory blow, then B has the ability to deter A. For mutual deterrence, A's capability must be comparable to B's.

As events showed, both Germany and France had the ability to hurt each other severely, but to do the damage would take considerable time. How that time could be used was a question of immense importance. Armies were the means of attack; they were also the means of defense. Both sides might initially mount an invasion, as in fact they did, but either side (France, it turned out) could be forced to abandon its invasion and go on the strategic defensive by the success of the other's offensive strike. Each side could hope that its offensive first strike would eliminate the other side's offensive power — and thus its ability to retaliate. The initial success of one side would then determine the course of the war. Therefore, worries about preemption dominated, and mutual offensive capabilities and strategies had little deterrent effect.

A defensive strategy, had anyone adopted one, would have changed the situation. It would have, that is, if two conditions could have been met: first, that defensive preparations not also appear to be preparations for an attack and, second, that a smaller number of troops dug in to defend be able to hold off a larger number attacking. As has just been indicated, the first of these conditions was not satisfied in the years immediately before 1914; and neither was the second one, for reasons that can easily be stated.

It may be true that "a good offense is the best defense." Depending on circumstances, however, it may instead be true that a good defense is the best means of dissuading an enemy from launching an attack. Until the latter part of the nineteenth century, the defense was thought to have an advantage in land warfare of 3 to 2 or even of 3 to 1.[19] A favorable ratio for the defense has a stabilizing

[19] B. H. Liddell Hart gives the even higher estimate of 5:1 for the Normandy campaign in World War II. For a historical sketch of the increasingly favorable ratios that the defense has enjoyed since 1800, see his *Deterrent or Defense* (London: Stevens and Sons, 1960), pp. 97–110.

effect, for any increase of one country's offensive capability can be negated by a lesser increment of its adversary's defensive strength. If state *A* adds three army corps, for example, state *B* can counter this conservatively by adding only two. To play such a game is expensive (and perhaps futile) for *A*, and that should make an arms race less likely. It should also make a first strike appear less beneficial. If victory is state *A*'s aim, then *B*'s construction of a powerful defense may dissuade state *A* from actively seeking it. In eras in which strategic emphasis falls upon defense and victory, a state may be dissuaded from attacking because the quality of the opponent's defense makes the achievement of victory unlikely.

French and German military planners, dazzled by Bismarck's lightning victories over Denmark, Austria, and France, forgot Clausewitz's demonstrations of the advantages of defense. The conviction that the defense enjoyed little if any advantage increased their impatience to strike the first blow and made the avoidance of war more difficult.

DETERRENCE IN THE NUCLEAR AGE

A state unprepared to counter a weapon invites the use of that weapon against itself. In the nuclear age, the problem has been to devise a strategy that will discourage the use of weapons against which no defense yet exists.[20] Economically most capable and technologically most advanced, the United States has been the fashion leader in nuclear strategy, with the Soviet Union following along after some few years have elapsed.[21] To look at recent American strategy and problems attendant upon it will illustrate some strategic principles and show how strategy has responded to changes in technology.

The Soviet Union did not explode an atomic device until 1949 and had no intercontinental atomic capability until the early 1950s. In these years, American strategy emphasized preparation for victory should war occur, rather than deterrence of it. With little conventional force in being, the strategy relied on bombing capability plus the nation's vast mobilization potential. World War III, if it came, would look like World War II, but with American atomic bombs added. Coherence of strategy, however, was not achieved. The military's emphasis on B-36 bombers and supercarriers clashed with President Truman's persistent and unavailing advocacy of Universal Military Training.

[20] See the selection by Donald G. Brennan in Part V for a discussion of the defensive value of ABM systems.

[21] See the speeches by John Foster Dulles and Nikita S. Khrushchev in Part I.

The Eisenhower administration's New Look shifted American doctrine abruptly from a war-fighting to a war-deterring strategy. One stimulant to change was the desire to find a strategy that the country could afford and could stick to without gearing its responses to the wayward actions of other states. The Korean war was another stimulant to change. In his claim that we would never fight another one like that, Defense Secretary Wilson succinctly conveyed the intention. Never again would America fight a war in which she denied herself the use of her best (i.e., atomic) weapons. The threat to drop A-bombs, as various statements of Secretary Dulles made clear, was intended to deter other states from starting wars or carrying them through.[22] The threat of "massive retaliation" would bring a halt to all aggression, whether undertaken by big or small states, by conventional troops or guerrilla warriors.

The New Look was a radical military strategy propounded for the sake of serving conservative ends at home: balancing the budget at a low level of federal expenditure. With unbalanced forces and a simple program of action, radical strategies seek to meet all the important contingencies a nation is likely to face. Strong strategies make bold bets. The Schlieffen Plan, the Maginot Line, Japan's initial plan for war against the United States, and America's New Look policy — all of these fall into the same category, and none of them worked very well.[23]

Deterrent strategies, whether or not they are strong ones, encounter two basic problems. The first is the threatener's credibility. To be effective, a deterrent threat has to be believed. One state must believe that the other can deliver the threatened punishment and that under certain circumstances it may do so. Otherwise the state that is threatened will not be deterred. The second problem is posed by the actions that a threatened state may take. Confronted with a strong defense, a would-be aggressor may attempt to outflank the defense or to overcome it. Confronted with a powerful deterrent, a would-be aggressor may seek to reduce its effect by taking measures to protect its population or by striking to destroy a large part of the adversary's deterrent force.

The deterrent threat is a threat to punish someone if he undertakes certain loosely specified acts. The state to which the threat is addressed must at least believe that the punishment *may* be administered. In the old Indochina war, the threats made in 1954 by President Eisenhower, Secretary Dulles, and others to retaliate massively neither stopped the advance of Ho Chi Minh's forces nor

[22] See Dulles's statement in Part I.
[23] On the strategic intention of Japan, see Sir George Sansom's essay in Part II.

slowed the flow of supplies to them. Would Moscow or Peking be bombed because artillery pieces were shipped to Ho's forces through Russia and China? To make a nuclear threat against such actions plausible, the country issuing the threat would have to make itself look like a monster. The threat of wreaking massive destruction would be credible only against actions of the utmost evil. The problem of making the punishment fit the crime bedeviled the New Look doctrine. Could the credibility of the threat be established despite the wide disparity between action and threatened reaction? This question could not be affirmatively answered.

A further difficulty soon emerged. The New Look doctrine was formulated in the presence of the Soviet Union's growing nuclear arsenal, and this brought into question the credibility of nuclear threats made to deter conventional aggression in a bilateral nuclear world. Why should Russians credit American retaliatory threats once the Soviet Union had developed the ability to respond in kind?

The existence of two nuclear countries raised questions about the design and the vulnerability of the bomber forces and, later, the missile forces by which nuclear warheads would be delivered. Would they be directed at cities or at the other fellow's delivery systems? If bombers and missiles might become targets, how could they be protected? Mutual vulnerability of forces would lead to mutual fear of surprise attack by giving each nuclear power a strong incentive to strike first. If either country could eliminate the other's bombers and missiles in one surprise blow, then both of them would be encouraged to mount a sudden attack if only for fear that if one did not the other one would. Here the temptation to preempt appears in extreme form. It is as though the two cowboys confronting each other were armed with hair-trigger revolvers. Put differently, the situation is like the one just before World War I, but now with the problem compounded by fantastic increases in destructive power and in the speed of its deliverability.[24]

To reduce or eliminate the temptation to preempt, offensive forces must be protected. They must be made invulnerable, or nearly so, for example, by keeping bomber forces dispersed, and alert, and a portion of them airborne, by placing missiles under the sea in order to render them invisible, by putting them in concrete silos, or by placing anti-ballistic missiles around them. If neither of two countries can knock out the other's means of delivery, then cities become

---

[24] Worries about the dangers in the vulnerability of delivery systems and about the consequent temptation to preempt were often expressed in the middle and later 1950s. See especially Albert Wohlstetter, "The Delicate Balance of Terror," *Foreign Affairs*, XXXVII (January, 1958).

the main targets. A strike by one country at the other country's cities leaves its missiles intact, and they can then be expected to destroy the first country's cities in a retaliatory blow. From about 1956 onward, both the United States and the Soviet Union have sought, apparently with considerable success, to maintain second-strike countercity capabilities at a minimum. Insofar as they succeeded, both were deterred from unleashing their strategic nuclear forces. The invulnerability of retaliatory weapons to destruction by a first strike is the surest guarantee against such a strike. Thus both superpowers are pressed to spend huge sums designing and deploying weapons so that neither will ever have to use them. The "assured destruction" of cities that would be wrecked by the retaliatory blow becomes the keystone of deterrence.[25]

With large portions of their delivery systems in a state of near invulnerability, both states can afford to wait to see whether acts that might ambiguously threaten vital interests were in fact designed to do so. In contrast, vulnerability of missile forces would produce mutual fear of preemption, obviously a highly unstable and dangerous condition. The incentive to avoid it is strong. This urge, which represents a general requirement of any nuclear deterrent strategy, is one of the two major impulses of America's (and Russia's) military policies. In American policy, it is concretely expressed in the insistence upon maintaining multiple weapons systems with each of them able to deliver the amount of destructive force deemed sufficient to deter the Soviet Union — long-range bombers, land-based missiles (Minutemen), and sea-based missiles (Polaris and Poseidon). If a Russian technological breakthrough should make one system vulnerable, the other two would still be available. Thus, multiple assured destruction (or MAD, to use Warner Schilling's acronym) is maintained. More generally, of course, the premium placed on the invulnerability of missiles is expressed in the ceaseless efforts made in research and development lest someone else's innovations exceed one's own in ingenuity and destructiveness.[26]

The second major impulse of American military policy is found in the commitments made by the United States to the countries of NATO and in the extension of security commitments of some sort to forty-odd countries. In a condition of mutual deterrence, the United States cannot rely on strategic nuclear threats to dissuade

[25] See the selections on countercity and counterforce strategies in Part I.
[26] See the selections by Samuel P. Huntington and George W. Rathjens in Parts IV and V.

the Soviet Union from acting in ways that are damaging, say, to Western European states. As Undersecretary of State Herter said in April of 1959:

> I can't conceive of the President involving us in an all-out nuclear war unless the facts showed clearly that we are in danger of devastation ourselves, or that actual moves have been made toward devastating ourselves.[27]

The conditions that make nuclear deterrence credible also make it nearly incredible that either state will launch a nuclear strike at the other in response to actions it has taken against third countries. What protection, then, do these states gain from America's nuclear arsenal? The Soviet Union would presumably still be deterred by its fear that the United States would retaliate massively, not only in response to blows aimed at America, but also in response to large-scale attacks on America's major allies. America's strategic deterrent would then cover only those actions which Americans might view as endangering their basic security. One can well imagine that some acts of aggression would impress allied states as intolerable and yet not be severe enough threats to the United States to merit her retaliating at the risk of her own destruction. To say that two states deter each other means that they create a condition of strategic stability. Strategic stability, however, makes it possible to use force on a fairly large scale without much danger of anyone's pressing the nuclear buttons. Strategic strikes are deterred but not conventional actions.

One who follows this reasoning carefully will understand why the establishment in the late 1950s of an American-Russian system of mutual second-strike deterrence had the following consequences: the decreased confidence of allies in the protection afforded by American or Russian nuclear weapons, the loosening of alliances, and the increased desire of lesser powers to have their own nuclear weapons. If American and Russian forces are secure against each other's first strike and if their cities are vulnerable to each other's second strike, then neither of them can be expected to use its strategic weapons on behalf of third states. Neither of the superpowers can fire its missiles without the near certainty of being struck in return. Only if a country's survival is directly at stake is it at all possible to believe that the act will be performed that may well result in the country's destruction. Once two states possess invulnerable delivery systems, deterrence can only cover their homelands,

---

[27] Quoted in Dean Acheson, "The Practice of Partnership," *Foreign Affairs*, XLI (January, 1963), pp. 251–252.

as Secretary Herter rightly perceived. The smaller states of the world then have good reason to want nuclear weapons of their own. Strategic stability for the superpowers can be purchased only at the expense of increasing the incentives for nuclear proliferation. The more America's allies have questioned her commitments to them, the more they have wanted to find other means of guaranteeing their security.

The late Hugh Gaitskell, for example, once said in the House of Commons: "I do not believe that when we speak of our having to have nuclear weapons of our own it is because we must make a contribution to the deterrent of the West." As he indicated, no contribution of consequence was made. Instead, he remarked, the desire for a nuclear force derives in large part "from doubts about the readiness of the United States Government and the American citizens to risk the destruction of their cities on behalf of Europe."[28]

The nuclear superiority enjoyed by America in the early 1950s created a fear in Europe that the United States would too easily succumb to a temptation to retaliate massively. The arrival of strategic stability produced the opposite worry. In the words of a senior British general: "McNamara is practically telling the Soviets that the worst they need expect from an attack on West Germany is a conventional counterattack."[29] The countries of Europe, separate or united, have an incentive to adopt destabilizing military programs. Thus, in the 1964 *Statement on Defence*, the "unique contribution" of Britain's V-bombers and Polaris submarines was described as being to dissuade a potential enemy from attacking Europe "in the mistaken belief that the United States would not act unless America herself were attacked."[30] The contribution of Britain's nuclear force, it appears, has consisted in placing a British finger firmly on the American trigger. Where Britain led, France soon followed. The French Institute of Strategic Studies has justified nuclear diffusion in part with the argument that the uncertainty produced by a third power's nuclear force "considerably augments the opponent's belief in the possibility of a *first* strike" (italics added).[31] It is understand-

---

[28] *House of Commons Debates,* Vol. 618 (March 1, 1960), cols. 1136–1138. Cf. Hugh Gaitskell, *The Challenge of Co-Existence* (London: Methuen, 1957), pp. 45–46.

[29] Quoted by Eldon Griffiths, "The Revolt of Europe," *Saturday Evening Post,* CCLXIII (March 9, 1963), 19.

[30] *Statement on Defence: 1964,* Cmnd. 2270 (London: HMSO, 1964), p. 6, par. 7.

[31] The conclusion is reported by André Beaufre, retired general and director of the Institute, in his essay on "Nuclear Deterrence and World Strategy," in Karl H. Cerny and Henry W. Briefs, eds., *NATO in Quest of Cohesion* (New York: Praeger, 1965), p. 221.

able that lesser powers should, by mounting nuclear weapons, want
to be able to decide when the United States should risk destruction,
but it is also easy to see that the United States will resist such an
outcome. A force well protected will, for example, be less easily
triggered, whether by allied or enemy action.

The military motives for nuclear independence arise from the
doubtful durability of alliances in the nuclear age. The multiplication of nuclear establishments makes alliances less durable still. A
third country, however, can neither trigger its ally's weapons nor
deter an aggressor by its own threats to retaliate unless those threats
are credible.

A British threat to use nuclear force in order to deter a conventional attack launched by a nuclear great power is a threat to do
limited damage to the invading state at the risk of Britain's own
annihilation. Is this credible? The Defence Statement of 1955 spoke
of a policy that would "demonstrate that we have both the will to
survive and the power to ensure victory." But the 1957 Statement
said bluntly that "there is at present no means of providing adequate protection for the people of this country against the consequences of an attack with nuclear weapons."[32] The British, and the
French as well, have too readily assumed that if the homeland is
directly in danger, retaliation will be undertaken even at high risk
of national suicide. What the Americans call "finite deterrence"
(second strike, countercity), the British call "passive deterrence," a
term which implies that nuclear response would be automatic.
Though England may or may not choose suicide in the event, the
defenders of the policy claim that even a slight possibility of British
nuclear retaliation will deter an aggressor. The willingness of the
Soviet Union to run the risk of seeing several of its cities destroyed
will be proportionate, among other things, to the size of the prize.
Notice, however, that the small nuclear power would be put in the
position of *initiating* nuclear warfare; the superpower adversary,
with a rich variety of military instruments at his command, could
(if he wished) undertake actions none of which seemed to call for
national suicide but all of which would be damaging. Retaliation by
a small power, which is almost incredible, can be made entirely so
by the would-be aggressor's own policy. One must then wonder
what the deterrent value of an incredible threat will be. America's
massive-retaliation doctrine was to make a "New Look" in military
forces possible by permitting the substitution of nuclear for con-

---

[32] *Statement on Defence: 1955*, Cmnd. 9391 (London: HMSO, 1955),
p. 7, par. 21; *Defense: Outline of Future Policy*, Cmnd. 124 (London:
HMSO, 1957), pp. 2–3, par. 12.

ventional forces; the difficulties that doctrine encountered now plague the builders of independent nuclear establishments.[33]

The steps taken by the superpowers to ensure mutual strategic invulnerability have increased the pressures on third states to acquire nuclear weapons. Those very same steps have made it hard to believe that such weapons would be used against the superpowers. Although each superpower may have only a second-strike capability versus the other, against minor nuclear states both of them possess effective first-strike capabilities. A superpower's second-strike forces could be used on first strike to destroy a small country's offensive missiles or to shatter its command and control facilities. And should the superpowers build defenses effective against missiles fired in small numbers, that would compound the difficulties faced by any third country that sought to create a nuclear force useful against America or Russia.[34]

The United States and the Soviet Union have taken the insecurity of third states to be a part of the problem of their own foreign and military policies. If each worried only about what the other could do to its own homeland, then both might well be content with the stability promised by mutual possession of second-strike deterrent forces. What is described above as the first impulse of American military policy would exhaust their motivations. But because their interests extend beyond their boundaries (concern for the security of allies; desire to dampen the enthusiasm of smaller states for the acquisition of nuclear weapons), either may develop a desire to do more than deter the other by means of second-strike forces. If either does so, then the military policies of both will be affected — simply because each must react to the other. They must do so because grievous harm can be done to either of them only by the other. Let us again carry through the reasoning for the American case since,

[33] The point can be carried further. The Eisenhower administration freely chose unbalanced military forces in order to cut the costs of defense. It did not have to do so. The United States could easily have spent more on defense, as the early Kennedy-McNamara years demonstrated. Countries like Britain, however, are forced to unbalance their military forces — to cut back conventional power — because the costs of nationally owned nuclear forces are so high. Thus the pursuit of a new look by middle-rank powers locks them into a strategic posture whose deterrent value is dubious.

[34] The nuclear weapons of minor nuclear powers are, in short, possibly useful for deterrent or other purposes only against other such states or against non-nuclear states. For a summary of the possibilities, see Kenneth N. Waltz, *Foreign Policy and Democratic Politics* (Boston: Little, Brown, 1967), pp. 145–148, upon which the above discussion is based. Also see the selection by Donald Brennan in Part V.

as previously indicated, America's strategic revisions have usually come first, to be followed later by Russia's.

From the desire to cater to interests beyond the national domain, either or both of two military requirements arise: to increase the country's strength in conventional arms and to create a first-strike capability. To protect client states, an alliance leader needs either a war-fighting or a first-strike capability. If both of these should be lacking, then, say, a conventional Russian thrust into Europe would pose the choice of appeasement or annihilation. Weakness on the ground makes fighting a war impossible; mutual invulnerability inhibits making a strategic strike. If appeasement or annihilation are the choices, the former is likely to be preferred.

McNamara's policy of flexible response was designed to remedy both tactical and strategic weakness. American troops in Europe created a tangible identification of America's fate with Europe's. With at least several thousand tactical nuclear warheads and more than one hundred medium range missiles in the area of the European command, the forces available to NATO's European area also represented something of a war-fighting capability. Facing it, Russia would either have to move with considerable force and thus raise the risk of American strategic retaliation, or she would have to forgo the use of force entirely. At the same time, the enlargement and the improvement of American missile forces created a qualified first-strike capability: that is, an ability to destroy enough Russian missiles on first strike to reduce significantly the amount of damage done by her expected retaliatory blow.

If both had second-strike deterrent forces, the Soviet Union would find it difficult to believe that the United States would initiate a nuclear strike in response to a move — even a severely damaging one — by the Soviet Union against a third country. So long as the United States had only a second-strike capability, its European allies would also find it difficult to believe that the United States could generate from its expensive nuclear arsenal the ability to protect them. A first-strike (i.e., counterforce) capability would spread the deterrent benefits of the American nuclear force from the homeland to countries abroad. Just as a second-strike force may be unleashed in response to an attack on the homeland, so a first-strike force may be unleashed in response to one abroad.

To extend the coverage of America's nuclear weapons beyond the national borders requires the ability to reduce the damage that can be done by the Soviet Union in retaliation. A first-strike capability will do this, and protection of population by ballistic missile defenses and shelters would add to the effect. Expected damage would nevertheless still be extensive. A first strike would obviously be made only in the face of extreme provocation; the war-fighting capability would take care of other cases. The United States with its varied arsenal could then choose to use just the right amount and type of force for the occasion and would presumably have the Russians stopped at all levels.

Nowadays, obviously, a first-strike capability is hard to achieve. Moreover, even when its achievement is claimed, the claim is necessarily problematic. An American first strike at the Soviet Union's weapons would reduce the amount of damage that could be done in retaliation. But no one can ever know in advance either how great that retaliatory damage would still be or how much expected damage responsible officials could contemplate and still be willing to order a first strike. In McNamara's early years in the Defense Department, some claims to an American first strike capability were made. That the United States reached such a position of superiority because of conscious efforts to calm the doubts of its allies is unlikely.[35] It is more likely that the United States achieved this position almost accidentally as a byproduct of conscious efforts to maintain its second-strike capability vis-à-vis the Soviet Union. To describe superiority in weapons as constituting a first-strike capability may help in catering to the interests of allies. It is also a way of heightening competition in armaments.

ARMS RACES IN THE NUCLEAR AGE

A brief look at developments from 1957 to 1970 will make clear how military capabilities, strategic policy, foreign-policy ends, and national apprehensions interacted to bring about an arms race. The launching of Sputnik in 1957 created great fears in America that Russia's lead in rocketry would enable her to build a missile force large enough to give her a first-strike capability within a few years. This view was widely publicized by the Gaither Committee, a blue-ribbon panel appointed by President Eisenhower to assess the significance of Sputnik's launching for the United States.[36] Predicating their estimates on what the Russians could build (their capability)

[35] That it used such a position in order to try to calm those doubts is clear.

[36] Strategists at the RAND Corporation and within the Defense Department were also worried about the vulnerability of America's strategic nuclear force. They worried, however, about its present vulnerability, not about the number of missiles that Russia might be able to fire at America's bombers in the future; and they worried about the absence of any system that could give adequate warning of attack. See Albert Wohlstetter, "Vietnam and Bureaucracy," in Morton A. Kaplan, ed., *Great Issues in International Politics* (Chicago: Aldine Publishing Company), pp. 280–292; and Morton H. Halperin, "The Gaither Committee and the Policy Process," *World Politics*, XIII (April, 1961), pp. 360–384.

rather than on what they were likely to build (their intentions), the Committee predicted that a missile gap would materialize — one that the United States would not be able to overcome until 1960 or 1961, even were it to begin immediately to make strenuous efforts to redress the balance.[37] The Eisenhower administration, looking at Russia's intentions instead of her capabilities, differed with the Committee's conclusions, but it never succeeded in dispelling the doubts cast by its critics. John F. Kennedy used the predicted missile gap against Richard Nixon in the campaign for the presidency. Upon coming into office, Kennedy accelerated the efforts begun by the previous administration to ensure America's retaliatory capability and initiated new ones.[38]

Near the end of 1961, it became apparent to defense officials that the predicted missile gap had failed to materialize. In fact, a missile gap had opened up in America's favor. Beginning with a statement in October of 1961 by Deputy Secretary of Defense Roswell Gilpatric, the Kennedy administration began to stress America's overwhelming superiority. In December of 1961, Paul Nitze, then Assistant Secretary of Defense for International Security Affairs, put the case for American superiority very clearly:

> ... It appears to be the consensus of the intelligence community, both in the United States and in the United Kingdom, that the Soviet deployment of ICBM's has proceeded less rapidly than it was once feared it might. There has never been any doubt that the West possesses by far the greater nuclear force, including delivery capability. ... We believe that this force ... and the NATO forces ... give the West a definite nuclear superiority. We further believe this superiority can be maintained into the future. ... Furthermore, we believe this superiority, particularly when viewed from the Soviet side, to be strategically important in the equations of deterrence and strategy.[39]

Evidently the Soviet Union agreed with Nitze, for in September of 1962 it began to introduce medium range and intermediate range ballistic missiles into Cuba. The various motives that the Russians may have had at that time are not completely clear. But one point seems certain: by introducing missiles into Cuba, they were resorting to a "quick fix" to redress their strategic inferiority.[40] As a result of American statements, the Russians knew that the Americans

[37] The same situation occurred nearly fifty years earlier when, in 1909, the British were seized by fears of a possible "dreadnought gap" vis-à-vis Germany. See the selection by Kenneth L. Moll in Part V.

[38] See William W. Kaufmann, *The McNamara Strategy* (New York: Harper and Row, 1964), pp. 47–56.

[39] Quoted in *ibid.*, pp. 108–109.

[40] See the selection by Albert and Roberta Wohlstetter in Part II.

now knew what the Russians had always known: they had not built as many ICMB's as they could have. Moreover, the showdown and retreat from Cuba in October of 1962 apparently convinced the Russian leaders that such inferiority vis-à-vis the United States was extremely dangerous. The Chinese may have been correct in asserting that the Soviet Union was "adventuristic" when it put missiles into Cuba and "cowardly" when it took them out. Adventurousness and cowardice, however, were both born of strategic inferiority. To avoid these two extremes in the future, the Soviet Union would have to increase drastically its strategic nuclear forces. It did so. By the end of the decade, it was approaching parity with the United States. In late 1969, the United States had 1,054 land-based ICBM's and 656 sea-based missiles; the Soviet Union, 1,050 and 160, respectively.[41]

The American response after 1957 to a predicted missile gap, and the Russian response after 1961 to a real missile gap, clearly demonstrate that each superpower will refuse to accept a situation in which the other might have a first-strike capability. From the standpoint of the balance of terror, such a refusal is conducive to stability because it reduces the likelihood of preemption. From the standpoint of arms control, such a refusal can be disastrous. Both countries have an interest in taking measures to discourage preemption. Both also have an interest in holding down defense expenditures. The difficulty lies in trying to figure out how much is enough to ensure a second-strike capability and how much is so much as to create fear that a first-strike capability is being sought. In their efforts to determine how much to have, the two superpowers have not helped each other. Russian boasts of superiority from 1957 onward did little to restrain America's fears and to discourage her from looking at capabilities rather than intentions in her intelligence estimates. American boasts of superiority from 1961 onward did little to inhibit the Russians from undertaking a massive land-based and sea-based missile buildup. Each boasted, however, because each found itself in a situation where boasts could serve other interests. After 1957, the Soviet Union found it advantageous to use a presumed superiority in order to undertake a general political offensive in its foreign policy. After 1961, the United States found it advantageous to use a known superiority to try to convince her allies that they did not need national nuclear establishments.

In the nuclear arms race from 1957 to 1970, then, the two super-

[41] These figures are taken from the Institute of Strategic Studies, *The Military Balance, 1969–70* (London: The Institute of Strategic Studies, 1969), p. 55.

powers experienced intense and conflicting pressures.[42] For their own protection, they had to maintain retaliatory capabilities at the least. For their alliance commitments and other interests, they were tempted to strive for superiority and to make full diplomatic use of any real or presumed advantage. Complicating matters even further were the difficulties inherent in trying to infer each other's unknown strategic intentions from well-known strategic capabilities. If the two superpowers had been interested solely in preserving their respective second-strike capabilities, the arms race would have been easier to manage. The problem, of course, is that each has interests beyond the dissuasion of an attack by the other on its homeland. Both have used their strategic nuclear forces to serve larger political purposes.

STRATEGY AND FOREIGN POLICY

A strategy is a plan to gain maximum advantage from resources that are insufficient to provide complete security for the nation and to serve all its positive ends. The implementation of a good strategy then increases the benefits to be gained from a given expenditure or, holding expected benefits constant, decreases the costs of attaining them. McNamara's policy of flexible response was not so much a strategy as it was the transcendence of strategy. Flexible response amounted to this: Be prepared to meet any adversary at every level of warfare from irregular through conventional to nuclear force. In the good old American way, the United States sought to use high technological skill and immense productive capacity to equip forces that would be able to counter any weapon, to meet every tactic, and to cope with all imaginable contingencies. As the cliché has it, states do what they can and suffer what they must. If this is true, then by increasing mightily what the nation could do, McNamara's policy correspondingly increased the temptations to pursue interventionist military policies. Capability may have fathered policy.

Looking weak at one level of force increases the adversary's fear that force at the next higher level will be used. Weakness in conventional force in Western Europe, for example, adds to the deterrent effect of tactical nuclear weapons. But deterrent strategies always raise (as they have at the strategic level) the possibility of the adversary's making moves that, though damaging, do not justify the escalation required by the forces available. That is the trouble with deterrent strategies. At times, deterrence has been emphasized in American policy to the neglect of war-fighting capability. The

---

[42] For more general discussions of arms races, see the three selections in Part IV.

reaction from Europe has then always been — your policy is one of suicide or surrender, and surely in a showdown you will opt for the latter. At other times, as in the McNamara years, war-fighting capability has received more attention. Europeans were not made much happier. Increased ability to fight lessens the credibility of deterrence. Why risk widespread destruction if one is able to fight on the ground and forgo the use of nuclear weapons? Since miscalculation is possible, strategic deterrence risks the destruction of much of the world. A policy of flexible response, in lessening reliance on strategic deterrence, increases the chances of actually fighting a war and promises to destroy only the arena of battle. That, as Europeans have seen, is little comfort to the people who live in the arena. The dilemmas of strategy, especially of one intended to encompass a number of standpoints and interests, are not easily transcended.

The logic in the evolution of strategy is highlighted in the above summary. It indicates how strategic choices interact with foreign-policy decisions and with international political conditions. It sets forth the terms in which strategic debates are conducted and thus serves as a guide to the present and the future. Ballistic missile defenses (BMD) and multiple independently targeted reentry vehicles (MIRV), for example, are fiercely debated partly out of fear that their deployment will set off a new round of the arms race. But the chances of sparking an arms race cannot be reasonably assessed unless one realizes that arguments about the development of MIRV and about the building of BMD are basically arguments about military and political strategies. A wide deployment of MIRV plus the building of a heavy BMD for the protection of population would shift a country's policy toward reliance upon war-fighting capability. BMD restrictively deployed so as only to protect offensive missiles would indicate, in contrast, a policy of betting heavily on deterrence. Strategic decisions are also foreign-policy choices.

**PART I
Capabilities
and Doctrines:
Theories on the
Use of Force**

States coexist in a condition of anarchy. If one state is attacked by another, no means of protection are available other than those which the attacked state is able to muster. No authoritative agency can be called upon to resolve disputes among states. In conducting their foreign policies, therefore, statesmen often find it convenient or necessary to use force or to threaten to do so. Military force is important, if not central, to international relations. It brings some order out of chaos, and it helps to make and enforce the rules of the game.

Since force is so important in international politics, the following questions arise: How can states most effectively employ military force in pursuit of national goals? What effects has the growth in national military power had on the ways in which force has been used? What kinds of military threats are productive, and what kinds counterproductive? Have nuclear weapons changed the nature of international politics or drastically altered the ways in which states can use military power? These are the questions that the authors of the selections in Part I explore. Robert E. Osgood provides a historical analysis of the changes in the military capabilities of states and of the effects that these changes have had on the ways in which force has been used. Glenn H. Snyder distinguishes between the functions of pre-attack deterrence and post-attack defense in his discussion of the dilemmas that nuclear technology has created for strategists. With conventional weapons, deterrence and defense had tended to become fused; Thomas C. Schelling shows how nuclear weapons have separated these two functions. Henry A. Kissinger spells out the constraints on using force that nuclear weapons have imposed on national leaders. And finally, the selections under "Deterrent Postures and Targeting Strategies" deal more specifically with the kinds of choices that statesmen have made in their use of nuclear weapons.

The Expansion of Force

ROBERT E. OSGOOD

THE TRANSFORMATION OF FORCE

Sources of the expansion of force. Between the full establishment of the modern military state in the eighteenth century and the dawn of the nuclear age, military power underwent a transformation as remarkable as its transformation in the nuclear age. As in the nuclear age, the chief impetus of this transformation came from the tremendous expansion in the destructive power available to the most advanced states; but the sources of expansion were rooted deeply in social and political changes. . . .

One can sum up the sources of the expansion of military power in the following terms, arranged in the approximate chronological sequence of their initial impact upon international politics: the rationalization, centralization, popularization, professionalization, and modernization of military power.

In many ways these developments have fostered disorder and complicated the problem of controlling and restraining military power. But since they seem as irreversible as modern Western civilization, we must wonder whether they condemn us to novel and terrible destruction or whether they may provide the foundation of a new international order of unprecedented stability.

The rationalization of force under the state. The modern state, applying a rational, instrumental approach to power and war in the wake of the relatively disorganized conflict of the Middle Ages, became the primary agent of the expansion of force. Man's approach to war had been highly rationalized in relatively orderly periods before. It did not become entirely divorced from motives of glory, adventure, and mission in the eighteenth century. When transferred to the nation-state after the French Revolution, these motives were more compelling than during the Crusades. Nevertheless, a signifi-

From *Force, Order and Justice* by Robert Osgood and Robert Tucker, pp. 41–70 and 118–120. Copyright 1967 by The Johns Hopkins Press. Reprinted by permission. Portions of the text and some footnotes have been omitted.

cant change in man's approach to war took place with the state's establishment of internal order in the eighteenth century. As military power became the instrument of state policy, the religious and messianic, the social or agonistic, and the personal motives of war became subordinate to a utilitarian approach oriented toward using power with studied efficiency. This rationalization of military power has become increasingly comprehensive, calculated, and technical since the last part of the nineteenth century. Although we take this approach for granted as part of our civilization, this was not always the prevailing attitude.

In the Middle Ages, from roughly the eleventh century through much of the fourteenth, war was more a way of life than a calculated instrument of policy. It was virtually a continuous but small-scale activity that men took for granted.[1] The small scale resulted from the smallness of the armies, the short term of service, and the physical difficulty of keeping forces in the field for more than a few weeks at a time. Moreover, armies lacked the weapons and logistics to overcome the defensive advantage of castles and fortresses or to hold territory. The most successful commanders relied on maneuver, while generally avoiding pitched battles, where all might be lost in a day. Strategic direction was weak or entirely missing, although some commanders displayed great tactical skill.

Battles were, in effect, extensions of personal disputes arising primarily from the network of conflicting jurisdictions and loyalties involved in feudal obligations and dynastic claims. They needed no other justification. Except for the Crusades and the later years of the semi-national Hundred Years' War (1338–1452), wars were fought for the security, status, and enrichment of kings and for the emotional and economic gratification of the nobility. They were permeated by the chivalric values of personal honor, glory, and vengeance. We need not enter the controversy over the extent to which these values — especially the gentler ones of magnanimity and fair play — were actually lived up to. There are many examples in the Middle Ages of the mutual observation of rules of fair contest and of ceremonial restraints in the conduct of warfare. There are also many examples of one or both sides violating such rules and restraints. The important point here is that social and personal motives were so pervasive that war was more like a continuing enterprise or recreation than a recurrent political necessity. Consequently, boldness, vengeance, adventure, plunder, and sometimes

[1] In perhaps the greatest battle of the Middle Ages, Bouvines (1214), the French had 11,000 cavalry and about 20,000 militia infantry, fighting a coalition with 11,000 cavalry and over 70,000 infantry. . . .

even generosity frequently overrode tactical or strategic considerations. In the spirit of knight-errantry, kingdoms went to war in the most reckless and unpremeditated way; armies fought in the most amateurish and capricious fashion.[2]

Chivalry as a code of military conduct was largely destroyed during the fourteenth through sixteenth centuries by infantries with crossbows and longbows, by Swiss pikemen, gunpowder, and the growth of national allegiance. Still, the instrumental approach to war remained subordinate to its social or agonistic aspect. The chaotic Religious Wars of the sixteenth and seventeenth centuries dissolved what was left of the old codes of combat and injected a new intensity into warfare. Yet war did not become an instrument of policy in the modern sense.

War was scarcely under the effective control of rulers. Armies were often little more than undisciplined bands of marauders living off the land, since states lacked organizational control of them and were unable to provide logistical support. War was a clash of dynastic and religious sectarian allegiances. Above all, it was, in Sir George Clark's words, a "general melee," a "collision of societies."[3] Even in fifteenth- and sixteenth-century Italy, which saw the origins of modern diplomacy, the formation of military coalitions, and the consolidation of several fairly cohesive political units absorbed in Machiavellian competition, war was governed by feudal and dynastic interests rather than by the interests of nations or modern states.

In the second half of the seventeenth century, as the religious issues waned, monarchs began to construct internal order by establishing effective control over economic and political life. The growing internal power of governments facilitated their control of war and gave war political direction. In the coalitions formed against Louis XIV's drive toward Continental hegemony, diplomacy became absorbed in efforts to shape the configurations of state interest and power. Concomitantly, effective control of the military establishments, marked by improved military discipline, the formulation of military codes restraining plunder and piracy, and the creation of more efficient and larger standing armies, laid the foundation for

---

[2] . . . A lack of planning and calculation continued to characterize warfare after the Hundred Years' War. For example, France's repeated costly military adventures in Italy in the sixteenth century were undertaken without any calculation of possible material gains and losses. Her expeditions against Naples were militarily impossible tasks undertaken with neither naval supremacy nor effectual control of Lombardy and central Italy. . . .

[3] Sir George Clark, *War and Society in the Seventeenth Century* (Cambridge: Cambridge University Press, 1958), pp. 25ff.

the war system of the eighteenth century, in which force and the threat of force were to serve as instruments of state policy. Through these developments modern *Realpolitik,* foreshadowed in Renaissance Italy, emerged on a larger scale than ever before, backed by the organized power of the state.

In the eighteenth century kings became identified with modern sectarian states, yet states transcended the monarchy to encompass the people and the land as well. The development of centralized authority and of financial and bureaucratic structures capable of raising revenue enabled the state to create and control professional standing armies in order to enforce civil order and support external policies. In the aftermath of Louis XIV's failure to establish a European order based on French hegemony, the ambitions and rivalries of military states led to a pattern of calculated, circumspect relations based upon alignments of countervailing power. The stakes of politics were predominantly dynastic, turning largely upon marriages and inheritances, territory and commerce, but the common unit of political currency was now more clearly the power of the state to make war. This currency was freely exchanged in limited quantities for limited ends. Yet these limitations were, in a sense, the result of the weakness as well as the strength of the state.

The constraints on force. The rulers of eighteenth-century Europe lacked the mobility and firepower and the base of mass enthusiasm that were essential to wage Napoleonic war. Equally important, they lacked the political system and the administrative capacity to mobilize the whole nation and its resources for war. The expensive standing armies and artillery of the period imposed a severe strain on the limited capacity of governments to tax the people and finance protracted campaigns. The stringencies upon seapower were even greater, since no state could afford to train seamen in time of peace, and the quantity and quality of seamen that could be dragged into the service by press gangs were not conducive to large-scale warfare. Throughout the eighteenth century, war on land and at sea had to be attenuated or terminated because it threatened financial ruin, owing to the destruction of commerce at sea and to the expense of keeping armies and navies fighting.

These limiting conditions were in accord with the political necessities of the ruling classes. To have waged war for larger purposes with greater violence would have required popular states (whether autocratic or representative) and, therefore, the end of the Old Regime. Besides, the stilted tactics and clumsy logistics of warfare seemed appropriate to the social differences of the time. They reflected on the one hand the aristocratic and mercantilist outlook of the ruling classes, who liked their battlefield amenities and wished to limit the expenditure of life and money, and on the other hand the apathy and unreliability of the soldiery, who, having been drawn from the nonproductive segments of society and feeling little allegiance to the state, had to be disciplined to the stylized, drill-like maneuvers of the time in order to be kept reasonably efficient.

Yet the social and political constraints upon war would not have been so limiting without the material and technological constraints, which, in fact, persisted for decades after the French Revolution. The military inventions of the eighteenth century did not notably increase the scope, tempo, or intensity of warfare. The important changes in weapons since the Middle Ages — notably the development of muskets and artillery, fortresses, and heavily armed sailing ships — were assimilated only very gradually. The relative strength of the defense continued to retard the pace of war. Indeed, the greater use of artillery further encumbered logistics; and material shortages, especially in metal, fuel, and saltpeter, hampered exploitation of the new technology. The nearest thing to a modern arms race was the competitive establishment and enlargement of standing armies, but this competition was not accompanied by comparable competition in weapons.

European industry, still mainly dependent on craftsmanship, had not yet developed much standardization or mass production, either in civilian or military technology. Transportation and communication did not become significantly faster and cheaper. There was little or no pressure for innovations in military technology from monarchs, and there was considerable resistance to it on the part of the nobility and soldiery: the nobility, because innovations threatened their supremacy as a fighting class; the soldiery, because they feared the destructiveness of new weapons. Military inventions were not the product of a systematic response to military needs; they were largely a by-product of civilian technology. Science was not oriented toward practical invention, even for civilian uses; and scientists were generally hostile to the thought of applying their learning to military uses.[4]

These basic material, technological, political, economic, and social constraints enable us to speak of the eighteenth century before the French Revolution as a century of limited wars. The generaliza-

---

[4] . . . In the eighteenth century the sailing warship was technologically the most complicated military machine, but it remained substantially unchanged, and its effectiveness continued to depend on relative skill of operation rather than on technological advantage. . . .

tion is too sweeping, since these wars were not notably different from those of the seventeenth century in their number, frequency, scope, duration, intensity, and deadliness to combatants. Indeed, when the typical wars of maneuver and position were punctuated with pitched battles, the improved discipline of the armies, together with the continuing low level of medical science, produced extremely high casualty rates. In one important respect, however, the limited wars of the eighteenth century were comparatively moderate: they caused significantly less destruction of civilian life, property, and welfare, with the exception of the devastating Seven Years' War in Prussia. This limitation distinguished them from the *grande mêlée* of the Religious Wars and made them a discriminating tool of statecraft.

In this respect kings and statesmen, anxious to avoid the excesses of the Thirty Years' War and determined to employ no more force than necessary to achieve modest and well-defined objectives, kept war limited. Limited war in turn generally served them as a means of policy commensurate with their ends. Thus the limited scope of land warfare was well suited to the limited territorial goals that states usually sought. War at sea was frequently little more than commercial war with an admixture of violence. Diplomatic bargains resolved what force could not decide.

Harbingers of military dynamism. Yet even in this century of limited war there were harbingers of a new military dynamism. The rulers of Prussia, despite the many limitations on military power, demonstrated the capacity of the state to improve its relative position in the hierarchy of states by generating military power. By the end of the seventeenth century Frederick William, the Great Elector of Brandenburg-Prussia, had already shown the capacity of an absolute monarch to utilize the material, human, and administrative resources of the state to build a superior standing army.[5] In the eighteenth century his successors, Frederick William I and Frederick the Great, added limited military conscription, intensive tactical training, efficient artillery barrages, and skillful generalship to raise Prussia through conquests and diplomacy to the front rank of states, although France, Russia, and Austria had from ten to twenty

[5] ... The greatest organizer of an efficient standing army in the seventeenth century was Sweden's King Gustavus Adolphus, although great advancements in rationalizing military organizations were also made by Richelieu in the army and by Colbert in the navy, under Louis XIV. Where Gustavus had about 30,000 men under arms in 1631, Louis XIV is said to have maintained a military establishment of 400,000, with field armies approaching 100,000 — a size not to be duplicated until the French Revolution. ...

times the population and corresponding advantages in wealth, resources, trade, and territory.[6]

England provides the other striking example of an eighteenth-century state capitalizing upon military superiority based on efficient use of natural and human resources. By concentrating on naval power and a merchant marine and keeping military adventures on the Continent to a minimum, England compensated for her scarce native material resources by using her strategic geographical position, her substantial population, and her financial and trading prowess to become the dominant commercial and colonial power, with hegemony on the seas.

As Prussia based its military ascendance on the army and the control of land, England based its hegemony on the navy and control of overseas commerce. Through its army Prussia acquired and controlled land and population, which in turn were major ingredients in strengthening the army. Through its navy England acquired colonies and controlled commerce, which in turn provided the money to hire soldiers and subsidize allies on land while supporting a navy that could strangle the commerce of adversaries. Both were pre-eminent examples of states operating as successful military organizations, although the relatively unobtrusive impact upon domestic life of a standing navy, as compared to a standing army, helped England avoid the conspicuous militarism that arose in Prussia. Both provided impressive examples of the internal expansion of military power, which subsequent generations would emulate in the nineteenth century.

Moreover, in the rationalism of the eighteenth century there was also a harbinger of the technological explosion that transformed the scale of military power in the half century before World War I. In this century modern materialism — faith in the inevitable progressive increase of man's mastery of inanimate things for practical ends — became a sacred standard. The standard eroded the remnants of medieval moral and aesthetic constraints upon weaponry and lay the cultural foundation for the uninhibited advancement of military technology. The invention of more powerful weapons was presumed to be a mark of advancing civilization. The perfection of firearms, some hoped, would make wars so destructive that they

[6] ... In size of population, Prussia, with 2½ million, was twelfth among European states in 1740, but largely through conquest this population had doubled by 1786. The Prussian army under Frederick the Great grew to about 200,000, with a field army of about 53,000, at the beginning of the Seven Years' War (as compared to an average size of 47,000 among first-rank field armies in the eighteenth century). Four-fifths of Prussia's revenue went into the army.

would be quickly terminated or avoided altogether. Thus Europe was being prepared for a revolution in military technology that would be the counterpart of the industrial revolution — that astonishing explosion of man's ingenuity and productivity ignited in England two hundred years ago.[7]

Yet before the rise of popular nationalism and the onset of the industrial-technological revolution, military power could not approach the volatility, dynamism, mass, and intensity it attained in the nineteenth and twentieth centuries. Consequently, the military managers of the eighteenth century were spared the problems of control which afflicted their successors and were permitted the illusion of mastering the still latent energy of destruction. In the hands of enlightened statesmen and generals, military establishments seemed to be calculable and safe instruments of policy.[8]

Confidence in the calculability of war was consonant with the stress on rigid tactical principles of maneuver and position and with elaborate rules of siege and surrender. It reflected the prevalent faith in the ability of men to rationalize all human activity by discovering the precise, mechanical laws of its operation. Some analysts foresaw a universal military science that would be so exact as to render war futile and unnecessary. There was reason for such confidence, for although the outcome of war depended on many imponderables, the principal elements of military power were sufficiently ponderable to facilitate roughly accurate comparisons in advance of war. In war itself they remained fairly stable, and victory turned upon the most skillful use of largely unchanging weapons and tactical rules known to everyone.

In reality, of course, war was not as precisely calculable as its theorists professed. The vicissitudes of physical environment and human skill on the battlefield and especially at sea, where weather and unreliable communications interfered more with command and control, repeatedly led to miscalculations. The chief significance of

[7] Among the civilian innovations of the eighteenth-century industrial revolution which transformed military technology in the latter part of the nineteenth were the steam engine, iron metallurgy, the shift from wood to coal for fuel, the rise of industrial chemistry, the establishment of a machine tool industry, and the beginnings of the science of electricity. . . .

[8] "By and large a statesman in 1750 or 1815, if he possessed information on the size of armies, on the men who led them, and on the relative wealth of the rulers, probably had a better chance of estimating the power of a foreign state than he would have today. Much of the necessary information was actually common knowledge in the chancelleries of Europe." Edward V. Gulick, *Europe's Classical Balance of Power* (Ithaca: Cornell University Press, 1955), p. 28.

the limitations on armed forces was that, together with the rough equality of combinations of opposing forces, they rendered the consequences of miscalculations less serious.

Thus Frederick II, who was increasingly impressed by the role of chance in war and diplomacy as he gained experience, reflected upon the results of the War of the Austrian Succession (1740–48) with a certain melancholy satisfaction: "Since the art of war has been so well understood in Europe, and policy has established a certain balance of power between sovereigns, grand enterprises but rarely produce such effects as might be expected. An equality of forces, alternate loss and success, occasion the opponents at the end of the most desperate war, to find themselves much in the same state of reciprocal strength as at the commencement."

The wars of the French Revolution and Napoleon's military adventures would reveal a dynamism and decisiveness in war that Frederick II could not have imagined. But this new dimension of force also created a new dimension of miscalculation — and new efforts to master force.

The wars of the French Revolution showed what unprecedented concentration of military energy the popularization of war could produce even before the technological transformation preceding World War I. Although Carnot, as Minister of War in 1799, directed the first concerted effort to mobilize scientific talent for war, Napoleon was indifferent to technological innovations. Nevertheless, Napoleon magnified the force of war tremendously by exploiting the new sources of organized violence released by popular nationalism and ideological fervor. Following the course of the revolutionary leaders who preceded him, he transformed warfare into a national crusade, involving not just tactical maneuver and attrition of the enemy's supply lines but annihilation of the enemy's forces, occupation of his territory, and even political conversion of his people. With universal military conscription and comprehensive material and economic mobilization, he created a "nation in arms." To the revolutionary tactics of offensive mobility, surprise, the concentration of overwhelming numbers on a single point, massed artillery fire, and destructive pursuit, he added the extravagant ambition of a bold field commander, to give war a terrible new impact and momentum.

Truly, "The wars of Kings were at an end; the wars of peoples were beginning."[9] The sheer scale of the resulting violence made

[9] This is Marshal Foch's pronouncement occasioned by the famous cannonade at Valmy (1792), which marked the end of the Prussian offensive. Foch, *The Principles of War*, trans. Hilaire Belloc (New York:

the impact of war as unpredictable and uncontrollable as it was momentous. In Clausewitz's terms, it made war more nearly "a thing in itself."

Yet, although the potential autonomy and dynamism of popular, massive war had been revealed, the European wars of the following century, from 1815 to 1914, were relatively limited. Indeed, there were fewer significant wars in the European state systems than in the period from the defeat of Louis XIV to the French Revolution.[10] There were none of the scope or duration of the Seven Years' War and only one, the Crimean War, that was a general war involving several major powers. In the Crimean and Franco-Prussian Wars the field armies were several times larger than those of the seventeenth and eighteenth centuries — in the hundreds of thousands instead of twenty or thirty thousand — but the percentage of combat casualties was not much different, and civilian destruction was localized. The wars of this period are notable for their short duration and the small number of battles and participating states, as compared to the eighteenth or twentieth centuries. They were fought and settled for limited objectives, they were localized, and they were quickly terminated. . . .

The explanation of limited war in the period between the Napoleonic Wars and World War I, as in the eighteenth century, seems to lie in circumstances that were partly fortuitous, partly technological and economic, and partly the result of deliberate restraints upon the political objectives of war. Although the material and technical limits upon war were not so constraining as before the French Revolution, the destructive potential of armies was still sufficiently restricted to enable states to keep combat within bounds in the absence of a political occasion for fighting a general war of annihilation.

The Austro-Prussian War and the Franco-Prussian War were

Henry Holt & Co., 1918), p. 29. Much earlier, Goethe and Clausewitz, among others, had interpreted the battle at Valmy as the end of the old warfare and the beginning of the new. Actually, Valmy was tactically insignificant, but it was strategically and politically significant because a citizen army withstood a model eighteenth-century army and permitted the Revolutionary forces to go on to future victories. . . .

[10] Of course, what one regards as a militarily and politically significant war is somewhat subjective. By our reckoning there were either nine or sixteen such wars in the eighteenth century and either seven or thirteen in the latter period, depending upon what criteria are used. However, the number of belligerents and the duration of wars were markedly greater in the eighteenth century. In the eighteenth century the period from 1763 to the French Revolution was generally peaceful in the sense that there was no more than one large war and only a few small wars. In nineteenth-century Europe the periods 1815–1854 and 1871–1914 were equally peaceful.

limited chiefly by Prussia's ability to bring superior force to bear quickly and by Bismarck's willingness to negotiate a limited victory consistent with a new equilibrium of power. The Russo-Japanese War of 1904-05 was limited chiefly by Japan's sudden naval victory, by its satisfaction with a local victory, and by the material incapacity of both belligerents to carry the war to the other's homeland. The Crimean War was limited by its location — the same war in Austria might well have become a world war — and by the incompetence and inefficiency of the belligerents. These and other wars in this period remained local largely because the European system of political alignments, as in the eighteenth century, was relatively fragmented and loosely knit before the emergence of the two great alliances that clashed in 1914.

The new management of force. Although war itself remained limited in the period after the Napoleonic Wars and before World War I, military power expanded greatly. The professionalization and modernization of military power in the latter half of this period created an unprecedented peacetime war potential. But the success of states in preserving a relatively peaceful and orderly international system while greatly expanding its military basis concealed the latent dangers of the new military potential.

In the latter half of the nineteenth century, military power in Europe came under the systematic direction of a new class of specialists in military organization and planning. Professionally dedicated to maximum military efficiency, these specialists directed their nation's human, material, technological, and economic resources toward the creation in peacetime of military machines capable of inflicting maximum destruction upon the enemy's forces in war. The systematic training of these military specialists, with their highly developed staffs and administrative procedures, codes of professional conduct, formulation of war plans, conduct of war games, and development of strategic and tactical doctrine marked the application to the management of force of those methods of modern production that were transforming private industry.

The outstanding model of military management was the Prussian General Staff. By capitalizing on two great new military resources, universal compulsory peacetime conscription and the railways-and-telegraph system, the Staff led Prussia to two rapid, stunning victories over Austria in 1866 and France in 1871.[11] The quickness and

[11] The conscription system introduced by the Prussian military reformers enabled Prussia to combine a relatively small, highly professional standing army with a large military potential and thereby to join numbers with skill at a tolerable cost. The system entailed compulsory universal service for several years with the regular army and the regular reserve and then with a civilian militia. The military organization of the

completeness of Prussia's destruction of the fighting capacity of the dominant military power in Europe were particularly remarkable. It convincingly demonstrated to the rest of Europe the necessity of systematically developing peacetime military potential under professional, scientific management. Thereafter all the major states on the Continent created general staffs, railway networks, and systems of universal peacetime military service.

As we shall see in examining the political consequences of the expansion of military power, the new military machines provided statesmen with a powerful political instrument; but, unfortunately, the statesmen permitted the machines to follow a logic of their own — the narrow logic of military efficiency held by the professional managers. Thus instead of becoming a flexible instrument of policy short of war, the new peacetime military potential became, in effect, an independent force largely divorced from political control. Because the military machines were geared so strictly to fighting a war, they tended to foreclose new opportunities for using force short of war. . . .

The expanded function of strategy called for a systematic integration of military plans with foreign policy. In the hands of military professionals, however, strategy tended, on the one hand, to exalt the romantic emphasis of Foch on *will* and the all-out offensive and, on the other hand, to emphasize meticulous operational planning for military efficiency measured by the maximum force that could be brought to bear upon the enemy. The result was a kind of strategic monism that simplified planning but did not serve policy.

Thus the war mobilization plans of the general staffs in the years of armed peace after the Franco-Prussian War seriously limited the opportunities for diplomatic accommodation and committed governments in certain contingencies to an almost automatic shift into general war, as though their war machines had only one forward gear and no brakes. The prevailing military assumption that a future war would be swift and decisive like the Franco-Prussian War and that a long war would ruin a nation's economy and incur the danger of revolution put a premium on striking first with superior

---

railways entailed first constructing a railway network, then mobilizing the army, transporting it with weapons and supplies to the right spot at the right time, and finally deploying the forces properly. Prussia made many mistakes in conscription and railway organization in the war with Austria, but the General Staff studied the experience and profited from it. Michael Howard, *The Franco-Prussian War* (New York: Macmillan, 1961), pp. 18–29. Howard's study shows how substantially Prussia's success depended upon superior organization of mobilization and railway utilization.

forces. This requirement in turn led military staffs to commit their governments to plans for total mobilization only and to regard mobilization as an inevitable prelude to all-out war. When mobilization began, diplomacy would stop. For the sake of military efficiency, military plans were directed toward meeting a single contingency with one kind of response. The whole machinery was inflexibly geared to the complicated, exacting logistics of the railway networks, with the object of concentrating the maximum force at a single military point as quickly as possible. Consequently, when Austria declared war against Serbia in 1914, Austria, Russia, and Germany forfeited the diplomatic opportunities for avoiding war that partial mobilization against each other might have afforded, lest they lose precious time in fully mobilizing for the war that their military staffs considered inevitable.[12]

Actually, despite their commitment to full mobilization, each of these governments, at the behest of statesmen, tried to resist and, except in Germany, temporarily succeeded in resisting the prescribed automatic response by undertaking partial mobilization so as not to provoke the potential adversary into war or draw others into war. In the end, however, the military, pleading military necessity, prevailed and full mobilization was instituted, thereby turning military foresight into a self-fulfilling prophecy. In this way the attempt to manage military power more precisely and calculably made it more autonomous and less subject to control.

Thus mobilization plans seriously limited opportunities for diplomatic accommodation and, once they had been put into effect, virtually assured general war. In the end, the ineffective political control of peacetime military preparations proved to be even more dangerous to international order than the tremendous increase of destructive power that accompanied the outburst of industrial and technological energy. On the other hand, the modernization and hence increasing complexity of military power created a far more serious problem of peacetime political control than had existed before.

The technological revolution in military power. Competitive arming in a dynamic military technology further enhanced the role of

[12] Thus Dobrorolski, in charge of mobilization in Russia, insisted, "The whole plan of mobilization is worked out ahead to its end in all its details. When the moment has been chosen, one only has to press the button, and the whole state begins to function automatically with the precision of a clock's mechanism. . . . Once the moment has been fixed, everything is settled; there is no going back; it determines mechanically the beginning of war." Quoted in Sidney B. Fay, *The Origins of the World War* (2d ed. rev.; New York: Macmillan, 1930), p. 481.

military power as an autonomous political force. The modern arms race originated in an unprecedented surge of military invention in the last quarter of the nineteenth century.

The rifled gun barrel, together with improvements in gunpowder and firing mechanisms, led to tremendous improvements of range and accuracy. The development of breech-loading rifles and artillery, along with improved recoil mechanisms late in the century, greatly increased rapidity of fire. As significant as the accelerated rate of invention was the reduction of time between invention, mass production, and tactical assimilation of weapons, due to the effective co-ordination of economic and technological-scientific resources and to systematic battlefield experimentation and analysis.[13]

As land warfare was transformed by the utilization of railways and the telegraph, maritime warfare was transformed by the invention of the iron-hulled, steam-propelled warship. The rapid development of the battleship and the profusion of offensive and defensive naval technology to counter it were unprecedented in the history of military innovation. This weapon system changed more in the latter half of the nineteenth century than it had in the preceding ten centuries.

The development of the battleship altered the distribution of power, stimulated far-reaching rivalries, and shaped new political alignments. More than ever before a single weapon became the pre-eminent test and symbol of national greatness. It was integrally linked to foreign policy in the gospel of seapower according to Mahan. Mahan's great popularity as a strategist (particularly in England, Germany, and France) was based on his view that seapower was the royal road to national wealth and prestige. It would enable states to enlarge and protect overseas imperial holdings and commerce with an integrated system of colonies, bases, and merchant marine, supported by a fleet of line-of-battle ships designed to control the sea lanes, not merely to raid commerce and protect ports.

The rapid improvement of battleships created the first modern technological arms races. The arms race is a somewhat misleading metaphor for a competitive advancement of the type, quantity, and quality of weapons between adversaries seeking an advantageous

[13] . . . Despite the increased rate of assimilation, the French, although they developed the machine gun shortly before the Franco-Prussian War, failed to exploit its potentialities because they used it like artillery instead of like rifles against infantry at close range. Improved models by the Americans Gatling and Browning and the Englishman Maxim were developed in the last half of the century, but the full significance of the machine gun was not demonstrated until World War I.

ratio of military strength. In the latter part of the nineteenth century it became a major form of power politics and greatly enhanced the role of military power in peacetime.

From the 1850s through the 1880s France precipitated an arms race with Britain by attempting to offset numerical inferiority in warships with superiority in ironclad battleships, guns, and commerce-destroying torpedo boats and light cruisers, in accordance with the strategic concepts of the *Jeune École* navalists.[14] The resulting competition was most conspicuous in the contest between offensive guns and defensive armor. France eventually abandoned the competition without approaching naval equality chiefly because of disorder in French politics, growing fear of the German army, and friendlier political relations with Britain.

Germany launched another naval race with Britain in 1898, primarily to compete with her as a colonial world power. The British naval program, based on the famous two-power standard, had been designed to offset a Franco-Russian combination. Germany's program, coinciding with an alleviation of the Russian threat by virtue of the Anglo-Japanese Alliance and the Russo-Japanese War, shifted the focus of Britain's naval program to Germany. In October, 1905, Britain laid down the original *Dreadnought* and in February, 1906, launched it. The *Dreadnought* had greater speed and several times greater long-range firepower than previous battleships. Germany soon followed suit, and in 1912 First Lord of the Admiralty Churchill announced a British naval standard of 60 per cent superiority over Germany in dreadnoughts, while threatening to lay two keels for every one German keel unless Germany would reciprocally slow down or freeze construction without any political conditions. By 1914 the German government had abandoned this competition for fear of encouraging further British naval expansion and pressing German taxpayers too heavily, as well as because of more urgent demands imposed by military preparations on land.

The role of dreadnoughts foreshadowed the revolutionary role of submarines and airpower in that they were intended not merely to defeat the enemy's forces but to exert a far-reaching effect upon its livelihood and status. They would do this, moreover, not merely by harassing commerce directly but primarily by securing or deny-

[14] This school of navalists, echoing the old view of naval warfare as an extension of commercial warfare, did not anticipate starving England but only cutting off enough food and raw materials to cause an economic panic by raising insurance rates. The British decided to counter this danger by providing national insurance and devising new tactics to protect merchant vessels. Arthur J. Marder, *The Anatomy of British Sea Power* (New York: Alfred A. Knopf, 1940), chap. vi.

ing control of sea lanes vital to a nation's welfare and greatness. What is more, they were admirably suited to sustaining in peacetime a world policy and position through the conspicuous representation of a nation's might in distant places. This had been the more or less conscious strategy of British seapower since the latter part of the eighteenth century, but Mahan made it explicit and popularized it, and the modern battleship dramatized its efficacy.

The development of steamships with screw propellers relieved sea maneuvers from dependence on the vagaries of the wind and currents and completely outmoded sailing vessels. It greatly enhanced the defensive strength of advanced industrial nations, especially such insular powers as Japan and the U.S. It also greatly enhanced the geographical extension of the power of nations that could develop coaling bases and colonies. Therefore it became the mainstay of the great imperial contests and the virtually global struggles for hegemony that agitated international politics in the two decades or so preceding World War I.

In these ways the dreadnought exemplified the momentous impact of technological innovation upon international politics. It demonstrated the growing impact of armed forces, as well as their growing dependence, upon the nation as a whole.

It also posed the question of whether the new technology could be controlled. This question was posed in one form by the new factor of uncertainty in warfare and military planning, injected by the accelerated rate of technological innovation. The dreadnought complicated the calculation of relative military power and made more difficult the control and prediction of the outcome of war. To integrate the new battleships into war plans and production programs, certain assumptions had to be made about their military function. The assumption that a surprise attack with naval forces-in-being would be decisive provided the strategic impetus for naval competition, just as the assumption that the army that struck first with the most firepower would have a decisive advantage impelled the arms race in land weapons. Yet forces-in-being at the moment of a hypothetical war would depend not only on existing weapons but, equally, on future weapons produced by the building programs in the shipyards — programs that were complex and, in the case of challenging states, shrouded in secrecy.

In 1909 official and private British sources indicated that Germany might build 17 or even 21 dreadnoughts by 1912 instead of the officially announced 13. This estimate turned out to be wrong. It was based on information concerning an increase in German shipbuilding capacity; an increase in Krupp's capacity to produce gun mountings; the secret accumulation of nickel for use in guns, armor, and mountings; and an acceleration of contracts for ships. In effect, the alarmists based estimates of production on their view of Germany's capabilities, whereas more moderate advocates of a naval build-up credited Germany's announced intentions. England, unlike Germany, did not keep production details secret. The details of its naval program were publicly debated in Parliament and in the press. On the other hand, the public debate was often a confusing guide to those concerned with estimating the future of England's naval program.

The secrecy, complexity, and dynamism of building programs meant that naval programs had to be based on uncertain estimates not only of an adversary's relative capacity but also of its *intentions* to increase the quantity and quality of its navy. Yet the adversary's intentions could be affected by many imponderable internal and external considerations, including its estimate of one's own capacity and intentions. Therefore one state might try to alter the other's intentions by threatening and bargaining with a construction program and, perhaps, by linking this game with political proposals.

After some controversy, the British built the more powerful dreadnoughts, although they knew that this would lead to expensive and possibly dangerous competition with Germany in a weapon in which British superiority would not be as great as in pre-dreadnought battleships. The decisive argument for doing so was simply that Britain's refraining from building dreadnoughts would not prevent Germany from building them but only give Germany a head start. After competitive building started, however, the British tried to induce the Germans to agree to a reciprocal reduction of the tempo of competition or at least to an exchange of construction information in order to mitigate exaggerated suspicions of rates of construction. But the German government was unwilling thus to concede British superiority without some political *quid pro quo*, such as British neutrality in the event of a Franco-German war. The British government, on the other hand, was unwilling to break the Anglo-French entente. Winston Churchill, First Lord of the Admiralty, tried in vain to get German agreement to proportional reductions or to a joint holiday in construction of dreadnoughts while threatening, otherwise, to outbuild Germany by a precise ratio or number of ships. In the end, Germany defeated its political purpose by driving Britain closer to France. At the same time, it had to concede British superiority in the naval competition.

The difficulties of using the new peacetime power of weapons as a finely calculated instrument of policy were demonstrated in the failure of Admiral Tirpitz's too-clever "risk" strategy, which foundered on miscalculations of British policies and capabilities. Tirpitz developed his "risk theory" as a strategy for advancing Germany's political status and security vis-à-vis Britain by improving its relative naval power without obtaining naval equality. According to this strategy England would prefer to make concessions to Germany in the colonial field or possibly even enter into a military commitment with Germany rather than risk a clash with a smaller German navy, if, in the event of such a clash, that navy were strong enough to leave England inferior in the face of a Franco-Russian naval combination. The underlying assumptions of this strategy, if they ever had any merit, were invalidated by the Anglo-Russian entente, the Anglo-French rapprochement, the Admiralty's decision to concentrate the British fleet in the North Sea, and England's decision to build dreadnoughts. But the German government continued to pursue Tirpitz's strategy and brought about the very political result — consolidation of the Triple Entente — that it was intended to prevent, while inciting Britain to enter a competition Germany could not win.

As the Anglo-German naval competition illustrates, the nature of the new technology gave arms races a kind of self-generating impetus based on the interaction of opposing military capabilities and intentions, real and estimated. This interaction produced a mode of peacetime power politics that resembled the maneuvering and bargaining of eighteenth-century wars, except that the stakes of the game were larger, the rules less reliable, and the whole game more volatile and subjective.

Moreover, because the game was expensive, because it impinged upon national pride and affected international tensions and the prospect of war, and because even nondemocratic governments felt the need to elicit popular consent for arms policies, arms races were also deeply involved in the vagaries of public opinion and internal politics — an involvement which the armed services and the armaments manufacturers stimulated and exploited. Thus during both the Anglo-French and Anglo-German naval races there were a number of naval scares in England, causing widespread, although unwarranted, fears of sudden naval attack and invasion. News of French and German naval increases created considerable public apprehension and touched off controversies with political overtones in the government and press. There were lively public disputes over future German naval strength and the proper number of ships to be built in the British program.

In England, as elsewhere, it was widely assumed that the outcome of crises like the two in Morocco depended upon naval superiority. Therefore all governments that could afford a navy, as well as some that could not, pointed to the navy as a symbol of national might and pride. The involvement of the public in military policies through arms races, demonstrations of military prowess, and crises added a further dimension of subjectivity and incalculability to the use of military power short of war.

The difficulties of planning in peacetime for the effective use of military power in war were no less severe. For in addition to all the other complicating factors in arms races, the new high rate of technological innovation and obsolescence deprived the military managers of one of the crucial, though increasingly inadequate, criteria for determining military requirements: wartime experience. Thus the London *Times* of November 19, 1895, noted: "A modern navy is a totally untried weapon of warfare. It is the resultant of a host of more or less conflicting theories of attack and defense. The seaman, the gunner, the torpedoist, the engineer, and the naval constructor each has his share in the creation of the modern man-of-war, each presses the paramount claim of his own department, and the result is a marvel of theory, compromise, and complication."[15]

To some extent, formulation of strategic doctrine, conduct of war games, and mathematical calculations of projected operations compensated for lack of experience,[16] but they also tended to foster a dangerous illusion of precision and predictability. The meticulous planning and rehearsal of complex military operations and the single-minded pursuit of maximum wartime efficiency tended not only to overlook the contingent and unpredictable elements of war; equally important, the inflexibility of military plans had unexpected and often quite adverse political consequences. Germany's Schlieffen Plan, before World War I, is the most notable case in point.

Under Chief of Staff Von Schlieffen's command, this plan followed his predecessor Waldersee's crucial assumption that a full-scale two-front war with France and Russia was inevitable. The elder Moltke had planned a quick war and a settlement with Russia in the East while offering France neutrality or fighting her with a holding action if necessary. But Waldersee, coming into office after the formation of the Franco-Russian Alliance, planned a full-scale

---

[15] Quoted in Marder, *The Anatomy of British Sea Power, op. cit.,* p. 9.
[16] War games, however, often led to false conclusions. Thus the British Royal Navy's maneuvers of 1892 supported the belief that torpedo boats had little chance of success against fleets at sea. *Ibid.,* p. 166. But the first real example of this new technology in battle, provided by Japan against Russia in the war of 1904–5, contributed much to Japan's astonishing victory when torpedo boats attacked the Russian squadron in Port Arthur and sank a Russian flagship and three other ships in the decisive Battle of Tsushima.

war against Russia, preceded by a quick knockout blow against France. This foreclosed the possibility of keeping a Balkan war localized, since even if a war with the Russians were to originate in the Balkans, Germany would have to strike first against France. Moreover, the Schlieffen Plan envisaged an attack through Belgium even if, as proved to be the case, France were to refrain from invading Belgium first and England were to regard the invasion of Belgium as requiring her intervention.

Strategic prognostications in other countries showed the same lack of foresight. On the eve of World War I the general staffs of the major European antagonists were universally convinced that their forces, with the help of allied forces, would be victorious and that victory would come from a quick, decisive contest like the Prussian victory over France in 1871.[17] They believed in Marshal Foch's mystical doctrine of *l'offensive brutale et à outrance*. Foch's stress on offensive action went along with his advocacy of "absolute" or total war, in opposition to the eighteenth-century limited wars of maneuver and position. It was associated with his belief in the decisiveness of the moral factor in war: the will to victory. It was in accord with the widespread belief that a modern war of attrition would be such a severe strain on industrial economies that nations would have to end a war quickly rather than face bankruptcy and revolution.

The military staffs were, therefore, completely unprepared for the war of stalemate and attrition that ensued when the devastating firepower unleashed by the new weapons, unaccompanied by comparable innovations in tactical mobility, drove troops into the trenches and exacted unimagined casualties for negligible advances.[18]

World War I. In World War I the principal object of war was conceived to be the annihilation of the enemy's forces. Yet the British

[17] The Elder Moltke and Joffre were exceptions in foreseeing a war of attrition, but neither undertook preparations for such a war. Only Lord Kitchener, who became war minister after war was declared, urged preparation for a long war of attrition. England's War Council, however, regarded his views as extravagant whimsy.... The most detailed and well-reasoned prophecy of a war of attrition was made by Ivan S. Bloch in his six-volume work, *The Future of War in Its Technical, Economic, and Political Relations* (1897–99), which predicted that the increased firepower of guns would force entrenchment and stalemate. However, Bloch shared the consensus that modern war would be economically and socially catastrophic, or "impossible," as he put it. . . .

[18] . . . According to the official French history of the war, *Les Armées Françaises dans la grande guerre* (1922–25), French casualties in the month of August alone amounted to about 300,000 out of a field army of 1,600,000.

blockade and the German submarine campaign put whole nations under siege as never before. In the end Britain was bankrupted, France and Britain had lost a terrible portion of their youth, Italy was on the brink of political chaos, Russia and Germany were racked with revolution, the Austro-Hungarian Empire had vanished, and the Ottoman Empire was dismembered. Only the American Civil War, the first conflict to reveal fully the momentous destructive power generated by modern technology and the popularization of war, could have prepared the world of 1914 for the protracted, profligate expenditure of lives, homes, and money; but the lessons of that war were largely ignored in Europe.

Thus, contrary to the illusion of precision and calculability conveyed by advanced professional management — but contrary also to the conviction that sheer morale and the will to victory would be decisive — total war proved to be far more intractable to intelligent direction than the managers expected. This was partly the result of unwarranted faith in the simple military axioms that led armies into massive assaults in the expectation of quick, decisive victories and partly the result of the enormous dimensions of force and the immense complexity of military establishments, which multiplied the frequency and repercussions of unanticipated developments.

World War I precipitated a torrent of technological innovations, fostered for the first time by a comprehensive mobilization of scientific talent. These innovations included not only the improvement of previous weapons but also the introduction of new weapons: the airplane, the tank, poison gas, and the submarine. Each of these weapons and the interaction of all of them with other weapons, with tactical innovations, and with new factors of logistics and materiel affected the conflict in unexpected ways. The submarine, which had been only an ineffective novelty in previous wars, came close to being a truly decisive weapon.

Of course, all these innovations provided only a faint foretaste of the proliferation of decisive technology in World War II,[19] in which the participants were as unprepared for mechanized, mobile, blitzkrieg warfare as they had been unprepared for trench warfare in 1914. In the interwar period mechanized mobile warfare had been

[19] In World War II the mobilization of scientific and engineering talent for military purposes was especially comprehensive and effective in England. The British program grew into a gigantic co-ordinated international effort including Canada and the U.S. A great part of this effort went into the perfection of weapons developed in previous wars; but new inventions — most notably radar, the proximity fuse, and the atomic bomb — played an even more significant role than in World War I.

espoused by a few prophets in England and France — notably, Fuller, Liddell Hart, and De Gaulle — but only the Nazis put it into practice.

The fact that the marvelous ingenuity of technology and military management resulted in such unexpected destruction of life and property produced a deep agony and revulsion in the world, in many ways deeper than that created by World War II. The unprecedented loss of life and the massive devastation of material civilization, compressed into a few years, intensified the psychological shock caused by the sharp contrast with prewar expectations of a quick, decisive, exhilarating contest. The wholesale inhumanity and suffering inflicted by modern nations geared to war seemed like a cruel refutation of the general optimism in the preceding decades that industrial-technological and sociopolitical progress marched together.

It is true that if one measures the destructiveness of war by economic and demographic statistics covering the immediate postwar period of recuperation as well as the war itself, World War I seems much less pernicious as a whole than its reputation — indeed, almost beneficent in some countries. For the same factors of modern civilization that made massive violence possible also facilitated a rapid restoration of population and national incomes. But this measurement, of course, is irrelevant to the lasting psychological and political effect of an immense, violent upheaval in modern civilization inflicted by man's own monstrous military machines running amuck.

A new dimension of force. Man's enthusiasm for war and the whole war system was deeply shaken by World War I, yet his underlying confidence in technological solutions to warfare was not undermined. On the contrary, the war aroused hope that some single new weapon might prove overwhelming, that some technological breakthrough might simplify the problem of exerting calculable, decisive force. This hope centered above all on the strategic bomber, which promised to attain victory by striking directly at the enemy's homeland, avoiding massive, inconclusive encounters on the ground and obviating the travails of attrition.

Actually, although the development of strategic airpower greatly enhanced the peacetime effects of force, it showed as dramatically as World War I the difficulty of controlling the wartime effects of the volatile new technology. Indeed, the very characteristic of strategic airpower that enhanced its political impact short of war complicated its control in war: its capacity to inflict sudden punishment directly upon civilians at a range far beyond the battlefield. This characteristic, although analogous to the indirect punitive effect of the naval blockade, distinguishes airpower from all other kinds of military power.

In the midst of the stalemate during World War I, the development of the military airplane inspired a small but influential group of advocates to propound a doctrine of strategic bombing long before the bomber was technically capable of playing its purported role. The doctrine promised victory by inflicting decisive damage on the basic civilian sources of enemy power without having to defeat the enemy's armed forces or occupy his territory.

In April, 1918, British political leaders, over the opposition of the highest ranking military officers, succeeded in establishing a separate Royal Air Force in their search for an alternative to sending the flower of British manhood to "chew barbed wire in Flanders," as Churchill put it. The public shock over the German attacks on London with Zeppelins, and later Gotha bombers, provided the immediate impetus. The prevailing strategic doctrine at the time contemplated the use of bombers against military targets directly related to the war on the ground, but the general impression that punitive air raids on cities could exert great psychological effects injected a significant ambiguity in the nascent doctrine of airpower. The heavy casualties inflicted by the daylight raids on undefended London raised great popular and professional expectations about the efficacy of strategic bombing. On the basis of these casualties it was calculated that in a future war London might be made almost uninhabitable in the first weeks of bombing. Furthermore, the one-sided emphasis on offensive uses of airpower in World War I fostered the conviction that there was no effective defense against such devastation except bombing the enemy's bases and factories and inflicting reprisal damage upon his cities. These assumptions and the strategic doctrine that was based upon them had a powerful effect upon international politics after World War I.

In the years after the war the writings of the Italian prophet of airpower, Giulio Douhet, broadcast the doctrine of victory-through-strategic-bombing throughout Europe and beyond. In essence this doctrine held that victory depended first on obtaining "command of the air," which in turn depended on destroying air bases and air factories, and then on shattering the enemy's will to fight by inflicting maximum damage on his cities, transportation centers, and industries. The doctrine assumed that war among major powers must aim at annihilating the enemy before he annihilates you, that there would be no defense against the bomber, and that victory would come quickly (and, incidentally, therefore humanely) to the force that could strike first by surprise and inflict the greatest damage in the shortest time. The logical defense against this danger would be either to strike first in a pre-emptive or preventive attack or else to depend on the threat of reprisal to deter the enemy from striking first.

As in the case of a prospective naval or ground attack, the supposition that a sudden first strike from the air could be decisive added an element of tension to international conflict and a new danger of pre-emptive or preventive attack. It also gave states a mighty instrument of intimidation and deterrence. With the integration of airpower into military establishments, the whole nation became the direct object as well as the source of military power — in peacetime as well as in war. In short, strategic bombing put the nation-in-arms in the front line. This further complicated the problem of calculating and controlling military power.

Success in exploiting military power for its psychological and political effects short of war depended heavily on the credibility of a government's and, indirectly, a whole nation's will to use its power of devastation, especially when the enemy was assumed to have the power of counter-devastation. But what determined credibility? It depended partly on the relative material capabilities of opposing air forces; but, because of the subjective nature of governmental and national will, the relation of capabilities to credibility was less direct and more complicated than in the case of weapons that exerted their effect only against armed forces.

Moreover, the estimate of air capabilities was also uncertain. Not only was the efficacy of untried weapons in doubt, but, as in the case of naval competition, plans and preparations for weapons that would be produced only years hence were a crucial factor in capabilities; yet these plans and preparations were obscured by secrecy and the diffuseness of the production process. Thus after the British decided in 1934 to seek air "parity" as a "deterrent" to German aggression, they discovered not only that parity was difficult to define in quantitative and qualitative terms but that attaining it required a rearmament effort based on quite uncertain and fallible estimates of Germany's rate of production, which in the early stages of German rearmament depended heavily on such obscure auxiliary preparations as the manufacturing of machine tools. In May, 1935, Prime Minister Baldwin publicly confessed that his government had completely underestimated the rate of German rearmament. Britain's task then became to expand her aircraft industry and rate of production so as to obtain parity with the air force that Germany was expected to have by 1940.

Britain's whole air rearmament program was based on the assumption that Germany could deliver a knockout blow against England. Baldwin's pronouncement that "the bombers will always get through" was taken as axiomatic. The fact that the Germans had no intention, plan, or capability for such an attack did not change the significance of the British assumption. Indeed, Germany capitalized on this psychological reality by encouraging British apprehensions of a knockout blow and by exploiting them to paralyze British diplomatic and military resistance to piecemeal aggression. Consequently, Britain's strategic doctrine stressed the deterrent effect of a capability for offensive reprisals against Germany, and her rearmament program stressed heavy bombers. Nevertheless, when the government belatedly discovered the magnitude of Germany's air superiority after 1938, it shifted from a strategy of massive civilian bombing to one of confining bombing to military objectives in the hope that Germany would spare British cities. Then, shortly before the war, the Air Staff, having previously failed to base air strategy on operational possibilities, discovered the limited penetration ability of bombers; so it shifted the strategic priority to defending France on the ground, although there were no concerted plans to fulfill this priority.

War itself was the great school of strategy and tactics, but wartime trial and error provided unexpected lessons. Strategic bombing turned out to be even more volatile and less subject to foresight and control than the contest between massive armies had been in World War I. At first both sides confined bombing to tactical and industrial targets. The air war demonstrated that both sides had unprecedented incentives for contrived reciprocal restraints. And for a while such restraints were practiced.[20] But, contrary to claims of great precision, the inaccuracy of bombing and the collateral civilian damage, combined with the unexpected vulnerability of bombers engaged in precision bombing, eventually broke down reciprocal restraints and led to raids designed chiefly to inflict terror and reprisals upon civilians and things of civilian value, culminating in the senseless bombing of cities like Dresden.

The actual effect of such bombing upon civilian morale and the national will to fight proved to be almost negligible in Germany, as in England, although similar attacks on Japanese cities were apparently more effective in helping to induce surrender. But in both cases civilian bombing signified that an ultimate stage had been reached in the expansion of military power — a stage in which the whole nation had become a direct target of psychological pressure

[20] In view of common assumptions about Hitler's "irrationality," it is interesting to note that he felt special incentives to avoid city bombing, such as the fear of the adverse effect of British retaliatory bombings on his domestic support; and that he was generally more anxious to preserve reciprocal restraints than the British. . . .

and physical punishment. Before the nuclear age airpower revealed both the possible utility of modern force short of war and its potential uselessness in war. . . .

THE POLITICS OF FORCE

The changing attitude toward force. In the whole melancholy tale of misadventures accompanying the expansion of force through the period of two world wars, perhaps something as simple yet as imponderable as the prevailing attitude toward force and war affected international order more decisively than the structure and organization of power or the nature of military technology — although, of course, these factors were closely related.

The prevailing attitude toward force did not change as dramatically or as uniformly as military technology; yet there is a tremendous gap between the attitude of the eighteenth century and that of the period following World War I. In the eighteenth century, when the instruments of force were inherently quite limited and power politics was no concern of national publics, war was largely taken for granted as a normal recourse of statecraft. Those who deplored war did so more for its wastefulness, its control by the aristocracy, its cruelty, and its irrationality than for its material destruction of civilian life and its threat to national survival. . . .

During the last quarter of the nineteenth century governments became very receptive to an influential group that exalted war, the military virtues, and national expansion. In a kind of reversion to preindustrial attitudes and in reaction to the rising spirit of bourgeois liberal pacifism, this movement extolled international conflict and war as instruments of progress and expressed a strong preference for "total" war and the all-out offensive in contrast to unheroic and inconclusive limited wars. But it is important to note that this glorification of war and the war system still assumed that war was either so quick and decisive as to be moderate in its destructiveness or else so intense as to be increasingly rare. . . .

The romanticization of the military ethic reached its ultimate political expression in imperialism, rationalized by the Darwinian doctrine of the survival of the fittest through constant struggle. Yet political Darwinism was really the dying, though vociferous, gasp of laissez faire in international theory. While the militant spirit continued to grow more popular and vocal, the liberal opposition to war and power politics also grew stronger. By the beginning of the twentieth century, the organized peace movement, now appealing directly to governments, had become a powerful voice in political life and diplomacy — witness the two Hague disarmament conferences and the active concern of governments with arbitration treaties. The argument about war's wastefulness and irrationality (by then called "obsolescence") had gained new force with the spectacular advance of industrialism and commerce and the growing interdependence of military preparedness and the civilian economy.

To be sure, on the eve of World War I public spokesmen could still rattle the national sword with an exuberant spirit of military adventure and glory without being considered eccentric or evil. The patriotic thirst for military pageantry and excitement reached its height. Nations could face war with unabashed crusading zeal, exulting in the prospect and then in the reality with a passion more intense than was ever attained in the real Crusades. Yet this was probably the final spasm of massive military enthusiasm in the advanced democratic states. World War I killed the romance in war — except in a tragic or personal sense — and destroyed man's confidence in the beneficence of military laissez faire. The Fascist glorification of war was an evil aberration and seemed so at the time.

One should not depreciate the practical significance of the spreading popular aversion to force and the declining legitimacy of acquisitive war, which has been voiced so conspicuously since World War I, simply because of the continuing discrepancy between the ideal and reality of international politics. The widespread revulsion against the Religious Wars and the Napoleonic Wars probably had more to do with the moderation of war and politics in the eighteenth century and the resolution of crises short of war in the nineteenth than any of the so-called objective factors of international politics. Similarly, the widespread revulsion against war, international laissez faire, and military preparedness after World War I had a decisive impact upon international order. Its impact, unfortunately, was largely negative because it was accompanied by an aversion to the calculated management of force as an instrument of policy.

In the nuclear age preoccupation with the avoidance of war between nuclear powers and their allies has tempered the aversion to war with a novel respect for deterrence and the contrived control of force. It remains to be seen whether it has also created a more stable international order, or only the complacent illusion of self-sustaining order that has eventually proved the nemesis of every other period of equilibrium.

Deterrence and Defense

GLENN H. SNYDER

National security still remains an "ambiguous symbol," as one scholar described it almost a decade ago.[1] Certainly it has grown more ambiguous as a result of the startling advances since then in nuclear and weapons technology, and the advent of nuclear parity between the United States and the Soviet Union. Besides such technological complications, doctrine and thought about the role of force in international politics have introduced additional complexities. We now have, at least in embryonic form, theories of limited war, of deterrence, of "tactical" vs. "strategic" uses of nuclear weapons, of "retaliatory" vs. "counterforce" strategies in all-out war, of "limited retaliation," of the mechanics of threat and commitment-making, of "internal war," "protracted conflict," and the like. Above all, the idea of the "balance of terror" has begun to mature, but its relation to the older concept of the "balance of power" is still not clear. We have had a great intellectual ferment in the strategic realm, which of course is all to the good. What urgently remains to be done is to tie together all of these concepts into a coherent framework of theory so that the end-goal of national security may become less ambiguous, and so that the military means available for pursuance of this goal may be accumulated, organized, and used more efficiently. This book can claim to make only a start in this direction.

The central theoretical problem in the field of national security policy is to clarify and distinguish between the two central concepts of *deterrence* and *defense*. Essentially, deterrence means discouraging the enemy from taking military action by posing for him a

From *Deterrence and Defense: Toward a Theory of National Security* by Glenn H. Snyder, pp. 3–16, 31, 33–40, 50. Copyright © 1961 by Princeton University Press for the Center of International Studies, Princeton University. Reprinted by permission of Princeton University Press. Portions of the text and some footnotes have been omitted.

[1] Arnold Wolfers, " 'National Security' as an Ambiguous Symbol," *Political Science Quarterly*, Vol. LXVII, No. 4 (December 1952), pp. 481ff.

prospect of cost and risk outweighing his prospective gain. Defense means reducing our own prospective costs and risks in the event that deterrence fails. Deterrence works on the enemy's *intentions;* the *deterrent value* of military forces is their effect in reducing the likelihood of enemy military moves. Defense reduces the enemy's *capability* to damage or deprive us; the *defense value* of military forces is their effect in mitigating the adverse consequences for us of possible enemy moves, whether such consequences are counted as losses of territory or war damage. The concept of "defense value," therefore, is broader than the mere capacity to hold territory, which might be called "denial capability." Defense value is denial capability plus capacity to alleviate war damage.

It is a commonplace, of course, to say that the primary objectives of national security policy are to deter enemy attacks and to defend successfully, at minimum cost, against those attacks which occur. It is less widely recognized that different types of military force contribute in differing proportions to these two objectives. Deterrence does not vary directly with our capacity for fighting wars effectively and cheaply; a particular set of forces might produce strong deterrent effects and not provide a very effective denial and damage-alleviating capability. Conversely, forces effective for defense might be less potent deterrents than other forces which were less efficient for holding territory and which might involve extremely high war costs if used.

One reason why the periodic "great debates" about national security policy have been so inconclusive is that the participants often argue from different premises — one side from the point of view of deterrence, and the other side from the point of view of defense. For instance, in the famous "massive retaliation" debate of 1954, the late Secretary of State Dulles and his supporters argued mainly that a capacity for massive retaliation would deter potential Communist mischief, but they tended to ignore the consequences should deterrence fail. The critics, on the other hand, stressed the dire consequences should the threat of massive retaliation fail to deter and tended to ignore the possibility that it might work. The opposing arguments never really made contact because no one explicitly recognized that considerations of reducing the probability of war and mitigating its consequences must be evaluated simultaneously, that the possible consequences of a failure of deterrence are more or less important depending on the presumed likelihood of deterrence. Many other examples could be cited.

Perhaps the crucial difference between deterrence and defense is that deterrence is primarily a peacetime objective, while defense is a wartime value. Deterrent value and defense value are directly enjoyed in different time periods. We enjoy the deterrent value of our military forces prior to the enemy's aggressive move; we enjoy defense value after the enemy move has already been made, although we indirectly profit from defense capabilities in advance of war through our knowledge that if the enemy attack occurs we have the means of mitigating its consequences. The crucial point is that *after* the enemy's attack takes place, our military forces perform different functions and yield wholly different values than they did as deterrents prior to the attack. As deterrents they engaged in a psychological battle — dissuading the enemy from attacking by attempting to confront him with a prospect of costs greater than his prospective gain. After the enemy begins his attack, while the psychological or deterrent aspect does not entirely disappear, it is partly supplanted by another purpose: to resist the enemy's onslaught in order to minimize *our* losses or perhaps maximize *our* gains, not only with regard to the future balance of power, but also in terms of intrinsic or non-power values. That combination of forces which appeared to be the optimum one from the point of view of deterrence might turn out to be far inferior to some other combination from the point of view of defense should deterrence fail. In short, maximizing the enemy's cost expectancy may not always be consistent with minimizing our own. Thus we must measure the value of our military forces on two yardsticks, and we must find some way of combining their value on *both* yardsticks, in order accurately to gauge their aggregate worth or "utility" and to make intelligent choices among the various types of forces available.

Before launching into a theoretical analysis of the concepts of deterrence and defense, it may be useful to present a sampling of policy issues involving a need to choose between deterrence and defense; the examples will be treated in more detail in subsequent chapters.

EXAMPLES OF CHOICES AND CONFLICTS BETWEEN DETERRENCE AND DEFENSE

A strategic retaliatory air force sufficient only to wreak minimum "unacceptable" damage on Soviet cities — to destroy, say, 20 cities — after this force has been decimated by a surprise Soviet nuclear attack, would have great value for deterring such a surprise attack and might be an adequate deterrent against that contingency. But if deterrence were to fail and the Soviet attack took place, it would then not be rational to *use* such a minimum force in massive retaliation against Soviet cities, since this would only stimulate the Soviets to inflict further damage upon us and would contribute nothing to our "winning the war." If we are interested in defense — i.e., in winning the war and in minimizing the damage to us — as well as in deterrence, we may wish to have (if technically feasible) a much larger force and probably one of different composition — a force which can strike effectively at the enemy's remaining forces (thus reducing our own costs) and, further, either by actual attacks or the threat of attacks, force the enemy to surrender or at least to give up his territorial gains.

The threat of massive nuclear retaliation against a Soviet major ground attack in Western Europe may continue to provide considerable deterrence against such an attack, even if actually to carry out the threat would be irrational because of the enormous costs we would suffer from Soviet counterretaliation. Strategic nuclear weapons do not provide a rational means of defense in Western Europe unless they not only can stop the Russian ground advance but also, by "counterforce" strikes, can reduce to an acceptable level the damage we would suffer in return. We may not have this capability now and it may become altogether infeasible as the Soviets develop their missile technology. For a means of rational defense, therefore, NATO may need enough ground forces to hold Europe against a full-scale attack by Soviet ground forces. This does not mean, however, that we necessarily must maintain ground forces of this size. If we think the probability of attack is low enough, we may decide to continue relying on nuclear deterrence primarily, even though it does not provide a rational means of defense. In other words, we might count on the Soviet uncertainties about whether or not nuclear retaliation is rational for us, and about how rational we are, to inhibit the Soviets from attacking in the face of the terrible damage they *know* they would suffer if they guessed wrong.

An attempt to build an effective counterforce capability, in order to have both a rational nuclear defense and a more credible nuclear deterrent against ground attack in Europe, might work against the *deterrence* of direct nuclear attack on the United States. Since such a force, by definition, would be able to eliminate all but a small fraction of the Soviet strategic nuclear forces if it struck first, the Soviets might, in some circumstances, fear a surprise attack and be led to strike first themselves in order to forestall it.

Tactical nuclear weapons in the hands of NATO forces in Europe have considerable deterrent value because they increase the enemy's cost expectation beyond what it would be if these forces were equipped only with conventional weapons. This is true not only because the tactical weapons themselves can inflict high costs on the enemy's forces, but also because their use (or an enemy "preemptive" strike against them) would sharply raise the probability that the war would spiral to all-out dimensions. But the defense value of tactical nuclear weapons against conventional attack is comparatively low against an enemy who also possesses them, because their use presumably would be offset by the enemy's use of them against our forces, and because in using such weapons we would be incurring much greater costs and risks than if we had responded conventionally.

For deterrence, it might be desirable to render automatic a response which the enemy recognizes as being costly for us, and communicate the fact of such automation to the enemy, thus reducing his doubts that we would actually choose to make this response when the occasion for it arose. For example, a tactical nuclear response to conventional aggression in Europe may be made semi-automatic by thoroughly orienting NATO plans, organization, and strategy around this response, thus increasing the difficulty of following a non-nuclear strategy in case of a Soviet challenge. But such automation would not be desirable for defense, which would require flexibility and freedom to choose the least costly action in the light of circumstances at the time of the attack.

The Continental European attitude toward NATO strategy is generally ambivalent on the question of deterrence vs. defense; there is fear that with the Soviet acquisition of a substantial nuclear and missile capability, the willingness of the United States to invoke massive retaliation is declining, and that therefore the deterrent to aggression has weakened. Yet the Europeans do not embrace the logical consequence of this fear: the need to build up an adequate capacity to defend Europe on the ground. A more favored alternative, at least in France, is the acquisition of an independent strategic nuclear capability. But when European governments project their imaginations forward to the day when the enemy's divisions cross their borders, do they really envisage themselves shooting off their few missiles against an enemy who would surely obliterate them in return? One doubts that they do, but this is not to say that it is irrational for them to acquire such weapons; they might be successful as a deterrent because of Soviet uncertainty as to whether they would be used, and Soviet unwillingness to incur the risk of their being used.

Further examples easily come to mind. For the sake of deterrence in Europe, we might wish to deploy the forces there as if they intended to respond to an attack with nuclear weapons; but this might not be the optimum deployment for defense once the attack has occurred, if the least-cost defense is a conventional one. For deterrence of limited aggressions in Asia, it might be best to deploy troops on the spot as a "plate-glass window." But for the most efficient and flexible defense against such contingencies, troops might better be concentrated in a central reserve, with transport facilities for moving them quickly to a threatened area.

As Bernard Brodie has written,[2] if the object of our strategic air forces is only deterrence, there is little point in developing "clean" bombs; since deterrence is to be effected by the threat of dire punishment, the dirtier the better. But if we also wish to minimize our own costs once the war has begun, we might wish to use bombs producing minimum fall-out, to encourage similar restraint in the enemy.

For deterrence, it might be desirable to disperse elements of the Strategic Air Command to civilian airfields, thus increasing the number of targets which the enemy must hit if he is to achieve the necessary attrition of our retaliatory power by his first strike. However, this expedient might greatly increase the population damage we would suffer in the enemy's first strike, since most civilian airfields are located near large cities, assuming that the enemy would otherwise avoid hitting cities.

THE TECHNOLOGICAL REVOLUTION

The need to *choose* between deterrence and defense is largely the result of the development of nuclear and thermonuclear weapons and long-range airpower. Prior to these developments, the three primary functions of military force — to *punish* the enemy, to *deny* him territory (or to take it from him), and to *mitigate damage* to oneself — were embodied, more or less, in the same weapons. Deterrence was accomplished (to the extent that military capabilities were the instruments of deterrence) either by convincing the prospective aggressor that his territorial aim was likely to be frustrated, or by posing for him a prospect of intolerable cost, or both, but both of these deterrent functions were performed by the *same* forces. Moreover, these same forces were also the instruments of defense if deterrence failed.

Long-range airpower partially separated the function of punishment from the function of contesting the control of territory, by making possible the assault of targets far to the rear whose relation to the land battle might be quite tenuous. Nuclear weapons vastly increased the relative importance of prospective *cost* in deterring the enemy and reduced (relatively) the importance of frustrating his aggressive enterprise. It is still true, of course, that a capacity to deny territory to the enemy, or otherwise to block his aims, may be a very efficient deterrent. And such denial *may* be accomplished by

[2] Bernard Brodie, *Strategy in the Missile Age,* Princeton: Princeton University Press, 1959, p. 295.

strategic nuclear means, though at high cost to the defender. But it is now conceivable that a prospective aggressor may be deterred, in some circumstances at least, solely or primarily by threatening and possessing the capability to inflict extreme punishment on his homeland assets and population, even though he may be superior in capabilities for contesting the control of territory. Nuclear powers must, therefore, exercise a conscious choice between the objectives of deterrence and defense, since the relative proportion of "punishment capacity" to "denial capacity" in their military establishments has become a matter of choice.

This is the most striking difference between nuclear and pre-nuclear strategy: the partial separation of the functions of pre-attack deterrence and post-attack defense, and the possibility that deterrence may now be accomplished by weapons which might have no rational use for defense should deterrence fail.

DETERRENCE

Deterrence, in one sense, is simply the negative aspect of political power; it is the power to dissuade as opposed to the power to coerce or compel. One deters another party from doing something by the implicit or explicit threat of applying some sanction if the forbidden act is performed, or by the promise of a reward if the act is not performed. Thus conceived, deterrence does not have to depend on military force. We might speak of deterrence by the threat of trade restrictions, for example. The promise of economic aid might deter a country from military action (or any action) contrary to one's own interests. Or we might speak of the deterrence of allies and neutrals as well as potential enemies — as Italy, for example, was deterred from fighting on the side of the Dual Alliance in World War I by the promise of substantial territorial gains. In short, deterrence may follow, first, from any form of control which one has over an opponent's present and prospective "value inventory"; secondly, from the communication of a credible threat or promise to decrease or increase that inventory; and, thirdly, from the opponent's degree of confidence that one intends to fulfill the threat or promise.

In an even broader sense, however, deterrence is a function of the *total* cost-gain expectations of the party to be deterred, and these may be affected by factors other than the apparent capability and intention of the deterrer to apply punishments or confer rewards. For example, an incipient aggressor may be inhibited by his own conscience, or, more likely, by the prospect of losing moral standing, and hence political standing, with uncommitted countries. Or, in the specific case of the Soviet Union, he may fear that war will encourage unrest in, and possibly dissolution of, his satellite empire,

and perhaps disaffection among his own population. He may anticipate that his aggression would bring about a tighter welding of the
Western alliance or stimulate a degree of mobilization in the West
which would either reduce his own security or greatly increase the
cost of maintaining his position in the arms race. It is also worth
noting that the benchmark or starting point for the potential aggressor's calculation of costs and gains from military action is not his
existing value inventory, but the extent to which he expects that inventory to be changed if he refrains from initiating military action.
Hence, the common observation that the Russians are unlikely to
undertake overt military aggression because their chances are so
good for making gains by "indirect" peaceful means. Conceivably
the Soviets might attack the United States, even though they foresaw greater costs than gains, if the alternative of not attacking
seemed to carry within it a strong possibility that the United States
would strike them first and, in doing so, inflict greater costs on the
Soviet Union than it could by means of retaliation after the Soviets
had struck first. In a (very abstract) nutshell, the potential aggressor presumably is deterred from a military move not simply when
his expected cost exceeds his expected gain, but when the net gain
is less or the net loss is more than he can expect if he refrains from
the move. But this formulation must be qualified by the simple fact
of inertia: deliberately to shift from a condition of peace to a condition of war is an extremely momentous decision, involving incal-
culable consequences, and a government is not likely to make this
decision unless it foresees a very large advantage in doing so. The
great importance of *uncertainty* in this context will be discussed
below.

In a broad sense, deterrence operates during war as well as prior
to war. It could be defined as a process of influencing the enemy's
intentions, whatever the circumstances, violent or non-violent. Typically, the outcome of wars has not depended simply on the clash of
physical capabilities. The losing side usually accepts defeat somewhat before it has lost its physical ability to continue fighting. It is
deterred from continuing the war by a realization that continued
fighting can only generate additional costs without hope of compensating gains, this expectation being largely the consequence of the
previous application of force by the dominant side. In past wars,
such deterrence usually has been characteristic of the terminal
stages. However, in the modern concept of limited war, the intentions factor is more prominent and pervasive; force may be threatened and used partly, or even primarily, as a bargaining instrument
to persuade the opponent to accept terms of settlement or to observe
certain limitations. Deterrence in war is most sharply illustrated in

proposals for a strategy of limited retaliation, in which initial strikes, in effect, would be *threats* of further strikes to come, designed to deter the enemy from further fighting. In warfare limited to conventional weapons or tactical nuclear weapons, the strategic nuclear forces held in reserve by either side may constitute a deterrent against the other side's expanding the intensity of its war effort. Also, limited wars may be fought in part with an eye to deterring future enemy attacks by convincing the enemy of one's general willingness to fight.

The above observations were intended to suggest the broad scope of the concept of deterrence, its non-limitation to military factors, and its fundamental affinity to the idea of political power. In the discussion following, we shall use the term in a narrower sense, to mean the discouragement of the *initiation* of military aggression by the threat (implicit or explicit) of applying military force in response to the aggression. We shall assume that when deterrence fails and war begins, the attacked party is no longer "deterring" but rather "defending." Deterrence in war and deterrence, by military action, of subsequent aggressions will be considered as aspects of defense and will be treated later in this chapter.

The logic of deterrence. The object of military deterrence is to reduce the probability of enemy military attacks, by posing for the enemy a sufficiently likely prospect that he will suffer a net loss as a result of the attack, or at least a higher net loss or lower net gain than would follow from his not attacking. If we postulate two contending states, an "aggressor" (meaning potential aggressor) and a "deterrer," with other states which are objects of conflict between these two, the probability of any particular attack by the aggressor is the resultant of essentially four factors which exist in his "mind." All four taken together might be termed the aggressor's "risk calculus." They are (1) his valuation of his war objectives; (2) the cost which he expects to suffer as a result of various possible responses by the deterrer; (3) the probability of various responses, including "no response"; and (4) the probability of winning the objectives with each possible response. We shall assume, for simplicity's sake, that the deterrer's "response" refers to the deterrer's entire strategy of action throughout the war precipitated by the aggressor's move — i.e., not only the response to the initial aggressive move, but also to all subsequent moves by the aggressor. Thus the aggressor's estimate of costs and gains is a "whole war" estimate, depending on his image of the deterrer's entire sequence of moves up to the termination of the war, as well as on his own strategic plans for conducting the war, plans which may be contingent on what moves are made by the deterrer during the war.

Obviously, we are dealing here with factors which are highly subjective and uncertain, not subject to exact measurement, and not commensurate except in an intuitive way. Nevertheless, these are the basic factors which the potential aggressor must weigh in determining the probable costs and gains of his contemplated venture.

Certain generalizations can be made about the relationship among these factors. Factor 3 in the aggressor's calculus represents the "credibility" of various possible responses by the deterrer. But credibility is only one factor: it should not be equated with the deterrent *effectiveness* of a possible or threatened response, which is a function of all four factors — i.e., the net cost or gain which a response promises, discounted by the probability (credibility) of its being applied. An available response which is very low in credibility might be sufficient to deter if it poses a very severe sanction (e.g., massive retaliation) or if the aggressor's prospective gain carries very little value for him. Or a threatened response that carries a rather high credibility but poses only moderate costs for the aggressor — e.g., a conventional response, or nuclear retaliation after the aggressor has had the advantage of the first strategic strike — may not deter if the aggressor places a high value on his objective and anticipates a good chance of attaining it.

The credibility factor deserves special attention because it is in terms of this component that the risk calculus of the aggressor "interlocks" with that of the deterrer. The deterrer's risk calculus is similar to that of the aggressor. If the deterrer is rational, his response to aggression will be determined (within the limits, of course, of the military forces he disposes) largely by four factors: (1) his valuation of the territorial objective and of the other intangible gains (e.g., moral satisfaction) which he associates with a given response; (2) the estimated costs of fighting; (3) the probability of successfully holding the territorial objective and other values at stake; and (4) the change in the probability of future enemy attacks on other objectives which would follow from various responses. Variations on, and marginal additions to, these factors may be imagined, but these four are the essential ones. The deterrer will select the response which minimizes his expectation of cost or maximizes his expectation of gain. (As in the case of the aggressor's calculus, we assume that the deterrer's estimates of cost and gain are "whole war" estimates — i.e., the aggregate effects not only of the deterrer's initial response, but also of all the aggressor's counter-moves, combined with the deterrer's counter-countermoves, over the entire progress of the war.) The credibility of various possible responses by the deterrer depends on the aggressor's image of the deterrer's risk calculus — i.e., of the latter's net costs and gains from each response — as well as on the aggressor's assessment of the deterrer's capacity to act rationally.

The aggressor, of course, is not omniscient with respect to the deterrer's estimates of cost and gain. Even the deterrer will be unable to predict in advance of the attack how he will visualize his cost-gain prospects and, hence, exactly what response he will choose once the aggression is under way. (Witness the United States response to the North Korean attack in 1950, which was motivated by values which apparently did not become clear to the decision-makers until the actual crisis was upon them.) Nor can the aggressor be sure the deterrer will act rationally according to his own cost-gain predictions. Because of these uncertainties, the aggressor's estimate of credibility cannot be precise. More than one response will be possible, and the best the aggressor can do is attempt to guess how the deterrer will visualize his gains and losses consequent upon each response, and from this guess arrive at a judgment about the likelihood or probability of each possible response.

The deterrer evaluates the *effectiveness* of his deterrent posture by attempting to guess the values of the four factors in the aggressor's risk calculus. In estimating the credibility factor, he attempts to guess how the aggressor is estimating the factors in *his* (the deterrer's) calculus. He arrives at some judgment as to whether the aggressor is likely to expect a net cost or net gain from the aggressive move and, using this judgment and his degree of confidence in it as a basis, he determines the probability of aggression. Happily, the spiral of "guesses about the other's guesses" seems to stop here. In other words, the aggressor's decision whether or not to attack is not in turn affected by his image of the deterrer's estimate of the likelihood of attack. He knows that once the attack is launched the deterrer will select the response which promises him the least cost or greatest gain — at that point, the deterrer's previous calculations about "deterrence" of that attack become irrelevant.

Denial vs. punishment. It is useful to distinguish between deterrence which results from capacity to deny territorial gains to the enemy, and deterrence by the threat and capacity to inflict nuclear punishment. Denial capabilities — typically, conventional ground, sea, and tactical air forces — deter chiefly by their effect on the fourth factor in the aggressor's calculus: his estimate of the probability of gaining his objective. Punishment capabilities — typically, strategic nuclear power for either massive or limited retaliation — act primarily on the second factor, the aggressor's estimate of possible costs, and may have little effect on his chances for territorial gain. Of course, this distinction is not sharp or absolute: a "denial" response, especially if it involves the use of nuclear weapons tactically, can mean high direct costs, plus the risk that the war may get out of hand and ultimately involve severe nuclear punishment for both sides. This prospect of cost and risk may exert a significant deterring effect. A "punishment" response, if powerful enough, may foreclose territorial gains, and limited reprisals may be able to force a settlement short of complete conquest of the territorial objective. However, there are some differences worth noting between these two types or strategies of deterrence.

Apart from their differential impact on the cost and gain elements of the aggressor's calculations, the two types of response are likely to differ also in their credibility or probability of application. As a response to all-out nuclear attack on the deterrer, the application of punishment will be highly credible. But for lesser challenges, such as a conventional attack on an ally, a threat to inflict nuclear punishment normally will be less credible than a threat to fight a "denial" action — assuming, of course, that denial capabilities are available. While the making of a *threat* of nuclear punishment may be desirable and rational, its *fulfillment* is likely to seem irrational after the aggressor has committed his forces, since punishment alone may not be able to hold the territorial objective and will stimulate the aggressor to make counterreprisals. The deterrer therefore has a strong incentive to renege on his threat. Realizing this in advance, the aggressor may not think the threat a very credible one. A threat of denial action will seem more credible on two counts: it is less costly for the deterrer and it may be effective in frustrating the aggressor's aims, or at least in reducing his gains. A denial response is more likely than reprisal action to promise a rational means of *defense* in case deterrence fails; this consideration supports its credibility as a deterrent.

A related difference is that the threat of denial action is likely to be appraised by the aggressor in terms of the deterrer's *capabilities;* threats of nuclear punishment require primarily a judgment of *intent.* It is fairly certain that the deterrer will fight a threatened denial action if he has appropriate forces;[3] the essential question for the aggressor, therefore, is whether these forces are strong enough to prevent him from making gains. In the case of nuclear reprisals, however, the capability to inflict unacceptable punishment is likely to be unquestioned, at least for large nuclear powers; here the aggressor must attempt to look into the mind of the deterrer and guess whether the will to apply punishment exists. Thus a denial threat is

[3]It is possible that the aggressor may be able to deter "denial" resistance by theatening to take punitive action if resistance occurs. This is perhaps most feasible with respect to allies of the country attacked whose troops are not deployed on the territory of the victim.

much more calculable for the aggressor than a reprisal threat —
assuming that a comparison of military capabilities is easier than
mind-reading. This may make a denial strategy the more powerful
deterrent of the two if the deterrer has strong denial forces; but if
he obviously does not have enough ground and tactical forces to
block conquest, the threat may be weaker than a nuclear reprisal
threat. Even if there is doubt in the aggressor's mind that the reprisals will be carried out, these doubts may be offset by the possible severity of his punishment if he miscalculates and the threat
is fulfilled. . . .

DEFENSE[4]

The deterrer, in choosing his optimum military and threat posture
in advance of war, must estimate not only the effectiveness of that
posture for deterrence, but also the consequences for himself should
deterrence fail. In short, he is interested in defense as well as in
deterrence; his security is a function of both of these elements.
Capabilities and threats which produce a high level of deterrence
may not yield a high degree of security because they promise very
high costs and losses for the deterrer should war occur. . . .

Strategic value and deterrent value. Much of the inconclusive-
ness of the recurring "great debates" about military policy might
be avoided if the concept of "strategic value" could be clarified and
clearly separated from the deterrent effects of military action. The
strategic value of a particular piece of territory is the effect which its
loss would have on increasing the enemy's *capability* to make various future moves, and on decreasing our own capacity to resist
further attacks. The deterrent value of defending or attempting to
defend that piece of territory is the effect of the defense on the
enemy's *intention* to make future moves. The failure to recognize
this distinction contributed to the apparent about-face in United
States policy toward South Korea, when we decided to intervene
after the North Korean attack in June 1950. Earlier, the Joint Chiefs
of Staff had declared that South Korea had no strategic value — apparently meaning that its loss would have no significant effect on
the U.S. capacity to fight a general war with the Soviet Union. This
determination was thought to justify — or at least was used as a
rationalization for — the withdrawal of U.S. combat forces from

---

[4] The reader is reminded that I am using the word "defense" in a
rather special sense, which is narrower than one ordinary usage of the
term and broader than another. Obviously it is narrower than the usage
which makes "defense" synonymous with all military preparedness. It
is broader, however, than "capacity to hold territory in case of attack,"
which I would prefer to call "denial capability."

the Korean peninsula in 1948 and 1949. Secretary of State Dean Acheson strengthened the impression that "no strategic value" meant "no value" when, in a speech early in 1950, he outlined a U.S. "defense perimeter" in the Far East which excluded Korea. Then when the North Koreans, perhaps encouraged by these high-level U.S. statements, attacked in June 1950, the United States government suddenly discovered that it had a deterrent interest, as well as strong political and intrinsic interests, in coming to the rescue of South Korea. The dominant theme in the discussions leading up to the decision to intervene was that if the Communists were "appeased" this time, they would be encouraged to make further attacks on other areas.[5] The chief motive behind the intervention was to prevent such encouragement from taking place, and positively to deter similar attempts in the future.

Another case in point was the debate about the desirability of a United States commitment to defend the Chinese offshore islands of Quemoy and Matsu. Those who took the negative in this debate stressed that these two small islands held no "strategic value" for the United States, that they were not "vital" to the defense of Formosa,

---

[5] As former President Truman has stated: "Our allies and friends abroad were informed through our diplomatic representatives that it was our feeling that it was essential to the maintenance of peace that this armed aggression against a free nation be met firmly. We let it be known that we considered the Korean situation vital as a symbol of the strength and determination of the West. Firmness now would be the only way to deter new actions in other portions of the world. Not only in Asia but in Europe, the Middle East, and elsewhere the confidence of peoples in countries adjacent to the Soviet Union would be very adversely affected, in our judgment, if we failed to take action to protect a country established under our auspices and confirmed in its freedom by action of the United Nations. If, however, the threat to South Korea was met firmly and successfully, it would add to our successes in Iran, Berlin and Greece a fourth success in opposition to the aggressive moves of the Communists. And each success, we suggested to our allies, was likely to add to the caution of the Soviets in undertaking new efforts of this kind. Thus the safety and prospects for peace of the free world would be increased." Harry S. Truman, *Years of Trial and Hope*, New York: Doubleday and Co., 1956, pp. 339–40.

The primary political value of the intervention, as U.S. decision-makers saw it, was that it would give other free nations confidence that they could count on U.S. aid in resisting aggression. The most salient intrinsic values were moral value in opposing the aggressive use of force, support for the "rule of law" in international affairs, support for the collective security system embodied in the United Nations Charter, and the special responsibility the United States felt for the Republic of Korea, whose government it had played a major role in establishing. "Support for the collective security system" of course had deterrent and political as well as moral overtones.

etc. Former Secretary of State Dean Acheson declared that the islands were not worth a single American life.[6] Administration spokesmen, on the other hand, emphasized the political and deterrent value of defending Quemoy and Matsu. President Eisenhower, for example, said that this country's allies "would be appalled if the United States were spinelessly to retreat before the threat of Sino-Soviet armed aggression."[7] Secretary of State Dulles asserted that the stakes were not "just some square miles of real estate," but the preservation of confidence in other countries — both allies and enemies — that the United States would resist aggression. It was better to meet the challenge at the beginning, Mr. Dulles said, than after "our friends become disheartened and our enemies overconfident and miscalculating."[8]

Power values are sometimes discussed in terms of the "falling domino" theory. According to this reasoning, if one objective is lost to the enemy, other areas contiguous to the first one inevitably will be lost as well, then still additional areas contiguous to these, etc., as a whole row of dominoes will fall when the first one is knocked over.[9] In its extreme form, the domino thesis would value any objective, no matter how small, as dearly as the value which the United States placed on the continued independence of all other non-Communist countries. Thus we should be as willing to fight for one place as another, since a failure to resist once inevitably means future losses. The important thing is to "draw a line" and resist violations of the line, whatever their dimensions and wherever and whenever they may occur.

The domino theory tends to overstate power values: since the enemy may have limited aims and may be satisfied with a small gain, his increase in capability from a single small conquest may not significantly shift the balance of capabilities in his favor, and the loss of single small areas may not have adverse political effects

[6] *New York Times,* October 3, 1958, p. 3.
[7] *Ibid.,* October 5, 1958, p. 1.
[8] *Ibid.,* September 26, 1958, p. 1.
[9] Apparently the domino theory was first given public expression by President Eisenhower on April 7, 1954, when he said, in reply to a request that he explain the strategic value of Indo-China to the United States: "You had a row of dominoes set up, and you knocked over the first one, and what would happen to the last one was the certainty that it would go over very quickly. So you could have a beginning of a disintegration that would have the most profound influences." The President then referred to "the possible sequence of events, the loss of Indo-China, of Burma, of Thailand, of the peninsula, and Indonesia following." *Ibid.,* April 8, 1954, p. 18.

among neutrals and allies.[10] Nevertheless, the domino image does highlight an important truth: the strategic and intrinsic value of the immediate territorial prize is not a sufficient criterion for evaluating the wisdom of resisting aggression, or for estimating the forces necessary for successful resistance. The enemy's possible ultimate objective must also be considered, as well as the effect of resistance in discouraging him from attempting further progress toward that objective, and in forestalling political changes among other countries which would tend to further that ultimate objective.

There is a relationship between the strategic, political, and intrinsic value which the enemy believes one attaches to a given objective, and the deterrent value which can be realized by responding to an attack on that objective. For example, a failure to resist effectively a Communist attack on the offshore islands of Quemoy and Matsu might not increase perceptibly the chances of Chinese Communist attacks on other non-Communist countries in Asia, if the Communists did not believe we placed a high intrinsic and strategic value on these islands. On the other hand, it could be argued that a determined and costly response to an attack on an objective which the enemy thinks means little to us in strategic and intrinsic terms is likely to give him greater pause with respect to his future aggressive intentions. Thus, if the objective is to "draw a line" to deter future aggression, perhaps the best place to draw it is precisely at places like Quemoy and Matsu. The enemy would reason that if the United States were willing to fight for a place of such trivial intrinsic and strategic value to itself, it must surely be willing to fight for other places of greater value. Thus, the deterrent value of defending any objective varies inversely with the enemy's perception of its value to us on other accounts. There is a further consideration: if it is thought necessary to fight a certain amount of war, or risk a certain amount of war, to convince the other side of our willingness to fight generally, what better place to do it than at places like Quemoy and Matsu, where it is least likely that the war will spiral to all-out dimensions?

Mutually shared expectations are extremely important in determining the deterrent value of military actions. The United States did not lose much in deterrent utility by failing to intervene in Hungary in 1956, because both sides regarded Hungary as part of

[10] It is hard to believe, for example, that a Communist Chinese conquest of Quemoy and Matsu would have reduced the confidence of the European allies in the willingness of the United States to defend Europe. The solidarity of NATO might have been weakened by a U.S. attempt to defend the islands.

the Communist camp. But a failure to defend Berlin would severely undermine the U.S. capability to deter future Communist incursions in Europe or elsewhere.

The consequences of enemy moves, and the defense value of forces for resisting them, are subject to modification by policy declarations. Threats and commitments may involve one's honor and prestige in a particular area or objective, and this involvement increases the deterrent, political, and intrinsic value of defending such places and the value of forces which are able to defend. Thus the adverse consequences of an unresisted Communist attack on Quemoy and Matsu were increased by the various official statements, including the Formosa Resolution passed by Congress, to the effect that these offshore islands were "related" to the defense of Formosa. But these consequences were not increased as much as they might have been, had the United States made an unequivocal commitment to defend the islands.

Of course, losses of power values through the loss of an ally or neutral to the enemy may be offset by increased mobilization of domestic resources. The cost of the additional mobilization required might be taken as a measure of the power value of the territory in question. Thus the defending power might ask itself: "If I let this piece of territory or this ally be taken over by the enemy, how many additional resources will I have to spend for military weapons to have the same degree of security I have been enjoying?"

Once war is entered into, consideration of deterrent possibilities may call for a different strategy than would be the case if we were interested only in the strategic and intrinsic values of the particular area attacked. If the latter were our only interest, our war aims might be limited to restoration of the *status quo ante;* deterrence of future aggressions, however, might dictate more ambitious aims. In the Korean War, for example, it is possible that if closer consideration had been given to deterrent benefits, the U.N. armies might have pushed on farther than they did — if not to the Yalu, then perhaps at least to the "narrow neck" of the Korean peninsula. The opportunity was not taken to show the Communists that their aggressions were likely to result in losses not only of manpower but also of territory; that in future limited wars they could not hope to end up at least where they started.

In general, we will be willing to suffer higher costs in fighting a limited war if deterrence is an objective than if it is not. In other words, it may be desirable to fight on longer and in the face of a higher cost expectancy if an important objective is to assure the enemy of our willingness to suffer costs in future contingencies.

The objective of deterrence may call for the use of different

weapons than would the simple objective of blocking enemy conquest of an area at least cost. Our use of nuclear weapons probably
would support the Communist estimate of our willingness to use
them in the future; and, conversely, to refrain from using them
when such use would be militarily advantageous would weaken that
estimate. However, as in the decision whether or not to fight at all,
the strategic and intrinsic value of the immediate objective is relevant to the deterrent effects: the use of nuclear weapons to defend
highly valued objectives might support but little the probability that
they would be used to meet lesser challenges;[11] the failure to use
them when the prize was small would not necessarily signal a reluctance to do so when the object of the conflict was vital.

Finally, for deterrent reasons it might be desirable to *attempt*
resistance against a particular limited enemy attack even though we
knew in advance that our resistance would fail. The purpose would
be to inform the enemy, for future reference, that although he could
expect to make gains from limited aggression in the future, these
gains could be had only at a price which (we hoped) the enemy
would not want to pay. Proposals for limited nuclear retaliation
against one or a few enemy cities in response to limited ground
aggression may draw on this kind of reasoning.

Of course, the concept of "deterrence by action" has no relevance
in determining the appropriate response to a direct thermonuclear
attack on the United States, or in valuing the forces for the response. In that event there would be no future contingencies which
would seem worth deterring or worrying about at all, compared with
the magnitude of the catastrophe which had already taken place.
The primary values would be intrinsic values associated with reducing war damage, perhaps limiting the enemy's territorial gains
in Eurasia, and preserving the independence of the United States
itself.[12]

Power values lost by the defender represent power values gained
by the attacker, although the values may not be equally important
to each side. For example, the Middle East has strategic value for
the United States because its geographic location and resources add

[11] On the other hand, any use of nuclear weapons would set a precedent. The symbolic or psychological barrier to their use which had
rested on their previous non-use would be eroded. The Russians might
believe, after they had been used once, that the probability of their use
in *any* future conflict had increased.

[12] We might, of course, attempt to "deter" the enemy from continuing
his attacks, thus reducing our war costs and perhaps preserving our independence and the essential fabric of our society, by a discriminating
use of the weapons we had left after absorbing a surprise attack, accompanied by appropriate bargaining tactics. . . .

significantly to the West's capacity to fight limited war in Europe and elsewhere, and because the area, in the hands of the Soviets, would increase the Soviets' capacity to fight such wars — because of its position athwart vital transportation routes if not because of its oil resources. Our strategic loss if the Middle East should fall under Communist control would be the sum of the deprivation to the West's future military capabilities and the increment to the Soviet capabilities. Similarly, the strategic gain to the Soviets would be the sum of their own direct gain in military resources plus the losses for the West.

It is less obvious that deterrent values also have this reciprocal character. When, by fighting in Korea, we demonstrated our willingness to defend free institutions in Asia, not only did we gain "deterrent value" with respect to other possible Communist moves in Asia; the Communists lost something analogous to it in their own value system. Presumably they became less confident that overt aggression could be attempted again without U.S. intervention. Their "expected value" from future aggressive moves declined perhaps below what it was before Korea, and certainly below what it would have been if the North Korean aggression had been unopposed by the United States.

When an aggressor state successfully completes a conquest, or has its demands satisfied short of war, its willingness in the future to make war, or to make demands at the risk of war, presumably is strengthened by the reduction of expected cost or risk which it perceives in such future moves. This reduction in the perceived chances of being opposed in the future we might label "expectational value," to differentiate it from "deterrent value," which is peculiarly associated with *status quo* powers. Deterrent and expectational values are in obverse relationship — i.e., when the defender loses deterrent value by failing to fight or to carry out a threat, the aggressor gains expectational value, and vice versa — although again the gain or loss may have a stronger psychological impact on one side than on the other, since the value in question is highly subjective.

This distinction is similar to Thomas Schelling's distinction between "compellent" and "deterrent" threats.[13] A compellent threat is used in an aggressive way; it is designed to persuade the opponent to give up some value. A deterrent threat, on the other hand, is intended to dissuade the opponent from initiating some positive action. A successful conquest would increase an aggressor's com-

[13]Thomas C. Schelling, *The Strategy of Conflict*, Cambridge: Harvard University Press, 1960, pp. 195–196.

pellent power with respect to other possible victims, especially if the fighting had included the use of nuclear weapons; other countries would lose deterrent power, since their psychological capacity to resist demands would be weakened by the aggressor's demonstration of willingness to risk or to undertake nuclear war.

Strategic gains by the Soviets might appear in their risk calculus as an increased probability that future attacks on other areas would be successful, or perhaps as a decreased expectation of cost in making future conquests. Gains in expectational value would appear as a decreased probability of resistance to future attacks, or perhaps as a reduced probability of a high-cost response by the defender or its allies. The aggregate of strategic gains and expectational gains produces an increase in "expected value" to be gained from future moves (or a reduction in "expected cost").

This might not always be the case if the consequence of a successful aggression were to stimulate an increased level of military mobilization by the United States and its allies and/or an increased determination to resist future attacks. Thus a successful limited attack might backfire and *reduce* the Soviets' strategic position as well as their expectational value, although of course they would retain whatever intrinsic values they had gained by their conquest. . . .

THE NEW BALANCE OF POWER

. . . The existence of a balance of power, or the capabilities requirements for balancing, can hardly be determined without attempting to look into the "mind" of the enemy. One might say that a subjective "balance of intentions" has become at least as important as the more objectively calculable "balance of capabilities."

A corollary of the increased relative importance of intentions is that methods of communicating intent have become more important *means* in the balancing process than they have been in the past. First, nations are becoming more sensitive to what they say to each other about their intentions; the psychological importance of threats and other declarations is on the increase. Secondly, the function of military forces themselves may be shifting in the direction of a demonstrative role: the signaling of future intentions to use force in order to influence the enemy's intentions, as opposed to being ready to use, or using, force simply as a physical means of conquest or denial. Hence the enhanced importance of *deterrence* in the modern balance of power as compared with *defense*. We are likely to see more imaginative and subtle uses of "force demonstration" in time of peace. . . . Warfare itself may in the future become less a raw physical collision of military forces and more a contest of wills, or a bargaining process, with military force being used largely to demonstrate one's willingness to raise the intensity of fighting, with the object of inducing the enemy to accept one's terms of settlement. While direct conflict or competition is going on at a low level of the spectrum of violence, selective force demonstrations using means appropriate to higher levels may take place as threats to "up the ante." . . .

The Diplomacy of Violence

THOMAS C. SCHELLING

The usual distinction between diplomacy and force is not merely in the instruments, words or bullets, but in the relation between adversaries — in the interplay of motives and the role of communication, understandings, compromise, and restraint. Diplomacy is bargaining; it seeks outcomes that, though not ideal for either party, are better for both than some of the alternatives. In diplomacy each party somewhat controls what the other wants, and can get more by compromise, exchange, or collaboration than by taking things in his own hands and ignoring the other's wishes. The bargaining can be polite or rude, entail threats as well as offers, assume a status quo or ignore all rights and privileges, and assume mistrust rather than trust. But whether polite or impolite, constructive or aggressive, respectful or vicious, whether it occurs among friends or antagonists and whether or not there is a basis for trust and goodwill, there must be some common interest, if only in the avoidance of mutual damage, and an awareness of the need to make the other party prefer an outcome acceptable to oneself.

With enough military force a country may not need to bargain.

Some things a country wants it can take, and some things it has it can keep, by sheer strength, skill, and ingenuity. It can do this *forcibly*, accommodating only to opposing strength, skill, and ingenuity and without trying to appeal to an enemy's wishes. Forcibly a country can repel and expel, penetrate and occupy, seize, exterminate, disarm and disable, confine, deny access, and directly frustrate intrusion or attack. It can, that is, if it has enough strength. "Enough" depends on how much an opponent has.

There is something else, though, that force can do. It is less military, less heroic, less impersonal, and less unilateral; it is uglier, and has received less attention in Western military strategy. In addition to seizing and holding, disarming and confining, penetrating and obstructing, and all that, military force can be used *to hurt*. In addition to taking and protecting things of value it can *destroy* value. In addition to weakening an enemy militarily it can cause an enemy plain suffering.

Pain and shock, loss and grief, privation and horror are always in some degree, sometimes in terrible degree, among the results of warfare; but in traditional military science they are incidental, they are not the object. If violence can be done incidentally, though, it can also be done purposely. The power to hurt can be counted among the most impressive attributes of military force.

Hurting, unlike forcible seizure or self-defense, is not unconcerned with the interest of others. It is measured in the suffering it can cause and the victims' motivation to avoid it. Forcible action will work against weeds or floods as well as against armies, but suffering requires a victim that can feel pain or has something to lose. To inflict suffering gains nothing and saves nothing directly; it can only make people behave to avoid it. The only purpose, unless sport or revenge, must be to influence somebody's behavior, to coerce his decision or choice. To be coercive, violence has to be anticipated. And it has to be avoidable by accommodation. The power to hurt is bargaining power. To exploit it is diplomacy — vicious diplomacy, but diplomacy.

THE CONTRAST OF BRUTE FORCE WITH COERCION

There is a difference between taking what you want and making someone give it to you, between fending off assault and making someone afraid to assault you, between holding what people are trying to take and making them afraid to take it, between losing what someone can forcibly take and giving it up to avoid risk or damage. It is the difference between defense and deterrence, between brute force and intimidation, between conquest and blackmail, between action and threats. It is the difference between the unilateral, "undiplomatic" recourse to strength, and coercive diplomacy based on the power to hurt.

The contrasts are several. The purely "military" or "undiplomatic" recourse to forcible action is concerned with enemy strength, not enemy interests; the coercive use of the power to hurt, though, is the very exploitation of enemy wants and fears. And brute strength is usually measured relative to enemy strength, the one directly opposing the other, while the power to hurt is typically not reduced by the enemy's power to hurt in return. Opposing strengths may cancel each other, pain and grief do not. The willingness to hurt, the credibility of a threat, and the ability to exploit the power to hurt will indeed depend on how much the adversary can hurt in return; but there is little or nothing about an adversary's pain or grief that directly reduces one's own. Two sides cannot both overcome each other with superior strength; they may both be able to hurt each other. With strength they can dispute objects of value; with sheer violence they can destroy them.

And brute force succeeds when it is used, whereas the power to hurt is most successful when held in reserve. It is the *threat* of damage, or of more damage to come, that can make someone yield or comply. It is *latent* violence that can influence someone's choice — violence that can still be withheld or inflicted, or that a victim believes can be withheld or inflicted. The threat of pain tries to structure someone's motives, while brute force tries to overcome his strength. Unhappily, the power to hurt is often communicated by some performance of it. Whether it is sheer terroristic violence to induce an irrational response, or cool premeditated violence to persuade somebody that you mean it and may do it again, it is not the pain and damage itself but its influence on somebody's behavior that matters. It is the expectation of *more* violence that gets the wanted behavior, if the power to hurt can get it at all.

To exploit a capacity for hurting and inflicting damage one needs to know what an adversary treasures and what scares him and one needs the adversary to understand what behavior of his will cause the violence to be inflicted and what will cause it to be withheld. The victim has to know what is wanted, and he may have to be assured of what is not wanted. The pain and suffering have to appear *contingent* on his behavior; it is not alone the threat that is effective — the threat of pain or loss if he fails to comply — but the corresponding assurance, possibly an implicit one, that he can avoid the pain or loss if he does comply. The prospect of certain death may stun him, but it gives him no choice.

Coercion by threat of damage also requires that our interests and our opponent's not be absolutely opposed. If his pain were our greatest delight and our satisfaction his greatest woe, we would just proceed to hurt and to frustrate each other. It is when his pain gives us little or no satisfaction compared with what he can do for us, and the action or inaction that satisfies us costs him less than the pain we can cause, that there is room for coercion. Coercion requires finding a bargain, arranging for him to be better off doing what we want — worse off not only doing what we want — when he takes the threatened penalty into account.

It is this capacity for pure damage, pure violence, that is usually associated with the most vicious labor disputes, with racial disorders, with civil uprisings and their suppression, with racketeering. It is also the power to hurt rather than brute force that we use in dealing with criminals; we hurt them afterward, or threaten to, for their misdeeds rather than protect ourselves with cordons of electric wires, masonry walls, and armed guards. Jail, of course, can be either forcible restraint or threatened privation; if the object is to keep criminals out of mischief by confinement, success is measured by how many of them are gotten behind bars, but if the object is to *threaten* privation, success will be measured by how few have to be put behind bars and success then depends on the subject's understanding of the consequences. Pure damage is what a car threatens when it tries to hog the road or to keep its rightful share, or to go first through an intersection. A tank or a bulldozer can force its way regardless of others' wishes; the rest of us have to threaten damage, usually mutual damage, hoping the other driver values his car or his limbs enough to give way, hoping he sees us, and hoping he is in control of his own car. The threat of pure damage will not work against an unmanned vehicle.

This difference between coercion and brute force is as often in the intent as in the instrument. To hunt down Comanches and to exterminate them was brute force; to raid their villages to make them behave was coercive diplomacy, based on the power to hurt. The pain and loss to the Indians might have looked much the same one way as the other; the difference was one of purpose and effect. If Indians were killed because they were in the way, or somebody wanted their land, or the authorities despaired of making them behave and could not confine them and decided to exterminate them, that was pure unilateral force. If *some* Indians were killed to make *other* Indians behave, that was coercive violence — or intended to be, whether or not it was effective. The Germans at Verdun perceived themselves to be chewing up hundreds of thousands of French soldiers in a gruesome "meatgrinder." If the purpose was to eliminate a military obstacle — the French infantryman, viewed as a military "asset" rather than as a warm human being — the offensive at Verdun was a unilateral exercise of military force. If instead the object was to make the loss of young men — not of impersonal "effectives," but of sons, husbands, fathers, and the pride of French manhood — so anguishing as to be unendurable, to make surrender a welcome relief and to spoil the foretaste of an Allied victory, then it was an exercise in coercion, in applied violence, intended to offer relief upon accommodation. And of course, since any use of force tends to be brutal, thoughtless, vengeful, or plain obstinate, the motives themselves can be mixed and confused. The fact that heroism and brutality can be either coercive diplomacy or a contest in pure strength does not promise that the distinction will be made, and the strategies enlightened by the distinction, every time some vicious enterprise gets launched.

The contrast between brute force and coercion is illustrated by two alternative strategies attributed to Genghis Khan. Early in his career he pursued the war creed of the Mongols: the vanquished can never be the friends of the victors, their death is necessary for the victors' safety. This was the unilateral extermination of a menace or a liability. The turning point of his career, according to Lynn Montross, came later when he discovered how to use his power to hurt for diplomatic ends. "The great Khan, who was not inhibited by the usual mercies, conceived the plan of forcing captives — women, children, aged fathers, favorite sons — to march ahead of his army as the first potential victims of resistance."[1] Live captives have often proved more valuable than enemy dead; and the technique discovered by the Khan in his maturity remains contemporary. North Koreans and Chinese were reported to have quartered prisoners of war near strategic targets to inhibit bombing attacks by United Nations aircraft. Hostages represent the power to hurt in its purest form.

COERCIVE VIOLENCE IN WARFARE

This distinction between the power to hurt and the power to seize or hold forcibly is important in modern war, both big war and little war, hypothetical war and real war. For many years the Greeks and the Turks on Cyprus could hurt each other indefinitely but neither could quite take or hold forcibly what they wanted or protect themselves from violence by physical means. The Jews in Palestine could not expel the British in the late 1940s but they could cause pain and fear and frustration through terrorism, and eventually influence somebody's decision. The brutal war in Algeria was more a contest in pure violence than in military strength; the ques-

[1] Lynn Montross, *War Through the Ages* (3rd ed., New York, Harper, and Brothers, 1960), p. 146.

tion was who would first find the pain and degradation unendurable. The French troops preferred — indeed they continually tried — to make it a contest of strength, to pit military force against the nationalists' capacity for terror, to exterminate or disable the nationalists and to screen off the nationalists from the victims of their violence. But because in civil war terrorists commonly have access to victims by sheer physical propinquity, the victims and their properties could not be forcibly defended and in the end the French troops themselves resorted, unsuccessfully, to a war of pain.

Nobody believes that the Russians can take Hawaii from us, or New York, or Chicago, but nobody doubts that they might destroy people and buildings in Hawaii, Chicago, or New York. Whether the Russians can conquer West Germany in any meaningful sense is questionable; whether they can hurt it terribly is not doubted. That the United States can destroy a large part of Russia is universally taken for granted; that the United States can keep from being badly hurt, even devastated, in return, or can keep Western Europe from being devastated while itself destroying Russia, is at best arguable; and it is virtually out of the question that we could conquer Russia territorially and use its economic assets unless it were by threatening disaster and inducing compliance. It is the power to hurt, not military strength in the traditional sense, that inheres in our most impressive military capabilities at the present time. We have a Department of *Defense* but emphasize *retaliation* — "to return evil for evil" (synonyms: requital, reprisal, revenge, vengeance, retribution). And it is pain and violence, not force in the traditional sense, that inhere also in some of the least impressive military capabilities of the present time — the plastic bomb, the terrorist's bullet, the burnt crops, and the tortured farmer.

War appears to be, or threatens to be, not so much a contest of strength as one of endurance, nerve, obstinacy, and pain. It appears to be, and threatens to be, not so much a contest of military strength as a bargaining process — dirty, extortionate, and often quite reluctant bargaining on one side or both — nevertheless a bargaining process.

The difference cannot quite be expressed as one between the *use* of force and the *threat* of force. The actions involved in forcible accomplishment, on the one hand, and in fulfilling a threat, on the other, can be quite different. Sometimes the most effective direct action inflicts enough cost or pain on the enemy to serve as a threat, sometimes not. The United States threatens the Soviet Union with virtual destruction of its society in the event of a surprise attack on the United States; a hundred million deaths are awesome as pure damage, but they are useless in stopping the Soviet attack — especially if the threat is to do it all afterward anyway. So it is worth while to keep the concepts distinct — to distinguish forcible action from the threat of pain — recognizing that some actions serve as both a means of forcible accomplishment and a means of inflicting pure damage, some do not. Hostages tend to entail almost pure pain and damage, as do all forms of reprisal after the fact. Some modes of self-defense may exact so little in blood or treasure as to entail negligible violence; and some forcible actions entail so much violence that their threat can be effective by itself.

The power to hurt, though it can usually accomplish nothing directly, is potentially more versatile than a straightforward capacity for forcible accomplishment. By force alone we cannot even lead a horse to water — we have to drag him — much less make him drink. Any affirmative action, any collaboration, almost anything but physical exclusion, expulsion, or extermination, requires that an opponent or a victim *do* something, even if only to stop or get out. The threat of pain and damage may make him want to do it, and anything he can do is potentially susceptible to inducement. Brute force can only accomplish what requires no collaboration. The principle is illustrated by a technique of unarmed combat: one can disable a man by various stunning, fracturing, or killing blows, but to take him to jail one has to exploit the man's own efforts. "Come-along" holds are those that threaten pain or disablement, giving relief as long as the victim complies, giving him the option of using his own legs to get to jail. . . .

The fact that violence — pure pain and damage — can be used or threatened to coerce and to deter, to intimidate and to blackmail, to demoralize and to paralyze, in a conscious process of dirty bargaining, does not by any means imply that violence is not often wanton and meaningless or, even when purposive, in danger of getting out of hand. Ancient wars were often quite "total" for the loser, the men being put to death, the women sold as slaves, the boys castrated, the cattle slaughtered, and the buildings leveled, for the sake of revenge, justice, personal gain, or merely custom. If an enemy bombs a city, by design or by carelessness, we usually bomb his if we can. In the excitement and fatigue of warfare, revenge is one of the few satisfactions that can be savored. . . . Pure violence, like fire, can be harnessed to a purpose; that does not mean that behind every holocaust is a shrewd intention successfully fulfilled.

But if the occurrence of violence does not always bespeak a shrewd purpose, the absence of pain and destruction is no sign that violence was idle. Violence is most purposive and most successful when it is threatened and not used. Successful threats are those that do not have to be carried out. By European standards, Denmark was virtually unharmed in the Second World War; it was violence that made the Danes submit. Withheld violence — successfully threatened violence — can look clean, even merciful. The fact that a kidnap victim is returned unharmed, against receipt of ample ransom, does not make kidnapping a nonviolent enterprise. The American victory at Mexico City in 1847 was a great success; with a minimum of brutality we traded a capital city for everything we wanted from the war. We did not even have to say what we could do to Mexico City to make the Mexican government understand what they had at stake. (They had undoubtedly got the message a month earlier, when Vera Cruz was being pounded into submission. . . .)

Whether spoken or not, the threat is usually there. . . .

THE STRATEGIC ROLE OF PAIN AND DAMAGE

Pure violence, nonmilitary violence, appears most conspicuously in relations between unequal countries, where there is no substantial military challenge and the outcome of military engagement is not in question. Hitler could make his threats contemptuously and brutally against Austria; he could make them, if he wished, in a more refined way against Denmark. It is noteworthy that it was Hitler, not his generals, who used this kind of language; proud military establishments do not like to think of themselves as extortionists. Their favorite job is to deliver victory, to dispose of opposing military force and to leave most of the civilian violence to politics and diplomacy. But if there is no room for doubt how a contest in strength will come out, it may be possible to bypass the military stage altogether and to proceed at once to the coercive bargaining.

A typical confrontation of unequal forces occurs at the *end* of a war, between victor and vanquished. Where Austria was vulnerable before a shot was fired, France was vulnerable after its military shield had collapsed in 1940. Surrender negotiations are the place where the threat of civil violence can come to the fore. Surrender negotiations are often so one-sided, or the potential violence so unmistakable, that bargaining succeeds and the violence remains in reserve. But the fact that most of the actual damage was done during the military stage of the war, prior to victory and defeat, does not mean that violence was idle in the aftermath, only that it was latent and the threat of it successful. . . .

. . . The Russians crushed Budapest in 1956 and cowed Poland and other neighboring countries. There was a lag of ten years between military victory and this show of violence, but the principle was the one [just] explained. . . . Military victory is often the prelude to violence, not the end of it, and the fact that successful violence is usually held in reserve should not deceive us about the role it plays.

What about pure violence during war itself, the infliction of pain and suffering as a military technique? Is the threat of pain involved only in the political use of victory, or is it a decisive technique of war itself?

Evidently between unequal powers it has been part of warfare. Colonial conquest has often been a matter of "punitive expeditions" rather than genuine military engagements. If the tribesmen escape into the brush you can burn their villages without them until they assent to receive what, in strikingly modern language, used to be known as the Queen's "protection." . . .

Pure hurting, as a military tactic, appeared in some of the military actions against the plains Indians. In 1868, during the war with the Cheyennes, General Sheridan decided that his best hope was to attack the Indians in their winter camps. His reasoning was that the Indians could maraud as they pleased during the seasons when their ponies could subsist on grass, and in the winter hide away in remote places. "To disabuse their minds from the idea that they were secure from punishment, and to strike at a period when they were helpless to move their stock and villages, a winter campaign was projected against the large bands hiding away in the Indian territory."[2]

These were not military engagements; they were punitive attacks on people. They were an effort to subdue by the use of violence, without a futile attempt to draw the enemy's military forces into decisive battle. They were "massive retaliation" on a diminutive scale, with local effects not unlike those of Hiroshima. The Indians themselves totally lacked organization and discipline, and typically could not afford enough ammunition for target practice and were no military match for the cavalry; their own rudimentary strategy was at best one of harassment and reprisal. Half a century of Indian fighting in the West left us a legacy of cavalry tactics; but it is hard to find a serious treatise on American strategy against the Indians or Indian strategy against the whites. The twentieth is not the first century in which "retaliation" has been part of our strategy, but it is the first in which we have systematically recognized it.

Hurting, as a strategy, showed up in the American Civil War, but as an episode, not as the central strategy. For the most part, the

[2] Paul I. Wellman, *Death on the Prairie* (New York, Macmillan, 1934), p. 82.

Civil War was a military engagement with each side's military force pitted against the other's. The Confederate forces hoped to lay waste enough Union territory to negotiate their independence, but hadn't enough capacity for such violence to make it work. The Union forces were intent on military victory, and it was mainly General Sherman's march through Georgia that showed a conscious and articulate use of violence. "If the people raise a howl against my barbarity and cruelty, I will answer that war is war. . . . If they want peace, they and their relatives must stop the war," Sherman wrote. And one of his associates said, "Sherman is perfectly right. . . . The only possible way to end this unhappy and dreadful conflict . . . is to make it terrible beyond endurance."[3]

Making it "terrible beyond endurance" is what we associate with Algeria and Palestine, the crushing of Budapest, and the tribal warfare in Central Africa. But in the great wars of the last hundred years it was usually military victory, not the hurting of the people, that was decisive; General Sherman's attempt to make war hell for the Southern people did not come to epitomize military strategy for the century to follow. To seek out and to destroy the enemy's military force, to achieve a crushing victory over enemy armies, was still the avowed purpose and the central aim of American strategy in both world wars. Military action was seen as an *alternative* to bargaining, not a *process* of bargaining.

The reason is not that civilized countries are so averse to hurting people that they prefer "purely military" wars. (Nor were all of the participants in these wars entirely civilized.) The reason is apparently that the technology and geography of warfare, at least for a war between anything like equal powers during the century ending in World War II, kept coercive violence from being decisive before military victory was achieved. Blockade indeed was aimed at the whole enemy nation, not concentrated on its military forces; the German civilians who died of influenza in the First World War were victims of violence directed at the whole country. It has never been quite clear whether blockade — of the South in the Civil War or of the Central Powers in both world wars, or submarine warfare against Britain — was expected to make war unendurable for the people or just to weaken the enemy forces by denying economic

---

[3] J. F. C. Fuller reproduces some of this correspondence and remarks, "For the nineteenth century this was a new conception, because it meant that the deciding factor in the war — the power to sue for peace — was transferred from government to people, and that peace-making was a product of revolution. This was to carry the principle of democracy to its ultimate stage. . . ." *The Conduct of War: 1789–1961* (New Brunswick, Rutgers University Press, 1961), pp. 107–12.

support. Both arguments were made, but there was no need to be clear about the purpose as long as either purpose was regarded as legitimate and either might be served. "Strategic bombing" of enemy homelands was also occasionally rationalized in terms of the pain and privation it could inflict on people and the civil damage it could do to the nation, as an effort to display either to the population or to the enemy leadership that surrender was better than persistence in view of the damage that could be done. It was also rationalized in more "military" terms, as a way of selectively denying war material to the troops or as a way of generally weakening the economy on which the military effort rested.

But terrorism — as violence intended to coerce the enemy rather than to weaken him militarily — blockade and strategic bombing by themselves were not quite up to the job in either world war in Europe. (They might have been sufficient in the war with Japan after straightforward military action had brought American aircraft into range.) Airplanes could not quite make punitive, coercive violence decisive in Europe, at least on a tolerable time schedule, and preclude the need to defeat or to destroy enemy forces as long as they had nothing but conventional explosives and incendiaries to carry. Hitler's V-1 buzz bomb and his V-2 rocket are fairly pure cases of weapons whose purpose was to intimidate, to hurt Britain itself rather than Allied military forces. What the V-2 needed was a punitive payload worth carrying, and the Germans did not have it. Some of the expectations in the 1920s and the 1930s that another major war would be one of pure civilian violence, of shock and terror from the skies, were not borne out by the available technology. The threat of punitive violence kept occupied countries quiescent; but the wars were won in Europe on the basis of brute strength and skill and not by intimidation, not by the threat of civilian violence but by the application of military force. Military victory was still the price of admission. Latent violence against people was reserved for the politics of surrender and occupation.

The great exception was the two atomic bombs on Japanese cities. These were weapons of terror and shock. They hurt, and promised more hurt, and that was their purpose. The few "small" weapons we had were undoubtedly of some direct military value, but their enormous advantage was in pure violence. In a military sense the United States could gain a little by destruction of two Japanese industrial cities; in a civilian sense, the Japanese could lose much. The bomb that hit Hiroshima was a threat aimed at all of Japan. The political target of the bomb was not the dead of Hiroshima or the factories they worked in, but the survivors in Toyko. The two bombs were in the tradition of Sheridan against the Comanches and

Sherman in Georgia. Whether in the end those two bombs saved lives or wasted them, Japanese lives or American lives; whether punitive coercive violence is uglier than straightforward military force or more civilized; whether terror is more or less humane than military destruction; we can at least perceive that the bombs on Hiroshima and Nagasaki represented violence against the country itself and not mainly an attack on Japan's material strength. The effect of the bombs, and their purpose, was not mainly the military destruction they accomplished but the pain and the shock and the promise of more.

THE NUCLEAR CONTRIBUTION TO
TERROR AND VIOLENCE

Man has, it is said, for the first time in history enough military power to eliminate his species from the earth, weapons against which there is no conceivable defense. War has become, it is said, so destructive and terrible that it ceases to be an instrument of national power. "For the first time in human history," says Max Lerner in a book whose title, *The Age of Overkill,* conveys the point, "men have bottled up a power . . . which they have thus far not dared to use." And Soviet military authorities, whose party dislikes having to accommodate an entire theory of history to a single technological event, have had to re-examine a set of principles that had been given the embarrassing name of "permanently operating factors" in warfare. Indeed, our era is epitomized by words like "the first time in human history," and by the abdication of what was "permanent."

For dramatic impact these statements are splendid. Some of them display a tendency, not at all necessary, to belittle the catastrophe of earlier wars. They may exaggerate the historical novelty of deterrence and the balance of terror.[4] More important, they do not help

[4] Winston Churchill is often credited with the term, "balance of terror," and the following quotation succinctly expresses the familiar notion of nuclear mutual deterrence. This, though, is from a speech in Commons in November 1934. "The fact remains that when all is said and done as regards defensive methods, pending some new discovery the only direct measure of defense upon a great scale is the certainty of being able to inflict simultaneously upon the enemy as great damage as he can inflict upon ourselves. Do not let us undervalue the efficacy of this procedure. It may well prove in practice — I admit I cannot prove it in theory — capable of giving complete immunity. If two Powers show themselves equally capable of inflicting damage upon each other by some particular process of war, so that neither gains an advantage from its adoption and both suffer the most hideous reciprocal injuries, it is not only possible but it seems probable that neither will employ that means. . . ."

to identify just what is new about war when so much destructive energy can be packed in warheads at a price that permits advanced countries to have them in large numbers. Nuclear warheads are incomparably more devastating than anything packaged before. What does that imply about war?

It is not true that for the first time in history man has the capability to destroy a large fraction, even the major part, of the human race. Japan was defenseless by August 1945. With a combination of bombing and blockade, eventually invasion, and if necessary the deliberate spread of disease, the United States could probably have exterminated the population of the Japanese islands without nuclear weapons. . . .

It is a grisly thing to talk about. We did not do it and it is not imaginable that we would have done it. We had no reason; if we had had a reason, we would not have the persistence of purpose, once the fury of war had been dissipated in victory and we had taken on the task of executioner. If we and our enemies might do such a thing to each other now, and to others as well, it is not because nuclear weapons have for the first time made it feasible.

Nuclear weapons can do it quickly. . . . To compress a catastrophic war within the span of time that a man can stay awake drastically changes the politics of war, the process of decision, the possibility of central control and restraint, the motivations of people in charge, and the capacity to think and reflect while war is in progress. It *is* imaginable that we might destroy 200,000,000 Russians in a war of the present, though not 80,000,000 Japanese in a war of the past. It is not only imaginable, it is imagined. It is imaginable because it could be done "in a moment, in the twinkling of an eye, at the last trumpet."

This may be why there is so little discussion of how an all-out war might be brought to a close. People do not expect it to be "brought" to a close, but just to come to an end when everything has been spent. It is also why the idea of "limited war" has become so explicit in recent years. Earlier wars, like World Wars I and II or the Franco-Prussian War, were limited by *termination*, by an ending that occurred before the period of greatest potential violence, by negotiation that brought the *threat* of pain and privation to bear but often precluded the massive *exercise* of civilian violence. With nuclear weapons available, the restraint of violence cannot await the outcome of a contest of military strength; restraint, to occur at all, must occur during war itself.

This is a difference between nuclear weapons and bayonets. It is not in the number of people they can eventually kill but in the speed with which it can be done, in the centralization of decision, in the divorce of the war from political processes, and in computerized programs that threaten to take the war out of human hands once it begins.

That nuclear weapons make it *possible* to compress the fury of global war into a few hours does not mean that they make it *inevitable*. We have still to ask whether that is the way a major nuclear war would be fought, or ought to be fought. Nevertheless, that the whole war might go off like one big string of firecrackers makes a critical difference between our conception of nuclear war and the world wars we have experienced.

There is no guarantee, of course, that a slower war would not persist. The First World War could have stopped at any time after the Battle of the Marne. There was plenty of time to think about war aims, to consult the long-range national interest, to reflect on costs and casualties already incurred and the prospect of more to come, and to discuss terms of cessation with the enemy. The gruesome business continued as mechanically as if it had been in the hands of computers (or worse: computers might have been programmed to learn more quickly from experience). One may even suppose it would have been a blessing had all the pain and shock of the four years been compressed within four days. Still, it was terminated. And the victors had no stomach for doing then with bayonets what nuclear weapons could do to the German people today.

There is another difference. In the past it has usually been the victors who could do what they pleased to the enemy. War has often been "total war" for the loser. With deadly monotony the Persians, Greeks, or Romans "put to death all men of military age, and sold the women and children into slavery," leaving the defeated territory nothing but its name until new settlers arrived sometime later. But the defeated could not do the same to their victors. The boys could be castrated and sold only after the war had been won, and only on the side that lost it. The power to hurt could be brought to bear only after military strength had achieved victory. The same sequence characterized the great wars of this century; for reasons of technology and geography, military force has usually had to penetrate, to exhaust, or to collapse opposing military force — to achieve military victory — before it could be brought to bear on the enemy nation itself. The Allies in World War I could not inflict coercive pain and suffering directly on the Germans in a decisive way until they could defeat the German army; and the Germans could not coerce the French people with bayonets unless they first beat the Allied troops that stood in their way. With two-dimensional warfare, there is a tendency for troops to confront each other, shielding their own lands while attempting to press into each other's. Small penetrations could not do major damage to the people; large penetrations were so destructive of military organization that they usually ended the military phase of the war.

Nuclear weapons make it possible to do monstrous violence to the enemy without first achieving victory. With nuclear weapons and today's means of delivery, one expects to penetrate an enemy homeland without first collapsing his military force. What nuclear weapons have done, or appear to do, is to promote this kind of warfare to first place. Nuclear weapons threaten to make war less military, and are responsible for the lowered status of "military victory" at the present time. *Victory is no longer a prerequisite for hurting the enemy.* And it is no assurance against being terribly hurt. One need not wait until he has won the war before inflicting "unendurable" damages on his enemy. One need not wait until he has lost the war. There was a time when the assurance of victory — false or genuine assurance — could make national leaders not just willing but sometimes enthusiastic about war. Not now.

Not only *can* nuclear weapons hurt the enemy before the war has been won, and perhaps hurt decisively enough to make the military engagement academic, but it is widely assumed that in a major war that is *all* they can do. Major war is often discussed as though it would be only a contest in national destruction. If this is indeed the case — if the destruction of cities and their populations has become, with nuclear weapons, the primary object in an all-out war — the sequence of war has been reversed. Instead of destroying enemy forces as a prelude to imposing one's will on the enemy nation, one would have to destroy the nation as a means or a prelude to destroying the enemy forces. If one cannot disable enemy forces without virtually destroying the country, the victor does not even have the option of sparing the conquered nation. He has already destroyed it. Even with blockade and strategic bombing it could be supposed that a country would be defeated before it was destroyed, or would elect surrender before annihilation had gone far. In the Civil War it could be hoped that the South would become too weak to fight before it became too weak to survive. For "all-out" war, nuclear weapons threaten to reverse this sequence.

So nuclear weapons do make a difference, marking an epoch in warfare. The difference is not just in the amount of destruction that can be accomplished but in the role of destruction and in the decision process. Nuclear weapons can change the speed of events, the control of events, the sequence of events, the relation of victor to vanquished, and the relation of homeland to fighting front. Deterrence rests today on the threat of pain and extinction, not just on the threat of military defeat. We may argue about the wisdom of announcing "unconditional surrender" as an aim in the last major war, but seem to expect "unconditional destruction" as a matter of course in another one.

Something like the same destruction always *could* be done. With nuclear weapons there is an expectation that it *would* be done. . . . What is new is . . . the idea that major war might be just a contest in the killing of countries, or not even a contest but just two parallel exercises in devastation.

That is the difference nuclear weapons make. At least they *may* make that difference. They also may not. If the weapons themselves are vulnerable to attack, or the machines that carry them, a successful surprise might eliminate the opponent's means of retribution. That an enormous explosion can be packaged in a single bomb does not by itself guarantee that the victor will receive deadly punishment. Two gunfighters facing each other in a Western town had an unquestioned capacity to kill one another; that did not guarantee that both would die in a gunfight — only the slower of the two. Less deadly weapons, permitting an injured one to shoot back before he died, might have been more conducive to a restraining balance of terror, or of caution. The very efficiency of nuclear weapons could make them ideal for starting war, if they can suddenly eliminate the enemy's capability to shoot back.

And there is a contrary possibility: that nuclear weapons are not vulnerable to attack and prove not to be terribly effective against each other, posing no need to shoot them quickly for fear they will be destroyed before they are launched, and with no task available but the systematic destruction of the enemy country and no necessary reason to do it fast rather than slowly. Imagine that nuclear destruction *had* to go slowly — that the bombs could be dropped only one per day. The prospect would look very different, something like the most terroristic guerilla warfare on a massive scale. It happens that nuclear war does not have to go slowly; but it may also not have to go speedily. The mere existence of nuclear weapons does not itself determine that everything must go off in a blinding flash, any more than that it must go slowly. Nuclear weapons do not simplify things quite that much.

In recent years there has been a new emphasis on distinguishing what nuclear weapons make possible and what they make inevitable in case of war. The American government began in 1961 to emphasize that even a major nuclear war might not, and need not, be a simple contest in destructive fury. Secretary McNamara gave a controversial speech in June 1962 on the idea that "deterrence" might operate even in war itself, that belligerents might, out of self-interest, attempt to limit the war's destructiveness. Each might feel the sheer destruction of enemy people and cities would serve no decisive military purpose but that a continued *threat* to destroy them might serve a purpose. The continued threat would depend on their not being destroyed yet. Each might reciprocate the other's restraint, as in limited wars of lesser scope. Even the worst of enemies, in the interest of reciprocity, have often not mutilated prisoners of war; and citizens might deserve comparable treatment. The fury of nuclear attacks might fall mainly on each other's weapons and military forces.

"The United States has come to the conclusion," said Secretary McNamara,

> that to the extent feasible, basic military strategy in a possible general war should be approached in much the same way that more conventional military operations have been regarded in the past. That is to say, principal military objectives . . . should be the destruction of the enemy's military forces, not of his civilian population . . . giving the possible opponent the strongest imaginable incentive to refrain from striking our own cities.[5]

This is a sensible way to think about war, if one has to think about it and of course one does. But whether the Secretary's "new strategy" was sensible or not, whether enemy populations should be held hostage or instantly destroyed, whether the primary targets should be military forces or just people and their source of livelihood, this is not "much the same way that more conventional military operations have been regarded in the past." This is utterly different, and the difference deserves emphasis.

In World Wars I and II one went to work on enemy military forces, not his people, because until the enemy's military forces had been taken care of there was typically not anything decisive that one could do to the enemy nation itself. The Germans did not, in World War I, refrain from bayoneting French citizens by the millions in the hope that the Allies would abstain from shooting up the German population. They could not get at the French citizens until they had breached the Allied lines. Hitler tried to terrorize London and did not make it. The Allied air forces took the war straight to Hitler's territory, with at least some thought of doing in Germany what Sherman recognized he was doing in Georgia; but with the bombing technology of World War II one could not afford to bypass the troops and go exclusively for enemy populations —

[5] Commencement Address, University of Michigan, June 16, 1962.

not, anyway, in Germany. With nuclear weapons one has that alternative.

To concentrate on the enemy's military installations while deliberately holding in reserve a massive capacity for destroying his cities, for exterminating his people and eliminating his society, on condition that the enemy observe similar restraint with respect to one's own society, is not the "conventional approach." In World Wars I and II the first order of business was to destroy enemy armed forces because that was the only promising way to make him surrender. To fight a purely military engagement "all-out" while holding in reserve a decisive capacity for violence, on condition the enemy do likewise, is not the way military operations have traditionally been approached. Secretary McNamara was proposing a new approach to warfare in a new era, an era in which the power to hurt is more impressive than the power to oppose.

FROM BATTLEFIELD WARFARE TO THE DIPLOMACY OF VIOLENCE

Almost one hundred years before Secretary McNamara's speech, the Declaration of St. Petersburg (the first of the great modern conferences to cope with the evils of warfare) in 1868 asserted, "The only legitimate object which states should endeavor to accomplish during war is to weaken the military forces of the enemy." And in a letter to the League of Nations in 1920, the President of the International Committee of the Red Cross wrote; "The Committee considers it very desirable that war should resume its former character, that is to stay, that it should be a struggle between armies and not between populations. The civilian population must, as far as possible, remain outside the struggle and its consequences."[6] His language is remarkably similar to Secretary McNamara's.

The International Committee was fated for disappointment, like everyone who labored in the late nineteenth century to devise rules that would make war more humane. When the Red Cross was founded in 1863, it was concerned about the disregard for noncombatants by those who made war; but in the Second World War noncombatants were deliberately chosen as targets by both Axis and Allied forces, not decisively but nevertheless deliberately. The trend has been the reverse of what the International Committee hoped for.

In the present era noncombatants appear to be not only deliberate targets but primary targets, or at least were so taken for granted

---

[6] International Committee of the Red Cross, *Draft Rules for the Limitation of the Dangers Incurred by the Civilian Population in Time of War* (2d ed., Geneva, 1958), pp. 144, 151.

until about the time of Secretary McNamara's speech. In fact, non-combatants appeared to be primary targets at both ends of the scale of warfare; thermonuclear war threatened to be a contest in the destruction of cities and populations; and, at the other end of the scale, insurgency is almost entirely terroristic. We live in an era of dirty war.

Why is this so? Is war properly a military affair among combatants, and is it a depravity peculiar to the twentieth century that we cannot keep it within decent bounds? Or is war inherently dirty, and was the Red Cross nostalgic for an artificial civilization in which war had become encrusted with etiquette — a situation to be welcomed but not expected?

To answer this question it is useful to distinguish three stages in the involvement of noncombatants — of plain people and their possessions — in the fury of war. These stages are worth distinguishing; but their sequence is merely descriptive of Western Europe during the past three hundred years, not a historical generalization. The first stage is that in which the people may get hurt by inconsiderate combatants. This is the status that people had during the period of "civilized warfare" that the International Committee had in mind.

From about 1648 to the Napoleonic era, war in much of Western Europe was something superimposed on society. It was a contest engaged in by monarchies for stakes that were measured in territories and, occasionally, money or dynastic claims. The troops were mostly mercenaries and the motivation for war was confined to the aristocratic elite. Monarchs fought for bits of territory, but the residents of disputed terrain were more concerned with protecting their crops and their daughters from marauding troops than with whom they owed allegiance to. They were, as Quincy Wright remarked in his classic *Study of War*, little concerned that the territory in which they lived had a new sovereign.[7] Furthermore, as far as the King of Prussia and the Emperor of Austria were concerned, the loyalty and enthusiasm of the Bohemian farmer were not decisive considerations. It is an exaggeration to refer to European war during this period as a sport of kings, but not a gross exaggeration. And the military logistics of those days confined military operations to a scale that did not require the enthusiasm of a multitude.

Hurting people was not a decisive instrument of warfare. Hurting people or destroying property only reduced the value of the things that were being fought over, to the disadvantage of both sides. Furthermore, the monarchs who conducted wars often did not want to discredit the social institutions they shared with their enemies.

[7] Chicago, University of Chicago Press, 1942, p. 296.

Bypassing an enemy monarch and taking the war straight to his people would have had revolutionary implications. Destroying the opposing monarchy was often not in the interest of either side; opposing sovereigns had much more in common with each other than with their own subjects, and to discredit the claims of a monarchy might have produced a disastrous backlash. It is not surprising — or, if it is surprising, not altogether astonishing — that on the European continent in that particular era war was fairly well confined to military activity.

One could still, in those days and in that part of the world, be concerned for the rights of noncombatants and hope to devise rules that both sides in the war might observe. The rules might well be observed because both sides had something to gain from preserving social order and not destroying the enemy. Rules might be a nuisance, but they restricted both sides the disadvantages might cancel out.

This was changed during the Napoleonic wars. In Napoleon's France, people cared about the outcome. The nation was mobilized. The war was a national effort, not just an activity of the elite. It was both political and military genius on the part of Napoleon and his ministers that an entire nation could be mobilized for war. Propaganda became a tool of warfare, and war became vulgarized.

Many writers deplored this popularization of war, this involvement of the democratic masses. In fact, the horrors we attribute to thermonuclear war were already foreseen by many commentators, some before the First World War and more after it; but the new "weapon" to which these terrors were ascribed was people, millions of people, passionately engaged in national wars, spending themselves in a quest for total victory and desperate to avoid total defeat. Today we are impressed that a small number of highly trained pilots can carry enough energy to blast and burn tens of millions of people and the buildings they live in; two or three generations ago there was concern that tens of millions of people using bayonets and barbed wire, machine guns and shrapnel, could create the same kind of destruction and disorder.

That was the second stage in the relation of people to war, the second in Europe since the middle of the seventeenth century. In the first stage people had been neutral but their welfare might be disregarded; in the second stage people were involved because it was *their* war. Some fought, some produced materials of war, some produced food, and some took care of children; but they were all part of a war-making nation. When Hitler attacked Poland in 1939, the Poles had reason to care about the outcome. When Churchill said the British would fight on the beaches, he spoke for the British and not for a mercenary army. The war was about something that mattered. If people would rather fight a dirty war than lose a clean one, the war will be between nations and not just between governments. If people have an influence on whether the war is continued or on the terms of a truce, making the war hurt people serves a purpose. It is a dirty purpose, but war itself is often about something dirty. The Poles and the Norwegians, the Russians and the British, had reason to believe that if they lost the war the consequences would be dirty. This is so evident in modern civil wars — civil wars that involve popular feelings — that we expect them to be bloody and violent. To hope that they would be fought cleanly with no violence to people would be a little like hoping for a clean race riot.

There is another way to put it that helps to bring out the sequence of events. If a modern war were a clean one, the violence would not be ruled out but merely saved for the postwar period. Once the army has been defeated in the clean war, the victorious enemy can be as brutally coercive as he wishes. A clean war would determine which side gets to use its power to hurt coercively after victory, and it is likely to be worth some violence to avoid being the loser.

"Surrender" is the process following military hostilities in which the power to hurt is brought to bear. If surrender negotiations are successful and not followed by overt violence, it is because the capacity to inflict pain and damage was successfully used in the bargaining process. On the losing side, prospective pain and damage were averted by concessions; on the winning side, the capacity for inflicting further harm was traded for concessions. The same is true in a successful kidnapping. It only reminds us that the purpose of pure pain and damage is extortion; it is *latent* violence that can be used to advantage. A well-behaved occupied country is not one in which violence plays no part; it may be one in which latent violence is used so skillfully that it need not be spent in punishment.

This brings us to the third stage in the relation of civilian violence to warfare. If the pain and damage can be inflicted during war itself, they need not wait for the surrender negotiation that succeeds a military decision. If one can coerce people and their governments while war is going on, one does not need to wait until he has achieved victory or risk losing that coercive power by spending it all in a losing war. General Sherman's march through Georgia might have made as much sense, possibly more, had the North been losing the war, just as the German buzz bombs and V-2 rockets can be thought of as coercive instruments to get the war stopped before suffering military defeat.

In the present era, since at least the major East-West powers are capable of massive civilian violence during war itself beyond anything available during the Second World War, the occasion for restraint does not await the achievement of military victory or truce. The principal restraint during the Second World War was a temporal boundary, the date of surrender. In the present era we find the violence dramatically restrained during war itself. The Korean War was furiously "all-out" in the fighting, not only on the peninsular battlefield but in the resources used by both sides. It was "all-out," though, only within some dramatic restraints: no nuclear weapons, no Russians, no Chinese territory, no Japanese territory, no bombing of ships at sea or even airfields on the United Nations side of the line. It was a contest in military strength circumscribed by the threat of unprecedented civilian violence. Korea may or may not be a good model for speculation on limited war in the age of nuclear violence, but it was dramatic evidence that the capacity for violence can be consciously restrained even under the provocation of a war that measures its military dead in tens of thousands and that fully preoccupies two of the largest countries in the world.

A consequence of this third stage is that "victory" inadequately expresses what a nation wants from its military forces. Mostly it wants, in these times, the influence that resides in latent force. It wants the bargaining power that comes from its capacity to hurt, not just the direct consequence of successful military action. Even total victory over an enemy provides at best an opportunity for unopposed violence against the enemy population. How to use that opportunity in the national interest, or in some wider interest, can be just as important as the achievement of victory itself; but traditional military science does not tell us how to use that capacity for inflicting pain. And if a nation, victor or potential loser, is going to use its capacity for pure violence to influence the enemy, there may be no need to await the achievement of total victory.

Actually, this third stage can be analyzed into two quite different variants. In one, sheer pain and damage are primary instruments of coercive warfare and may actually be applied, to intimidate or to deter. In the other, pain and destruction *in* war are expected to serve little or no purpose but *prior threats* of sheer violence, even of automatic and uncontrolled violence, are coupled to military force. The difference is in the all-or-none character of deterrence and intimidation. Two acute dilemmas arise. One is the choice of making prospective violence as frightening as possible or hedging with some capacity for reciprocated restraint. The other is the choice of making retaliation as automatic as possible or keeping deliberate control over the fateful decisions. The choices are determined partly by governments, partly by technology. Both variants are characterized by the coercive role of pain and destruction — of threatened (not inflicted) pain and destruction. But in one the threat either succeeds or fails altogether, and any ensuing violence is gratuitous; in the other, progressive pain and damage may actually be used to threaten more. The present era, for countries possessing nuclear weapons, is a complex and uncertain blend of the two.

Coercive diplomacy, based on the power to hurt, was important even in those periods of history when military force was essentially the power to take and to hold, to fend off attack and to expel invaders, and to possess territory against opposition — that is, in the era in which military force tended to pit itself against opposing force. Even then, a critical question was how much cost and pain the other side would incur for the disputed territory. The judgment that the Mexicans would concede Texas, New Mexico, and California once Mexico City was a hostage in our hands was a diplomatic judgment, not a military one. If one could not readily take the particular territory he wanted or hold it against attack, he could take something else and trade it. Judging what the enemy leaders would trade — be it a capital city or national survival — was a critical part of strategy even in the past. Now we are in an era in which the power to hurt — to inflict pain and shock and privation on a country itself, not just on its military forces — is commensurate with the power to take and to hold, perhaps more than commensurate, perhaps decisive, and it is even more necessary to think of warfare as a process of violent bargaining. This is not the first era in which live captives have been worth more than dead enemies, and the power to hurt has been a bargaining advantage; but it is the first in American experience when that kind of power has been a dominant part of military relations.

The power to hurt is nothing new in warfare, but for the United States modern technology has drastically enhanced the strategic importance of pure, unconstructive, unacquisitive pain and damage, whether used against us or in our own defense. This in turn enhances the importance of war and threats of war as techniques of influence, not of destruction; of coercion and deterrence, not of conquest and defense; of bargaining and intimidation.

Quincy Wright, in his *Study of War,* devoted a couple of pages (319–320) to the "nuisance value" of war, using the analogy of a bank robber with a bomb in his hand that would destroy bank and robber. Nuisance value made the threat of war, according to Wright, "an aid to the diplomacy of unscrupulous governments." Now we need a stronger term, and more pages, to do the subject justice, and need to recognize that even scrupulous governments often have little else to rely on militarily. It is extraordinary how many treatises on war and strategy have declined to recognize that the power to hurt has been, throughout history, a fundamental character of military force and fundamental to the diplomacy based on it.

War no longer looks like just a contest of strength. War and the brink of war are more a contest of nerve and risk-taking, of pain and endurance. Small wars embody the threat of a larger war; they are not just military engagements but "crisis diplomacy." The threat of war has always been somewhere underneath international diplomacy, but for Americans it is now much nearer the surface. Like the threat of a strike in industrial relations, the threat of divorce in a family dispute, or the threat of bolting the party at a political convention, the threat of violence continuously circumscribes international politics. Neither strength nor goodwill procures immunity.

Military strategy can no longer be thought of, as it could for some countries in some eras, as the science of military victory. It is now equally, if not more, the art of coercion, of intimidation and deterrence. The instruments of war are more punitive than acquisitive. Military strategy, whether we like it or not, has become the diplomacy of violence.

The Problems of Limited War

HENRY A. KISSINGER

Perhaps the basic problem of strategy in the nuclear age is how to establish a relationship between a policy of deterrence and a strategy for fighting a war in case deterrence fails. From the point of view of its impact on the aggressor's actions, maximum deterrence can be equated with the threat of maximum destructiveness. From the point of view of a power's readiness to resist aggression, the optimum strategy is one which is able to achieve its goals at minimum cost. The temptation of strategic doctrine is to seek to com-

Reprinted from *Nuclear Weapons and Foreign Policy* by Henry A. Kissinger by permission of W. W. Norton and Company, Inc., pp. 114–129 and 139–144. Copyright © 1957, 1958 by Council on Foreign Relations, Inc. Copyright © 1969 by W. W. Norton and Company, Inc.

bine the advantages of every course of action: to achieve maximum deterrence but also to do so at minimum risk.

Ever since the end of our atomic monopoly, however, this effort has been thwarted by the impossiblity of combining maximum destructiveness with limited risk. The greater the horror of our destructive capabilities, the less certain has it become that they will in fact be used. In such circumstances deterrence is brought about not only by a physical but also by a psychological relationship: deterrence is greatest when military strength is coupled with the willingness to employ it. It is achieved when one side's readiness to run risks in relation to the other is high; it is least effective when the willingness to run risks is low, however powerful the military capability. It is, therefore, no longer possible to speak of military superiority in the abstract. What does "being ahead" in the nuclear race mean if each side can already destroy the other's national substance? What is the strategic significance of adding to the destructiveness of the nuclear arsenal when the enormity of present weapons systems already tends to paralyze the will?

Given the power of modern weapons, a nation that relies on all-out war as its chief deterrent imposes a fearful psychological handicap on itself. The most agonizing decision a statesman can face is whether or not to unleash all-out war; all pressures will make for hesitation, short of a direct attack threatening the national existence. And he will be confirmed in his hesitations by the conviction that, so long as his retaliatory force remains intact, no shift in the territorial balance is of decisive significance. Thus both the horror and the power of modern weapons tend to paralyze action: the former because it will make few issues seem worth contending for; the latter because it causes many disputes to seem irrelevant to the over-all strategic equation. The psychological equation, therefore, will almost inevitably operate against the side which can extricate itself from a situation *only* by the threat of all-out war. Who can be certain that, faced with the catastrophe of all-out war, even Europe, long the keystone of our security, will seem worth the price?

As the power of modern weapons grows, the threat of all-out war loses its credibility and therefore its political effectiveness. Our capacity for massive retaliation did not avert the Korean war, the loss of northern Indo-China, the Soviet-Egyptian arms deal, or the Suez crisis. Moreover, whatever the credibility of our threat of all-out war, it is clear that all-out thermonuclear war does not represent a strategic option for our allies. Thus a psychological gap is created by the conviction of our allies that they have nothing to gain from massive retaliation and by the belief of the Soviet leaders that they have nothing to fear from our threat of it.

This gap may actually encourage the Soviet leaders to engage in aggression. The destructiveness of nuclear weapons having made it unlikely that any responsible statesman will lightly unleash a general war, one of the gravest dangers of all-out war lies in miscalculation. This is the only war which it is within our power to avoid, assuming we leave no doubt concerning our capabilities and our determination. But even this "avoidable" war may break out if the other side becomes convinced that we cannot interfere locally and that our threats of all-out war are bluff. If that should happen, the Soviet bloc may then decide, as its nuclear arsenal grows, to absorb the peripheral areas of Eurasia by means short of all-out war and to confront us with the choice of yielding or facing the destruction of American cities. And because the Sino-Soviet leaders may well be mistaken in their assessment of our reaction to such a contingency, the reliance on "massive retaliation" may bring about the total war it seeks to prevent.

To be sure, a threat to be effective need not be *absolutely* credible. An aggressor may be reluctant to stake his national existence for a marginal gain even if he should have some doubts about whether a threat will in fact be implemented. It has even been argued that a reduction of our forces around the Soviet periphery would multiply Soviet hesitations because it would make clear to the Soviet leaders, beyond doubt, that *any* aggression may involve all-out war. And for purposes of deterrence, so the argument goes, what we *may* do will prove as effective as what we *will* do.

Such a strategy, however, would be highly risky and demoralizing. It would widen the gap between the psychological and physical components of policy even more. It is a strange doctrine which asserts that we can convey our determination to our opponent by reducing our overseas commitments, that, in effect, our words will be a more effective deterrent than our deeds. It overlooks that all Soviet and Chinese aggressive moves have occurred in areas where our commitment of resources was small or nonexistent: Korea, Indo-China and the Middle East. Above all, a strategy which sought to compensate for its lack of plausibility by posing ever more fearful threats would be demoralizing. It would place control over our survival entirely in the hands of another power, for any Soviet move, however trivial, would force us to respond, if at all, by what may amount to national suicide. It ignores the contemporary revolution which, as events in the Middle East and the satellite orbit have shown, may create its own tensions independent of the plans of the major powers and which may force the United States and the U.S.S.R. to contest certain areas despite themselves.

The power of modern weapons has thus set our statesmanship a problem unique in our history: that absolute security is no longer possible. Whatever the validity of the identification of deterrence with maximum retaliatory power, we will have to sacrifice a measure of destructiveness to gain the possibility of fighting wars that will not amount to national catastrophe. Policy, it has been said, is the science of the relative. The same is true of strategy, and to understand this fact, so foreign to our national experience, is the task history has set our generation.

What strategic doctrine is most likely to enable us to avoid the dilemma of having to make a choice between all-out war and a gradual loss of positions, between Armageddon and defeat without war? Is limited war a conceivable instrument of policy in the nuclear period? Here we must analyze precisely what is meant by limited war.

It is a historical accident reflecting the nature of our foreign involvements that we should have come to consider limited war an aberration from the "pure" case and that we have paid little attention to its strategic opportunities. In a sense this is due, too, to the manner in which we have legitimized the limited wars which we *have* fought. Every war in which we have been engaged in the Western Hemisphere was a limited war, in the sense that it did not involve a mobilization of all our material resources. But since we generally justified them as expeditions, punitive or otherwise, they rarely entered our national consciousness as part of the phenomenon of limited war.

The debate which has raged since Korea on the subject of limited war has tended to confuse the issues because it has not sufficiently distinguished between the various forms of limited war. Some wars are inherently limited because of the disparity in power between the protagonists. A war between the United States and Nicaragua would not require more than a fraction of our strength whatever the objectives we set ourselves. Such a war would be all-out in relation to Nicaragua, but limited with respect to us. Another variation of this form of limited war occurs when the stronger power is restrained from exerting its full potential by moral, political or strategic considerations. This was the case in the Korean war, in which the Chinese probably made the maximum military effort of which they were capable while we, for a variety of reasons, limited our commitments. Still another kind of limited war is one between major powers in which the difficulty of supply prevents one side from making a total effort. An example of this is the Russo-Japanese war of 1905 in which the Russian commitment was limited to the forces that could be supplied over a single-track railway. Finally there may occur limited wars between major powers which are kept from spreading by a tacit agreement between the contestants and not by difficulties of technology or of logistics.

If one inquires which of these types of limited war are possible in the present situation, four broad categories can be distinguished. The first includes wars between secondary powers, such as between Israel and Egypt or between India and Pakistan, whether or not they involve the danger of the major powers joining in. The second type consists of wars involving either the Western powers or the Soviet bloc against powers which are clearly outmatched and under circumstances in which outside intervention is not likely. Examples of this would be Soviet intervention in the satellites, or United States military action in the Western Hemisphere. A third category are conflicts which begin as struggles between a major and a minor power but which may evolve the prospect of spreading as in the case of a Chinese move against South Vietnam or the Anglo-French "police action" against Egypt. Finally, there is the problem of limited war which begins explicitly as a war between the major powers. This is obviously the most explosive situation. If a war between major powers can be kept limited, it is clear that the first three situations would also stand a good chance of being kept from expanding.

In the history of warfare, limited wars between major powers have been a frequent occurrence. For a long time, however, they remained limited less by conscious choice than by considerations of domestic policy. In the seventeenth century Louis XIV employed almost his entire army for a period of close to twenty-five years. But his military establishment utilized only a small proportion of the national resources because of a domestic structure which prevented him from conscripting his subjects, levying income taxes, or confiscating property. [France's army was] therefore limited by the availability of resources and so were the wars [it] fought. On the other hand, the wars of Prussia, without exceeding those of France in scope, required a far greater mobilization of the national resources. Because of Prussia's limited resources, it was able to survive as a major power only by organizing the entire state for war. But Prussia's exertions only gave it a precarious parity with the other powers; it did not force them to emulate it. Wars remained limited because the major powers were able to mobilize only a small proportion of their national resources for war and because Prussia, the one power which was not so restrained, did not thereby gain a decisive advantage.

Since the French Revolution the domestic restrictions on the capacity of governments to mobilize national resources have increasingly disappeared. And this has occurred simultaneously with an industrial revolution which has made it technically possible to devote a substantial proportion of the national product to war without imposing a degree of privation which would shake the social order. To be sure, there still exist differences in *the willingness* of governments to exact sacrifices. One of the sources of Soviet strength is the readiness to devote a much larger proportion of the national income to military expenditures than the United States. But for purposes of present strategy it is clear that no major power will be forced to adopt a strategy of limited objectives because of insufficient resources. With modern weapons, a limited war becomes an act of policy, not of necessity.

What, under modern conditions, is a limited war? One can think of many models. It may be a war confined to a defined geographic area, or a war that does not utilize the entire available weapons system (such as refraining from the use of thermonuclear weapons). It may be a war which utilizes the entire weapons system but limits its employment to specific targets. But none of these military definitions seems adequate. A war may be confined to a geographic area and yet be total in the sense of draining the national substance, as happened to France in World War I. The fact that the most destructive weapons are not employed, or that the destructiveness of weapons used is small, is no guarantee against excessive suffering. In the Thirty Years' War the power of weapons was negligible compared to modern armaments and the number of men in each army was small by present-day standards — the Austrian Field Marshal Montecuccoli put at 15,000 the absolute maximum that could be commanded efficiently in one army. Yet it is estimated that the population of Germany was reduced by 30 percent during its course. A new world war fought with what are now called conventional weapons would also produce appalling casualties since the destructive power even of these weapons has increased between five- and tenfold since World War II. In short, there exists no way to define a limited war in purely military terms. The end result of relying on purely military considerations is certain to be all-out war: the attempt to render the enemy defenseless.

A limited war, by contrast, is fought for specific political objectives which, by their very existence, tend to establish a relationship between the force employed and the goal to be attained. It reflects an attempt to *affect* the opponent's will, not to *crush* it, to make the conditions to be imposed seem more attractive than continued resistance, to strive for specific goals and not for complete annihilation.

Limited war presents the military with particular difficulties. An all-out war is relatively simple to plan because its limits are set by military considerations and even by military capacity. The targets for an all-out war are fixed, and the force requirements are determined by the need to assemble overwhelming power. The characteristic of a limited war, on the other hand, is the existence of ground rules which define the relationship of military to political objectives. Planning becomes much more conjectural, much more subtle, and much more indeterminate, if only because a war against a major enemy can be kept limited only if both parties so desire, and this desire in itself tends to introduce a factor which is outside the control of planning officers. Since the military can never be certain how many forces the opponent will in fact commit to the struggle and since they feel obliged to guard against every contingency, they will devise plans for limited war which insensibly approach the level of all-out conflict.

From a purely military point of view they are right, for limited war is essentially a political act. Its distinguishing feature is that it has no "purely" military solution. The political leadership must, for this reason, assume the responsibility for defining the framework within which the military are to develop their plans and capabilities. To demand of the military that they set their own limits is to set in motion a vicious circle. The more the military plan on the basis of crushing the enemy even in a limited area, the more the political leadership will recoil before the risks of taking *any* military action. The more limited war is conceived as a "small" all-out war, the more it will produce inhibitions similar to those generated by the concept of massive retaliation. The prerequisite for a policy of limited war is to reintroduce the political element into our concept of warfare and to discard the notion that policy ends when war begins or that war can have goals distinct from those of national policy.

To what extent can the nuclear age leave room for a policy of intermediate objectives? Do any of the factors apply today which in the past made possible a diplomacy of limited objectives and a military policy of limited wars?

In the great periods of European cabinet diplomacy, between the Treaty of Westphalia and the French Revolution and between the Congress of Vienna and the outbreak of the first World War, wars were limited because there existed a political framework which led to a general acceptance of a policy of limited risks. This political framework was based on several factors. There was, to begin with, a deliberate decision that the upheavals of the Thirty Years' War and the Napoleonic wars should not be allowed to recur. While most effective in the period immediately following these conflicts, this decision gave the newly established international orders a breathing spell in which the major powers became convinced that none of the outstanding disputes involved their survival. More important was the fact that the international order did not contain a revolutionary power. No state was so dissatisfied with the peace settlement that it sought to gain its ends by overthrowing it, and no power considered that its domestic notion of justice was incompatible with that of the other states. Finally, in an era of stable weapons technology both the strength of the powers and the assessment of it were relatively fixed; the risks of surprise attack and of unforeseen technological developments were relatively small. All this did not make conflicts impossible, but it limited them to disputes within a given framework. Wars occurred, but they were fought in the name of the existing framework and the peace was justified as a better arrangement of a basically unchanged international order.

Today, as we have seen, we lack both stable power relationships and a legitimate political order on whose tenets all major powers are agreed. But these shortcomings may be outweighed by a third factor, the fear of a thermonuclear war. Never have the consequences of an all-out war been so obvious, never have the gains seemed so out of relation to the sacrifices.

It is often argued that since limited wars offer no inherent guarantee against their expansion, they may gradually merge into all-out war. On purely logical grounds, the argument is unassailable. But it assumes that the major protagonists will be looking for an excuse to expand the war whereas in reality both sides will probably grasp at every excuse, however illogical, to keep a thermonuclear holocaust from occurring. [That], in fact, [is] what happened in the Korean war, at a time when the weapons technology was much less horrendous. We refused to retaliate against the Manchurian air bases from which enemy planes were attacking our forces. And the Chinese made no effort to interfere with our aircraft-carriers, or with our bases in Japan, or even to launch an attack against our only two big supply ports, Pusan and Inchon.

These limitations were not brought about by logic or agreement but by a mutual reluctance to expand the conflict. It is clear that war cannot be limited unless both sides wish to keep it limited. The argument in favor of the possibility of limited war is that both sides have a common and overwhelming interest in preventing it from spreading. The fear that an all-out thermonuclear war might lead to the disintegration of the social structure offers an opportunity to set limits to both war and diplomacy.

The conduct of limited war has two prerequisites: a doctrine and a capability. So long as we consider limited war as an aberration from the "pure" case of all-out war we will not be ready to grasp its opportunities, and we will conduct the wars we do fight hesitantly and ambiguously, oscillating between the twin temptations to expand them (that is, to bring them closer to our notion of what war should be like), or to end them at the first enemy overture.

A doctrine for limited war will have to discard any illusions about what can be achieved by means of it. Limited war is not a cheaper substitute for massive retaliation. On the contrary, it must be based on the awareness that with the end of our atomic monopoly it is no longer possible to impose unconditional surrender at an acceptable cost.

The purpose of limited war is to inflict losses or to pose risks for the enemy out of proportion to the objectives under dispute. The more moderate the objective, the less violent the war is likely to be. This does not mean that military operations cannot go beyond the territory or the objective in dispute; indeed, one way of increasing the enemy's willingness to settle is to deprive him of something he can regain only by making peace. But the result of a limited war cannot depend on military considerations alone; it reflects an ability to harmonize political and military objectives. An attempt to reduce the enemy to impotence would surely lead to all-out war.

Nevertheless, a strategic doctrine which renounces the imposition of unconditional surrender should not be confused with the acceptance of a stalemate. The notion that there is no middle ground between unconditional surrender and the *status quo ante* is much too mechanical. To be sure, a restoration of the *status quo ante* is often the simplest solution, but it is not the only possible one. The argument that neither side will accept a defeat, however limited, without utilizing every weapon in its arsenal is contradicted both by psychology and by experience. There would seem to be no sense in seeking to escape a limited defeat through bringing on the cataclysm of an all-out war, particularly if all-out war threatens a calamity far transcending the penalties of losing a limited war. It simply does not follow that because one side stands to lose from a limited war, it could gain from an all-out war. On the contrary, both sides face the same dilemma: that the power of modern weapons has made all-out war useless as an instrument of policy, except for acts of desperation.

The West has accepted several contractions of its sphere without resorting to all-out war. If the military position of the Soviet leadership became untenable and it were offered face-saving alternatives short of surrender, it too might accept local withdrawals without resorting to all-out war. Even if limited war offered no more than the possibility of local stalemates, it would represent a strategic improvement, for our current problem is our inability to defend major areas except by the threat of a thermonuclear holocaust which we should make every effort to avoid.

The development of a wide spectrum of capabilities would be of crucial importance even should it be assumed that any war between us and the U.S.S.R. or China will inevitably be all-out. For, unless the exchange of nuclear and thermonuclear blows leads to the social collapse of both contenders — a distinct possibility — the side which has in being superior forces for other forms of conflict may win out in the end. If the Red Army, for example, should succeed in overrunning Eurasia during or after an exchange of all-out blows, we would probably not have sufficient resources remaining to undertake a reconquest. As stockpiles of the largest modern weapons are exhausted or delivery vehicles are used up, an increasing premium is placed on a diversified military capability and not only vis-à-vis the enemy but toward hitherto secondary powers as well. In the absence of forces for other forms of conflict, all-out war may merely pave the way for the dominance of the world by states whose social structure and forces-in-being have remained more or less intact during the struggle-to-death of the superstates.

There exist three reasons then, for developing a strategy of limited war. First, limited war represents the only means for preventing the Soviet bloc, at an acceptable cost, from overrunning the peripheral areas of Eurasia. Second, a wide range of military capabilities may spell the difference between defeat and victory even in an all-out war. Finally, the intermediate applications of our power offer the best chance to bring about strategic changes favorable to our side.

For while a balance can be maintained along existing lines on the Eurasian continent, it will always be tenuous. So long as Soviet armies are poised on the Elbe, Western Europe will be insecure. So long as Chinese might presses upon free Asia, the uncommitted powers will seek safety in neutralism. The United States faces the task not only of stemming the Soviet expansion, but also of reducing Soviet pressures and demonstrating the limitations of Soviet power and skills. The resolution of the free world, now assailed by a sense of its impotence, will improve to the extent that it realizes that the Soviet bloc, behind its façade of monolithic power, also shrinks from certain consequences. When we have achieved this capability and this understanding, we may be in a position to reduce the Soviet sphere.

A strategy of limited war is more likely to achieve this objective than the threat of a total nuclear war. Either the threat of an all-out war will be considered a bluff or it will turn every dispute into a question of prestige, inhibiting any concessions. Actions short of total war, on the other hand, may help restore fluidity to the diplomatic situation, particularly if we analyze precisely what is meant by the concept of reducing the Soviet sphere. The Sino-Soviet bloc can be turned back short of a general war in one of two ways: by a voluntary withdrawal or by an internal split. The former is unlikely and depends on many factors beyond our control, but the latter deserves careful study.

While it is impossible to predict the precise circumstances of a possible split within the Soviet orbit, its general framework can be discerned. The U.S.S.R. may be forced to loosen its hold on its European satellites if it finds that the effort to hold them in line absorbs ever more of its strength. And relations between China and the Soviet Union may become cooler if the alliance forces either partner to shoulder risks for objectives which are of no benefit to it. Tito's break with Moscow was caused at least in part by his disenchantment over the Soviet Union's lukewarm support on the Trieste issue, and that in turn was due to the unwillingness of the Kremlin to risk an all-out war for the sake of a peripheral objective. Similarly, it is not clear how much China would risk to rescue the U.S.S.R. from embarrassments in Europe or in the Middle East, or to what lengths the U.S.S.R. is prepared to go to increase the power of China in Asia. A test of our strategy is, therefore, its ability to bring about situations which accentuate potential differences within the Soviet bloc. In these terms, one of the basic indictments of an excessive emphasis on a strategy of all-out war is that its inability to differentiate and graduate its pressures may actually contribute to the consolidation and the unity of the Soviet bloc.

It is therefore misleading to reject a strategy of limited war on the ground that it does not offer a military solution to our strategic problem. Its merit is precisely that it may open the way to a political solution. Had we defeated the Chinese Army in Korea in 1951, the U.S.S.R. would have faced the problem of whether the risk of expanding the war was worth keeping China from suffering a limited defeat. Had we followed up our victory with a conciliatory political proposal to Peiping, we could have caused it to reconsider the wisdom of being too closely tied to the U.S.S.R. Even if we had failed in our primary task of dividing the U.S.S.R. and China, we would have greatly improved our position toward our allies and even more toward the uncommitted nations in Asia. The best counterargument to the charge of colonialism is political moderation after a military victory. A military stalemate, on the other hand, always leaves open the question whether what is advanced as a proof of moderation is not in reality a sign of weakness or at least of irresolution. Thus, if limited actions are implemented as part of a policy which offers the other side a way out short of unconditional surrender, they may bring about local reversals. These in turn may set off chain reactions which will be difficult to control and which may magnify the tensions within the Soviet bloc. A strategy of limited war, then, would use our retaliatory power as a means to permit us to fight local actions on our own terms and to shift to the other side the risk of initiating all-out war.

Whatever the theoretical advantages of limited war, is it practical? Does not a policy of limited war run up against the geographic reality that the Soviet bloc possesses interior lines of communication and may therefore be able to assemble a superior force at any given point along its periphery? Can we afford a policy of limited war or will it not overstrain our resources just as surely as would all-out war? Does not the concern with local resistance mistake the real security problem which, in major areas, is political instability and a standard of living considered oppressively low by the majority of the population?

Admittedly, we alone cannot possibly defend the Soviet periphery by local actions and the present period of revolutionary change will not be managed solely by reliance on a military doctrine. Our task also includes strengthening the will to resist among the peoples threatened by Communist expansionism. In the underdeveloped third of the world this means pursuing a variety of measures: a political program to gain the confidence of local populations and to remove the stigma of colonialism from us, together with a degree of economic assistance which will help bring about political stability. But such programs, although essential, will in the end be ineffective unless we improve our capacity for local defense. We have a weakness for considering problems as "primarily" economic or "primarily" military rather than as total situations in which political, economic and military considerations merge, which is the way the Soviet leadership regards policy.

Thus one of the conditions of political stability is our capacity to react to local aggression at the place of its occurrence. Few leaders of threatened countries will wish to rely for protection on our strategic superiority in an all-out war. Victory in a general war will mean little to a country which meanwhile has undergone the moral and physical ravages of Soviet occupation.

Can the non-Soviet countries of Eurasia be defended, assuming the willingness of the threatened countries to resist and an ability on our part to help them? In support of a negative answer such factors are cited as the "unlimited" Soviet manpower and the vast distances of the threatened areas from the centers of our strength. Absolute numbers are important, but only the part of them that can be utilized effectively is strategically significant. The value of Sino-Soviet manpower is limited by the capacity of the Soviet bloc to equip and train it, and its effectiveness is reduced by the power of modern weapons and by difficulties of communications and supply.

The particular danger zone for limited wars is the arc which stretches from the eastern border of Turkey around the periphery of Eurasia. Within that area the Indian subcontinent is protected by mountain barriers and by extremely difficult communications. Aggression against the Middle East would have to count on the flanking position of Turkey and, despite the Suez fiasco, Great Britain would probably join in resistance. An attack on Burma would antagonize India and would be difficult to supply, and the same would be true of the remainder of Southeast Asia. An attack in the Far East would have to take place either across water or against indigenous forces, as in Korea. Moreover, if we utilize nuclear weapons there will be an inherent upper limit to the number of troops that can be profitably employed in threatened areas. Thus if we could develop forces capable of conducting limited war and of getting into position rapidly, we should be able to defeat the Soviet Union or China in local engagements despite their interior position.

If we commit ourselves to a strategy of local defense, do we not run the risk of having our forces always at the wrong place? Cannot the Soviet bloc utilize its interior position to keep us constantly off balance? To be sure, the Soviet bloc is able to pick the initial point of attack, but the greater mobility of its interior position is illusory because of the difficulties of communication. Once the Soviet armies are committed in one area, they cannot be shifted at will against our air power or with greater speed than we can shift ours by sea or air. The Chinese Communists, for example, cannot draw us into Indo-China and then attack in Burma with the same army. They can, of course, build up two armies, but we should be able to learn of this in time and then decide to defend one or the other area, or both, depending on the strategic situation. . . .

Limited war is not simply a question of appropriate military forces and doctrines. It also places heavy demands on the discipline and subtlety of the political leadership and on the confidence of the society in it. For limited war is psychologically a much more complex problem than all-out war. In an all-out war the alternatives will be either surrender or resistance against a threat to the national existence. To be sure, psychological factors will largely determine the relative willingness to engage in an all-out war, and the side more willing to run risks may gain an important advantage in the conduct of diplomacy. However, once the decision to fight is taken, a nation's physical ability to conduct war will be the most important factor in the outcome.

In a limited war, on the other hand, the psychological equation will be of crucial importance not only with respect to the decision to enter the war but throughout the course of military operations. A limited war among major powers is kept limited by the conscious choice of the protagonists. Either side has the physical power to expand it, and, to the extent that each side is willing to increase its commitment in preference either to a stalemate or to a defeat, the war will gradually become an all-out one. The restraint which keeps a war limited is a psychological one: the consequences of a limited victory or a limited defeat or a stalemate — the three possible outcomes of a limited war — must seem preferable to the consequences of an all-out war.

In a limited war the choices are more varied than in an all-out conflict and their nature is more ambiguous. Victory offers no final solution and defeat does not carry with it the penalty of national catastrophe. As a result, the psychological correlation of forces in a limited war is not stable; it depends on a series of intangibles. The side which is more willing to risk an all-out war or can convince its opponent of its greater readiness to run that risk is in the stronger position. Even when the willingness of both sides to run risks is equal at the beginning of the war, the psychological equation will constantly be shifting, depending on the course of military operations. Because the limitation of war is brought about by the fear of unleashing a thermonuclear holocaust, the psychological equation is, paradoxically, constantly shifting *against* the side which seems to be winning. The greater the transformation it seeks, the more plausible will become the threat by its opponent of launching an all-out war. The closer defeat in the limited war brings the losing side to the consequences which it would suffer by defeat in an all-out war, the less it will feel restrained from resorting to extreme measures.

At the same time, the winning side may become increasingly reluctant to test the opponent's willingness to resort to all-out war. For while the winning side is staking its chance for obtaining a favorable transformation, the losing side is risking an adverse change of position. The better the position of the winning side, the more secure it will feel and the less it will be willing to take the risks of an all-out war. The more precarious the position of the losing side becomes, the more insecure it will feel and the more likely it is to raise its commitment toward the level of an all-out war. The prerequisite of victory in a limited war is therefore to determine under what circumstances one side may be willing to run greater risks for winning than its opponent will accept to avoid losing. A calculation of this character must pay special attention to the importance of diplomatic overtures which make clear that national survival is not at stake and that a settlement is possible on reasonable terms. Otherwise the result is almost certain to be either stalemate or all-out war.

If an opponent attaches great importance to an area in dispute — or is thought to attach great importance to it — he will have a distinct psychological advantage in a limited war. This was the case with China's role in Korea. Some areas may be thought so important to one of the contenders that they will be protected by the belief of the opponent that any attack on them will lead to a general war. Protection for these areas will be achieved less by local defense than by over-all strategic balance. This has been the case up to now with Western Europe with respect to the United States, or with the satellite regions with respect to the U.S.S.R. As total war poses increasingly ominous prospects, however, the over-all strategic balance will be a less and less adequate protection to threatened areas, for ever fewer regions will seem worth this price. As the implications of all-out war with modern weapons become better understood, security for many areas will increasingly depend on the capability for local action. Limited war would thereby become a test of the determination of the contenders, a gauge of the importance they attach to disputed issues. If one side attaches greater importance to an area or an issue and is willing to pay a higher price, and if it possesses a capability for waging a limited war, it may well achieve a favorable shift in the strategic equation.

The key to a successful policy of limited war is to keep the challenge to the opponent, whether diplomatic or military, below the threshold which would unleash an all-out war. The greater the risk in relation to the challenge, the less total the response is likely to be. The more the challenge approximates the risks posed by all-out war, the more difficult it will be to limit the conflict. A policy of limited war therefore presupposes three conditions: the ability to generate pressures other than the threat of all-out war; the ability to create a climate in which survival is not thought to be at stake in each issue; and the ability to keep control of public opinion in case a disagreement arises over whether national survival is at stake. The first condition depends to a considerable extent on the flexibility of our military policy; the second on the subtlety of our diplomacy; the third will reflect the courage of our leadership. . . .

But assuming that it will be possible to create a spectrum of military capabilities to meet the widest range of Soviet challenges, will our diplomacy be able to bring about a framework in which national survival is thought not to be at stake? Pressures severe enough to cause withdrawal or stalemate may, after all, seem severe enough to threaten survival, especially to a regime like that of Soviet Russia. It must be admitted that the challenge to our diplomacy is formidable. It would be hopeless except against the background of a retaliatory capability which can make the Soviet leadership recoil from the prospect of an all-out war. As long as we maintain a powerful strategic striking force, an all-out conflict is likely in only two contingencies: if the Soviets see an opportunity to achieve hegemony in Eurasia by peripheral actions which we would be unable to counter except by all-out war; or if the U.S.S.R. should misunderstand our intentions and interpret each military move on our part as a prelude to a thermonuclear holocaust.

Provided our military policy equips us with a wide spectrum of capabilities, the task of our diplomacy will be to convey to the Soviet bloc what we understand by limited war, at least to some extent. This becomes all the more important because Soviet reactions to our measures will depend less on what we intend than on what we are thought by the Soviet leaders to intend. The power and speed of modern weapons make too much obscurity dangerous. Unless there has been some degree of comprehension of the nature of limited war on both sides, it may be impossible to improvise it in the confusion of battle. Diplomacy should therefore strive to insure that the opponent obtains the information he requires to make the correct decisions. To be sure, such a course will not restrain an enemy determined on a showdown. It may, however, prevent him from stumbling into an all-out war based on miscalculation or on the misinterpretation of our intentions.

The same program which may reduce the danger of miscalculation by the enemy would also go a long way toward educating public opinion in the realities of the nuclear age. This is, of course, less of a problem in the Soviet bloc where dictatorship confers a much greater freedom of action. In the Western world, however, and particularly in the United States, a considerable change in the concept of war is required. It is important for our leadership to understand that total victory is no longer possible and for the public to become aware of the dangers of pressing for such a course.

A long history of invulnerability has accustomed our public opin-

ion to look at war more in terms of the damage we can inflict than
of the losses we might suffer and to react to frustrations abroad by
a demand for absolute solutions. The American people must be
made aware that, with the end of our atomic monopoly all-out war
has ceased to be an instrument of policy, except as a last resort,
and that for most of the issues likely to be in dispute our only choice
is between a strategy of limited war or inaction. It would be tragic
if our Government were deprived of its freedom of maneuver by the
ignorance of the public regarding the consequences of a course before which it would recoil if aware of all its implications. This is
all the more true since the same ignorance which underlies the demand for all-or-nothing solutions might well produce panic if our
people were unexpectedly brought face-to-face with consequences
of an all-out war. Conversely, a public fully aware of the dangers
confronting it and forearmed psychologically by an adequate civil
defense program will be better prepared to support a more flexible
national policy.

Whatever aspect of our strategic problem we consider — mitigating the horrors of war, creating a spectrum of capabilities to
resist likely Soviet challenges — we are brought to recognize the
importance of developing a strategy which makes room for the
possibility of limited war. Creating a readiness for limited war
should not be considered a problem of choice but of necessity. It
results from the impossibility of combining both maximum force
and the maximum willingness to act.

A strategy which makes room for the possibility of fighting
limited wars will not eliminate the precariousness of our situation.
In the nuclear age the best strategy can provide only a relative
security, for the threat of all-out war will always loom in the background as a last resort for either side. Moreover, as nuclear technology becomes more widely diffused, other and perhaps less
responsible powers will enter the nuclear race. The fear of mutual
destruction, today the chief deterrent to all-out war for the major
powers, may prove less effective with nations who have less to lose
and whose negotiating position might even be improved by a threat
to commit suicide.

Even among the major powers the strategy outlined in this chapter will not be easy to implement. It presupposes a military capability which is truly graduated. It assumes a diplomacy which can
keep each conflict from being considered the prelude to a final
showdown. And it requires strong nerves. We can make a strategy
of limited war stick only if we leave no doubt about our readiness
and our ability to face a final showdown.

Deterrent Postures and Targeting Strategies

Since 1953, strategists have differed widely over the best ways of using strategic nuclear weapons. The differences have occurred because of the conflicting answers they have given to three questions. First, what kinds of forces and targeting strategies are most effective for discouraging a preemptive attack? Second, how effective can nuclear weapons be for uses other than deterrence of an attack on one's homeland? And third, if deterrence were to fail, how should nuclear weapons be used in order to minimize casualties? The selections below present some of the answers that have been given. Glenn H. Snyder analyzes the requirements for a stable balance of terror, in which preemption is not likely to occur. John Foster Dulles argues that nuclear weapons can be used, not only to deter attacks on one's homeland, but also to dissuade an opponent from attacking the other states that one is pledged to defend.[1] Nikita S. Khrushchev concludes that mutual possession of second-strike capabilities makes peaceful coexistence between the superpowers not only possible but necessary. Robert S. McNamara asserts that if a nuclear war were to break out between the NATO alliance and the Soviet Union, only the management of the alliance's strategic nuclear forces by a central authority could keep casualties to a minimum.[2] Such management would keep casualties down because it would make the extension of deterrence into war possible. Each side could hold the other's cities as hostages. The "no-cities" doctrine would then require counterforce targeting. Thomas C. Schelling and Hans J. Morgenthau present pro and con arguments, respectively, for counterforce targeting.

[1] The use of nuclear threats to dissuade a Russian attack on Europe is not dealt with here. See the Editors' Introduction, pp. 12–21. See also Robert E. Osgood, *NATO: The Entangling Alliance* (Chicago: University of Chicago Press, 1962) and Henry A. Kissinger, *The Troubled Partnership* (New York: McGraw-Hill, 1965).

[2] McNamara also used the centralized-management argument to discredit the efficacy of nationally owned, middle-power nuclear forces. See William W. Kaufmann, *The McNamara Strategy* (New York: Harper and Row, 1964), pp. 114–120.

The Conditions of Stability

GLENN H. SNYDER

We may say that a "balance of terror" exists when each side has somewhat more than the minimum strike-back requirement — i.e., when neither side, in striking first, can destroy enough of the opponent's forces to make the latter's retaliation bearable. But the *existence* of a deterrent balance is something different from the *stability* of the balance. Stability in one sense refers to the degree of change in the military, technological, or political situation which is necessary to give one side a sufficient first-strike capability or sufficient incentive to strike first. For example, the balance would be unstable if either side required only a small additional expenditure of resources to achieve a first-strike capability which could reduce the opponent's retaliation to acceptable proportions. It would also be unstable if some moderately conceivable technological or scientific breakthrough — say, in air defense or in devices for tracking mobile missile launchers — suddenly gave one side a first-strike capability. Or it might be unstable if the commitment of one side's honor and prestige in a policy declaration made it willing to accept significantly greater retaliatory damage, so that a first-strike capability which previously had been insufficient became sufficient to justify a first strike.

A second form of instability would be a force relationship which produced strong fears on one or both sides that the other was about to strike first, thus creating an incentive to strike first to pre-empt the other's attack.

Stability, at any given time, is a function of two factors: the extent to which either side's strike-back capability exceeds the necessary minimum, and the "attacker-to-target ratio." The latter refers to the amount of attacking forces required to eliminate a given amount of the defender's forces; it may also be called the degree of "structural stability." Both factors together determine the degree of

From *Deterrence and Defense: Toward a Theory of National Security* by Glenn H. Snyder, pp. 97–109. Copyright © 1961 by Princeton University Press for the Center of International Studies, Princeton University. Reprinted by permission of Princeton University Press. Some footnotes have been omitted.

effort required of the attacker to achieve a sufficient first-strike capability.

Stability is highest when both sides have much more than the minimum strike-back capability and when the attacker-to-target ratio is high. Then a very large increase in either side's forces would be necessary to obtain a sufficient first-strike capability; only a very major and rather fantastic scientific discovery would overcome the deterrent balance; and no political commitment or threat would be likely to increase either side's values at stake to a degree necessary to offset the costs of all-out war. And with such a configuration of forces, neither side would be likely to fear a first strike by the other, so there could be no incentive for pre-emptive attack.

At the other extreme, the balance would be very unstable if both sides just barely had a minimum strike-back capability and if the attacker-to-target ratio were low, so that only a slight increase in one side's forces, or a minor technological breakthrough, or a small rise in political tension, would create a situation in which one side felt it could rationally strike first. Incentives to pre-empt would be high because of mutual fears that the opponent had, or would soon develop, a sufficient first-strike capability.

Of course, there could be many intermediate degrees of stability between these extremes. For example, if one side could muster a wide margin of forces over its minimum deterrent, while the other side just barely met this criterion, stability would be fairly high if the stronger country were a status quo power with little incentive to strike first. But stability would depend on the continuance of benevolent intentions on the part of the stronger side.

Even with a high degree of structural and over-all stability in the sense just discussed, there may be countervailing factors which make for instability. For example, even though a very major unilateral scientific breakthrough would be required to give one side a first-strike capability, if such breakthroughs are possible or likely, the situation may be unstable. The sudden perfection of a good anti-missile defense system by one side would drastically shift the balance of terror in its favor, whatever the previous degree of structural and over-all stability. Or if one or both sides entertain a policy of firing missiles on warning alone, there may be serious dangers of accidental war. However, . . . the danger of accidental war is closely related to the degree of stability on other counts; when neither side has anything approaching a sufficient first-strike capability, there is little likelihood of their being "trigger-happy."

It is instructive to consider the degree of structural stability which would seem likely to exist with various types and combinations of weapons.

If both sides were to rely entirely on fixed land-based missiles, reasonably well-hardened and dispersed, the attacker-to-target ratio would depend largely on the accuracy of the attacking missiles and their lethal radius, the latter defined as distance from the point of impact within which the target would be destroyed.[1] For example, if accuracy were such that there was a .50 chance of a single missile landing within the lethal radius, four missiles would have to be fired to achieve upward of a .90 chance of killing the target and the situation would be, structurally, very stable. The attacker would need many more missiles than the defender to be sure of getting off with acceptable retaliatory damage. But if there were a .50 chance of an attacking missile landing within a circle of only half the lethal radius, the attacker would have a .94 chance of destroying the target with a single missile. Then the balance of terror would be structurally unstable; one side might be willing to strike, for example, if its missile stocks only equaled the defender's and if it were willing to accept the retaliatory destruction which approximately 6 per cent of the defender's missiles could inflict.

The degree of preponderance, if any, which the attacker needs, is sensitive not only to the attacker-to-target ratio, but also to the absolute number of missiles which the defender has. This follows from the fact that the damage which the attacker will accept is constant, while the number of defending missiles which escape the first strike, with given accuracy and lethal radius, varies with the total number of defending missiles. For example, suppose retaliation against cities by 25 missiles is just unacceptable damage for the attacker, the defender has 50 missiles, and the attacker has a .5 chance of killing any particular missile site with any one missile. Then the attacker needs only 50 missiles for a sufficient first-strike capability. If both sides are symmetrical in their accuracies and willingness to accept damage, each has a sufficient first-strike capability and the situation is unstable. But if one side increases to 100, the other must fire 200 (two at each of the defending sites) to be confident of retaliation by only 25 missiles. If the defender increases to 200, the attacker needs 600. If the defender increases to 300, the attacker needs 1,200, and so on.[2] The less accurate the

---

[1] Lethal radius is a function of the "hardness" of the target — the amount of blast pressure it can withstand — and the yield of the warhead. . . .

[2] The mathematical reason for this "multiplier effect" is that increasing numbers of attacking missiles are wasted in "overkills" as the defender's launching sites increase in number. When both have 50 missiles, the attacker reduces the retaliating force to 25 by firing one missile at each defending site. When the defender has 100, the attacker must reduce the probability of missing each target to .25, to have a statistical likelihood of reducing the number of retaliating missiles to 25. The attacker

attacker's missiles, the faster his first-strike requirement multiplies as the defender increases his stocks. Thus, when the number of missiles on both sides is reasonably large, the requirement for a sufficient first-strike capability will be some multiple of the requirement for a minimum strike-back capability, and the multiple itself will be greater, the larger the number of the defender's missile sites. It is thus characteristic of the missile arms race, in seeming contrast to traditional arms races with conventional weapons, that it becomes more stable as it proceeds. The incentives to continue the arms race diminish rapidly as the numbers of weapons increase on both sides. The country which wishes to have only a minimum deterrent need have one that amounts to only a fraction of the opponent's striking force when the former's number of dispersed weapons is large relative to the number of weapons which would cause unacceptable damage to the opponent's cities.[3] By similar reasoning, the country which contemplates a first strike can provide itself with the necessary capability only by resource expenditures very much larger than the expenditures the opponent must make to counter and re-establish the deterrent balance.

Of course, improvements in accuracy, reliability, and payload of missiles would work against the stabilizing effect of increased numbers. On the other hand, increased hardening and dispersal would be stabilizing.[4] In general, it does not seem that a system of numerous hardened and well-dispersed sites at fixed bases would ever become seriously unstable in a structural sense (barring a substantial breakthrough in active defense against missiles), since it is hard to believe any aggressor would be so sure of the accuracy and

---

must fire two missiles per target: the probability that both will hit the target is .25, the probability that one or the other will hit is .50, and the probability of a miss by both is .25. When more than one missile is fired at a target, the probability that the target is missed is the product of the probabilities of a miss with each missile. When the defender has 200, the attacker must fire three per target to reduce the probability of a miss per target to .125 ($.50 \times .50 \times .50$). With 300 defending missiles, the probability of a miss must be reduced to .0625 or $(.50)^4$, requiring four missiles per target.

[3] A further conclusion might be that, as missile stocks increase, the "competition" between numbers of missiles and passive defense measures as means of preserving a minimum punitive deterrent comes more and more to favor the former, provided the accuracy and reliability of the enemy's missiles do not increase proportionally.

[4] Hardening and dispersal are complementary measures. The greater the hardening, the lesser the degree of dispersal which is necessary to make sure a single attacking missile does not destroy more than one defending missile site. Thus hardening can produce administrative and logistical economies by allowing the closer clustering of missile sites.

reliability of his missiles and target intelligence as to be confident of eliminating each of the defending sites with a single missile. Two missiles per site would seem about the minimum for any aggressor who is not a pathological risk-taker. Even with this ratio, over-all instability could of course occur if the aggressive-minded side were allowed to gain a very large preponderance in weapons.

Statements of comparable precision regarding mobile systems, both land- and sea-based, are more difficult to make. A land-based mobile system may be highly invulnerable, and hence may contribute to overall stability, if methods for continuous aerial surveillance of its movements are not devised. However, if space photography develops to the point where surveillance becomes possible, missile trains may become more vulnerable than fixed-base missiles. Since they are "soft" installations, lethal radius against them will be high; a moving train might not be able to get out of range of the blast between the time an enemy space satellite transmits a "fix" and the enemy fires a missile with a high-yield warhead against that fix. If missile trains carry several missiles (as in current U.S. plans) one successful attacking missile could eliminate more than one defending missile, in which case the mobile system might be considerably less stable than the fixed-base system. Also the generalization made above, about the balance of terror becoming more stable as it proceeds to higher levels of armament, might not hold if both sides relied heavily on rail-mobile missiles. At some point in his accumulation of missiles, an aggressor would reach the point where he could simply blanket the defender's railroad system with enough blast "overpressure" to destroy all trains.

Missile-firing submarines are in a somewhat different category, since they are not subject to attack by missiles, but rather by other submarines and other ships, as well as by aircraft. Here the crucial first-strike requirement is not for numbers of attacking weapons, but rather for the development of technical means of identification, tracking, and coordinated attacks. Since the enemy may develop such means in secret, sole reliance on Polaris submarines might create an unstable situation. Also, Polaris submarines do not benefit from the stabilizing effect of numbers, since each successful attack on a submarine would mean the loss of 16 missiles.

With aircraft against aircraft, stability depends on the degree to which defending aircraft are protected and dispersed, the efficiency of the defender's warning systems, and the efficiency of the attacker's air defenses. If the defender's warning system is not reliable, and if his aircraft are unsheltered and only moderately dispersed, the situation may be very unstable, since one attacking bomber can destroy several bombers which are caught on the ground. But if the defender does have a very good warning system which cannot be penetrated by sneak attacks or evaded by "end runs," a minimum strike-back capability can be assured by an ability to get enough aircraft into the air, after receipt of warning, to penetrate the attacker's air defenses in sufficient strength to inflict unacceptable damage. The number of attacking bombers is virtually irrelevant. With reliable warning, the balance is likely to be stable unless the attacker is confident that his air defenses can achieve a very high kill rate against the retaliating bombers.[5]

When the prospective attacker has large numbers of missiles and the defender relies entirely on aircraft, similar reasoning applies. If the defender does not have a good warning system against missiles, if his aircraft are unprotected and undispersed, and if the attacker has enough missiles to hit all the defender's airbases, the defender must have enough bombers on continuous airborne alert to inflict unacceptable damage after attrition by the attacker's air defenses. If the defender does have a good warning system against missiles, he needs the same number of aircraft on ground alert, but the degree of alertness must be much higher than when the attacker uses aircraft, because of the very short flight-time of missiles.

When both sides have mixed forces, as we must expect in the foreseeable future, stability depends, of course, on some combination of the factors just discussed.

Both structural stability and over-all stability are ultimately economic functions. Structural stability depends on the amount of economic resources which an incipient attacker must invest to gain a capacity to eliminate a given amount of the defender's forces, compared with the amount of resources which the defender must invest to counter the attacker's increase. For example, if the cost of building a "hardened" missile site, requiring three enemy firings for a sure kill, were substantially less than the cost to the enemy of building three additional missiles, the balance would be fairly stable structurally. It is conceivable that the cost of building the three attacking missiles would be less than the cost of the hardened missile, since missiles designed for attack do not have to be protected. Then the balance would be structurally unstable, since the defender would have to spend more than the attacker to offset the attacker's increase. Or if a 10 per cent increase in the attacker's air defense kill rate would cost him considerably more than a 10 per cent in-

---

[5] Of course, warning systems are vulnerable to destruction. The situation could be unstable if the attacker were willing to gamble that destruction of the defender's warning system would not cause immediate retaliation.

crease in the defender's aircraft on air alert or high ground alert, this would make for stability. But *over-all* stability depends not only on structural stability but also on the *total amount* of expenditure which the attacker must make to gain a sufficient first-strike capability. This, of course, is a function of the margin of insurance which the defender has provided himself in building his strike-back force.

We have left the question of pre-emptive attack for separate consideration because it involves certain factors not pertaining to other forms of instability — principally its incentive, which does not stem from the prospect of gain, but from the desire to forestall losses from a first strike by the opponent which is believed to be imminent. In the usual analysis of pre-emptive war, a spiral of mutual reinforcing fears and counterfears is postulated: A begins to fear that B intends to strike first, from which A derives some incentive to deliver a forestalling strike; B, realizing that A is subject to such fears, begins to fear A's forestalling attack, from which B develops some incentive to strike first even if, originally, it had entertained no such intention; A, recognizing that B fears a pre-emptive strike by A, has its fears of B's first strike reinforced, and feels even greater pressure to strike first; B, guessing that A feels this pressure, develops still greater fears and incentives to strike first, . . . and so on for as many regressive steps as either side might wish to contemplate. If such a spiral of expectations and incentives did occur, either side might be willing to accept much greater retaliatory damage after its own first strike than it would accept if the pre-emptive motivation did not exist.

The following analysis will attempt to show that although pre-emptive attack is at least conceivable when manned bombers are the mainstay of each side's strategic nuclear power, it is unlikely even then, and it becomes increasingly unlikely as both sides come to rely more and more on long-range ballistic missiles.

If there were to be a serious danger of pre-emptive attack, it would have to follow from the existence of two conditions: (1) that there is a substantial if not decisive first-strike advantage — i.e., that if war is expected with certainty, it is much better to strike first than second; and (2) that one side believes the other side is very likely to strike first.

The first condition is often taken as axiomatic. The advantage of getting in the first blow in all-out war is said to follow from the benefits of surprise;[6] from the advantage of being able to choose

[6] Although surprise is usually mentioned among the advantages of striking first, surprise would be minimal under conditions conducive to

the most propitious time of attack; and, above all, from the effect of the first blow in establishing an asymmetry of surviving forces favoring the attacker. The defender must strike back with a disorganized and badly decimated force, in the face of air defenses and civil defenses which are alerted. Although the defender can inflict some damage in retaliation, this damage is as nothing compared with the damage which the "defender" could have inflicted if he had been allowed to strike first.

The "advantage of striking first" which we are presently discussing is not the advantage which follows from having a sufficient first-strike capability. When a country bent on aggression has such a capability, it has an incentive to strike, simply because the victim's retaliatory blow would be tolerable — tolerable when measured against the expectation of gains from the attack. The "advantage of striking first," as it relates to the question of pre-emptive attack, means that even though a retaliation blow would be unacceptable when measured against objectives other than pre-emption, it is nevertheless preferred to the costs of taking the opponent's first strike. It implies simply that if war is believed to be imminent, one's own losses are minimized by getting in the first blow.

Whether there is an advantage in getting in the first blow depends on a combination of *strategic* and *intrinsic* considerations. In strategic terms, there is a strike-first advantage when the side striking first can destroy more of the opponent's strategic nuclear capability in doing so than it loses of its own. In intrinsic terms, a strike-first advantage exists when the destruction to one's population and economy which would be suffered in the opponent's first strike is greater than the destruction which the opponent could inflict in a retaliatory blow.

There may be a strategic advantage in striking first when the bulk of each side's striking forces is made up of manned bombers, if one assumes that a considerable number of the defender's aircraft will be caught on the ground. One attacking airplane can eliminate several on the ground, since the defender is likely to have several planes at each base and since each attacking aircraft may be able to hit several bases in succession, carrying, as it may, a multiple bomb load. So the side which strikes first may be able to achieve a considerable preponderance of forces even though it may have struck from a prewar position of inferiority. However, even if such a strike-first advantage did exist in this sense, it would hardly trigger off a spiral of fears and counterfears leading to pre-emptive

---

pre-emption — i.e., when both sides have strong fears of impending attack by the opponent.

attack unless each side had a first-strike capability which could be construed by the other as being sufficient or nearly sufficient to make a first-strike rational for non-pre-emptive reasons. And even if this condition did exist, either side, rather than striking first because of uncertain fears that the other intended to strike, would be more likely to take measures — such as putting more aircraft on a high alert status — which would reduce the other's first-strike capability.

There may not be a first-strike advantage in an all-missile or predominantly missile environment if one makes four quite plausible assumptions: that the targets of a first strike would be the opponent's missile bases; that missile sites are well dispersed and hardened, or mobile; that a given number of missiles aimed at missile bases would cause less damage to the population and economy than a smaller number of retaliating missiles aimed at cities; and that the primary targets of a retaliatory blow would be cities.

Consider first a situation in which both sides rely entirely on fixed-base ICBM's, and missiles on both sides are equally accurate, reliable, and vulnerable. Suppose each side has 100 ICBM's. If accuracies, reliabilities, and vulnerabilities are all very high, we might imagine an extreme case in which each protagonist would feel absolutely confident that a single attacking missile could eliminate one of the opponent's launching sites before its missile was fired. Then of course there would be an advantage in striking first, since, although the attrition of forces on both sides would be equal and complete, all the war damage would be concentrated on the side which received the first (and only) blow.

But this is an extreme case which is hardly likely to be realized. The attacker probably will always have to lose more missiles in attacking than he is able to destroy of the defender's. Let us suppose, to give technology and the attacker's confidence the benefit of every doubt, that the missile-to-target ratio drops as low as 2:1. Then, with equal numbers of missiles on each side, it *may* not be advantageous to strike first. The attacker would lose two missiles for every one of the defender's which is destroyed. Firing off his entire stock of 100 missiles, the attacker would have to expect retaliation by at least 50 missiles against his cities. Rather than accept this result, the "attacker" might prefer to let the other side strike first against his missile sites. For either side, a first-strike advantage would *not* exist if the damage from 50 retaliatory missiles on its cities were expected to be greater than the by-product damage to population which would be expected from the enemy's first strike with 100 missiles directed at missile sites, not cities. Or, following another line of reasoning, each side might well believe that it would be best to let the other use up all its striking power, leaving the attacked side with a residual force which could be used to compel the attacker to capitulate. Thus, even with the low missile-to-target ratio of 2:1, there may be disadvantages in striking first. Obviously, with higher missile-to-target ratios, the supposed "strike-first advantage" becomes even more doubtful.

It is sometimes overlooked, in discussions of pre-emptive attack, that the act of pre-emption tends to convert the other side's target system from primarily counterforce to primarily countercity. If pre-emption cannot virtually eliminate the opponent's striking forces, this conversion may result in the pre-emptor's suffering more damage than he would have absorbed as the result of the opponent's first strike. Although pre-emption then would reduce the number of missiles landing on one's own territory, the ones which did arrive would hit where they would do maximum damage.

The primary object of getting in the first blow is to reduce the damage to oneself, as compared with what it would be if the opponent were allowed to strike first. But if it takes two or more missiles to eliminate one, missiles may be more useful for reducing the enemy's damage-producing capacity when they function as targets than when they are used as instruments of attack. With a missile-to-target ratio of 2:1 for both sides, two missiles destroy one in attacking, but "destroy" four as targets. The strategic advantage in *not* striking first varies as the square of the missile-to-target ratio, when the latter is greater than 1:1, and roughly equal for both sides. The strategic disadvantage may be enough in itself to discourage pre-emption if an important objective is to gain the best possible position in the post-strike balance of forces for bargaining purposes. But there may also be an intrinsic disadvantage in striking first if the gain from reducing the number of missiles impacting on one's own territory is overwhelmed by the extra costs incurred in making cities rather than forces the enemy's primary targets.

Let us suppose, however, that each side prefers to strike first rather than accept a first strike by the other, possibly because neither can be sure that the other would avoid cities on a first strike. Continuing to assume a 2:1 missile-to-target ratio and equal forces on each side, the strength of the incentive for either side to launch a pre-emptive first strike would then depend on its estimate of the likelihood that the other intended to strike, as well as on the amount by which the damage suffered from the other side's first strike was expected to exceed the damage from the other side's retaliatory blow after one's own first strike. In other words, neither side would contemplate pre-emption unless it believed that the probability of a first strike by the other (p), times the population-economic costs which this strike would cause (c), was greater than the retaliatory damage (d) which would follow its own pre-emptive strike. Thus the *minimum* condition for "incentive to pre-empt" can be expressed by the formula: $pc > d$.

It must be emphasized, however, that this is a minimum condition. Even if pc were very much larger than d, the estimated probability of the other side's first strike probably would have to approach unity to create a very strong incentive to pre-empt. It is very hard to believe that any country would deliberately accept the *certainty* of severe retaliatory damage in preference to the *uncertain* prospect of being the recipient of a first strike. As long as there existed any significant chance of avoiding war altogether, inaction would be preferred to striking first.

It is possible, however, that one side — let us say, the Soviet Union — might have other than pre-emptive motivation for striking first, so that the addition of even uncertain fears of a first strike by the United States to the motives already existing might be enough to trigger a Soviet first strike. The greater the Soviets' non-pre-emptive incentives to strike, the less certain they would have to be of a U.S. intent to strike first in order to be willing to strike first themselves.

But a pre-emptive motivation is hardly likely to arise unless *both* sides have a very substantial first-strike counterforce capability. Neither side can develop an incentive to pre-empt unless the other side appears to have enough strength to be willing to strike first for non-pre-emptive reasons. And if one side does begin to fear attack by the other, it cannot consider pre-emption unless it also has a large first-strike counterforce capability. In an all-missile environment, it would be possible for both sides simultaneously to have a sufficient first-strike capability only when the total number of missiles on each side was relatively low — relative, that is, to the number of retaliating missiles which each would tolerate as a price for the non-pre-emptive gains which it could expect from striking first — and when the missile-to-target ratio was also low. This condition would exist in the hypothetical case just presented: when each side has 100 missiles, when the missile-to-target ratio is $2:1$, and when each is willing to accept retaliatory damage by 50 missiles. Then either might begin to fear an attack and might decide to pre-empt. But again, for pre-emption to seem rational, the pre-emptor would have to prefer 50 missiles on his cities to 100 missiles aimed at his missile-launching sites. If each side had 500 missiles, neither would have any fear of surprise attack (because each would know the other would not willingly accept a retaliatory blow by 250 or more missiles), so there would be no incentive to pre-empt.

We must conclude that when both sides' strategic arsenals are composed primarily of missiles, the danger of pre-emptive war is very small — first, because there may be no advantage in striking first even if one is sure the other intends to strike; and, secondly, because of the unlikelihood that both sides simultaneously will have a capability approaching sufficient first-strike proportions. Pre-emptive war would be more likely if both sides relied chiefly on manned bombers, but even in this case the danger would be rather small because neither side would be likely to trade the certainty of retaliation for the uncertainty of a first strike by the other, even if both sides had a substantial first-strike capability.

We have assumed equal striking forces on each side. When the forces are unequal, there might still be no advantage for either side in striking first in a predominantly missile environment, so long as a first strike by the other side would be less costly than its retaliatory strike. Of course, the greater the preponderance achieved by one side, the less retaliatory damage it would have to expect, and the more likelihood that it would see an advantage in striking first. On the other hand, the greater its preponderance, the less need for the stronger side to fear a first strike by the other; hence if it does strike first, it is not likely to be for pre-emptive reasons. . . .

Massive Retaliation

JOHN FOSTER DULLES

. . . As a loyal member of the United Nations, we had responded with force to repel the Communist aggression in Korea. And when that effort exposed our military weakness, we rebuilt rapidly our military establishment, and we helped to build quickly new strength in Western Europe.

Excerpts from a speech delivered before the Council on Foreign Relations, New York City, January 12, 1954.

KOREA

These were the acts of a nation which saw the danger of Soviet communism; which realized that its own safety was tied up with that of others; and which was capable of responding boldly and promptly to emergencies. These are precious values to be acclaimed. And also, we can pay tribute to the congressional bipartisanship which puts politics second and the nation first.

But we need to recall that what we did was in the main emergency action, imposed on us by our enemies.

Let me illustrate.

We did not send our Army into Korea because we judged, in advance, that it was sound military strategy to commit our Army to fight land battles in Asia. Our decision had been to pull out of Korea. It was a Soviet-inspired decision that pulled us back.

We did not decide in advance that it was wise to grant billions annually as foreign economic aid. We adopted that policy in response to the Communist efforts to sabotage the free economies of Western Europe.

We did not build up our military establishments at a rate which involved huge budget deficits, a depreciating currency and a feverish economy because this seemed, in advance, to be good policy. Indeed, we decided otherwise until the Soviet military threat was clearly revealed. . . .

. . . It is necessary also to say that emergency measures — however good for the emergency — do not necessarily make good permanent policies. Emergency policies are costly, they are superficial and they imply that the enemy has the initiative. They cannot be depended upon to serve our long-time interests.

Now this "long time" factor is of critical importance.

SOVIET PLANS

The Soviet Communists are planning for what they call "an entire historical era," and we should do the same. They seek through many types of maneuvers gradually to divide and weaken the free nations by over-extending them in efforts which, as Lenin put it, are "beyond their strength, so that they come to practical bankruptcy." Then, said Lenin, "our victory is assured." Then, said Stalin, will be "the moment for the decisive blow."

In the face of such a strategy, our own measures cannot be judged adequate merely because they ward off an immediate danger. That, of course, needs to be done. But it is also essential to do this without exhausting ourselves.

And when the Eisenhower Administration applied this test, we felt that some transformations were needed.

It is not sound military strategy permanently to commit United States land forces to Asia to a degree that gives us no strategic reserves.

It is not sound economics to support permanently other countries; nor is it good foreign policy, for in the long run, that creates as much ill will as good.

It is not sound to become permanently committed to military expenditures so vast that they lead to what Lenin called "practical bankruptcy."

Change was imperative to assure the stamina needed for permanent security. But also it was imperative that change should be accompanied by understanding of what were our true purposes. There are some who wanted and expected sudden and spectacular change. That could not be. That kind of change would have created a panic among our friends, and our enemies might have miscalculated and misunderstood our real purposes and have assumed that we were prepared to tolerate their aggression.

So while we had to change also we had to change carefully.

We can, I believe, make a good report in these respects.

NATIONAL SECURITY

Take first the matter of national security. We need allies and we need collective security. And our purpose is to have them, but to have them on a basis which is more effective and on a basis which is less costly. How do we do this? The way to do this is to place more reliance upon community deterrent power, and less dependence upon local defensive power.

This is accepted practice so far as our local communities are concerned. We keep locks on the doors of our homes; but we do not have armed guards in every home. We rely principally on a community security system so well equipped to catch and punish any who break in and steal that, in fact, would-be aggressors are generally deterred. That is the modern way of getting maximum protection at bearable cost.

INTERNATIONAL SECURITY

What the Eisenhower Administration seeks is a similar international security system. We want for ourselves and for others a maximum deterrent at bearable cost.

Local defense will always be important. But there is no local defense which alone will contain the mighty land power of the Communist world. Local defense must be reinforced by the further deterrent of massive retaliatory power.

A potential aggressor must know that he cannot always prescribe the battle conditions that suit him. Otherwise, for example, a potential aggressor who is glutted with manpower might be tempted to attack in confidence that resistance would be confined to manpower. He might be tempted to attack in places where his superiority was decisive.

The way to deter aggression is . . .

MORE SECURITY, LESS COST

. . . To depend primarily upon a great capacity to retaliate instantly by means and at places of our choosing. . . . Now the Department of Defense and the Joint Chiefs of Staff can shape our military establishment to fit what is our policy instead of having to try to be ready to meet the enemy's many choices. And that permits of a selection of military means instead of a multiplication of means. And as a result it is now possible to get, and to share, more security at less cost.

Now let us see how this concept has been practically applied to foreign policy, taking first the Far East. In Korea this Administration effected a major transformation. The fighting has been stopped on honorable terms.

That was possible because the aggressor, already thrown back to and behind his place of beginning, was faced with the possibility that the fighting might, to his own great peril, soon spread beyond the limits and the methods which he had selected.

The cruel toll of American youth, and the nonproductive expenditure of many billions has been stopped. Also our armed forces are no longer committed to the Asian mainland. We can begin to create a strategic reserve which greatly improves our defensive posture.

This change gives added authority to the warning of the members of the United Nations which fought in Korea that if the Communists renewed the aggression, the United Nations' response would not necessarily be confined to Korea.

I have said, in relation to Indo-China, that if there were open Red Chinese aggression there, that would have "grave consequences which might not be confined to Indo-China."

I expressed last month the intention of the United States to maintain its position in Okinawa. This is needed to ensure adequate striking power to implement our new collective security concept.

All this is summed up in President Eisenhower's important statement of Dec. 26. He announced the progressive reduction of the United States ground forces in Korea. And in doing so, he pointed out that United States military forces in the Far East will now feature "highly mobile naval, air and amphibious units"; and he said that in this way, despite some withdrawal of land forces, the United States will have a capacity to oppose aggression "with even greater effect than heretofore."

The bringing home of our land forces also provides a most eloquent rebuttal to the Communist charges of "Western imperialism" in Asia.

EUROPEAN SECURITY

Let us turn now to Europe. . . .

Last April, when we went to the meeting of the NATO Council, the United States put forward a new concept which is now known as that of the "long haul." That meant a steady development of defensive strength at a rate that will preserve and not exhaust the economic strength of our allies and ourselves. This defensive strength would be reinforced by the striking power of strategic air based upon internationally agreed positions.

At this April meeting our ideas met with some skepticism. But when we went back as we did last month, December, we found that there had come about general acceptance of this "long haul" concept, and recognition that it better served the probable needs than an effort to create full defensive land strength at a ruinous price. . . .

FOREIGN AID

Turning now to foreign aid we see that new collective security concepts reduce nonproductive military expenses of our allies to a point where it is desirable and practicable also to reduce economic aid. There was need of a more self-respecting relationship, and that, indeed, is what our allies wanted. Trade, broader markets and a flow of investments are far more healthy than intergovernmental grants-in-aid.

There are still some strategic spots where local governments cannot maintain adequate armed forces without some financial help from us. In these cases we take the judgment of our military advisers as to how to proceed in the common interest. For example, we have contributed largely, ungrudgingly, and I hope constructively, to help to end aggression and advance freedom in Indo-China.

We do not, of course, claim to have found some magic formula that insures against all forms of Communist successes. It is normal that at some times at some places there may be setbacks to the cause of freedom. What we do expect to insure is that any setbacks will only be temporary and local because they will leave unimpaired those free world assets which in the long run will prevail.

If we can deter such aggression as would mean general war, and that is our confident resolve, then we can let time and fundamentals work for us. Under these conditions we do not need self-imposed policies which sap our strength.

Mutual Deterrence

NIKITA S. KHRUSHCHEV

While visiting the USA we became convinced that the most far-sighted statesmen, businessmen, representatives of the American intelligentsia — not to speak of workers and farmers — desire not a continuation of the armament race, not a further increase in nervous tension, but calm and peace.

After the launching of the Soviet artificial satellites and cosmic rockets which demonstrated the possibilities of modern technology, the fact that the USA is now by no means less vulnerable in the military sense than any other country has firmly entered the mind of the American people.

I believe that nobody will suspect me of the intention of intimidating anybody by such words. No, this is the actual state of affairs, and it is evaluated in this way not only by us but also by Western statesmen of the USA herself. . . .

We cannot as yet give up completely the production of nuclear arms. Such decisions must be the result of an agreement among countries possessing nuclear arms.

Our state has at its disposal powerful rocket equipment. The air force and navy have lost their previous importance in view of the modern development of military equipment. This type of arms is not being reduced but replaced.

Almost the whole of the air force is being replaced by rocket equipment. We have by now cut down sharply and it seems will continue to cut down and even discontinue the manufacture of bombers and other obsolete machinery.

In the navy, the submarine fleet assumes great importance, whilst abovewater ships can no longer play the part they did in the past.

In our country, the armed forces have been to a considerable extent transferred to rocket and nuclear arms. These arms are being perfected and will continue to be perfected until the time they are banned.

The proposed reduction will in no way reduce the firepower of our armed forces, and this is the main point.

Excerpt of an address to the Supreme Soviet, January 14, 1960.

I am emphasizing once more that we already possess so many nuclear weapons, both atomic and hydrogen, and the necessary rockets for sending these weapons to the territory of a potential aggressor, that should any madman launch an attack on our state or on other Socialist states we would be able literally to wipe the country or countries which attack us off the face of the earth.

The Central Committee of the Communist Party and the Soviet Government can inform you, Comrade Deputies, that, though the weapons we have now are formidable weapons indeed, the weapon we have today in the hatching stage is even more perfect and more formidable.

The weapon, which is being developed and is, as they say, in the portfolio of our scientists and designers, is a fantastic weapon.

The following question arises, however, inevitably: if the possibility is not excluded that some capitalist countries will draw level with us in the field of contemporary armament, will they not, possibly, show perfidy and attack us first in order to make use of the factor of the unexpectedness of attack with such a formidable weapon as the rocket-atomic one and thus have an advantage to achieve victory?

No. Contemporary means of waging war do not give any country such advantage.

The "No-Cities" Doctrine

ROBERT S. MC NAMARA

... What I want to talk to you about here today are some of the concrete problems of maintaining a free community in the world

Excerpts from a speech delivered at the Commencement Exercises, University of Michigan, Ann Arbor, Michigan, June 16, 1962.

today. I want to talk to you particularly about the problems of the community that bind together the United States and the countries of Western Europe. . . .

Today, NATO is involved in a number of controversies, which must be resolved by achieving a consensus within the organization in order to preserve its strength and unity. . . .

It has been argued that the very success of Western European economic development reduces Europe's need to rely on the U.S. to share in its defenses.

It has been argued that the increasing vulnerability of the U.S. to nuclear attack makes us less willing as a partner in the defense of Europe, and hence less effective in deterring such an attack.

It has been argued that nuclear capabilities are alone relevant in the face of the growing nuclear threat, and that independent national nuclear forces are sufficient to protect the nations of Europe.

I believe that all of these arguments are mistaken. . . . In our view, the effect of the new factors in the situation, both economic and military, has been to increase the interdependence of national security interests on both sides of the Atlantic, and to enhance the need for the closest coordination of our efforts.

A central military issue facing NATO today is the role of nuclear strategy. Four facts seem to us to dominate consideration of that role. All of them point in the direction of increased integration to achieve our common defense. First, the Alliance has over-all nuclear strength adequate to any challenge confronting it. Second, this strength not only minimizes the likelihood of major nuclear war, but it makes possible a strategy designed to preserve the fabric of our societies if war should occur. Third, damage to the civil societies of the Alliance resulting from nuclear warfare could be very grave. Fourth, improved non-nuclear forces, well within Alliance resources, could enhance deterrence of any aggressive moves short of direct, all-out attack on Western Europe.

Let us look at the situation today. First, given the current balance of nuclear power, which we confidently expect to maintain in the years ahead, a surprise nuclear attack is simply not a rational act for any enemy. Nor would it be rational for an enemy to take the initiative in the use of nuclear weapons as an outgrowth of a limited engagement in Europe or elsewhere. I think we are entitled to conclude that either of these actions has been made highly unlikely.

Second, and equally important, the mere fact that no nation could rationally take steps leading to a nuclear war does not guarantee that a nuclear war cannot take place. Not only do nations sometimes act in ways that are hard to explain on a rational basis, but even when acting in a "rational" way they sometimes, indeed disturbingly often, act on the basis of misunderstandings of the true facts of a situation. They misjudge the way others will react, and the way others will interpret what they are doing. We must hope, indeed I think we have good reason to hope, that all sides will understand this danger, and will refrain from steps that even raise the possibility of such a mutually disastrous misunderstanding. We have taken unilateral steps to reduce the likelihood of such an occurrence. . . .

For our part, we feel and our NATO allies must frame our strategy with this terrible contingency, however remote, in mind. Simply ignoring the problem is not going to make it go away.

The U.S. has come to the conclusion that to the extent feasible, basic military strategy in a possible general nuclear war should be approached in much the same way that more conventional military operations have been regarded in the past. That is to say, principal military objectives, in the event of a nuclear war stemming from a major attack on the Alliance, should be the destruction of the enemy's military forces, not of his civilian population.

The very strength and nature of the Alliance forces make it possible for us to retain, even in the face of a massive surprise attack, sufficient reserve striking power to destroy an enemy society if driven to it. In other words, we are giving a possible opponent the strongest imaginable incentive to refrain from striking our own cities.

The strength that makes these contributions to deterrence and to the hope of deterring attack upon civil societies even in wartime does not come cheap. . . .

. . . Relatively weak national nuclear forces with enemy cities as their targets are not likely to be sufficient to perform even the function of deterrence. If they are small, and perhaps vulnerable on the ground or in the air, or inaccurate, a major antagonist can take a variety of measures to counter them. Indeed, if a major antagonist came to believe there was a substantial likelihood of it being used independently, this force would be inviting a pre-emptive first strike against it. In the event of war, the use of such a force against the cities of a major nuclear power would be tantamount to suicide, whereas its employment against significant military targets would have a negligible effect on the outcome of the conflict. Meanwhile, the creation of a single additional national nuclear force encourages the proliferation of nuclear power with all of its attendant dangers.

In short, then, limited nuclear capabilities, operating independently, are dangerous, expensive, prone to obsolescence, and lacking in credibility as a deterrent. Clearly, the United States nuclear contribution to the Alliance is neither obsolete nor dispensable.

At the same time, the general strategy I have summarized magnifies the importance of unity of planning, concentration of executive authority, and central direction. There must not be competing and conflicting strategies to meet the contingency of nuclear war. We are convinced that a general nuclear war target system is indivisible, and if, despite all our efforts, nuclear war should occur, our best hope lies in conducting a centrally controlled campaign against all of the enemy's vital nuclear capabilities, while retaining reserve forces, all centrally controlled.

We know that the same forces which are targeted on ourselves are also targeted on our allies. Our own strategic retaliatory forces are prepared to respond against these forces, wherever they are and whatever their targets. This mission is assigned not only in fulfillment of our treaty commitments but also because the character of nuclear war compels it. More specifically, the U.S. is as much concerned with that portion of Soviet nuclear striking power that can reach Western Europe as with that portion that also can reach the United States. In short, we have undertaken the nuclear defense of NATO on a global basis. . . .

The Logic of Counterforce

THOMAS C. SCHELLING

As a doctrine, "massive retaliation" (or rather, the threat of it) was in decline almost from its enunciation in 1954. But until 1962 its final dethronement had yet to be attempted. All-out, indiscriminate, "society-destroying" war was still ultimate monarch, even though its prerogative to intervene in small or smallish-to-medium conflicts

From *Arms and Influence* by Thomas C. Schelling, pp. 190–198. Copyright © 1966 by Yale University. Reprinted by permission of the publisher, Yale University Press.

had been progressively curtailed. Beyond some threshold all hell was to be unleashed in a war of attempted extermination, a competition in holocaust, a war without diplomacy and without "options" yet unused, a war in which the backdrop of ultimate deterrence had collapsed on the contenders — a war that would end when all weapons were spent. But in his speech at Ann Arbor, Michigan, in June 1962 — a speech reportedly similar to an earlier address in the NATO Council — Secretary McNamara proposed that even in "general war" at the highest level, in a showdown war between the great powers, destruction should not be unconfined. Deterrence should continue, discrimination should be attempted, and "options" should be kept open for terminating the war by something other than sheer exhaustion. "Principal military objectives . . . should be the destruction of the enemy's military forces, not of his civilian population . . . giving the possible opponent the strongest imaginable incentive to refrain from striking our own cities."*

The ideas that Secretary McNamara expressed in June 1962 have been nicknamed the "counterforce strategy." They have occasionally been called, as well, the "no-cities strategy." As good a name would be "cities strategy." The newer strategy at last recognized the importance of cities — of people and their means of livelihood — and proposed to pay attention to them in the event of major war.

Cities were not merely targets to be destroyed as quickly as possible to weaken the enemy's war effort, to cause anguish to surviving enemy leaders, or to satisfy a desire for vengeance after all efforts at deterrence had failed. Instead, live cities were to be appreciated as assets, as hostages, as a means of influence over the enemy himself. If enemy cities could be destroyed twelve or forty-eight hours later and if their instant destruction would not make a decisive difference to the enemy's momentary capabilities, destroying *all* of them at once would abandon the principal threat by which the enemy might be brought to terms.

We usually think of deterrence as having failed if a major war ever occurs. And so it has; but it could fail worse if no effort were made to extend deterrence into war itself.

Secretary McNamara incurred resistance on just about all sides. The peace movements accused him of trying to make war acceptable; military extremists accused him of weakening deterrence by making war look soft to the Soviets; the French accused him of finding a doctrine designed for its incompatibility with their own "independent strategic force"; some "realists" considered it impractical; and some analysts argued that the doctrine made sense only

*[Editors' Note: See pp. 118–121.]

to a superior power, yet relied on reciprocity by an inferior power for which it was illogical. The Soviets joined in some of these denunciations and have yet to acknowledge that they share the American government's interest in limiting such a war — though their reaction acknowledges receipt of the message.

This was the first explicit public statement by an important official that deterrence should be extended into war itself and even into the largest war; that any war large or small might have the character of "limited war" and ought to; that (as live captives have often been worth more than enemy dead on the battlefield) live Russians and whole Russian cities together with our unspent weapons might be our most valuable assets, and that this possibility should be taken seriously in war plans and the design of weapons. The idea was not wholly unanticipated in public discussion of strategy; but suggestions by analysts and commentators about limiting even a general war had never reached critical mass. Secretary McNamara's "new strategy" was one of those rare occurrences, an actual policy innovation or doctrinal change unheralded by widespread public debate. Still, it was not altogether new, having been cogently advanced some 2,400 years earlier by King Archidamus of Sparta, a man, according to Thucydides, with a reputation for both intelligence and moderation.

"And perhaps," he said,

> when they see that our actual strength is keeping pace with the language that we use, they will be more inclined to give way, since their land will still be untouched and, in making up their minds, they will be thinking of advantages which they still possess and which have not yet been destroyed. For you must think of their land as though it was a hostage in your possession, and all the more valuable the better it is looked after. You should spare it up to the last possible moment, and avoid driving them to a state of desperation in which you will find them much harder to deal with.[1]

ENEMY FORCES AND ENEMY CITIES

There were two components of the strategy that Secretary McNamara sketched. Most comment has implied that they are two sides of the same coin, and whether we call it heads or tails we mean the same. But they are distinct. "Counterforce" describes one of them, "cities" (or "no-cities") the other. The two overlap just enough to cause confusion.

Badly expressed they sound alike. In "counterforce" language the principle is to go for the enemy's military forces, not for his cities

[1] Thucydides, *The Peloponnesian War*, pp. 58–59.

(not right away, anyhow). In "no-cities" language, the principle is to leave the cities alone, at least at the outset, and confine the engagement to military targets. If we were at a shooting gallery, had paid our fee and picked up the rifle and could shoot either the clay pipes or the sitting ducks, "shoot the pipes" would mean the same as "don't shoot the ducks." But we are not talking about a shooting gallery. The reason for going after the enemy's military forces is to destroy them before they can destroy our own cities (or our own military forces). The reason for not destroying the cities is to keep them at our mercy. The two notions are not so complementary that one implies the other: they are separate notions to be judged on their separate merits.

There is of course the simple-minded notion that war is war and if you are not to hit cities you have to hit something. But that comes out of the shooting gallery, not military strategy. The idea of using enemy cities as hostages, coercing the enemy by the threat of their destruction, can make sense whether or not the enemy presents military targets worth spending our ammunition on.

It may not make sense; the enemy may be crazy, he may not be equipped to know whether or not we have yet destroyed his cities, he may not be able to control his own conduct according to the consequences we confront him with. But if it does make sense, or is worth trying at the outset, it makes sense whether or not we can simultaneously conduct an effective campaign to reduce his military capabilities.

The counterforce idea is not simply that one has to shoot something, and if cities are off limits one seeks "legitimate" targets in order to go ahead with a noisy war. It is a more serious notion: that a good use of weapons is to spend them in the destruction of enemy weapons, to disarm the enemy by trading our weapons for his. If we can forestall his attack on our cities by a disarming attack on his weapons, we may help to save ourselves and our allies from attack.

The "counterforce" idea involves the destruction of enemy weapons so that he cannot shoot us even if he wants to. The "cities" idea is intended to provide him incentive not to shoot us even if he has the weapons to do it. (It can also, with no loss of manliness, be recognized as a decent effort to keep from killing tens of millions of people whose guilt, if any, is hardly commensurate with their obliteration.)

The two notions complement each other, of course, in that both are intended to keep the enemy from using his weapons against us, one through forcible disarmament and the other through continued deterrence. There is some incompatibility, though. The city-hostage strategy would work best if the enemy had a good idea of what was happening and what was not happening, maintained control over his own forces, could perceive the pattern in our action and its implications for his behavior, and even were in direct communication with us sooner or later. The counterforce campaign would be noisy, likely to disrupt the enemy command structure, and somewhat ambiguous in its target selection as far as the enemy could see. It might also impose haste on the enemy, particularly if he had a diminishing capability to threaten our own cities and were desperate to use it before it was taken away from him.

Nevertheless, a furious counterforce campaign would make the enemy know there was a war on, that things were not completely under control and that there was no leisure for protracted negotiations. If his cities were to be threatened more than verbally, so that he knew we meant it, it might be necessary to inflict some damage; doing it in a counterforce campaign that caused a measure of civilian damage might be better than doing it in a cold-blooded demonstration attack on a few population centers.

There are, then, different strategies that somewhat support each other, somewhat obstruct each other, and somewhat compete for resources. Either alone could make sense. A completely reliable and effective counterforce capability would make it unnecessary to deter the enemy's use of his weapons by keeping his cities conditionally alive; it would simply remove his weapons. And a completely successful threat against his cities would immobilize his weapons and induce capitulation. (In the latter case the "war" would not look like a big one, in noise and damage, but the sense of commitment and showdown could make it "all-out" in what was at stake.)[2]

The question is often raised whether a counterforce strategy is not self-contradicting: it depends on a decisive military superiority over the enemy and yet to succeed must appeal equally to the enemy, to whom it cannot appeal because he must then have a decisive inferiority. This widespread argument contains a switch between the two meanings, "counterforce" and "cities." A decisive capability to

[2] The nearest the Administration came to making the distinction emphasized here is in an address of John T. McNaughton, General Counsel of the Department of Defense, at an Arms Control Symposium in December 1962. "There is the assertion that *city avoidance* must equal *disarming first strike*" *(his italics)*. "This is wrong. The United States does not think in terms of hitting first. The city-avoidance strategy is no more nor less than an affirmation that, *whatever other targets may be available*" (my italics), "and whoever initiates the use of nuclear weapons, the United States will be in a position to refrain from attacking cities. But it will have in reserve sufficient weapons and it will have the targeting flexibility to destroy enemy cities if the enemy strikes cities first." . . . *Journal of Conflict Resolution*, 7 (1963), 232.

disarm the enemy and still have weapons left over, in a campaign that both sides wage simultaneously, is not something that both sides can exploit. Both may aspire to it; both may think they have it; but it is not possible for both to come out ahead in this contest. (It could be possible for *either* to come out ahead according to who caught the other by surprise. In that case we should say that each had a "first-strike counterforce capability," superiority attaching not to one side or the other but to whoever initiates the war. This is an important possibility but not one the United States government aspired to in its counterforce strategy.)

It can, however, make sense for both sides to take seriously a "cities" strategy that recognizes cities as hostages, that exploits the bargaining power of an undischarged capacity for violence, threatening damage but only inflicting it to the extent necessary to make the threat a lively one. In fact, this "cities" aspect of the so-called "counterforce" strategy should appeal at least as much to the side with inferior strategic forces. If the inferior side cannot hope to disarm its enemy, it can survive only by sufferance. It can induce such sufferance only by using its capacity for violence in an influential way. This almost surely means not exhausting a capacity for violence in a spendthrift orgy of massacre, but preserving the threat of worse damage yet to come.

Some commentators calculated that the Soviets would merely "disarm" themselves by directing their weapons at American forces. Having observed that a "counterforce" campaign made no sense they concluded, on the analogy of the shooting gallery, that the Soviets naturally had to fire all their weapons somewhere else. And where else could that be but cities? A facetious answer that brings out the speciousness of the argument is that the Soviets could just as well fire their missiles at their own cities. By firing all their weapons at American cities they virtually guarantee the destruction of their own, and historians would not much care whether the Soviet cities were destroyed by weapons produced domestically or abroad. The idea that restraint in warfare, if it favors the United States, could not be in the Soviet interest has about the same compelling appeal as the idea that a Japanese surrender in 1945, if it favored the United States, could not make sense to the Japanese.[3]

___

[3] Evidently a counterforce campaign that did not destroy cities and populations would require that weapons not be located so near to cities as to merge with them into a single system of targets, and require some protection against radioactive fallout to keep people from being merely destroyed more silently, a little later, by weapons exploded at a distance. The United States conspicuously located Minuteman missiles, for the most part, in the less populous parts of the country, although it did not

Separating the two components of this strategy is also necessary in dealing with whether a "counterforce" strategy is of transient or enduring interest. There has been a genuine argument whether the United States can reliably expect a capability to disarm the Soviet Union by an offensive campaign, bolstered by defense of the homeland. By "genuine," I mean an argument in which either side could be right depending on the facts and neither can win by sheer logic or casuistry. It is going to depend on technology, intelligence, costs, and the sizes of budgets; and the actual facts may never be reliably clear. By the middle of the 1960s neither side had any clear-cut win in the argument. Testimony of the Defense Department hinted that the United States could not count on a good counterforce capability indefinitely. But if we distinguish the "counterforce" from the "city-threatening" components of the strategy, it is evident that one part of the strategy does, and the other does not, depend on the outcome of this argument. If it is going to turn out as a result of technology, budgets, and weapon choices, that we do not have a capability to disarm the enemy forcibly, then of course a strategy that depends on doing so becomes obsolete — at least until some later time when that capability is available. But there is no reason why that makes the "cities" strategy obsolete. In fact, it virtually yields front rank to the "cities" strategy.

One might pretend, in order to make war as fearsome as possible, that the obvious way to fight a war if we cannot successfully destroy military forces is to destroy the enemy's cities, while he does the

---

go to the expense of relocating bomber bases away from the population centers that, for historical reasons, they tended to be close to. It has been argued that the Soviet Union, if it continues to have a numerically inferior missile force and wants to deny the United States a capacity to attack Soviet missiles in a "clean," no-cities war, might choose to keep missiles and bombers near cities; a reciprocated counterforce *and* no-cities war would then be physically impossible, and war might seem less inviting to the United States. A "massive retaliation" would be guaranteed by the lack of any Soviet motive to spare cities and to bargain. If this were done it would not be the first time a government used its own population as a "shield" for its military forces, daring an enemy to do his worst. There are things to be said both for and against the idea – in my opinion much more against, even for the Soviet Union — but the point that needs emphasis here is that, though this could frustrate a counterforce city-avoidance campaign, it would not make city destruction a more sensible mode of warfare. It is simply a precarious means of making Soviet weapons less vulnerable by reducing American motives to attack them — confronting the American government with a choice *between* "counterforce" and "city-threatening" strategies, and no opportunity to combine them — and if war should come the motives for restraint should be no less, possibly greater, than if weapons were segregated from people.

same to us with the weapons that we are powerless to stop. But, once the war started, that would be a witless way to behave, about as astute as head-on collision to preserve the right of way. And general nuclear war is probably fearsome enough anyway to deter any but a most desperate enemy in an intense crisis; making it somewhat less fearsome would hardly invite efforts to test just how bad the war would be. And in the intense crisis, belief that the war could be controlled if it broke out, and stopped short of cataclysm, might actually help to deter a desperate gamble on preemption. So the alleged hard choice between keeping deterrence as harsh as possible and making war, if it should occur, less harsh may not be the dilemma it pretends to be. . . .

The Illogic of Counterforce

HANS J. MORGENTHAU

. . . The most consistent attempt thus far at conceiving a nuclear war after the model of a conventional one is the conception of counter-force strategy. As Secretary of Defense McNamara put it in his Commencement Address at the University of Michigan on June 16, 1962: "The United States has come to the conclusion that to the extent feasible, basic military strategy in a possible general nuclear war should be approached in much the same way that more conventional military operations have been regarded in the past. That is to say, principal military objectives, in the event of a nuclear war stemming from a major attack on the Alliance, should be the destruction of the enemy's military forces, not of his civilian population."

It is the distinctive characteristic of counter-force strategy that it

From the *American Political Science Review*, March 1954, pp. 28–30. Reprinted by permission of the American Political Science Association.

expands the sphere of attempted rationalization from tactical into strategic nuclear war. It seeks to use nuclear bombs for pin-point attacks after the model of conventional ones and assimilate the strategic use of missiles to that of long-range artillery. An all-out nuclear war would then be fought, to quote Mr. McNamara again, "against all of the enemy's vital nuclear capabilities." The belligerents would then emerge from such a war shaken and wounded but with their societies essentially intact. If such a counter-force strategy were feasible the belligerents at the end of a nuclear war fought on such principles would be better off than Germany was at the end of World War II, subjected as she had been to conventional saturation bombing. However, four arguments militate against the feasibility of a counter-force strategy.

First of all, World War II showed that the expansion of the list of legitimate military targets under the impact of total war has made the traditional distinction between military and non-military targets tenuous in theory and untenable in practice. Railroad stations and factories, for instance, have become legitimate military targets, and they were attacked and destroyed as such during the Second World War. Yet, as a rule, large expanses of non-military targets in the surrounding areas were destroyed as well. It can of course be argued that missiles are more reliable instruments for pin-point attack than bombs dropped from airplanes by humans, who during the Second World War frequently dropped their bombs in the vicinity of, rather than on, the military target because of the hazards of the latter's antiaircraft protection. But the greater precision of the missiles is offset by the enormously increased range of the destructiveness of their warheads. For this reason alone, counter-force strategy would be feasible only on the assumption that all military targets were isolated from population centers by the number of miles sufficient to protect the latter from the destructive effects of a nuclear attack upon the former.

Yet even if one assumes for the sake of argument that all Russian military targets are of that nature, an obvious asymmetry differentiates their location from the location of our nuclear installations. Thus, supposing it were technically feasible for us to pursue a counter-force strategy against the Soviet Union, the Soviet Union would be unable to do so even if it wanted to. Many of our nuclear installations are in the vicinity of cities, and it could not attack the former without risking the destruction of the latter. It could not attack — to give only one concrete example — our missile installations in the vicinity of Cheyenne and Phoenix without for all practical purposes attacking these cities. . . .

Second, another asymmetry which renders counter-force strategy unfeasible concerns the nuclear arsenal at the disposal of the United States and the Soviet Union. Counter-force strategy is predicated upon the availability of a highly diversified nuclear arsenal, each weapon appropriate in kind and yield to its target. The United States is supposed to possess such a nuclear arsenal while the Soviet Union is not. The Soviet Union is supposed to have compensated for the lack of diversity and quantity of its nuclear arsenal by relying for intercontinental strategic purposes upon a relatively small number of high-yield weapons in the tens-of-megatons range. So although it may be possible to limit destruction from, say, a one-megaton weapon to an isolated military target — provided such a target is available — there is no American nuclear installation which could be made the target for a Russian ten-, twenty- or fifty-megaton device without increasingly large civilian centers being affected. Thus, assuming we were technically able, in view of the location of our targets and the quantity and diversification of our nuclear arsenal, to pursue a counter-force strategy, the Soviet Union, because of the location of its targets and the nature of its nuclear weapons system, would be unable to do so even if it had a mind to. Since counter-force strategy is predicated upon reciprocity — in the words of Mr. McNamara. "We are giving a possible opponent the strongest imaginable incentive to refrain from striking our own cities" — this dual asymmetry makes it impossible for the Soviet Union "to refrain from striking our own cities" and, hence, makes the conduct of a counter-force strategy unprofitable on our part.

Third, apart from the asymmetry of targets and weapons, counter-force strategy is also negated by an asymmetry in fundamental strategic position. An effective counter-force strategy is inseparable from a first-strike strategy. The nuclear installations of the two major nuclear powers are composed of two types: those that are vulnerable and, hence, lend themselves as targets for the counter-force and those that are relatively invulnerable, because of their location in hardened sites or, more particularly, their mobility, and can provide but marginal targets for counter-force. Nation A which pursues a counter-force strategy against Nation B through a first strike will be able to cripple, if not destroy completely, B's vulnerable nuclear installations by using primarily its own vulnerable nuclear installations for that purpose. B, committed to a counter-force strategy against A through a second strike, would have to use its invulnerable nuclear installations. But against what targets of A could it use them? It could destroy soft launching sites without missiles, empty submarine berths, airfields, and factories. The damage it could do to A through a second strike would certainly be far inferior to the damage it suffered from A's first strike, and it could do so only at the price of committing unilaterally at least a fraction of its remaining and invulnerable nuclear reserve. Thus after the first nuclear exchange carried out within the limits of counter-force strategy, A has a great advantage by virtue of having been the first to strike.

The advantage of A results from a peculiarity of nuclear weapons. A launching installation, such as a gun, a cannon, or a missile pad, is an active element in the military equation only as long as ammunition is available for it to fire. The launching mechanism has lost its military usefulness when it runs out of ammunition, and the availability of ammunition stands in inverse ratio to its potency. At one extreme, the carrier of a pistol can fire his weapon hundreds of times with the ammunition he is able to carry. At the other extreme, a mobile missile carrier can be fired only once and must rely for each successive firing upon a fresh supply, which in case of war may at best be forthcoming only at uncertain and prolonged intervals. A Polaris submarine, after it has fired its salvo, loses its function as a weapons carrier until it has access to a fresh supply of missiles. Thus the active usefulness of a mobile nuclear weapon is enormous but limited to an instant, while the active usefulness of conventional weapons is much inferior in potency but extends over considerable spans of time. Or to put it into the language of conventional warfare: conventional infantry or artillery may temporarily run out of ammunition under exceptional circumstances and may lose for the time being its active military usefulness; but that mobile nuclear installations will run out of ammunition instantaneously or at least after a relatively few firings is inherent in the nature of nuclear weaponry.

By virtue of this peculiarity of nuclear weapons, A gains a military advantage if he can compel B to expend unilaterally a fraction of its invulnerable deterrent. Let us suppose — to take an oversimplified but illustrative example — that A and B each possess ten Polaris submarines and that after A's first strike B commits six of its submarines to counter-force retaliation. If A were to start the second nuclear exchange by committing four of its Polaris submarines to a selective counter-city strategy and if B were to retaliate in kind with its remaining Polaris submarines, the quantitative relationship between A and B in terms of Polaris submarines at the end of the second round would be six to zero. In other words, the unilateral commitment of B's invulnerable deterrent would have resulted in a clear nuclear superiority for A. It would be irrelevant to this argument that B might have a nuclear stockpile quantitatively and qualitatively the equal or even superior to that of A.

What is decisive is the destructive power of nuclear weapons deliverable at a particular moment. It is here that A's advantage lies, regardless of what B might be able to deliver a week or a month hence.

Since A and B must be aware of the advantage of a first strike before the war starts, both have an incentive to be the first to strike. Counter-city strategy would allow A and B to wait for the other side to make the first move, secure in their possession of an invulnerable nuclear deterrent and their knowledge of the unacceptable damage it could inflict upon the other side. Thus counter-city strategy, through the mechanics of mutual deterrence, minimizes the possibility of nuclear war. Counter-city strategy, as it were, expresses the inner logic of nuclear war. On the other hand, counter-force strategy, by presuming to superimpose upon the dynamics of nuclear war a pattern appropriate to conventional war, increases the likelihood of nuclear war. For it puts a premium upon preventive war and thus stimulates not the desire to prevent nuclear war but rather competition for starting one.

However, even if A did not have the advantage after its first strike — and this is the fourth and last argument against counter-force strategy — what would A and B do after the nuclear exchange? They have destroyed what counter-force strategy allows them to destroy and they now find themselves in a political and military blind alley. Wars are fought for the purpose of breaking the will of the opponent through victory in battle. Yet the predictable outcome of a nuclear war fought within the limits of counter-force strategy is stalemate. After the nuclear exchange the belligerents will find themselves — as to weapons — in the same relative position they occupied before the outbreak of the war, minus their vulnerable nuclear installations. They can of course make peace on the basis of the *status quo ante bellum,* and then the counter-force strategy will have revealed itself as a complete waste of human and material resources. Or they can continue the war with conventional means, supplemented by tactical nuclear weapons. But then they will be up against the insoluble problems posed by tactical nuclear war. . . .

There is still another, and perhaps the most likely, alternative. Even if one assumes — quite unrealistically in view of the first two arguments presented here — that counter-force strategy will work during the initial nuclear exchange, the very fact of that exchange will conjure up the possibility of escalation into counter-city strategy. A will have an incentive to embark upon that course in order to exploit the advantage the first strike has given it. A may reason, rightly or wrongly, that B, by committing unilaterally a part of its invulnerable deterrent, has been at least temporarily weakened to such an extent as to give A a chance of victory. B, on the other hand, has an incentive to dissuade A from pursuing a counter-city strategy by demonstrating its ability and resolution to embark upon one itself.

Thus counter-force strategy turns out to be unfeasible as a conventional and rationally limited version of nuclear war, first, because of the inherent asymmetry of targets and weapons, secondly, because of the asymmetry between the likely effects of a first and second strike, and finally, because of the impossibility of following up the initial nuclear exchange with a politically and militarily satisfactory conclusion. . . .

**PART II
Case Studies
in the Use
of Force**

The selections in Part II illustrate the general principles explored in Part I. The six studies are taken from the twentieth century and are arranged in chronological order. The authors deal with different types of military technologies, ranging from chemical to nuclear weapons, and treat the use of military force in both wartime and peacetime. In all these examples, military power was essential to the successful pursuit of national goals or was thought to be so. Each of these selections either demonstrates a specific way of using military power — in an offensive, defensive, or deterrent fashion — or identifies the factors that restrained states in their use of force.

Leonard Wainstein examines Britain's strategic use of seapower in the early years of this century and describes the deterrent role of the Royal Navy's dreadnoughts. Frederic J. Brown explains why restraint prevailed in the use of chemical weapons in World Wars I and II. George H. Quester explores the effects that fears of strategic bombing had on foreign policy in Europe in the 1930s and makes explicit why these fears were not realized in the first few years of World War II. Sir George Sansom explains why the Japanese decided to launch what they considered to be a preventive war against the United States and indicates why their strategic calculations were faulty. Morton H. Halperin describes the evolution of a system of mutual restraints in the American and Chinese use of force during the Korean War and speculates on why the two countries accepted the restraints. Finally, Albert and Roberta Wohlstetter discuss the reasons why the Soviet Union put missiles into Cuba in September 1962 and why it took them out in October and November of that same year.

The Dreadnought Gap

LEONARD WAINSTEIN

We tend to think of our strategic problems as being unique. In scale, they most certainly are; in essence, they have been seen before. Many of the problems and fears of our era were met by the British in the decade before World War I — the problems of democratic military establishment versus totalitarian military machine; deterrence; surprise attack; technological obsolescence.

We even think the compression of time a unique feature of our age. However, the world slid from comparatively unruffled peace to total war in just 13 days in 1914.

In examining history for analogies as a basis for generalization or projections, however, one must be careful not to read into the thoughts of persons of past periods viewpoints and concepts which are based upon the current phenomena one is investigating, and about which persons of the past could not have known. The idea of deterrence, for example, existed before World War I, but it has today acquired a quite new intellectual and emotional content and form which obviously varies from the concept as understood by the men who controlled the destinies of the British Empire 50 years ago.

Of the supreme importance of the Royal Navy, the British never had any doubt. Their ability to command the seas near Britain and beyond had been a cardinal point of faith for generations. Their strategic evaluation always assumed the prime need of that sea supremacy. From Trafalgar to the turn of the century, however, the problem seemed almost an academic one. There were simply no serious naval challenges. It was around 1901–1902 that the Admiralty first became seriously concerned about the German Navy. The rapid growth of that concern, immeasurably inspired by unbelievable German moves, was whipped up by the press and popular writers on both sides. Above all, there was the strangely

From *United States Naval Institute Proceedings*, September 1966, pp. 78–91. Copyright © 1966 by U.S. Naval Institute. Reprinted by permission.

determined anti-British spirit evinced by the Germans and especially by the officers of the new German Navy.

Consequently, the Royal Navy seemed to become acutely self-conscious at this time. Certainly this was long overdue. The Royal Navy in 1900 was in a century-old rut. The fortunate arrival on the scene of the flamboyant Admiral Sir John Fisher as First Sea Lord provided a much needed impetus. He made the Royal Navy realize that the object of its existence was fighting, and not fighting pirate junks in distant Oriental waters but a first class European battle fleet close to home.

He made the Royal Navy think. There had been little or no tactical or especially strategic thinking for many years before his arrival. The commanders of the Royal Navy were primarily sailors and not strategists. There was little understanding of the broader strategy of a naval power, and what there was was derived mostly from the works of the American naval officer, Rear Admiral Alfred Thayer Mahan.

The German decision to be at least the second naval power as well as the first military power was the message that the German Navy Bill of 1900 seemed to signal to the world. To the Navy Bill of 1900, the Germans added the amending measure of 1906 and then the increases of 1908. The Kaiser began his series of fantastic off-the-cuff comments, typical of which was one at Reval in 1904 when he styled himself "Emperor of the Atlantic." The British soon realized that it was useless to try to turn Germany aside from its purpose by abstaining from countermeasures. Reluctance to do so would obviously be taken only as weakness.

From the story of the next decade two interesting points can be drawn. The total effect of the German Navy on the British was immense. Yet, the German Navy was a relatively cheap force when viewed as a fraction of the total German military budget.

In 1909 occurred the famous "Navy Scare," when for months a furious public debate raged in Britain as to respective British and German dreadnought building rates. Admiralty estimates indicated that, by 1920, the Germans would have a far stronger battle fleet than anything the British had, up to then, possessed. This estimate was accompanied by the assumption that such a force would be used against Britain and was indeed designed primarily for use against Britain.

In other words, the British before World War I were confronted by what might be called a dreadnought gap. The British presumed that the Germans would produce at their maximum, while the Royal Navy would continue to grow at the then scheduled rates. This assumption showed the fallacy of basing policy upon a problem solution examined in *vacuo*, of examining military-scientific capability without reference to possible intention or objective. At any rate, the British suddenly became very conscious of their critical military force, as a hostile battle line grew only 400 miles away across the North Sea.

A critical military force may be defined as one upon which the defeat or survival of a nation depends, although it may [not] necessarily represent a means to victory. A critical military force may have either defensive or offensive aspects. The force may be critical in that it alone can defend the nation, but it may also be incapable of defeating an enemy nation.

The Royal Navy was primarily a defensive force, no matter how offensively minded it was in terms of the specific mission of pursuing and destroying enemy fleets and ships. Its main role was to control the seas in order to protect the United Kingdom from invasion by larger continental forces or to prevent such powers from reaching out to seize British overseas territories and British merchant ships. The Royal Navy was viewed by the British as a threat to no other nation. Proof of this belief was found in the absence of any large standing army that could be used to invade a Continental power or to conduct major land operations. The British position was once summarized by Sir Edward Grey to King Edward VII in these words, "If the German Fleet ever becomes superior to ours, the German Army can conquer this country. There is no corresponding risk of this kind to Germany; for however superior our Fleet was, no naval victory would bring us any nearer to Berlin."

Under these circumstances, the German fleet was seen as only for aggressive purposes, since there was no defensive role for it. That it was primarily a powerful and necessary adjunct to German foreign policy was, with much reason, doubted by the British at that time.

In 1913, Winston Churchill, First Lord of the Admiralty, pointed out some basic truths in a Cabinet paper:

> Our naval standards and the programmes which give effect to them must also be examined in relation not only to Germany but to the rest of the world. We must begin by recognizing how different the part played by our Navy is from that of the Navies of every other country. Alone among the great modern States we can neither defend the soil upon which we live nor subsist upon its produce. Our whole regular Army is liable to be ordered abroad for the defense of India. . . .
>
> All the world is building ships of the greatest power. . . . None of these powers need, like us, Navies to defend their actual safety or independence. They build them so as to play a part in the world's affairs. It is sport to them. It is death to us.

One can, of course, question whether or not the British belief was based upon realities. In a case of Britain against Germany alone, the results of a naval defeat could well have been invasion. However, even then such a war seemed most unlikely. The two alliance structures ensured that other countries would be drawn in and that Britain would have Continental Armies on its side. The German Army would not, therefore, be available for an invasion, except in some small portion even if the British battle fleet had been smashed. This line of reasoning only goes to prove the significance of "appearances" in foreign and strategic policy matters.

Because of this keen awareness of the critical nature of the Royal Navy, the British became increasingly sensitive to its preservation as the years moved on toward 1914. It would seem, then, that the more critical a critical military force is, the more the nation is dependent upon it, the greater will be the sensitivity of the nation to the preservation of that force. This is especially so when the critical military force is of such a character that it could conceivably be in large part destroyed quickly and in a single action.

Consequently, in times of serious crisis the very existence of a critical force tends to increase tension through fear of surprise attack by one's antagonist. In turn, the precautionary steps taken to alert the critical force act to alarm the antagonist, and so fears are magnified on both sides. The British faced this problem when it came to concentrating their battle squadrons at a time of crisis. An utterly indispensable naval strategic readiness move was also an extremely provocative political gesture.

While recognizing the problem of provocation, Fisher, early in the period under review, began concentrating the fleet in home waters in place of the three separate fleets which then had existed. His justification for this action was: "Germany keeps her *whole* fleet always concentrated within a few hours of the United Kingdom. We must therefore keep a fleet twice as powerful concentrated within a few hours of Germany."

German reaction to any warlike deployment of the British fleet was inevitable. When, in the very last hours of peace in 1914, it became known that the Grand Fleet had been quietly concentrated in the North Sea, the German ambassador vigorously complained to the Foreign Office. The Foreign Secretary, Sir Edward Grey, tried to prevent the deployment from heightening tension by claiming the move was free from all offensive character and would not take the fleet near German waters. The British never fully solved the problem of "desensitizing" their critical military force — of making it simultaneously alert, responsive, secure, and yet non-provocative.

Another characteristic of a critical military force is the limited number of roles it can play. In fact, it would appear such a force can by its very nature have but one role. The mission of the British Grand Fleet was to find and destroy the enemy battle line. Beyond that, the war was to show it had no role but to lie and wait. It was thereby unable to exert its influence directly into military and naval operations anywhere else in the world. Its sole "beat" was the North Sea, its sole objective the German High Seas Fleet.

Once German cruisers and shipping had been swept from the seas, the Grand Fleet had little role in the other main mission of British sea power, that of blockade. After the rise of mass continental armies in the 19th century British sea power ceased to be able to fight continental powers directly. The small British military expeditions which in other years had been able to exert an influence out of all proportion to their size would now be swallowed by the armed millions on the Continent.

In the century after Waterloo, the British had not further developed their sea power as a means of influencing the land battle by amphibious operations. Big ships were meant to fight big ships, and basically all ships were meant to fight other ships. The failure of the British to develop more versatile theories of sea power before 1914 was to cost them dearly. The tragic story of Gallipoli was directly attributable to this failure, and the one truly great strategic alternative of that war was thrown away by the inability of the world's greatest naval power to exploit it, leaving only the endless attrition of the Western Front.

There was the matter of cost, too. Concentration on any one branch of the military forces can be accomplished only at the expense of another. The vast expense of the one-purpose Grand Fleet reduced British capabilities in other naval and amphibious fields.

Once a nation that is aware of its dependence upon a critical military force recognizes a threat, its concern over the safety of that force naturally becomes almost obsessive. The British began to react by 1905 or 1906 to the rapidly growing German fleet.

In terms of the peacetime existence of a critical force, there are three main categories of problems concerning its preservation. These derive from fears of surprise attack, the security of the critical force's bases, and the possibility of unexpected destabilizing influences such as new technological developments. The British experienced all three.

Churchill spoke for the British when he wrote that of all the dangers that menaced the British Empire in this period, none was comparable to a surprise of the Fleet. If the Fleet or any vital part of it were caught unaware or unready and British naval predominance destroyed, Britain had already lost the war. On the Continent rapid decision — surprise — was not possible. Warning was inevitable. The automatic safeguard against surprise was the need for mobilization, and it took a fortnight to raise Continental armies to a major segment of their total strength.

There existed no such assurance for the Royal Navy. No naval mobilization was needed on either side to enable the best and most powerful ships to attack each other. Admiral Sir John Fisher, who was violently hostile to Germany and regarded war as inevitable, believed that "suddenness is now the characteristic feature of sea fighting." In late 1906, Fisher told the King, "The German Empire is the one power in political organization and in fighting efficiency where one man (the Kaiser) can press the button and be confident of hurling the whole force of the empire instantly, irresistibly, and without warning on its enemy."

Fisher was convinced that the Germans would bide their time until they could catch the Fleet unprepared, since they could not hope to match its numbers. At the selected moment and without warning, they would attack. He believed the "selected moment" would be a weekend, probably one with a bank holiday. War with Germany did, in fact, come on a weekend with a bank holiday.

Preparation against a surprise attack without a formal declaration of war was the foundation of defensive strategy at the Admiralty in the pre-war decade. The Directorate of Naval Intelligence prophesied with uncanny insight in 1905 that "if history is any guide, a sudden and dramatic outbreak would be distinctive of future wars, especially the war at sea. The advantages . . . are so enormous as to quite outweigh any lingering scruples of international comity."

The Committee of Imperial Defence formally stated in 1908 that the possibility of a surprise attack during normal diplomatic negotiations was not sufficiently remote to be ignored. They felt that if the German government believed that the adoption of such a method made the crucial difference between failure and success in a general war, it was conceivable that they might resort to it. This statement became policy. In short, the option was open to the Germans of mounting a "disarming," or to use another contemporary term, "counterforce" strike.

British fears are illustrated by an episode of the Agadir Crisis of 1911. After Lloyd George's blunt, and unequivocal warning to Germany on 21 July that Britain would fight if Germany pushed too far, the Germans kept their silence for four days. It seemed extremely ominous. On 25 July, Churchill recalls, he and Lloyd George were out walking when they were urgently summoned to the Foreign Secretary. Grey told them, "I have just received a communication from the German Ambassador so stiff that the Fleet might be attacked at any moment. I have sent for McKenna [then First Lord of the Admiralty] to warn him."

Captain Maurice Hankey, the influential Assistant Secretary of the Committee of Imperial Defence, speculated shortly thereafter on the possibilities of that weekend of 21 July 1911, in a way most illustrative of what sort of thing the British feared:

> What a chance for our friends across the water! Supposing the High Sea Fleet (German), instead of going to Norway as announced, had gone straight for Portland, preceded by a division of destroyers, and after a surprise night torpedo attack had brought the main fleet into action at dawn against our ships without steam, without coal, and without crews. Simultaneously, another division of destroyers might have gone for the Atlantic Fleet at Cromarty, leaving only the Berehaven Division and the scattered segments of the 3rd and 4th Divisions to deal with.

Churchill expresses his thoughts on that same weekend in a notable passage of his great work, *The World Crisis*. Noting the cool, cautious, correct but deadly tones of the diplomatic communications, he says:

> With less warning cannons had opened fire and nations been struck down by this same Germany. So now the Admiralty wireless whispers through the ether to the tall masts of ships, and captains pace their decks absorbed in thought. It is nothing. It is less than nothing. It is too foolish, too fantastic to be thought of in the 20th Century. Or is it fire and murder leaping out of the darkness at our throats, torpedoes ripping the bellies of half awakened ships, a sunrise on a vanished naval supremacy, and an island well guarded hitherto, at last defenseless. . . . Common sense has rendered such nightmares impossible. Are you quite sure? It would be a pity to be wrong. Such a mistake could only be made once — once for all.

Of course, if Germany had no will to war, all the fears and speculations were so many bad dreams. If Germany had the will and intention, it was clear that there would be no difficulty in finding a pretext to create a situation in which war was inevitable and to create it at the most opportune moment.

Torpedo attack was the menace most feared by the British. So far as gunfire was concerned, the principal danger was for the Fleet to be caught divided and to have a vital wing of it destroyed without inflicting proportionate damage on the enemy. This danger was greatly reduced by the introduction of wireless, permitting fleet concentrations and avoidance of action at will. Besides, it was hard

to imagine that the main strength of the fleets would even be allowed to come within range of each other without taking proper
precautions. The torpedo, on the other hand, was essentially a
weapon of surprise or even treachery, and all that was true of a
torpedo in a surface ship applied manyfold to a torpedo in a
submarine.

There were obviously limits beyond which it was impossible to
protect the Fleet. It was recognized that absolute security against
the worst conceivable treachery was physically impossible. The
British thus realistically recognized that the "worst possible case,"
could not be a genuine basis for planning, but could serve only to
indicate the number and type of circumstances possible in the
event of attack. Churchill, who was highly alert to the possibilities,
nevertheless said that, "On the other hand, even treachery, involving and requiring co-ordination of large numbers of people in
different stations and the setting in motion of an immense and
complicated apparatus was not easy to bring about." Thus the
British aimed at a reasonable and constant level of security.

An additional factor in this concern over surprise attack was
related to the matter of a possible German invasion of the British
Isles. It was considered not at all infeasible for the Germans to rush
a force of picked troops across the North Sea and land them before
being intercepted. In early 1912, the Navy assured the Committee
of Imperial Defence's invasion committee that, once the Fleet were
concentrated, nothing over 70,000 Germans could get ashore. However, they could not guarantee keeping out forces of 20,000–30,000.
Since the whole regular army was to be rushed to France by D+13,
even small German forces could be troublesome. Those who believed invasion not only possible but probable always began with
the premise of a successful German surprise attack on the Fleet in
order to clear the way for the invasion. The debate on the true
seriousness of the threat raged on for many years, and concern was
felt right up through the opening days of the war. The matter became, in fact, one of the major strategic issues debated in Britain
in the period under review, with the Army and Foreign Office representing the "bolt from the blue" school who considered invasion
a major danger, and the Navy who insisted that major invasion
was impossible.

The result was an interesting and familiar inter-service wrangle.
The Army's position called for a larger army and different disposi-
tions for the Navy. The Navy, in the person of Fisher, maintained
that, "The whole of this question rests upon naval surprise. . . . We
keep reiterating and reiterating that you cannot have this naval
surprise; it is inconceivable." It is interesting to note that Fisher,

who fully expected the Germans to begin their war with a surprise attack and was making strenuous efforts to avoid just such an event, would deny the relevance of the issue when it came to the inter-service wrangle.

Churchill, as First Lord of the Admiralty, adopted some innovations to increase the alert status and readiness of the Fleet as soon as he took office in October 1911. He immediately had the protection of all the vital naval magazines assigned to Admiralty control and guarded them heavily. Previously, these had been under the watch of a few constables! He arranged for continuous residence of naval officers, plus resident clerks, at the Admiralty at all times to give alarms. One of the Sea Lords was always to be on duty in or near the Admiralty building to act with authority. Churchill himself kept a large map of the North Sea behind his desk, indicating the disposition of the German Fleet, at which he carefully looked once a day, less to keep informed than to inculcate in himself and his subordinates a sense of ever-present danger.

The Grand Fleet did not annually cruise to warm waters near Spain until it was known that the German High Seas Fleet was having its winter refits. When grand maneuvers were held, schedules for coaling and leave were arranged so as to secure the power of meeting any blow that could possibly reach the British fleet in a given time.

Herbert Asquith, then Prime Minister, recalled that in July 1912, Churchill, told the Committee of Imperial Defense of the two "safety signals" which the Royal Navy watched most carefully. In the winter the German fleet was largely immobilized, owing to the fact that large numbers of new recruits had to be absorbed. Thus, the strain of watching was relaxed and the British fleet could be sent away on training cruises or could undertake repairs of the best ships.

Another indicator of safety was when the British noted some of the German great ships of the newer types on the Baltic side of the Kiel Canal. If surprise had been afoot against the British fleet, valuable naval units would not likely be in the Baltic where a long voyage was needed before they could reach the theater of action.

However, both these intelligence indicators, Churchill revealed, would soon be extinguished. The deepening of the Kiel Canal would permit rapid passage of the largest ships between the Baltic and the North Seas. Also, the new German Navy Law would allow them to keep four-fifths of their fleet permanently in full operation. German potential for achieving surprise was thereby measurably increased.

Fear of surprise attack remained right up until the actual outbreak of war. The concentration of the Grand Fleet at Scapa Flow was ordered by Churchill on 28 July 1914, when the crisis was rapidly approaching the critical point. The Fleet was ordered to go from Portland to Scapa Flow on a schedule which took it through the Straits of Dover during darkness. The 18-mile long column of ships moved out on the 29th, and Churchill, wishing to avoid the appearance of a provocative move detrimental to the few remaining slim chances for peace, told only the Prime Minister what he had ordered. Even with these precautions, there was considerable concern that the Germans might have learned of the move and would lay a mine or submarine trap across the route of the Grand Fleet.

The Fleet was safely into the North Sea by the morning of the 30th, however, and the danger of a surprise torpedo attack before or simultaneous with the outbreak of war was now past. Nevertheless, the British remained uneasy over the sudden unexpected German blow right up to the last minutes of peace.

Lloyd George recalled a curious incident on 4 August. The British ultimatum to Germany had been sent and was due to expire at 2300 hours London time. At 2105 hours, a message from the German Foreign Office to the German Embassy in London was intercepted. It informed the German ambassador that the British ambassador in Berlin had asked for his passports at 1900 hours and had announced the British declaration of war. This was four hours ahead of the expiration of the ultimatum.

London had not heard from the British ambassador, and was at a loss to know the meaning of all this. Immediately it was suspected that this was a move on the part of the Germans to anticipate the hour of the declaration of war in order to effect some coup against the British Fleet or British coasts. It raised the issue as to whether the British should accept the intercept as evidence of the commencement of hostilities or wait until the ultimatum actually expired.

The interesting point in this episode is that, despite the fact that their critical military force was concentrated and presumably safe from surprise attack, the British, far from being confident, were still haunted by nameless fears of the unknown.

One of the greatest problems facing a critical military force lies in the area of new technological developments. Obviously, new offensive devices coming into the hands of an enemy, especially those which enhance surprise attack, will be viewed with the greatest alarm. The same can be said of certain defensive weapons.

There is another interesting and indeed ironic way in which a critical military force can be agitated and an international military equilibrium thrown out of kilter. This is through the introduction of a new and radically better weapon to one's own force. The effect can well be to make obsolescent all the existing critical military force.

The appearance of HMS *Dreadnought* in 1906 tended to do just that. She unstabilized the whole situation as far as her creators were concerned. The new ship raised the standard for a battleship from four big guns and many smaller caliber ones to ten or twelve big guns and a minimum of smaller weapons. She was Fisher's brainchild, and as such she was attacked from the day she was launched. Beyond that, however, she was attacked on the very genuine grounds that she swept away British superiority (at that time more than three to one over Germany in capital ships) in pre-*Dreadnought* vessels. The Germans were given the priceless opportunity to start almost equal in the competition.

Many saw the move as effectively wiping out the beneficial effects of Fisher's many reforms. One furious critic put it, "The whole British Fleet was morally scrapped and labeled obsolete at the moment when it was at the zenith of its efficiency." The view was widely expressed that the *Dreadnought* was Fisher's greatest mistake and that her real effect had been to bring about a period of enhanced strain in the arms race.

Here was a curious situation and yet one with many historical parallels. Once any nation achieves a predominance in any branch of military strength, it will inevitably wish to freeze technology and technique at that point so as to perpetuate its advantage. By various forms of self-delusion, it can convince itself that any technological innovation is no good, immoral, or that an enemy is incapable of producing it.

Undeniably, the effects were as the critics said. The British had wiped out their lead; the naval race with Germany was intensified as the Germans saw a heaven-sent chance to catch up. The British critical force automatically became smaller, and the margin of superiority henceforth was to be measured by a handful of dreadnoughts. All the British fears regarding their critical force were only increased. The smaller their critical force, the easier it would be for the Germans to surprise and destroy the greater part of it. Furthermore, the loss of a few ships or even a single ship became a matter of much greater concern. The fewer the ships that counted, the easier it would be to wrest supremacy away by their destruction. The British seemed to be putting a much reduced number of eggs into one basket.

However, Fisher was really only anticipating the inevitable. The trend toward increased tonnage had been going on for 20 years. As a result of the Russo-Japanese War, the all-big-gun ship was being considered by several powers — the Germans, Russians, and Japanese. As early as 1904, the U. S. Navy was planning to build two dreadnought-type ships and in early 1905 the two, *Michigan* and *South Carolina,* were authorized by Congress, although not completed until 1909. HMS *Dreadnought* was laid down in October 1905 and was completed, in very fast time, in December 1906. Thus, there were fully sound military and technological reasons for her development, fortified by the lessons of the Russo-Japanese War and by the knowledge that other powers were contemplating development of the type.

One of the main arguments used against the dreadnought was that a larger number of small battleships was preferable to a fleet of dreadnoughts. The British were said to be forcing the game against themselves. The larger the battleships, the fewer could be built, and the fewer there were to patrol the wide reaches of the Empire.

There was sense to these points, especially that pertaining to the fewer ships to cover the Empire. On the other hand, the Royal Navy under Fisher had already begun to pull back its battleships and, as we have seen, to concentrate in the North Sea. The dreadnought was not designed for the old patrol function. It was designed to meet a new type of threat, a powerful battle fleet near Britain. Thus strategic reasons and not merely technological fertility wrought the change. The weapon was designed for a specific need, and there was a high price to be paid. Whether that price tag was too high could not have been foretold at that time. That it was inevitable seems certain. The only question was whether the British should have built the first dreadnought and thus wiped out their own overwhelming supremacy or waited until another power did so first. This might have brought them several more years of the old supremacy, but the price tag would have been in the material and moral advantages that would have gone to another naval power.

These, then, were the concerns and fears of the British in preserving their critical military force. But what of its employment? We have earlier discussed its prime role in peacetime — as the great balancing element which Britain had to wield in dealing with the Continental land powers. The primarily defensive role of the Grand Fleet has been pointed out. Having thus amassed this great aggregation of power at Scapa Flow, how could the British profitably employ it? How many options were open to them?

The watchwords of the Grand Fleet were, "Guard against surprise! Guard against division! Increase the strength of forces available for the supreme sea battle!" No stage was felt to be so difficult or dangerous as this initial one. If the Fleet could successfully pass through this period and fulfill its preparatory requirements, it would be in a position to control events.

But what events? Suppose the German High Seas Fleet did not choose to fight a great sea battle and the war went on for years? There were two obvious ways the situation could go. The preferred, from the British viewpoint, was for the Germans to seek a pitched battle. The second was a war of harassments in which both fleets looked about for some means of waiting on the other without undue risk until a decisive opportunity presented itself.

Schools of thought on this problem were curiously ambiguous among the British. On the one hand, the whole spirit and tradition of the Royal Navy was geared to offensive action, of achieving their objectives in the quickest and surest manner by destroying the enemy's naval forces. This spirit fitted the "tactical" frame of mind into which the Navy had fallen during the long peace since Waterloo, from which not even Fisher's best efforts were enough to rouse them fully by 1914.

However, the realities of the European strategic situation showed the grave inadequacies of this point of view. Even Jellicoe, whose view was no broader than most of his naval colleagues, at least sensed it:

> But history has always shown that it is a very difficult matter to impose our will upon a weaker naval adversary, and that instead of giving us the opportunity of destroying his armed naval force, he usually keeps the main body of those forces — his Battle Fleet — in positions of safety in fortified harbors, where they are a constant threat. . . .

In short, there was a general expectation in spite of the lessons of history, of a great fleet action early in the war. Most people found it hard to believe that the German High Seas Fleet, built at such effort and expense, would adopt from the outset a purely passive role. The Germans, however, feared a general fleet action, since, among other things, a perilous weakening of the High Seas Fleet might lead to loss of control of the Baltic to the Russians. Also, they realized that a defensive policy created by far the most difficult situation for the British. While the High Seas Fleet remained in being, the British could not afford to undertake operations elsewhere that tended to weaken the Grand Fleet, especially in the earlier part of the war when the margin of superiority, at whatever moment the Germans might choose for an all-out fight, was not great.

The British thus found themselves on the outbreak of the greatest war in their history with a superb and massive engine of war with only one purpose, and that purpose could only be fulfilled with the willing co-operation of the enemy. At the same time, there were many other purposes to be fulfilled in a global war and the means for these were painfully slim. The critical military force was displaying another of its cost tags.

Of course, the process of concentration of effort in the battle fleet had begun a decade before 1914 when Fisher began his policy of scrapping large numbers of small ships around the world. It was a case of "covering the heart and leaving the arteries to care for themselves on the outbreak of war." Certainly the submarine as a serious menace to British shipping was unforeseen until the very eve of the war, and no convoy planning was done until well along in the war. Then, the vital small ships needed for convoy work were missing.

Even Fisher was concerned during the prewar decade over the criticism that, by weeding out the small ships of no great power, the whole policy concentrated too much attention on the Grand Fleet as an engine of fighting at sea and ignored the possibility of influencing operations on shore. Fisher himself did not see how ships could influence land operations except by forbidding the enemy free transit of men and supplies. Under no conditions were naval vessels to be used to attack forts or towns. The war was to prove Fisher wrong, and he did his best to develop and accelerate a program of auxiliary construction that cut down dreadnought building.

Naval attitudes and strategic outlooks had already appeared in conflict with the accepted strategy of the British Government during a 1911 review of Army and Navy plans. The Navy was utterly opposed to sending the entire expeditionary force out of the United Kingdom to France, since this threw added burden on them. Transporting of the expedition plus the increased burden of defending the Isles against a possible German invasion tended to interfere with the Navy's plans for its preferred type of war in which the enemy fleet would come out and be smashed, thus allowing a close blockade by the total British naval resources.

However, national strategy made new demands on the Navy and the first six weeks of the war saw a larger British Army than had ever before been on the Continent grappling with the Germans. The struggle to save Belgium and the effort to hold the coasts threw unexpected tasks on the Navy. Through all these novel and titanic events the Grand Fleet sat in Northern Scotland or cruised the North Sea, removed from the furor to the south.

Whether or not the British fears of a surprise attack on their critical military force were justified is probably something that can never be proven. Churchill himself, writing in 1923, did not believe that either the Kaiser or the German Government ever contemplated such a course of action. The Germans may not have considered a surprise attack on the British battle fleet for the simple reason that Germany did not really believe the British would ever enter a Continental war against them. Certainly they were aware of British fears but may have considered them only so much anti-German propaganda. Yet, fear is an infectious disease, and the very thing the British feared began very early to be feared by the Germans too.

This may in part have been the result of guilty conscience. A large and influential section of German public opinion looked on a preventive war as a legitimate means of defense, a grave act of policy that might be forced on a nation. Such a preventive war might prove to be a political blunder, but it was not necessarily a crime or an offense against civilization.

Grand Admiral Tirpitz believed that the British attitude in 1904–1905 was inclined toward a preventive strike, although the question had arisen in German minds at the time of the first Navy Bill as to whether or not the British might not want to nip the new German fleet in the bud. He was convinced that this danger was not far off in that two-year period when the seriousness of the German naval effort was fully recognized by the British, but while German strength was still low. Tirpitz felt it was only the unpreparedness of France to stand up to a land war with Germany and of the British Army to assist France which prevented the British from striking.

Certainly some British actions gave a suspicious people cause for alarm. The concentration of British forces in the North Sea area, for example, was seen as threatening. There were other elements too, more flamboyant ones which received much greater attention in Germany. In February 1905, the Civil Lord of the Admiralty, Arthur Lee, made a tactless public declaration that, were war to be declared against Germany, the Royal Navy "would get its blow in first, before the other side had time even to read in the papers that war had been declared." Lee's comment led to a war scare in Germany, as a suspicious combination of factors seemed to lead the Germans to believe a British attack was in the wind.

The personality of Fisher was another source of German fear. His zeal and the ferocity with which he pursued his goals were matched by the violence of his words, many of which reached German ears. For example, during the 1904 fleet redistribution debate, Fisher let loose a blast which, in its essence, was a very apt description of the theory of deterrence:

> My sole objective is PEACE in doing all this! Because if you rub it in both at home and abroad that you are ready for instant war with every unit of your strength in the first line and intend to be "first in" and hit your enemy in the belly and kick him when he's down and boil your prisoners in oil (if you take any!) and torture his women and children, then people will keep clear of you.

Fisher believed it was the job of the Navy to hit first, hit hard, and keep on hitting, so that by one huge initial effort the enemy would be destroyed and Britain spared a long drawn-out series of contests. His belligerence was supposedly proven by his "plans" for a preventive war. Undeniably, in private conversations with intimates, he had put forth the belief that it would be a good thing to attack the German fleet before it became too strong. On at least two occasions he claimed to have raised the subject with King Edward. On the first occasion in late 1904, Fisher delightedly recalled, the King replied, "My God, Fisher, you must be mad!" In early 1908, Fisher again made the suggestion and this time reported the King was more receptive.

In May or June 1905, Fisher was reported to have said to the First Lord of the Admiralty, "Sir, if you want to smash up the German Fleet, I am ready to do so now. If you wait five or six years, it will be a much more difficult job." The First Lord was supposed to have taken the proposition to the Prime Minister who asked that Fisher be told "we don't want to smash up the German Navy — but to keep in readiness." Fisher replied, "Very well, remember I have warned you."

Nevertheless, despite Fisher's convictions, and he was certainly not alone in these beliefs, there is no proof that the idea was ever really formally proposed by him. He simply realized that such an action was impossible for a British Government. His "suggestions" were apparently never considered by the Board of the Admiralty and certainly no such plan was ever part of British naval policy in this period.

However, the legend had much greater weight than the fact. Many responsible Germans, apparently including both the Kaiser and Tirpitz, really believed Fisher planned to attack. Occasional press outbursts in England or appearance of the preventive war theme in speeches only fanned German alarm. The Kaiser in 1905 told the British naval attaché that many German naval officers believed that Fisher's great aim was to fight Germany. In early 1907, a rumor that "Fisher was coming" spread out of proportion and actually caused a panic at the main German base town of Kiel. Alarmed parents even kept their children out of school for two days and the panic also affected the Berlin stock exchange. In 1910, Tirpitz told the British ambassador that Fisher was an arch rascal who wanted to commemorate his leaving the Navy with a "Trafalgar" against Germany.

A truly serious basis for alarm, as far as the Germans were concerned, was their fear around 1906–1907 that Britain was finding the economic strain of the naval race too much to bear and might be tempted to end the strain by striking. German naval strategy at this time was a deterrent one, the so-called "risk theory," which was predicated upon the assumption that the British would not risk a naval war with the Germans, since the losses incurred by them in destroying the German fleet would excessively weaken British strength vis-à-vis the rest of the world. If the British had chosen to begin a naval war against the Germans in the 1907–1910 period, however, the risk theory would not have acted as a deterrent. The British superiority was too overwhelming then, since the head start in dreadnoughts was added to the huge advantage in older battleships. The Germans thus looked upon these years as a "danger zone," an often repeated expression. Once the danger zone had been passed and the dreadnought ship was available in numbers, the coming of the all-big-gun ship would clearly have been to the advantage of the Germans. The reduced size of battle lines, as older battleships grew obsolescent, made the risk very effective.

Thus, these years saw two naval powers facing each other, one initially vastly stronger than the other. The weaker naval power commenced and continued to build its fleet apparently in full awareness of its provocative and threatening appearance to the stronger power. Because it was weaker, the weaker power feared a preventive surprise attack by the stronger before the growing strength of the weaker power made such a coup no longer feasible.

The stronger power lived in fear of a surprise attack from the weaker one, since surprise attack was the only means by which the weaker power could actually defeat the stronger. The weaker power followed a deterrent strategy, building a fleet which it must surely have known could never overtake in strength and destroy in combat the fleet of the stronger power, if both maintained full building rates. Having provoked British hostility by starting their new fleet in the first place, the Germans thereafter used this very hostility to justify the fleet and to call it a deterrent against British attack.

Chemical Warfare:
A Study in Restraints

FREDERIC J. BROWN

. . . [World War I] was [a] war without limits — the brains and muscle of modern industrial nations applied without restriction to the art of war. In the minds of expert and layman alike, World War I was about to pass a threshold into new levels of violence when it ended. It was the mind that could speculate not the eye that had seen which would project World War I as it could have been in 1919.

MILITARY PERSPECTIVES

Speculation would play a significant role in determining the future of gas warfare; however, there were more substantial factual inputs that would influence subsequent decision-makers — the lessons learned from the experiences of World War I.

Tactical characteristics. The tactical military lessons were mixed, a potpourri of individual or unit experiences extremely difficult to evaluate in the aggregate in order to rate gas as "effective" or "noneffective." More important to military analysts than an imprecise evaluation of effectiveness were the characteristics of poison gas as observed on the battlefield. By November 1918, it was apparent that chemical warfare had three central characteristics: it was an extremely versatile weapon, tractable to almost any tactical situation; the logistic requirements complicated the battlefield enormously; and its employment demanded unprecedented sophistication of individual and unit training.

The tactical versatility of gas was derived from the diverse properties of the gases employed. Gas could be persistent or nonpersistent over a wide range of lethality — from an extremely toxic cyanic compound to a nonlethal, harassing tear or sneezing gas.

From *Chemical Warfare: A Study in Restraints* by Frederic J. Brown, pp. 32–48 and 290–298. Copyright 1968 by Princeton University Press. Reprinted by permission. Portions of the text and some footnotes have been deleted.

The effect of the gas could be immediate or delayed for several hours.

These properties gave chemical warfare a role in the offensive or defensive, in mobile or position warfare. A lethal, nonpersistent agent could be placed on enemy positions just before an attack and it would be dissipated before friendly troops arrived. A persistent agent such as mustard could be placed to protect a flank during an attack, to deny an area to the enemy, or as a very effective barrage in front of a defensive position. Such flexibility applied, of course, to all belligerents, provided that each could support the logistic requirements of gas warfare.

The logistic demands were enormous. Gas substituted for nothing. Its requirements were an additional load to an already overloaded battlefield. To be effective, a high concentration of gas had to be maintained over the enemy position. The Germans found that 12,000 kilograms of Green Cross [nonpersistent] shells were necessary to gas an area one kilometer square. Similar consumption figures were experienced by the other belligerents.[1]

Graver problems were presented to both logisticians and tacticians by the requirements for individual and collective protection in a toxic environment. In addition to the other stresses and dangers of war, the very air the soldier breathed and the harmless inanimate objects he touched had become potential weapons against him. The range of problems posed was infinite: How would the soldier eat, drink, sleep, perform bodily functions, use his weapon, give and receive commands; how would he protect horses, pigeons, and watch dogs; how would he know when his immediate area was contaminated? By November 1918, many of these issues had been broached but they had not been solved. The battlefield had experienced a quantum jump in sophistication; it had become too "complicated."

Nothing indicated the spectrum of new problems better than the gas mask. A highly personal symbol of gas warfare, it was awkward, heavy to carry, and uncomfortable to wear. An officer in the 3rd Division, AEF, described it:

> The mask is safe but it is the most uncomfortable thing I ever. experienced. If . . . [anyone wants to] know how a gas mask feels, let him seize his nose with a pair of fire tongs, bury his face in a hot

---

[1] . . . High ammunition expenditure rates were not unique to gas; however, gas required a special infrastructure — meteorological stations, special purpose units with specialized training, etc. — that was not required for conventional warfare.

feather pillow, then seize a gas pipe with his teeth and breathe through it for a few hours while he performs routine duties. It is safe, but like the deadly poison which forced its invention, it is not sane.[2]

It was not just that the mask was uncomfortable. The survival of the individual was determined by the quality of the mask. Either it worked faultlessly or the soldier died. Life was dependent upon 100 per cent reliability. This unique and disquieting reliance on science and industry, was not the only psychological problem related to wearing the mask. There was the added trauma of divorcement from the external environment. The gas mask "makes the soldier blind and deaf when he enters into material warfare, despoils him of his feed and drink, his nicotine and alcohol, and then makes war a fearful means for the destruction of morale."[3]

As well as indirect psychological effects derived from protective measures, fears of gas warfare produced other reactions. One was a psychoneurosis, "Gas Fright." Soldiers, hearing a report that gas was in the area, would acquire all of the symptoms of gas poisoning although they had not been gassed. Gas could induce severe morale problems among troops already fatigued and dispirited by a difficult tactical situation. The First Army of the AEF was in such a situation facing the Kriemhilde Stellung in October 1918. The history of the 42nd Division commented:

> . . . an important cause of the low morale was the mounting fear of the enemy's use of gas . . . it was largely responsible for creating so great a straggler problem that, as Bullard said, a solid line of MP's back of the fighting front had become necessary to keep the men in the line. The basis of that fear was the gas atmosphere that the enemy maintained over much of the front by his regulated gas fire each day. When it did not cause real casualties, it supported apprehension and panic, and hastened the onset of battle fatigue and gas mask exhaustion.[4]

The combined effects of tactical flexibility, logistical complexity, and adverse psychological response to an alien environment required highly trained units. For front-line troops, instantaneous reaction was required twenty-four hours per day. If the unit was not properly trained, it suffered debilitating casualties.[5]

[2] R. Cochrane, *Gas Warfare in World War I*, 20 Studies (Army Chemical Center: Chemical Corps Historical Office, 1957–1960), Study 14, p. 34. . . . The mask also reduced vision and muffled the voice — two essential requirements to command on the battlefield. . . .

[3] Maj. G. Soldan, *Der Mensch und die Schlacht der Zunkuft* (Oldenberg: Verlag Stalling, 1925). . . .

[4] Cochrane, *op. cit.*, Study 17, pp. 40–41. . . .

[5] All armies experienced roughly equivalent gas-casualty rates, dependent upon the training of troops. Casualties at Ypres in 1915 were

In summary, chemical warfare was an enigma from the perspective of tactical military employment. It it could be used unilaterally, there was no question that it was effective. Unfortunately, however, it could not be used unilaterally. Once the enemy retaliated, the game did not appear worth the candle. No transitory advantage justified the difficulties of a chemical battlefield. The problems of fighting in an alien environment appeared insoluble. Science and technology might develop an answer but this was a mixed blessing at best.

Science and technology. If it can be said that science and the industrial revolution approached the battlefield in the American Civil War, it can be said to have arrived during World War I. In no other area was this as apparent as chemical warfare. A General could improve upon or detract from the capabilities of the chemical warfare equipment given to him; but the life and death decisions of strategic magnitude were made in laboratories and industrial plants.

Throughout the war there was a scientific race between belligerents. The Germans seized the initiative when they introduced chlorine gas at Ypres in April 1915; six months passed before the Allies could retaliate. In July 1917, the Germans introduced mustard gas; it was June 1918 before the Allies could retaliate in kind,[6] and not until the last month of the war that they had sufficient stocks of mustard gas. This provided a significant advantage to the Germans in the spring-summer offenses of 1918.

Thirty different chemical substances were tested in combat during the war,[7] each of which posed a unique problem for defense. Since no army could afford to find itself in a defenseless position due to a new enemy gas, there were continual efforts at improvement. The British alone issued 7 different masks to their troops — a total of 50 million masks. . . .

The role of science was equal to if not greater than the traditional value of physical courage in determining success on the battlefield. As toxic agents and their methods of delivery became more sophisticated in 1917 and 1918, the necessity for professional-military assimilation of science and technology became more pronounced. It was not a comforting thought to realize that an enemy with a superior technical expertise and industrial capability

---

estimated at over 30 per cent. Later in the year, the gas-casualty rate declined to less than 3 per cent as training improved. Yet the first attack on U.S. troops in 1918 produced over 30 per cent casualties — not a glowing testimonial to U.S. preparations. . . .

[6] Due to a brilliant manufacturing feat of the French. The British did not have mustard gas until September 1918.

[7] . . . Over 3,000 substances were investigated for war use.

could introduce a weapon which would overcome one's own superior training and leadership. This was a disturbing reality that the military profession faced in looking back at World War I. Chemical warfare was the most striking example.

A question of honor. However, there was more to disturb the military profession than science and technology. Chemical warfare did not fall within the limits of the honor of the profession. The code of war was unwritten, but it was understood. Essentially based upon the code of chivalry, it had varied as mores changed and as the increasing range of weapons changed the nature of the battlefield. In 1914, it was represented by the Rules of Land Warfare in the Hague Conventions. Violation could be tolerated only through necessity of war and even here the accountability rested with the Head of State.

Two hallmarks of the profession were that war would be limited in its efforts to combatants only, and that the most honorable and heroic way to defeat the enemy was in hand-to-hand combat. In the minds of certain World War I military leaders, gas violated these customs and typified the contemporary degeneration of the profession in the face of unlimited war.

General Peyton March, the Chief of Staff of the United States Army during and after the war, recalled a visit to a hospital in France:

> [The hospital contained] . . . over one hundred French women and children who had been living in their homes in rear of and near the front and who were gassed. The sufferings of these children, particularly, were horrible and produced a profound impression on me. War is cruel at best, but the use of an instrument of death, which, once launched, cannot be controlled, and which may decimate noncombatants — women and children — reduces civilization to savagery.[8]

While March was primarily concerned about the gassing of noncombatants, two general officers more closely connected with the initiation at Ypres condemned the effect on troops. General von Deimling, Commanding General of a German Corps at Ypres, commented: "I must confess that the commission for poisoning the enemy just as one poisons rats struck me as it must any straightforward soldier; it was repulsive to me."[9] Lord French, the British Commander in France, expressed the "deepest regret and some

---

[8] Gen. P. March, *The Nation at War* (Garden City, N.Y.: Doubleday-Doran, 1932), p. 333. This passage was written in 1931, but it was not inconsistent with his immediate postwar attitude.

[9] Gen. von Deimling, *Reminiscences* (Paris: Montaigne, 1931). . . .

surprise" that the German Army claiming to be "the chief exponent of the chivalry of war should have stooped to employ such devices against brave and gallant foes. . . ."[10] Reactions such as these would be reinforced with time as the rationale of wartime necessity faded from view. A sense of guilt for past actions combined with the natural desire to enhance the image of one's profession could make gas an exceedingly unpopular subject for military discussion.

At the end of World War I, the prospects of military acceptance of chemical warfare were unfavorable. On balance, the military characteristics of gas warfare did not justify its use unless the situation ensured unilateral employment. Unless some nation made a significant technological breakthrough in protection, a mutual exchange of gas would create a toxic battle environment causing more problems to be raised than could be solved. Nevertheless, the rewards for a breakthrough would be high. . . .

The question was complicated, however, by the side issues that gas introduced. Gas symbolized the encroachment of science and technology into military decision-making, and became "an affair of honor" to the military profession. If the military continued to view gas from these perspectives, its future would not be promising.

FEARS FOR THE FUTURE — ESCALATION

The issues that gas posed to the military were dwarfed by the problems it presented to the makers of national security policy. The history of the use of toxic agents in World War I made a near perfect model of escalation: escalation of delivery systems, of weapon capabilities, and of targets selected. . . .

By the time of the 1918 offensive, at least 50 per cent of the artillery shells fired by the Germans were gas shells. The last ominous increment to delivery capability was never employed. In 1918, the British contracted for 250 bombing aircraft each with a 7,500-pound bomb load. . . .

The last and most foreboding input to the model of escalation was target selection. The initial use of gas was confined to a military target, but as the war developed and the use of gas increased in intensity, it was impossible to avoid noncombatants. One of the objections to the release of clouds of gas from cylinders was that the size of the cloud produced significant gas concentrations at undesired locations. In discussing this problem, Hanslian referred to effects as far as 20 kilometers behind the front and deaths at a

---

[10] *The Despatches of Lord French* (London: Chapman and Hull Ltd., 1917), p. 360. In the British Army, the Gas Brigade and gas itself were referred to as "frightfulness. . . ."

distance of 15 kilometers. There is no indication, however, that the belligerents did not tacitly agree that a certain "spillover" of gas into towns was an inevitable accompaniment to its tactical use in a congested countryside.

The strategic use of gas was an entirely different question. The delivery system could only be by airplane and the implications were truly frightening. The Germans initiated strategic bombing on Christmas Eve 1914 — one aircraft with one bomb. The bombing effort gradually escalated to two serious raids on London (June 13, 1917 and July 7, 1917) causing 832 casualties. After the July 7th raid, the English War Cabinet appointed a committee headed by Jan Christian Smuts to study the air defense of the United Kingdom. In its report, this committee gave serious consideration to the "probability" of the Germans using gas to attack London. Thus by the fall of 1917, the Germans had initiated unrestricted city bombing and the British had matched the capability of gas with the potential of the airplane, at least in defensive contingency planning.

By late 1918, the potential of the airplane was becoming real capability. The bomber force would be available in 1919. There was no shortage of toxic agent. The Allies were prepared.[11] As the capability was being gathered, the Allies made plans for the forthcoming air offensive. The order called for unrestricted bombing. In addition to authorizing the use of high explosives, the order provided a ready case for gas bombing.

There is no indication that a decision was ever made to initiate strategic gas bombing. The mere fact that it had quite obviously been seriously considered was enough to complete a rather terrifying model of escalation that would haunt the makers of postwar policy.

During the war there had been two attempts to halt the spiral of escalation. The first was offered by the United States in May 1915 — after German initiation at Ypres but before British retaliation at Loos. President Wilson proposed that Germany discontinue submarine warfare against merchant ships and the use of poison

[11] In the spring of 1918, Colonel Fries suggested to General Pershing that the Allies deliver gas by airplane. As the incident was related by General Harbord, Chief of Staff, AEF, General Pershing refused the idea because the AEF would not initiate and "at that time" the enemy was not using gas against civilian populations, although the situation could change. "While our aviators were not allowed to initiate such warfare, *we were not unprepared to retaliate if it came to that*" (Maj. Gen. J. Harbord, *The American Army in France, 1917–1919* [Boston: Little, Brown, 1936], p. 223 [italics mine]).

gas, while England would terminate the blockade of neutral ports. The offer was refused by both powers.[12]

The other attempt was an appeal against the use of gas by the International Committee of the Red Cross on February 6, 1918. The Red Cross put its finger on the root of the problem when it predicted that the use of gas "threatens to increase to a never foreseen extent."[13] The appeal was rejected by both sides in notes designed more for propaganda effect than for serious negotiation. The atmosphere of distrust could not be overcome despite a mutual interest in terminating gas warfare.

Viewed in retrospect, the image of gas was no more encouraging to the decision-maker than it was to the military professional. The other group whose impressions would influence the future of poison gas was the general public. It will be recalled that the Allies had changed the focus of gas propaganda several times during the war. By 1918, poison gas was being represented as an unwanted but German-introduced feature of the war in which Allied science and technology were proving their superiority.

Under the circumstances, gas was being presented quite rationally, and it apparently was not the subject of any more unfavorable reaction than that directed at all the new weapons of war. The situation could change rapidly, however, if interest groups, including decision-makers and the military, desired to use gas as a *cause célèbre* to promote a particular want.

Only the future would tell. . . .

SUMMARY AND CONCLUSIONS

To advocates of chemical warfare, World War II repeated the pattern of World War I. Toxic agents had been on the verge of acceptance as a major strategic weapons system but then were not employed. In both cases, the war ended before chemical warfare had the opportunity to display its potential. In the former case, realization of the potential effectiveness of gas was impeded due to the unavailability of a delivery system (the long-range bomber) commensurate with the capabilities of the weapon.

The situation was totally different in World War II. The supporting infrastructure required for effective employment had been developed. Non-use resulted from the interaction of a variety of

[12] E. Franklin, "Chemical Warfare — Its Possibilities and Probabilities," *International Conciliation*, No. 248 (March 1929), p. 57.

[13] Comité International de la Croix-Rouge (CICR), *Documents relatifs à la Guerre Chimique et Aérienne* (Genéve: CICR, 1932), p. 6. Trans. by author.

objective and subjective restraints. For the first time since the advent of the nation at arms a major weapon employed in one conflict was not carried forward to be used in a subsequent conflict. Can this be considered a favorable indicator of inhibitions on the employment of nuclear weapons in general war, or is it an accident unlikely to recur?

It is extremely difficult to predict the future employment of nuclear weapons. Nevertheless, I believe that a study of American chemical warfare policy can provide an understanding of the nature of restraints which should prove as valid in the present and future as it has in the past. . . .

Three general areas of restraint have emerged in this study. First, there are those forces which were expected to restrain but which were proven generally ineffective in the heat of war. Second, there is the problem of non-assimilation by the professional military — a significant but little-appreciated subjective inhibition on employment. Last are the agreed components of deterrence — cost, capability, and credibility; this study evaluates their effectiveness as an element of restraint and emphasizes several critical aspects of deterrence developed from the study of chemical warfare.

Overestimation of the influence of public opinion was a serious fallacy of interwar prognostication. In the belief that adverse public sentiment was a major hope of preventing war, the United States actively encouraged anti-gas propaganda in the immediate post-World War I period. During World War II, however, this restraint was ineffective. Without government encouragement, American public attitudes toward the employment of gas shifted from opposition to passive acceptance if not support of initiation. The combination of bitter, costly island invasions in the Pacific Theater, and the identification of the entire enemy population as evil created an environment wherein the primary criterion for weapon use was rapid termination of the conflict rather than the "humanity" of a particular weapon.

Although public opinion per se was not a direct restraint on the use of gas, indirect effects of public attitudes in the interwar period were operative throughout the war. Due in significant measure to its awareness of the abhorrence with which the public viewed gas during the twenties and thirties, the Army never seriously pressed for gas warfare readiness; an Army desiring integration into the mainstream of American life would not burnish its image by meaningful support of a weapon so distasteful to the public. Public opinion, therefore, contributed to the nation's low state of readiness for chemical warfare at the outbreak of war.

Public opinion also had an impact on the decision-making elite of

World War II. Profoundly influenced by the anti-gas propaganda, President Roosevelt would not even consider the possibilities of American initiation or preparation beyond the minimum amount required for retaliation. Anti-gas propaganda conditioned the attitudes of other leaders, both military and civilian, as well. Chemical warfare was consistently associated with a normative qualifying expression. State Department as well as JCS* papers on chemical warfare referred to "this inhuman method of warfare" or "this particularly inhuman form of warfare."

The other great hope of opponents of gas warfare lay in the creation of legal restraints, which turned out to have no greater direct effect than had public opinion. No power considered any treaty restriction or limiting declaration of a belligerent to be more than a statement of intent, which could be violated if the exigencies of unlimited war required.

The legal restraint was moderately effective; but in an unanticipated sense. The numerous interwar attempts to codify prohibition served to focus public and elite group attention on the problems and prospects of chemical warfare. Due to extensive conferences, specific national decisions had to be made on chemical warfare policy at times when national capability and popular sentiment created environments of unreality. Particularly in the United States, ratification of the chemical warfare prohibition of the Washington Conference established a questionable precedent for future negotiation and made it exceedingly difficult to promote actual chemical warfare readiness.

A comparable effect developed in Germany. Readiness was impeded by the legal prohibition of Versailles and the Geneva Protocol; in addition, there were the specific arms control measures of the Peace Treaty. The Germans lost ten years in the international race to develop more effective chemical warfare weapons, and this hiatus provoked a serious "crisis of confidence." Ironically, the Germans made the major offensive chemical warfare breakthrough of the interwar period — nerve agents — yet forfeited the advantage by presuming that the Allies had made a similar advance. Thus, a former legal restraint helped indirectly to negate a major technological breakthrough.

Similar to the case with public attitudes, the legal restraint gained its limited effectiveness in an indirect and unanticipated manner. Based upon this experience, it would appear that the primary value of the legal restraint rests in its tendency to reinforce other existing restraints. Treaty prohibition, though imperfect, re-

*[*Editors' note:* Joint Chiefs of Staff.]

inforced both public and military dislike and fear of chemical warfare and provided a ready excuse for lack of substantive preparation. Any legal restraint derived from custom or a general principle of law prohibiting weapons causing unnecessary suffering — if such exists and can be applied — should be even more effective, in that each would represent a more universal consensus of expert and lay attitudes.

Acceptance of a weapon within the military establishment is a prerequisite to employment. Influenced by the counter-propaganda writings of articulate military proponents of chemical warfare, most civilians assumed that the military accepted and was eager to employ chemical weapons. This assumption was false. Aside from those military leaders institutionally committed to toxic agents, the military establishment as a whole was opposed to their use. As an area weapon developed by scientists to strike insidiously and from afar, gas did not accord with the honor of the profession. In addition, the immense logistical and training burden unique to gas warfare required greater battlefield effect than could be attained with other weapons in order to justify resort to such a high-cost weapon. It could not be proven that the use of gas would provide any quantum jump in probability of battlefield success, particularly when the enemy could be expected to retaliate in kind. With major financial restraints imposed throughout the Depression, no national military establishment was inclined to emphasize weapons of doubtful effectiveness when Artillery, Infantry, and the Air Force were faced with acute shortages in conventional weapons.

Since gas warfare was not assimilated into the military establishment of any major power, its use was precluded in World War II. Without professional support for meaningful gas warfare readiness, no nation was prepared to employ toxic agents when it entered the war. For the Axis Powers, during the successful first half of the war, there was no incentive to commit the resources required for increased chemical warfare preparedness when other weapons of proven utility were in constant demand. The same logic, albeit reversed in its time sequence, applied to the Allied Powers.

This lack of assimilation was particularly evident in the United States response to the extreme asymmetry of readiness existing between the United States and Japan toward the end of World War II. Despite its awareness that the Japanese could not retaliate, the United States did not employ toxic agents. The central reason for this lay in the general military disinterest in gas which had retarded readiness sufficiently to preclude timely, serious consideration of initiation. Decades of conditioning to a second-strike philosophy prevented such logistic preparedness in the forward areas which could have provided an incentive to striking the first blow.

The implication here is that lack of assimilation is a more fundamental inhibition to initiation than fear of retaliation. No major belligerent in World War II accepted gas warfare. As a result, a defensive aura surrounded the entire area of toxic chemical warfare. Aside from Japan, each nation maintained a credible retaliatory capability, yet the capability was in each case more potential than real. There was never sufficient readiness to provide the incentive for immediate initiation.

Even if any nation had developed a material capability adequate to make initiation feasible, fear of the costs of enemy retaliation would have remained as a restraint sufficient to deter it. Whether the prospective victim actually possessed sufficient retaliatory capability to inflict intolerable levels of punishment is essentially irrelevant. Partially due to poor chemical warfare intelligence on the part of all belligerents, which credited the enemy with a capability commensurate with the assumed diabolical nature of his intentions, each nation saw asymmetrical chemical warfare capabilities as favoring the enemy. When the potential initiator realized his superiority and his invulnerability to direct enemy retaliation, as was the case of the United States, in the last stages of the Pacific War, initiation was deterred by threat of retaliation against an ally, China. In World War II, the restraint of enemy retaliation was magnified in effect by the demands of coalition warfare. The presence of allies that were hostages for the good conduct of the coalition leader increased the stability of mutual deterrence.

These restraints, proven in war, varied considerably from inter-war predictions. Neither public opinion nor legal restriction was directly effective; but, on the other hand, lack of assimilation and fear of retaliation proved to be significant restraints. In World War II, the lesson was clear; the loci of decision-making with respect to gas warfare lay within the professional military establishments themselves. Military lack of interest kept the issue of initiation from reaching civilian elite groups.

American experience with toxic agents during World War II revealed several general characteristics of successful deterrence. Readiness to retaliate was communicated through statements of heads of government backed up with overt chemical warfare preparations. The unrestricted nature of war, exemplified by the unlimited bombing policy, gave credibility to the threat to employ toxic agents in response to enemy initiation. No nation doubted that the potential target nation possessed a retaliatory capability sufficient to punish the initiator, directly, or indirectly, through a coalition partner, and general military dislike of toxic agents was sufficient to restrain any inclination to develop a possible disarming first-strike capability.

Each belligerent saw escalation of toxic agent employment as an inevitable effect of initiation. Once World War II began, there does not appear to have been any serious consideration of initiation solely for tactical success. It was tacitly assumed that any use of gas would immediately escalate to the strategic level and, therefore, that any initiation should itself be at the strategic level. Essentially the same logic applied to the choice of chemical agents. It was assumed that there was no effective limiting point between the employment of nonlethal and lethal agents. For this reason, nontoxic chemical agents were not employed in a combat environment.

Based upon Japanese actions, however, the validity of both assumptions is questionable. The Japanese employed nontoxic and toxic agents against the Chinese both before and after United States entry in the war, yet the United States ignored the situation. Due to lack of readiness and unwillingness to employ, the United States preferred to overlook a situation that, in terms of declaratory policy, would have required retaliation. As long as Japanese violation of tacitly agreed limits did not affect a core interest of the United States as defined by decision-makers or by reaction of the general public, there was no automaticity of escalation. The effect of this American response was to diminish the credibility of the American policy which enabled the Japanese to reallocate their chemical warfare readiness resources.[14]

World War II also saw in the United Kingdom and Germany the establishment of the most extensive and costly passive defense systems yet developed. In neither case did civil defense measures act as a destabilizing element in the maintenance of mutual deterrence. Each accepted civil protection as a necessary component of readiness for a nation continuously under the threat of surprise strategic attack. If it had any specific effect, the existence of effective civil defense acted as a stabilizing element by reducing the expected reward, and thus incentive, for a surprise first strike.

A further element of restraint demonstrated in the Second World War was the impact on decision-making of an irrational leader.

[14] There is no indication that, despite attendance at interwar international conferences, the Japanese thought that in initiating they were doing anything other than field testing a new weapon. One can only speculate that it was their inexperience with chemical warfare which prevented them from realizing the implications of initiating employment.

Hitler was accepted by the Allied Powers as a national leader likely to make irrational decisions. This image was in itself a stimulant to British preparations for gas warfare and thus indirectly contributed to deterrence. With his back to the wall, Hitler apparently decided to initiate gas warfare, but the inevitability of defeat was so obvious by early 1945 that he had lost authority over his key military subordinates. The result was failure to implement his decision.

This development would suggest that the critical time for one belligerent's initiation of a mass-casualty weapon is during that period when it is becoming obvious that eventual victory is improbable unless a new element is introduced into the war to restore the momentum of the offensive, but before it is obvious to the military establishment that the initiative has passed to the enemy and that eventual defeat is certain. In short, the decision would have to be made before the national leader has, by failure, undermined his power to have such a momentous decision implemented.

It remains one of the ironies of the Second World War that toxic agents, considered sufficiently humane to be used for the execution of convicted prisoners, were not employed in a war which saw the extensive use of another weapon with enormous destructive powers — the atomic bomb. The heritage of World War I was responsible — poison gas was a weapon too technologically demanding and psychologically disquieting to be assimilated by the military profession. It was an unacceptable anachronism, born too early out of a unique marriage of science and war. Added to this primary and most effective restraint of nonassimilation was mutual possession of a credible deterrent force. . . .

*Strategic Bombing
in the 1930's and 1940's*

GEORGE H. QUESTER

THE CONTEST FOR BOMBER SUPERIORITY, 1933–1937

The Nazi assumption of power in January of 1933 forced an almost immediate shift of Britain's attention from the more hypothetical French air threat to the real menace of Germany. An increasingly visible German air potential, coupled with the open Nazi challenge to the settlements of 1919, made an upward revision of British air procurement plans almost inevitable. Yet the failure of the British government to fully underwrite aircraft development in the 1920's or to implement the expansion plans of 1923 left the RAF with great technological obstacles in its rearmament schemes, which were to be seen as a real handicap to any staving off of German equality or superiority.

For the ensuing six years, three broad observations hold true. First, British air expenditures, for reasons of economy, and for lingering hope of some accommodation with Germany, were never to satisfy the requests of the RAF leadership, although these expenditures were, in fact, to rise markedly through this period. Second, the RAF thus found itself, by Allied intelligence estimates, steadily falling behind the supposed strength of its opponent, the German Luftwaffe. Third, these intelligence estimates were generally exaggerated, to the point that the RAF was never in anything like the supposed position of inferiority. . . .

. . . At no time was the German potential to be what British observers feared it to be. The German aircraft industry was never rationalized until 1943 and 1944, and even the major retooling for the production of World War II quality aircraft did not occur until 1937 and 1938. Such German effort as was expended, moreover, was not channeled into a really strategic weapon. Proponents of a broad

From *Deterrence Before Hiroshima* by George Quester. Reprinted by permission of the publisher, John Wiley and Sons, Inc., pp. 82–122. Portions of the text and some footnotes have been omitted.

strategic development in the German Air Force, such as Milch and Wever, were overruled by Goering and Hitler, and the long-range bomber, in which Germany might have moved ahead of Britain in 1937, was canceled in that year, as the interest of the Luftwaffe leadership shifted to tactical support and dive bombers. . . .

[In Britain] the general issue of instability and pre-emption was again a source of some concern. Philip Noel Baker, a leading Labor spokesman on disarmament in the 1920's, now warned that the offensive efficacy of large bomber forces would increase the likelihood of their use, since pre-emption would seem so necessary if war threatened. The larger the matching bomber forces, the greater would be the incentive to striking first rather than second, and the greater the destruction when war came. . . .

Thus, continued effort to achieve a reliable reduction or abolition of air weapons (and of offensive bombers in particular) was held to be desirable. Analysts concerned about strategic stability in the 1930's once more urged the transfer of funds from great inventories of bombers (which were threatening to Germany) to active or passive defenses (which would cancel the threat from Germany). This position, in many ways consistent with that of the appeasement school, implied that German military growth was somewhat justified, and that the British response should not be such as to bait the Germans into fears which would force further growth. By such a policy, a mutual deterrence was sought, based both on the painfulness and on the fruitlessness of air war. In the words of a persistent British critic of bomber procurement, Jonathan Griffin, whose language is impressively modern:

> One is the fact that war is becoming so destructive as to be its own deterrent: so much so that already even the rashest of rulers are coming to see that only a short war can pay anyone. This gives us a new chance of permanent peace, if we will use it; for by making a successful short war clearly impossible we can make any war highly improbable. The way to do this is for each country that wants peace — but especially for Great Britain — to concentrate mainly on making itself less vulnerable to attack from the air, not (as now) on competitive counter-measures.[1]

The maintenance of deterrence was seen to require some inhibition of the bomber's offensive advantage, since this advantage in symmetrical confrontations was likely to offer both sides the

[1] Jonathan Griffin, *Glass Houses and Modern War* (London: Chatto and Windus, 1938), p. 3.

prospect of quick victory, or more importantly, threaten them both with an apparently quick defeat.

> . . . Even if all the countries were equally vulnerable and if all were neglecting home front defence, still to concentrate on bombers would be folly, because bombers, though they may in time deter, must in the end precipitate attack. Competitive rearmament concentrating mainly on weapons of unprecedented power for sudden devastation at long ranges will, if it goes on, create a situation in which every country is defenceless, yet has one chance of a decisive victory — to get in first with a knockout blow from the air. There may be cases where in the short run this or that country by rearming mainly with weapons of offence will lessen the risk of war; but when all the Great Powers vie hysterically in mainly menacing rearmament, the upshot is bound to be an explosive situation, even if each of them means to use those terrific armaments against aggression only.[2]

Any attempt at a deterrence based primarily on threats of retaliation was seen to be too precarious, when the means of retaliation also threatened to be a means of violent disarmament, and when the "retaliatory" city-bombing tools could be used to pre-empt and cripple an enemy's war machine. A "balance of terrors," according to Griffin, could not be a stable one:

> It would be a balance of terrors — for that is what the balance of power, loaded with bombs, should truly be called. In the end one group must strike.[3]

An equality of large bombing forces would not be as stable as an equality of small forces coupled with the bolstering of the domestic societies involved. An assumption was again made that the disabling capability or offensive superiority is enhanced as bomber forces increase in size.

> Deadly mutual menaces are more likely to deter attack in proportion as neither side is reasonably sure of getting in first with a crushing offensive and making retaliation impossible. From this it is often concluded that it will be enough to get equality between the air forces of the Great Powers. Such thinking is hasty; it leaves out several steps — steps which lead to a far different conclusion. In the first place, with the scale and swiftness of air forces already so great and growing so quickly, an aggressor may soon find half his air force enough to crush the cities, leaving the other half free to damage and delay the opposing air-power.[4]

---

[2] *Ibid.*, p. 178.
[3] Jonathan Griffin, *Alternative to Rearmament* (London: Macmillan and Co., 1936), p. 75.
[4] *Ibid.*, pp. 62–63.

. . . The strengthening of defenses, with resources drawn away from the offensive, was thus held to be the ideal over-all policy; an essentially unilateral act would suffice both for the protection of national sovereignty and for the prevention of war. If defensive research removed the destabilizing influence of air weapons, it would make possible a safe reduction of total retaliatory forces in an early version of a "finite deterrence" policy.

Awesome bombing capabilities for aircraft were almost taken for granted now; relatively few observers felt driven to scrutinize these pessimistic assumptions more closely, or to doubt that war would indeed be so horrible as to be unthinkable. . . .

THE ALLIED ACCEPTANCE OF INFERIORITY, 1937–1939

As the months rolled on and Axis air strength seemed to grow, some alteration, almost inevitably, had to come in the RAF operational strategy which had been based for so long on 1918 force ratios. By early 1937, a significant slippage had begun to show itself, as relatively abstract airpower theories were compared with real aircraft inventories; in May of that year the Air Staff expressed grave doubts as to whether a "knockout blow" against Germany could still be possible, if only because no city in Germany now seemed to hold the great significance that London apparently held for Great Britain.

> Any attempt to demoralise the German people before German air attacks could demoralise our own people would operate under severe handicap. London is an objective of far greater national importance than Berlin, and for many reasons presents an easier and more effective target for German attack than Berlin does for the Allied air forces. . . . Germany covers twice the geographical area of Great Britain, so that opportunities for dispersion are correspondingly greater. German preparations to meet air attack are much in advance of our own. Moreover, a military dictatorship is likely to be less susceptible to popular outcry than a democratic Government. It is, consequently, unsafe to assume that under our present programme our air force, even with the co-operation of the French, will be able, by attacking the morale of the German people, to produce an effect in any way comparable with that which would result from German air attack against our own.[5]

The RAF bomber force was now rated as being so weak that its bases could not even draw the expected German air assault away

---

[5] Text in Charles Webster and Noble Frankland, *The Strategic Air Offensive Against Germany* (London: H.M.S.O., 1961), IV, p. 89.

from British cities, no matter what the British bombers were trying
to do over Germany.

> So far, we have been unable to discover any air objective to attack
> which would be likely to force Germany to divert her own air offensive
> from the relatively more vulnerable points in our own organisation.
> Unless, therefore, we discover some unexpected weakness in Germany,
> it is certain that mutual air attack, even at equal intensity, upon each
> other's vulnerable points would only lead to a far quicker reduction of
> the war effort in England than in Germany.[6]

Counterforce raids against the strictly "military" German air
bases would now replace attacks on the enemy's civilian "heart."
Such a shift might spare German civilians and thus leave some un-
spoiled "value" to the German government; more importantly, this
shift offered the only physically significant prospect — mere damage limitation for British cities, hardly an optimistic outlook:

> While we are forced to admit that there seems to be no satisfactory
> answer to the problem on such *premises,* nevertheless we are here
> concerned with doing the best we can with the forces we have pre-
> sumed to be at our disposal.
> It appears that in these circumstances we should be forced . . . to
> direct the bulk of our counter air offensive against the enemy's air
> striking force and its maintenance organisation as the most immedi-
> ate method of reducing, however inadequately, the scale of enemy air
> attack.[7]

While the British government had been expanding its air programs steadily since the advent of Hitler's power, it had not, at any
time, appropriated as much as the RAF leadership had requested.
Operational plans that might have been appropriate on the basis of
a once-achievable RAF bomber superiority now had to be dropped,
with a dramatic descent, in fact, to the alarmist assumption of a
marked German bomber superiority. The increasing anxiety of the
British civilian leadership made greater resources now available at
last, but these had for the time to flow into a quite different and
more restricted strategy — into a large step-up in British active and
passive defenses. The apparent shift in bomber superiority would
indeed be politically significant.

As the prospect of German territorial expansion became more
immediately threatening, with the seizure of Austria in 1938, the
development and procurement of interceptor fighters were now accelerated. Shelter and gas mask programs were also set in motion,

---

[6] *Ibid.*
[7] *Ibid.,* p. 90 (italics in original).

and plans were made again for the evacuation of cities.[8] Remembering the disorders of 1917, British planners expected a panicky and disorderly mass exodus from cities, the control of which would require a substantial reserve of police manpower. Steps had to be taken both to spare the British people unnecessary suffering and to keep such suffering from hamstringing the government. By June of 1938, the British Prime Minister had publicly announced to Parliament that in the event of war the RAF would bomb only such German targets as were separate from civilian residences. As a crisis developed in the ensuing months over German claims on the Sudetenland, the RAF command remained resigned to the limitations implied by such announcements, in the face of its supposed inability to deliver a serious blow against the heart of Germany or to blunt a Luftwaffe attack; implicitly, therefore, the counterforce blow at Luftwaffe bases would only come if (and *after*) air raids on Britain were begun.[9]

Similarly intense fears of German bombing capability began to be expressed at this time in the French Cabinet. For causes not traceable to any particular government, France had completely lost her earlier advantage in air strength, as she passed through a series of eleven air force reorganizations in ten years; moreover, the nationalization of the aircraft industry in 1936 had proved disastrously disruptive to aircraft production. The reports of British liaison officers in Paris, at the time of Munich, pointed to the threat of German bombing as the primary deterrent to any French aid for the Czechs. French estimates of German bombing capability seem to have been as extravagant as those of the British intelligence estimates, having been inflated in part by the pessimistic reports of Charles Lindbergh.

> But pointed at Paris (and at London) is the threat of the German Air Force, and the Fuhrer found a most convenient ambassador in Colonel Lindbergh, who appears to have given the French an impression of its might and preparedness which they did not have before, and who at the same time confirmed the view that the Russian Air Force was worth almost exactly nothing.
> . . . Colonel Gauche replied, "Of course there will be no European War, since we are not going to fight." He went on to say that they could not face the risk of the German air threat — since their material was so superior that they (the French) were powerless to deal with it.
> To sum up, then, the military situation is that the German Army is

[8] Terence H. O'Brien, *Civil Defence* (London: H.M.S.O., 1955), pp. 117–19; R. M. Titmuss, *Problems of Social Policy* (London: H.M.S.O., 1950), pp. 16–22.
[9] Webster and Frankland, *op. cit.,* I, pp. 99–100.

mobilised, and that it has completed its concentration against Czecho-slovakia. The "couverture" in the West is very thin because Hitler is convinced, in spite of all statements to the contrary, that the threat of his Air Force is sufficient to keep the French, and consequently our-selves, quiet under all circumstances.[10]

I said "What then, since you don't intend to fight?" and went on to suggest that the situation had deteriorated since Colonel Lindbergh's visit and his stories of the German Air Force. General Dentz did not react; he merely pointed out that French cities would be laid in ruins and that they had no means of defence. They were now paying the price of years of neglect of their Air Force.[11]

Aerial bombardment was thought to threaten a demoralization of the French civilian population, or even some sort of a revolt. . . .

While France had set little store by airpower when she was pre-occupied with tactical victory at the front, the security of the Maginot Line and the stalemate it promised had now allowed the French imagination to wander to the air, precisely at a time when French air superiority seemed irretrievably lost.

Both Britain and France thus went into September of 1938 quite concerned about the German air threat. During the Munich crisis itself, trenches were dug in London parks, and nearly a third of the population of Paris evacuated the city. Yet the evacuations could promise to reduce civilian suffering only somewhat, and the willing-ness of both Allies to accede to Hitler's demands reflected the continuing concern about the Luftwaffe's potential. When the pos-sibility arose that Czech intransigence or Hitler's bellicosity might still produce war, Chamberlain pleaded with Hitler to spare Prague. Hitler responded with promises that no air attack would be made on that city and reaffirmed a general feeling that cities should not be bombed at all.

> *Mr. Chamberlain:* . . . in particular, he trusted that there would be no bombardment of Prague or killing of women and children by attacks from the air.
>
> *Herr Hitler:* Before answering that specific question, he would like to say something on a point of principle. Years ago he made proposals for the restriction of the use of the air arm. He himself fought in the Great War and has a personal knowledge of what air bombardment means. It had been his intention, if he had to use force, to limit air action to front line zones as a matter of principle, but even if the Czechs were mad enough to reject the terms and he had consequently to take forcible action, he would always try to spare the civilian popu-

[10] *Documents on British Foreign Policy* (Third Series, Vol. II [London: H.M.S.O., 1949]), p. 439.
[11] *Ibid.*, p. 474.

lation and to confine himself to military objectives. He hated the thought of little babies being killed by gas bombs.[12]

Hitler reiterated a proposal he had first advanced in 1935 for a combat zone or artillery range limitation on air raids, while suggesting the more general abolition of all bombers, where other nations could, somehow, be brought to comply.

> It would be just the same if one tried to abolish bombing aircraft. It could only be accepted if all did the same. He himself had proposed years ago —
> 1. The abolition of bombing aircraft;
> 2. If *1* could not be accepted, the abolition of bombing outside a zone of 15 to 20 km from the front line;
> 3. If neither *1* nor *2* were accepted, the limitation of bombing to a zone which could be reached by heavy artillery.
> He himself was particularly attached to *1*, which was, in his view, in line with the Geneva Agreement providing for the exemption of non-combatants from the effects of warfare. The development of bombing from the air extends the horrors of war to the non-combatant population and is therefore a barbarism.[13]

While German endorsements of abstentions from terror bombing had not been lacking, in fact, after the Nazi ascendance to power, relatively little significance had been attached to such declarations by observers monitoring the supposedly burgeoning Luftwaffe, especially since Goering and others still were fond of boasting that Germany had a decisive "knockout blow" capability that could be directed against any of its neighbors. In actuality, the Luftwaffe planners saw no such possibilities in the 1930's, the potential of long-range bombardment now having been considerably more soberly appraised than it had been by the Zeppelin officers at the outbreak of World War I. At the time of the Munich crisis, Hitler's contingency directives to his air force had clearly forbidden any attack on Czech cities until he should direct such an attack;[14] as late as 1939, Hitler privately expressed his continuing skepticism about the possibility of any victory through air attack alone, refusing to believe that bombing could completely incapacitate an enemy's war-making potential.

> If the German Air Force attacks English territory, England will not be forced to capitulate in one day. But if the fleet is destroyed, immediate capitulation will be the result.

---

[12] *Ibid.*, pp. 636–38.
[13] *Ibid.*, p. 638.
[14] *Nazi Conspiracy and Aggression* (Washington: U.S.G.P.O., 1946), III, p. 388.

A country cannot be brought to defeat by an Air Force. It is impossible to attack all objectives simultaneously and the lapse of time of a few minutes would evoke defensive counter-measures.[15]

Despite its independent status and a tendency to revel in its aerial accomplishments, the Luftwaffe, in actuality, was now satisfied with the functions of close support to ground forces, and of the maintenance of tactical air superiority. It saw little more to be achieved by air. Moreover, as the German leadership did not believe in the feasibility of the counterforce knockout blow against its enemies, it similarly did not fear any such blow against Germany. Yet Hitler was, nevertheless, very anxious to avoid any bombing of Germany at all, not for fear of the total military breakdown envisaged in London and Paris, but because of his personal desire to spare Germany all possible wartime hardship, and because of his fear that the enthusiasm of the German people for his regime might not survive the rigors of war. Hitler's policies on the production of consumer goods and on the mobilization of women show a great unwillingness to impose a real austerity on Germany, and his aversion to an aerial exchange of strategic attacks sprang from the same motive. Anxious, therefore, to avoid an actual exchange of blows, the German leadership strove to build up the deterring fears of the Allies, fears which the Luftwaffe did not feel itself capable of fulfilling.

Nonetheless, the possibility was left open to the world that foreign cities might yet come to be bombed even if German cities had not already been attacked. For reasons of personal psychological satisfaction, it may well have suited Hitler and Goering to play with, and be the object of, fears that lacked real justification; more rationally such vague allusions to a strategic instability could, in fact, be exploited for minor diplomatic victories. Aggressive German initiatives, until Munich, were often accompanied by subtle references to "total destruction" inevitably raining down from the air, if German demands should be militarily resisted; during the final takeover of Bohemia-Moravia, the threat (entirely a bluff) of a bombing of Prague was conveyed to Dr. Hacha, with significant influence on his decision not to resist. While Hitler thus saw little possibility of victory in an aerial assault on the population centers of the Allies, and, for several reasons, was extremely reluctant to have his own population centers bombed, we find, nonetheless, the German leadership until 1939 playing the somewhat dangerous game of predicting a course of events which it, in fact, hoped to avoid.

Since bombers could not be totally abolished (even though Ger-

---

[15] *Nazi Conspiracy and Aggression* (Washington: U.S.G.P.O., 1946), VII, pp. 852–53.

many had been responsive to this proposal), they could be harnessed by Hitler to deter both all-out war *and* any more-restrained resistance. If such a restrained conflict should break out, however, the German advantage would lie again with a limited bombing zone immediately along the line of combat, which would mean that only foreign towns would be damaged when the Germans were on the offensive. Such a set of limits still had some hope of acceptance because of its resemblance to the traditional rules of international law limiting damage to "combat areas," and because the initiative of any escalation from this level could be thrown to the defending Allied nations, who had now lost confidence in their ability to terror-bomb Germany into submission. The German operational assumption, here, seemed to be that the use of aircraft in a limited sense would favor the tactical offense, and would (if kept restrained) be preferable even to an absolute ban on bombing.

Thus, we have three simultaneous Nazi objectives: to deter any Allied conventional military operations by issuing warnings of strategic instability; to deter any Allied all-out air attack, by promises of restraint and threats of retaliation; but to allow for German combat zone air attack if any Allied military resistance did arise. The interaction of these goals created an obscurity which may have later contributed to Germany's undoing.

The aftermath of Munich saw no relaxation of Britain's air augmentation, but rather an intensification of the program. Partially because the chances of striking a real blow at Germany had come to be seen as depending on a tremendous and temporarily unachievable bomber force, and because of the extreme exposure of Britain to air attack, the emphasis was now predominantly shifted to the buildup of fighter forces. The lingering argument that a bomber expansion would provoke Germany still drew some support; but more important were the assumptions that no strikes against Germany itself could be powerful enough in the near future to blunt an attack on London, and that defenses at the site might be more helpful to the city against an attack now rated as quite likely to come. . . .

Where Germany could expand against minor satellites of France, the military initiative could be thrown back to the presumably deterred Allies; yet, while this stratagem worked in 1938, it failed in 1939 when the Allies decided to risk all-out air war rather than to acquiesce in the demise of Poland.

In light of the vague German threats and of the earlier British strategic theories, it is not surprising that the Allies did indeed expect an offensive against their cities as the likely price of military action in the Munich crisis and later. But the apparently overwhelming superiority of the German Air Force left few advantages to a pre-emptive Allied air attack; it was not high hopes of wartime German abstinence that held back the French and British bomber forces, but an awareness of these forces' impotence, which made even a small hope of German restraint seem preferable to the meager projected results of any bombing of Germany.

The years up to 1939, therefore, are remarkable for the abandonment of some implicit assumptions of post-1918 airpower theorists. On the German side there is a realistic skepticism about the pre-emptive panacea of aerial bombardment; on the Allied side one finds an acceptance of a numerical inferiority, which similarly invalidated the pre-emptive strategies of the past. Yet the Allies still had to fear the imaginary Luftwaffe offensive strategy. Hitler's awareness of these Allied fears, and his willingness to exploit such fears, completed the setting for the war that was about to ensue.

THE PHONEY WAR: SEPTEMBER, 1939–MAY, 1940

It is clear that Hitler was disappointed when his aggression against Poland of September 1, 1939 led to British and French declarations of war, and thus to World War II. The German leadership had hoped that the dismemberment of Poland might yet be so handled that the Allies would prefer continued peace to intervention, with the threat of air attack perhaps solidifying their preference for peace.

But Hitler's hopes may not have been so unrealistic. At Munich the Allied leaders had rejected intervention on the side of Czechoslovakia, even when their civil defense measures and some evacuations had been implemented to reduce the costs of an all-out air war. By the summer of 1939, some further progress had presumably been made in these preparations for the protection of Allied populations; but this could not have sufficed to change the Allied expectation that the inevitable wartime German city busting would be very painful. If the Allied aversion to war was now less pronounced, therefore, it was only because Hitler's territorial appetites seemed so very much less appeasable than before.

The German invasion of Poland had been scheduled for August 25, and then postponed, as Hitler strove to ease Britain and France out of their commitments to the Poles. Evacuations of Paris and London were begun. As the German invasion began, at last, on September 1, the Allied response was certainly not immediate; Italian suggestions for mediation were examined, warnings delivered, and positions coordinated; several days passed with declarations of war coming neither from Britain nor France. It was without enthusiasm that Chamberlain at last delivered his final ultimatum and declaration of war on September 3, after much of his Parliament had in fact feared that he would again concede to Hitler. The French government had pleaded again for a delayed ultimatum, for time to complete the evacuation of its cities, and, perhaps, to negotiate. Expecting severe bombing as the price of intervention, the British and French leaderships declared war without eagerness or haste, and might well not have done so had Hitler staged his Polish operation more carefully. No Allied land or air offensives were set in motion; the Allied governments, having resolved to risk declaration of war, braced themselves now for the initiative they had felt forced to concede to the Luftwaffe.

Despite the many dire prewar predictions of a terroristic conflict, leaving no sanctuary for civilian populations, and despite these British expectations of an immediate "knockout blow" attempt by the Luftwaffe, the opening rounds of World War II now witnessed no bombing raids at all on the populated areas of Britain and France or of Germany.

On September 1, 1939, President Roosevelt had addressed an appeal to the belligerent powers for a restriction of aerial warfare to strictly military targets, the formal acceptance of which appeal was announced on the 2nd by the Allies and, on September 18 by the German government. But orders to this effect had been issued to each of the air forces in question even before the appeal; while many expected otherwise, Luftwaffe operations against Britain and France were forbidden by Hitler himself. . . .

THE BLITZ: AUGUST, 1940–MAY, 1941*

. . . The "Blitz" was now about to be triggered. On August 24, 1940, the Luftwaffe, still concentrating its daytime attack on the installations and supporting industries of the RAF, added a series of night attacks on aircraft factories and other industrial targets in

*[Editors' note: Prior to the "Blitz," air warfare went through three phases: (1) The Phoney War, September, 1939–May, 1940; (2) The Fall of France, May–June, 1940; and (3) The Battle of Britain, June–August, 1940. In the first phase mutual restraints were observed, and bomber missions were confined to reconnaissance. In the second phase bomber operations on both sides expanded but were confined to military targets. The Germans spared Paris from bombing and made only a few raids on RAF fighter strips in southeastern England. Beginning May 15, the British began to bomb selected military targets at night in and around northwestern German cities. In the third phase the restraints on bomber operations weakened still more. The Germans continued to observe a "no-cities" policy, but began a heavy assault on English coastal shipping, RAF airfields, and the British aircraft industry. In effect, the Germans were pursuing a counterforce campaign to destroy British air power. The Blitz begins the fourth major phase of the bomber war when all restraints were ended.]

cities around England. Although London was not programmed as a target, navigation and accuracy inevitably suffered at night, and several planes (by any account less than twelve) did drop bombs on London unintentionally on the 24th (London had, in fact, been accidentally bombed before, as early as June 18).[16] The extension and change in form of the Luftwaffe raids once more increased the exposure of the British populace to aerial attack, if only because of the lesser accuracies of night bombing. . . .

On August 25, however, 95 aircraft of RAF Bomber Command were dispatched on the first mission against Berlin (of which 81 found the target), a mission executed as usual by night, described, nonetheless, as a precision bombing of industrial targets.[17] Berlin was now on the regular target list alongside the invasion ports and the Ruhr, and five similar raids were flown against the German capital in the succeeding two weeks. The German response came soon. On September 7, the Luftwaffe halted most of its attack on the airdromes and began a heavy assault on the city of London, an assault which was to continue for two months, until the middle of November. While the orders to the German crews were still to bomb carefully and not indiscriminately, the sheer weight of the night attacks tended to mitigate the effects of such orders. After November 14, attacks were extended again to areas outside of London. Targets and aiming points still were chosen for industrial potential as the new phase opened with a severe raid on Coventry. Intensive raids alternating between London and the lesser cities of Britain continued through the winter and spring, until the middle of May of 1941, with close to 40,000 British civilians losing their lives.

Over the period of the "Blitz," Bomber Command continued to hit an assortment of targets including the Ruhr, northern Italy, Berlin, invasion shipping, German naval bases, and various special industrial sites around northwestern Germany. On October 30, 1940, it was decided, moreover, to seek targets with a supplementary effect for stray bombs, that is, targets surrounded by populated areas. On December 12, an attack experimentally designed to inflict maximum destruction on a German town was ordered, the "area

[16] Accounts of the August 24th bombing of London are not very clear. All now agree that London was not intended as a target, but the number of planes participating is left vague. Apparently, twelve planes were programmed for targets near London, and *some* of these dropped bombs within the city limits. . . .

[17] Arthur Bryant, *The Turn of the Tide* (London: Collins, 1957), p. 213; B. Collier, *The Defence of the United Kingdom* (London: H.M.S.O., 1957), p. 234.

bombing" attack being executed on Mannheim on the night of the 16th, with disappointing results. Early 1941 saw attacks on German U-boat bases, and another area attack on Bremen, followed by similar attacks on a series of German North Sea ports through the rest of the spring. Yet as British bomber forces were drawn away to the Middle East and to anti-submarine patrols at sea, the British bombload of 15,000 tons in this period failed to match the 67,000 tons of the German assault.

The winter of 1940–1941 thus saw all possible military and industrial targets opened to attack in both Britain and the Axis homelands. No deliberate "terror-maximizing" attacks had as yet been launched against Britain, and only a few with limited resources had as yet been launched against Germany, but the inaccuracies of navigation and bombardment on night flights made the results of "terror" attacks seem not very different from "discriminate" or "precision" attacks. Meaningful limits on the air war were at an end, and the explanation is not so obvious.

Winston Churchill in his memoirs cites the bombs dropped on London on August 24, 1940 as his moral justification for the British raids beginning on the 25th, and he further indicates that he expected a serious German assault on London sooner or later in any event:

> The sporadic raiding of London towards the end of August was promptly answered by us in a retaliatory attack on Berlin. . . . He [Hitler] took, of course, full advantage of our reprisal on Berlin, and publicly announced the previously settled German policy of reducing London and other British cities to chaos and ruin.[18]

But it was clear that the bombs dropped on the 24th were not the all-out Luftwaffe terror attack for which Britain had been braced since 1939, and a serious German assault on London, in the absence of provocation, could by no means be a certainty. If Churchill was writing off further German restraints, he was writing off quite a lot, for most of London still stood untouched. There was, therefore, a reason why Churchill took the step which indeed made an early German attack on London more likely, and it was not simply a desire for revenge for the stray bombs that had fallen; it is remarkable how even the words of 1914 are echoed:

> *Far more important to us than the protection of London* from terror-bombing was the functioning and articulation of these airfields and the squadrons working from them. In the life-and-death struggle of

[18] Winston Churchill, *Their Finest Hour* (Boston: Houghton Mifflin Co., 1949), p. 342.

the two air forces, this was a decisive phase. We never thought of the struggle in terms of the defence of London or any other place, but only who won in the air.

The War Cabinet were much in the mood to hit back, to raise the stakes, and to defy the enemy.

It was therefore with a sense of relief that Fighter Command felt the German attack turn on to London on September 7, and concluded that the enemy had changed his plan.

The night attacks on London for ten days after September 7 struck at the London docks and railway centres, and killed and wounded many civilians, but they were in effect for us a breathing space of which we had the utmost need.[19]

In fact, Churchill's decision to bomb Berlin almost certainly was a conscious effort to bait Hitler into an immediate shifting of the Luftwaffe attack on to London, away from the RAF Fighter Command bases which were beginning to collapse under the strain. The decision was made in the context of the threat of a German invasion, which was, indeed, expected momentarily. A continuing Luftwaffe assault on the airdromes threatened not only to weaken the bases as flying strips, but also to destroy enough on-base communications and control centers (the "Sector-Stations," which digested radar information and guided the fighter groups in the air) to make southern England untenable for the RAF. A withdrawal of the RAF to the north would have given the Luftwaffe the superiority it needed over the Channel to support an invasion. Churchill's assessment, therefore, of the value of sparing London from attack may not have declined seriously from May to August, but his estimation of the value of inducing Hitler to bomb London instead of the airdromes had risen, indeed.

Churchill admits his desire, in late August, for an immediate shifting of the massive Luftwaffe offensive from the RAF airstrips to London, and he admits his personal responsibility for the bombings of Berlin, begun on August 25; it seems quite likely that he was aware of the probable connection between the two. While the RAF Air Staff opposed the bombing of Berlin on military grounds, since strikes at the invasion ports seemed far more pressing at this crucial moment, Churchill himself overruled its objections.

Before the war, the RAF had contemplated using its bombers to draw the expected German assault on to its air bases, away from London; now, ironically, it was directed to divert the Germans in exactly the opposite direction. Similarly, while efforts had earlier been made to separate British defense industries from cities, the

[19] *Ibid.*, pp. 330–331, 331 (italics added) 342. . . .

closeness of "legitimate" Luftwaffe targets to London now had given Churchill the pretext for an escalation.

The German reaction to the attacks on Berlin was not long in coming. Hitler had desired to deter all air attacks on German cities, and he had, by his restraining directives to the Luftwaffe, been bargaining since May for an end to the Bomber Command offensive. As the program of conquering Britain got under way, some of these restraints began to be deferred (at least for a time) to the requirements of winning superiority over RAF Fighter Command, and the decision prior to the 24th to open a German night offensive was such a deferment. But a great deal of the bargaining restraint was still in effect; Berlin, in particular, was of great value to Hitler, for while the minor raids being executed in the Ruhr could be ignored or explained away, a bombing of Berlin would spoil completely the illusion of "perfect safety" for the German people, an illusion for which Hitler still showed himself willing to spare London. While the attack on the German capital was not the only factor in the assault on London, it was, therefore, the critical factor, and Hitler made his decision on the morning after Berlin was first bombed.

Since the real weakness of Fighter Command was not, however, known to the Germans, the decision to bomb London cannot be viewed merely as an instance of the revenge motive (or "punishing of a contract-breaker") irrationally overriding all other practical considerations. The Luftwaffe command was not, in fact, aware of the critical state of Fighter Command's communications, and it had been hitting the "Sector-Station" communication centers as part of its general bombardment of RAF airdromes. The invasion of Britain still was pending, still requiring the achievement of air superiority over the coasts, but the Luftwaffe command was far from agreement on tactical policy at this time; some planners had been advocating raids on London as a means of forcing a British commitment of Fighter Command's remaining reserves, while others urged a continued bombing of the airdromes to catch fighters on the ground.

By removing the sparing of Berlin from the German prospects, Churchill tipped the scales in the multi-elemented German calculations and induced a shifting of attack which spared Fighter Command. By exposing London to attack, he led the Germans to see a net advantage where they did not have one, and to miss the real opportunity available to them.

The German motives in continuing the bombing of London, after the "Operation Sea Lion" invasion plan was finally given up on September 17, hinged on the possibility (now, for the first time seriously contemplated by the Luftwaffe) that painful air attack, alone, might induce the British to surrender. Yet this assumption was accepted only with strong reservations, reservations which, in fact, required that bombing continue to be programmed for industrial targets, regardless of what effects on the national will were expected, reservations which, moreover, still could allow the attack to be labeled as less than a deliberate antipopulation "terror" assault, for fear of more severe British retaliation. Having moved up to a strategically significant counterforce operation, the originally "tactical" Luftwaffe now moved on to a morale campaign, but still with some show of restraint.

The British reaction to the heavier bombings (especially of London and Coventry) was nonetheless to interpret them as meaningfully equivalent to all-out terror attacks, which seemed to leave little prospect of gain in any further RAF restraints. At about the same time (although for reasoning processes which now seem slightly suspect), British target planners began again to speculate that German morale might be the key target whose significance had been overlooked, and that an "area" bombing offensive might in any event be more effective than a precision attack, on purely practical considerations. This conclusion, still quite tentative, stemmed largely from the disappointing accuracies shown in missions against precision targets, and also from a flood of advice that German morale would never equal the performance of the British under the Blitz, and that heavy bombing of the German populace might lead to a breakdown of German civilian life, or even to a revolt.

> The evidence at our disposal goes to show that the morale of the average German civilian will weaken quicker than that of a population such as our own as a consequence of direct attack. The Germans have been under-nourished and subjected to a permanent strain equivalent to that of war conditions during almost the whole period of Hitler's regime, and for this reason also will be liable to crack before a nation of greater stamina. . . .
>
> Morale as a main target is one which it may prove profitable to turn to as a long-term objective for our expanded bomber force, and when the state of German morale is less robust than it is at the moment. We think that there is not sufficient justification to concentrate upon it with our present strength, although we believe that the undermining of enemy morale must be an aim which we must always keep in mind.[20]

Yet British capabilities were still to be so limited as to preclude any really effective "terror raids," and the paradoxical result thus obtained that neither side correctly interpreted the other's intentions

[20] Text in Webster and Frankland, *op. cit.*, IV, p. 190.

of attack in 1941, the German "limited" attack not being seen as such in Britain because of its inaccuracy by night, and the few British "terror" or "area" attacks being misinterpreted because of their weakness.

The "Blitz" thus represented the end of effective bargaining on the question of aerial bombardment, for while certain later German moves could possibly be interpreted as "feelers" aimed at re-establishing restraints for the exchange, September of 1940 marked the end of British desires for such restraints. A bargain, to be consummated, requires that both partners see themselves as better off by it; after September of 1940 this could not be the case.

As the bombings went on through the winter of 1940–1941, the British government slowly resigned itself to a complete destruction of London and the other cities of southern England. British civilian life made its adjustment to the bombings far more successfully than it had in 1917. The contrast between the two world wars is remarkable in this regard. Enthusiasm for a quick successful war had been manifest in both Germany and Britain in 1914, and the prolonged suffering endured thereafter had come as an unpleasant shock. In 1939, by contrast, inhabitants of all major cities in Europe had expected a severe punishment. In Britain, the worst fears were not realized. The need for hospital beds, the number of casualties, the destruction of cities, all had been overestimated, and these overestimates widely circulated and accepted. When the expected pain clearly did not materialize, the public proved to be more able to bear the suffering actually inflicted. Some planners began almost cheerfully to contemplate the complete urban redevelopment of the British capital. With no prospect for an end to the bombings in sight, this prospect ceased to be a powerful incentive for any British concessions.

It is probably fair to say that Nazi Germany held an interest in limits to aerial warfare longer than Britain did. Unfortunately, for the Germans, their bargaining for such limits had been poorly executed. German propaganda under Goebbels had not been fully enough harnessed to the communication of the nation's intent; Luftwaffe complaints of misinterpretations and distortions of its campaigns were recurrent, and on crucial questions of fine distinction, such as Warsaw and Rotterdam, broadcasts threatening other cities with similar imminent fates served to undermine the general German purpose. The deliberate prewar tendency (in pursuit of lesser objectives) to hint at all-out air attack if German wishes were not granted similarly had made dangerously ambiguous the wartime German intention to abstain from such attack except in retaliation.

Beyond the distortions of propaganda, however, the German decision at several points to interpret borderline opportunities in their own favor was incautious, for these opportunities did not seem "tactical" or "strictly military" to the other side. For a nation as averse to bombing as Germany, the severity of the final raid on Warsaw and the dive-bomber attack on Rotterdam were precarious moves, as was the decision to add a night offensive against Britain, based, as it was, on a serious overestimation of bombing accuracy and of the separability of "military" and "civilian" targets.

If the Germans still hoped to limit the war, after they had seemed to acquire a chance to eliminate RAF's Fighter Command, a more careful measure of the values of their opponent had to be taken. While France proved willing to surrender before expanding the air war, Britain preferred, under Churchill, to drop limits when military force survival (and the national existence) were threatened, when a dropping of such limits offered a contribution to force survival. By threatening to disarm or to invade Britain, Germany exposed herself to air assault.

Finally, since the German ability to restrain the war depended so much on a British fear of the Luftwaffe, it was unwise to demonstrate the limits of its capabilities. Indeed, if the British had known in 1938 what the Blitz would be like, it seems unlikely that they would have been restrained by fear of air attack.

In the battle of Britain and the Blitz, some 67,000 tons of bombs were delivered to England by the Luftwaffe, considerably less than had been expected, but still roughly 2500 times as much as had been delivered in all of World War I. Much more physical damage was now inflicted on the city, and 30 times as many people were killed. The inaccuracy of the forecast linear relationship of casualties to bomb tonnage is interesting here; yet the psychological effects on the British public in fact were *absolutely* less than in 1916 and 1917, and this is much more remarkable.

The severity of the later Allied air offensive was to come as a surprise to Hitler, and would greatly overshadow the tonnage and casualty figures of the Blitz. Perhaps the German aversion to air attack would indeed have been fortified if there had been foreknowledge of its actual severity, and perhaps the bargaining for limits might then have been conducted with more care. As it was, the Germans had sought restraints fairly consistently, but also quite ineptly.

The first year of the war thus saw two factors push the powers into a campaign of all-out air attack; the German tendency to misjudge the values of Britain, and then the emergence of an apparently decisive opportunity for the Luftwaffe to disarm the RAF. The knowledge that this last opportunity might not quite be decisive still imposed some caution on the Germans, but apparently not enough.

Japan's Fatal Blunder

SIR GEORGE SANSOM

In the light of what we know today the decision of the leaders of Japan to make war upon the United States appears as an act of folly, by which they committed themselves to a hopeless struggle against a Power with perhaps ten times their own potential industrial and military strength. But was that decision in fact as reckless as it now seems, or can it be regarded as the taking of a justifiable risk in the circumstances in which it was made?

Perhaps it is too soon to expect a complete answer to this question, but there is already available a good deal of useful information upon which a preliminary judgement can be based. There is, for instance, an interesting series of reports published by the United States Strategic Bombing Survey,* which was conducted (by civilians) primarily for the purpose of ascertaining the degree to which air-power contributed to the defeat of Japan. During this enquiry there was collected a mass of statistical and other information regarding political and economic conditions in Japan prior to and during the war. These studies, together with two volumes of Interrogations compiled by the United States Navy,† include valuable data based upon oral and documentary evidence obtained in Japan in 1945, not long after the surrender, when memories were fresh. It should be understood that the answers elicited by interrogations cannot all be taken at face value. Allowance must be made for certain factors of error. Thus, the "Summaries" of the Bombing Survey, in which general conclusions are drawn, naturally tend to place emphasis on the part played by aircraft in reducing Japan to the point of surrender and, by implication, to underestimate the importance of the general strategic conduct of the war and the particular effectiveness of submarine action on vital Japanese lines of com-

Reprinted by permission from *International Affairs,* October 1948, pp. 543–555. One footnote has been omitted.

* [*Editors' note:* United States Strategic Bombing Survey, *Japan's Struggle to End the War* (Washington, D.C.: Government Printing Office, 1946).]

† [*Editors' note:* United States Strategic Bombing Survey, *Interrogations of Japanese Officials,* 2 vols. (Washington, D.C.: Government Printing Office, 1946).]

munication by sea. Moreover, the interrogations were not always skillfully conducted and the replies sometimes betray a desire to please the questioners, if not to mislead them. Different and more reliable results might have been obtained from really searching cross-examination by experienced persons. Nevertheless, the documents are extremely interesting and suffice to establish beyond reasonable doubt a number of important facts. The following tentative appraisal draws freely upon information which they contain, though it is supplemented at a few points by knowledge derived by the writer from other sources during a visit to Japan early in 1946.

There is no doubt that Japan was preparing for war at least a decade before 1941, but this does not necessarily mean that she had decided before that year to make war upon the United States or the British Commonwealth. The most that can be safely said is that certain influential army leaders and their civilian supporters contemplated war if the European situation should so develop as to make it feasible and advantageous. There was no concealment of Japan's intention to get ready for war. But during 1940 there was still no agreement in influential circles as to the course which Japan should take in international affairs, or even as to the lines upon which her economy should be further developed and controlled. The full powers which the Government had progressively acquired in preceding years were exercised only partially; a medley of State controls existed side by side with autonomous direction in separate branches of production and trade; and, in general, conflict between the military and the leaders of industry and finance continued unabated and unresolved.

It is sometimes stated by British and American writers that Big Business in Japan — the so-called *Zaibatsu* — co-operated enthusiastically in preparations for war or at least meekly gave way to military pressure. The evidence for this view is poor. On the contrary, during the early part of 1940 the influential Economic Federation of Japan (*Nihon Keizai Remmei*) resisted the Government's plans for industrial expansion, arguing that they were basically unsound. Their opposition was, it is true, based on technical rather than political grounds, but it cannot be said that they co-operated freely with the military leaders in the development of an economy designed for warlike purposes.

In fact, under the Yonai Government, which was in power until July 1940, there were still elements in the Cabinet that favoured a cautious if not a pacific foreign policy, and were inclined to take the side of the industrialists in resisting totalitarian trends. It was at this point that the military used their strongest political weapon.

By withdrawing the War Minister, they forced the resignation of the Yonai Cabinet, in which the relatively liberal Mr. Arita was Foreign Minister. The second Konoye Cabinet was then formed, with Tojo, a convinced expansionist, as War Minister. Its announced policy was the development of a highly organized National Defence State and the consolidation of an Asiatic "Co-Prosperity Sphere." This was definitely a war Cabinet, and its immediate purpose was to bring the industrialists to heel. Once the Government reached a firm decision the resistance of the industrialists was sooner or later bound to collapse. The close concentration of industrial power in Japan, having historically been achieved largely under official direction or with official support, had never acquired true independence or substantial political strength. It could struggle against this measure or that, but in matters of high policy it could not successfully challenge the authority of the bureaucracy with which it was so organically related.

In September 1940, Tojo let it be known that national mobilization required an intensified control which was inconsistent with the old liberal economic structure. But still the struggle continued and, surprisingly, the resistance of the industrial and financial leaders, represented by the Economic Federation, increased rather than diminished. The planned economy which was the object of Hoshino and Ohashi — two officials who had gained experience in Manchuria — was fought with some success by members of the *Zaibatsu* who, whatever their views as to war and peace, realized the limitations of the Japanese economy. But they were at length forced to execute plans in which they had little faith.

These facts are cited as showing that as late as 1941, despite long preparation, there was yet no effective centralized control of the Japanese industrial structure; and, quite apart from the conflict between Government and private enterprise, there was another defect in the country's war-making capacity, for the administrative machine, seemingly so efficient in normal times, turned out to be rigid and unmanageable. It was even necessary for Tojo, when he became Prime Minister in 1941, to seek legislation which would compel the various ministries to obey his orders. Such a diagnosis of the radical weaknesses in Japan's governmental structure at a juncture when her national existence was about to be staked upon its efficiency may seem too sweeping, but it could be supported by further evidence. It is sufficient to say here that the subsequent course of events, in both the economic and military spheres, shows that part of the failure of the Japanese economy to meet the demands made upon it in time of war can be traced back to faulty arrangements in time of peace. That governments or individuals should contract bad habits is not surprising, but it is surprising that the rulers of Japan should not have realized how inadequate, even by their own standards, was their country's organization for a war of their own choosing against powerful enemies.

The degree of their economic miscalculations is easy to measure by results. More difficult is an assessment of their political judgement. There can be no doubt that the coalition which began to rule Japan in July 1940 was determined to make use of the European war to further an expansionist policy in Asia and, if possible, to settle the conflict with China on favourable terms. When France was defeated and England appeared to the Japanese to be about to follow her in disaster, the Konoye Government began to feel confident enough to probe the weaknesses of possible antagonists by such measures as flouting British and American interests in China, blackmailing the United Kingdom into closing the Burma Road, pressing the Netherland Indies for economic concessions and moving troops into northern Indo-China. In the summer of 1940 it even looked as if an attack upon British possessions in the Far East was imminent. But action was postponed, partly because the progress of the Battle of Britain raised doubts about the expected collapse of the United Kingdom, but also because the Japanese army and navy wished to complete their armament and to collect further stocks of basic materials. They appear to have decided that, tempting as it was, an attack upon British and Dutch territories alone would be strategically unsound, because it would leave on their flank unimpaired American strength which might intervene at a moment chosen by the United States. They were, moreover, not yet satisfied that they had the whole country with them, for despite their vigorous domestic propaganda there were still dissidents in high places and doubtless also among the people. The distribution of political influence within Japan was traditionally such that any decisive move required much bargaining and persuasion. The firmly established system of checks and balances was customary rather than constitutional, but it had the effect of delaying political action. Even within the ruling coalition there were differences of opinion on the timing and the length of each step taken on the road to war, and there were cautious or conservative elements whose hesitations had to be overcome.

This was the condition reached by the summer of 1941. The extremists continued to strengthen their position step by step, by committing Japan to engagements from which it was difficult if not impossible to withdraw. Perhaps this period was the most crucial in Japanese history, since a vital decision on war or peace is not a simple choice of alternatives at a given moment, but is influenced by the cumulative effect of previous commitments, none of which is separately decisive. The extremists had in July 1941, by a series of gradual manoeuvres, gone far towards creating a situation in which their voice would be dominant. They then took a long step by establishing bases in Southern Indo-China. All available evidence goes to show that they did not expect this move to evoke strong reactions from the United States or the United Kingdom. It was represented as nothing but a strategical development in the war against China, but its implications were perfectly clear. It was the first phase of a projected southward movement. It is interesting to note, from the captured German documents published in January 1948 by the United States Government, that the draft secret protocol of November 1940 to the agreement between the U.S.S.R. and the Tripartite Powers states that "Japan declares that her territorial aspirations centre in the area of Eastern Asia to the south of the Island Empire of Japan."[1] The sharp counter-measures of the United States and the United Kingdom came as a surprise to the extremists and threw the moderates into confusion, though they must have had some warning from the Japanese Embassy in Washington. The situation is well described in the Summary Report of the United States Bombing Survey, as follows:

> Though the conservative wing of the ruling coalition had endorsed each move of its coalition partners, it hoped at each stage that the current step would not be the breaking-point leading to war. It arranged and concluded the Tripartite Pact (September 1940) and hoped that the Western Powers would be sufficiently impressed with the might and solidarity of the Axis to understand the futility of further resistance. It approved of the Indo-China adventure, assuming that Japan would get away with this act of aggression as easily as with previous ones.

But while the freezing of Japanese assets and the embargo upon the export of strategic materials to Japan imposed by the Western Powers shocked the conservatives and frightened the moderates, they had already gone too far in their acquiescence. They could not now suggest any course but negotiations with the United States, and over the terms of these negotiations they could exercise no control, since the power of final decision had already passed into the hands of the extremists. All they could now hope for was that the extremists would make enough concessions to satisfy the United States, and this was a vain hope, because to make any effective

---

[1] J. Sontag and J. S. Beddie, eds., Declaration 3, Draft Secret Protocol No. 1, *Nazi Soviet Relations, 1939–40* (U.S.A. Department of State, 1948), p. 257.

concessions would be to admit that the whole of Japanese policy since 1931 had been a blunder, for which the military party and its civilian allies were responsible. The Army's prestige would never recover from such a blow. War was inevitable. The only question now was what kind of war.

Such in broad outline was the political background of the decision to go to war. It remains to consider on what grounds the military leaders of Japan based their judgement that Japan could successfully challenge the United States and the British Commonwealth. It cannot be assumed that they blindly led their country into war with no prospect of success. Theirs was a considered policy, attended by calculated risks. Examined in retrospect it proves to have been based upon mistaken assumptions, and executed with insufficient skill and foresight; but it was not, as conceived, irrational. It must also be remembered that the economic sanctions imposed upon Japan in 1941 were such as to make war appear a reasonable, if dangerous, alternative.

The planners who decided that the risk of war could be taken were not blind to the frightful disparity between their own strength and that of their enemies. They counted upon certain favourable circumstances to balance their own deficiencies. Late in the summer of 1941 they were convinced that Germany would be victorious and that within a few months, Russia having been defeated, the United States and the United Kingdom would be obliged to accept supremacy of Germany in Europe. This outlook, though it promised them membership of a successful alliance, was in one respect not entirely pleasing to them, since they felt some distrust of their Axis partners, which the Germans in Japan by their arrogant behaviour did nothing to diminish. Some Japanese expansionists therefore felt that their plans might be upset by a premature settlement of the European conflict, which would leave them without any spoils of war in the Pacific; and this fear probably, though not certainly, was an additional motive for the rapid seizure of territories in Asia from which they could derive supplies of oil and rubber, and strategic bargaining power. As they saw the position, those objectives — stepping stones to further expansion — could be attained by a short and restricted campaign. They would engage in hostilities in the Pacific for a strictly limited purpose. First they would conquer an area enclosed within a perimeter including Burma, Malaya, Sumatra, Java, Northern New Guinea, the Bismarck Archipelago, the Gilbert and Marshall Islands, Wake and the Kuriles. This, they calculated, could be achieved in a few months if American sea and air power could be weakened by surprise attacks upon Pearl Harbor and the Philippines. The United States, preoccupied with the European situation, would be unable to take the offensive before Japan had accomplished the necessary strengthening of the perimeter and established forward air and sea bases. Once firmly entrenched on that perimeter they could obtain from the occupied areas what they required to sustain and expand their deficient economy — oil, rubber, bauxite, metals, food. Thus supplied, they could wage defensive warfare which, it was supposed, would within a year or two weaken the American purpose and so lead to a compromise peace. Negotiation would leave to Japan a substantial portion of her gains and a dominant position in Eastern Asia.

This was not at that time a strategy which could be condemned out of hand as unrealistic. It could be regarded, and presented to the Japanese people, as a reasonable and honourable alternative to submitting to sanctions. It aroused misgivings in some circles in Japan, and even its proponents knew that it would throw a great strain upon Japan's capacity; but they counted upon the shock of rapid conquests, and upon the fighting qualities of their soldiers and sailors. Certainly in the first few months of the war nothing happened to make them revise their opinions. Their successes were greater and easier than they had foreseen.

So encouraged were they by their achievement that they began to consider an extension of their perimeter. They planned an advance into the Solomons and Port Moresby, to be followed by a further advance into New Caledonia, Samoa, and the Fijis, the capture of Midway and the occupation of the Aleutians. It was here that they made their first cardinal blunder, for . . . "by stretching and overextending her line of advance, Japan was committed to an expensive and exacting supply problem. She delayed the fortification of the perimeter originally decided upon, jeopardised her economic program for exploiting the resources of the area already captured and laid herself open to early counter-attack in far advanced and, as yet, weak positions."[2]

This blunder in execution also laid bare certain weaknesses in the original conceptions of the Japanese planners. Perhaps the most important of these was their misjudgement of the temper of the United States, for the attack on Pearl Harbor had a stimulating psychological effect upon the American people which in military importance far outweighed the losses sustained at Pearl Harbor. The Japanese army had persuaded the Japanese people that the democratic states were materialistic, irresolute, incapable of match-

[2] United States Strategic Bombing Survey, Summary Report, *Pacific War* (Washington, United States Government Printing Office, 1946), p. 4.

ing the unique Japanese spirit. They had argued, not without some plausibility, that the United States had for a decade or more shown a strong aversion to protecting its interests in the Far East by war-like measures, despite repeated provocation. They inferred that those interests were not regarded as of vital importance and that consequently in the long run a spirit of compromise would prevail. They seem to have been deceived by their own propaganda, for even after their initial reverses in the first half of 1942 at Midway and towards the end of the year at Guadalcanal, they appear still to have supposed that they could fight the war on their own terms. They did not yet realize that their original plan of restricted war-fare, which could be sustained for a limited period by their 1941 economy was no longer feasible.

It was not until 1943 that they had fully grasped the fact that they could no longer dictate the scale or location of hostilities, but were involved in total war in which the initiative had already passed to the American forces. That they made this mistake is in-dicated by their failure to carry out complete economic mobilization until 1943. An index of the gross national product (computed by the United States Bombing Survey with the assistance of Japanese experts) shows a rise from 100 in 1940 to only 101 in 1941 and 102 in 1942. It was not until 1943 that a substantial increase was gained by a production drive which raised the figure to 113 for 1943 and 124 for 1944. This was the peak of Japanese production, and it was reached by forcing an ever-growing proportion of the total economy into direct war purposes, while straining the civilian population almost to breaking point. It was a remarkable perform-ance, but it was too little and too late. No effort was made to carry out a coherent plan of overall expansion of the Japanese economy, perhaps because a balanced development was impossible in view of its previous distortion. Even if the foregoing explanation of the delay in carrying out full economic mobilization errs in placing too much emphasis upon a tardy appreciation of the strategic position, it is clear that the Japanese tradition of government depending upon slow and cautious compromise was ill-adapted for times of emer-gency that demanded bold decision and quick performance.

The subsequent course of the Pacific war needs no detailed recital here. It is enough to say that although the Japanese made after 1942 immense military and economic efforts to meet conditions for which they had not originally planned, both were insufficient to stem the tide which began to flow against them. Nearly all their calculations had gone wrong. The British Isles were not invaded, the Soviet Union did not collapse, the United States showed not the least disposition to compromise, but began to plan the outright de-

feat of Japan. The prospect of a negotiated peace vanished. Plans
to draw upon the occupied territories for essential materials could
not be executed, because submarine and air attacks upon Japanese
shipping prevented not only the carriage of needed supplies to
Japan, but also the full support of Japanese forces in the field.
Japanese commanders have testified that only 20 per cent of the
supplies despatched to Guadalcanal reached their destination, and
that of 30,000 troops landed, 10,000 died of starvation or disease
and 10,000 were evacuated early in 1943 in a debilitated condition.
Though Japanese troops everywhere fought stubbornly and well, inflicting heavy losses upon their opponents, by the opening months
of 1943 not only had the Japanese advance been stopped, but their
overall strategic plan had been upset. This was the result of an
overwhelming superiority of American power, and it revealed a
basic error in the initial premises of that plan. It had been supposed
that the perimeter could be held indefinitely, but American experience showed after the engagements of 1942 that it was not necessary to reduce the whole perimeter. The widely spread Japanese
positions were dependent upon supply by sea, and it was necessary
to destroy them only at points selected by the American command.
So long as attacks upon Japanese shipping were maintained, other
points could be by-passed as a general advance was begun towards
bases within striking distance of Japan.

It was after the evacuation of Guadalcanal, in February 1943,
that thoughtful Japanese began to suspect that their prospects of
victory had disappeared, while those who knew all the facts saw
that the situation was desperate. It is surprising that, to quote the
words of Hoshino, Chief Secretary of the Tojo Cabinet, "the real
Japanese war economy only began after Guadalcanal." Perhaps
even more surprising is the confusion which is revealed in the direction both of the war economy and the national strategy after that
date. Full credit must be given to the Japanese people for their efforts to restore and develop their war potential after 1942, but their
leaders seem never to have reached a clear and comprehensive view
of their country's situation. Some rough estimates of national
strength were compiled before the war. They were tentative and
incomplete, and perhaps this was in the circumstances unavoidable.

But it is strange that, so far as is known, a full re-appraisal in
the light of the new conditions was not attempted until September
1943. This was made not by the Government for its own purposes,
but by Takagi, an officer of the Naval General Staff, at the request
of Admiral Yonai, who had been out of office since his Cabinet fell
in 1940. This influential statesman, when asked in 1945 what he
considered the turning point of the war replied: "To be very frank,

I think the turning point was the start. I felt from the very beginning that there was no chance of success." Takagi's report strengthened Admiral Yonai's fears that the prosecution of the war by the
Tojo Government was unsatisfactory. It confirmed his judgement
that Japan should seek a compromise peace before she suffered a
crushing defeat. Yonai was not alone in this feeling. It was shared
by certain influential persons outside the Government and a number of naval officers. They had indeed good reason for their anxiety.
The circumstances beyond Japan's control were grave enough —
the growing shortages of materials, losses of aircraft, warships and
merchant vessels, and the certainty of long-range air attacks upon
the centres of production at home. And, added to these, was growing confusion within Japan.

Nominally, by 1943 the Japanese Government had achieved full
control of all national organs and activities, but Japan had evidently
not become a solid authoritarian state. Animosity between Army
and Navy was such that the submarine service resented the diver-
sion of its vessels from combatant functions to army transport duties, and towards the end of the war the Army began to build
submarines for its own use and declined naval advice. Army and
Navy details, it is said, would fight outside factories for supplies
designated for one or the other service. Ginjiro Fujihara, an industrial magnate who at a critical juncture became director of aircraft
production, even alleged (no doubt untruthfully) that army and
navy rivalry was responsible for keeping down the total output by
about 50 per cent. In addition to their inter-service quarrels, the
armed forces displayed hostility towards civilian organs. The director of the General Mobilization Bureau testified on interrogation
that they would never disclose their stocks or discuss their requirements with him, would not submit demands through the appropriate ministry and thus thwarted all attempts at co-ordination of
supply. Control bodies set up by the Government for key materials
tried to enforce a system of priorities, but the Army and Navy would
help themselves to supplies without troubling to obtain priority-
certificates. Civilian manufacturing firms were, it is reported,
obliged to resort to black market transactions in order to secure
material or machines. It is of course easy to exaggerate the extent
and importance of such abuses, which are common enough in all
countries at war; but it is clear that there was a serious lack of
harmony between the two fighting services. Admiral Toyoda (Commander-in-Chief Combined Fleet, and later Chief of Naval General
Staff) said upon interrogation: "There was not full understanding
and agreement between Army and Navy prior to and during the
war." This discord he ascribed to the great political power of the
Army, which the Navy did not share. It showed itself, he thought,

not so much in operational matters as in the division of supplies. But General Yamashita, the Japanese commander in the Philippines, was only apprised of the intended naval strike on Leyte Gulf in a *written* communication from Tokyo which was two weeks on the way and reached him on the day of the operation.

Uneasy relations between Army and Navy were paralleled by quarrels between civilian organs. It is remarkable that, despite their reputed gift for careful and strict organization, the Japanese authorities were not in practice able to exercise their unlimited powers of control. Under a surface appearance of national unity, old divisions of opinion, old patterns of influence, persisted with very little change. It is perhaps comforting to discover that what appears to be a solid monolithic state can hide grave structural weaknesses behind a forbidding exterior.

By July 1944, the invasion of Saipan had succeeded and Tojo's Cabinet had collapsed. The strenuous efforts made to raise production in Japan had led to a considerable increase in capacity, yet by late in the summer output had begun to decline because shipping losses had cut down essential imports. National morale was still high but by the autumn of 1944 Japan was on the verge of economic collapse, and that was before the heavy strategical bombing of the home islands. Tojo was succeeded as Prime Minister by Koiso, a retired general, whose Government set up a Supreme War Direction Council intended ostensibly to strengthen national defence, but in fact obliged to consider ways of terminating the war. The story of the steps by which most of its members at length reached a decision in favour of surrender is a long and complicated one. Not much progress was made at first, but certain members of the Cabinet were cautiously working for peace and carrying on discussions with senior statesmen who, though out of office, retained great personal influence. High naval officers were predominant among the service men who favoured attempts to secure a negotiated peace, while the Army command still thought in terms of prolonged resistance, hoping that they could inflict such losses upon an invading force that a compromise could be secured, which would leave to Japan something better than the prospect of unconditional surrender. The peace party was growing in confidence, but only slowly, and was hampered by the fear that, since the Japanese people were still ignorant of the true state of affairs, a premature move might bring about internal chaos.

Meanwhile, with the loss of the Philippines and the intensification of bombing, which affected both military targets and urban populations, the situation became more and more desperate in the eyes of the peace party, less and less hopeful in the eyes of the last-ditchers. But it seems that there was little prospect of obtaining the agreement of any substantial portion of the Army leaders so long as Germany continued to resist. It was not until April 8, 1945 that the Koiso Government fell and was succeeded by a Cabinet under Admiral Suzuki, whose mission was to bring the war to an end, though publicly both Government and people were still committed to a continued resistance. Progress towards peace was still slow, for nobody would come out with an open declaration that the war was lost. Early in May, however — shortly after the end of the European war — the balance began to turn in favour of peace. Appraisals of the economic situation showed that the country was utterly incapable of continuing effective resistance, and there were even some signs of a decline in public morale. Still no specific proposals for ending the war were made, though on June 6 the Supreme War Council definitely stated to the Emperor that it was necessary to bring it to an end. On June 20, the Emperor summoned the Council, and showed himself in favour of positive steps, including an approach to the Soviet Union with a request for mediation. Discussions with Russia made no progress, the Soviet Government temporized and the Japanese ambassador in Moscow reported that in his opinion there was no alternative to unconditional surrender.

Time went by, and still no firm decision had been reached when the Potsdam Declaration was issued on July 26, 1945. The Prime Minister, the Foreign Minister and the Navy Minister (Yonai) were in favour of accepting its terms, the War Minister and the Chiefs of Staff were opposed. It is interesting to note, as illustrating the nature of the opposition, that Toyoda had not approved of the war from the beginning, yet was unable to agree to unconditional surrender, which he thought dishonourable. A strong military group still held out for resistance to invasion. Differences of opinion continued until August 9, 1945, by which time an atomic bomb had been dropped on Hiroshima (August 6) and the Soviet Union had declared war upon Japan (August 9). After repeated meetings on August 9, just before midnight the Inner Cabinet appealed to the Emperor for a final expression of his wish and the Emperor declared in favour of peace. There were further cabinet discussions as to the interpretation of the Potsdam terms, but they were finally accepted on August 14. This was more than twelve months after the fall of the Tojo Government, and four months after the formation of the Suzuki Cabinet, which was certainly intended to bring an end to hostilities. It may well be asked why, in the light of Japan's inability, so manifest after the end of 1944, to carry the war to a successful conclusion, the discussion was prolonged well into 1945, while her factories and her houses were being destroyed, her warships sunk and her armies cut off from their homes? The answer is not clear, but it seems as if the delay was something dictated by the nature of Japanese institutions. The slow process by which an apparently unanimous will to war was created before 1941 had to be repeated in reverse before a will to peace could be announced.

The fact that the decision to accept the Potsdam terms was reached soon after the explosion of the atomic bomb and the Russian declaration of war has been interpreted as showing that the bomb and the Russian action were what produced Japan's surrender. This is a view which it is difficult to accept. It might be correct to say that these two menacing events accelerated a decision which was being reached by slow and devious processes characteristic of Japanese political life. But it cannot be truthfully said that any one single cause brought about the surrender; at the same time there is good reason for thinking that, even had no atomic bombing attacks been delivered, the disintegration of Japan's economic life, under sustained blockade and continued aerial and naval bombardment, would within a few months — perhaps weeks — after June 1945 have brought about unconditional surrender, even without the need for invasion. But all this is in the realm of conjecture, and not even the participants themselves can say with certainty what course the debates in the War Council would have taken in hypothetical conditions. Even if we were today certain that it was not the atomic bomb which caused the surrender, it would not follow that the decision to use the bomb was wrong. That decision was necessarily taken in the light of such sure knowledge as was then at the disposal of our Governments; and although intelligence reports on conditions in Japan were remarkably good, that knowledge was not sufficient to justify abstaining from the use of a weapon which might end the war quickly, and save the lives of thousands of allied prisoners, possibly hundreds of thousands of allied soldiers, to say nothing of great numbers of enemy soldiers and civilians. Discussion of the rights and wrongs of the use of the atomic bomb at Hiroshima frequently confuses two separate issues. If the question is whether it was immoral to use such a destructive weapon, then one must bring into consideration incendiary raids, such as that of the night of March 9, 1945, which killed probably 100,000 people and destroyed over 250,000 homes, in circumstances of appalling terror. If the question is whether the use of the atomic bomb was strategically unnecessary or (in the light of subsequent history) politically mistaken, then moral considerations are irrelevant so long as the right of a belligerent to attack civilian targets is admitted. There cannot by any rational standard of morals be a valid distinction between methods of killing civilians in which one is right and the other is wrong because it is quicker and more effective.

The Korean War

MORTON H. HALPERIN

FOREIGN-POLICY OBJECTIVES

Prior to the outbreak of the Korean War, the United States believed that a major objective of the Soviet Union was to expand the area under its control. Thus, in responding to the North Korean attack — which had not been anticipated — American objectives were developed in the framework of the belief that the attack was part of a general plan for expansion and perhaps a prelude to general war. The United States sought to prevent the success of this Communist attempt to expand by the use of force in the belief that allowing the Soviets to succeed in Korea would encourage aggression elsewhere. General Omar Bradley expressed this purpose at the MacArthur hearings in describing Korea as "a preventive limited war aimed at avoiding World War III."[1] President Harry Truman later described his objectives in intervening in the Korean War in similar terms:

> Communism was acting in Korea just as Hitler, Mussolini, and the Japanese had acted ten, fifteen, and twenty years earlier. I felt certain that if South Korea was allowed to fall Communist leaders would be emboldened to override nations closer to our own shores. If the Communists were permitted to force their way into the Republic of Korea without opposition from the free world, no small nation would have the courage to resist threats and aggression by stronger Communist neighbors. If this was allowed to go unchallenged it would mean a third world war, just as similar incidents had brought on the second world war.[2]

The defense of Korea was partly motivated by the feeling that the action was necessary to convince the West Europeans that the

From *Limited War in the Nuclear Age* by Morton H. Halperin, pp. 39–58. Reprinted by permission of the publisher, John Wiley and Sons, Inc. Some footnotes have been omitted.

[1] Hearings before the Committee on Armed Services and the Committee on Foreign Relations, *Military Situation in the Far East,* U.S. Senate, 82nd Congress, 1st Session, 1951, five parts, p. 154.

[2] Harry S. Truman, *Memoirs,* Vol. II: *Years of Trial and Hope.* Garden City, N.Y.: Doubleday & Co., 1956, p. 333.

United States would come to their aid. The Administration was wary of committing its military power, thereby leaving itself exposed to Soviet aggression in Europe. During the latter stages of the Korean War, in fact, the major American buildup occurred in Europe and not in the Far East. The Administration was also aware of the danger of splitting the NATO alliance in a dispute over Far Eastern policy. A major objective throughout the war was to prevent adverse repercussions in Europe while using the episode to strengthen NATO and build up its military capability. America's NATO allies, particularly the British, constantly applied pressure on the United States to prevent expansion of the war and to bring it swiftly to a conclusion. Following an almost inadvertent reference by President Truman at a press conference to the possibility of using atomic weapons, British Prime Minister Clement Attlee flew to the United States to confer with Truman and to propose the seeking of a cease fire in Korea to be followed by the admission of Communist China to the United Nations. Partly because the defense effort in Korea was carried on under UN auspices, the United States felt obliged constantly to consult its allies on policy and was influenced by their continuous efforts to halt the expansion of the war and to bring about its conclusion.

Soviet objectives were more closely related to the situation in the Far East. The Soviets were interested in the capture of South Korea for its own sake and probably expected a relatively quick and easy North Korean victory. In addition, the Soviets probably hoped to prevent Japan's alignment with the Western powers. Allen Whiting has suggested the nature of the Soviet Far Eastern objective:

> In view of the multiple pressures directed at Japanese foreign policy, the Communist leaders may have conceived the Korean War as serving ends beyond the immediate control of the peninsula. Military victories in Taiwan and Korea could be heralded as ushering in the Communist era in Asia, and as demonstrating the impotence of America's "puppets," Chiang Kai-shek and Syngman Rhee. The resultant effect upon Japan might swing opportunistic groups behind existing neutralist opposition to Yoshida and prevent his supporting American policy.[3]

This interpretation of Soviet strategy in the Korean War was offered by John Foster Dulles right after the North Korean attack. Dulles, who was at the time the State Department planner for the Japanese Peace Treaty, suggested that the Korean attack may have been motivated in part by a desire to block American efforts to make Japan a full member of the free world. He conjectured also that the

---

[3] Allen S. Whiting, *China Crosses the Yalu: The Decision to Enter the Korean War.* (New York: Macmillan Co., 1960), p. 37.

attack may have been ordered because the Communists could not tolerate the "hopeful, attractive Asiatic experiment in democracy" that was under way in South Korea.[4]

The Chinese objectives in entering the Korean War were also based on general political considerations, but of a defensive nature. According to Whiting the Chinese also hoped to influence the course of United States-Japanese relations. Moreover they were worried about the loss of prestige they would suffer if they allowed the Western "imperialists" to march unhindered to their borders. And they were perhaps most concerned with the beneficial effects of United Nations success in Korea on the many opponents of the Communist regime still active in China and on Taiwan. Whiting concluded:

> In sum, it was not the particular problems of safeguarding electric-power supplies in North Korea or the industrial base in Manchuria that aroused Peking to military action. Instead, the final step seems to have been prompted in part by general concern over the range of opportunities within China that might be exploited by a determined, powerful enemy on China's doorstep. At the least, a military response might deter the enemy from further adventures. At the most, it might succeed in inflicting sufficient damage to force the enemy to compromise his objectives and to accede to some of Peking's demands. Contrary to some belief, the Chinese Communist leadership did not enter the Korean War either full of self-assertive confidence or for primarily expansionist goals.[5]

The Chinese apparently entered the war with the aim of saving at least some of North Korea. Their minimal objective was to preserve the identity of Communist North Korea rather than its total territorial integrity.

In an effort to secure the political effects discussed, American battlefield objectives and war-termination conditions underwent considerable fluctuation during the course of the war. When the United States first intervened, its objective was simply to restore peace and the South Korean border. Very early in the war and after the Chinese intervention, the United States considered a total withdrawal from Korea.[6] Later its battlefield objective expanded to include the unification of Korea. But in the end, the United States accepted a truce line which closely approximated the *status quo ante*. As Richard Neustadt has pointed out, Truman's original de-

---

[4] *New York Times,* July 2, 1950.

[5] Whiting, *op. cit.,* p. 159.

[6] Courtney Whitney, *MacArthur: His Rendezvous with History.* New York: Alfred A. Knopf, 1956, pp. 429–431, 438.

cision to seek the unification of Korea failed to take into account the political-effects objectives that the United States was pursuing, and in the end the recognition of this forced the abandonment of the unification effort.

Had the unification of Korea been Truman's dearest object, its announcement as a war aim would have been another matter. But it was among the least of the objectives on his mind. In July and August 1950, in December after Chinese intervention, in his struggles with MacArthur, and thereafter through his last two years of office, his behavior leaves no doubt about the many things he wanted more than that. He wanted to affirm that the UN was not a League of Nations, that aggression would be met with counterforce, that "police actions" were well worth their cost, that the "lesson of the 1930's" had been learned. He wanted to avoid "the wrong war, in the wrong place, at the wrong time," as General Bradley put it — and any "War," if possible. He wanted NATO strengthened fast, both militarily and psychologically. He wanted the United States rearmed without inflation, and prepared, thereafter, to sustain a level of expenditure for military forces and for foreign aid far higher than had seemed achievable before Korea.[7]

Once the Soviets recognized that they could not easily secure their objective of demonstrating American weakness and unwillingness to use force, they seemed to have abandoned the battlefield objective of capturing all of Korea. They may have been willing to accept an end to the war with part or perhaps even all of North Korea in Western hands, and ultimately settled for a virtual restoration of the *status quo ante*.

RISK OF CENTRAL WAR

The Korean War was fought before the era of intercontinental ballistic missiles and fusion weapons. Thus, while both sides could have expanded the war quickly and decisively, there was not the danger that now exists of a sudden unleashing of nuclear missiles which within an hour could destroy a large part of both the United States and the Soviet Union.

Even without this threat of a mutually devastating strategic exchange, the danger of a world war was nevertheless present, and both sides seem to have been determined to prevent its occurrence. Truman has reported that the major American aim in Korea was to prevent a third world war. The Russian decision to remain out of the war seemed to be partly motivated by a fear of igniting a global war. In this situation where neither side could gain a decisive ad-

[7] Richard E. Neustadt, *Presidential Power: The Politics of Leadership.* New York: John Wiley and Sons, 1960, p. 126.

vantage by going first, both sides seemed to recognize that, no matter who started the global war, both would suffer major losses. Though the United States could have attacked the Soviet Union with its very limited stockpile of atomic weapons, it probably could not have prevented a Soviet ground attack in Western Europe which might have resulted in Communist domination of the European continent. The Soviets had almost no capacity to attack the United States and could not have prevented an American attack on the Soviet Union. Though both sides avoided forcing the other into starting a global war, neither was constantly concerned with the possibility of "preemption" by its adversary.

The United States, however, was concerned that the Korean War should not lead it to expend those military capabilities which were considered an important deterrent to general war. In Korea the United States was employing the troops and the matériel which it felt were necessary to deter general war. At the MacArthur hearings, Air Force General Vandenburg rejected a senator's suggestion that the United States should commit a major part of the American Air Force to the Korean War effort. He argued instead that the United States must get a cease fire

> without endangering that one potential that we have which has kept the peace so far, which the United States Air Force; which, if utilized in a manner to do what you are suggesting, would [sic], because of attrition and because the size of the Air Force is such and the size of the air force industry is such that we could not still be that deterrent to [general] war which we are today.[8]

Soviet action during the war, including the failure to commit combat forces, suggests that they shared with the United States the desire to avoid a global war.

IMAGES OF THE ROLE OF FORCE

The North Korean attack on South Korea suggested the willingness of the Communists to seek a limited objective by a limited use of force. The Soviets probably intended to seize South Korea with the use of North Korean forces and then to halt their military operations. When the United States intervened, they recognized their miscalculation of American intentions, but proceeded on the assumption that American intervention need not lead to world war. The attack into South Korea, moreover, seems to have been motivated by the Soviet compulsion to fill power vacuums. In view of the specific United States declaration that South Korea was outside its defense perimeter, the Soviets reasonably could have counted

---

[8] *Military Situation in the Far East, op. cit.,* p. 1385.

on a quick and easy victory by the North Koreans. But, while Communist conduct during the war reflected a doctrine that included the limited use of military force and limited objectives, neither the Chinese nor the Russians seemed to have any idea of the optimum methods of communicating intentions and capabilities to the other side in the course of such a war.

American images of the role of force, on the other hand, seem to have been much less hospitable to the limitation of warfare. It would appear that the United States had not foreseen the possibility of Soviet military action in South Korea or any other local area unconnected with a general Soviet military offensive. The result was the American decision not to prepare for the defense of South Korea in view of the low estimate of its value in a general war. Thus the decision of June 1950 to defend South Korea was not based on a reestimate of South Korea's military importance, but on a recognition that something had occurred for which American military doctrine had not been prepared. In making its policy decisions throughout the war, the United States was operating without any general theoretical notions of the nature of local war in the atomic age, and its decisions were probably affected by the lack of such theory.

Each side's image of the other's intentions influenced its decisions. The Soviets clearly underestimated the likelihood of American intervention. In the Soviet view American action in withdrawing its troops from Korea and the American declarations that it would defend South Korea only as part of its United Nations obligations had meant that the United States would not in fact defend South Korea. The Soviets failed to anticipate the partly moral and partly political American reaction to aggression. They were insensitive to the importance that the United States would attach to repelling "illegal" aggression, as opposed to less clear-cut violations of international law.

The American decision to intervene in Korea and the subsequent decisions were also based on and influenced by estimates of Soviet intentions.[9] In assessing the motives of the North Korean attack, American policy makers gave consideration and, to some extent, credence to five different interpretations, as follows:

1. The "diversionary move" interpretation. In view of the number of other areas, particularly Western Europe, that appeared more militarily significant than South Korea, the North Korean

---

[9] This discussion of the American image of Soviet doctrine is based on Alexander L. George, "American Policy-Making and the North Korean Aggression," *World Politics*, VII (January 1955), pp. 209–232.

attack was seen as a diversionary move, aimed to draw American resources away from the areas where they were most important. Truman reports that he shared this view in part and was determined not to leave Europe vulnerable to Soviet aggression.

2. The "soft-spot probing" interpretation. By this image of Soviet doctrine, the Soviet compulsion to fill power vacuums had led to the attack on South Korea which had been abandoned by the United States and which was clearly incapable of defending itself.

3. The "testing" interpretation. This was the view that seemed to influence most Truman's image of the North Korean attack. It recalled the progress of Hitler's aggressive moves and asserted that the North Korean attack should be seen as a prelude to attacks in other areas if that aggression were allowed to succeed. This view differed from the "soft-spot probing" interpretation in its assumption that the Communists' success in Korea would encourage them to attempt aggression in the other areas where Western defense capabilities were far stronger. In short the purpose of the Korean attack was to probe the firmness of Western intentions, and not simply to fill a power vacuum.

4. The "demonstration" interpretation. By this interpretation, the Soviets were mainly concerned with demonstrating their own strength and American weakness in order to promote, on a long-term basis, important shifts in political allegiance throughout the world.

5. The "Soviet-Far-East-strategy" interpretation. This interpretation put emphasis on the idea, already discussed, that the Soviets hoped to prevent the entrance of Japan into the Western camp and to pave the way for further Communist expansion in the Far East.

. . . The inclination of American policy makers toward the "testing" interpretation of Soviet doctrine — in which the Korean attack was equated with Hitler's early expansionist moves — may have reinforced the likelihood that the United States would intervene in Korea. If the "soft-spot probing" interpretation of Soviet conduct had been accepted instead, the United States might have been more prone to cede South Korea while taking steps to prevent the existence of power vacuums elsewhere. The belief that successful aggression would embolden the Soviets made the defense of South Korea seem crucial.

DOMESTIC POLITICAL PRESSURES

During the Korean War the Truman administration continued to pursue its domestic political goals. Despite the war there was politics-as-usual on both sides of the political fence. The President was constantly concerned with promoting his Fair Deal program, consolidating the position of the Democratic Party, strengthening his northern and western liberal support in Congress, and calming the political crises raised by such men as Senator Joseph McCarthy. Nor was the Administration immune to criticism from the Republican Party, which felt that it was possible, necessary, and desirable to attack the Administration's conduct as well as to question the basic concept of limiting war.

After the MacArthur hearings, a Republican minority report declared:

> We believe that a policy of victory must be announced to the American people in order to restore unity and confidence. It is too much to expect that our people will accept a limited war. Our policy must be to win. Our strategy must be devised to bring about decisive victory.[10]

These few sentences suggest a number of important assumptions about the nature of wartime politics. The first is the notion that the unity of the American people can be achieved only with a declaration that victory is the goal. A further implication is that, after such a declaration, the method of achieving a battlefield victory becomes a "military" problem that is beyond the realm of partisan domestic politics. On the other hand, once the government admits that there are other political considerations that affect and moderate the goal of a strictly military victory, then, according to this Republican statement, it is legitimate to criticize the particular policy adopted. Unity will come only when the country is asked to back an absolute goal. If there is no such goal, then the opposition has a duty to examine and critically appraise the war effort.

Congress, as a whole, also felt itself free to criticize. The hearings into the firing of General Douglas MacArthur were striking in that they required the Administration, *during the war,* to justify its conduct and to explain what it hoped to accomplish in the war and how the war was being conducted, as well as to explicate a host of particulars which must have been of as much interest to the Communists as they were to the senators across the table. Actually the the Chinese and the Russians. However, the senators' questions at hearings provided a unique and invaluable opportunity for the Administration to communicate what it wanted to communicate to this hearing did not have that motivation. Congress forced the Administration to discuss its strategy and objectives during the war without any apparent consideration of the effect this would have on the American war effort.

The quotation from the report of the Republican senators also

[10] *Military Situation in the Far East, op. cit.,* p. 3590.

reflects the then still strong American opposition to fighting a local war. The Senators stated flatly that the American people would not accept a strategy of limiting war, and indicated their rejection of the strategy as well. The implication is that during a local war the American government will be subjected to attacks from the political opposition, from Congress, and from public citizens on two grounds: the legitimacy of fighting such a war and the particular strategy employed in the war.

The general public seems to have shared the Republican senators' dissatisfaction with the course of the Korean War, at least in its later stages. On the other hand, the public apparently approved the decision of the Eisenhower administration to end the war short of victory as it had approved the initial decision to intervene. The public's frustration with the continuing war probably added to the margin of Eisenhower's victory in 1952; his ending the war enhanced the Republican image as the party of peace and increased the Eisenhower plurality in 1956. The Korean War does not seem to have had a major or lasting impact on popular political attitudes.[11] In this respect, American political leaders seem to have overestimated the effect of the war on the voting public. Korea is taken as demonstrating — as to some extent it did — that extended local wars which cannot be decisively won are not popular with the American public. Leading the United States into a major local war or expanding the war without securing a clear victory is likely to be perceived as a political liability; ending a war on almost any terms may be a political asset.

All these domestic pressures undoubtedly influenced the manner in which the Truman administration conducted its Korean operations, both by hampering its freedom of action and by increasing the costs of various actions.

ATOMIC WEAPONS

The most dramatic limit on the Korean War was that neither side used its atomic weapons. According to Brodie there were four reasons why these weapons were not used by the United States:[12]

1. The Joint Chiefs of Staff and civilian policy makers continued to feel that the war in Korea was basically a Soviet feint. There was, therefore, a strong case for conserving the then relatively limited stockpile of atomic weapons for the principal war which, they

[11] Angus Campbell et al., *The American Voter.* New York: John Wiley and Sons, 1960, pp. 49, 50, 527, 546, 555.

[12] Bernard Brodie, *Strategy in the Missile Age.* Princeton, N.J.: Princeton University Press, 1959.

thought, would come in Europe. Their fear was not that the employment of nuclear weapons would lead to an expansion of the war and a Soviet attack on Europe, but rather that Korea was deliberately designed as a decoy to get the United States to exhaust its nuclear stockpile and conventional military resources so that the Soviets could later attack with impunity in Europe. It was the desire, then, to save resources and not the fear of provoking the enemy that was one of the main causes of the American decision not to use nuclear weapons in Korea.

2. American policy was also affected by the reports of local Air Force commanders that there were no suitable targets for atomic weapons in Korea. While the impact of this view was considerable, it apparently reflected an uninformed attitude about the possible uses of atomic weapons. Commanders in the field came to think, for example, that atomic bombs were of little use against bridges, a belief which Brodie explained as follows:

> This odd idea probably resulted from a mis-reading of the results at Hiroshima and Nagasaki. Some bridges were indeed badly damaged at those places and some were not, but for the latter it was generally forgotten that a bridge only 270 feet from ground zero at Hiroshima was actually 2,100 feet from the point of explosion, and also that it received its blast effect from above rather than from the side.[13]

Nuclear weapons were still relatively new and had not been extensively tested, and it is probable that commanders in the field were too busy to search out potential targets for nuclear weapons.

3. American allies, particularly the British, were strongly and emotionally opposed to the use of atomic weapons in the Korean War. This pressure from allies strengthened America's own anxieties and moral doubts about again using these weapons.

4. A subsidiary reason for the failure to use atomic weapons in the Korean War was the fear of the retaliatory employment by the Soviets of the few atomic weapons in their possession against Pusan or Japan, despite the American near monopoly of these weapons. Brodie doubts, however, whether this fear played a conscious part in the relevant decisions.

The first two motives just discussed will not be important in the future. The American stockpile of tactical nuclear weapons is now so great that military commanders may urge their use precisely because they are a nonscarce military resource, and certainly no argument can be made that they should not be used because they are scarce. Military officers now have a much better understanding of

[13] *Ibid.*, p. 319n.

the capabilities of nuclear weapons, which, moreover, now come in much smaller packages. Thus it will be clear to military commanders that there would be suitable targets for their use in any conceivable future major limited war. While we can expect continued pressure from our allies against the use of nuclear weapons, certain allies might advocate their use in some situations. There will, however, be other international political pressures — for example, from the uncommitted or neutral states — against nuclear weapons, and the possibility of a Soviet nuclear response will be a much more important determinant of the decision.

We know much less about the details of the Russian decision not to use atomic weapons in Korea. The Russians seemed determined not to supply any matériel to the forces fighting in Korea which could clearly be labeled as having been supplied by them after the war began. This would certainly be the case with atomic weapons.[14] In addition, the Soviet stockpile of such weapons was so small that its use in a localized military encounter might have seemed wasteful.

The limit observed by both sides seems not to have resulted from an attempt — or even an awareness of the need — to bargain with the enemy. However the Soviets were probably more restrained than the United States by the fear that the initiation of nuclear attacks would be met by a response in kind.[15]

The Chinese Communists seem genuinely to have feared the possibility of the American use of atomic weapons when they intervened in the Korean War. According to Whiting the Chinese felt that a nuclear response was a real possibility; intervention was considered risky and every effort was made to delay it and to minimize its consequences. The extent of this Chinese concern was reflected both in its shelter-building program and in domestic Chinese Communist propaganda. But Peking was reassured by the three-week testing period of relatively small Chinese intervention which revealed that United States aircraft, though authorized to bomb the Korean ends of the Yalu bridges, were forbidden to venture into Chinese territory.

The background of the limit on the use of atomic weapons in the Korean War, then, suggests a failure of both sides to understand what the other side was likely to do and what the other side's fears and goals were. It also suggests that, to a large extent, the

---

[14] It was also true, however, of the MIGs which the Soviets supplied probably with Russian pilots.

[15] However, if the use of atomic weapons had been confined to the Korean theater — that is, if the decision to use these weapons was not coupled with a decision to expand the war in some other way — it is not clear who would have gained from an atomic exchange.

determination of limits is based on considerations other than those that result from the battlefield interaction. Some of the other limiting points established in the war reveal the same pattern.

CHINESE INTERVENTION

One of the major expansions of the Korean War was the decision of the United Nations Command to cross the thirty-eighth parallel. This decision was based partly on the military consideration that one could not stand by and allow the enemy forces to regroup for renewed attack just beyond the border, but also on political grounds — when the battlefield conditions changed in its favor, the United States decided to pursue the unification of Korea by military means. In crossing the parallel the United States was aware of the risk that it might trigger Chinese Communist intervention, and tried by reassuring statements to prevent it. But it apparently underestimated the Chinese reaction and, at the same time, failed to develop a concurrent strategy which, by retaliatory threats or other sanctions, could succeed in preventing Chinese intervention. As Whiting has suggested the threat to use atomic weapons on the Chinese mainland if the Chinese intervened might have been a much more effective deterrent than the attempt to reassure them that a march to the border did not presage an attack on mainland China.[16] The threat to use atomic weapons would have involved major political costs for the United States, and the American government might not have threatened to launch an atomic attack even if it had recognized that the threat might be effective. Had the Administration been aware of the fact that the fear of greater expansion might have deterred Chinese intervention, an alternative course might have been to threaten to expand the war to China with conventional weapons. But even this was not done. In fact, a decision was made before the intervention that Chinese intervention would not lead to conventional bombing beyond the Yalu. MacArthur reportedly believed that this decision had been leaked to the Chinese.[17]

In choosing, instead, to inform the Chinese of its limited objectives, the United States also considered it important to reassure the Chinese that their hydroelectric plants would not be jeopardized by a march up to the Yalu. But, as Whiting has pointed out:

> It was widely believed in Western circles that a determining factor in Chinese Communist concern over North Korea was the reliance of Manchurian industry upon power supplies across the border as well as along the Yalu River. This belief prompted explicit reassurances

[16] Whiting, *op. cit.*, p. 162. Panikkar, the Indian ambassador in Peking, reported that the Chinese expected an atomic attack, but were nonetheless prepared to intervene.
[17] Whitney, *op. cit.*, pp. 455–456.

from Western spokesmen, both in Washington and at Lake Success, concerning "China's legitimate interests" near the frontier. Yet we have seen that Peking ignored this issue completely in its domestic as well as its foreign communications. The absence of propaganda about the protection of the hydroelectric installations, despite the need to maximize popular response to mobilization of "volunteers," suggests that this consideration played little if any role in motivating Chinese Communist intervention.[18]

In its advance through North Korea, then, the United Nations Command was attempting to communicate two points to the Chinese Communists: first, that it was prepared to go up to but not beyond the Yalu; and second, that it was prepared to respect China's legitimate interests in the northern regions of North Korea. The United States sought, therefore, to establish its limited objectives: that United Nations forces would take all North Korea, that the North Korean government would cease to exist, but China's legitimate industrial interests would be protected. An effort was made to assure the Chinese that the capture of North Korea would not be used as a springboard for an attack into China. The United States assumed that the limits were ones that the Chinese were interested in, and that these limits would serve to keep the Chinese out of the war. But Chinese interests were different and could only be satisfied by different boundary conditions to the war.

Neustadt argues that the Chinese were not in any way affected by the announcement of the United Nations' aim to destroy the North Korean government.

> To judge from what the Chinese said, and later did, Peking's concern was with MacArthur's military progress, never mind its foreign policy objective. Chinese concern was not confined to anything so simple as a buffer zone along the border; an entity called North Korea, not the border, was at stake (perhaps in roughly the same sense that South Korea, under reverse circumstances, was for Washington). Even had the UN promised restoration of an independent North once all resistance ceased — which, naturally, no one proposed — I know of nothing to suggest that Peking would have withheld intervention. The communist world does not take kindly, it appears, to the dismantling of a member state's facilities for governance: the party and the army. MacArthur's military progress threatened both, no matter what came after. In short, the military risks and diplomatic dangers usually associated with MacArthur's march across the parallel existed independent of the words used in the UN resolution. MacArthur's march was authorized before the words were seen, much less approved, at Lake Success.[19]

[18] Whiting, *op. cit.*, pp. 151–152.
[19] Neustadt, *op. cit.*, p. 125.

Washington was apparently convinced even in retrospect that its declarations did not influence the Chinese decision to enter the war and that no other declaratory policy could have altered the Chinese decision. American policy makers concluded that once the decision was made to cross the thirty-eighth parallel, nothing could be done to affect the Chinese decision. In fact, the State Department reportedly argued in December of 1950 that the Chinese decision to intervene was made prior to the crossing of the thirty-eighth parallel. In one sense, at least, this conclusion may be wrong: the Chinese position might have been altered by threats to expand the war with the use of atomic weapons against China. Moreover it is by no means certain that the Chinese were concerned with the preservation of the total territorial integrity of North Korea. As Whiting suggests an American commitment to advance only part way up the peninsula — that is, to permit the maintenance of the North Korean government in some part of its territory — might have been sufficient to deter the Chinese entrance into the war.

> Neither before nor during the first three months of war [Whiting wrote] did the degree of interest in Pyongyang evinced by Peking warrant acceptance at face value of its concern for a "just" peace, based upon the *status quo ante bellum.*
>
> This is not to say that the Chinese Communist leadership was prepared to accept with equanimity the total defeat of North Korea. As a minimal goal, intervention must have been attempted to preserve an entity identifiable as the DPRK, and to prevent unification of all Korea under U.N. supervision. The late date of Chinese Communist entry into the war suggests that it was the political importance of the North Korean government, rather than its territorial integrity, that was at stake. Although intervention was officially predicated upon U.N. crossing of the thirty-eighth parallel, no Chinese People's Volunteers and Democratic People's Republic of Korea defense lines were established during the August-October period, not even to protect Pyongyang. To Peking, a "just" Korean peace was not an end in itself but rather a means towards fulfilling other related goals of policy.[20]

Thus, even after the crossing of the thirty-eighth parallel, Chinese intervention might have been prevented had the United States acted differently. Although trying to impose limits on expansion, the United States failed to grasp adequately either the reasons that the Chinese felt intervention was necessary or the threats that might have deterred their intervention. Both sides expanded the war, the United Nations by crossing the thirty-eighth parallel and the Chinese by entering the war. Each side failed to convey to the other the kind of counteraction to be expected which might have deterred

[20] Whiting, *op. cit.,* pp. 155–156.

expansion. China attempted to prevent the crossing of the thirty-eighth parallel by declaring her intention to intervene, but this intention, relayed by the Indian ambassador, was not taken seriously by the United Nations Command. The United Nations sought to prevent the Chinese entrance, not by threatening a further expansion but by attempting to satisfy the Chinese security interests that, it was assumed, might lead her to enter the war.

PORTS AND TROOPS

Despite the fact that United States planes, taking off from airfields in South Korea and Japan and from aircraft carriers, consistently bombed targets in North Korea, the Communists engaged in almost no bombing south of the thirty-eighth parallel. This was one of the major asymmetries of the war both from a legalistic point of view and in terms of interfering with the military operations of the enemy. Both sides apparently devoted considerable attention to the question of what targets to attack, and a variety of motives affected the relevant decisions.

The American decision to bomb targets in North Korea was made prior to the commitment of American ground troops in June 1950. A month later permission was given to bomb industrial targets in North Korea, but the use of incendiary bombs was not allowed because of the civil damage that would have resulted. The Air Force was not authorized to bomb areas close to the Soviet and Chinese borders. Rashin was the single industrial center within the forbidden area and it was the only industrial target in North Korea which was not destroyed by mid-September when an end to strategic bombing was ordered by the Joint Chiefs. Not until June 1952 were attacks on the hydroelectric plants in North Korea authorized; within two weeks almost 90 per cent of the North Korean power capacity was destroyed.[21]

American attacks on targets in North Korea steadily expanded. The attacks were aimed at affecting the immediate military situation. The restraints observed had several motives: (1) to avoid extensive civilian destruction considered undesirable on both humanitarian and propaganda grounds; (2) to avoid a spillover of the war into China or the Soviet Union (the spillover into China prior to her entry into the war probably did not have a major impact on Chinese policy, but the incursion did create propaganda and political difficulties); (3) to avoid damaging, in the case of the hydroelectric plants, targets considered vital to the Chinese so as to avoid their entrance into the war, presumably in retaliation.

[21] Robert Frank Futrell, *The United States Air Force in Korea 1950–1953*. New York: Duell, Sloan and Pearce, 1961, pp. 449–452.

The Communists exercised far greater restraint on their air forces. Except for a few night "heckling" attacks from small biplanes in the spring of 1951 no air attacks were made on any targets in South Korea. The Communist restraint was not the result of the absence of inviting military targets. The port of Pusan was an extremely inviting target for bombardment and mining. It was the key to the American logistic effort and frequently was lighted up all night. American logistic convoys and troops in the field also could have been hampered by air attacks. A number of factors seem to have influenced the Communist decision not to respond in kind to United Nations air attacks on North Korea:

1. The Communists might have believed that it would have been very difficult, if not impossible, for the United Nations to continue its operations in Korea if Pusan came under heavy attack, and that, once the United Nations committed itself to the defense of South Korea, it was no longer in a position to accept complete withdrawal. Therefore, if attacks on logistic lines made impossible the continued conduct of an effective ground war in Korea, the United States might have been forced to engage in strategic strikes against the Chinese, if not the Russian, homeland.[22] If the Communists found this supposition credible, they may have concluded that, once their initial grab for South Korea failed, they could not afford to do anything that would lead to their complete control over South Korea.[23] They may have recognized that American confinement of the war to the Korean peninsula was dependent on her ability to fight there effectively.

2. In order to avoid attacks on Chinese air bases just north of the Yalu, Red airmen were not allowed to attack United Nations positions from these bases. Although the Communists were permitting the United States the sanctuary of bases in Japan and on aircraft carriers, they apparently were afraid that they would not be granted a similar sanctuary for bombing operations. United States planes managed to keep the North Korean airfields out of commission almost continuously throughout the war. Thus, given that the Chi-

---

[22] The United States had secured British concurrence to bomb bases in China in the event of heavy air attacks from Chinese bases on United Nations troops (*H. C. Debs.*, 5th Series, CDXCVI, 970, Feb. 26, 1952) and this was probably communicated to the Chinese. However, Truman reported that he was convinced that Russia would come in if Manchurian bases were bombed.

[23] This thesis implies that the Chinese would not have driven the United Nations forces off the Korean peninsula by ground action even if they had the capability. There is no evidence to substantiate or invalidate this point.

nese limited the use of their fields to staging operations and to fighter planes, the Communists were incapable of bombing operations.

3. There is some evidence to suggest that Soviet pilots constituted a significant part of the "Chinese" air force during the Korean War.[24] If this is true the explanation for target restraint may have been the desire to avoid the capture of Soviet airmen. This proof of direct Soviet involvement in the war would at the least have been politically damaging and, from a Soviet point of view, might have created an intolerable risk of American retaliation.

By the end of the war the United States was exercising almost no target restraint in North Korea and the Communists were doing no bombing in South Korea. Each side was guided by a complex series of motives and incentives. However, despite the asymmetry of the actions, there is nothing to suggest that either side treated its decisions on targeting as being closely related to, affected by, or likely to affect, the opponent's decisions on these questions.

EXPANSION AND LIMITATION

Decisions on expanding the United Nations operations resulted from the rejecting or approving of the field commanders' proposals by the Joint Chiefs of Staff or civilian officials. In some cases, particularly on the question of using atomic weapons, the military never made the request, and so, in some sense, no decision was made. On three occasions General MacArthur was refused his requests: to employ Chinese Nationalist troops, to impose a naval blockade on China, and to bomb bases and supply lines in China. But a number of MacArthur's requests for permission to expand the war were approved. These included the commitment of American ground forces, the Inchon offensive, and the crossing of the thirty-eighth parallel.

President Truman states that the National Security Council recommended the consideration of three factors relevant to the decision of whether to go on the offensive: action by the Soviet Union and the Chinese Communists, the views of friendly members of the United Nations, and the risk of general war.[25] These and other decisions were also influenced by American doctrine as well as by domestic political pressures. The balancing of the factors varied from decision to decision, but all played a role in the major decisions to limit or expand the war.

Much less is known about the Communist decision-making pro-

---

[24] Futrell, *op. cit.*, pp. 370, 651–652.
[25] Truman, *op. cit.*, p. 359.

cess or the factors which influenced their decisions to limit or expand the war. The initial decision to keep the Chinese out of the war seems to have been based largely on domestic conditions in China, particularly the desire of the Chinese to implement their program of economic growth and development, and their desire to avoid military entanglements at a time when they had not yet consolidated their hold over their own country.[26] The reasons for the Russians' abstention from open intervention in the war are less clear. The Soviets were determined not to do anything that directly labeled them as participants; they did not publicize the participation of any Russian "volunteers" in the war, nor provide any atomic capability, although they did supply large amounts of conventional military equipment. One likely explanation is the Russian fear that intervention would lead to general war. The United States had the capability of inflicting great destruction on the Soviet homeland with its stock of atomic weapons, while the Soviets had no capability of directly attacking the United States, although they might have been able to capture a large part of Western Europe with ground forces. Thus the Soviets, aware of their inferior strategic position, were probably determined to keep out of the war and to provide no excuse for a direct American attack on the Soviet Union.

Each side apparently made its decisions to limit the war for different reasons and with minimal attention to the battlefield interaction. In addition the two sides observed very different limits. What the United States did in North Korea was quite different from what the Communists did in South Korea, but the Chinese used a much greater percentage of their gross national product than the United States did. Nevertheless, while the United States used naval vessels and airplanes to bomb troops and airfields within Korea, the Communists did not. The United States engaged in logistical interdiction; the Communists did not. Each side, then, observed its own series of limits and restraints only in some very general way related to, and dependent on, the limits of the other side.

At least a few of the limits were symmetrical. Both sides restricted their military operations almost entirely to Korea, and neither used nuclear weapons. There was lack of symmetry in that all the military targets in North Korea were attacked but most in South Korea were not. The United States attacked the Chinese points of entry — the Yalu bridges; but the Chinese did not attack the United States' points of entry — the ports. Both sides observed

[26] It was probably based also on the belief that the United States would not intervene and that the North Korean army would capture all of South Korea. . . .

a number of what Schelling has called "legalistic" limitations.[27] The United Nations carefully observed both the Chinese and Russian borders and tried to avoid crossing them inadvertently. There was symmetry in the absence of official declaration of war. The United Nations troops participated in the war in a "police action" capacity, and none of the countries involved, including the United States, declared war. The Chinese used "volunteers," and the Russians supplied equipment and presumably technicians, but little manpower for the battle.

In some cases the limits represented a recognition of the battle-field interaction. But the origin of many of the limits observed, and part of the explanation for others, lay not within the dynamics of the war itself, but within the domestic and international context in which the war was fought.

Controlling the Risks in Cuba

ALBERT AND ROBERTA WOHLSTETTER

The environment in which smaller powers face large ones, has, it is clear, changed drastically. The intensive development of nuclear and other modern weapons, the vast expansion of communications linking remote parts of the world have on the one hand increased the level of violence possible in a world conflict, and on the other seem to have made minor and local violence a world-wide public concern. It is not easy, however, to trace the implications of this changed environment. Public light on local violence does not pass with equal speed in both directions through the Iron and Bamboo

From *Controlling the Risks in Cuba* (Adelphi Paper No. 7, April 1965), pp. 3–24. Reprinted by permission of the authors. Some footnotes have been omitted.

[27] Thomas C. Schelling, *Nuclear Weapons and Limited War*. RAND P-1620, Feb. 20, 1959, p. 1.

Curtains. Though one striking movement of our time has been the multiplication of realigned, non-aligned, and partly aligned nations and their use of many international forums, shifting modes of rivalry and co-operation continue to be dominated by the two principal centres of force: a many-centred East against a not-very-completely allied West. Overwhelming nuclear capabilities, in spite of the many hopeful or ominous predictions of rapid diffusion during the last twenty years, and in spite of the search for independence by the United Kingdom, France, China, and possibly others, still are concentrated in the United States and the Soviet Union.

How does the threat of great power violence increase the risks for the smaller powers? And how might the smaller powers affect the nuclear risks? In a contest between the great powers does the very size of their weapons of destruction inhibit, as it is said, any use of force? What is the role of non-nuclear force? And what are the uses of great power bases on foreign soil?

It is much easier to ask these questions than to answer them; and too much to hope that an analysis of the crisis over the Russian bases in Cuba can provide the answers. However a look at this crisis may illuminate a little the issues and so at least help make the questions more precise. All of the questions at any rate were raised in Cuba. There the two big powers and a small one were engaged in a three-cornered partial conflict (and partial co-operation); and nuclear weapons and their future, if not immediate, launching from these Russian bases outside the Soviet Union were at the very heart of the matter. It is frequently said that we were very close to nuclear war, that Russia and the United States played a desperate game of "Chicken," with the risks nearly out of control. Threats and warnings were signalled, and not always understood. And we now hear that the resolution of the crisis will affect all future risk-taking, that the crisis was a "turning point."

It is perhaps worth one more look then at this much inspected event, to see how some of the standard sayings about constraints and risks in the use of force apply. What were the interests and what were the dangers in the various policy alternatives open to each of the three powers directly engaged? And how did they affect allies less directly engaged?

THE VIEW FROM CUBA

From the standpoint of Cuba the basing of nuclear weapons there had some clear values. Mr. Theodore Draper,[1] an acute analyst of the development of Castro's Cuba, suggested rather early that Cuba

[1] Interview, 6 December, 1962.

may have invited the Russians to put their bombardment missiles there. Castro himself has fluctuated between attributing the idea to the Cubans and to the Russians. On our count, out of some half a dozen major mentions, the score is about even.[2] Whoever got the idea first, strategic bases in Cuba would have had their uses for Castro as well as for Khrushchev. For one thing there was the prestige; modern weapons impress neighbours and can raise the political status of the country which harbours them, especially if the neighbours are misinformed or uninformed. The prestige, to be sure, is precarious, as the United Kingdom, in spite of its great scientific competence, has found, first with *Blue Streak,* then with *Skybolt,* and now with the recently aired difficulties in the *Valiant* and TSR-2 programmes. However, in the less developed countries and even in secondary industrial powers, arms may be valued more for their flourish than their actual power. It seems that the sheer magnitude of the capabilities of the United States and the Soviet Union has outclassed the nuclear potential of others in ways that were quite unexpected by those who predicted nuclear weapons would be equalizers on the world scene. Yet France and China would scarcely agree, and a less developed country like Cuba might place a sizeable symbolic value on being only the host to nuclear installations.

For another thing, the symbol had its important domestic uses. Within Cuba the presence of these bases, while essentially alien and forbidden to Cuban citizens, reinforced and confirmed Castro's defiance of the Northern colossus, made more persuasive his warnings of an American invasion, and distracted attention from gathering difficulties at home. These difficulties had been political as well as economic. 1962 had witnessed an open break in March between Castro and the old guard Communists, followed by a purging and reorganization of Cuba's single political party.[3] A severe drop (the first of several) in the sugar harvest from the preceding year (from 6.8 to 4.8 million tons) was among the early results of an ill-conceived attempt to diversify agriculture quickly at the expense of Cuban comparative advantage. Troubles had also begun to plague

[2] Claude Julien, *Le Monde,* 22 and 23 March, 1963; followed by Castro's denial to *Prensa Latina,* 23 March, 1963; Jean Daniel, "Unofficial Envoy: An Historic Report from Two Capitals," *The New Republic,* 14 December, 1963, pp. 15–20; Herbert Matthews, "Return to Cuba," *Hispanic American Report,* Special Issue, January, 1964, p. 16; Juanita Castro, Speech to the World Affairs Council, Los Angeles, 8 February, 1965.

[3] The ORI (Integrated Revolutionary Organization), now PURS, a fusion of the Cuban Communist Party and Castro's own 26 July Organization.

the industrial programme. The Cuban planners had left out of their plans the provision of raw materials for the factories they ordered, and were discovering to their dismay that in many cases it cost as much to import the raw materials as to buy the finished products abroad. An extraordinarily rapid collectivizing and statification of farms and even small commercial and manufacturing enterprises, at a pace unequalled in Russia, Asia, or middle Europe, had begun to affect production incentives and to require a large increase in managerial skills; meanwhile Cuba had been losing professionals through emigration. As these internal threats to the Revolution appeared, distraction may have been welcome.

In any case the move had international relevance for the future of Castro's variety of Communism, particularly in Latin America. The missile installation was seen by the Cubans as a great and unprecedented gesture of protection and solidarity by the most powerful country in the Communist world. Inevitably some of this power might be expected to rub off on Castro. By increasing his prestige, it could be expected to serve as an aid in his programme for spreading insurgency throughout Latin America. And it suggested that, like Castro's own communism, successful coups on the same model might be protected against counter-revolution and external attack. One of Castro's explanations for accepting Moscow's offer of long-range missiles could also support this interpretation. It was, he said, "not in order to assure our own defence, but foremost in order to reinforce Socialism on the international plane."[4]

Speeches in September and early October, 1962, by Cuban communist leaders hammered at the theme, "Cuba is not alone," and Castro's public expressions of thanks to the Soviet Union were emotional to an extreme. Read today, with our present knowledge of the timing of arrangements to install the rockets, these pre-crisis speeches seem to contain implied threats of rocket fire against the United States in case of an invasion, and an identification of Cuba's fate with the final catastrophe. *Goetterdaemmerung.* Castro explained on 20 April, 1963, the second anniversary of Playa Giron, "When the missiles were installed here, it was no longer a problem of six or seven divisions, it was . . . a problem (for the United States) of

[4] Claude Julien, *Le Monde,* 22 March, 1963, reporting an interview which took place in January of that year. Castro repudiated some statements of this interview, but in view of Julien's reputation as an accurate journalist and some of the confirmable details of the setting and circumstances, there is much to suggest this account is authentic. The role of long-range missiles in his insurgency programme has been confirmed by his sister, Juanita Castro, in a talk 8 February, 1965, to the World Affairs Council, Los Angeles.

having to confront the risk of a thermonuclear war." In a recent interview with Barnard L. Collier he made this more explicit. "The missiles were very logical to us. We were running the danger of conventional war . . . The conventional war would be most dangerous to us. We would be destroyed alone."[5]

Cuba was not alone in another sense, because the missile bases supplied hostages. They were a visible symbol that Russia was "contracting in," just as their withdrawal, Castro feared, might make it easier for the United States to underestimate the Soviet Union's solidarity with Cuba. Castro's statement to Collier suggests that the rationalization he had given earlier to the French reporter, Jean Daniel, for accepting missiles hardly represented his actual motives and estimates. To Daniel he had implied that if Russia extended only conventional military aid, the United States would not be deterred from invading, even though Russia would, in spite of American doubts, actually retaliate with thermonuclear weapons and so touch off world war;[6] Russian nuclear missiles in Cuba, however, would deter a US invasion and therefore prevent nuclear war altogether. To Collier, on the other hand, Castro made clear that he himself did not believe the Soviet Union would retaliate with nuclear weapons in the event of US conventional attack, and that if Cuba were to go down he would prefer that it be destroyed not alone, but on a grand scale along with a good deal of the rest of the world. As he said, "For us the danger of a conventional war and a world war were the same, the destruction of Cuba."[7]

The presence of the missiles meant that the Soviet Union was more obviously engaged — in Castro's phrase, "highly compromised" — in the fate of Cuba. Though not, as it turned out, irretrievably; not at any rate when Russia was caught in the process of installation. If a substantial number of missiles had been installed and made operational before discovery, forcing withdrawal might have been somewhat harder. The quarantine of missiles and ground support equipment on their way to Cuba would, of course,

[5] *New York Herald Tribune*, 17 August, 1964.

[6] According to Daniel's account of Castro's beliefs (*The New Republic*, 14 December, 1963, p. 18), Russia "recognized that if conventional military aid was the extent of their assistance, the United States might not hesitate to instigate an invasion, in which case Russia would retaliate and this would eventually touch off a world war." Russia therefore decided to install the missiles, and Castro accepted them as a matter of "honour." The passage just quoted was omitted from the *New York Times* version of the interview, but appears in the original in *L'Express*, 6 December, 1963.

[7] *New York Herald Tribune*, 17 August, 1964.

no longer have been open to the United States. Something less focussed on the actual process of installing missiles would therefore have been necessary; perhaps a more general blockade or a still broader and more violent measure. Moreover, though this is arguable, it might have been somewhat more difficult psychologically for the Russians to withdraw immediately after the installation of the missiles than during the process. Perhaps this difficulty would have faded rapidly with time; after some years, surely withdrawal would again be easier. In any case, Chairman Khrushchev was caught *in flagrante*, in a difficult position to maintain.

In the event of conflict between the United States and Cuba, a considerable number of Russian missiles and bombers, at least twenty odd thousand Russian troops[8] and, still more, Russian prestige would have been put in jeopardy. To avoid Russian casualties in some of the attacks that might have been made at the end of October (for example, the non-nuclear bombing of Cuban bases manned by Russian forces) there would have had to be extreme selectivity in the American attack; or evacuation by the Russians on receipt of explicit warning; or some combination of the two. Russian forces in Cuba then, like American forces in Europe, though to a very much lesser extent, would have been hostage to the Cubans in the event of an attack by the United States. This point should not be pushed too far or regarded simply in formal terms. The United States forces which are hostage in Europe number now perhaps 350,000 men and many of their dependents. By comparison, a Russian force of 20 odd thousand, is a token. Nonetheless, a distinctly visible token. As Castro puts it today, "The Soviet Union is seriously compromised in the world with Cuba. That is important. It is like the US in Berlin."[9] But he observes that the "compromising" was even more serious with the surface-to-surface missiles in Cuba.

It was not simply the presence of Soviet troops in Cuba, but their manning and guarding of the long-range rockets that seems to have faced the United States with a dilemma in October 1962. If the United States undertook some hostile action against Cuba, would it dare leave these lethal weapons alone? Would it not have

[8] The estimate by President Kennedy in January, 1963, was 16,000 to 17,000 in Cuba, after a withdrawal of 4,500. 25 January, 1963, Press Conference, as reported in the *New York Times*, 26 January, 1963. The official American figure for the crisis period has stayed around 22,000. Castro now claims the number was much larger.

[9] Interview with Barnard Collier, *New York Herald Tribune*, 19 August, 1964.

to destroy them? And would this not bring Russia's intercontinental missiles down on the United States?

The line of argument suggested by these questions without a doubt is plausible. However, it persuades mainly by its vagueness. The precise circumstances and nature of the United States action and the risks to the Russians of their own alternative responses need to be specified, and these are only some of the things which would require examination. We shall not assess how the risks would have looked in connection with the various actions open to the United States, if the installations had been completed. We shall ask: What were the risks involved in the actions taken by the United States and in alternatives it considered during the process of the missile installation by the Russians? Much has been said about this, but how close *were* we to the brink?

Whether or not the Russians might have used their medium and intermediate range missiles located in Cuba or their intercontinental missiles based at home in retaliation against an attack on Cuba, desperate action by the Cubans themselves was another matter. Could the Cubans have used the Russian's missiles based in Cuba? If the surface-to-surface missiles had been in their charge, they may well have been more tempted than the Russians to use them. At least the threat to use these missiles against the United States in any of a number of circumstances might from the standpoint of the Cubans have had a considerable appeal. For one thing, the Cubans know less about the consequences of nuclear exchange: these are sobering, as Chairman Khrushchev used to keep telling Chairman Mao; and there is no reason to suspect that Khrushchev's successors — or ultimately Mao's —would be less sober. (Familiarity breeds respect.) For another, we are told, the Cuban Communists and the Russian ones are rather different. We even had some hints from Chairman Khrushchev on this subject. The Cubans are Southerners, impulsive, romantic revolutionaries; and they would put their own fate (or at least that of the current Cuban government) at stake in an American attack or an American-supported resistance. The Russians are Northern and more controlled (though there are those embarrassing nineteenth century Dostoievskian Russians); they are disciplined Bolsheviks (whose character was formed in conscious contrast to such Dostoievskian Russians); and for all of their twenty odd thousand, clearly much less intimately engaged in Cuba.

Whatever faith we attach to these contrasting characterizations, we have some actual observations on the contrasting behaviour of Chairman Khrushchev and the Cuban Communists. Or more exactly, we can at the very least contrast how the Russians behaved in the crisis and how the Cubans say they would have behaved. In the clutch the Chairman was eminently cautious and controlled about the triggering of Russian missiles in Cuba. The Cubans on the other hand suggested considerably more abandon. Che Guevara apparently had a beady eye on New York, and said later that he would have pulled New York down with Cuba. "If the rockets had remained, we would have used them all and directed them against the very heart of the United States, including New York, in our defence against aggression. But we haven't got them, so we shall fight with what we've got. In the face of an aggressor like the United States, there can be no solution other than to fight to the death, inflicting the maximum damage on the enemy."[10]

This sort of threat might be compared with that posed by a small nuclear power, according to General Pierre Gallois and other enthusiasts for the spread of nuclear weapons. In the writings of these theorists the precise service performed by nuclear weapons for the small powers is seldom very clear. If one of the two major powers planned a nuclear first strike against a small nuclear power, such as Cuba might have become, or for that matter, a secondary industrial power like France, the small power's arsenal might not offer much of a deterrent. To deter a first strike, a nuclear force must be able to survive it. And a second strike capability is a more complicated matter than enthusiasts for diffusion have understood.

However, sometimes the use of nuclear weapons by a small power is contemplated as response to lesser attacks by the great power: a massive retaliation theory, in short, with the smaller power appearing in the role of miniature massive retaliationist. Such nuclear retaliation against a non-nuclear move by a great power would of course be suicidal. The small power is not likely to have a genuine second strike capability against Russia or the United States; if these countries are careful, it is still less likely to have a "preclusive" first strike capability, that is, an ability to prevent the great nuclear power from retaliating. From a responsible leader of a smaller power, then, the threat of a miniature massive retaliation might not be very convincing. It is not clear that Guevara, for example, who has a reputation for disciplined intelligence, would be as abandoned in fact as he claims in retrospect. After all, Chairman Khrushchev tried to sound rather reckless in advance of the crisis. In mid-September of 1962 he called the attention of the governments of the world and world opinion to "the provocations which might plunge the world into the disaster of a universal world war with the

---

[10] Interview, 28 November, 1962, with a London *Daily Worker* correspondent, reported in the *Los Angeles Times*, 11 December, 1962.

use of thermonuclear weapons. . . ." "Bellicose reactionary elements of the United States have long since been conducting in the United States Congress and in the American press an unbridled propaganda campaign against the Cuban Republic, calling for an attack on Cuba, an attack on Soviet ships carrying the necessary commodities and food to the Cuban people, in one word, calling for war." ". . . One cannot now attack Cuba and expect that the aggressor will be free from punishment for this attack. If this attack is made, this will be the beginning of war."[11] In short, interception of Russian ships carrying arms to Cuba would mean the start of World War III.

On the other hand, some leaders in small countries have earned a reputation for recklessness. Guevara's uncompromising speed in nationalizing industry, and immediate full implementation of what he regards as communist principles, have an element of ruthlessness and lack of realism which is not the same as recklessness, but which should make us thoughtful. And it may be that Castro himself could convince us with a suicidal threat. The *Venceremos* ("We shall win") with which all Cuban letters now are signed might be hollow, but Castro might just mean the *Patria o Muerte* ("Fatherland or Death") which precedes it.[12] He has had a long personal history of near suicidal defiance of big forces; his casual and disastrous assault on the Moncada barracks on 26 July, 1953; his landing on the *Gramma* in Oriente in 1956, announced in advance to Batista, calamitous not only to most of his companions but to the inhabitants who expected him two days earlier; to say nothing of some hair-raising student escapades. *Frente a Todos* ("Against Everybody") has been his slogan.[13] One can understand that more than the traditional guerilla doctrine of protecting the leader might have influenced Fidel's subordinates to keep him home in the headquarters of the Sierra Maestra when they went out on a raid. When he was in charge, casualties were prohibitive. His own life has been charmed, but not that of his followers. It should give any prospec-

[11] *New York Times,* 12 September, 1962. (Soviet Government Statement released by *Tass.*)

[12] He describes the Cubans manning the surface-to-air missiles today in precisely these terms. They are "disciplined and fatherland-or-death types" (Speech, 21 January, 1965). If he had surface-to-surface missiles, he might very well man them with the same "types" and, at the least, almost certainly so describe them.

[13] *Frente a Todos* is the title Fidel gave to his reply in Mexico in 1955 to charges against him of corruption and usurpation of power by the Ortodoxo Party and other groups fighting Batista in Cuba.

tive father figure — or even a brother figure, Russian or otherwise — considerable pause.[14]

Castro in charge of nuclear rockets might be convincingly reckless.[15] It is precisely this case which would appear to be intolerable to both of the two opposing great powers. It is clear that a persisting threat by Cuba to use nuclear weapons in response to unspecified or vaguely specified non-nuclear moves by the United States would be very hard for the US to bear. But it would also raise grave problems for the Soviet Union. Russia would have every motive to preclude or stop such a threat or, if this were not possible, to separate herself as clearly as could be from the threatener.

From the standpoint of the Cuban people a miniature massive-retaliation policy would place them in double jeopardy. It would raise the stakes and conjure up the possibility of nuclear destruction either before or after a Cuban move. However, the hazards to Cubans were increased considerably by the presence even of Russian-controlled missiles.

The issue of Russian control is raised very acutely by the nightmare vision of Cuba pulling Russia down along with New York. No doubt with exactly this in mind Mr. Khrushchev made every attempt to assure Mr. Kennedy that there was nothing whatsoever to worry about from those romantic Cubans. Good, solid, stolid, sensible Russians were guarding the safety catches on the missiles in Cuba: "The means which are located on Cuba now, about which you are talking and which as you say concern you, are in the hands of the Soviet officers. That is why any possibility of accidental usage of

[14] Fidel's actual father had trouble. When Fidel was 13 years old he organized a strike of sugar workers against his father, and later when he was 18, his mother reports in a biography written with one of Castro's sisters, that she permitted him to call his father an exploiter and a landlord, one of "those who abuse the powers they wrench from the people with deceitful promises." While the father reacted in rage, Fidel apparently still expected (and received) his financial support even after his marriage, demanded $1,000 to buy weapons for the Moncada attack, left the house finally with $100. Castro's vilification and attack of big forces may have aimed at a continued dependence rather than an absolute break in relations. The United States turned out to be a less tolerant father, withdrawing economic support, intending damage, and even inflicting some, when Castro carried on too long, too noisily, too roughly.

[15] Some European analyses of the crisis suggest that Castro and the Cubans differed from Khrushchev in that the Cubans do not believe in nuclear threats in response to less than nuclear attack. The claim cannot survive an examination of Castro's and Guevara's speeches. Such suicidal nuclear threats were not only contemplated by Castro, but might be more persuasive issuing from him than from Khrushchev.

those means, which might cause harm to the United States, is excluded."[16] During the crisis as well as earlier, Chairman Khrushchev indicated that he subscribed to the analysis of the Cubans as temperamental Southerners. "The Cubans are very volatile people, Mr. Khrushchev said, and all of the sophisticated hardware provided for their defence was entirely under the control of Soviet officers . . . and it would never be fired except on his orders as Commander in Chief of all of the armed forces of the Soviet Union."[17]

Of course this raises some interesting questions. How sure could Khrushchev be? What about the use of force by Castro to jump Big Brother (*Frente a Todos*)? Mightn't he try to get hold of Russian nuclear weapons for use against the United States and so ultimately to ensure the engagement of Russia? (To say nothing of the rather grandiose plans he has expressed for spreading his revolution beyond the Andes.) That, we may surmise, was what a good many of those 22,000 Russian troops were there to prevent: they were there to see that the weapons and in particular the war heads, if they were on the island, would be totally inoperable when seized. Newspaper reports have made clear that the Russian bases were heavily guarded and the Cubans, with the possible exception of a few of the elite, never got near the weapons.

But could these Russian forces be relied on? We know that the Russian troops in the satellites wavered during the revolts in Eastern Europe in the 1950s. The Russians have since rotated their security forces more frequently. However, seeing to it that nuclear weapons would not fall into the hands of irresponsible Cuban users is a much simpler job than preventing sympathetic collusion between rebels and an occupying force. It requires only a very small elite force whose loyalty could be relied on. And the loyalty of even a random sample of Russians might be trusted here: letting Cubans get hold of these weapons would mean placing all of Russia and a good deal else in jeopardy. In any case, there are more sophisticated methods of assurance available. The United States, on 5 July, 1962, announced that it was initiating a programme to install electronic locks (the Permissive Action Link) on its weapons to protect them against unauthorized use. These locks would require release from a central source, possibly very distant. Analogous remote keys conceivably could be held in Moscow itself. And while there is no public evidence whatsoever of mechanical or electronic devices so used in

[16] 27 October, 1962, message to President Kennedy, published 28 October, 1962, *New York Times*.

[17] Interview with W. E. Knox, American industrialist, *New York Times* Magazine, 18 November, 1962, "Close Up of Khrushchev During a Crisis," described as taking place "a little more than three weeks ago."

the Soviet Union, a tight political control seems most probable, given the structure of Soviet society; physical possession of these potent weapons would be dangerous in the hands of a dissident internal faction. The interests of the larger powers clearly coincide in preventing unauthorized firings by their own citizens. And both want to keep the keys out of the desperate hands of a smaller power. In the event it was the interests of the major powers that dominated.

So far we have treated the crisis mainly from the viewpoint of the small power. How did these missile bases figure in the calculations of the big powers?

THE VIEW FROM THE SOVIET UNION

Much ink has been spilled over whether the Soviet move into Cuba had a purely political significance for the Russians, or whether Soviet bases in Cuba had also a military worth to them. But Soviet objectives can be both political and military; these purposes are not separate, and neither the political nor military is very simple or pure. If the "purely political" is somewhat nebulous, the "purely military," a kind of art-for-art's-sake, has no meaning at all.

The leaders of the Soviet Union in any case, when they address the communist world, have never made the separation. In fact, the shift in the balance of forces, which according to Mr. Khrushchev had come drastically to favour the Socialist countries, was clearly linked in his pronouncements to the development of Soviet military power, and was accompanied by a drum fire of rocket threats against the United States, and all of the countries in which the United States bases its military forces. And this supposed shift in military power is not unrelated to a vision of a future, totally communist world, whether this be single or many-centred. Many American and British writers recently have assured us that the Soviet Union is a *status quo* power, a "have" or satisfied power. This is all very well, but Chairman Khrushchev did not seem to know it. The *status quo* he was looking for seemed to be, as he had told it to Walter Lippmann, the *status quo post* rather than *ante* a major transformation. And there is no evidence that Khrushchev's successors look on the matter more comfortably for the West. To say that they would prefer this to be a peaceful transformation and indeed believe that it may well be, does not exclude latent military power as a major element in the expected transformation. Otherwise one would have to count every acquiescence to a threat of force as a peaceful change. Latent or actual communist military force monitored the early take-overs in Eastern Europe at the end of the war and prevented a reversal of the revolutions in 1953 and 1956. The possibility of its use defined the rules of behaviour both for internal opposition and outside aid. The possible use or threat to use military force is an operative element in many political transformations. In any case, it is apparent that the military build-up in Cuba had a considerable number of entwined political-military functions.

First it should be recalled that the introduction of strategic bombardment vehicles, MRBMs, IRBMs, and IL 28s, capped a vast piling up, started considerably earlier, of active defences and ground forces which could be used to defend Cuba against internal as well as external attack, and the building of a base in Cuba which could serve as a centre of weapons transfer and material aid to insurgency in Latin America. From the standpoint of the Soviet Union the purposes of such a build-up partially coincide with some of the Cuban interests we have sketched. The important split between the Russians and the Red Chinese is not accurately represented as an ideological contrast between the foreswearing of any use of revolutionary violence by the Russians and its reckless advocacy by the Chinese. There are of course important differences in national interests. But the Chinese are considerably less reckless and the Russians more flexible and opportunistic than the conventional picture suggests.

Specifically for the Russians, the military build-up was in part a reaffirmation of the relationship between Russia and Cuba, a healing of wounds after the rift in March, 1962, that had resulted in the flight of Escalante, the old line Communist Party bureaucrat. It was a visible demonstration to those who were unaligned or falling out of line that for a small power to line up with the Soviet Union even near the centre of American power was safe, that a changeover to communism would not be reversed and that the power of the Soviet Union was committed as safeguard against any threat of reversal. More than this, by successfully defying the United States, forcing it to accept this major move into Cuba, the Soviet Union could powerfully influence the expectations of the rest of the world, most obviously those of the Latin Americans, but also those expectations and hopes that affect the outcome in Berlin and in more remote regions of Southeast and Southern Asia. And the expectations affected were specifically about relative strength and the will to use that strength. The large-scale Russian introduction of nuclear bombardment vehicles would have appeared also directly to answer the persuasive official American analyses of US superiority published in 1961 and 1962. The tendencies toward division within the communist world only reinforced some of these purposes. For the move was a Soviet blow in competition with the Chinese for leadership of the Socialist countries, and for leading the way in transforming the uncommitted world — and eventually that part of the world now committed to what they regard as the wrong side.

We have been discussing functions objectively served rather than Soviet conscious motivation, which must necessarily remain obscure. If, for example, the move had been successful, if the Soviet Union had gone before the United Nations to defend it, and the United States had acquiesced in the accomplished fact, it might have served any or all of the preceding military-political functions. On the other hand, if the success had been less complete, if the United States had not acquiesced, Soviet withdrawal might then have exacted as a price American withdrawal from some of its military bases on the territory of allies. The tentative skirmishing in the Khrushchev-Kennedy correspondence on the Turkish-Cuban base swap indicated one line of Soviet interest. But elimination of military bases is a directly military as well as political fact. This has been somewhat obscured, because the significance of overseas bases themselves for the 1960s has been understood only in a rather cloudy and sometimes quite erroneous fashion in the current Western discussions. How about the Cuban bombardment bases themselves? Some commentators have stated in rather unqualified fashion that they had essentially no military worth.[18]

Perhaps the first thing to be said is that it is not very sensible to talk with great confidence on these subjects. Responsible judgment here is difficult even with complete access to privileged information. The classified data are uncertain, the public data still more so, and few of the commentators have looked carefully at the quantitative implications of even the public data. Many who doubted the Russians would install bombardment vehicles in Cuba simply took at face value Chairman Khrushchev's statement that such weapons would add nothing to the capabilities provided by their intercontinental rockets. And then when it was clear that Khrushchev had gambled a great deal on precisely such installations, they persisted in dismissing their military significance. As we have already suggested, such bases have a variety of functions, but Khrushchev's gamble should at least have raised some doubts in the minds of those who dismiss their strategic value out of hand.

Part of the confusion comes from the fact that the military value of these Russian installations was not likely to consist in their efficiency as an addition to the Russion deterrent to American nuclear attack. Because of their proximity, their known position, and their lack of shelter, warning, or protected reliable communications, they

[18] See, for example, *The New Republic*, 3 November, 1962, pp. 3ff; *The Reporter*, 22 November, 1962, pp. 21ff; *The Bulletin of the Atomic Scientists*, Vol. 19 (February, 1963), pp. 8ff.

would not have been hard to eliminate in an opening blow, nor would they have severely complicated an attack by a large reliable missile force;[19] and so they were not likely to be an economic way to increase a Russian second strike capability. The more likely strategic value concerned their significance for a possible Russian preclusive first-strike, as weapons that, in case of need during a grave crisis of escalation, would help to blunt an American retaliation. Resolution of such an issue would involve a detailed analysis of the entire complex mechanism of American retaliation, as it existed in 1962, including not merely the vehicles (that is, the missiles and aircraft), their physical disposition, their protection and degree of readiness, but also the system for commanding and controlling their response and penetrating enemy defences. For good reason, data on this subject are not publicly available. And overall statements on capability by public officials necessarily must be designed not simply to convey information to the public, important though that is, but also to limit information to the enemy and to affect his estimates favourably to ourselves. A resolution of this complex issue cannot therefore be made one way or the other. Even the much simpler partial question, the comparative vulnerability of our bombardment vehicles to distant as distinct from close, land-based attack, is necessarily shrouded with secrecy. Recognition of these limitations on analysis is the beginning of wisdom.

Take the partial problem of protecting the vehicles against the initial blow, from far-off or near-by. This is a quantitative matter demanding more than the standard caution. The probability that a vehicle will survive depends among other things on the number of attacking vehicles, their reliability, their average aiming accuracy, the kiloton yield of their nuclear warheads, and the degree of resistance of the vehicles under attack. This dependence moreover is not simply linear. The number of weapons, for example, required to destroy a vehicle sheltered to a sufficient degree will within relevant limits vary as the square of the average aiming accuracy. That is, double the inaccuracy and four times the number of attacking vehicles are required; triple the inaccuracy and nearly ten times the number of attackers are needed. Requirements are sensitive also to yield and degree of resistance, though less so. Changes in requirement are something less than proportionate to changes in yield or resistance: they vary as the two-thirds power: if a shelter is 8 or 27 times harder, the number of attackers required for a given probabil-

[19] During the 1950s the belief was widespread that even very vulnerable unprotected bases, if widely separated, would present insuperable co-ordination problems for a missile attack. . . .

ity of destruction would increase by factors of 4 or 9 respectively. But the average inaccuracy, for example, of even our own weapons can only be uncertainly estimated with complete access to classified tests. Our estimates of the performance of Russian weapons must be still more uncertain. Estimates are in any case not public and are frequently misrepresented with great confidence in the press. Moreover they change rather rapidly. A careful reading of the public press will confirm that the publicly stated average inaccuracies of bombardment missiles have decreased in the last few years by very large amounts; public estimates have been divided by at least five. Yet a factor of 3 reduction in inaccuracy can lower requirements to destroy hard targets by a factor of 9; a factor of 5 reduction, by 25. Even estimates of the number of vehicles of various types in the Russian force, we know from experience, have been in error. And the errors have not always been in one direction. The Cuban example illustrates some of the uncertainties. Here in a small area close by, under the most intense and continuous air reconnaissance, we counted some 30 missiles; and the Russians removed 42.[20] These comments suggest the limits of our own discussion.

The point to be made then is that some of these sensitive performance characteristics for the offensive vary with distance and improve significantly with close proximity: the important parameter of guidance accuracy, for example. Reliability is another performance characteristic which can improve with the simplified missiles possible at close range. A typically blithe argument assessing the military worth of Cuban bases states that while accuracy is improved in the shorter ranges, on the other hand bomb yields are necessarily smaller. Unfortunately, as we have indicated, changes in accuracy affect requirements much more sensitively than changes in yield. And, what is more, there is no law of nature suggesting that a missile payload declines at shorter ranges. For a given thrust, other things being equal, the opposite is true. It is possible to throw larger payloads at shorter distances. All of this is relevant for an exclusive choice between distant and close-in attack.

However, the second point to be noted is that *in the short run* this was not the choice open to the Russians. In the long run they could choose to build intercontinental missiles and base them in Russia, say, or spend an equal amount of resources for missiles based in Cuba. But in the years 1962 and 1963 the Russian bombardment force capable of reaching the United States was sharply limited.

[20] ". . . we never knew how many missiles were brought into Cuba. The Soviets said there were 42. We have counted 42 going out. We saw fewer than 42." Roswell L. Gilpatric, 11 November, 1962. ABC's Issues and Answers, telecast.

The missiles they sent to Cuba were a net addition to this force, since, based in Russia or in one of the European satellites, they could not reach the United States. Moreover the number of MRBMs — 48 — and the IRBMs — apparently between 24 and 32 — which were already installed or on the way[21] was quite sizeable in relation to the public Western and American government estimates of the Russian intercontinental missile force and approximately equalled the Institute of Strategic Studies' estimate of 75 Soviet ICBMs.[22]

Third, our short run need not be so short as to stop in mid-December, 1962 — the time the Department of Defence indicated as the operational date for the IRBMs of 2200 nautical mile range. In fact, it appears that the Russians had in addition to the roughly 75 medium and intermediate range missiles shipped to Cuba in 1962 hundreds more that could acquire by location in Cuba the ability to bomb American targets. The ISS estimate suggests a force of MRBMs alone ten times as large as the total number of MRBMs and IRBMs emplaced in Cuba, and beyond this, a growing total force of IRBMs. Further shipments of medium and intermediate range missiles could have been installed in Cuba, if the United States offered no interference, with the same impressive speed that characterized the installation of the first 75. The MRBMs were activated "with the passage of hours." (For example, two sets of photographs separated by less than 24 hours, displayed an increase of perhaps 50 per cent in the amount of equipment.[23] There has been almost universal agreement on the logistic efficiency of the Soviet operation.) Such a change in location might have corrected at a stroke what appears to be a great imbalance in the composition of the Russian strategic force: it is heavily weighted towards attacking European theatre targets and by comparison neglects American forces based outside Europe, though these make up the principal retaliatory strength of the alliance.

Fourth, the axis of attack from Cuba outflanked the Ballistic Missile Early Warning System. Unlike submarine launched missiles, of the range estimated to be available to the Soviet Union, these Cuban based missiles would have covered essentially all of the

[21] On the CIA and DOD public accounts, there were 48 MRBMs for which launch positions had been prepared (there were 24 launchers). For the IRBMs, 17 erectors were counted on the way out, with the 17th reckoned by the Americans as a spare. Briefing, 6 February, 1963, by Mr. John Hughes, Special Assistant to General Carroll, reprinted in *Department of Defence Appropriations for 1964.* US Congress, House of Representatives 88th Session, Part I, Washington, DC, 1963.

[22] "The Military Balance," 1962–1963.

[23] According to a Defence Department spokesman, 22 October, 1962.

United States, with little or no warning.[24] The co-ordination problems for the Russians are less severe than were suggested by some writers at the time of the crisis, and in fact on the whole before attacking it is easier to communicate at a great distance with land based missiles than with distant submerged submarines.

All of the above is in the short or fairly short run. For a long run in which the Russians were free to spend resources, to build new ICBMs based in Russia or new medium or intermediate range ballistic missiles based in Cuba, the choice this opens up to them cannot be dismissed out of hand. As some of the commentators suggested, the shorter range missiles are cheaper. If they are drastically cheaper for a desired level and type of performance, they would offer the Russians a significantly larger destruction capability for a given budget. Some long run mixture of close and distant basing then might be optimal for a Russian force, providing their decision makers with an improved option in a crisis to strike first.

In sum, Cuba offered to the Russians the means for a very large and immediate expansion of the forces capable of hitting elements of the American retaliatory force based in the United States. Moreover further large increments were readily available. The effect of such a rapid increase in power on the actual military balance could not be lightly dismissed; and the political uses of even an apparent change seemed evident.

THE VIEW FROM THE UNITED STATES

The sudden installation of a sizeable number of nuclear bombardment vehicles in Cuba, and the long-term prospects of such a base very near American shores, offered much foundation for sober thought about significant alterations in the military balance. This balance is not a simple one-dimensional matter and neither were the effects of such an installation. However, as we have already indicated, the Russian military build-up touched many problems of defence other than the preservation of a United States second-strike capability in the event of a thermonuclear war. It affected the political and military stability of Cuba and Latin America. And President Kennedy was acutely conscious of the political effects of

[24] Doubts about this coverage persist in some European and American analyses. They appear to be based on a poorly reasoned uncritically sceptical commentary by Roger Hagan and Bart Bernstein, "The Military Value of Missiles in Cuba," *Council for Correspondence Newsletter,* 22 November, 1962. Hagan and Bernstein relied on newspaper and magazine accounts of intelligence data that themselves confused the MRBMs and IRBMs installed in Cuba with the shorter range T–1 and T–2 and they misread the public statements about the expected operational date and number of IRBMs.

even the *appearance* of a vast Soviet increase in military power. "The Cuban effort," he commented after the crisis, with Russian deception in mind, "has made it more difficult for us to carry out any successful negotiations, because this was an effort to materially change the balance of power . . . not that [the Soviets] were intending to fire [the missiles] . . . But it would have politically changed the balance of power. It would have appeared to, and appearances contribute to reality."[25]

One of the least understood aspects of the crisis from the standpoint of American as well as Russian interests concerned the role of overseas bases. It was the building of a Russian overseas base of course that prompted the crisis. Our discovery of the installation was preceded by Khrushchev's public deprecation of its utility, his statement that it would add nothing to his long-range rockets based in the Soviet Union. In Western discussion, during the crisis and since, of concessions or disengagements, the possibility of giving up American bases overseas was prominent. The issue was somewhat blurred by the focus on the Turkish-based *Jupiters* whose removal had been planned before the crisis and ironically was delayed by Soviet demand for their removal during the crisis itself. For good reason. Whether or not the *Jupiter* installations were useful, it was apparent that their removal under pressure would be a very different thing from the dismantling of the *Thors* in England, initiated sometime before because they were not worth their keep. (In fact one of the writers of this essay had written a series of critical analyses of the *Thors* and *Jupiters* beginning in 1957; but was clear that October 1962 would have been a poor date for a change.) In any case, the deficiencies of the *Thor* and *Jupiter* bases should not be taken as an example of the general worthlessness or for that matter of the lessening value of overseas bases.

In the West, liberal and conservative opinion sometimes meet on common ground in the depreciation of the role of overseas bases in the 1960s. Suggestions that modern developments in missilery make them unnecessary might be quoted from the surviving massive retaliationists, but also from *The Liberal Papers*.[26]

[25] *Washington Post,* 18 December, 1962. The right contrast with mere appearance is not a steady intent to fire, but a contingent choice in future crises.

[26] "The United States may find that it will no longer need bases around the periphery of the USSR and Communist China, and that instead, pending effective arms reduction, it should place its chief reliance on long-range missiles to be delivered from its own territory," p. 268, *The Liberal Papers,* ed. James Roosevelt, Anchor Books, Doubleday and Co., Garden City, New York, 1962.

And "The question would then arise whether the security of Japan

Such suggestions are a vast over-simplification of the military implications of current and future states of the art of war. It is true that the deterrent function of some American weapons in a big thermonuclear war was much more dependent on overseas bases when the predominant part of the US force was the short-legged B-47. However, thermonuclear war is not the only problem of national and alliance defence or of the defence of non-aligned powers. US defence programmes have stressed more and more the threat of non-nuclear, conventional and unconventional warfare — moreover, thermonuclear war itself is a lot more complicated than this deprecation of overseas bases suggests.

In brief, overseas bases have vital roles in a possible central war in the 1960s and 1970s — both for deterrence and for limiting damage in case deterrence fails. They do dilute and can dilute even more Soviet offensive preparations by posing the need to set up a *variety* of defensive barriers. They are an important source of continuing information on the enemy. They can be made to complicate the design of his attack — for example, with the extension of the present bomb alarm system. Under several plausible contingencies of outbreak they can help spoil his attack. All this for a thermonuclear war.

But even more obviously today overseas bases have a dominant role in non-nuclear wars. They affect the speed with which the West can react and the cost and size of reaction to aggressions in remote parts of the world. The role of Japan in fighting the Korean war, the movements in May 1962 from various stations to Thailand, and later movements of weapons from Thailand in support of the Indians in their battle with the Chinese all illustrate the continuing importance of overseas bases.

For the Russians also overseas bases in the 1960s and 1970s might conceivably come to have an important role. And this role would have principally to do with non-nuclear internal and external wars. Dr. Guy Pauker suggested a while ago that the massive Russian military aid to Indonesian or other overseas base areas might be the only way Russia has of influencing events in Southeast Asia directly rather than through the agency of its quarrelsome Chinese sometime partner and rival. Whatever the case for the Soviet Union, recent American policy unambiguously requires distant logistic support. The explicit shift in the last four years to stress conventional and unconventional non-nuclear war makes it more necessary

---

would be more effectively safeguarded by the use of United States long-range missiles in case of an emergency than by the presence of American troops and/or weapons on Japanese territory." p. 269, *ibid.*

than ever, and yet the importance of overseas bases seems to be less and less understood. Perhaps the recent troubles in India and Malaysia, with the demands they may place on British bases east of Suez as well as some American ones, will make their worth more generally appreciated. Less than nuclear contests remote from one or both of the great powers may nevertheless engage their interests in conflict, but such contests are hard to influence without overseas bases.

Our discussion of Cuba suggests that not all the interests of the United States conflict with those of the Soviet Union. Mr. Khrushchev and Mr. Kennedy were both clear about their mutual interest in keeping Castro's finger off a nuclear trigger. On the other hand, the view from the Soviet Union indicates that, in spite of talk about "overriding" interests of both sides in avoiding nuclear war, there are many fundamental points at issue between the great powers. And while there is hardly a doubt that both sides would be worse off in the event of a nuclear war, and that they do and should spend considerable energies and resources in avoiding it, the dubious note in the phrase "overriding interests . . ." is struck by the adjective "overriding." It suggests that the opposing interests are negligible, well understood, and easily resolved or likely to be resolved in the near-term future, if only, we are told, the politicians are sincere.

President Kennedy did not take the Soviet build-up in Cuba as an act unrelated to the future of the world. He related it to Chairman Khrushchev's desire to see the world transformed, to sponsor struggles of liberation, and to revise what the Russians regard as "abnormal" situations, such as West Berlin. In his October 22 speech announcing the American blockade of arms shipments to Cuba, President Kennedy warned that any hostile acts at other points on the globe (he mentioned West Berlin specifically) would meet with equal American determination, and he called upon Mr. Khrushchev to "abandon this course of world domination."

The encounter over this small island, then, on the American view, had to do with the future of the world. However, in this encounter, not only Cuba, but the rest of the aligned and non-aligned world — the OAS, NATO, China, the United Nations — were subordinated to a passive role. The chief actors were the opposing nuclear powers. Castro could obstruct, delay and complicate the resolution of the issue, but in the end he was hardly able to affect it centrally. Members of the OAS and NATO were apprised of the President's decision to institute a quarantine a few hours before it was announced to the public, and the actual signing of the Presidential proclamation of quarantine, was delayed to obtain the formal approval of the OAS members. These friends of the United States without exception rallied to its support and in the week of unrelenting pressure to get the missiles out, their consensus played a part. To assess its importance one should contemplate what might have been the effect of dissent. Can we be sure that a welter of doubts and alternative proposals might not have altered Khrushchev's estimate of the singleness of American resolve? If it had, the crisis might not have ended where it did.

Mr. Khrushchev had worse luck in his dealings with some of his allies. But in the end it was President Kennedy's and Chairman Khrushchev's decisions that determined events. The difficulty in sharing such momentous decisions raises important domestic issues in a democracy, but it has even more obvious problems for allies whose fate may be affected by those decisions.

Nonetheless what transpired was by no means a game of nuclear "Chicken," as the advocates of unilateral disarmament suggest; both President Kennedy and Mr. Khrushchev showed acute consciousness and care about the risks. (Some sober and excellent analysts accept the analogy of "Chicken," but the differences seem to us more significant than the identities. Bertrand Russell, who introduced the parallel in the 1950s as a paradigm of international behaviour today, meant precisely to suggest the recklessness of the statesmen, and the triviality and childishness of what was at issue — a kind of loss of face with the other children in the neighbourhood.) Nor was Cuba a case in which there was no danger of military action. There were possibilities of escalation, of the spread and intensification of violence. The risks of nuclear war are never zero. But the President was aware also of the risks of escalation in *inaction*. Inaction in Cuba would have invited, for example, a spiralling series of actions over Berlin.

From the timing of Mr. Khrushchev's move in Cuba it seems likely that he was conscious of the relation between Cuba and a climax to East-West disagreements over Berlin. President Kennedy at any rate was explicit about the connection. Retreat from a prominent public and formal stand that the United States had taken as recently as mid-September would have invited Mr. Khrushchev to believe that the United States would retreat also in Berlin. (This might also have come to be the belief of the allies of the United States.) However, the risks that Mr. Khrushchev would have undertaken in Berlin are, for a variety of reasons, considerably larger than the risks he undertook in Cuba. The government of the United States had tried to make it clear that if the Soviet Union moved on Berlin or on the Central European front, then NATO in spite of local communist superiority, would throw into the breach a very large conventional force, including perhaps a half dozen American divisions. If these were destroyed or in danger of destruction, it is evident that the risks of an American nuclear response would be raised enormously.

One cliche and over-simple view that seems to have a special appeal in crisis has it that the threat of force or the use of a low level of violence, including even a partial blockade, leads naturally to higher levels of violence. But in Cuba a very rudimentary and limited use of force, reversed the direction, started it down. There was in fact at no time during the crisis any suggestion on the part of President Kennedy and his immediate staff that this was a careless game of bluff, in which they incautiously might let a war get started by chance or unauthorized acts. On the contrary there was every attempt to resist the acts of desperation proposed from both the left and the right. "We have been determined," President Kennedy said on 22 October, "not to be diverted from our central concerns by mere irritants, and fanatics." Newspaper accounts during the crisis and a Senate Report published at the end of January, 1963, stressed the extreme concern of the President and his executive committee with even the minute details of actions taken at the lowest levels of government.[27] There was no dearth of management of the crisis.

Some of the statements of President Kennedy and even more those of Chairman Khrushchev may be a little misleading in this respect. In the case of Mr. Khrushchev, up to a certain point he may have wanted to convey an impression of recklessness. When confronted with the threat of having a Russian freighter boarded and searched, he asserted that this "would make talks useless" and bring into action the "forces and laws . . . of war";[28] it would have "irretrievably fatal consequences."[29]

In other words he was indicating to President Kennedy that interception of a freighter would involve thermonuclear massive retaliation, either as a deliberate act of the Russians or because he would not be able to restrain and control his own forces. Not he, but

[27] Senator Henry M. Jackson (Democrat, State of Washington), *Los Angeles Times*, 29 January, 1963, and "The Administration of National Security: Basic Issues" for the Committee on Government Operations, 1963.

[28] Message to President Kennedy on 27 October, 1962: "you, in your statement, said that the main aim is not only to come to an agreement [but also to] undertake measures to prevent a confrontation of our ships and thus aggravate the crisis and thus [ignite the fires] of a military conflict in such a confrontation, after which any talks would be already useless as other forces and laws would go into action, the laws of war." *New York Times*, 28 October, 1962.

[29] *Ibid.*

the laws of war would be in charge. After the crisis had receded, moreover, Chairman Khrushchev was anxious to represent his retreat as a statesman's action to save the world from the imminent peril, "the direct threat of world thermonuclear war which arose in the Caribbean area."[30] "If one or the other side had not shown restraint, not done everything needed to avert the outbreak of war, an explosion of irreparable consequences would have followed."[31] He made more than a suggestion after the event that the danger of recklessness arose from "the ruling circle of the United States who are rightly called 'madmen.' The madmen insisted and insist now on starting a war as soon as possible against the Soviet Union."[32] Mr. Khrushchev's open and bitter contest with the Chinese and Albanian Communists also required pointed reference to the imminent dangers of thermonuclear war. However, at the peak of the crisis and in fact in the same letter in which he tried for the last time to suggest an inevitable and uncontrollable thermonuclear response to the interception of a Soviet freighter, Chairman Khrushchev made it very plain that he was in careful, thorough and self-conscious charge of the decision on whether or not to respond with nuclear weapons. It was here in fact that he in particular stressed that the Cuban missiles were under his control. And in the following day he emphasized again that "the Soviet government will not allow itself to be provoked."[33] Finally in his *post-mortem* speech to the Supreme Soviet on 12 December, 1962, he indicated that both the Russian and American "sides displayed a sober approach, and took into account that unless such steps were taken that could help overcome the dangerous development of events, a third World War might break out." The madmen in the ruling circle of the United States then were very sober lunatics; and the sober Russians understood that.

Some of President Kennedy's statements in the crisis and after may also have overstated the likelihood of a nuclear exchange. He was appropriately anxious to express the gravity of his concern about such a catastrophe. Theodore Sorensen makes clear that President Kennedy was aware of the pitfalls of public utterance at this time. "His warnings on the presence of Soviet missiles in Cuba had to be sufficiently sombre to enlist support around the world without creating panic here at home."[34] And so on 22 October, 1962,

[30] Speech of 12 December, 1962, to the Supreme Soviet, *New York Times*, 13 December, 1962.
[31] *Ibid.*
[32] *Ibid.*
[33] Message to President Kennedy of 28 October, 1962.
[34] *Decision-Making in the White House*, Columbia University Press, New York, 1963, p. 47.

he talked of the world "at the abyss of destruction." In his acceptance of Mr. Khrushchev's retreat on 28 October, 1962, he seemed also to accept the validity of Mr. Khrushchev's earlier threat of uncontrollability. "Developments were approaching a point where events could have become unmanageable." Though control was evident in every one of his moves, President Kennedy's statements did not stress in words that he was in control. It has therefore been possible to misconstrue just what were the risks in the crisis.

The matter is of great importance. The fact that Cuba could be isolated makes a great contrast with the problem in Central Europe. But even on the Central European front American policy differs markedly from that of a dictator who uses a reputation for irresponsibility and apparent willingness to usher in *Goetterdaemmerung* for even minor gains. Threats of uncontrollability should be administered by prescription, against special dangers, and in small doses. Its use except *in extremis* is not compatible with a reputation for being both sane and meaning what one says.

In fact the main risks were of a local, non-nuclear action involving the United States and Russian forces. The possibilities of isolating a limited conflict have seldom been clearer. The situation is very different from Berlin. Remote islands are better than enclaves in satellite territory in this respect. Cuba, surrounded by water rather than East Germans, very distant from the centre of Russian conventional power, did not represent, nor was it contiguous to, any interests that the Soviet Union had dominated for many years. How likely was Chairman Khrushchev to launch missiles at the United States to retrieve a gamble for a quick expansion of this communist foothold in the Western Hemisphere, itself a windfall? Retreat in fact has not even meant the loss of the foothold.

What was threatened was a local non-nuclear action, a measure of very limited violence, only the boarding of ships. On the staircase of ascending steps in the use of force there would have been many landings, many decision points, at which either side could choose between climbing higher or moving down. The United States' nuclear retaliatory force would have made a Soviet missile strike against the United States catastrophic for Russia. But the United States also had an immense local superiority in conventional forces. The Soviet Union clearly would have lost the non-nuclear exchange. Chairman Khrushchev stepped down to avoid a clash of conventional forces in which he would have lost. To avoid this level of loss he would have had irresponsibly to risk very much higher levels.

Some distinguished American analysts tell us that our local superiority in conventional force was an inessential convenience affecting our self-confidence, but not Khrushchev's. Without a deep psychoanalysis of the former Chairman, this would be rather hard to prove or disprove. However, so bald a separation of the determinants of decision on the two sides seems most implausible. Each side strained to affect the anticipations of the other by act as well as word, and its own expectations depended in part on how it read the other's. The American leadership knew that Khrushchev had no basis for confidence in the outcome of any clash with conventional arms in the Caribbean; and a world to lose if he resorted to nuclear weapons.

Inevitably, the question of how nuclear and how conventional arms figured in forcing Khrushchev's withdrawal was much disputed once the crisis had passed, although it is doubtful whether many of the disputants changed their views as a result either of the crisis or the post-crisis debate. Witnesses at the Congressional hearings in the following spring at any rate interpreted events according to their predispositions.[35] Those who had held before the crisis that a strategic nuclear threat can credibly and safely deter all but rather minor border incursions testified that "strategic superiority" was the major factor forcing Khrushchev's withdrawal. Those who had believed that nuclear force — in particular a clear-cut second-strike nuclear capability — is vital, but inadequate as a response to an important range of provocations, took the withdrawal as illustrating "the cutting edge" of the conventional sword. This single encounter where the United States had both the capability to dominate in a conventional conflict and also to inflict overwhelming nuclear damage could not demonstrate once and for all that conventional superiority will always have a major utility; still less could it show that it might easily be dispensed with. Witnesses such as Secretary McNamara who valued and had greatly increased useable conventional capability in the preceding two years, were in charge of controlling the risks during the crisis. They deployed and prepared to use a vast conventional force, including several hundred thousand men poised for invasion. While continuing to deter nuclear action by the Russians, they prepared a mounting sequence of threats short of nuclear war. The dispensability of these moves can only be conjectured. Relying on more desperate threats might have worked, but would clearly have been a greater gamble.

The relevance to Berlin of the Cuban crisis was, as we have said, immediately recognized by the President and the other members of

[35] *Military Procurement Authorization, Fiscal Year 1964*, Committee on Armed Services, US Senate, 88th Congress, First Session, 1963, pp. 507, 896 and *passim*, Cf. also *Hearings on Military Posture*, House Armed Services Committee, 1963.

the EXCOM, for a retreat in Cuba would have been evidence of a likely retreat in Berlin. But our firmness in Cuba cannot conclusively show the opposite. Some Americans are concerned to play down our conventional superiority in Cuba lest it suggest, illogically to be sure, that we would be firm *only* where we have conventional superiority. But for us as for the Russians the stakes as well as the risks are larger in Berlin.

Not that the risks were small in Cuba. The menace of actual conflict between American and Russian forces even in battle with conventional weapons was emphasized by the long history of debate on the massive retaliation theory. As General Maxwell Taylor's account makes clear, much of the doctrinal dispute among the Joint Chiefs had taken the form of a seemingly scholastic argument over the definition of "general war."[36] "General war" had been defined as a conflict between the forces of the United States and those of the Soviet Union, and the definition assumed and made explicit that nuclear weapons would be used from the outset. The definition was an attempt to enforce by semantics, so to speak, a belief that any hostile contact between American and Russian troops would bring immediate nuclear devastation, and so to discourage such a contact. But in Cuba it was apparent that conventional attack on the Russian missile bases was one of the alternatives contemplated and that therefore the United States was separating the decision to do battle with the Russians from the decision to initiate a nuclear war. Decisions to board Russian ships were even more obviously kept distinct from a nuclear decision.

Chairman Khrushchev was right in his later assertion that the United States and the Soviet Union were both in full control of their nuclear forces.

CONTROL AND AUTOMATIC STAIRS

We stress the point only because, in this respect, some of the American official statements made at the height of the crisis did less than justice to American policy. Any suggestion that the United States could not control its responses even in boarding a Russian freighter, would be bound to raise disturbing questions at home. And under some circumstances it would be self-defeating. If Chairman Khrushchev had thought that American decision makers themselves believed their next move would push events out of control, that they had, in the legal phrase, the last clear chance to avoid nuclear war, he might very well have doubted the desperate move

---

[36] *The Uncertain Trumpet,* Harper Brothers, New York (1959), 1960, pp. 7ff, 39, 117.

and so have been rather less deterred and less alarmed than the American public and America's allies. He might have found it inconceivable that the American President would deliberately let matters get unmanageable. In fact well before the Cuban crisis the President and Secretary McNamara and Secretary Rusk had declared, and their subordinates had elaborated, a thoughtful doctrine of controlled response, up to and including the conduct of a nuclear war. Yet, as we have mentioned, President Kennedy's statement of 22 October, excellent as it was on the whole, focussed, for understandable reasons, on "the abyss of destruction." And in attempting to get across the essential message of the American nuclear guarantee for neighbours in Latin America, it indicated that "any nuclear missile launched from Cuba against any nation in the Western Hemisphere" would evoke "a *full* retaliatory response upon the Soviet Union" (our italics). This does not sound like a controlled response. The attempt, it appears, was to say that the United States would respond to a missile against its neighbours as it would respond to one against itself. This latter policy would leave open the possibility of controlled reaction. The United States has made clear that a single nuclear missile launched against the United States need not trip an uncontrolled "full" response.

However, it was even more important to make clear, and in American behaviour it was evident, that the United States did not exclude the possibility of control in the non-nuclear spectrum. In fact it insisted upon it. It responded in a carefully limited way to an aggression which involved the installation, but not the firing, of a nuclear weapon. Against such a move the Cuban crisis demonstrated the relevance and the adequacy of the lowest non-nuclear moves in an ascending series of non-nuclear threats and actions: the threat to board and search freighters for military equipment, a single actual boarding of a chartered Lebanese ship, the imposition of a selective economic blockade, a general blockade, the threat or the actual use of bombing with high explosives against strategic missile bases, the threat or actual use of paratroops, and so forth. The later steps in the sequence never had to be more than latent. But one of the reasons the limited American threat worked was that the United States was willing to take the next steps, if necessary, and had the power to do so — to make each next step less profitable for the Soviet Union.

Before the crisis, the alternatives for policy were discussed in terms of a few bare possibilities: a pure American military invasion, a total blockade, or doing nothing. In the crisis it appeared the world was richer in alternatives than had been conceived by extremists of the left or right. There is a good deal between doing nothing and all-out nuclear war, and an appropriate intermediate response could make a nuclear war less rather than more likely. President Kennedy observed that these alternatives became apparent in the course of five days of discussion, that without this time for hammering out alternatives, he might have chosen less wisely and more extremely.[37] The history of this crisis should be an important corrective for the loose assumption that the only time available for decision in the nuclear age is 15 minutes — a magic number supposed to represent the time from radar intercept to impact of an ICBM following a least energy path.

Professor Richard Neustadt, who has written most perceptively about the use, the limits, and the risks of using American presidential power, has taken the Cuban missile confrontation to illustrate the President's extreme awareness of the new dimensions of these risks, of the fact that somewhere in a succession of decisions he may make one that can neither be reversed nor repaired.[38] It has probably always been true that at some time in a sequence of diplomatic acts, warnings of possible military actions, and military acts themselves, statesmen have felt "things in the saddle," events taking over. It then becomes extremely unlikely that adversaries will back away from the contest or its intensification. Even though the new level of violence is likely to leave both of them worse off than *before* the sequence of threats and pre-war manoeuvres had started, nonetheless, there may be some point of no return in the sequence. At that point the outcome may appear to be better than the risk of stopping. The fact that today decisions taken in crisis might precipitate a disaster on a scale without precedent in history is sobering.

There is a sense of course in which any large scale war does enormous, irreparable harm. Population growth and economic recovery after the war replace the lives lost, the wealth annihilated and the suffering, only in a statistical sense that ignores precisely who died and what treasures were destroyed. Some nuclear conflicts might start by miscalculation and end by being quickly brought under control, and conceivably could do less material damage than World War II and I. Nonetheless such a standard is terrible enough and a nuclear war could be enormously worse. This new sense of the possibility of irreparable harm says a good deal about the psychological burden of the Presidency. And not only the Presidency. The Chairman of the CPSU explicitly referred to the "irrep-

---

[37] *Washington Post,* 18 December, 1962.

[38] *Administration of National Security. Hearings Before the Subcommittee on National Security Staffing and Operations of the Committee on Government Operations,* United States Senate, 88th Congress, 1st Session. Part I, 1963, p. 76ff.

arable" consequences of a failure in restraint by either side. It makes clear why neither Nikita Khrushchev nor John Kennedy behaved like the irrational juvenile delinquents who are sometimes presumed to occupy the seats of power today, strapped by their seatbelts in a carefree game of Chicken.

Where the alternative is to be ruled by events with such enormous consequences, the head of a great state is likely to examine his acts of choice in crisis and during it to subdivide these possible acts in ways that make it feasible to continue exercising choice. This sort of behaviour does not fit an increasingly popular and professional picture which has it that political leaders may be thoughtful, responsible and close to reality in between crises, but overreact passionately during the crises themselves. However, there is a good deal of professional evidence as well as common sense opinion to indicate that, as Dewey put it, when any thinking is going on, it is likely to be because there has been some trouble. Routine experience may lead us imperceptibly to ignore a slowly changing or suddenly new reality, but we do sometimes rise to a challenge with heightened alertness and an increased sense of responsibility, especially on matters of great moment. The behaviour of the decision makers in the Cuban crisis at any rate provides a counter example to a good many pessimistic predictions derived from studies by behavioural scientists concerned with reducing international tension.[39]

A process of escalation is usually thought of simply as an increase in violence growing out of a limited conflict in which an adversary may act to stave off his loss or an opponent's prospective success. The aspect of "escalators" that inspired its use in this connection, we suspect, is the fact that moving stairways carry a passenger on automatically without any effort of his will. However, as we have

---

[39] Generalising from 1914, some studies predict that as tensions rise in a crisis, decision makers will tend to decide emotionally rather than by calculation. The range of alternatives they see will narrow and they will be less able to assess the likely consequences of each possible choice. They will see less time before the enemy strikes and this will lead to still greater tension, to a tendency to value early action and dislike delay, to depreciate the dangers of violent action and the rewards of non-violent action, and to accept suspicions and fears as facts. These predictions are necessarily somewhat vague. None of them, however, appears to have been borne out by the behaviour of decision makers in the missile crisis. See *Content Analysis, a Handbook with Applications for the Study of International Crisis* by Robert C. North, Ole R. Holsti, M. George Zaninovich, and Dina A. Zinnes, Northwestern University Press, 1963, Appendix B, for the hypotheses derived from 1914 and contrast with materials derived from the Cuban crisis and presented by Holsti, North and Brody in *Peace Research Society (International) Papers*, Vol. 2, Oslo, 1965.

suggested there are down-escalators as well as up-escalators, and there are landings between escalators where one can decide to get off or to get on, to go up or down, or to stay there; or take the stairs. Just where automaticity or irreversibility takes over is an uncertain but vital matter, and that is one of the reasons a decision maker may want to take a breath at a landing to consider next steps. It is apparent from President Kennedy's own descriptions of the Cuban crisis as well as Mr. Sorensen's that he gave enormous value to the cautious weighing of alternatives made possible by the interval of almost a week; to the five or six days mentioned for hammering out the first decision. And the decision made was precisely one that left open a variety of choices. Finally the availability of less desperate choices than acquiescence or holocaust had been prepared before the crisis by the deliberate policy of preserving options, developing a force capable of flexible response.

One way in which the overhanging possibility of an irreversible disastrous decision might operate today is to bring on an immobility that, paradoxically, reduces the alternatives to a few extremes. The irreversible sequence might be started then by a desperate act to avoid the loss that looms in the extreme of retreat. But there is more than one way to arrive at a paralysis and gross reduction of choice. The opposite path, proceeding on the perception that commitment is inevitable, can advance commitment to a much earlier stage than necessary in the process of coercion and resisting coercion. This is the danger inherent in threats of massive retaliation. That war can be so massive a disaster tempts us to use the threat of this disaster to paralyse an adversary bent on aggression; but it may end in our own paralysis. The Cuban missile crisis at any rate illustrated an intensive search among alternatives to find a threat that could be executed with a minimal risk, and a slowly ascending sequence of threats which could not be challenged by the Soviet Union without making its position still worse.

There is an important class of situations in which a crisis may be precipitated as the result of an unfounded or exaggerated mutual distrust. These are cases where, in the words of the most brilliant analyst of such reciprocal fears, "people may vaguely think they perceive that the situation is inherently explosive, and respond by exploding."[40] But some of the time guns go off because we do not know they are loaded; grenades explode because we think they are duds; or enemies attack because we are so sure they will not attack that we are unprepared for it. The Cuban missile crisis should remind us of these equally important situations in which an excess of

[40] T. C. Schelling, *The Strategy of Conflict*, p. 208.

trust or self-confidence causes the trouble, and a sharp awakening to the possibilities of explosion helps bring the trouble under responsible control. Tactics of deception typically attempt to induce trust where it is not warranted. Khrushchev and Gromyko during the prelude to the crisis simply lied. And the traditional confidence man feeds on the guillibility and wishfulness of his target. "Never give a sucker an even break" evokes a long history of cases where it is not mutual distrust that is explosive, but fond belief on the one side, a willingness to exploit it on the other, and a violent sense of outrage by the victim at having his innocence exploited. But the victim need not explode. He can carefully signal the danger to his adversary.

The resolution of the missile crisis may be regarded as in the main a brilliant example of a successful communication of a precise and firm intention. However, in some of its aspects, and especially in its generation, the crisis illustrates the possibilities of miscommunication. Under other circumstances, such miscommunication might not have had so fortunate an ending. Moreover, the misunderstandings do not fit one current wishful stereotype: that our troubles stem only from our failure to realize how like us our adversaries really are. Our estimates and those of the Russians, just before the missile confrontation, resembled each other mainly in that they each too easily assumed an identity in modes of thought and valuation. They illustrate rather the difficulty one always has in breaking out of the circle of one's own notion of what is normal in national behaviour.

The missile crisis was precipitated by some poor Russian and American estimates of each other's willingness to take risks. The American leaders did not believe the Russians would be foolhardy enough, in the face of President Kennedy's explicit warning against it, to put into Cuba missiles which were capable of hitting the United States. The Russians on the other hand did not think the Americans would risk a direct confrontation.

The false estimates on both sides did not concern whether the United States had clearly warned the Russians not to put in place in Cuba surface-to-surface missiles with a significant capability to hit the United States. They had to do with Russian disbelief that the President would act in case they ignored his warning, and an American judgment that the Russians would recognize that the President meant what he said. Yet one curious aftermath of the crisis is a rewriting of history, especially in Europe, that questions not merely whether it was obvious that President Kennedy meant what he explicitly stated in September, but doubts even that he had said it.

The situation is somewhat confused by the interminable wrangle over the distinction between "offensive" and "defensive" weapons. There is of course no sharp distinction between the two and there are many interconnections. An aggressor can defend himself, limit the destruction wreaked against his own territory, among other subtler ways, by using surface-to-surface missiles or bombers to reduce his victim's retaliatory forces before they take off; and once his victim's retaliatory forces are launched on their way, he can use active and passive defences, such as surface-to-air missiles, jet fighters and civil defence to reduce his victim's retaliation further. Moreover, the Cuban surface-to-air missiles and fighters themselves illustrate that active defences can be used to prevent or to impede surveillance and so help to cover the build-up of a force of surface-to-surface missiles and manned bombers. Even the direct use of fighter aircraft or short-range missiles with the help of torpedo boats would provide some minimal capability to hit American coastal targets. All of this ignores still subtler interconnections between the threats or the use of "offensive" or "defensive" weapons.

However, the distinction the President made between offensive and defensive weapons served the purpose of warning well enough, because he made very clear what weapons he had in mind as "offensive." On 4 September he said, ". . . the Soviets have provided the Cuban government with a number of anti-aircraft defence missiles with a slant range of 25 miles which are similar to early models of our Nike. . . . There is no evidence . . . of the presence of offensive ground-to-ground missiles; or of other significant offensive capability either in Cuban hands or under Soviet direction and guidance. Were it to be otherwise, the gravest issues would arise."

In other words the President drew a line with a broad and hairy brush between offensive and defensive weapons in general, but he clearly classed Russian medium and intermediate range surface-to-surface missiles in the offensive category. Emplacing them in Cuba would be strategic trespass. Moreover, the Russians understood him. Their government authorized *Tass* to state on 11 September ". . . there is no need for the Soviet Union to shift its weapons . . . to any other country, for instance Cuba . . . the Soviet Union has rockets so powerful to carry . . . nuclear warheads that there is no need to search for sites for them beyond the boundaries of the Soviet Union . . . the Soviet Union has the capability from its own territory to render assistance to any peace-loving state and not only to Cuba."

The President knew that the message had been understood. He believed it would be respected. It was this last conviction, supported by Soviet reassurances, "both public and private," in September, that proved illusory in the following month. In President Kennedy's words,

> I don't think that we expected that he (Khrushchev) would put the missiles in Cuba, because it would have seemed such an imprudent action for him to take, as it was later proved. Now, he obviously must have thought that he could do it in secret and that the United States would accept it. So that he did not judge our intentions accurately.

The Americans assumed in short that the Russians understood that Americans are tolerant but cannot be pushed beyond a certain point, especially when that point has been clearly and publicly announced. But just how imprudent it was for the Russians to put missiles in Cuba depended on whether the Americans were willing to force a showdown. So the American estimate that the Russians would not emplace the missiles depended on an American judgment about how the Russians thought Americans would act. Moreover, there is no doubt that President Kennedy's judgment of the American character was right. His own behaviour, with its brief explosion of anger at Gromyko's continuing deception, and the bitter repetition in the 22 October speech "That statement was false" was in a long tradition of sharp moral reactions at confidence betrayed. In more controlled form, it repeated the indignation of acting Secretary Polk and President Wilson at the decoded German message showing that while the German foreign minister had been talking peace he had plotted to encourage a Mexican attack on the United States. Or the fury of Secretary Hull and President Roosevelt at the Japanese representatives Kurusu and Nomura at the time of Pearl Harbour.

On the other hand, to the Russians surely President Kennedy's response was an extraordinary over-reaction. Chairman Khrushchev had enunciated and withdrawn a succession of ultimata on Berlin beginning in 1958, and done so with distinct disappointment, but with comparative equanimity. He could hardly have understood either the enormous importance conferred by domestic party debate (with the Bay of Pigs disaster in the background) on the specific line the President had drawn between offensive and defensive weapons, or the great to-do over the deception. (Khrushchev's experience with cases in which Americans themselves had used deception might have suggested the accompanying sense of guilt and half-heartedness with which this is done. The American response to the shooting down of the U2 piloted by Powers in 1960 forms an interesting cultural contrast with the indignant denial by the Soviet government in the United Nations of actions revealed by the detailed reconnaissance photos of the missiles in Cuba.) Each side in short tended to project its own psychology or certain stereotypes about the behaviour of the other. The Russians acted on the assumption that the Americans were so driven by domestic politics as to be unlikely to react in any decisive way; or that they would act like Russians.

In the period of withdrawing the missiles, once again, Americans tended to project American behaviour on to the Russians. Just as they had exaggerated the Russian estimate of risks and underestimated Russian daring, they now overestimated Russian reluctance to withdraw after a nice try. But here too Russian behaviour is very different from American. The prospect of humiliation was of enormous importance to President Kennedy. It did not have quite the same importance for Khrushchev. Serious students of Russian behaviour with such different approaches as George Kennan and Nathan Leites have long observed that "the Kremlin has no compunction about retreating in the face of superior force."[41] After the withdrawal, many journalists recalled Brest-Litovsk and Lenin's phrase about the good revolutionary being willing to crawl in the mud. But that recollection was much rarer in the actual week of quarantine and crisis. By December, 1962, Khrushchev himself was referring to Lenin's "sensible" and "temporary" concession. The Albanian dogmatists who criticized the withdrawal of missiles, he claimed, were sliding down Trotsky's path of unyielding infantilism at Brest. But the missile withdrawal was not even a temporary retreat, much less a capitulation. The concessions, Khrushchev said, were "mutual."[42]

Such cultural contrasts are of course a matter of degree; but nonetheless real. Ruth Benedict's *The Chrysanthemum and the Sword* offers a brilliant analysis of Japanese feelings toward retreat and humiliation — as far exceeding in depth and range American emotions on the subject. And there are limits to Bolshevik tolerance in withdrawal.

INTERESTS AND INFLUENCE OF THE
TWO PRINCIPALS AND THEIR ALLIES

This retrospect of the interests and policy alternatives open to the three powers in the crisis indicates the need for refining some of the questions with which we started. When we say that in the

[41] George Kennan, *American Diplomacy*, 1900–1950, p. 112. See also Nathan Leites, *Study of Bolshevism,* Chapter 19, and his recent "Kremlin Thoughts: Yielding, Provoking, Rebuffing, Retreating." RM 3618-ISA, the RAND Corporation, May, 1963, pp. 24ff.
[42] Speech, 12 December, 1962.

nuclear age force is no longer an instrument of policy, it is not clear whether this is description or exhortation. In fact a blockade, it was generally agreed in September, 1962, was an act of war. Attitudes and definitions changed in October. This is a delicate matter of semantics. The American interdiction of ships carrying arms to Cuba was called a "quarantine." Nonetheless it was an act of force. And threats of higher levels of violence were implicit at every stage in the developing crisis. The questions at issue directly affected Soviet, Cuban, and United States military power.

The availability of nuclear weapons to the great powers had a double aspect. The weapons imposed the need for great responsibility and careful, very conscious control over the limited encounters that took place. On the other hand the use of lower levels of violence in such encounters is in a certain sense encouraged by the knowledge that a decision to escalate to nuclear weapons would be irrational and inappropriate for either of the participants and, for the prudent men in control, uncharacteristically irrational. And prudent antagonists can co-operate to insulate nuclear weapons from less prudent third parties. These encounters were rather clearly isolable from a decision to use nuclear weapons. Each of the nuclear powers took the time and had the information to see that the initiation of nuclear weapons would badly worsen its own position.

American nuclear power immobilized Russian nuclear power. And American local superiority in non-nuclear force together with a demonstrated willingness to use it discouraged further destabilizing moves. The familiar saying that overwhelming nuclear force simply disables its possessor from using any force at all is a rather shallow paradox. Nevertheless thermonuclear weapons clearly suit only the gravest purposes. And while small nations are less able to affect events than big ones, they do have an effect. There are serious limits to the control even a great nuclear power has over its non-nuclear allies. This applies more obviously to relations between the United States and its allies than it does to Russia's relations with its friends. Even allies whose defence and economy depend almost wholly on the United States are, as the headlines continually remind us, far from being its puppets. A variety of South Korean and South Vietnamese regimes in the last few years has made this point vivid. And the point is much more obvious for allies that are themselves great nations.

But in this crisis at any rate a small communist power was the object of contention between its protector and its adversary and could not decisively affect the outcome. It had some capability for mischief, but even this was limited. Close and receding allies of the Soviet Union and the United States as well as the non-aligned countries could do little more than endorse or criticize after the fact. In the climactic encounter it was the United States and the Soviet Union who determined events.

The loneliness of the President's decision in such a crisis raises essential problems for allies, whose fates might be affected by it. They have an interest in sharing and influencing the decision. But also in seeing to it that the decision can be made — in avoiding paralysis. This is an essential dilemma of nuclear control. In some sense the problem is quite as acute from the standpoint of American citizen as it is from that of a Briton, or an Italian, or a Frenchman, or a citizen of any of the NATO or OAS countries. In the five or six days in which the course of quarantine was selected, only an extremely small number of people (the President himself suggested a maximum of 15) had any share in the choice.

In spite of the very just allied as well as domestic concern, this is not the sort of problem that can be neatly "solved." It can be softened somewhat, and essentially the same methods can widen both allied and domestic participation. The crises themselves and the time for decision in crises are, we have suggested, likely to occupy a good deal longer interval than the magic 15 minutes frequently referred to when nuclear dangers are in mind. The small group concerned with the actual management of the crisis conceivably could then include a few high level allied political figures. It is notable that in the missile crisis, while allies were not notified of the American quarantine until the day before its public announcement, the decision itself undertook a very minimal use of force, leaving many decision points still open in the future conduct of the affair.

More important, one can prepare for a variety of contingencies in advance of crises; one can determine what might be done, if they occur. In fact, the quadripartite planning for Berlin at the very least strongly influenced President Kennedy and his immediate associates, predisposed them to the consideration of firm but carefully measured responses to any local action, and also made them more highly conscious of the world-wide repercussions inherent in many such "local" crises.

Unfortunately, however, acute perception of the importance of far off points in space tends to be highly localized in time — to be mostly limited, in fact to times of crisis.[43] The problem of sharing

[43] There was a strand of European opinion that seized on the Americans' firm response to Cuba as somehow a verification of the thesis that United States interests are also high localized; it would act strongly in its own interests, when threatened close to home, but not in Europe, not, for example, in Berlin. We may leave aside the rather curious inference from the fact of positive reaction to a strong provocation close to

contingency planning is complicated by the fact that allies are notoriously ambivalent about distant troubles. Before the crisis itself, they are likely to feel that the remote problem is not very important from their point of view; they may believe either that the chances of disaster are small; or that the disaster will be local. They are almost sure to feel their resources are limited and they have troubles "of their own." Indeed America's troubles with Cuba tended to be deprecated by its allies as something of an American obsession. The United States on the other hand naturally often felt that its allies underestimated the depth and complexity of the threat of communism in Latin America, and its possible ultimate worldwide importance.

NATO collaboration in shaping policy for future crises is not easy for crises in the NATO treaty area. It is a good deal harder for any of the multiplicity of crises that, arising outside the NATO periphery, may ultimately be of concern to NATO. Nonetheless it seems that, for those allies that feel a concern, rather more contingency planning in common, formal or informal, bilateral or multilateral, could be done.

The interests of Latin American governments and people in the outcome of the missile crisis was most obvious. It was the first time that these countries had come directly in the shadow of a nuclear war. And the discovery of the missiles and their forced withdrawal in a dangerous crisis had a large emotional impact. While some of the concern was directed against the United States, on the whole Castro lost ground. By pulling Latin America into the centre of a confrontation between the two principal nuclear powers, he appeared to an increased number of Latin Americans to be dangerously irresponsible. Even Goulart's Brazil and Mexico, which had opposed OAS concert against Castro, backed the President's blockade; and there is no doubt that such effects lasted long beyond the crisis. The losses Castro suffered contrast with his exalted hopes before the crisis that Russian missiles in Cuba would fortify his prestige and influence in Latin America. But they do not show that his hopes were unfounded; just that he had gambled. Smaller countries may feel a great deal of ambivalence about the acquisition of nuclear weapons by their neighbors. So the mingled fear, pride, respect, and distrust inspired in Asia today by the first Chinese nu-

---

home — to the conclusion that there would be no reaction to a more distant challenge. However, a careful scrutiny of the American response to Cuba would suggest that far from showing that the United States would not defend Berlin, the defence of Cuba from the very first revelation of the Soviet move was recognized to be a vital part of the defence of Berlin, and the fate of Berlin was prominent in the contingency planning.

clear test. The main trouble with Castro's gamble from his stand-point was that it failed; at least for the time.

Finally a note of caution: it is easy to read too much into events, even those of outstanding importance. Once the crisis had passed, perhaps inevitably it was greeted as the herald of a new era — a testing and final stabilization of "the balance" of nuclear power between the Soviet Union and the United States, an essential elim-ination of the danger of nuclear war for the foreseeable future. Especially in Europe the notion seems widespread that the Cuban missile crisis represented a "turning point." But such an interpreta-tion should be suspect in particular when advanced by those who before the missile crisis had felt the era of effortless stability and already arrived, and then during the crisis swung to the opposite extreme of panic in exaggerating the likelihood of war. In fact the "balance" is too vaguely defined, too complex and too changeable for any such assurance. The hazards of change are political as well as technical and military. It would be a mistake to regard the Soviets' emplacement of missiles in Cuba as something like a crucial experiment deliberately conducted by the Russians and es-tablishing for them definitely once and for all that the West is determined to resist any changes in the balance — however the "balance" is defined. Khrushchev himself quickly rejected Lord Home's hopeful declaration that the Russians, sobered by their re-cent experience in Cuba, might from that time revise their interna-tional role.

The Western show of determination in the missile crisis had its effects. Perhaps, as has been said, it made easier the conclusion of the test ban. Perhaps it contributed to the ultimate fall of Khrush-chev. At least it provided both Khrushchev's foreign and domestic rivals with a sequence of two misdeeds to cite — "adventurism" followed by "capitulationism."[44] In spite of the ready vocabulary of abuse available to describe the sequence, such an apparently op-portune advance followed by a prudent withdrawal in the face of superior force is entirely consistent with a marxist canon of be-haviour, which fixes no time-table for communist expansion. The effects of the Western determination, however, in the long run are uncertain and are hardly likely to be definitive. It is most im-plausible to suppose that this one major Communist failure will foreclose all future significant attempts, should opportunities arise, to make further advance.

The world has changed then; but not completely. It is surely no

[44] Statement by the People's Government of China of 1 September, 1963.

simpler now than it was before. There are many possible dangers to the West other than a precisely timed world conspiracy of a perfectly unified, permanently hostile communist camp. Some have to do with intense communist rivalries and the great variety of "communisms" today. Even an abating hostility impels caution, so long as the change is uncertain, patchy, intermittent and slow. The transformation of the whole world need hardly be at stake, only substantial parts of it. Castro is no Tito, nor a satellite, nor an immediate military threat, nor simply a minor nuisance, but a persistent source and model for insurgency and terror in the hemisphere.

Inevitably, one extreme reading of the missile crisis took it as proving that Communists in a showdown will always retreat, that we need only face them in the future with the alternative of nuclear disaster for them to abandon any use of force to transform the world. This simple view fortunately is not very influential. Yet, if it is dangerously implausible to suppose that a few future military confrontations are capable of having this happy result, it is at least equally implausible to hold that a single encounter has already had it.

PART III
Innovation and Obsolescence in the Use of Force: Adjusting Strategy to Capability

The four studies in Part III deal with two of the perennial tasks involved in using military power. The first task is to discover how to use a new weapon most effectively; the second, to determine when an old weapon has become obsolete. These two tasks are not easy for strategists to perform. Because of the nature of their work, these men come to believe firmly in certain doctrines. The difficulty they will have in adjusting strategy to capability depends in part on just how tenaciously they hold to those doctrines. If they have become so committed to fixed paths that they are not likely to change, then they will not be receptive either to experimentation with new weapons that may prove to be extremely valuable or to elimination of old weapons that have become obsolete. Strategists do not necessarily become committed to particular doctrines. In the past, they have often cast off old modes of thought and, in doing so, have been quite effective in developing techniques designed to use new weapons effectively.

The selections below deal with both types of cases: those in which strategists have stubbornly clung to old weapons long after their utility had ended and those in which they have made good use of new weapons. The selections by Katzenbach and Stone treat the first case — obsolescence; those by May and Morton, the second — innovation. Edward L. Katzenbach, Jr., describes the innumerable rationalizations used to extend the life of the horse cavalry well into the twentieth century. Jeremy J. Stone argues that missiles have made manned bombers obsolete and that therefore bombers should be done away with. Ernest R. May shows why in 1914 the German Navy evolved a bold, new, central role for the submarine, a weapon that, before then, the Navy had considered to be experimental and of limited value. Louis Morton discusses the reasons why the United States decided to use the atomic bomb against Japan.

The Horse Cavalry
in the Twentieth Century

EDWARD L. KATZENBACH, JR.

THE PROBLEM

Lag-time, that lapsed period between innovation and a successful institutional or social response to it, is probably on the increase in military matters. Moreover, as the tempo of technological change continues to quicken, it is likely that lag-time will increase as well. . . .

Of course, at first there would seem to be a paradox here. As weapons systems have become more complex, the lead-time needed to bring them from the drawing board to the assembly line has become markedly longer. On the basis of the longer lead-time one might hypothesize that the institutional lag might lessen inasmuch as prior planning would seem eminently more possible. It might even be surmised that the institutional response might be made to coincide with the operational readiness of new weapons. To date, however, military institutions have not been able to use this lead-time effectively because real change has so outdistanced anticipated change. Moreover, there is not the urgency that there should be in the military to make major institutional adjustments in the face of the challenge of new weapons systems, if for no other reason than that the problem of testing is so difficult. . . . It is quite impossible to *prove* that minor adjustments in a traditional pattern of organization and doctrine will not suffice to absorb technological innovations of genuine magnitude.

Furthermore the absence of any final testing mechanism of the military's institutional adequacy short of war has tended to keep the pace of change to a creep in time of peace, and, conversely, has whipped it into a gallop in time of war. The military history of the past half century is studded with institutions which have managed to dodge the challenge of the obvious. . . . The most curious of all was the Horse Cavalry which maintained a capacity for survival

From *Public Policy* (1958), pp. 120–149. Reprinted by permission of the publisher and the author. Portions of the text and some footnotes have been omitted.

277

that borders on the miraculous. The war horse survived a series of challenges each of which was quite as great as those which today's weapons systems present to today's traditional concepts. . . . It continued to live out an expensive and decorous existence with splendor and some spirit straight into an age which thought it a memory. . . .

The horse cavalry has had to review its role in war four times since the end of the nineteenth century in the face of four great changes in the science of war: the development of repeating automatic and semi-automatic weapons, the introduction of gasoline and diesel-fueled engines, the invention of the air-borne weapon, and the coming of the nuclear battlefield. Each new challenge to the horse has been, of necessity, seriously considered. Each has demanded a review of doctrine, a change in role and mission. And in each review there have been, of necessity, assumptions made as to the relevance of experience to some pattern of future war . . . [for] the paradox of military planning is that it must be reasonably precise as to quite imprecise future contingencies.

THE WEAPONS PROBLEM

By the year 1900, or thereabouts, the clip-fed breech-loading repeating rifle was in the hands of the troops of all the major powers. . . . Self-firing automatic weapons were also on the assembly lines of the world's armament makers. Hiram Maxim had registered the last of a famous series of machine gun patents in 1885. By the time (1904–1905) of the Russo-Japanese War the guns of Maxim and Hotchkiss were in national arsenals everywhere, or almost everywhere, for the expense of new weapons was rapidly shrinking the ranks of those powers which could be considered "great." At roughly the same time it had been found that the use of glycerine in the recoil mechanism of artillery pieces enabled these to remain aimed after being fired. This in turn meant that the artillery piece itself became a rapid fire (20 rounds per minute) weapon. . . . Firepower, in short, had a new meaning.

For the elite of the armies of the world, the cavalry, each of these developments would seem to have been nothing short of disaster. For that proud and beautiful animal, the horse, has a thin skin and a high silhouette, and its maximum rate of speed on the attack is only 30 m.p.h. Especially in conjunction with barbed wire, automatically manufactured since 1874 and in military use at the end of the century, it is difficult to imagine a target more susceptible to rapid fire.

The cavalry had always considered itself to have a variety of missions. The cavalry was the good eye of the infantry. It was taught to collect, and if necessary to fight for information about the enemy. The cavalry protected friendly, and harried enemy flanks and rear. It covered any necessary withdrawal. It was used in pursuit of defeated enemy. And above and beyond all else, the cavalry was used to charge the faltering, the weary, or the unwary, to deliver the *coup de grâce* with the *arme blanche:* with cold steel, with saber or lance, to "crown victory" as the proud phrase went.

It was clear that the introduction of the automatic and the semiautomatic weapon would make some cavalry missions more difficult. But there was no doubt in any cavalryman's mind, and there was little doubt in the minds of most others, that most cavalry missions would have to continue simply because there was no viable substitute. The horse was transport, and the horse was mobility. A group of horsemen could cover a hundred miles in twenty-four hours with a load of around 225–250 pounds. The beast was reasonably amphibious; at least it could swim rivers. To scout, to patrol, to cover flank, rear and withdrawal, to raid — these missions remained untouched.

There remained, however, one really great problem area. Did automatic fire relegate the horse to a transport role or should it still be considered as part of a weapons system? At the time the problem was never stated quite this simply. Indeed it was never stated simply at all, but in essence this was the issue from roughly the end of the Boer War until World War I. The reason why the question so divided men was this: Cavalry as an arm was an integrated weapon made up of horse, man and cold steel fighting as one. If horses were to be considered simply as transportation, and if man and horse were to be separated for the fire fight, then the cavalry as an arm would no longer exist. Only mounted infantry would remain.[1]

On the issue of the relationship between horse and man hung a number of subsidiary issues. Should the horseman be armed with the new automatic weapons? If so, he would have to be dismounted in action, for the horse, as differentiated from the elephant, is a most unsatisfactory gun platform. Yet to deprive cavalry of the new weapons would be to deprive the weapons of mobility. And if the horse could no longer be used to charge the new guns, then of what possible use was honed steel, e.g., lance and sword, even if one took into serious account the last ditch defense of it, to wit that it was "always loaded"? Finally, and here one comes to the most burning question in any issue of military policy — the effect of change on

---

[1] Perhaps this will be better understood if a modern analogy is cited — the substitution of missile for manned aircraft, for example.

morale. If the cavalry were deprived of its cold steel, would it lose that fine edge of morale, that elan without which of course it simply would not be "cavalry," no matter what its mission?

There should have been some way to learn through experience just what could and could not be done with the cavalry with and against the new weapons. There were, after all, two wars of some importance during the period under consideration — the Boer War (1898–1901) and the Russo-Japanese (1904–1905). In both, cavalry and repeating and automatic weapons were used. Each fall, moreover, there were great maneuvers in each country of Europe. Present at each were foreign observers with, at least by modern standards, a free run of the field of action. Why was it then that there could be no final decisions on these matters?

The answer lies in the number of variables. For instance, before the problem of the cavalry armament could even be tackled, the difficult question had to be answered as to what the rapid-fire weapons could do and should be doing.

. . . For each demonstrable fact there was an awkwardly intangible "if" which could neither be properly accounted for nor possibly forgotten. If into the balance of judgment concerning the machine gun was thrown the urgent problem of its resupply and its vulnerability to long-range artillery fire, then a rational conclusion might be reached that the weapon was primarily defensive in character and should be dug into the earth, into a well sandbagged bunker, there to pour forth its withering fire into an attacking force. Yet if, on the other hand, it was concluded that the withering fire of the weapon made it ideal to use on the surprise target, the target of opportunity on the enemy flank, then the weapon became offensive. If an offensive weapon, then the machine gun could well be designated a cavalry weapon. If defensive, then was it not an infantry, or even an artillery weapon? Of course this initial decision was a serious one for it might well determine the future of the weapon. Once assigned to an organization, a branch or arm of a service, it was at least likely that the weapon's development would be stunted except in line with the mission of the unit to which it was assigned.

Within the military staff of all nations the machine gun raised many more problems than it solved — as can be expected of any new weapons system. These problems were, furthermore, broadly intellectual rather than narrowly technical. Indeed the mechanical improvement of a given weapons system is usually less urgent and almost always less baffling than deciding a proper and fitting target for it, and then solving the galaxy of problems of organization and control which hinge on this basic decision. . . .

So in the period between 1900 and 1914 the immediate problem was to conceptualize the mission or missions of the machine gun and the tactics of the new clip-fed, bolt-action rifle and the automatic gun. The second problem was to decide the future tactics and armament of cavalry in view of the concept arrived at. What actually happened was that the new was absorbed into old organizational and tactical concepts, and nothing of the old was rejected. The reasoning from country to country may, however, be of lasting interest. The matter of the cavalry *charge* provides an excellent focal point.

THE CHARGE

It is hard to see where there was room for claim and counter-claim in so substantive an issue as this — the charge of a wave of horsemen, gaily colored (except in the United States), helmets shining, plumes flying, sabers drawn or lances at the ready. Surely a comprehensive and conclusive study of the charge and its role, if any, in modern war was not outside the bounds of logical possibility. Yet just as it was impossible in the 1930s to analyze the role of the battleship in the air age and is now impossible to assess the relationship between the naval aircraft carrier and the nuclear bomber, so it was impossible to evaluate the charge — and for much the same reasons.

The reasons why the charge was continued varied from one country to another. But basically it was continued because the cavalry liked it. In virtually all countries the cavalry was a club, an exclusive one, made up at the officer level of those who could afford to ride when young, hunt, dress and play polo when older. The impression that one absorbs from contemporary cavalry reviews, from the pictures, the social columns, the interests expressed in the less than serious articles, together with the portrait of the cavalryman in the contemporary novel, is of a group of men who were at once hard-riding, hard-drinking, and hard-headed. Its leadership was derived from the countryside rather than from the city. The cavalry was the home of tradition, the seat of romance, the haven of the well-connected. New York City's Squadron A, the proud majors in the Prussian Cavalry Reserve, the French Horse Breeders' Association, all had a built-in loyalty to the cavalry, and if the Chief of Cavalry said that the charge was still feasible, he had important backing. So it was that in Europe the charge was still considered not only feasible, but a future way of war.

American cavalrymen, however, thought that European cavalry had much to learn. And in many respects the U.S. "Red Necks" were quite the most realistic of the world's cavalries in the period just prior to World War I. To be sure, they retained the saber charge, executing it with the same straight saber, a thrust weapon, used by the Canadian cavalry. But in the years from just before World War I until just after World War II the U.S. Cavalry preferred to practice the charge with the Colt semi-automatic .45 pistol. (The pistol charge was never actually used in battle. The last battle charge of the U.S. Cavalry seems to have been in the Philippines during the insurrection of 1901.) Of course it might be argued that to put a .45 in the hands of a man on a horse was simply to mount the inaccurate on the unstable, but given the argument that the essence of the charge was its psychological impact, the sound of the .45 might have had an effect comparable to the sight of saber or lance.

But what the U.S. Cavalry did have that others did not was a genuine appreciation of the importance of dismounted action. It is this which is given the more elaborate treatment in the regulations, and it is this that the trooper really expected to be the rule in combat. But was this the result of a thoughtful analysis of the new weapons or something else?

Certainly the articles in the *Journal of the U.S. Cavalry Association* are the most sophisticated in regard to the new repeating arms and their impact on cavalry. In the years just after the turn of the century the great argument in U.S. Cavalry circles was whether or not the saber should be retained at all. But it seems to have been generally admitted that while "Mounted charges may yet be used on rare occasions when the enemy is demoralized, out of ammunition, or completely taken by surprise . . ," nonetheless "for cavalry to make a mounted charge against enemy troops who are dismounted and armed with the present magazine gun, would be to seek disaster." The corollary that ". . . the trooper must bear in mind that in fighting his carbine is his main reliance"[2] was also accepted.

Were it not that certain European cavalry groups were at the time tending to reject the thesis to which the U.S. subscribed, there would be nothing in any way remarkable about the U.S. position, so patently obvious and right does it seem in retrospect. Yet in the early nineteen hundreds U.S. doctrine was different, and hence needs a word of explanation.

The U.S. cavalryman had a tradition quite different from that of any of the Europeans. He had always done the bulk of his fighting on his feet. Therefore there was no break in tradition for him to

<hr>

[2] "Comment and Criticism," *Journal of the U.S. Cavalry Association* (*JUSCA*), Vol. 13, No. 48, April 1903, pp. 720, 721.

recognize the revolution in firepower for the great change it was. Cavalry during the Civil War most frequently fought dismounted, although clashes between cavalry were fought with the sword, and in the wars against the Indians cavalrymen also dismounted to fight with the aimed accurate fire quite unattainable on horseback. Horses were considered transportation, and the ground was considered a respectable substance on which to fight a battle. U.S. cavalrymen did not feel morally obligated to die on a horse — which European cavalrymen did. In short, the U.S. Cavalry reacted to the new firepower as it did because its history and its tradition made it quite natural for it to do so. In Europe the cavalry history of the U.S. Civil War was scarcely known until the very late nineteen hundreds, and hence the relevance of that war to cavalry problems was largely overlooked. Or given European experience and tradition, would a study of the Civil War have made any real difference?

Of all the cavalry arms of the world that which seems in retrospect to have been the furthest behind the times was that of the German Empire. The German Cavalry had adopted the lance for all ninety-three of its cavalry regiments in 1890 instead, as was true in the mid-nineteenth century, of having only one in four so armed. The lance was, of course, much more than a shaft of wood taller than a man, one tipped with steel and pennant decked: a lance was a state of mind. And it was a reminder that those who carried it still believed that the cavalry really was an arm to be reckoned with. . . .

Why was it that such serious students of war as the Germans are reputed to have been were in general quite so oblivious to the impact of the new firepower? There seem to have been several reasons. The first and most important was the attitude of Emperor William II towards cavalry. A young U.S. Cavalry lieutenant who witnessed German maneuvers in the fall of 1903 was frankly appalled by it. He noted the total lack of realism in the great rolling charges of the cavalry against both rifle and artillery. And he noted too the fact that the Kaiser was so proud of his cavalry that his umpires, knowing their place, pronounced the charges successful!! In Germany, in short, the well-known penchant of the Emperor for the charge undoubtedly did much to insulate the Germans from any serious thought of change.

There was, however, another reason as well. Even after seeing machine guns fired in the late 1880s, the German General Staff refused to take them seriously. Their reason lay in their mis-reading of their own experience with the *mitrailleuses* during the war of 1870–71 when these were badly misused. The fact that past experience happened to be irrelevant did not make it any less important, however, and it was not until 1908 that the machine gun was given the serious attention in Germany that it so obviously deserved. Even then it was only the infantry that recognized the importance of the new automatic weapons. Cavalry units, although armed with them, did not take them very seriously. German cavalry went trotting off to war in 1914, pennons flying from their lances, just as units of French infantry went off to war in red trousers, and for much the same reason: psychological effect. For the real effect of cavalry was, when on the charge, a psychological one, and was generally admitted as such. It was the role of the charge to break the enemy's will, and what could do this more effectively than a charge by lancers? The same argument was used by those who wanted to keep the infantry in red pants. They advanced the proposition that the sense of belonging was the essence of group spirit, and group spirit in turn was the touchstone of the will to fight, the ingredient that won battles. They added the corollary that nothing gave units the sense of oneness that did red trousers, and that therefore camouflaged material would actually sabotage national security. . . .

So tradition, personal predilection, and misinterpreted past experience kept the cavalry charge alive in Germany. The experience of the British after the Boer War likewise suggests how difficult it is to test the relevance of one's own experience in war.

THE RELEVANCE OF EXPERIENCE

From the end of the Boer War to the beginning of World War I the great debate in the British Cavalry, as in other countries, dealt with the retention of the lance and the charge. The arguments put forward for their retention inevitably raise the question of whether faith was not interfering with reason. . . .

A U.S. Cavalry officer noted on a trip to Aldershot in 1903 that "Every change is made entirely with reference to the Boer War and the Boer country, as though future wars would be fought under the same conditions."[3] But what this observer should also have noted was that there was a wide division of opinion as to just what that war proved, and how genuinely relevant it really was. . . .

Like other modern wars the Boer War was made up of a series of actions no one of which was decisive. The Boers, fine shots and fine horsemen, used their horses as transportation. In effect they fought as mounted infantry, employing the mobility of the horse in combination with the aimed firepower of infantry. They possessed all the advantages of great space and a friendly and embattled popula-

[3] Frank R. McCoy, "Notes of the German Maneuvers," *JUSCA*, Vol. 14, No. 49, January 1904, pp. 30, 31.

tion, and the British were hard put to it to bring them to terms. But these were virtually the only points on which there was any agreement whatsoever. What did the facts mean, if anything?

Two of Great Britain's best known military figures, Lord Roberts, the British Chief of Staff, and Field-Marshal Sir John D. P. French, Cavalry Commander in Africa and, in 1914, Commander-in-Chief of the British Expeditionary Forces, led two factions within the army whose views of the future of cavalry were in direct opposition.

The Right Honorable Field-Marshal Earl Roberts placed the *imprimatur* of his authority on a book called *War and the Arme Blanche* by one Erskine Childers. In his introduction to this book Lord Roberts set forth his basic beliefs. . . . Lord Roberts believed simply that the "main lesson" to be learned from the Boer War and the Russo-Japanese War was that "knee to knee, close order charging is practically a thing of the past." He qualified his opinion somewhat. "There may be, there probably will be, mounted attacks, preferably in open order against Cavalry caught unawares, or against broken Infantry," he wrote. But even these mounted attacks, he said, should be carried out with the rifle, rather than with steel.[4] These ideas he actually wrote into the British regulations, *Cavalry Training*, in 1904.

. . . The general argument, as one can imagine, was first that lances and sabers were not killing men in war, and, second, that infantry and mounted infantry were killing, when dismounted, cavalrymen. Three wars, the U.S. Civil War, the Boer War, and the Russo-Japanese War, were cited as proof of the contention. In retrospect this point of view hardly needs explanation. It seems quite obvious to think that the armaments which took the warrior off his feet and put him on his belly would by the same token take him off his charger and put him on the ground.

For a time Lord Roberts was Commander-in-Chief of the British Army, and his views were thus imposed for a brief moment on the generals. What this meant in effect was that the lance disappeared in Britain between 1903 and 1906. But Lord Roberts proved unpopular, and as is the way with unpopular leaders, he was eased gently out of office in quite short order, to become a disturbing shadow amongst their eminences in the House of Lords. And the lance came back into use in 1906 to remain for better than two decades — until 1927, to be precise.

Sir John French, an officer whom one of the most distinguished

---

[4] Erskine Childers, *War and the Arme Blanche* (London, 1910). With an introduction by the Right Hon. Field-Marshal Earl Roberts, V.C., K.G., p. xii.

of Great Britain's War Secretaries, Lord Haldane, called "a real soldier of the modern type"[5] was an old Hussar. He had entered the army through the Militia and had thus avoided Sandhurst and the mental training this would have involved. For Sir John the experience of the Boer War was disturbing only because a number of his colleagues had been disturbed by it. As he thought over this experience, his final assessment as of the very eve of World War I was that "It passes comprehension that some critics in England should gravely assure us that the war in South Africa should be our chief source of inspiration and guidance, and that it was not normal."[6]

The Field-Marshal's reasoning was very simple. First, he said, "The composition and tactics of the Boer forces were as dissimilar from those of European armies as possible," and he added that "Such tactics in Europe would lead to the disruption and disbandment of any army that attempted them."[7] Second, he noted that in South Africa both unlimited space and the objective of complete submission of the enemy made it a most unusual war. Third, he maintained that the British had not at the time developed proper means for remounting the cavalry with trained horses. But to say this is really to say nothing at all. It is only by uncovering Sir John's basic premises that there is really any possibility of understanding his view of his own experience.

Perhaps Sir John summarized his own thinking best when he wrote sometime during the course of 1908 that "The Boers did all that could be expected of Mounted Infantry, but were powerless to crown victory as only the dash of Cavalry can do."[8] It was the "dash of Cavalry" of which Sir John was thinking. There is ample evidence to document the point. If cold steel were thrown away as "useless lumber," he wrote, ". . . we should invert the role of cavalry, turn it into a defensive arm, and make it a prey to the first foreign cavalry that it meets, for good cavalry can always compel a dismounted force of mounted riflemen to mount and ride away, and when such riflemen are caught on their horses they have power neither of offence nor of defence and are lost."[9] Based on this analysis of the effect of rapid fire on mounted cavalry action, he deduced that the proper role of cavalry was first to fight the battlefield's greatest

---

[5] Richard Burdon Haldane, *An Autobiography* (London, 1929), p. 295.

[6] General Friedrich von Bernhardi, *Cavalry* (New York, 1914), with a preface by Field-Marshal Sir J. D. P. French, p. 9.

[7] *Ibid.*, p. 9.

[8] From his introduction to the English edition of Lt. Gen. Friedrich von Bernhardi, *Cavalry in Future Wars* (London, 1909), p. x.

[9] Bernhardi, *Cavalry, op. cit.*, p. 11.

threat, i.e., the enemy cavalry. "The successful cavalry fight confers upon the victor command of the ground."[10] This, he said, was a job for cold steel. Only when the enemy cavalry was out of action did he think that the cavalry would rely more on the rifle than on steel — which is not to say that he ruled "out as impossible, or even unlikely, attacks by great bodies of mounted men against other arms on the battlefield."[11]

So it was that Sir John and his followers decided that the experience of recent wars was irrelevant. The Boer War was not relevant because it had not been fought in Europe and because the Boers had not been armed with steel as were cavalries in Europe. The war in Manchuria between the Russians and the Japanese was irrelevant not only because it had not been fought in Europe, but also because the cavalry used there had been badly mounted, rode indifferently, and, above all, were poorly trained, i.e., in dismounted principles. "They were," wrote Sir John, "devoid of real Cavalry training, they thought of nothing but of getting off their horses and shooting. . . ."[12] From one principle, note, Sir John never deviated: *Unless the enemy cavalry was defeated, the cavalry could not carry out its other responsibilities.* And there was a corollary of this, to wit: *"Only cavalry can defeat cavalry,"* cavalry being defined of course as "a body of horsemen armed with steel."

Sir John, however wrong he may have been in his estimate of the firepower revolution of his day, made one point of real consequence when he insisted that the cavalry should keep its mind on a war likely to be fought — which a war in Manchuria, the United States, or South Africa was not. To talk about wars which are likely seems eminently sensible, although there are times when the unlikely ones are given rather more attention than they warrant depending on what set of premises are in search of some wider acceptance. To cite a recent example, the war in Korea in 1950–1952 provided what seemed to the U.S. Air Force to be irrelevant experience because bombers were not effectively used. To the U.S. Navy and Marine Corps, on the other hand, it seemed very relevant indeed because Korea was a peninsula admirably suited to the projection of naval power. To the U.S. Army it presented a whole new way of thinking: that limited war involving ground troops might well be the way of the future despite and because of the horrors of nuclear exchange.

[10] *Ibid.*, p. 13.
[11] *Ibid.*, p. 15. See also A. P. Ryan, *Mutiny at the Curragh* (London, 1956), pp. 97–100 for a further elaboration of Sir John's views.
[12] Bernhardi, *Cavalry in Future Wars, op. cit.* p. xxiii.

THE LIMITS OF A WEAPONS SYSTEM EVALUATION

But even if history in terms of recent war experience seemed irrelevant for one reason or another to the problem of the charge, it is
hard to believe that war is a science so limited that means could not
be found to test in practice the effectiveness of the charge, that a
conclusive study could not be made of charges made in a variety of
patterns, in different formations, and with different weapons
against simulated "enemy formations." But the simple truth is that
nothing is more difficult to test than a weapon's effectiveness. . . .

There is a grievously large number of intellectual stumbling
blocks in first setting up and then later evaluating any test experience. For example, during the summer of 1936[13] the U.S. Infantry
maneuvered against the U.S. Cavalry at Fort Benning, Georgia. As
the problem started, the cavalry rode and the infantry trucked to
the given maneuver area. The motor vehicles being rather faster
than the horses the infantry had ample time to get into position first.
This proved a most frightening advantage. The infantry, well
camouflaged, waited with some excitement while the cavalry were
allowed to pass concealed forward infantry units. Only when the
advance units of cavalry hit the main units of infantry did the infantry's stratagem become apparent. It was at that moment that the
infantrymen rose shouting from entrenched positions waving bed
sheets. The horses thought their Day of Judgment had arrived as
ghosts rose over the battlefield, and what followed is best left to the
imagination.

To infantrymen the maneuver proved conclusively that trucks
gave the infantry a mobility with which the cavalry could not hope
to compete and that when minus multicolored uniforms and not
drawn up in drill formation, the infantry made unsatisfactory cavalry targets. Yet to the cavalrymen — and this raised a furor that
still stays in men's minds — the whole exercise only proved that
infantrymen were practical jokers. The problem, that is to say, of
"proving out" doctrine in the field of maneuver is distressingly
difficult.

Essentially the problem lies in one's estimate of that appalling
obscurity, "the nature of man." The cavalryman knows, as he
charges "the enemy designate," that if this were really the enemy,
he would be quite too frightened to fire accurately. And he knows
this because it is part of a credo without which he would never be
induced to charge in the first place. Therefore the "effect of fire"
becomes a subjective instead of an objective judgement, mitigated

[13] The story is from eye-witness reports and there is a date problem.

by one's belief in a concatenation of other effects — of surprise, of fear, of the use of the defilade. So while all will call for more realism in testing, getting a consensus as to what "realism" is, more frequently than not, quite outside the realm of possibility.

FACTORS IN INSTITUTIONAL SURVIVAL

The role of history. On the morrow of victory after World War I, a member of the House of Commons rose to criticize the Secretary of War, Mr. Winston Churchill. He noted that the cavalry was at "practically the same figure as before the war, and yet if I should have thought anything had been proved by the War, it was that cavalry was less useful (than) we had previously thought it was going to be."[14]

Shortly thereafter, in 1930 to be precise, there appeared a history of the French Cavalry in the World War by a Professor of Tactics at l'École Militaire et d'Application du Génie, a most prolific writer by the name of Capitaine F. Gazin. The next to the last paragraph reads as follows:

> Today, really more than yesterday, if the cavalry is to have power and flexibility, following along with technical progress, it must have horses with better blood lines, cadres filled with burning faith, and above all well trained troops conscious of the heavy weight of past glory.[15]

There would seem to be no reasonable doubt but that in the minds of the doughboy, the *poilu* or Tommy Atkins, the day of the horse was over. The cavalryman had been called a number of things during the war, "Pigsticker," the "Rocking Horseman," etc., which indicated what the infantry thought of his contribution. But to the cavalryman himself the cavalry was not dead, and the history of the Great War was never written really in meaningful terms. To him the role of the horseman in the victory became swollen with the yeast of time. Indeed, in cavalry historiography, the role of the horse in World War I was most emphasized at that moment in time when the cavalry was most threatened in army reorganization plans, between 1934 and 1939.

The cavalry had been used in the First World War. The Germans used it extensively on that last stronghold of the cavalryman, the eastern frontier. The British and French used it extensively in 1914 during the retreat from Le Mans during late August and early September. Indeed the largest item of export from Great Britain to

[14] *125 H.C. Deb.* 25, pp. 1366 ff.

[15] F. Gazin, *La Cavalerie dans la Guerre Mondiale* (Paris, 1930), p. 325.

its forces on the Continent for the war as a whole was horse fodder.
. . . For the most part the cavalry fought dismounted, but it did
fight mounted as well. It did charge machine guns. In one case the
Canadians charged a group of German machine guns, and came
out unscathed, so great was the surprise achieved when the horsemen charged, blades bared. And it was used mounted as late as
1918. Indeed this claim has been made for its work at that time —
by a cavalryman: "It may or may not be true to say that we (the
allies) should have defeated the Germans just the same in the
autumn of 1918, even without our cavalry. But it is certainly true
that, had it not been for that same cavalry, there would have been
no autumn advance at all for the Germans would have defeated us
in the spring."[16]

But the campaign which did more to save the horse cavalry than
any other was not fought in Europe at all. It was fought on the
sands of Palestine, at Gaza, at Beersheba, at Jerusalem, and it was
fought in part, and indeed in large part, with the lance. It was as
dashingly romantic as anything that happened during that singularly drab war, and strong drink it was to the cavalry. In a sense, it
kept the cavalry going for another quarter century. There was irony
in this for the most eager of the cavalrymen, men of the stamp of
Sir John French, had for a decade defended the cavalry regulations
on the basis of the forecast of their utility for the big war on the
continent, only to have the cavalry successfully used only on the
periphery of the great battlefields.

So experience, that most revered of teachers, continued to couch
the "lessons" of war in a certain studied ambiguity. The horse retained that place in warfare which it had had for a thousand years
— in the minds of its military riders.

Mission justification for the future, 1920–1940. On the eve of
World War II the General Officers of the U.S. Army were, next to
those of Poland, Rumania and possibly the USSR, most convinced
of the continuing utility of the horse. The French had four divisions
of mixed horse and mechanized cavalry. The Germans had a debated number of horses and mechanized cavalry, for use largely as
reconnaissance. The British were converting from oats to oil as
rapidly as possible.

A number of problems immediately present themselves. A first
very general question must be asked of the cavalrymen themselves:
What did they consider their mission to be in the period between
1920 and roughly 1935 when the development of both plane and

[16] Lt. Col. T. Preston, "Cavalry in France," *Cavalry Journal* (British),
No. 26 (1936), p. 19.

tank had reached the stage at which their future development could be foreseen with some clarity, and at which therefore some reasonable readjustment of forces to the fact of their existence could be expected? How can one account for those great differences in thinking between the responsible staffs of the larger nations during the years between 1935 and the outbreak of war in 1939? . . .

The basic argument of the cavalrymen in their journals and in their manuals in the period between the great wars was an absolutely sound one. They argued in essence that new weapons obviated only those with like characteristics. They argued that while a better tank scrapped a worse one, the tank as a weapons system could not replace the horse until such time as it could perform all the missions of a horse. Whether these missions were worthwhile was seldom considered.

Many of the arguments which cavalrymen of all nations advanced to substantiate their claims as to their future role in war will be recognized by any student of recent military history as a version of what one can only describe as standardized clap-trap. One was the argument that, since most of the world was roadless, "To base our transportation needs solely upon conditions existent in the comparatively tiny proportion of the earth's surface containing roads . . . is putting too many eggs in the same basket."[17] This will be recognized as a cavalry variant on the navy contention that "since the world is 60 per cent water . . .," and the air contention that "since air surrounds the earth and the shortest distance between two points. . . ." Another argument familiar to all military historians came up again and again in the journals. This one was to the effect that mechanical aids and auxiliaries end by neutralizing each other, an argument which in its most outrageous form had the anti-tank weapon returning the battlefield to the horse.[18] "It is quite within the bounds of possibility that an infantry anti-tank weapon may be produced which will make tanks useless as weapons of attack," wrote one enthusiast[19] in a vein not unlike that used by airmen against seamen at roughly the same moment in time. The difficulty of supplying tanks was brought up as the supply problem is brought up as a limitation on each new weapons system.[20] And, of course, the essentially experimental nature of tanks

[17] Major Malcolm Wheeler-Nicholson, *Modern Cavalry* (New York, 1922), p. vii.

[18] Anonymous, "Oil and Oats," *Cavalry Journal* (British), Vol. 28, No. 107, Jan. 1938, p. 31; Col. Sir Hereward Wake, "The Infantry Anti-Tank Weapon," *Army Quarterly*, Vol. 17, No. 2, Jan. 1929.

[19] Wake, *op. cit.*, p. 349.

[20] Lt. F. A. S. Clark, "Some Further Problems of Mechanical Warfare," *Army Quarterly*, Vol. 6, No. 2, July 1923, p. 379.

— "as yet untried" is the term — raised its head perennially and everywhere.

But there were other problems and more serious ones. If the tank could be made to replace the cavalry on the charge, did that mean that the tank could take over all the other cavalry missions: reconnaissance, raids, flank protection in rough country? Could the plane be made to supplement the tank in such a way that the two used in combination could effectuate a complete substitution for the horse? Or would some kind of combination of horse and tank, and plane and tank be a future necessity? And if this were so with whom would the control lie, with tankmen or horsemen or pilots? And finally if this was a problem of phasing out the horse, what factors should govern the timing of this phasing?

These questions do not seem to have been asked with any precision largely perhaps because they edged too closely on the emotion-packed matter of prestige, on the one hand, and on an essentially insoluble organizational problem on the other. Naturally armor wanted maximum independence as do those who service and fire any weapon. The tankman wanted a command of his own, just as the machinegunner wanted his own battalion, the artillery its own regiment, the horse cavalry its own division and the airman his own service. And this is logical for in a decentralized structure growth is faster as imagination is given a freer rein. But the difficulty is that, war being all of one cloth, each weapon component also wishes to control elements of the others. And this is why the sparks flew between arms in the period between the World Wars, and before the First and after the Second. Where, as in Germany and Great Britain, armor was given its independence, it thrived. Where, as in the United States and Poland, the Cavalry (Horse) remained in control, tank doctrine never grew roots. But where, as in France, mechanized and horse were joined together in what at first blush seemed to be a happy marriage, a unity was forced which was pitifully inadequate from every standpoint.

For the man on the horse there was much greater difficulty in understanding the tank than in understanding the rapid fire weapon. Perhaps this could be expected since tank and horse were competitors for the same missions. Certainly the limpid eye and high spirit of the one and the crass impersonal power of the other was enough to render partisans of the one quite helpless when it came to understanding the military views of the other, quite as helpless indeed as the seabased fighter is to understand the landbased or the airbased and their view of world geography.

Practicality and the concept of the balanced force. One finds the horse cavalryman making the same points over and over again. He stressed the tanks' need for spare parts, without taking into consideration that one of the greatest difficulties of the cavalry was that horses do not have spare parts. He stressed the lack of mobility of the tank along mountain trails without mention of the appalling problem of getting horses overseas — they have a tendency to pneumonia, together with a soft breast which becomes raw and infected with the roll and pitch of the ship. Whereas the point was occasionally made that the Lord took care of the resupply of horses — i.e., that while factories could be bombed out, sex could not — no mention was ever made that in wartime as in peace He still took four or five years to produce each animal. And, finally, although the horse was claimed to have certain immunities to gas warfare, the peculiar problems of getting gas masks on the poor beasts were omitted.

Yet whether partisans were ankle deep in the sands of prejudice or not, there were certain aspects of the relationship between horses and planes, and horses and tanks which were so obvious that they could hardly be missed. However low and slow it flew, the plane would not be a substitute for a still lower and still slower man on a horse. And the plane could not penetrate forests and neither, within limits, could tanks. So there was, and indeed there still is, a gap between what the horse can do and what the plane and the tank can do. But admitting the gap, there still remained the most vexing problem of all, to wit whether that gap was worth filling and if so how. And this was something which each general staff decided somewhat differently and for itself.

The U.S. Cavalry was, in retrospect, as retrogressive in 1940 as it had been progressive in the years before World War I. It had never crossed the sea during World War I due to transportation difficulties, and spent its war chasing Mexicans. But it shared every confidence that its future role would be everything that it had not been in the recent past. As of 1940 it labored under the most embarrassing of illusions. The U.S. Cavalry believed that it had modernized itself. And it defended its horse cavalry on the sacred ground of "balanced force." "Each arm has powers and limitations," explained Major General John K. Herr, Chief of Cavalry, before the Subcommittee on Military Affairs of the House Committee on Appropriations on March 11, 1940, "The proper combination is that which arranges the whole so that the powers of each offset the limitations of the others." It was because the Poles did not have that balance that they were, said General Herr, overrun by the Germans.

> Judging from Spain, had Poland's cavalry possessed modern armament in every respect and been united in one big cavalry command with adequate mechanized forces included, and supported by adequate

aviation, the German light and mechanized forces might have been defeated.

Then General Herr went on to add these words of comfort:

> Mechanized cavalry is valuable and an important adjunct but is not the main part of the cavalry and cannot be. Our cavalry is not the medieval cavalry of popular imagination but is cavalry which is modernized and keeping pace with all developments.[21]

Yet it certainly does not seem that the U.S. cavalry was "keeping pace with all developments." Putting horses in trucks to give them mobility (this was the so-called "portée cavalry"), and adding inadequate anti-tank batteries can hardly be called modernizing. Is there any reasonable explanation for the illusion?

Concepts of modernization. One cannot help but be impressed with the intellectual isolation in which the U.S. armed forces operated in the 1930's. *The Journal of the U.S. Cavalry Association* paid almost no attention to mechanization throughout the period. Compared to the military periodicals on the continent, the U.S. journal seems curiously antiquated. And because there was so little critical thinking going on within the service, it is not surprising that there was virtually no thinking going on in Army ordnance either, for ordnance, after all, works on a demand basis and if there is no demand, there is likely to be no new hardware. In the United States there was in short no intellectual challenge.

Not only were there no pressures to change cavalry thinking from inside the arm, there were no pressures from outside either. United States industry was never anxious to sell to the services during the depression years or before. They were no more willing to put money into military research and development than were the services or the Congress. The few Secretaries of War who can be considered adequate were interested in the managerial aspects of their office and not in matters which they considered "purely military." And finally there was a not inconsiderable pressure for the *status quo* in the Congress. The U.S. had some ten millions of horses, and government spending in this direction, little though it was, was a chief source of revenue to all the many horse breeders, hay growers, and saddlemakers.

In Great Britain, the situation was markedly different. Although the British had their branch journals, — the tankers founded their own in 1937 — they also had one great advantage in having two journals which were more generally read. The first was the *Army*

---

[21] The text of General Herr's testimony before Congress may be found reprinted in *JUSCA,* Vol. 49, No. 3, May-June 1940. See p. 206. . . .

Quarterly which published on all topics of concern to the army as a whole, and the other was *The Journal of the Royal United Service Institution* which crossed service lines. Into these journals there poured articles from a singularly able, and remarkably prolific and dedicated group of publicists of whom J. F. C. Fuller and Captain Basil H. Liddell Hart are simply the best known. Officers in the British Empire were simply unable to escape, as were U.S. officers, from challenge. Thus from 1936 onwards there was an increasingly strong movement in favor of conversion to oil. Furthermore this was helped rather than hindered by the stand taken by many in Parliament. For Parliament was at least conscious of *The Times* military correspondent, Liddell Hart, and the battle he was waging for mechanized warfare, a form of warfare which would, so he thought, limit and shorten future wars by making them more rapid, hence shorter and cheaper than the war of the trenches. To be sure there were those who, like Admiral of the Fleet Sir Roger Keyes, took a position against the reduction of cavalry. But they were in the minority. Most felt that the Household Cavalry and two mounted regiments still left in Egypt in 1939 were probably two too many. . . .

After World War II the French, as is the wont of democracies, held an inquiry into the military disasters of some five years before. But the questions which were put to the generals and the questions which they wanted to answer were all in terms of why they had not understood and appreciated the role of the tank and the plane. Never does the question seem to have been asked in the converse, i.e., why was the horse thought to have been so useful circa 1939? It would have been interesting to know too what thinking had been done as to the circumstances under which Cavalry divisions, offensive forces, were to be used in conjunction with the Maginot Line, a defensive ideal. Perhaps they were to have been used in the second phase of the struggle in a counter-offensive after the enemy had partially defeated himself by throwing his troops against the defensive fires of the Line. . . .

However the overall development of French cavalry thinking between the wars is plain enough. What they did was to absorb the new machines of war into old doctrine. Instead of allowing the characteristics of new weapons to create new doctrine, the French General Staff simply gave them missions to fulfill that were within the old framework. Thus tanks were made subordinate and supporting weapons to the infantry, and subordinate and supporting weapons to the cavalry. In a sense the French achieved what General Herr of the U.S. Cavalry wanted to achieve, except that the French did look forward to complete mechanization at some future date, which Herr did not. And the *Revue de Cavalerie,* a strange hodge-podge of oats, history and oil, reflects this point of view.

The German experience was somewhat different again. Whereas the French looked back to the stalemate at Verdun, the great achievement of defensive weapons, the Germans looked back to the great offensives of 1918 and to the very near miss of the Schlieffen plan in 1914. Particularly in the case of the younger officers the great objective was regaining the lost means of offensive. A defeated army, the Germans were in a position to start once more from the beginning. To be sure there was a very difficult period of struggle with German horse cavalrymen, but those in Germany with an interest in tanks had an advantage which those in the democracies did not. They had the interest of the Chief of State. When Hitler saw Panzer units in action, he said repeatedly, "That's what I need! That's what I want to have!"[22] To Hitler they were the keystone in a concept of total war.

The *Revue de Cavalerie* stopped publication during the war and never appeared again. The British *Cavalry Journal* disappeared forever as well. Only the *Journal of the U.S. Cavalry Association* continued to appear. Its heroes were the horse-drawn artillery which landed on Guadalcanal, the animals flown over the Burma "Hump" into China, the U.S. units which were remounted on Italian Cavalry horses in Italy and German horses in Germany; the great heroes were the only real cavalry left — the Cossacks. Duly noted was how greatly needed were horse cavalry during the battles in Normandy and elsewhere.

In his closing chapter of *He's in the Cavalry Now,* Brig. Gen. Rufus S. Ramey, a former commander of the U.S. Cavalry School, concluded in 1944, "Currently we are organizing and training adequate mechanized horse cavalry for field employment."[23] His was the final testament. The last old Army mule, except for the West Point Mascot, was retired in 1956. The horse cavalry had been disbanded five years before.

New Item. In 1956 the Belgian General Staff suggested that for the kind of dispersed war which low yield atomic weapons necessarily create, the horse, which in Europe could be independent of depots, should be reintroduced into the weapons system.[24]

---

[22] General Heinz Guderian, *Panzer Leader* (New York, 1952), p. 30.

[23] Brig. Gen. Rufus S. Ramey, *He's in the Cavalry Now* (New York, 1944), p. 190. There were 60,170 animals in the U.S. Forces on December 31, 1943.

[24] "Belgians Hit U.S. Concept of Atomic War," *Christian Science Monitor,* August 25, 1956.

CONCLUSION

The military profession, dealing as it does with life and death, should be utterly realistic, ruthless in discarding the old for the new, forward-thinking in the adoption of new means of violence. But equally needed is a romanticism which, while perhaps stultifying realistic thought, gives a man that belief in the value of the weapons system he is operating that is so necessary to his willingness to use it in battle. Whether a man rides a horse, a plane or a battleship into war, he cannot be expected to operate without faith in his weapons system. But faith breeds distrust of change. Furthermore there is need for discipline, for hierarchy, for standardization within the military structure. These things create pressures for conformity, and conformity too is the enemy of change. Nor is there generally the pressure for the adoption of the new that is found in other walks of life. There is no profit motive, and the challenge of actual practice, in the ultimate sense of war, is very intermittent. Finally, change is expensive, and some part of the civilian population has to agree that the change is worth the expense before it can take place. What factors then make for change in situations short of war?

Surely the greatest instigation of new weapons development has in the past come from civilian interest plus industrial pressure. The civilian governors get the weapons system *they* want. Hitler gets his tanks, the French public their line of forts. When society shows an interest in things military, weapons are adopted — apparently in great part because of the appeal they make to a set of social values and economic necessities. The abolition of the horse cavalry came about first in those countries which could not afford to raise the horses and in which there were those with a hungry intellectual interest in the ways of war. When there was no interest in the military, as in the United States, there was no pressure to change and the professional was given tacit leave to romanticize an untenable situation. Thus the U.S. Horse Cavalry remained a sort of monument to public irresponsibility in this, the most mechanized nation on earth.

The U-Boat Campaign

ERNEST R. MAY

Far more important than the rebuff to Wilson's mediation hopes was the German decision to open a submarine campaign against merchant shipping. Other acts might have aroused moral disapproval by the United States, but little else could have generated a genuine antagonism. There were no American interests within reach of German land forces. The one method by which Germany could stir the United States to threaten war was by ordering submarines to attack neutral ships and belligerent passenger carriers. Yet the German government chose to issue such an order.

Unlike the decision to reject mediation, this action was only partly a product of necessity. It came about almost accidentally. Submarines achieved surprise successes at a time when no other German forces were making news. Certain naval officers elected to champion wider use of the weapon, deliberately stirring public hopes. Since other officials failed to look deeply enough into the implications of these proposals, the publicity was allowed to run unchecked. As a result of its success, coupled with the relative absence of reflective opposition, a decision in favor of a submarine campaign was taken almost in a fit of absence of mind.

The process that led to this decision commenced in September, 1914. Early in the month a submarine chanced upon the British cruiser *Pathfinder* and sank her.[1] In the latter part of the month, a combination of bad weather and administrative inefficiency in the British Admiralty threw three more cruisers into the path of a U-boat. The aged vessels *Cressy, Hogue,* and *Aboukir Bay* were torpedoed off the Broad Fourteens by the small, slow U-9, a gasoline-burning submarine already considered obsolete.

One consequence of these accidental successes was an arousal in

Reprinted by permission of the publishers from Ernest R. May, *The World War and American Isolation, 1914–1917,* Cambridge, Mass.: Harvard University Press, pp. 113–136. Copyright 1959 by the President and Fellows of Harvard College. Some footnotes have been omitted.

[1] Vice Admiral Eberhard von Mantey (ed.), *Der Krieg zur See herausgegeben vom Marine-archiv:* Capt. Otto Groos, *Der Krieg in der Nordsee* (5 vols.; Berlin, 1920–1925), I, 7.

the navy of enthusiasm for wider use of U-boats. Theretofore the vessels had been regarded as experimental and, at most, as auxiliary arms of the fleet. Hardly anyone had conceived of the U-boat as an independent weapon operating against enemy commerce. After the September exploits, this novel idea began to spread through the fleet. *Tirpitz** and various officers in the Navy Ministry became interested. By early November the Chief of the Naval Staff had decided to urge such a course upon the Chancellor† and the Emperor.‡ By the turn of the year nearly all the higher ranks of the navy had become engaged in energetic agitation for a U-boat campaign.

It is easy to understand this emergent enthusiasm. The navy had been useless in the early stages of the war. The High Seas Fleet had stood inactive while Britain cleared the oceans and established her dominance over the North Sea. While the army struggled to preserve and increase the Fatherland, the navy remained merely decorative, and its officers felt wounded not only in pride but also in hope. "If we come to the end . . . without the fleet having bled and worked," wrote Tirpitz, "we shall get nothing more for the fleet, and all the scanty money that there may be will be spent on the army. The great efforts of His Majesty the Emperor to make Germany a naval power will have been all in vain."[2] The September triumphs awakened hopes that the navy might be able, after all, to help win the war.

How these natural feelings overcame the judgment of so many officers is somewhat harder to understand. The U-boats available for operations in the North Sea area were but twenty-one in number. Twelve of these were slow, gasoline-powered, and capable of operating only in the Channel region. Only nine were diesel craft that could reach England's western coasts, and the largest carried but ten torpedoes. In view of the quantity of British shipping, it required considerable imagination to envision a successful blockade. The only prewar estimate, indeed, called for a force of two hundred and twenty-one submarines equipped with devices not yet designed. Some officers remained aware of the discrepancy between the idea and the means available to execute it.

But the majority submerged their doubts. Neutral shipowners, they reasoned, would be frightened away from English ports. If the campaign were masked as retaliation against British interference

---

*[*Editors' note:* Grand Admiral Alfred von Tirpitz, Minister of the Navy.]

†[*Editors' note:* Theobald von Bethmann Hollweg.]

‡[*Editors' note:* Kaiser Wilhelm II.]

[2] Tirpitz to Pohl, Sept. 6, 1914, in Alfred von Tirpitz, *Politische Dokumente* (2 vols.; Berlin, 1926), II, 105.

with trade, neutral governments might even cooperate in the blockade. A few sinkings would meanwhile strike such terror into English
shippers as to halt sailings. Many officers relied on a hypothetical
account, printed before the war, of England's strangulation by a
handful of submarines. This confidence-inspiring estimate had appeared in *The Strand* magazine over the name of Sir Arthur Conan
Doyle. When an admiral was asked after the war to explain the
Naval Staff miscalculations, he indicated blushingly that the navy
had put too much faith in Sherlock Holmes.

From this irrational enthusiasm in the navy grew a public cry for
the opening of a submarine campaign against British commerce.
The idea was thrown dramatically into the public arena by Tirpitz.
In an interview with an American journalist, Karl von Wiegand,
the Grand Admiral declared, "England wants to starve us. We can
play the same game. We can bottle her up and destroy every ship
that endeavors to break the blockade." When asked if Germany had
enough U-boats, he replied vehemently and misleadingly, "Yes, we
are superior to England in submarines of the larger types."[3] Published in late December, this interview attracted wide notice. The
idea of striking England's vitals with the U-boat weapon had received the authoritative imprimatur of the navy's elder statesman.

The seed dropped by Tirpitz rooted in fallow ground. It is unlikely that the desperate frustration of the government was widely
shared. Few knew the extent to which operations in the west had
failed. Official reports had so disguised the importance of the Marne
engagements that they had passed almost unnoticed. The clamor
aroused by Tirpitz's interview was probably not spontaneous; the
newspapers that most strongly supported his plan were those most
closely identified with the Navy Ministry. But a feeling must have
been growing that moated England was responsible for the war's
prolongation. There was thus a favorable atmosphere for a secret
weapon delusion.

The Grand Admiral's proposal soon found support among party
leaders. It appealed to the Anglophobia of the right. Offering also
a promise of swift triumph, it fitted in with annexationist dreams.
When the government seemed to delay adopting the proposal,
vexation developed. Even Erzberger, the left Centrist, published a
pamphlet, *No Sentimentality*, calling for immediate institution of
a ruthless submarine blockade. When Bethmann visited Berlin, he
found deputies accusing him of pro-British leanings. And not even
the left socialists opposed this clamor. By the spring of 1915, there

[3] Text in *Politische Dokumente*, II, 623–627. . . .

seemed to have risen a U-boat fervor comparable to the annexationist passion.

The government was not so powerless before this movement as it
was before the annexationist fever. The Foreign Ministry had an
opportunity to kill the Tirpitz interview, which it blunderingly failed
to seize. The text was sent to the Ministry for censorship. When the
responsible officer, Count Mumm, read it through, he received the
impression that Wiegand had already cabled it to America. It had,
in fact, gone in a diplomatic pouch, and its publication could still
have been stopped. But Mumm assumed that it would be printed
overseas and therefore could not be kept from German editors. After
telling Zimmermann about it, he authorized its release to the press.

Even after the interview's publication, there remained some
chance of cooling public enthusiasm. The truth about Germany's
limited capabilities could have been spread before party leaders as
it was later. But Bethmann and his associates did not oppose the
movement, partly from mistaken information, partly from irresolution, but largely from simple failure to foresee its consequences.

Chance played a part, too, in the ultimate approval of the blockade plan, but Bethmann was alerted by this time to the need for
careful calculation. Every political aspect of the proposal was sur-
veyed, at least superficially, in the Foreign Ministry and the
Chancellery. On various grounds Bethmann postponed its adoption.

He was concerned, first of all, about possible effects on neutrals,
especially those of southern Europe. Should a submarine campaign
pit Germany against all neutrals, Italy and the entire Balkan peninsula might fall into the Allied camp. Since the army General Staff
held that Germany could not stand such an addition to the number
of her enemies, this possibility threw a dark shadow over the Chancellor's thoughts on U-boat warfare.

The United States was secondary in his thinking. Bernstorff* and
his aides had faithfully reported America's strong sympathy for
the Allies. They had also made clear her dedication to profitable
trade. From Wilson's legalistic pronouncements against interference with business, Bethmann might foresee an American outcry
against a submarine decree, but he had little reason to fear war.
"President Wilson said to me," wrote Bernstorff in his first personal
report to Bethmann. " 'We must be absolutely neutral, because otherwise our mixed population would fall into another war.' "[4] The am-

---

*[Editors' note: J. H. Bernstorff, German Ambassador to the United
States.]

[4] Bernstorff to Bethmann, Sept. 6, 1914, German Foreign Ministry
Archives (Outbreak and Mediation).

bassador stressed time and again America's consuming desire for peace, and he reported continual though slight improvement in America's attitude toward Germany, crediting the improvement to fear of Japan, to Britain's heavy-handed censorship, to the mine war zone decree, and to the achievements of German arms: " 'Nothing succeeds like success' is still a fundamental principle of Americans, and he who has success will always find friends." Receiving this report in late December, Bethmann read it carefully and underlined sections. It suggested that a successful blockade of Britain might turn American sympathies toward Germany. But the United States remained a question mark.

Rendering his preliminary verdict on the blockade plan, Bethmann gave more weight to uncertainty about the neutrals than to arguments advanced by the admirals. Shortly after receiving the first recommendation from Admiral Hugo von Pohl, the Chief of the Naval Staff, he asked the Foreign Ministry for an estimate of neutral reactions and received a further warning that the small neutrals, Italy, and the United States were all unpredictable. The submarine blockade should be instituted, he was advised, only if the military situation were so favorable as to make it folly for any neutral to take the Allied side. Answering Pohl, the Chancellor gave due regard to this advice. Though conceding the desirability of striking England with any and all weapons, he detailed the possible political consequences. Italy and Rumania might declare war, and all the European neutrals might halt exports to Germany. "Although America, because of its lack of military forces, can hardly declare war on us," the Chancellor stated, "still it is capable of proclaiming a trade boycott against us, like that of England, as well as pushing forward, to some extent officially, the export of war material to our enemies." American antipathy toward Japan would no longer hinder the Allies from bringing Japanese troops to Europe, and the United States might join the campaign to destroy German commerce. "The thoughts of the Foreign Office," Bethmann assured Pohl, "are not of a legalistic nature, but they result from considerations of military-political opportunity. The question is not *if*, but *when* the measure may be taken without harm to our situation. . . . This moment seems today still not to have arrived."[5]

Bethmann clung to these doubts throughout most of January. Arguing the question before the Kaiser on January 9, Bethmann presented his case "very aptly and calmly." Although Pohl contested each of the Chancellor's reservations, he failed to overcome them.

[5] Memo by Bethmann, Dec. 27, 1914, *Politische Dokumente*, II, 292–295.

The Kaiser ruled, "U-boat commerce war shall for the time being be postponed, until the present uncertainty of the political situation has cleared. Then shall the All-Highest be asked anew for a decision. In the meantime the U-boats are to be readied for commerce warfare."[6] Bethmann was not fighting the admirals as he was to do later. He was simply holding them back until a propitious time.

Although the political air failed to clear, Bethmann's doubts began to yield. Italy and the Balkan governments grew steadily less friendly, and it came to seem as if restraint on Germany's part would not, in any case, hold them back from war. The United States meanwhile issued its protest against British interference with trade. Reports from Washington indicated a widening breach between the Allies and the United States. The pro-German Queen of Sweden urged the Kaiser to declare a U-boat blockade, and the Naval Staff passed on intelligence reports indicating passivity, if not enthusiasm, in Norway and the Netherlands.

Pressure on the Chancellor meanwhile grew fierce. It came, first of all, from the Naval Staff. Growing more and more insistent, Pohl proclaimed that the blockade had to come at once. England had only six or seven weeks of food supplies, he declared, but she would soon begin to receive Argentine grain. Once this grain was in her warehouses, England could hold out indefinitely against a blockade. Germany's own food stocks were meanwhile dwindling. The Interior Ministry had grossly overestimated the harvest, making it necessary for the government to ration food. Economists joined with the admirals, therefore, in urging a submarine blockade of Britain, just as Zimmermann and others of the Foreign Office ceased to advise against it. Impressed also with the enthusiasm of the public, Bethmann felt unable to resist any longer.

He capitulated quickly. After conferring with Tirpitz, he met with Pohl, Zimmermann, Falkenhayn, and Interior Minister Clemens von Delbrück. All insisted that the submarine blockade be imposed as soon as possible. Bethmann still worried whether Germany had enough U-boats for the purpose, but Pohl assured him categorically that the fleet was ready. The Chancellor felt concern about Belgium. If American relief shipments were halted, Germany would have to feed the Belgians from her own slender stocks. Delbrück eased his mind on this score, and Bethmann went home from this conference with most of his doubts suppressed. On the following day, February 2, his reservations broke entirely. After a conference with Zimmer-

---

[6] Memo by Müller, Jan. 9, 1915, *ibid.*, pp. 190–192; memo by Hugo von Pohl, Jan. 9, 1915, Pohl, *Aus Aufzeichnungen und Briefen während der Kriegszeit* (Berlin, 1920), 100–101.

mann and the Treasury Minister, Karl Helfferich, he telephoned
Pohl and told him to go ahead and submit to the Kaiser a decree
declaring all the waters around Britain a submarine war zone.

Since Pohl was leaving the Naval Staff to take command of the
High Seas Fleet, he moved quickly to secure the Kaiser's consent.
He wanted the decree to be his last official act. The imminence of
his departure from the Naval Staff had, in all probability, spurred
him during the entire month. It certainly led him to evade routine
in approaching the Emperor, for he did not clear the decree with
Tirpitz as he should have. Nor did he permit the cautious Chief of
the Naval Cabinet to hear of it. At Wilhelmshaven, where the Kaiser
came on February 4 to install Pohl in his new command, the admiral cornered the Emperor in the bow of a motor launch. With
Tirpitz, Müller, and the rest of the imperial entourage sitting in
the after-part of the boat, unable to hear above the motor's roar,
Pohl asked the Kaiser to approve a war zone decree. The Emperor
nodded his consent. Pohl published a notice that day, over his own
signature, and the Foreign Office sent a prearranged dispatch to the
neutral capitals.

The waters around Great Britain and Ireland, declared the Navy
and Foreign Ministries, were to become a war zone on February 18.
Germany "will endeavor to destroy every enemy merchant ship that
is found in this area of war," the dispatch warned, "without its always being possible to avert the peril, that thus threatens persons
and cargoes. Neutrals are therefore warned against further entrust-
ing crews, passengers and wares to such ships." Since English vessels sometimes hid under neutral flags, the warning went on, neutral
ships ought not to enter the war zone. "[T]heir becoming victims of
torpedoes directed against enemy ships cannot always be avoided.
. . . The German Government . . . ," the dispatch concluded,
"may expect that the neutral powers will show no less consideration
for the vital interests of Germany than for those of England and
will aid in keeping their citizens and the property of the latter from
this area. This is the more to be expected, as it must be in the interest of the neutral powers to see this destructive war end as soon
as possible."[7]

The decree of February 4 had been issued without full consideration of possible American reactions. When Wilson denounced it,
the government suddenly realized the danger of drawing America
into the war. Although the admirals expressed willingness to run
this risk, Bethmann disagreed, holding American intervention to be

[7] *Foreign Relations of the United States Supplement: The World War*
(7 Vols.; Washington, D.C., 1928–1932), *1915*, pp. 96–97.

a calamity which Germany should industriously avoid, and there commenced the running battle that was to continue for two years.

The issue arose almost as soon as the decree had been published, for dispatches from all neutral capitals indicated vexation and, in some cases, outrage. The Italian foreign minister spoke gravely to the German ambassador. From Norway, the Netherlands, and Denmark came reports of angry press comment and grim official silence. Bernstorff warned of anger in the United States, cabling "*A mistake could have the most serious consequences.*"[8] Hard on the heels of this message came the American note calling attention "very candidly and earnestly, to the very serious possibilities of the course of action apparently contemplated." Should American ships or lives be lost as a result, the United States "would be constrained to hold the Imperial German Government to a strict accountability."[9] Despite some friendly embroidery, the note had the stiff texture of an ultimatum.

Before Bethmann thus loomed the contingency which he had foreseen but discounted. Recognizing the enormous economic power of the United States, he realized belatedly that her hostility could be the worst of all events for Germany. Italy, the Balkan states, and even the northern neutrals might follow the United States in a declaration of war, and the American protest note sounded like a preface to such a declaration.

He and Jagow at once concluded that the decree had been a mistake and ought to be revoked. With the help of Johannes Kriege, the Foreign Office's legal expert, they hastened to draw up a soothing reply to the American note, designed to reassure Wilson that Germany intended no harm to neutrals and that, if necessary, U-boats would be ordered not even to molest neutral ships carrying contraband. Since danger to American vessels rose solely from Britain's misuse of neutral flags, they also wished to declare, Germany was delighted that America had concurrently protested to London against this practice. If Britain yielded to this demand, they were prepared "to assert conditionally a guarantee that merchant ships sailing under American flags will not be attacked."[10] The Chancellor and Foreign Minister were ready thus to suspend the decree insofar as it affected the United States.

The admirals, however, opposed. Learning somehow of the draft note, the Naval Staff objected with sailorly vigor. To frighten the neutrals was a chief object of the war zone decree, the staff insisted,

[8] Bernstorff to Jagow, Feb. 11, 1915, German Foreign Ministry Archives (U-boat War).

[9] *Foreign Relations, Supplement: 1915*, pp. 98–101.

[10] German Foreign Ministry Archives (U-boat war). . . .

and an exemption for American ships would vitiate the entire plan. "I am of the opinion," wrote Admiral Bachmann, the new Chief of the Naval Staff, "that the assurance asked for by the American government can in no wise be given, for such an assurance makes *absolutely ineffective* the U-boat action ordered." Tirpitz supported him, and so did Pohl, now Chief of the High Seas Fleet. Seeking to protect his earlier accomplishment, Pohl telegraphed: "Respect for the navy will in my opinion suffer terribly, if this loudly publicized undertaking, which has aroused great hope among the people, should be ineffectively carried out. Please present my opinion to His Majesty."[11] With one voice they insisted on ruthless prosecution of the U-boat war.

In view of the gravity of the issue, it seems extraordinary that the admirals should have taken such an uncompromising stand. Pohl, of course, felt some natural pride of sponsorship. Already a dying man, he may not have been entirely sound in mind. Bachmann and Tirpitz, on the other hand, remained healthy, and both confessed to private doubts as to the workability of the whole plan. Although Tirpitz had incited agitation in favor of U-boat warfare, he had advocated a scheme somewhat different from Pohl's, and he had been in favor of postponing operations until sufficient submarines could be built. When Pohl recklessly pushed through his own plan, Tirpitz was so infuriated that he considered resigning. No less disturbed was Bachmann, who thought it almost inconceivable that any real success could be achieved with only twenty-one U-boats. But he and Tirpitz chose, nevertheless, to disguise these doubts and make a resolute defense of Pohl's decree.

Having elected to defend the decree, they felt it necessary to fight against any compromise with the neutrals. Since the twenty-one submarines would not be able to sink many ships, any real reduction in British imports would have to result from fear on the part of shipowners. As soon as the decree was issued, therefore, Tirpitz and Bachmann commenced a drive to terrify neutrals. The Grand Admiral called Gerard into a clandestine meeting where he warned of the terrible danger that American ships would run by entering the war zone.[12] Bachmann brought about the dispatch of a supplementary note to neutral capitals, declaring: "[T]here can be no further assurance for the safety of neutral shipping in the English naval war zone. . . . Neutral vessels must therefore again be *most*

[11] Bachmann to Bethmann, Feb. 14, 1915, *Politische Dokumente*, II, 309–310; Pohl to Bachmann, Feb. 15, 1915, *ibid.*, 311.
[12] James W. Gerard, *My Four Years in Germany* (New York: 1917), pp. 217–218.

earnestly warned against venturing into this area."[13] When Bethmann and Jagow proposed assuring the United States that neutral
ships would not be damaged, the admirals naturally fought against
them.

When the issue was brought before the Kaiser, Wilhelm solicited
the views of Falkenhayn. Colonel Treutler, the Foreign Ministry's
representative at Supreme Headquarters, and Admiral Müller, the
Chief of the Naval Cabinet, were present. Treutler took it upon himself to represent the Chancellor's viewpoint. As he subsequently
reported to Bethmann:

> I declared that a promise of concession in the note was absolutely
> necessary, for no one could give assurance that America would not,
> upon receiving a firm response, have recourse immediately to strong
> measures against us. The stakes in this game are too high for any risk
> to be taken that is not absolutely necessary.
>
> Herr v. Falkenhayn agreed and declared, under all circumstances
> it must be assured that America should not enter the war, so long as
> England is not subdued or else until our position is secure. He pro-
> posed in this connection that the question . . . be placed squarely
> before the Naval Staff, to what degree it would give assurance that
> England could be brought to modify her attitude within about six
> weeks. . . . His Majesty thereupon ordered . . . that the note . . .
> should be sent when and if the Naval Staff, as he could not but take
> for granted, should admit that it could not guarantee such a prompt
> modification on the part of England.[14]

Falkenhayn had thus intervened to support the Chancellor.

The result, nevertheless, was a compromise, for Tirpitz and Bachmann evaded the question. Receiving a telegraphic inquiry from
the Emperor, they put their heads together. They were expected,
obviously, to state that the U-boat could not work its magic within
six weeks. To Tirpitz's suspicious mind, the inquiry seemed a trick.
Bethmann meant to secure a bald admission from the navy, the
Grand Admiral believed, and use it as evidence to support some
timid policy. Tirpitz and Bachmann framed their answer, therefore,
with a view to blocking the Chancellor. "A silly question," remarked
the Grand Admiral's deputy, "deserves a silly answer," and the admirals telegraphed the Kaiser, "Secretary of State and Chief of Naval
Staff are convinced that England will modify attitude within six
weeks of opening of new campaign if all available forces be energetically employed from start." Although the Kaiser noted on the

---

[13] . . . Memo by Foreign Ministry, Feb. 11, 1915, *Foreign Relations,
Supplement: 1915,* pp. 104–105.

[14] Treutler to Bethmann, Feb. 15, 1915, *Politische Dokumente,* II,
313–315.

margin of the telegram, "richly hedged," he directed the Foreign Office to recompose the note to America in collaboration with Tirpitz and the Naval Staff.[15]

Germany's reply to the United States, as a result, blended unassimilated strains. Although asserting the exclusive intention of damaging British commerce, the German government reiterated its earlier warning. Neutral shippers who ventured into the war zone assumed the responsibility for any accidents. Although submarine commanders had been instructed "to abstain from violence to American merchant vessels when they are recognizable as such," still American ships could be safe only if they avoided the war zone or proceeded through it under convoy. Three-fifths of the note exhaled the dusty doubts of the Chancellery and Foreign Office; the remainder snorted with quarterdeck determination.

Hardly had Germany's civilians and admirals put together this note before they faced the same questions once again. A message from the United States suggested a possible compromise between Germany and Britain. In order to protect the interests of neutrals, the German government was to withdraw its decree and refrain from submarine attacks on merchantmen, while the British in return were to suspend orders which prohibited foodstuffs from reaching Germany.

The proposal aroused enthusiasm in the Foreign Office. Distressed by a continuing flow of ominous dispatches from Washington and Rome, Jagow exulted, "It would constitute a moral victory over England's pretended mastery of the sea. In addition we would ensure the provisioning of Germany." For bargaining purposes, the Foreign Minister wished to ask that Britain admit raw materials as well as food and, at the same time, give up the use of neutral flags and the arming of merchantmen. But he was willing to settle for the compromise as proposed and to abandon submarine warfare altogether.

The admirals, of course, opposed such a compromise. In this case, however, they employed somewhat subtler tactics. Instead of attacking the proposal outright, they merely insisted on the addition of impossible conditions. The admission of raw materials as well as food should be demanded, not merely suggested, and Britain should be required to permit idle German merchantmen to take the seas under neutral flags and carry wares to German ports. Differing basically with the Foreign Minister, the admirals contended that Germany would give up an extraordinary advantage if

[15] Alfred von Tirpitz, *My Memoirs* (New York, 1919), Vol. 2, pp. 149–150. . . .

she restricted her U-boat campaign and that the compensation had to be equal to the sacrifice. To Bethmann and Jagow, the sacrifice already seemed bearable.

Once again, naturally, the civilians and admirals had to offer up their quarrel into the irresolute hands of the Kaiser. Bethmann, Jagow, Tirpitz, Bachmann, and Müller gathered with the Emperor at Schloss Bellevue in Berlin. The Chancellor opened the debate by asserting that all the conferees agreed in not wishing simply to reject the American proposal. The admirals, he intimated, had less desire than he to ask a genuine compromise, and their conditions were impossibly high. Arguing the case for a conciliatory answer to America, Bethmann "emphasized the necessity for us to bring in food and fodder from outside, even if only in small volume." Against the Chancellor stood Tirpitz and Bachmann. "The U-boat war," the Grand Admiral proclaimed, "was perhaps the only effective weapon we had against England."

Viewing this sharp conflict, the Kaiser wavered. He "declared that our entire people urgently demanded the U-boat war. The Chancellor had to reconcile himself to that." He "was obviously hesitating as to how he should decide," noted the admirals, and he turned to Müller, asking the Cabinet chief's advice. When Müller explained regretfully that he had to go against his uniform and side with the Chancellor, the Kaiser followed suit. He permitted Bethmann and Jagow to answer the compromise proposal as they desired.

Nothing came of this victory, since the British government rejected the compromise and the Americans declined to press the question. Submarines continued to operate under the decree of February 4. Although the Chancellor had acknowledged the importance of keeping America out of the war, he had tried but feebly to halt the U-boat campaign. It was his policy to impose only such limitations as the United States insisted upon and to do this only when it was necessary to prevent war. His attitude was largely governed, therefore, by estimates of neutral attitudes, and these estimates were determined in turn by the information that came through official channels.

During the spring of 1915 Bethmann's concern about the U-boat problem temporarily eased. He practically ceased to worry about adverse effects on the south European neutrals. Whether Russia's advance against the key Carpathian fortress of Przemyśl could be checked or not seemed much more likely to determine their attitudes. Since his concern over the United States rose partly from fear lest her policies influence those of European neutrals, his interest in America also waned. In any case, dispatches from Washington indicated that American antagonism toward the U-boat had ebbed. Bernstorff radioed quotations from the Washington *Post*, a newspaper hostile to Britain, thus giving the impression that Americans had forgotten the submarine in a new preoccupation with the British blockade. "Our diplomatic situation here has significantly improved in recent days . . . ," cabled the ambassador shortly after the English blockade announcement, "commercial circles begin to realize that England menaces American trade more than we, and, conclusively, commercial interests are always decisive here."[16] Backing up the ambassador's estimate were reports from the military attaché, Captain Franz von Papen, who also described America's attitude as harmless. "It is above all pleasing," wrote Papen in early March, "to note how after 7 months of warfare, democratic heads begin at last to wonder whether the hated Prussian militarism has not borne a share in the marvelous blossoming of the German people and the marshaling of all moral and economic forces for the maintenance of our existence. . . . [C]ontinuous propaganda has succeeded in offsetting the prejudices of the independent press in this country, and the lessons of German successes on land and water will also triumph here, slowly but surely!"[17] When the United States then hesitated to make representations about the sinking of an American ship, the estimates of Bernstorff and Papen seemed to be confirmed. A German auxiliary cruiser halted and sank the *William P. Frye,* a grain ship bound for Queenstown, Ireland. According to Bernstorff's dispatches, Wilson and Lansing wanted to settle the question informally, and their eventual note to Berlin asked only compensation for the shipowner. Such courtesy seemed evidence that earlier fears of the United States had been chimerae.

When House appeared in Berlin late in March, his soft language strengthened disbelief in American enmity. Seeking to redeem Wilson's reputation as an impartial mediator, the colonel underplayed all points of German-American contention. Attacking the chief complaint against the United States, the colonel explained away the munitions trade. "Mr. House declared the following:" noted Jagow, "America has almost no government munitions factories (or none at all), and for her army in case of a war, she will

---

[16] Bernstorff to Jagow, April 6, 1915, German Foreign Ministry Archives (Secret). In a message bearing no date, but received in Berlin on Feb. 18, 1915, German Foreign Ministry Archives (General), Bernstorff had commented on the excitement roused by the question of British use of neutral flags. In a message of Feb. 19, 1915, *ibid.*, he observed that the torpedoing of an American vessel might be settled peaceably by appeal to the Hague Conventions and protracted litigation. He passed on a friendly editorial from the Washington *Post* in a cable of Feb. 22, 1915, *ibid.*

[17] Papen to War Ministry, March 7, 1915, *ibid.*

have to rely upon private industry. Should the President now forbid exports, he would ruin the domestic munitions and arms factories. That would constitute a danger for the State." Without explaining the Pan-American pact that he and Wilson had been discussing, House mentioned one of the articles envisioned for such a treaty. "Mr. Wilson has thought of declaring," Jagow further paraphrased, "that the State would take over the private factories. Then the export could be prohibited." Should this socialization of the munitions industry not occur, House explained, it would be the fault of Congress and not that of the President.[18]

House endeavored thus to make Wilson appear a friend of Germany, and by talking of freedom of the seas, he made it seem possible that the United States and Germany could team up against England. In his effort to show a friendly disposition, he went so far as to suggest that German-American understanding need not be hindered even by the Monroe Doctrine. Talking with the Minister for Colonies, House advised economic but not political colonization of Brazil. Whether or not the colonel's pleasing words rebuilt Wilson's status as an impartial mediator, they certainly blurred any image of the United States as a potential enemy.

Relieved of their momentary fright, German officials became sneeringly critical of the United States. They badgered every available American on the subject of the arms trade. "It seems that every German that is being killed or wounded is being killed or wounded by an American rifle, bullet, or shell," House wrote wryly from Berlin. "I never dreamed before of the extraordinary excellence of our guns and ammunition. They are the only ones that explode or are so manufactured that their results are deadly."[19] This criticism of America's arms trade appeared in public statements from Supreme Headquarters. Reading one of Bernstorff's dispatches, the Kaiser himself vented extreme annoyance. The ambassador had written, "The policy of the American government is dominated by the sole idea of becoming enmeshed in no complications whatever. 'We want to stay out of everything' is the single rule." *"Then stop the ammunition!"* scrawled the Kaiser on the margin. *"Peace at any price,"* he added.[20]

Even Bethmann fell into this prevailing mood. In early April he

[18] Memo by Jagow, March 23, 1915, German Foreign Ministry Archives (Secret Mediation).

[19] House to Wilson, March 26, 1915, in Charles Seymour, ed., *The Intimate Papers of Colonel House* (4 Vols.; Boston, 1926–1928), I, 404. . . .

[20] Bernstorff to Jagow, April 6, 1915, . . . German Foreign Ministry Archives (General).

met with the Bundesrat Committee on Foreign Affairs, whose members were ministers president from other German states. Before this select and discreet audience he asserted, "The United States of America would be able to play an influential role if imaginative and strong men were at her head. That is not the case. The American politicians limit themselves to paper protests even against Japan in order that their businessmen may enrich themselves. American public attitudes toward Germany have improved but without attaining influence on policy."[21] The respect and fear briefly inspired by the strict accountability note had soured into scorn.

Partly as a result of this changed feeling, the U-boat offensive increased its tempo. Under the influence of Wilson's protest, the Kaiser had first postponed the offensive and then permitted it to go ahead under severe restrictions. Only ships positively identified as enemy were to be destroyed; "in no circumstances are ships under neutral flags to be attacked."[22] As the likelihood of any real American opposition seemed to diminish, admirals began to find the Kaiser more attentive when they suggested giving a freer hand to the U-boat commanders. When the U-29 was rammed and sunk because of the restrictive order, the admirals believed it time to demand a change. Going directly to the Kaiser, Tirpitz and Bachmann asked him to approve a new directive. The Kaiser did so, instructing U-boat commanders to make their first concern thenceforth not the safety of neutral shipping but the security of their own boats. Although this new directive in no way repealed earlier orders to spare neutrals, it provided a wider margin for error and unchained the zeal of U-boat commanders. Sinkings rose to more than one a day, and accidental torpedoings of neutral ships became common occurrences. Supporters of the navy expressed their enthusiasm, and even Tirpitz felt content. The leash of strict accountability had frayed and snapped.

The U-boat commanders themselves had chafed under the earlier orders. Although they had succeeded in sinking about 132,000 tons of shipping during February and March, their achievement represented a dent of less than a quarter of 1 per cent of the United Kingdom's shipping. The cost in U-boats, furthermore, had been fearful. Four out of the twenty-one failed to return, and the surviving commanders welcomed as only right the new imperial order to pay more regard to their own vessels than to neutral flags.

[21] Report on the session of April 7, 1915, Ernst Deuerlein, *Der Bundesratsausschuss für die Auswartigen Angelegenheiten, 1870–1918* (Regensburg, 1955), Appendix VI, pp. 280–281.
[22] Rear Admiral Arno Spindler, *Der Handelskriegmit U-Booten* (3 Vols.; Berlin, 1932–1934), I, 135.

Although the new order also gave them more discretion, the commanders still felt hampered by the duty of sparing neutrals. Hardly one had returned from a voyage without reporting the English approaches to be filled with neutral flags, nearly all concealing British ships. On board genuine neutral vessels, furthermore, search parties from submarines had invariably found contraband. Were it not for political restrictions, they declared, each submarine could sail to its assigned ground, discharge its torpedoes quickly into a sea of profitable targets, and shunt back to port for a reload. The potentialities of U-boat warfare seemed fully demonstrated. In the Dover Straits on February 24, the U-8 sent to the bottom three English ships totaling 11,047 tons. On March 12, the ill-fated U-29 repeated the exploit, sending down three ships off the Scilly Islands, and the U-28 matched this score on March 27. If given a free hand, the U-boat commanders felt, they could fulfill even the rash promises made by Germany's admirals.

Talk around submariners' wardrooms undoubtedly turned to the folly of weakling politicians in Berlin. Despite the quantity of newspaper comment on U-boat prospects, the submarine captains must have felt that the civil government was insufficiently aware of the U-boat. It does not seem far-fetched to suppose that conversation touched on the possibility of some dramatic awakening. It had taken the U-9's successful sinking of three British cruisers, after all, to open the eyes of big-ship admirals. If some new coup could be brought off, it might stir even the politicians. Suppose, for example, that the pride of England's merchant marine, the giant luxury liner *Lusitania*, should be sent to the bottom; would that not show the government, and the world, how powerful was this weapon which Germany held in her hand?

The possibility of an attack on the *Lusitania* had certainly been a subject of comment elsewhere. As early as August 5, 1914, a Manhattan newspaper had described the belligerent vessels in the port of New York. The German auxiliary cruiser *Vaterland* was flashing a light around the harbor, wrote an imaginative reporter for the New York *Herald*, and stopping it at intervals "to dwell covetously on the trim stern of the *Lusitania*." A German diplomat wrote to an influential American in March, 1915: "If one of our submarines should get the *Lusitania*, either under English or American flag, she would sink her, if she could, without a moment's hesitation."[23] Since the possibility was also a common subject of horrified specu-

[23] Unsigned letter to John Callan O'Laughlin, March 25, 1915, copy enclosed in O'Laughlin to Wilson, April 16, 1915, in Baker and Dodd, eds., *The Public Papers of Woodrow Wilson* (6 Vols.; New York, 1925–1927). . . .

lation in Washington and London, it seems not at all improbable that it provided matter for enthusiastic discussion among German submarine commanders.

One who could discuss the subject with realism was Lieutenant Commander Schwieger. An articulate champion of U-boat warfare, Schwieger commanded the late model, long-range U-20. In January he had sailed out to intercept troopships entering Le Havre. He sank three English vessels without warning and damaged a fourth, which turned out to be a privileged hospital ship. During February he simply moved his boat from Wilhelmshaven to the advanced base at Zeebrugge. In port most of the time, he had plenty of opportunity to hear superior officers in the fleet and staff damn the blindness of politicians. During March, he was out for about two weeks, rounding Land's End and sailing as far north as the Firth of Clyde. He torpedoed one fair-sized English steamer deep in the mouth of the Bristol Channel, another off the Liverpool lightships, and a third on the way home. Before he set out again late in April, he had returned to Wilhelmshaven, learned of the Kaiser's new orders, and received a much broader directive. He was to return to Irish waters and the St. George's Channel area. His orders were simply "to attack: transports, merchant ships, warships." No caution about neutral flags or passenger-carrying vessels inhibited his initiative.

Knowing these waters to be the routes for the *Lusitania* and her sister, the troopship *Mauretania*, Schwieger may have made an inward promise to keep a weather eye open for a four-stack silhouette. Rounding the Orkneys and coming down west of the Hebrides, he failed to spot a worthwhile target. Northwest of Ireland he launched a torpedo against a ship under Danish flag, but the shot missed and the ship skittered out of harm. His first real victim was a tiny sailing boat caught outside of Queenstown on May 5. The next day's bag was considerably more satisfying: two English steamers totaling almost 12,000 tons. But the sea was rough and the fog heavy. He crept back to the Old Head of Kinsale, preparing to vacate the St. George's Channel in hope of clearer targets west of Ireland. The sight of a cruiser forced him under water and caused a delay in his departure. At 1:45 p.m. he surfaced to find the weather clearing. At 2:30 he sighted on the horizon a silhouette with four stacks and four masts.

Since the silhouette was moving diagonally across the U-boat's bow at 14 knots and the U-20's highest submerged speed was only 9½ knots, Schwieger's chances seemed slight. But the giant target suddenly began swinging to starboard, toward Queenstown and the U-20's track. As six bells sounded in his tiny control room,

Schwieger ordered the engines to stop. At 3:10 he signaled away one torpedo. It spun through the water and struck amidships, just aft of the bridge. A spraying explosion followed. Wreckage lifted into the sky, higher than the ship's tallest mast. "Boiler or coal or powder?" jotted Schwieger in his log. The giant vessel heeled and began to settle. Watching it, Schwieger decided not to expend another torpedo. The ship was going under, and his binoculars could make out on the sinking stern which of the sisters he had sunk. The golden letters spelled out *Lusitania*. Schwieger set a course for Wilhelmshaven, to report his triumph.

The *Lusitania* was carrying 1,959 persons. The voyage across the Atlantic had been uneventful. Thinking of the passengers' comfort, the captain had been careful not to remind them of the war. He had maintained a moderate speed and steered a straight course. The 18-knot speed and zigzag course prescribed by Admiralty warnings would have upset glasses in the parlors and interfered with deck games and promenades. It might also have alarmed some of the hundreds of women and children on board. For these reasons the *Lusitania*'s side had glided so easily into the path of Lieutenant Schwieger's torpedo. The point of impact chanced to be some vulnerable point. It may have been a bunker; it may have been a cargo space stored with cartridges or fuses; or the torpedo may have penetrated to a midships boiler. Whatever the case, the explosion shuddered the entire ship. Passengers leaped from their bunks or deck chairs, and panic swirled across the decks. In the next eighteen minutes, nevertheless, more than seven hundred went over the side into boats. The trained crew of an amphibious transport can hardly do better. But many could not be saved. When the ship sank, 1,198 passengers and crew went down with her. Of these, 128 were United States citizens. The submarine had thus created a real issue between the United States and Germany.

The Decision to Use
the Atomic Bomb

LOUIS MORTON

It is now more than ten years since the atomic bomb exploded over Hiroshima and revealed to the world in one blinding flash of light the start of the atomic age. As the meaning of this explosion and the nature of the force unleashed became apparent, a chorus of voices rose in protest against the decision that had opened the Pandora's box of atomic warfare.

The justification for using the atomic bomb was that it had ended the war, or at least ended it sooner and thereby saved countless American — and Japanese — lives. But had it? Had not Japan already been defeated and was she not already on the verge of surrender? What circumstances, it was asked, justified the fateful decision that "blasted the web of history and, like the discovery of fire, severed past from present"?[1]

The first authoritative explanation of how and why it was decided to use the bomb came in February 1947 from Henry L. Stimson, wartime Secretary of War and the man who more than any other was responsible for advising the President.[2] This explanation did not answer all the questions or still the critics. During the years that have followed others have revealed their part in the decision and in the events shaping it. These explanations have not ended the controversy, but they have brought to light additional facts bearing on the decision to use the bomb. With this information and with the perspective of ten years, it may be profitable to look again at the decision that opened the age of atomic warfare.

Reprinted by special permission from *Foreign Affairs*, January 1957, pp. 334–353. Copyright 1957 by the Council on Foreign Relations, Inc., New York. Some footnotes have been omitted.

[1] James Phinney Baxter, 3rd, *Scientists Against Time* (Boston: Little, Brown, 1946), p. 419.

[2] Henry L. Stimson, "The Decision to Use the Atomic Bomb," *Harper's*, February 1947. The article is reproduced with additional comments in Henry L. Stimson and McGeorge Bundy, *On Active Service in Peace and War* (New York: Harper, 1948), chapter 13, and in *Bulletin of the Atomic Scientists*, February 1947.

THE INTERIM COMMITTEE

The epic story of the development of the atomic bomb is by now well known. It began in 1939 when a small group of eminent scientists in this country called to the attention of the United States Government the vast potentialities of atomic energy for military purposes and warned that the Germans were already carrying on experiments in this field. The program initiated in October of that year with a very modest appropriation and later expanded into the two-billion-dollar Manhattan Project had only one purpose — to harness the energy of the atom in a chain reaction to produce a bomb that could be carried by aircraft if possible, and to produce it before the Germans could.[3] That such a bomb, if produced, would be used, no responsible official even questioned. "At no time from 1941 to 1945," declared Mr. Stimson, "did I ever hear it suggested by the President, or by another responsible member of the Government, that atomic energy should not be used in the war." And Dr. J. Robert Oppenheimer recalled in 1954 that "we always assumed if they [atomic bombs] were needed, they would be used."[4]

So long as the success of the project remained in doubt there seems to have been little or no discussion of the effects of an atomic weapon or the circumstances under which it would be used. "During the early days of the project," one scientist recalled, "we spent little time thinking about the possible effects of the bomb we were trying to make."[5] It was a "neck-and-neck race with the Germans," the outcome of which might well determine who would be the victor in World War II. But as Germany approached defeat and as the effort to produce an atomic bomb offered increasing promise of success, those few men who knew what was being done and who appreciated the enormous implications of atomic energy became more and more concerned. Most of this concern came from the scientists in the Metallurgical Laboratory at Chicago, where by early 1945 small groups began to question the advisability of using the weapon they were trying so hard to build. It was almost as if they hoped the bomb would not work after it was completed.

[3] The one exception was the Navy's work in the field of atomic energy as a source of power for naval vessels. *Hearings Before the Special Committee on Atomic Energy*, Senate, 79th Cong., 1st Sess., S.R. 179, pt. 3, pp. 364–389, testimony of Dr. Ross Gunn.

[4] Stimson, *Harper's*, p. 98; U.S. Atomic Energy Commission, *Transcript of Hearings Before Personnel Security Board in the Matter of Dr. J. Robert Oppenheimer, 12 April–6 May 1954* (Washington: G.P.O., 1954), p. 33.

[5] *Senate Hearings*, pt. 2, p. 302, testimony of Dr. John A. Simpson.

On the military side, the realization that a bomb would probably be ready for testing in the summer of 1945 led to concrete planning for the use of the new weapon, on the assumption that the bomb when completed would work. By the end of 1944 a list of possible targets in Japan had been selected, and a B-29 squadron was trained for the specific job of delivering the bomb. It was also necessary to inform certain commanders in the Pacific about the project, and on December 30, 1944, Major-General Leslie R. Groves, head of the Manhattan District, recommended that this be done.[6]

Even at this stage of development no one could estimate accurately when the bomb would be ready or guarantee that, when ready, it would work. It is perhaps for this reason — and because of the complete secrecy surrounding the project — that the possibility of an atomic weapon never entered into the deliberations of the strategic planners. It was, said Admiral William Leahy, "the best kept secret of the entire war" and only a handful of the top civilian and military officials in Washington knew about the bomb.[7] As a matter of fact, one bright brigadier-general who innocently suggested that the Army might do well to look into the possibilities of atomic energy suddenly found himself the object of the most intensive investigation. So secret was the project, says John J. McCloy, that when he raised the subject at a White House meeting of the Joint Chiefs of Staff in June 1945 it "caused a sense of shock, even among that select group."[8]

It was not until March 1945 that it became possible to predict with certainty that the bomb would be completed in time for testing in July. On March 15, Mr. Stimson discussed the project for the last time with President Roosevelt, but their conversation dealt mainly with the effects of the use of the bomb, not with the question of whether it ought to be used. Even at this late date, there does not seem to have been any doubt at the highest levels that the bomb would be used against Japan if it would help bring the war to an early end. But on lower levels, and especially among the scientists at the Chicago laboratory, there was considerable reservation about the advisability of using the bomb.

After President Roosevelt's death, it fell to Stimson to brief the new President about the atomic weapon. At a White House meeting

[6] "Memo, Groves for CofS, 30 Dec. 1944, sub: Atomic Fission Bombs," printed in *Foreign Relations of the United States: The Conferences at Malta-Yalta, 1945* (Washington: G.P.O., 1955)....

[7] Admiral William D. Leahy, *I Was There* (New York: Whittlesey House, 1950), p. 434.

[8] John J. McCloy, *The Challenge to American Foreign Policy* (Cambridge: Harvard University Press, 1953), p. 42. See also ... James F. Byrnes, *Speaking Frankly* (New York: Harper, 1947), p. 257.

on April 25, he outlined the history and status of the program and predicted that "within four months we shall in all probability have completed the most terrible weapon ever known in human history."[9] This meeting, like Stimson's last meeting with Roosevelt, dealt largely with the political and diplomatic consequences of the use of such a weapon rather than with the timing and manner of employment, the circumstances under which it would be used, or whether it would be used at all. The answers to these questions depended on factors not yet known. But Stimson recommended, and the President approved, the appointment of a special committee to consider them.

This special committee, known as the Interim Committee, played a vital role in the decision to use the bomb. Secretary Stimson was chairman, and George L. Harrison, President of the New York Life Insurance Company and special consultant in the Secretary's office, took the chair when he was absent. James F. Byrnes, who held no official position at the time, was President Truman's personal representative. Other members were Ralph A. Bard, Under Secretary of the Navy, William L. Clayton, Assistant Secretary of State, and Drs. Vannevar Bush, Karl T. Compton and James B. Conant. Generals Marshall and Groves attended at least one and possibly more of the meetings of the committee.

The work of the Interim Committee, in Stimson's words, "ranged over the whole field of atomic energy, in its political, military, and scientific aspects."[10] During the first meeting the scientific members reviewed for their colleagues the development of the Manhattan Project and described vividly the destructive power of the atomic bomb. They made it clear also that there was no known defense against this kind of attack. Another day was spent with the engineers and industrialists who had designed and built the huge plants at Oak Ridge and Hanford. Of particular concern to the committee was the question of how long it would take another country, particularly the Soviet Union, to produce an atomic bomb. "Much of the discussion," recalled Dr. Oppenheimer, who attended the meeting of June 1 as a member of a scientific panel, "revolved around the question raised by Secretary Stimson as to whether there was any hope at all of using this development to get less barbarous [sic] relations with the Russians."[11]

The work of the Interim Committee was completed June 1, 1945,

---

[9] Stimson's memorandum of this meeting is printed in *Harper's*, pp. 99–100.

[10] Stimson, *Harper's*, p. 100.

[11] *Oppenheimer Hearings*, pp. 34, 257, testimony of Dr. Oppenheimer and Dr. Compton; Byrnes, *op. cit.*, pp. 260–261; Stimson, *Harper's*, pp. 100–101.

when it submitted its report to the President, recommending unanimously that:

1. The bomb should be used against Japan as soon as possible.

2. It should be used against a military target surrounded by other buildings.

3. It should be used without prior warning of the nature of the weapon.

(One member, Ralph A. Bard, later dissented from this portion of the committee's recommendation.)

"The conclusions of the Committee," wrote Stimson, "were similar to my own, although I reached mine independently. I felt that to extract a genuine surrender from the Emperor and his military advisers, they must be administered a tremendous shock which would carry convincing proof of our power to destroy the empire. Such an effective shock would save many times the number of lives, both American and Japanese, than it would cost."[12]

Among the scientists working on the Manhattan Project were many who did not agree. To them, the "wave of horror and repulsion" that might follow the sudden use of an atomic bomb would more than outweigh its military advantages. "It may be very difficult," they declared, "to persuade the world that a nation which was capable of secretly preparing and suddenly releasing a new weapon, as indiscriminate as the rocket bomb and a thousand times more destructive, is to be trusted in its proclaimed desire of having such weapons abolished by international agreement."[13] The procedure these scientists recommended was, first, to demonstrate the new weapon "before the eyes of representatives of all the United Nations on the desert or a barren island," and then to issue "a preliminary ultimatum" to Japan. If this ultimatum was rejected, and "if the sanction of the United Nations (and of public opinion at home) were obtained," then and only then, said the scientists, should the United States consider using the bomb. "This may sound fantastic," they said, "but in nuclear weapons we have something entirely new in order of magnitude of destructive power, and if we want to capi-

[12] Stimson, *Harper's*, p. 101. The same idea is expressed by Sir Winston Churchill, *Triumph and Tragedy* (Cambridge: Houghton, 1953), pp. 638–639.

[13] "Report of the Committee on Social and Political Implications," signed by Professor James Franck of the University of Chicago and submitted to the Secretary of War, June 11, 1945, *Bulletin of Atomic Scientists*, May 1, 1946, p. 3.

talize fully on the advantage their possession gives us, we must use new and imaginative methods."[14]

These views, which were forwarded to the Secretary of War on June 11, 1945, were strongly supported by 64 of the scientists in the Chicago Metallurgical Laboratory in a petition sent directly to the President. At about the same time, at the request of Dr. Arthur H. Compton, a poll was taken of the views of more than 150 scientists at the Chicago Laboratory. Five alternatives ranging from all-out use of the bomb to "keeping the existence of the bomb a secret" were presented. Of those polled, about two-thirds voted for a preliminary demonstration, either on a military objective or an uninhabited locality; the rest were split on all-out use and no use at all.[15]

These views, and presumably others, were referred by Secretary Stimson to a distinguished Scientific Panel consisting of Drs. Arthur H. Compton, Enrico Fermi, E. O. Lawrence and J. Robert Oppenheimer, all nuclear physicists of the first rank. "We didn't know beans about the military situation," Oppenheimer later said. "We didn't know whether they [the Japanese] could be caused to surrender by other means or whether the invasion [of Japan] was really inevitable. . . . We thought the two overriding considerations were the saving of lives in the war and the effect of our actions on the stability of the postwar world."[16] On June 16 the panel reported that it had studied carefully the proposals made by the scientists but could see no practical way of ending the war by a technical demonstration. Almost regretfully, it seemed, the four members of the panel concluded that there was "no acceptable alternative to direct military use."[17] "Nothing would have been more damaging to our effort," wrote Stimson, ". . . than a warning or demonstration followed by a dud — and this was a real possibility." With this went the fear, expressed by Byrnes, that if the Japanese were warned that an atomic bomb would be exploded over a military target in Japan as a demonstration, "they might bring our boys who were prisoners of war to that area."[18] Furthermore, only two bombs would be available by August, the number General Groves estimated would be

[14] *Ibid.*, pp. 3–4.

[15] *Ibid.*, p. 1; Leo Szilard, "A Personal History of the Bomb," in *The Atlantic Community Faces the Bomb*, University of Chicago Roundtable, No. 601, Sept. 25, 1949, p. 15. See also P. M. S. Blackett, *Fear, War, and the Bomb* (New York: Whittlesey House, 1949), pp. 114–116.

[16] *Oppenheimer Hearings*, p. 34.

[17] Quoted in Stimson, *Harper's*, p. 101. The Scientific Panel was established to advise the Interim Committee and its report was made to that body.

[18] *Ibid.*, Byrnes, p. 261.

needed to end the war; these two would have to obtain the desired effect quickly. And no one yet knew, nor would the scheduled ground test in New Mexico prove, whether a bomb dropped from an airplane would explode.[19]

Nor, for that matter, were all those concerned certain that the bomb would work at all, on the ground or in the air. Of these doubters, the greatest was Admiral Leahy, who until the end remained unconvinced. "This is the biggest fool thing we have ever done," he told Truman after Vannevar Bush had explained to the President how the bomb worked. "The bomb will never go off, and I speak as an expert on explosives."[20]

Thus, by mid-June 1945, there was virtual unanimity among the President's civilian advisers on the use of the bomb. The arguments of the opponents had been considered and rejected. So far as is known, the President did not solicit the views of the military or naval staffs, nor were they offered.

MILITARY CONSIDERATIONS

The military situation on June 1, 1945, when the Interim Committee submitted its recommendations on the use of the atomic bomb, was distinctly favorable to the Allied cause. Germany had surrendered in May and troops from Europe would soon be available for redeployment in the Pacific. Manila had fallen in February; Iwo Jima was in American hands; and the success of the Okinawa invasion was assured. Air and submarine attacks had virtually cut off Japan from the resources of the Indies, and B-29s from the Marianas were pulverizing Japan's cities and factories. The Pacific Fleet had virtually driven the Imperial Navy from the ocean, and planes of the fast carrier forces were striking Japanese naval bases in the Inland Sea. Clearly, Japan was a defeated nation.

Though defeated in a military sense, Japan showed no disposition to surrender unconditionally. And Japanese troops had demonstrated time and again that they could fight hard and inflict heavy casualties even when the outlook was hopeless. Allied plans in the spring of 1945 took these facts into account and proceeded on the assumption that an invasion of the home islands would be required to achieve at the earliest possible date the unconditional surrender of Japan — the announced objective of the war and the basic assumption of all strategic planning.

Other means of achieving this objective had been considered and,

[19] *Ibid., Oppenheimer Hearings*, p. 163, testimony of General Groves.
[20] Harry S. Truman, *Year of Decisions* (Garden City: Doubleday, 1955), p. 11. Leahy in his memoirs frankly admits this error.

in early June, had not yet been entirely discarded. One of these called for the occupation of a string of bases around Japan in order to increase the intensity of air bombardment. Combined with a tight naval blockade, such a course would, many believed, produce the same results as an invasion and at far less cost of lives. "I was unable to see any justification," Admiral Leahy later wrote, ". . . for an invasion of an already thoroughly defeated Japan. I feared the cost would be enormous in both lives and treasure." Admiral King and other senior naval officers agreed. To them it had always seemed, in King's words, "that the defeat of Japan could be accomplished by sea and air power alone, without the necessity of actual invasion of the Japanese home islands by ground troops."[21]

The main arguments for an invasion of Japan — the plans called for an assault against Kyushu (Olympic) on November 1, 1945, and against Honshu (Coronet) five months later — are perhaps best summarized by General Douglas MacArthur. Writing to the Chief of Staff on April 20, 1945, he declared that this course was the only one that would permit application of the full power of our combined resources — ground, naval and air — on the decisive objective. Japan, he believed, would probably be more difficult to invade the following year. An invasion of Kyushu at an early date would, moreover, place United States forces in the most favorable position for the decisive assault against Honshu in 1946, and would "continue the offensive methods which have proved so successful in Pacific campaigns."[22] Reliance upon bombing alone, MacArthur asserted, was still an unproved formula for success, as was evidenced by the bomber offensive against Germany. The seizure of a ring of bases around Japan would disperse Allied forces even more than they already were, MacArthur pointed out, and (if an attempt was made to seize positions on the China coast) might very well lead to long drawn-out operations on the Asiatic mainland.

Though the Joint Chiefs had accepted the invasion concept as the basis for preparations, and had issued a directive for the Kyushu assault on May 25, it was well understood that the final decision was yet to be made. By mid-June the time had come for such a decision and during that period the Joint Chiefs reviewed the whole problem of Japanese strategy. Finally, on June 18, at a meeting in the White House, they presented the alternatives to President Truman. Also present (according to the minutes) were Secretaries

[21] Leahy, *op. cit.*, pp. 384–385. . . .
[22] This message is reproduced in *The Entry of the Soviet Union Into the War Against Japan: Military Plans, 1941–1945* (Department of Defense Press Release, September 1955), pp. 55–57.

Stimson and Forrestal and Assistant Secretary of War John J. McCloy.[23]

General Marshall presented the case for invasion and carried his colleagues with him, although both Admirals Leahy and King later declared they did not favor the plan. After considerable discussion of casualties and of the difficulties ahead, President Truman made his decision. Kyushu would be invaded as planned and preparations for the landing were to be pushed through to completion. Preparations for the Honshu assault would continue, but no final decision would be made until preparations had reached the point "beyond which there would not be opportunity for a free choice."[24] The program thus approved by Truman called for:

1. Air bombardment and blockade of Japan from bases in Okinawa, Iwo Jima, the Marianas and the Philippines.

2. Assault of Kyushu on November 1, 1945, and intensification of blockade and air bombardment.

3. Invasion of the industrial heart of Japan through the Tokyo Plain in central Honshu, tentative target date March 1, 1946.

During the White House meeting of June 18, there was discussion of the possibility of ending the war by political means. The President displayed a deep interest in the subject and both Stimson and McCloy emphasized the importance of the "large submerged class in Japan who do not favor the present war and whose full opinion and influence had never yet been felt."[25] There was discussion also of the atomic bomb, since everyone present knew about the bomb and the recommendations of the Interim Committee. The suggestion was made that before the bomb was dropped, the Japanese should be warned that the United States had such a weapon. "Not one of the Chiefs nor the Secretary," recalled Mr. McCloy, "thought well of a bomb warning, an effective argument being that no one could be certain, in spite of the assurances of the scientists, that the 'thing would go off.' "[26]

Though the defeat of the enemy's armed forces in the Japanese homeland was considered a prerequisite to Japan's surrender, it did not follow that Japanese forces elsewhere, especially those on the Asiatic mainland, would surrender also. It was to provide for just

---

[23] Forrestal says in his *Diaries* that neither he nor Stimson was present, while McCloy's definite recollection is that Stimson was present but Forrestal was not. A summary of this meeting is contained in *The Entry of the Soviet Union . . .*, pp. 77–85. . . .

[24] McCloy, *op. cit.*, p. 41. . . .

[25] *The Entry of the Soviet Union . . .*, p. 83. . . .

[26] McCloy, p. 43. . . .

this contingency, as well as to pin down those forces during the invasion of the home islands, that the Joint Chiefs had recommended Soviet entry into the war against Japan.

Soviet participation was a goal long pursued by the Americans. Both political and military authorities seem to have been convinced from the start that Soviet assistance, conceived in various ways, would shorten the war and lessen the cost. In October 1943, Marshal Stalin had told Cordell Hull, then in Moscow for a conference, that the Soviet Union would eventually declare war on Japan. At the Tehran Conference in November of that year, Stalin had given the Allies formal notice of this intention and reaffirmed it in October 1944. In February 1945, at the Yalta Conference, Roosevelt and Stalin had agreed on the terms of Soviet participation in the Far Eastern war. Thus, by June 1945, the Americans could look forward to Soviet intervention at a date estimated as three months after the defeat of Germany.

But by the summer of 1945 the Americans had undergone a change of heart. Though the official position of the War Department still held that "Russian entry will have a profound military effect in that almost certainly it will materially shorten the war and thus save American lives,"[27] few responsible American officials were eager for Soviet intervention or as willing to make concessions as they had been at an earlier period. What had once appeared extremely desirable appeared less so now that the war in Europe was over and Japan was virtually defeated. President Truman, one official recalled, stated during a meeting devoted to the question of Soviet policy that agreements with Stalin had up to that time been "a one-way street" and that "he intended thereafter to be firm in his dealings with the Russians."[28] And at the June 18 meeting of the Joint Chiefs of Staff with the President, Admiral King had declared that "regardless of the desirability of the Russians entering the war, they were not indispensable and he did not think we should go so far as to beg them to come in."[29] Though the cost would be greater he had no doubt "we could handle it alone."

The failure of the Soviets to abide by agreements at Yalta had also done much to discourage the American desire for further cooperation with them. But after urging Stalin for three years to declare war on Japan, the United States Government could hardly ask him now to remain neutral. Moreover, there was no way of keeping

[27] Letter, Stimson to Grew, May 21, 1945, reproduced . . . in *The Entry of the Soviet Union . . .*, pp. 70–71.
[28] Walter Millis, ed., *The Forrestal Diaries* (New York: Viking, 1951), p. 78.
[29] *The Entry of the Soviet Union . . .*, p. 85. . . .

the Russians out even if there had been a will to do so. In Harriman's view, "Russia would come into the war regardless of what we might do."[30]

A further difficulty was that Allied intelligence still indicated that Soviet intervention would be desirable, if not necessary, for the success of the invasion strategy. In Allied intelligence, Japan was portrayed as a defeated nation whose military leaders were blind to defeat. Though her industries had been seriously crippled by air bombardment and naval blockade and her armed forces were critically deficient in many of the resources of war, Japan was still far from surrender. She had ample reserves of weapons and ammunition and an army of 5,000,000 troops, 2,000,000 of them in the home islands. The latter could be expected to put up a strong resistance to invasion. In the opinion of the intelligence experts, neither blockade nor bombing alone would produce unconditional surrender before the date set for invasion. And the invasion itself, they believed, would be costly and possibly prolonged.[31]

According to these intelligence reports, the Japanese leaders were fully aware of their desperate situation but would continue to fight in the hope of avoiding complete defeat by securing a better bargaining position. Allied war-weariness and disunity, or some miracle, they hoped, would offer them a way out. "The Japanese believe," declared an intelligence estimate of June 30, ". . . that unconditional surrender would be the equivalent of national extinction, and there are as yet no indications that they are ready to accept such terms."[32] It appeared also to the intelligence experts that Japan might surrender at any time "depending upon the conditions of surrender" the Allies might offer. Clearly these conditions, to have any chance of acceptance, would have to include retention of the imperial system.[33]

How accurate were these estimates? Judging from postwar accounts of Japan, they were very close to the truth. Since the defeat at Saipan, when Tojo had been forced to resign, the strength of the "peace party" had been increasing. In September 1944 the Swedish Minister in Tokyo had been approached unofficially, presumably in the name of Prince Konoye, to sound out the Allies on terms for peace. This overture came to naught, as did another the following

[30] Statement to Leahy quoted in Leahy, p. 369. . . .

[31] *The Entry of the Soviet Union* . . ., pp. 85–88. . . .

[32] G-2 memorandum prepared for ODP and quoted in Ray S. Cline, *United States Army in World War II. The War Department. Washington Command Post: The Operations Division* (Washington: Department of the Army, Office of Military History, 1951), p. 347. . . .

[33] *Ibid.* . . .

March. But the Swedish Minister did learn that those who advocated peace in Japan regarded the Allied demand for unconditional surrender as their greatest obstacle.[34]

The Suzuki Cabinet that came into power in April 1945 had an unspoken mandate from the Emperor to end the war as quickly as possible. But it was faced immediately with another problem when the Soviet Government announced it would not renew the neutrality pact after April 1946. The German surrender in May produced another crisis in the Japanese Government and led, after considerable discussion, to a decision to seek Soviet mediation. But the first approach, made on June 3 to Jacob Malik, the Soviet Ambassador, produced no results. Malik was noncommittal and merely said the problem needed further study. Another overture to Malik later in the month also came to naught.

At the end of June, the Japanese finally approached the Soviet Government directly through Ambassador Sato in Moscow, asking that it mediate with the Allies to bring the Far Eastern war to an end. In a series of messages between Tokyo and Moscow, which the Americans intercepted and decoded, the Japanese Foreign Office outlined the position of the government and instructed Ambassador Sato to make arrangements for a special envoy from the Emperor who would be empowered to make terms for Soviet mediation. Unconditional surrender, he was told, was completely unacceptable, and time was of the essence. But the Russians, on one pretext and another, delayed their answer until mid-July when Stalin and Molotov left for Potsdam. Thus, the Japanese Government had by then accepted defeat and was seeking desperately for a way out; but it was not willing even at this late date to surrender unconditionally, and would accept no terms that did not include the preservation of the imperial system.

Allied intelligence thus had estimated the situation in Japan correctly. Allied invasion strategy had been reexamined and confirmed in mid-June, and the date for the invasion fixed. The desirability of Soviet assistance had been confirmed also and plans for her entry into the war during August could now be made. No decision had been reached on the use of the atomic bomb, but the President's advisers had recommended it. The decision was the President's and

[34] Robert J. C. Butow, *Japan's Decision to Surrender* (Stanford: Stanford University Press, 1954), pp. 40, 54–57. Other accounts of the situation in Japan are Toshikazu Kase, *Journey to the Missouri* (New Haven: Yale University Press, 1950); U.S. Strategic Bombing Survey, *Japan's Struggle to End the War* (Washington: G.P.O., 1946); Takushiro Hattori, *Complete History of the Greater East Asia War* (Japan: Masu Shobo Co., 1953), v. 4.

he faced it squarely. But before he could make it he would want to know whether the measures already concerted would produce unconditional surrender at the earliest moment and at the lowest cost. If they could not, then he would have to decide whether circumstances warranted employment of a bomb that Stimson had already labeled as "the most terrible weapon ever known in human history."

THE DECISION

Though responsibility for the decision to use the atomic bomb was the President's, he exercised it only after careful study of the recommendations of his senior advisers. Chief among these was the Secretary of War, under whose broad supervision the Manhattan Project had been placed. Already deeply concerned over the cost of the projected invasion, the political effects of Soviet intervention and the potential consequences of the use of the atomic bomb, Stimson sought a course that would avoid all these evils. The difficulty, as he saw it, lay in the requirement for unconditional surrender. It was a phrase that might make the Japanese desperate and lead to a long and unnecessary campaign of attrition that would be extremely costly to both sides. But there was no way of getting around the term; it was firmly rooted in Allied war aims and its renunciation was certain to lead to charges of appeasement.

But if this difficulty could be overcome, would the Japanese respond if terms were offered? The intelligence experts thought so, and the radio intercepts from Tokyo to Moscow bore them out. So far as the Army was concerned there was much to be gained by such a course. Not only might it reduce the enormous cost of the war, but it would also make possible a settlement in the Western Pacific "before too many of our allies are committed there and have made substantial contributions towards the defeat of Japan."[35] In the view of the War Department these aims justified "any concessions which might be attractive to the Japanese, so long as our realistic aims for peace in the Pacific are not adversely affected."[36]

The problem was to formulate terms that would meet these conditions. There was considerable discussion of this problem in Washington in the spring of 1945 by officials in the Department of State and in the War and Navy Departments. Joseph C. Grew, Acting Secretary of State, proposed to the President late in May that he issue a proclamation urging the Japanese to surrender and assuring them that they could keep the Emperor. Though Truman did not

---

[35] OPD Compilation for the Potsdam Conference, quoted in Cline, *op. cit.*, p. 345.
[36] Ibid., pp. 345–346.

act on the suggestion, he thought it "a sound idea" and told Grew to discuss it with his cabinet colleagues and the Joint Chiefs. On June 18, Grew was back with the report that these groups favored the idea, but that there were differences on the timing.

Grew's ideas, as well as those of others concerned, were summarized by Stimson in a long and carefully considered memorandum to the President on July 2. Representing the most informed military and political estimate of the situation at this time, this memorandum constitutes a state paper of the first importance. If any one document can be said to provide the basis for the President's warning to Japan and his final decision to use the atomic bomb, this is it.

The gist of Stimson's argument was that the most promising alternative to the long and costly struggle certain to follow invasion was to warn the Japanese "of what is to come" and to give them an opportunity to surrender. There was, he thought, enough of a chance that such a course would work to make the effort worthwhile. Japan no longer had any allies, her navy was virtually destroyed and she was increasingly vulnerable to air attack and naval blockade. Against her were arrayed the increasingly powerful forces of the Allies, with their "inexhaustible and untouched industrial resources." In these circumstances, Stimson believed the Japanese people would be susceptible to reason if properly approached. "Japan," he pointed out, "is not a nation composed of mad fanatics of an entirely different mentality from ours. On the contrary, she has within the past century shown herself to possess extremely intelligent people. . . ." But any attempt, Stimson added, "to exterminate her armies and her population by gunfire or other means will tend to produce a fusion of race solidity and antipathy. . . ."

A warning to Japan, Stimson contended, should be carefully timed. It should come before the actual invasion, before destruction had reduced the Japanese "to fanatical despair" and, if the Soviet Union had already entered the war, before Russian attack had progressed so far.[37] It should also emphasize, Stimpson believed, the inevitability and completeness of the destruction ahead and the determination of the Allies to strip Japan of her conquests and to destroy the influence of the military clique. It should be a strong warning and should leave no doubt in Japanese minds that they

[37] In his diary, under the date June 19, Stimson wrote: "The last-chance warning . . . must be given before an actual landing of the ground forces in Japan, and fortunately the plans provide for enough time to bring in the sanctions to our warning in the shape of heavy ordinary bombing attack and an attack of S-1 [the atomic bomb]." Stimson and Bundy, p. 624.

would have to surrender unconditionally and submit to Allied occupation.

The warning, as Stimson envisaged it, had a double character. While promising destruction and devastation, it was also to hold out hope to the Japanese if they heeded its message. In his memorandum, therefore, Stimson stressed the positive features of the warning and recommended that it include a disavowal of any intention to destroy the Japanese nation or to occupy the country permanently. Once Japan's military clique had been removed from power and her capacity to wage war destroyed, it was Stimson's belief that the Allies should withdraw and resume normal trade relations with the new and peaceful Japanese Government. "I personally think," he declared, "that if in saying this we should add that we do not exclude a constitutional monarchy under her present dynasty, it would substantially add to the chance of acceptance."

Not once in the course of this lengthy memorandum was mention made of the atomic bomb. There was no need to do so. Everyone concerned understood clearly that the bomb was the instrument that would destroy Japan and impress on the Japanese Government the hopelessness of any course but surrender. As Stimson expressed it, the atomic bomb was "the best possible sanction," the single weapon that would convince the Japanese "of our power to destroy the empire."[38]

Though Stimson considered a warning combined with an offer of terms and backed up by the sanction of the atomic bomb as the most promising means of inducing surrender at any early date, there were other courses that some thought might produce the same result. One was the continuation and intensification of air bombardment coupled with surface and underwater blockade. This course had already been considered and rejected as insufficient to produce surrender, though its advocates were by no means convinced that this decision was a wise one. And Stimson himself later justified the use of the bomb on the ground that by November 1 conventional bombardment would have caused greater destruction than the bomb. This apparent contradiction is explained by the fact that the atomic bomb was considered to have a psychological effect entirely apart from the damage wrought.[39]

Nor did Stimson, in his memorandum, consider the effect of the Soviet Union's entry into the war. By itself, this action could not be counted on to force Japan to capitulate, but combined with bombardment and blockade it might do so. At least that was the view of

[38] Stimson, *Harper's*, pp. 101, 104.
[39] *Ibid.*, p. 105.

Brigadier-General George A. Lincoln, one of the Army's top planners, who wrote in June that "probably it will take Russian entry
into the war, coupled with a landing, or imminent threat of landing,
on Japan proper by us, to convince them [the Japanese] of the hopelessness of their position."[40] Why, therefore, was it not possible to
issue the warning prior to a Soviet declaration of war against Japan
and rely on that event, together with an intensified air bombardment, to produce the desired result? If together they could not secure Japan's surrender, would there not still be time to use the bomb
before the scheduled invasion of Kyushu in November?

No final answer to this question is possible with the evidence at
hand. But one cannot ignore the fact that some responsible officials
feared the political consequences of Soviet intervention and hoped
that ultimately it would prove unnecessary. This feeling may un-
consciously have made the atom bomb solution more attractive than
it might otherwise have been. Some officials may have believed, too,
that the bomb could be used as a powerful deterrent to Soviet expansion in Europe, where the Red tide had successfully engulfed
Rumania, Bulgaria, Jugoslavia, Czechoslovakia and Hungary. In an
interview with three of the top scientists in the Manhattan Project
early in June, Mr. Byrnes did not, according to Leo Szilard, argue
that the bomb was needed to defeat Japan, but rather that it should
be dropped to "make Russia more manageable in Europe."[41]

It has been asserted also that the desire to justify the expenditure
of the two billion dollars spent on the Manhattan Project may have
disposed some favorably toward the use of the bomb. Already questions had been asked in Congress, and the end of the war would
almost certainly bring on a full-scale investigation. What more striking justification of the Manhattan Project than a new weapon that
had ended the war in one sudden blow and saved countless American lives? "It was my reaction," wrote Admiral Leahy, "that the
scientists and others wanted to make this test because of the vast
sums that had been spent on the project. Truman knew that, and
so did other people involved."[42]

This explanation hardly does credit to those involved in the Manhattan Project and not even P. M. S. Blackett, one of the severest
critics of the decision to use the bomb, accepted it. "The wit of
man," he declared, "could hardly devise a theory of the dropping of
the bomb, both more insulting to the American people, or more
likely to lead to an energetically pursued Soviet defense policy."[43]

[40] Quoted in Cline, p. 344.
[41] Szilard, *op. cit.*, pp. 14–15.
[42] Leahy, p. 441.
[43] Blackett, *op. cit.*, p. 138.

But even if the need to justify these huge expenditures is discounted — and certainly by itself it could not have produced the decision — the question still remains whether those who held in their hands a weapon thought capable of ending the war in one stroke could justify withholding that weapon. Would they not be open to criticism for failing to use every means at their disposal to defeat the enemy as quickly as possible, thereby saving many American lives?

And even at that time there were some who believed that the new weapon would ultimately prove the most effective deterrent to war yet produced. How better to outlaw war forever than to demonstrate the tremendous destructive power of this weapon by using it against an actual target?

By early 1945 the stage had been set for the final decision. Stimson's memorandum had been approved in principle and on July 4 the British had given their consent to the use of the bomb against Japan. It remained only to decide on the terms and timing of the warning. This was the situation when the Potsdam Conference opened on July 17, one day after the bomb had been successfully exploded in a spectacular demonstration at Alamogordo, New Mexico. The atomic bomb was a reality and when the news reached Potsdam there was great excitement among those who were let in on the secret. Instead of the prospect of long and bitter months of fighting the Japanese, there was now a vision, "fair and bright indeed it seemed" to Churchill, "of the end of the whole war in one or two violent shocks."[44]

President Truman's first action was to call together his chief advisers — Byrnes, Stimson, Leahy, Marshall, King and Arnold. "I asked for their opinion whether the bomb should be used," he later wrote. The consensus was that it should.[45] Here at last was the miracle to end the war and solve all the perplexing problems posed by the necessity for invasion. But because no one could tell what effect the bomb might have "physically or psychologically," it was decided to proceed with the military plans for the invasion.

No one at this time, or later in the conference, raised the question of whether the Japanese should be informed of the existence of the bomb. That question, it will be recalled, had been discussed by the Scientific Panel on June 16 and at the White House meeting with the JCS, the service Secretaries and Mr. McCloy on June 18. For a

[44] Churchill, *op. cit.*, p. 638.

[45] . . . Truman, *op. cit.*, p. 415. General Eisenhower was at Potsdam and his advice, Truman says, was asked. The various participants differ in their recollections of this meeting. . . .

variety of reasons, including uncertainty as to whether the bomb would work, it had then been decided that the Japanese should not be warned of the existence of the new weapon. The successful explosion of the first bomb on July 17 did not apparently outweigh the reasons advanced earlier for keeping the bomb a secret, and evidently none of the men involved thought the question needed to be reviewed. The Japanese would learn of the atomic bomb only when it was dropped on them.

The secrecy that had shrouded the development of the atomic bomb was torn aside briefly at Potsdam, but with no visible effect. On July 24, on the advice of his chief advisers, Truman informed Marshal Stalin "casually" that the Americans had "a new weapon of unusual destructive force." "The Russian Premier," he recalled, "showed no special interest. All he said was that he was glad to hear it and hoped we would make 'good use of it against the Japanese.' "[46] One cannot but wonder whether the Marshal was preoccupied at the moment or simulating a lack of interest.

On the military side, the Potsdam Conference developed nothing new. The plans already made were noted and approved. Even at this late stage the question of the bomb was divorced entirely from military plans and the final report of the conference accepted as the main effort the invasion of the Japanese home islands. November 15, 1946, was accepted as the planning date for the end of the war against Japan.

During the conference, Stalin told Truman about the Japanese overtures — information that the Americans already had. The Marshal spoke of the matter also to Churchill, who discussed it with Truman, suggesting cautiously that some offer be made to Japan. "Mr. Stimson, General Marshall, and the President," he later wrote, "were evidently searching their hearts, and we had no need to press them. We knew of course that the Japanese were ready to give up all conquests made in the war." That same night, after dining with Stalin and Truman, the Prime Minister wrote that the Russians intended to attack Japan soon after August 8 — perhaps within two weeks after that date.[47] Truman presumably received the same information, confirming Harry Hopkins' report of his conversation with Stalin in Moscow in May.

All that remained now was to warn Japan and give her an opportunity to surrender. In this matter Stimson's and Grew's views, as outlined in the memorandum of July 2, were accepted, but ap-

[46] Truman, p. 416. . . .
[47] Truman, p. 396; Churchill, p. 642. See also Byrnes, p. 205; Leahy, p. 420.

parently on the advice of the former Secretary of State Cordell Hull it was decided to omit any reference to the Emperor. Hull's view, solicited by Byrnes before his departure for Potsdam, was that the proposal smacked of appeasement and "seemed to guarantee continuance not only of the Emperor but also of the feudal privileges of a ruling caste." And should the Japanese reject the warning, the proposal to retain the imperial system might well encourage resistance and have "terrible political repercussions" in the United States. For these reasons he recommended that no statement about the Emperor be made until "the climax of Allied bombing and Russia's entry into the war."[48] Thus, the final terms offered to the Japanese in the Potsdam Declaration on July 26 made no mention of the Emperor or of the imperial system. Neither did the declaration contain any reference to the atom bomb but simply warned the Japanese of the consequences of continued resistance. Only those already familiar with the weapon could have read the references to inevitable and complete destruction as a warning of atomic warfare.

The receipt of the Potsdam Declaration in Japan led to frantic meetings to decide what should be done. It was finally decided not to reject the note but to await the results of the Soviet overture. At this point, the military insisted that the government make some statement to the people, and on July 28 Premier Suzuki declared to the press that Japan would ignore the declaration, a statement that was interpreted by the Allies as a rejection.

To the Americans the rejection of the Potsdam Declaration confirmed the view that the military was still in control of Japan and that only a decisive act of violence could remove them. The instrument for such action lay at hand in the atomic bomb; events now seemed to justify its use. But in the hope that the Japanese might still change their minds, Truman held off orders on the use of the bomb for a few days. Only silence came from Tokyo, for the Japanese were waiting for a reply from the Soviet Government, which would not come until the return of Stalin and Molotov from Potsdam on August 6. Prophetically, Foreign Minister Tojo wrote Sato on August 2, the day the Potsdam Conference ended, that he could not afford to lose a single day in his efforts to conclude arrangements with the Russians "if we were to end the war before the assault on our mainland."[49] By that time, President Truman had already decided on the use of the bomb.

Preparations for dropping the two atomic bombs produced thus

[48] *Memoirs of Cordell Hull* (New York: Macmillan, 1948), v. 2, p. 1593.
[49] Kase, *op. cit.*, p. 222.

far had been under way for some time. The components of the bombs had been sent by cruiser to Tinian in May and the fissionable material was flown out in mid-July. The B-29s and crews were ready and trained, standing by for orders, which would come through the Commanding General, U. S. Army Strategic Air Forces in the Pacific, General Spaatz. Detailed arrangements and schedules were completed and all that was necessary was to issue orders.

At General Arnold's insistence, the responsibility for selecting the particular target and fixing the exact date and hour of the attack was assigned to the field commander, General Spaatz. In orders issued on July 25 and approved by Stimson and Marshall, Spaatz was ordered to drop the "first special bomb as soon as weather will permit visual bombing after about 3 August 1945 on one of the targets: Hiroshima, Kokura, Niigata, and Nagasaki." He was instructed also to deliver a copy of this order personally to MacArthur and Nimitz. Weather was the critical factor because the bomb had to be dropped by visual means, and Spaatz delegated to his chief of staff, Major-General Curtis E. LeMay, the job of deciding when the weather was right for this most important mission.

From the dating of the order to General Spaatz it has been argued that President Truman was certain the warning would be rejected and had fixed the date for the bombing of Hiroshima even before the issuance of the Potsdam Declaration. But such an argument ignores the military necessities. For operational reasons, the orders had to be issued in sufficient time "to set the military wheels in motion." In a sense, therefore, the decision was made on July 25. It would stand unless the President changed his mind. "I had made the decision," wrote Truman in 1955. "I also instructed Stimson that the order would stand unless I notified him that the Japanese reply to our ultimatum was acceptable."[50] The rejection by the Japanese of the Potsdam Declaration confirmed the orders Spaatz had already received.

THE JAPANESE SURRENDER

On Tinian and Guam, preparations for dropping the bomb had been completed by August 3. The original plan was to carry out the operation on August 4, but General LeMay deferred the attack because of bad weather over the target. On August 5 the forecasts were favorable and he gave the word to proceed with the mission the following day. At 0245 on August 6, the bomb-carrying plane was airborne. Six and a half hours later the bomb was released over Hiroshima, Japan's eighth largest city, to explode 50 seconds later

[50] Truman, pp. 420–421.

at a height of about 2,000 feet. The age of atomic warfare had opened.

Aboard the cruiser *Augusta* on his way back to the United States, President Truman received the news by radio. That same day a previously prepared release from Washington announced to the world that an atomic bomb had been dropped on Hiroshima and warned the Japanese that if they did not surrender they could expect "a rain of ruin from the air, the like of which has never been seen on this earth."[51]

On August 7, Ambassador Sato in Moscow received word at last that Molotov would see him the next afternoon. At the appointed hour he arrived at the Kremlin, full of hope that he would receive a favorable reply to the Japanese proposal for Soviet mediation with the Allies to end the war. Instead, he was handed the Soviet declaration of war, effective on August 9. Thus, three months to the day after Germany's surrender, Marshal Stalin had lived up to his promise to the Allies.

Meanwhile, President Truman had authorized the use of the second bomb — the last then available. The objective was Kokura, the date August 9. But the plane carrying the bomb failed to make its run over the primary target and hit the secondary target, Nagasaki, instead. The next day Japan sued for peace.

The close sequence of events between August 6 and 10, combined with the fact that the bomb was dropped almost three months before the scheduled invasion of Kyushu and while the Japanese were trying desperately to get out of the war, has suggested to some that the bombing of Hiroshima had a deeper purpose than the desire to end the war quickly. This purpose, it is claimed, was nothing less than a desire to forestall Soviet intervention into the Far Eastern war. Else why this necessity for speed? Certainly nothing in the military situation seemed to call for such hasty action. But if the purpose was to forestall Soviet intervention, then there was every reason for speed. And even if the Russians could not be kept out of the war, at least they would be prevented from making more than a token contribution to victory over Japan. In this sense it may be argued that the bomb proved a success, for the war ended with the United States in full control of Japan.

This theory leaves several matters unexplained. In the first place, the Americans did not know the exact date on which the Soviet Union would declare war but believed it would be within a week

[51] The statement is published in *The New York Times,* August 7, 1945. . . .

or two of August 8. If they had wished to forestall a Soviet declaration of war, then they could reasonably have been expected to act sooner than they did. Such close timing left little if any margin for error. Secondly, had the United States desired above everything else to keep the Russians out, it could have responded to one of several unofficial Japanese overtures, or made the Potsdam Declaration more attractive to Japan. Certainly the failure to put a time limit on the declaration suggests that speed was not of the essence in American calculations. Finally, the date and time of the bombing were left to Generals Spaatz and LeMay, who certainly had no way of knowing Soviet intentions. Bad weather or any other untoward incident could have delayed the attack a week or more.

There is reason to believe that the Russians at the last moved more quickly than they had intended. In his conversations with Harry Hopkins in May 1945 and at Potsdam, Marshal Stalin had linked Soviet entry with negotiations then in progress with Chinese representatives in Moscow. When these were completed, he had said, he would act. On August 8 these negotiations were still in progress.

Did the atomic bomb accomplish its purpose? Was it, in fact, as Stimson said, "the best possible sanction" after Japan rejected the Potsdam Declaration? The sequence of events argues strongly that it was, for bombs were dropped on the 6th and 9th, and on the 10th Japan surrendered. But in the excitement over the announcement of the first use of an atomic bomb and then of Japan's surrender, many overlooked the significance of the Soviet Union's entry into the war on the 9th. The first bomb had produced consternation and confusion among the leaders of Japan, but no disposition to surrender. The Soviet declaration of war, though not entirely unexpected, was a devastating blow and, by removing all hope of Soviet mediation, gave the advocates of peace their first opportunity to come boldly out into the open. When Premier Suzuki arrived at the palace on the morning of the 9th, he was told that the Emperor believed Japan's only course now was to accept the Potsdam Declaration. The militarists could and did minimize the effects of the bomb, but they could not evade the obvious consequences of Soviet intervention, which ended all hope of dividing their enemies and securing softer peace terms.

In this atmosphere, the leaders of Japan held a series of meetings on August 9, but were unable to come to agreement. In the morning came word of the fate of Nagasaki. This additional disaster failed to resolve the issues between the military and those who advocated surrender. Finally the Emperor took the unprecedented step of calling an Imperial Conference, which lasted until 3 o'clock the next morning. When it, too, failed to produce agreement the Emperor told his ministers that he wished the war brought to an end. The constitutional significance of this action is difficult for Westerners to comprehend, but it resolved the crisis and produced in the cabinet a formal decision to accept the Potsdam Declaration, provided it did not prejudice the position of the Emperor.

What finally forced the Japanese to surrender? Was it air bombardment, naval power, the atomic bomb or Soviet entry? The United States Strategic Bombing Survey concluded that Japan would have surrendered by the end of the year, without invasion and without the atomic bomb. Other equally informed opinion maintained that it was the atomic bomb that forced Japan to surrender. "Without its use," Dr. Karl T. Compton asserted, "the war would have continued for many months."[52] Admiral Nimitz believed firmly that the decisive factor was "the complete impunity with which the Pacific Fleet pounded Japan," and General Arnold claimed it was air bombardment that had brought Japan to the verge of collapse.[53] But Major-General Claire Chennault, wartime air commander in China, maintained that Soviet entry into the Far Eastern war brought about the surrender of Japan and would have done so "even if no atomic bombs had been dropped."[54]

It would be a fruitless task to weigh accurately the relative importance of all the factors leading to the Japanese surrender. There is no doubt that Japan had been defeated by the summer of 1945, if not earlier. But defeat did not mean that the military clique had given up; the Army intended to fight on and had made elaborate preparations for the defense of the homeland. Whether air bombardment and naval blockade or the threat of invasion would have produced an early surrender and averted the heavy losses almost certain to accompany the actual landings in Japan is a moot question. Certainly they had a profound effect on the Japanese position. It is equally impossible to assert categorically that the atomic bomb alone or Soviet intervention alone was the decisive factor in bringing the war to an end. All that can be said on the available evidence is that Japan was defeated in the military sense by August 1945 and that the bombing of Hiroshima, followed by the Soviet Union's declaration of war and then the bombing of Nagasaki and the threat of

[52] Compton, "If the Atomic Bomb Had Not Been Dropped," *Atlantic Monthly*, December, 1946, p. 54.

[53] H. H. Arnold, *Global Mission* (New York: Harper, 1949), p. 598. . . .

[54] *The New York Times*, August 15, 1945. . . .

still further bombing, acted as catalytic agents to produce the Japanese decision to surrender. Together they created so extreme a crisis that the Emperor himself, in an unprecedented move, took matters into his own hands and ordered his ministers to surrender. Whether any other set of circumstances would have resolved the crisis and produced the final decision to surrender is a question history cannot yet answer.

The Strategic Role of
United States Bombers

JEREMY J. STONE

The strategic role of our bombers is severely limited by four characteristics. Bombers are vulnerable on the ground, slow to target, of uncertain penetration capability, and they must be committed at a very early stage in a war.

First, the bomber force cannot be depended upon for a high rate of survival from a surprise enemy attack because of its great vulnerability on the ground. In normal periods, in order to minimize this vulnerability, half of the SAC bomber force is maintained on a fifteen-minute ground alert with a small number on airborne alert. The fifteen-minute warning is supposed to be provided by BMEWS (Ballistic Missile Early Warning System) stations in Clear, Alaska, Thule, Greenland, and Fylingdales, Great Britain. Such notice would not be given if missiles were fired over the Antarctic — a widely discussed possibility that was mentioned by Premier Khrushchev (but which would be expensive in accuracy and in pay load)

Reprinted from *Containing the Arms Race* by Jeremy J. Stone by permission of The M.I.T. Press, Cambridge, Massachusetts, pp. 81–89. Some footnotes have been omitted.

— or if submarine-launched missiles were used. Similarly, the Cuban missiles would have "outflanked" the warning system.[1]

The submarine-launched missiles, especially, pose a potential threat to ground-based bombers. Secretary McNamara believes that "toward the latter part of this decade . . . we must anticipate that submarine-launched missiles or others coming with very little, if any, warning will very probably destroy the majority of aircraft on the ground."[2]

Against such problems the Department of Defense has maintained the capability to fly one-eighth of the B-52 force on airborne alert for about one year. (The Air Force had asked for one-fourth.)[3] And the number of SAC bases has steadily grown in number. SAC now presents 55 domestic airbase targets and 13 foreign targets, and, in times of immediate emergency, the force can be dispersed to 100 fields.[4]

Even after such dispersal, however, SAC would still provide a first-priority target. Consider, for instance, the situation in 1964. General Maurice Preston testified in 1960 that SAC's ultimate goal was one squadron (one-third of a wing of 45 bombers) of B-52's per base and one wing of B-47's per base. Since, in 1964 figures, there are about 15 wings of B-47's remaining (700 planes . . .),

[1] If there had been no heavy bombers in the U.S. force, the strategic concern over Soviet missiles in Cuba would have been diminished since the missiles would have had no highly profitable targets. This indicates one of the ways in which bomber disarmament will have a stabilizing effect.

[2] U.S. Congress, Senate, Subcommittee of the Committee Appropriations, *Department of Defense Appropriations for 1964* (88th Cong., 1st sess., 1963), p. 191.

[3] *Statement of Secretary of Defense Robert S. McNamara before the House Armed Services Committee on the Fiscal Year 1965–69 Defense Program and the 1965 Defense Budget* (Washington, D.C.: House Armed Services Committee Secretary, 1964), p. 33: U.S. Congress, House, Subcommittee of the Committee on Appropriations, *Department of Defense Appropriations for 1961* (86th Cong., 2nd sess., 1960), Part 7, p. 100.

[4] Such dispersal plans were described to Congress as far back as 1956.

"*Colonel Nichols:* Now we have a dispersal plan in SAC. It works like this: Each one of our bases, let's take the base at Fairchild, we have two wings there, each wing will have a plan and the plan will have the aircraft say take off from Fairchild and come down to these green areas. They are what we call orbit areas.

"At that position the aircraft will circle. He will await then instructions from his home base if it is not destroyed or from another source if his home base is destroyed, and then he will either land at what we call our dispersal base or go back to Fairchild, depending on what he is told." (U.S. Congress, Senate, Subcommittee of the Air Force Committee on Armed Services, *Air Power* [84th Congress, 2nd sess., 1956], Part 2, p. 146.)

42 squadrons of B-52's (14 wings . . .), and about 6 squadrons of B-58's (80 planes . . .), this would require 63 bases. Since the 55 domestic and 13 foreign bases referred to exceed this number, the goal has evidently been effectively achieved. Nevertheless, the "bonus" to enemy attack that catches the bombers on their bases would be somewhere between 15 to 1 (heavy-bomber bases) and 45 to 1 (medium-bomber bases), even assuming that the bombers carry nothing more than the single H-bomb that Secretary McNamara indicated would destroy every bomber on its base. With 100 fields, the average bonus would be at least 14 to 1 since there are about 1,400 bombers. It should be emphasized that the bombers with their expected BMEWS warning would not represent an adequate deterrent in the absence of protected missile systems. In this sense, they do not provide adequate backup protection for a situation in which our missiles could be successfully attacked.

The second limitation of bombers is that they are slow to target. If a bomber has a top speed of 500 mph and must travel 2,000, 4,000, or 6,000 miles, it will take 4, 8, or 12 hours to reach its target. Several different missile salvos can take place in this time. This means that bombers are especially unsuited to the "damage-limiting" strategy advocated by the Department of Defense. Only a "very, very, very, low percentage" of the effective forces will be bombers, despite the fact that they are capable of carrying a much larger number of megatons than are existing missiles. This was discussed by Secretary McNamara:

> SECRETARY McNAMARA: What percentage of the force that destroys the Soviet Union is delivered by bombers? The answer to that is a very, very, low percentage. . . .
>
> MR. FORD: If that is the case . . . why do you keep bombers in the force at all until 1968?
>
> SECRETARY McNAMARA: Because they add some insurance and because certain targets may be more effectively destroyed by bombers assuming the bomber can get there before the targets have been launched against the United States, *and that is quite an assumption*.[5] (Italics added.)

The third limiting characteristic of bombers is a "substantial range between the optimistic and pessimistic estimates" of the number that will penetrate the Soviet air defenses. (This uncertainty is itself undesirable since we should prefer to have our deterrent capability unequivocal.) And in both cases, "a higher proportion of the Minuteman force than of the B-52 force can be counted upon to reach targets in a retaliatory strike." Bombers are also rated lower

[5] U.S. Congress, House, *Department of Defense Appropriations for 1964*, Part 1, p. 318.

in "systems dependability," by which is meant that the uncertainties associated with them are harder to estimate. Thus the Secretary of Defense has noted that "we can predict the results of a missile attack with greater confidence than those of a bomber attack."[6] The extent of these uncertainties has been indicated by General Thomas White, who asserted, a few years ago, in reference to U.S. bombers: "All might get through in one case and then there might be a great loss in another."[7]

Speaking more generally of free-fall bombing, the Secretary of Defense termed it "nearly impossible" by the end of the sixties.[8] This means that planes would have to be dependent upon their own guided missiles which would permit an attack from a distance. But a missile of this type, Secretary McNamara noted in canceling one (the Skybolt),

> . . . could not make a worthwhile contribution to our strategic capability since it would combine the disadvantages of the bomber with those of the missile. It would have the bomber's disadvantages of being soft and concentrated and relatively vulnerable on the ground and the bomber's slow time to target. But it would not have the bomber's advantageous payload and accuracy, nor would it have the advantages usually associated with a manned system. It would have the lower payload and poorer accuracy of the missile. . . .[9]

The Secretary of Defense indicates as a fourth limitation that bombers must be "committed . . . very early" in a war and cannot be used "in a controlled and deliberate way."[10] In particular, the widely used argument that bombers can be "recalled" is quite misleading: invulnerably based missiles do not need to be fired in ad-

[6] *Statement of Secretary McNamara, op. cit.*, pp. 37–38.

[7] U.S. Congress, House, *Department of Defense Appropriations for 1960*, Part 1, p. 836.

[8] "SECRETARY MCNAMARA: . . . we will be in serious difficulty by the end of the decade if at that point our strategic force is dependent upon free-fall bombs as the primary weapon of attack, because no one in a responsible position at the Pentagon that I am aware of believes that free-fall bombs can be placed over the prime targets in the Soviet Union at the end of this decade.

"SENATOR STENNIS: Why?

"SECRETARY MCNAMARA: Because by that time the air defense systems of the Soviet Union will be such as to make it nearly impossible for an airplane to advance to a position over the target so that it would be in position to launch free-fall bombs against that target." (U.S. Congress, Senate, Committee on Armed Services, *Military Procurement Authorization Fiscal Year 1964* [88th Cong., 1st sess., 1963], p. 93.)

[9] U.S. Congress, House, *Department of Defense Appropriations for 1964*, Part 1, p. 114.

[10] U.S. Congress, House, *Department of Defense Appropriations for 1963*, Part 2, p. 15.

vance and hence the ability to be recalled is not an issue with them. Furthermore, recalling bombers is dangerous and difficult. They are not, in fact, very "recallable." The recalled fleet has tired, if not exhausted, crews, and somewhere in the system there must be low, if not empty, fuel tanks. If the recall is a mistake, the bombers may have been effectively neutralized. Bombers are, for this reason, not even very capable of accepting an enemy surrender — the risk of recalling them to vulnerable bases (if there were no missiles) could make it impossible. Most important, the time for recall is limited. Congress has been told that civilian decision makers would have to make some (recalling) decision within one and a half hours of the time the bomber force was launched toward its targets. (Obviously this does not refer to an airborne alert which might be maintained for relatively long periods.)

As a result of these restrictions, the utility of bombers is limited to certain special uses as "supplementary devices to the main force."[11] What are these supplementary uses? *Air Force and Space Digest* complained that

> No mention is [being] made of the position that manned strategic aircraft greatly enhance operational flexibility by allowing: recall of an attack; unmistakable displays of resolve, through stepped-up airborne alerts and large-scale maneuvers, such as were used in the Cuban crisis; wartime assessment of target damage; location and destruction of mobile targets; a close matching of the weapon to the target; and, when the occasion calls for it, the use of very-high-yield warheads.[12]

We have discussed recall of an attack. The threatening nature of a fleet of bombers on airborne alert is a more plausible but still quite dubious consideration. It has received wide attention.[13] In answer

[11] This comment of the Secretary of Defense was reinforced by the assertion that "There is no plan in the Air Force that I know of, or no thought of any plan to substitute air launch for sea and land launch for the great bulk of the megatonnage." (U.S. Congress, Senate, *Department of Defense Appropriations for 1964*, p. 192.)

[12] J. S. Buty, Jr., "The Future of Manned Bombers," *Air Force and Space Digest*, Vol. 46 (March 1963), p. 29.

[13] "SENATOR CANNON: When we get to the point that we are practically phased out without manned bombers under our present program we would have no method of making a visible display of strength insofar as SAC's posture is concerned, would we? (U.S. Congress, Senate, *Military Procurement Authorization Fiscal Year 1964*, p. 932.)

"GENERAL LEMAY: With missiles you cannot do anything except to say, 'I will shoot my missiles,' that is all.

"SENATOR CANNON: You cannot very well take a picture of a man with his thumb about 6 inches above the trigger and say, 'He is going to put it on down if you don't do such and such.' That doesn't give you much of a bargaining point, does it?

"GENERAL LEMAY: That is correct."

to a written question from Senator Margaret Chase Smith, Secretary McNamara said that the SAC bomber fleet's advanced state of readiness during the Cuban crisis was meant both "to avoid the possibility of surprise" and to "impress upon the Soviets our seriousness and determination."[14] In this latter effort it was presumably successful, although this was most clearly only one element among other considerations. In speaking to the Supreme Soviet of the U.S.S.R., Chairman Khrushchev reported on the Cuban crisis as follows:

> Events developed at a swift pace. The American command put all its armed forces, including troops stationed in Europe as well as the Sixth Fleet, in the Mediterranean, and the Seventh Fleet based in the Taiwan area, in a state of complete combat readiness. Several paratroop, infantry and armored divisions, numbering some 100,000 men, were allocated for the attack on Cuba alone. In addition, 183 warships, with 85,000 sailors on board, were moved toward the shores of Cuba. Several thousand warplanes were to cover the landing on Cuba. About 20% of all U.S. Strategic Air Command planes carrying atomic and hydrogen bombs were kept aloft around the clock. Reserves were called up.[15]

While analysts who emphasize air power tend to argue that the "20 per cent of SAC" was an important consideration leading to Soviet concessions, it is obviously impossible for anyone to say — perhaps even for Premier Khrushchev himself. It should be noted, however, that Soviet attitudes toward such displays of force are somewhat peculiar from an American analyst's point of view. For instance, during the Paris Summit Conference in 1960, Secretary of Defense Thomas S. Gates ordered the Joint Chiefs to institute an alert. This alert involved both the Continental Air Defense Command and the Strategic Air Command. It lasted for seven hours and was said to be justified by the need to check the ability of the President, while abroad, to keep in touch with U.S. forces.[16] (Nevertheless the action seems to have been most provocative. President Eisenhower argued that international negotiations had sometimes been used to conceal preparations for a surprise attack. This tends only to reinforce the seriousness of his act.) The reaction of American strategists, had they been in policy-making positions in the Soviet Union, would have been to put Soviet forces on alert to decrease Soviet vulnerability. Instead, at a Paris press conference, Malinovsky volunteered: "We have not declared any military alert."

[14] U.S. Congress, Senate, *Department of Defense Appropriations for 1964*, p. 932.

[15] Cited in *Current Digest of the Soviet Press*, Vol. 14 (January 16, 1963), p. 5.

[16] *The New York Times*, May 17, 1960.

And Khrushchev added: "Correct. We have not declared an alert and will not declare one. Our nerves are strong."[17]

Whatever the psychological impact of airborne bombers, it can hardly fail to decline rapidly. Our bombers, even from airborne alert stations, can hardly be within one half hour of their targets as our missiles are at all times.[18] Hence they do not add significantly to whatever threat of surprise attack exists. And even the implied threat deliberately to initiate a nuclear war will wear very thin in the face of the increasing invulnerability of Soviet forces.

The merits of most of the remaining arguments for bombers — wartime assessment of target damage, location and destruction of mobile targets, use of very-high-yield warheads, and so on — depend in part on U.S. strategy and in part on a host of cost-effectiveness considerations. The present strategy is a "damage-limiting" one.[19] The intention is to preserve the option of striking at many Soviet forces, after being attacked ourselves, so as to limit the size of a follow-on attack. Secretary McNamara argues, without giving details, that "comprehensive studies" show "under a wide variety of circumstances . . . forces in excess of those needed simply to destroy Soviet cities could significantly reduce damage to the U.S. and Western Europe." It can be assumed that the studies are based, in particular, on the assumption that a nuclear war will be fought to a finish. (For instance, the Secretary intends to attack weapon *storage* sites with bombers. This "limits" damage only if the war is not likely to be terminated quickly.) On the assumption that the Soviet Union achieves secure second-strike capabilities — a widely heralded expectation — these studies will become outmoded. The

---

[17] Hans Speier, *Divided Berlin* (New York: Praeger, 1961), p. 109.

[18] Congressman George Mahon, hypothesizing a situation in which war occurred after the bombers were approaching their targets, suggested that "probably the missile would hit its target before the bomber." General Curtis LeMay replied: "Under most circumstances, yes." (U.S. Congress, House, *Department of Defense Appropriations for 1964*, Part 2, p. 527.)

[19] "Thus, a 'damage-limiting' strategy appears to be the most practical and effective course for us to follow. Such a strategy requires a force considerably larger than would be needed for a limited 'cities only' strategy. While there are still some differences of judgment on just how large such a force should be, there is general agreement that it should be large enough to ensure the destruction, singly or in combination, of the Soviet Union, Communist China, and the Communist satellites as national societies, under the worst possible circumstances of war outbreak that can reasonably be postulated, and, in addition, to destroy their warmaking capability so as to limit, to the extent practicable, damage to this country and to our Allies." (Statement of Secretary McNamara, *op. cit.*, pp. 31–32.)

emphasis must then turn, in one way or another, to "war-termination strategies." If our enemy has secure second-strike forces, we will not be able to justify plans to eliminate quickly the residual forces of an aggressor. The tendency to do so now is reinforced by Soviet relative weakness, which permits the Secretary of Defense to state that "today, following a surprise attack on us, we would still have the power to respond with overwhelming force, and *they would not then have the capability of a further strike*."[20] (Italics added.)

When the Soviet Union can retain the "capability of a further strike," two different tendencies will discourage the use of bombers even if they exist. First, it will become relatively less likely that a Soviet attack would include American cities — since the Soviets would want and be able to hold these cities hostage with their secure force. (Our own policy takes this form.) Hence an unrestrained U.S. response to attack would not be in order. But bombers are difficult to use in a restrained fashion primarily because of penetration problems.

Second, there would be far less motivation to maintain the capability for such "bitter end" activities as assessment of target damage, destruction of weapon sites, location and destruction of mobile missiles, use of very-high-yield weapons, and so on.

Finally, there is the question of a "proper mix" in our offensive weapons. While such a mix is highly desirable, it is inevitably going to be a mix of missiles in the view of the Secretary of Defense. But missile-carrying bombers do not provide an especially good way to vary our missiles systems, for the reasons given previously.

In short, I believe that clearly foreshadowed changes in defense thinking will further reduce the utility of bombers, as Soviet second-strike capability increases. But in any case, it is clear that bombers are, by far, the most expendable portion of the strategic forces, whether judged by existing or anticipated doctrine. The bombers are simply insurance of a highly generalized kind. They have some unusual properties, which are not especially impressive. None of these calls for the approximately 700 bombers that will be in the force even after the B-47's have been phased out. From a strategic point of view, the United States should definitely be asking, "What can we get in return for dismantling our bombers?"

[20] Stewart Alsop, "Our New Strategy: The Alternative to Total War," *Saturday Evening Post* (December 1, 1962), p. 18.

PART IV

Constraints on the Use of Force: Reciprocal Interactions in Armament Races

In deciding where, when, and how to use military power, national leaders must calculate how much force they need in order to do what they wish. The calculation of how much is needed depends partially on what goals are being pursued. Coercion or conquest, for example, will usually require more force than would be needed to dissuade a foe from attacking one's country. The calculation of how much is needed also depends on the reactions of other states to the types and amounts of forces one procures. State *A* may have increased its forces only to find that any possible gains are soon negated by similar increases made by state *B*. State *A* may then decide that the prize is worth the payment of an extra price and may add still more to its forces. State *B* may decide likewise. State *A* may decide to up the ante again and so forth. Situations in which this action-reaction phenomenon occurs — where *B*'s actions depend on *A*'s and *A*'s on *B*'s — can be called "arms races."

Under what circumstances do such interactions occur? Are some types of weapons more likely to produce arms races than others? How can arms races be controlled? These are the questions that the three authors in this section explore. Hedley Bull specifies the circumstances likely to produce an arms race and the conditions required to achieve arms control. Samuel P. Huntington undertakes a historical comparison of arms races to determine whether quantitative or qualitative races are the more unstable. Malcolm W. Hoag examines different kinds of weapon technologies in order to lay bare the strategies making for stability in a nuclear arms race.

The Objectives of Arms Control

HEDLEY BULL

INTRODUCTION

This is an inquiry into the modern arms race and the measures by which it might be controlled. It is not a plea for disarmament, or against it, or for any particular military policy. If it contains a plea at all, this is for the recognition of complexity in the moral, military and political issues raised by modern war: for confronting this complexity, rather than turning away from it: for rigorous study and anxious questioning, in place of the pursuit of panaceas.

There are two ideas which have a central place in this study: disarmament and arms control. These are examined both in general and in the context of strategies, weapons and political tensions of the present time. It will be helpful to make clear at the outset what is meant by these terms.

Disarmament is the reduction or abolition of armaments. It may be unilateral or multilateral; general or local; comprehensive or partial; controlled or uncontrolled.

Arms control is restraint internationally exercised upon armaments policy, whether in respect of the level of armaments, their character, development or use.

Disarmament and arms control intersect with one another. They are not the same, for there can be disarmament which is not controlled, and control which does not involve a reduction of armaments. On the other hand they are not exclusive of one another. . . .

THE OBJECTIVES OF ARMS CONTROL

Before the first world war disarmament doctrine placed its chief emphasis on the economic objective. But since then it has had as its core the notion that armaments and, in particular, armaments races are a cause of war; and that to abolish or reduce and limit

Reprinted by permission of the Institute for Strategic Studies from Hedley Bull, *The Control of the Arms Race* (New York: Frederick A. Praeger, 1965), pp. vii, 4–12, 30–39, 65–69. Portions of the text and some footnotes have been omitted.

armaments, and to halt or otherwise control armaments races, is to contribute to international security.

The extent to which armaments and armaments races provoke international tension and war, and the extent to which arms control can provide guarantees of international security, are often exaggerated. The contribution of arms control to international security may be a modest one, and we must first reflect upon the source of its limitations.

The military factor is an important one in international politics, but it is not the only one. The view that international security is a matter of disarmament or arms control belongs to a group of opposed but closely related views, whose common theme is *peace through the manipulation of force*. According to one of these views, the maintenance of peace is a matter of securing a preponderance of force in the hands of a central authority, a world government or universal state. According to another, it is a matter of the pooling of force among right-minded nations, in a system of collective security. According to another, it is a matter of securing an equilibrium of force or balance of power throughout international society. According to yet another, security depends on neutralizing the advantages of resorting to force, in a system of mutual deterrence or general terror. Finally, there is the view that it depends on abolishing or reducing force, through disarmament; or on restraining and limiting force, through arms control.

All of these doctrines can be pursued a certain distance, and there are political and strategic circumstances in which each of them carries conviction. But the claims of each become absurd when they are pressed to the point of considering military in abstraction from political considerations. What happens in international politics is a matter of will as well as of weapons; or, in the language of the recent American strategic debate, of intentions as well as of capability. Armed power and the will to employ it is each itself and not the other thing. Each affects and limits the other, but neither can be regarded as the mere expression of the other.

This is as true of the doctrines of disarmament and arms control as of the others. Whatever contribution such phenomena as disarmament or arms control may have made in the past, or may come to make in the future, to international peace and order, it is a contribution whose bounds can be no greater than those set by the limited importance of the military factor in international relations. We may illustrate this limitation by considerng two of the characteristic assertions of disarmament doctrine: that arms races lead to war, and that disarmament or arms control halts arms races.

Arms races are intense competitions between opposed powers

or groups of powers, each trying to achieve an advantage in military power by increasing the quantity or improving the quality of its armaments or armed forces. Arms races are not peculiar to the present time or the present century, but are a familiar form of international relationship. Arms races which are qualitative rather than quantitative, which proceed more by the improvement of weapons or forces than by the increase of them, have grown more important with the progress of technology: and what is peculiar to the present grand Soviet-Western arms race is the extent to which its qualitative predominates over its quantitative aspect. However, there have not always been arms races, and they are in no way inherent in international relations, nor even in situations of international political conflict. Where the political tensions between two powers are not acute; where each power can gain an advantage over the other without increasing or improving its armaments, but simply by recruiting allies or depriving its opponent of them; where the economic or demographic resources to increase armaments, or the technological resources to improve them, do not exist, we do not find arms races. The prominent place which the Soviet-Western arms race occupies in international relations at the present time arises from the circumstance that the opportunities available to each side for increasing its relative military power lie very much more in the exploitation and mobilization of its own military resources, than in the attempt to influence the direction in which the relatively meagre military resources of outside powers are thrown, by concluding favourable alliances or frustrating unfavourable ones. It arises from the circumstance that the balance of military power can at present be affected very much more by armaments policy than by diplomacy.

It is seldom that anything so crude is asserted as that all wars are caused by arms races, but the converse is often stated, that all arms races cause wars: that in the past they have always resulted in war; or even that they lead inevitably to war.

It is true that, within states, armaments tend to create or to shape the will to use them, as well as to give effect to it; and that, between states, arms races tend to sustain or to exacerbate conflicts of policy, as well as to express them. Within each state, the military establishment, called into being by the policy of competitive armament, develops its own momentum: it creates interests and diffuses an ideology favourable to the continuation of the arms race, and generates pressures which will tend to resist any policy of calling it off. In this respect, that they display a will to survive, the armed forces, the armaments industries, the military branches of science and technology and of government, the settled habits of mind of those who think about strategy and defence, are like any great institution involving vast, impersonal organizations and the ambitions and livelihood of masses of men. Apart from these internal pressures of armaments establishments upon policy, it is possible to see in the pressures which each state exerts upon the other, in the action and reaction that constitute an arms race, a spiralling process in which the moving force is not, or not only, the political will or intention of governments, but their armaments and military capability. One nation's military security can be another's insecurity. One nation's military capability of launching an attack can be interpreted by its opponent as an intention to launch it, or as likely to create such an intention, whether that intention exists or not. Even where neither side has hostile intentions, nor very firmly believes the opponent to have them, military preparations may continue, since they must take into account a range of contingencies, which includes the worse cases. In so far as the competitors in an arms race are responsive to each other's military capabilities rather than to each other's intentions, in so far as they are led, by estimates of each other's capabilities, to make false estimates of each other's intentions, the arms race has a tendency to exacerbate a political conflict, or to preserve it where other circumstances are making towards its alleviation.

But the idea that arms races obey a logic of their own and can only result in war, is false; and perhaps also dangerous. It is false because it conceives the arms race as an autonomous process in which the military factor alone operates. The chief source of this error in recent years has been the belief in the importance of the various armaments competitions among the European powers, and especially the Anglo-German naval race, in contributing to the outbreak of the first world war. Even in this case, the importance of this factor is a matter of controversy. In the case of the origins of the second world war, the autonomous arms race cannot be regarded as having been important. On the contrary, we should say that the military factor which was most important in bringing it about was the failure of Britain, France and the Soviet Union to engage in the arms race with sufficient vigour, their insufficient response to the rearmament of Germany. In general, arms races arise as the result of political conflicts, are kept alive by them, and subside with them. We have only to reflect that there is not and has never been such a thing as a general or universal arms race, a war of all against all in military preparation. The context in which arms races occur is that of a conflict between particular powers or groups of powers, and of military, political, economic and technological circumstances in which an armaments competition is an appropriate form for his conflict to take.

Arms races have not always led to war, but have sometimes come to an end, like the Anglo-French naval races of the last century, and the Anglo-American naval race in this one, when, for one reason or another, the parties lost the will to pursue them. There is no more reason to believe that arms races must end in war than to believe that severe international rivalries, which are not accompanied by arms races, must do so. It is of course the case that wars are made possible by the existence of armaments. But the existence of armaments, and of sovereign powers commanding them and willing to use them, is a feature of international society, whether arms races are in progress or not. What is sometimes meant by those who assert that arms races cause wars is the quite different proposition that armaments cause wars. While armaments are among the conditions which enable wars to take place, they do not in themselves produce war, or provide in themselves a means of distinguishing the conditions of war from the conditions of peace. For all international experience has been accompanied by the existence of armaments, the experience of peace as much as the experience of war. To show why, in a context in which armaments are endemic, wars sometimes occur and sometimes do not; to show why, in this context, arms races sometimes arise, and either persist, subside or end in war, it is necessary to look beyond armaments themselves to the political factors which the doctrine of the autonomous arms race leaves out of account. . . .

The limitations of the view that arms races lead to war apply also to the view that the halting or reversing of arms races is a matter of arms control or disarmament. Just as the history of armaments and arms races is only one aspect of the history of international politics, so the history of disarmament and arms control can be only one aspect of the history of armaments. We cannot expect that a system of arms control will be brought into operation, nor that, if it is, it will persist, unless certain political conditions are fulfilled. It is, I believe, quite erroneous to suggest that disarmament cannot begin until political disputes have been removed, or that disarmament is something which follows automatically once they have been. On the contrary, it is only in the presence of political disputes and tensions serious enough to generate arms competitions that arms control has any relevance. Arms control is significant only among states that are politically opposed and divided, and the existence of political division and tension need not be an obstacle to it. On the other hand, the political conditions may allow of a system of arms control, or they may not. Unless the powers concerned want a system of arms control; unless there is a measure of political *détente* among them sufficient to allow of such a system; unless they are prepared to accept the military situation among them which the arms control system legitimizes and preserves, and can agree and remain agreed about what this situation will be, there can be little place for arms control.

This is indicated by the recent history of arms control agreements. The Rush-Bagot Treaty of 1817, under which the British Empire and the United States reduced and limited their naval armaments on the Great Lakes, made an important contribution to the development of confidence between these powers. The Washington Naval Treaty of 1922, under which the British Empire, the United States, Japan, France and Italy declared a ten-year "naval holiday" in the construction of new capital ships and aircraft carriers, limited each other's permitted total tonnage in these classes of vessel, and limited the size and armament of vessels in these classes and in the cruiser class, had a notable effect both on the course of armaments competition and on the course of international politics generally. So did the London Naval Treaty of 1930, under which the British Empire, the United States and Japan extended the "naval holiday" till 1936, and limited the maximum displacement of vessels in the destroyer and submarine classes, and the total tonnages permitted in the destroyer, submarine and cruiser classes. The treaty systems which preserved and made legitimate these levels and kinds of armaments or armaments ratios confirmed and strengthened the wider areas of agreement and mutual accommodation among these powers, on which peaceful and stable relations among them rested. But they also expressed, and were part of, these wider areas of agreement. Moreover, it was only in favourable political conditions that, once established, they continued to flourish. The Rush-Bagot Treaty, though it had to weather some political storms, survived in the temperate climate of Anglo-American and Canadian-American relations. On the other hand, when Japan determined to overthrow the political and territorial *status quo* in the Pacific, the Washington and London naval systems collapsed. The dependence of arms control systems for their survival on the continuance of those wider areas of political agreement of which they are a part is best illustrated by the most common form of arms control system, that contained in the military clauses of treaties of peace. It is characteristic of such systems that, like the disarmament clauses binding Germany in the Treaty of Versailles, they are part of wider political situations which the treaty makes legitimate and seeks to preserve, but are dictated by the victor and are inherently temporary.

Arms control systems, therefore, do not guarantee their own perpetuity. Theories of arms control often try to circumvent this difficulty by building into their projected systems some feature which purports to guarantee the permanence of the system, come what may politically. Thus the abolition of armaments is sometimes held to afford a means of making war physically impossible, whether nations have the will to wage it or not. Systems of inspection, supervision and sanctions are sometimes conceived of as means whereby arms control can be kept in operation, whatever the intention of the inspectors and the inspected. There are certainly means, formal and informal, of curbing or restraining the will to challenge or upset the military situation preserved in the system: if there were not, there would be no such thing as arms control. But arms control does not provide a technique of insulating a military situation from the future will of states to change it: it cannot bind, nor settle in advance, the future course of politics. There are no technical means of excluding the political factor.

If armaments and arms races are a threat to international security and disarmament or arms control a means of removing it, there are limits beyond which neither proposition can be pressed. However, these are limits which circumscribe not only the doctrine of disarmament, but also those military policies and doctrines with which it most frequently comes into collision. That armaments are causes as well as effects, and shape political motives and intentions as well as express them, is as much an assumption of the policy of "peace through strength" as it is of the policy of "peace through the reduction of armaments." It is no less a part of the policy of "deterrence" or the idea of "peace through terror," than it is a part of the ideas of disarmament or arms control. The limitations of disarmament doctrine to which I have drawn attention are not peculiar to this doctrine, but are the limitations of the whole field of strategic studies. . . .

THE CONDITIONS OF ARMS CONTROL

However desirable it may be, arms control can occur only if circumstances are such that governments both want it and can agree on its terms. . . . Unless the political conditions for arms control are present, the question of what method or procedure is appropriate in arms control negotiations, and the question how the technical problems involved in arms control can be solved, are of minor importance, and attempts to solve them in abstraction from political circumstances are of no significance. The view that international negotiations about arms control are concerned with the search for solutions to these problems, or that their failure to issue in agreements arises from the difficulty of finding these solutions, is, on the whole, mistaken. For the protracted public conversation of the powers about arms control should be viewed not as a cooperative attempt to solve a problem, but as a theme in their political relations.

Since the first world war, the ritual pursuit of disarmament has been part of the foreign policy of every important state. A nation's disarmament policy is, however, a subordinate part of its foreign policy, and expresses the general character of that policy. It is not necessarily shaped primarily, nor even at all, with a view to bringing about disarmament. At the World Disarmament Conference which began in 1932, for example, French disarmament policy was directed towards security against Germany, and German disarmament policy was directed towards equality with France. There was common ground between them as the policies of each included the alternative of some form of disarmament: an agreement, to this extent, was negotiable. But what determined the stance of each power in the conference chamber was not the range of ideas constituted by "the problem of disarmament," but the range of pressures and demands constituting its national policy. The most persistent objective of any nation's disarmament policy is that of demonstrating to opinion at home and abroad that efforts are being made towards disarmament, and that the reason why no agreement is arrived at lies in the policies of other nations, not in its own. The more radical and grandiose a disarmament proposal, the more it will satisfy this objective. Proposals which are radical and grandiose, moreover, are advanced in the knowledge that they will be rejected, and are an indication that the policy of the power advancing them is not directed towards disarmament.

But it would be quite mistaken to regard arms control negotiations as an elaborate charade enacted by the governments of the world for the benefit of the peoples of the world. Though they want other things more, most governments in most negotiations do want an agreement, if it can be had on their own terms. Usually, each government is divided as to how seriously an agreement should be sought: as the United States government has been regularly and publicly divided over the desirability of a ban on nuclear tests.

However, the question of establishing a system of arms control does not arise unless the powers concerned regard the pursuit of arms control, as distinct from the conduct of political warfare about arms control, as among the objectives of their policy. It cannot by any means be assumed that they do (nor should it be suggested without regard for other considerations, that they always should); and in fact many of them do not, except in the sense that they want other states to disarm. The conduct of political warfare about arms control, the cultivation of a favourable public image in relation to disarmament, is a constant preoccupation of all governments concerned in arms control negotiations or in making public pronouncements about them. The serious pursuit of arms control agreements, on the other hand, may be part of a nation's foreign policy, or it may not. Whether or not it is will depend upon the particular system of arms control, the general character of the nation's foreign policy, and the circumstances of the moment. We can say that powers which are bent at all costs on achieving or maintaining military supremacy over their opponents cannot contemplate the restraints of a comprehensive system of arms control. Powers that are weak, ambitious and frustrated, as Germany and the Soviet Union were in the years of the League disarmament negotiations, and as many Asian, African and Latin American nations are now, are adamant in their demands that the Great Powers should disarm, and would welcome a system of arms control which brought such disarmament about. But they would be hostile to the reduction of their own armaments or to the imposition of controls on the local arms races to which they are parties. The judgment that the serious pursuit of a particular arms control system does, or does not, form part of a nation's policy can be made only imprecisely and temporarily: for governments, as we know from public debates in Western countries on these matters, are often divided about the pursuit of a system of arms control, and the support for any such system within a government may ebb and flow.

If, however, the powers want a system of arms control, and present proposals which they believe might be accepted, arms control negotiations move out of the sphere of political warfare and into that of diplomacy. The obstacles to agreement in arms control negotiations are the same as in other kinds of negotiations, that in them each party seeks to promote its own advantage. It contemplates its own advantage, however, with a sensitivity and jealous regard that are peculiar even in diplomacy. For the subject-matter of arms control negotiations is the balance of military power. Treaties of arms control do not abolish military power, but stabilize a military situation. The central issue of arms control negotiations is: what military situation? No power is prepared to contemplate a treaty unless the situation that results from it is one in which its own military interest is firmly secured. Two facts stand persistently in the way of agreement: the inherent uncertainty as to what constitutes an equal balance between opponents, and the determination inherent in all military policy to err on the safe side. The imprecise and constantly changing balance that exists in the real world, and in the calculations and anxieties of statesmen, must be translated into the precision and fixity of a treaty. In all serious arms control negotiations, the proposals of any power express a closely reasoned (though not necessarily correct) estimate of its military interests. Thus in the

League period, the negotiators were unable to agree about what levels of military manpower a disarmament treaty should preserve, and about what categories of armament should be abolished or restricted by a scheme of qualitative disarmament, each power wishing to restrict those weapons most useful to its opponents. Britain and the United States, as the great naval powers, wished to abolish the submarine but retain battleships and aircraft carriers; the lesser naval powers wished to retain the submarine. France, as the great land power, wished to retain tanks and heavy guns, the lesser land powers favoured restriction of them, and so on. In the years of United States monopoly or superiority in nuclear weapons, there was a long debate concerning whether nuclear weapons should be abolished before the establishment of controls, as the Soviet Union insisted, or after, as the United States insisted. . . .

These reflections should not be the occasion of, nor do they express, cynicism about arms control negotiations, or despair about the possibility of agreements emerging from them. If governments did not consider disarmament proposals with a view to how they would affect their military security, they would be failing in their duty. Nor does their pursuit of military advantage mean that in principle agreement cannot be reached. All that follows from this interpretation is that an agreement, if it is reached, represents not the discovery of the solution to a problem, but *the striking of a bargain.* As in other kinds of bargaining agreements may emerge when proposals are worked out that advance the interests of both without injuring the interests of either. . . .

DISARMAMENT AND THE BALANCE OF POWER

The chief objective of arms control is international security. The contribution which arms control can make to international security is limited by the fact that it deals only with the military factor.

However, there is a military factor, and some military situations are more favourable to international security than others. . . . If arms control is concerned to foster military situations favourable to international security, what are these? In particular, how far is *disarmament,* or the reduction of armaments, the proper object of arms control? And how far is it the proper object of arms control to promote a stable *balance of power*? The purpose of this analysis is not to provide final answers to these questions; and not, in particular, to demonstrate that the proper object of arms control is to perfect a stable balance or equilibrium of armaments rather than to secure a reduction of armaments. Its purpose is to demonstrate the inadequacy of such prescriptions as "reduce!" or "abolish!" and the need to replace them with careful strategic analysis. It is not to be assumed (though cases could conceivably arise in which it could be shown) that the answer to the question, "what levels and kinds of armaments should arms control systems seek to perpetuate and make legitimate?" is the formula, "the lowest levels and the most primitive kinds." The conflict between this formula, and the doctrine of the balance of power, . . . indicates only one of the many respects in which it is inadequate. . . . We must be guided not by any such formula as this, nor by an exclusive concern with the maintenance of the military balance, but by addressing ourselves with determination to the complicated strategic and political calculation demanded by the question: what kinds, levels, deployments or uses of armaments would best promote security?

Disarmament is the reduction or abolition of armaments. The idea that the world is most secure when there is a *minimum* of armaments, the pursuit of the *maximum* disarmament, has been the central assumption of modern negotiations about arms control. . . .

But the idea that security lies in the minimum of armaments cannot be accepted uncritically. In considering this idea, we must examine separately two of the forms it takes: the stronger form, that the abolition of armaments makes war physically impossible; and the weaker form, that the reduction of armaments makes war less likely.

The stronger form is a doctrine which has great popular appeal, because it promises a form of security which is absolute and independent of the continuance of favourable political conditions. It suggests a world in which states cannot make war, even if they want to. It has played an important part in Soviet disarmament policy. Litvinov advocated total disarmament at a meeting of the preparatory commission of the League of Nations Disarmament Conference, on the occasion of the first appearance of Soviet delegates at Geneva, in 1927. All armed forces were to be disbanded and all armaments destroyed; military expenditure, military service, war ministers and chiefs of staffs were to be abolished; military propaganda and military instruction were to be prohibited; and legislation was to be passed in each country making infringement of any of these provisions a crime against the state. Litvinov contrasted the Soviet objective of "total disarmament" with the more modest objective of a "reduction and limitation of armaments," which was the formula on which the League of Nations negotiations proceeded. He repeated his proposal at the World Disarmament Conference in February 1932. The speech he made on this occasion, and those which followed later in the conference, were directed towards exposing the hypocrisy of the capitalist powers in their treatment of the subject of disarmament: the gap between their professions of intention and their actions; the dilatoriness and humbug of disarmament proceedings; the passing of problems from committee to committee; the endless vista of "preparation," the adoption now of this "method," now of that; the swathing of stark realities in a blanket of diplomatic nicety. His speeches are a brilliant critique of the diplomacy of disarmament and, indeed, of the most fundamental assumptions on which all diplomacy rests, and must rest. They contain a clarity of perception, a determination to call a spade a spade, to say what others only thought, that is extraordinary in the speeches of a foreign minister, and possible only because he himself was not taking part in diplomacy but in political warfare, and therefore saw the diplomatic process as an outsider. In defending his proposal for total disarmament, he advanced two main arguments. Total disarmament was "the only way of putting an end to war,"[1] something which the mere reduction and limitation of armaments could not do. And total disarmament was "distinguished from all other plans by its simplicity and by the ease with which it could be carried out and with which its realization could be controlled."[2] Total disarmament by-passed all those "thorny questions" which prevented agreement on any lesser measure of disarmament: what armaments were to be abolished and what not, how far were reductions to be carried out, which would be reduced first, how was the treaty to provide equal security for all, and so on.

Mr. Khrushchev proposed "total disarmament" in his speech to the United Nations Assembly in September 1959.

The objection is often made to proposals for "total disarmament," as it was made to those of Litvinov and has been to that of Mr. Khrushchev, that such a thing is impracticable: that nations will not in fact agree to it. It is true that agreement among heavily armed and hostile nations to implement such a proposal is as near to inconceivable as anything can be in the realm of politics. It is true also that actual proposals for total disarmament, like those advanced by Litvinov and Mr. Khrushchev, include the retention of internal security forces: forces which in authoritarian countries and countries with dissident overseas territories are often very powerful. The manpower of the French army, for example, is mainly devoted to internal security operations, or to what France, for the purposes of disarmament, would want to regard as internal security operations.

[1] *League of Nations: Conference for the Reduction and Limitation of Armaments*, Verbatim Records of Plenary Meetings, Vol. I, p. 82 (Geneva 1932).

[2] *Ibid.*, p. 85.

The objection that proposals for it are impracticable, however, concedes too much to the idea of total disarmament. The objection to total disarmament is not that it is impracticable, but that there can be, in principle, nothing of the kind: the physical capacity for organized violence is inherent in human society. Even the most thoroughgoing disarmament treaty must leave nations with the capacity to wage war on a primitive level; and, moreover, with the capacity to raise this level, to re-establish what has been dis-established, to remember or to re-invent what has been laid aside. Thus there is no force in Litvinov's first argument, that "total disarmament" will make war impossible in some sense in which lesser forms of disarmament will not: the physical possibility of war is not erased along with "armaments." Moreover, the most thoroughgoing disarmament treaty must leave some powers with a greater capacity for war than others: like lesser forms of disarmament, it must result in a definite ratio of military power. A nation's war potential does not reside merely in its "armaments," but in the whole complex of its economic and demographic resources, strategic position, technological and industrial skill, military experience and ingenuity, morale, commitments and more besides: a fact which emerges nowhere more clearly than in negotiations for disarmament, when the negotiators attempt to reach agreement by reference to armaments and armed forces alone. The removal of "armaments" does not disturb these other factors, but brings them further into play. Consequently there is equally no force in Litvinov's second argument, that the simplicity of total disarmament enables it to by-pass the difficulties of negotiation. His own proposals at the League Conference were brushed impatiently aside.

No system of disarmament can abolish the physical capacity to wage war, and the idea of an absolute security from war emerging from such a system is an illusion. However, it is at least logically and physically possible that the art of war might be rendered primitive: by the abolition of sophisticated weapons and the decay of sophisticated military organization and technique. There may be a great difference between an international society in which sovereign powers are bristling with modern weapons and organized military forces, and one in which they are not: just as there is a great difference between a society in which gentlemen carry swords, and one in which they do not. There is nothing contrary to logic, or nature either, in the idea of an international society not only without such weapons and forces, but with habits, institutions, codes or taboos which could impede the will to utilize the physical capacity for war inherent in it. We should have the imagination and the vision to contemplate the possibility of such a world, to recognize that the political and military structure of the world could be radically different from what it is now. But we should recognize that a world which was radically different from our own in respect of the primitiveness and extent of its national armaments would also be radically different in many other ways. If nations were defenceless, there could hardly be a political order worthy of the name unless there were an armed, central authority: the abolition of national military power appears to entail the concentration of military power in a universal authority. If a universal authority or world government were to be established in any other way than by conquest, and if, once established, it were to maintain itself in any other way than by the constant suppression of dissidence, the bitter political conflicts which now divide the world would have to have subsided. In a world fundamentally different from our own in all these respects, and in other respects, the reduction of national armaments to a primitive level might have a place. But the world in which we now find ourselves is not such as this: nor is it within the power of any political authority or combination of authorities to bring it about by *fiat*. The possession by sovereign powers of armaments and armed forces is not something extraneous to the structure of international society, something whose presence or absence does not affect other of its parts: it is, along with alliances, diplomacy and war, among its most central institutions. It is possible to conceive systems of world politics and political organization from which this institution is absent: but they are systems from which some of the most familiar and persistent landmarks of international experience are also absent; and which, though they might occur, cannot be legislated.

In a world such as our own it seems doubtful whether the reduction of national armaments to a primitive level, even if it could be brought about in isolation from other fundamental changes, would contribute to international security. It would carry within itself no guarantee that arms races would not be resumed. The resumption of an arms race from a primitive level, with its attendant circumstances of unpredictability and surprise, would be likely to lead to extreme instability in the balance of power, and might well produce greater insecurity than that attending a higher quantitative and qualitative level of armaments.

The weaker form of the doctrine of disarmament is that international security is enhanced when armaments are reduced to the lowest level that is practicable, given that there are limits to the reductions which the powers will entertain. This, rather than total disarmament, has been the formal object of most of the great multilateral disarmament negotiations: it may entail the abolition, rather than the reduction, of particular categories of armament, but falls short of the abolition of all categories. . . . The chief disarmament negotiations of the United Nations period have been concerned either with the abolition or centralized control of nuclear weapons, or with the reduction and limitation of non-nuclear weapons and forces, or both. The most radical form of the doctrine of the reduction of armaments is that according to which reductions should be carried out which are general and comprehensive: general in the sense that they affect all powers; comprehensive in the sense that they affect all categories of armaments and armed forces.

It is clear that if the objective of arms control were the economic one of reducing the resources devoted to armaments, it would have to comprise a reduction of armaments and armed forces, or, at all events, a reduction of expenditure on them. If, however, it is the objective of arms control to promote international security, it is far from clear that this is a mattter of reducing the quantity of forces or weapons, or restricting the sums spent on them. If in fact there is no question of the elimination of forces and weapons, it is not to be assumed that the level of forces and weapons most favourable to international security is the lowest one. The claims of the reduction of armaments clash with those of the balance of power, and must be weighed against them.

In international society as we know it, security is not provided by the concentration of military power in an authority superior to sovereign states, but rests on a balance of power among them.

The existence of a military situation in which no one power or bloc is preponderant is a most precarious and uncertain source of security. The idea of the balance of power, like that of disarmament, rests on the abstraction of the military factor. If there is a military balance between opposed powers, such as to leave them alike without prospect of decisive victory, there is no guarantee that they will act in accordance with an appreciation of this balance or even that they will be aware that it exists. The inherent uncertainty that surrounds estimates of military power, the play of the contingent in military operations themselves, the inadequacy of intelligence and its frustration by counter-intelligence, the willingness of governments to take risks despite unfavourable odds, their frequent failure even to weigh up the odds, render peace something precarious even where the balance of power is most stable. Military balances, moreover, do not remain stable for long periods but are inherently temporary. The technological, economic, demographic, political and other ingredients that go to make up the military strength of each side are subject to constant change, as is the attitude of each side towards the existing balance, which it may find satisfactory and accept, or find unsatisfactory and seek to overthrow.

The unsettling effect of changes on the balance of power is mitigated by the practice of making adjustments in the system of alliances: changes in the diplomatic combinations of the Powers enable the balance among them to accommodate changes in the intrinsic strength of each of them. But the recourse to the adjustment of alliances does not exist for two blocs between whom the world is divided. If, as now, in strictly military terms, neither antagonist can substantially affect the balance by throwing the strength of further powers into the scales, this balance is determined by the efforts of each in the arms race: in the event of the swing of the balance towards one of them, there are no new worlds the other can call into being in order to redress it. Military balances which are unstable and fluctuating are notoriously corrosive of international security: they give rise, in the power with a temporary preponderance, to the counsel of preventive war. The policy advocated in Germany in 1914, of striking first before the expansion of the Russian army got under way, the policy advocated by Churchill in Britain in the years when the power of Nazi Germany was feeble but gathering, the policy urged by a minority in the United States in the closing years of that country's nuclear superiority, the policy which Israel put into execution in 1956 in response to Egypt's amassing of armaments, are explicable in terms of this sense that the moment of fleeting preponderance is the moment of unique opportunity. Military balances have contributed to the avoidance of particular wars, but they are not a guarantee against war: on the contrary, war is one of the instruments by which the balance is maintained. The chief function of the balance of power in international society has not been to preserve peace, but to preserve the independence of sovereign states from the threat of domination, and to preserve the society of sovereign states from being transformed by conquest into a universal empire: to do these things, if necessary, by war.

But though it is no kind of panacea, the existence of a military balance between politically opposed powers and blocs is one of the chief factors making for peace and order among them. We shall be able to appreciate the importance of the balance of power if we consider carefully what, in the short run, the alternatives to it are. If — like the critics of the balance of power, from Richard Cobden to President Wilson to the present supporters of unilateral disarmament — we contrast the security provided by a military balance with that provided by some imagined political system that might arise in the long run, or with our image of some system that has occurred in the past, we shall be very conscious of its shortcom ings. If we examine the present military balance alongside our image of a just and liberal world government, or total disarmament, or free trade and universal brotherhood, or the Roman peace, we must be impressed with its dangers. But if we examine it alongside the alternatives to it that exist now, the alternatives that we by our action or inaction can bring about, we must form a very different impression. The alternative to a stable balance of military power is a preponderance of power, which is very much more dangerous. The choice with which governments are in fact confronted is not that between opting for the present structure of the world, and opting for some other structure, but between attempting to maintain a balance of power, and failing to do so. The balance of power is wrongly regarded as a synonym for international anarchy; rightly regarded as something which mitigates an anarchy which might otherwise be more rampant. It is not a panacea. But it exists now; and among those forces which make for international security and can be built upon by action that can be taken now it is one of the strongest. . . .

Arms Races:
Prerequisites and Results

SAMUEL P. HUNTINGTON

INTRODUCTION

Si vis pacem, para bellum, is an ancient and authoritative adage of military policy. Of no less acceptance, however, is the other, more modern, proposition: "Armaments races inevitably lead to war." Juxtaposed, these two advices suggest that the maxims of social science, like the proverbs of folklore, reflect a many-sided truth.

From *Public Policy* (1958), pp. 41–83. Reprinted by permission. Some footnotes have been omitted.

The social scientist, however, cannot escape with so easy an observation. He has the scholar's responsibility to determine as fully as possible to what extent and under what conditions his conflicting truths are true. The principal aim of this essay is to attempt some resolution of the issue: When are arms races a prelude to war and when are they a substitute for war?

Throughout history states have sought to maintain their peace and security by means of military strength. The arms race in which the military preparations of two states are intimately and directly interrelated is, however, a relatively modern phenomenon. The conflict between the apparent feasibility of preserving peace by arming for war and the apparent inevitability of competitive arms increases resulting in war is, therefore, a comparatively new one. The second purpose of this essay is to explore some of the circumstances which have brought about this uncertainty as to the relationship between war, peace, and arms increases. The problem here is: What were the prerequisites to the emergence of the arms race as a significant form of international rivalry in the nineteenth and twentieth centuries?

For the purposes of this essay, an arms race is defined as a progressive, competitive peacetime increase in armaments by two states or coalition of states resulting from conflicting purposes or mutual fears. An arms race is thus a form of reciprocal interaction between two states or coalitions. A race cannot exist without an increase in arms, quantitatively or qualitatively, but every peacetime increase in arms is not necessarily the result of an arms race. A nation may expand its armaments for the domestic purposes of aiding industry or curbing unemployment, or because it believes an absolute need exists for such an increase regardless of the actions of other states. In the 1880s and 1890s, for instance, the expansion of the United States Navy was apparently unrelated to the actions of any other power, and hence not part of an arms race. An arms race reflects disagreement between two states as to the proper balance of power between them. The concept of a "general" arms race in which a number of powers increase their armaments simultaneously is, consequently, a fallacious one. Such general increases either are not the result of self-conscious reciprocal interaction or are simply the sum of a number of two-state antagonisms. In so far as the arms policy of any one state is related to the armaments of other states, it is a function of concrete, specific goals, needs, or threats arising out of the political relations among the states. Even Britain's vaunted two-power naval standard will be found, on close analysis, to be rooted in specific threats rather than in abstract considerations of general policy.

PREREQUISITES FOR AN ARMS RACE

. . . Certain conditions peculiarly present in the nineteenth and twentieth centuries would appear to be responsible for the emergence of the arms race as a frequent and distinct form of international rivalry. Among the more significant of these conditions are: a state system which facilitates the balancing of power by internal rather than external means; the preeminence of military force-in-being over territory or other factors as an element of national power; the capacity within each state to increase its military strength through quantitative or qualitative means; and the conscious awareness by each state of the dependence of its own arms policy upon that of another state.[1]

Balancing power: external and internal means. Arms races are an integral part of the international balance of power. From the viewpoint of a participant, an arms race is an effort to achieve a favorable international distribution of power. Viewed as a whole, a sustained arms race is a means of achieving a dynamic equilibrium of power between two states or coalitions of states. Arms races only take place between states in the same balance of power system. The more isolated a nation is from any balance of power system the less likely it is to become involved in an arms race. Within any such system, power may in general be balanced in two ways: externally through a realignment of the units participating in the system (diplomacy), or internally by changes in the inherent power of the units. The extent to which the balancing process operates through external or internal means usually depends upon the number of states participating in the system, the opportunity for new states to

[1] Since an arms race is necessarily a matter of degree, differences of opinion will exist as to whether any given relationship constitutes an arms race and as to what are the precise opening and closing dates of any given arms race. At the risk of seeming arbitrary, the following relationships are assumed to be arms races for the purposes of this essay:

1.	France v. England	naval	1840–1866
2.	France v. Germany	land	1874–1894
3.	England v. France & Russia	naval	1884–1904
4.	Argentina v. Chile	naval	1890–1902
5.	England v. Germany	naval	1898–1912
6.	France v. Germany	land	1911–1914
7.	England v. United States	naval	1916–1930
8.	Japan v. United States	naval	1916–1922
9.	France v. Germany	land	1934–1939
10.	Soviet Union v. Germany	land	1934–1941
11.	Germany v. England	air	1934–1939
12.	United States v. Japan	naval	1934–1941
13.	Soviet Union v. United States	nuclear	1946–

join the system, and the relative distribution of power among the participating states.

The relations among the states in a balance of power system may tend toward any one of three patterns, each of which assigns somewhat different roles to the external and internal means of balancing power. A situation of *bellum omnium contra omnes* exists when there are a large number of states approximately equal in power and when there is an approximately equal distribution of grievances and antagonisms among the states. In such a system, which was perhaps most closely approximated by the city-states of the Italian Renaissance, primary reliance is placed upon wily diplomacy, treachery, and surprise attack. Since no bilateral antagonisms continue for any length of time, a sustained arms race is very unlikely. A second balance of power pattern involves an all-against-one relationship: the coalition of a number of weaker states against a single *grande nation*. The fears and grievances of the weaker states are concentrated against the stronger, and here again primary reliance is placed upon diplomatic means of maintaining or restoring the balance. European politics assumed this pattern in the successive coalitions to restrain the Hapsburgs, Louis XIV, Frederick II, Napoleon, and Hitler. At times, efforts may be made to bring in other states normally outside the system to aid in restoring the balance.

A third pattern of balance of power politics involves bilateral antagonisms between states or coalitions of states roughly equal in strength. Such bilateral antagonisms have been a continuing phenomenon in the western balance of power system: France vs. England, Austria vs. France and then Prussia (Germany) vs. France, Austria-Hungary vs. Russia, the Triple Alliance vs. the Triple Entente, and, now, the United States vs. the Soviet Union. In these relationships the principal grievances and antagonisms of any two states become concentrated upon each other, and, as a result, this antagonism becomes the primary focus of their respective foreign policies. In this situation, diplomacy and alliances may play a significant role if a "balancer" exists who can shift his weight to whichever side appears to be weaker. But no balancing state can exist if all the major powers are involved in bilateral antagonisms or if a single overriding antagonism forces virtually all the states in the system to choose one side or the other (bipolarization). In these circumstances, the balancing of power by rearranging the units of power becomes difficult. Diplomatic maneuvering gives way to the massing of military force. Each state relies more on armaments and less on alliances. Other factors being equal, the pressures toward an arms race are greatest when international relations assume this form.

In the past century the relative importance of the internal means of balancing power has tended to increase. A single worldwide balance of power system has tended to develop, thereby eliminating the possibility of bringing in outside powers to restore the balance. At the same time, however, the number of great powers has fairly constantly decreased, and bilateral antagonisms have consequently become of greater importance. Small powers have tended to seek security either through neutrality (Switzerland, Sweden) or through reliance upon broadly organized efforts at collective security. The growth of the latter idea has tended to make military alliances aimed at a specific common foe less reputable and justifiable. . . . Alliances were perhaps the primary means of balancing power in Europe before 1870. Between 1870 and 1914, both alliances and armaments played important roles. Since 1918 the relative importance of armaments has probably increased. The primary purpose of the military pacts of the post-World War II period, with the possible exception of NATO, generally has been the extension of the protection of a great power to a series of minor powers, rather than the uniting of a number of more or less equal powers in pursuit of a common objective. In addition, the development of democratic control over foreign policy has made alliances more difficult. Alignments dictated by balance of power considerations may be impossible to carry out due to public opinion. Rapid shifts in alliances from friends to enemies also are difficult to execute in a democratic society. Perhaps, too, a decline in the arts of diplomacy has contributed to the desire to rest one's security upon resources which are "owned" rather than "pledged."

Elements of power: money, territory, armaments. Arms races only take place when military forces-in-being are of direct and prime importance to the power of a state. During the age of mercantilism, for instance, monetary resources were highly valued as an index of power, and, consequently, governmental policy was directed toward the accumulation of economic wealth which could then be transformed into military and political power. These actions, which might take a variety of forms, were in some respects the seventeenth century equivalents of the nineteenth and twentieth century arms races. In the eighteenth century, territory was of key importance as a measure of power. The size of the armies which a state could maintain was roughly proportional to its population, and, in an agrarian age, its population was roughly proportional to its territory. Consequently, an increase in military power required an increase in territory. Within Europe, territory could be acquired either by conquest, in which case a surprise attack was probably desirable in order to forestall intervention by other states, or by agreement among the great powers to partition a smaller power. Outside of Europe, colonial territories might contribute wealth if not manpower to the mother country, and these could be acquired either by discovery and settlement or by conquest. Consequently, territorial compensations were a primary means of balancing power, and through the acquisition of colonies, states jealous of their relative power could strive to improve their position without directly challenging another major state and thereby provoking a war.

During the nineteenth century territory became less important as an index of power, and industry and armaments more important. By the end of the century all the available colonial lands had been occupied by the major powers. In addition, the rise of nationalism and of self-determination made it increasingly difficult to settle differences by the division and bartering of provinces, small powers, and colonies. By expanding its armaments, however, a state could still increase its relative power without decreasing the absolute power of another state. Reciprocal increases in armaments made possible an unstable and dynamic, but none the less real equilibrium among the major powers. The race for armaments tended to replace the race for colonies as the "escape hatch" through which major states could enhance their power without directly challenging each other.

The increased importance of armaments as a measure of national power was reflected in the new emphasis upon disarmament in the efforts to resolve antagonisms among nations. The early peace writers, prior to the eighteenth century, placed primary stress upon a federation of European states rather than upon disarmament measures. It was not until Kant's essay on "Eternal Peace" that the dangers inherent in an arms race were emphasized, and the reduction of armaments made a primary goal. In 1766 Austria made the first proposal for a bilateral reduction in forces to Frederick the Great, who rejected it. In 1787 France and England agreed not to increase their naval establishments. In 1816 the Czar made the first proposal for a general reduction in armaments. Thenceforth, throughout the nineteenth century problems of armament and disarmament played an increasingly significant role in diplomatic negotiations.[2]

Capacity for qualitative and quantitative increases in military power. An arms race requires the progressive increase from domestic sources of the absolute military power of a state. This may be done quantitatively, by expanding the numerical strength of its existing forms of military force, or qualitatively, by replacing its existing forms of military force (usually weapons systems) with new

[2] Merze Tate, *The Disarmament Illusion* (New York, 1942), p. 7.

and more effective forms of force. The latter requires a dynamic technology, and the former the social, political and economic capacity to reallocate resources from civilian to military purposes. Before the nineteenth century the European states possessed only a limited capacity for either quantitative or qualitative increases in military strength. Naval technology, for instance, had been virtually static for almost three centuries: the sailing ship of 1850 was not fundamentally different from that of 1650, the naval gun of 1860 not very much removed from that of 1560.[3] As a result, the ratio of construction time to use time was extremely low: a ship built in a few months could be used for the better part of a century. Similarly, with land armaments, progress was slow, and only rarely could a power hope to achieve a decisive edge by a "technological breakthrough." Beginning with the Industrial Revolution, however, the pace of innovation in military technology constantly quickened, and the new weapons systems inevitably stimulated arms races. The introduction, first, of the steam warship and then of the ironclad, for instance, directly intensified the naval competition between England and France in the 1850s and 1860s. Throughout the nineteenth century, the importance of the weapons technician constantly increased relative to the importance of the strategist.

Broad changes in economic and political structure were at the same time making quantitative arms races feasible. The social system of the *ancien régime* did not permit a full mobilization of the economic and manpower resources of a nation. So long as participation in war was limited to a small class, competitive increases in the size of armies could not proceed very far. The destruction of the old system, the spread of democracy and liberalism, the increasing popularity among all groups of the "nation in arms" concept, all permitted a much more complete mobilization of resources for military purposes than had been possible previously. In particular, the introduction of universal military service raised the ceiling on the size of the army to the point where the limiting factor was the civilian manpower necessary to support the army. In addition, the development of industry permitted the mass production and mass accumulation of the new weapons which the new technology had invented. The countries which lagged behind in the twin processes of democratization and industrialization were severely handicapped in the race for armaments.

In the age of limited wars little difference existed between a na-

[3] Bernard Brodie, *Sea Power in the Machine Age* (Princeton, 2nd ed., 1944), p. 181; Arthur J. Marder, *The Anatomy of British Sea Power* (New York, 1940), pp. 3–4.

tion's military strength in peace and its military strength in war. During the nineteenth century, however, the impact of democracy and industrialism made wars more total, victory or defeat in them became more significant (and final), military superiority became more critically important, and consequently a government had to be more fully assured of the prospect of victory before embarking upon war. In addition, the professional officer corps which developed during the nineteenth century felt a direct responsibility for the military security of the state and emphasized the desirability of obtaining a safe superiority in armaments. As a result, unless one of the participants possessed extensive staying power due to geography or resources, the outcome of a war depended almost as much upon what happened before the declarations of war as after. By achieving superiority in armaments it might be possible for a state to achieve the fruits of war without suffering the risks and liabilities of war. Governments piled up armaments in peacetime with the hope either of averting war or of insuring success in it should it come.

Absolute and relative armaments goals. A state may define its armaments goals in one of two ways. It can specify a certain *absolute* level or type of armaments which it believes necessary for it to possess irrespective of the level or type possessed by other states. Or, it can define its goal in *relative* terms as a function of the armaments of other states. Undoubtedly, in any specific case, a state's armaments reflect a combination of both absolute and relative considerations. Normally, however, one or the other will be dominant and embodied in official statements of the state's armaments goals in the form of an "absolute need" or a ratio-goal. Thus, historically Great Britain followed a relative policy with respect to the capital ships in its navy but an absolute policy with respect to its cruisers, the need for which, it was held, stemmed from the unique nature of the British Empire.

If every state had absolute goals, arms races would be impossible: each state would go its separate way uninfluenced by the actions of its neighbors. Nor would a full scale arms race develop if an absolute goal were pursued consistently by only one power in an antagonistic relationship: whatever relative advantage the second power demanded would be simply a function of the constant absolute figure demanded by the first power. An arms race only arises when two or more powers consciously determine the quantitative or qualitative aspects of their armaments as functions of the armaments of the other power. Absolute goals, however, are only really feasible when a state is not a member of or only on the periphery of a balance of power system. Except in these rare cases, the formulation by a state of its armaments goal in absolute terms is more likely to reflect the desire to obscure from its rivals the true relative superiority which it wishes to achieve or to obscure from itself the need to participate actively in the balancing process. Thus, its Army Law of 1893 was thought to give Germany a force which in quantity and quality would be unsurpassable by any other power. Hence Germany

> was, in the eyes of her rulers, too powerful to be affected by a balancing movement restricted only to the continent. . . . From this time on Germany considered herself militarily invulnerable, as if in a state of splendid isolation, owing to the excellence of her amalgam army.[4]

As a result, Germany let her army rest, turned her energies to the construction of a navy, and then suddenly in 1911 became aware of her landpower inferiority to the Dual Alliance and had to make strenuous last minute efforts to increase the size of her forces. Somewhat similarly, states may define absolute qualitative goals, such as the erection of an impenetrable system of defenses (Maginot Line) or the possession of an "ultimate" or "absolute" weapon, which will render superfluous further military effort regardless of what other states may do. In 1956 American airpower policy was consciously shaped not to the achievement of any particular level of air strength relative to that of the Soviet Union, but rather to obtaining an absolute "sufficiency of airpower" which would permit the United States to wreak havoc in the Soviet Union in the event of an all-out war.[5] The danger involved in an absolute policy is that, if carried to an extreme, it may lead to a complacent isolationism blind to the relative nature of power.

The armaments of two states can be functionally interrelated

---

[4] Arpad Kovacs, "Nation in Arms and Balance of Power: The Interaction of German Military Legislation and European Politics, 1866–1914" (Ph.D. Thesis, University of Chicago, 1934), p. 159.

[5] For the most complete statement of the sufficiency theory, see Donald A. Quarles, Secretary of the Air Force, "How Much is 'Enough'?" *Air Force*, XLIX (September, 1956), pp. 51–52: ". . . there comes a time in the course of increasing our airpower when we must make a determination of sufficiency. . . .

"Sufficiency of airpower, to my mind, must be determined period by period on the basis of the force required to accomplish the mission assigned. . . . Neither side can hope by a mere margin of superiority in airplanes or other means of delivery of atomic weapons to escape the catastrophe of such a [total] war. Beyond a certain point, this prospect is not the result of *relative* strength of the two opposed forces. It is the *absolute* power in the hands of each, and in the substantial invulnerability of this power to interdiction."

See also H. Rept. 2104, 84th Cong., 2d Sess., p. 40 (1956).

only if they are also similar or complementary. An arms race is impossible between a power which possesses only a navy and one which possesses only an army: no one can match divisions against battleships. A functional relationship between armaments is complementary when two military forces possessing different weapons systems are designed for combat with each other. In this sense, an air defense fighter command complements an opposing strategic bombing force or one side's submarine force complements the other's antisubmarine destroyers and hunter-killer groups. A functional relationship is similar when two military forces are not only designed for combat with each other but also possess similar weapons systems, as has been very largely the case with land armies and with battle fleets of capital ships. In most instances in history, arms races have involved similar forces rather than complimentary forces, but no reason exists why there should not be an arms race in the latter. The only special problem posed by a complementary arms race is that of measuring the relative strengths of the opposing forces. In a race involving similar forces, a purely quantitative measurement usually suffices; in one of complementary forces, qualitative judgments are necessary as to the effectiveness of one type of weapons system against another.

Even if both parties to an arms race possess similar land, sea and air forces, normally the race itself is focused on only one of these components or even on only one weapons system within one component, usually that type of military force with which they are best able to harm each other.[6] This component or weapons system is viewed by the states as the decisive form of military force in their mutual relationship, and competition in other forces or components is subordinated to the race in this decisive force. The simple principles of concentration and economy of force require states to put their major efforts where they will count most. The arms race between Germany and England before World War I was in capital ships. The arms race between the same two countries before World War II was in bombers and fighters. The current race between the Soviet Union and the United States has largely focused upon nuclear weapons and their means of delivery, and has not extended to the massing of conventional weapons and manpower. In general, economic considerations also preclude a state from becoming involved at the same time in two separate arms races with two different powers in two different forms of military force. When

---

[6] Other things being equal, this will probably be the "dominant weapon" in Fuller's sense, that is, the weapon with the longest effective range. See J. F. C. Fuller, *Armament and History* (New York, 1945), pp. 7–8.

her race in land forces with France slackened in the middle 1890s, Germany embarked upon her naval race with Great Britain, and for the first decade of the twentieth century the requirements of this enterprise prevented any substantial increase in the size of the army. When the naval race in turn slackened in 1912, Germany returned to the rebuilding of her ground forces and to her military manpower race with France.

Two governments can consciously follow relative arms policies only if they are well informed of their respective military capabilities. The general availability of information concerning armaments is thus a precondition for an arms race. Prior to the nineteenth century when communication and transportation were slow and haphazard, a state would frequently have only the vaguest notions of the military programs of its potential rivals. Often it was possible for one state to make extensive secret preparations for war. In the modern world, information with respect to military capabilities has become much more widespread and has been one of the factors increasing the likelihood of arms races. Even now, however, many difficulties exist in getting information concerning the arms of a rival which is sufficiently accurate to serve as the basis for one's own policy. At times misconceptions as to the military strengths and policies of other states become deeply ingrained, and at other times governments simply choose to be blind to significant changes in armaments. Any modern government involved in an arms race, moreover, is confronted with conflicting estimates of its opponent's strength. Politicians, governmental agencies and private groups all tend to give primary credit to intelligence estimates which confirm military policies which they have already espoused for other reasons. The armed services inevitably overstate the military capabilities of the opponent: in 1914, for instance, the Germans estimated the French army to have 121,000 more men than the German army, the French estimated the German army to have 134,000 more men than the French army, but both countries agreed in their estimates of the military forces of third powers.[7] Governments anxious to reduce expenditures and taxes pooh-pooh warnings as to enemy strength: the reluctance of the Baldwin government to credit reports of the German air build-up seriously delayed British rearmament in the 1930s. At other times, exaggerated reports as to enemy forces may lead a government to take extraordinary measures which are subsequently revealed to have been unnecessary. Suspicions that the Germans were exceeding their announced pro-

[7] Bernadotte E. Schmitt, *The Coming of the War: 1914* (New York, 2 vols., 1930), I, 54n.

gram of naval construction led the English government in 1909 to
authorize and construct four "contingency" Dreadnoughts. Subsequently revelations proved British fears to be groundless. Similarly,
in 1956 reports of Soviet aircraft production, later asserted to be
considerably exaggerated, influenced Congress to appropriate an
extra $900 million for the Air Force. At times, the sudden revela-
tion of a considerable increase in an enemy's capabilities may produce a panic, such as the invasion panics of England in 1847–48,
1851–53, and 1859–61. The tense atmosphere of an arms race also
tends to encourage reports of mysterious forces possessed by the
opponent and of his development of secret new weapons of unprecedented power. Nonetheless, fragmentary and uncertain though
information may be, its availability in one form or another is what
makes the arms race possible.

ABORTIVE AND SUSTAINED ARMS RACES

An arms race may end in war, formal or informal agreement
between the two states to call off the race, or victory for one state
which achieves and maintains the distribution of power which it
desires and ultimately causes its rival to give up the struggle. The
likelihood of war arising from an arms race depends in the first
instance upon the relation between the power and grievances of
one state to the power and grievances of the other. War is least
likely when grievances are low, or, if grievances are high, the sum
of the grievances and power of one state approximates the sum
of the grievances and power of the other. An equality of power and
an equality of grievances will thus reduce the chances of war, as
will a situation in which one state has a marked superiority in
power and the other in grievances. Assuming a fairly equal distribution of grievances, the likelihood of an arms race ending in war
tends to vary inversely with the length of the arms race and directly with the extent to which it is quantitative rather than qualitative in character. This section deals with the first of these
relationships and the next section with the second.

An arms race is a series of interrelated increases in armaments
which if continued over a period of time produces a dynamic equilibrium of power between two states. A race in which this dynamic
equilibrium fails to develop may be termed an abortive arms race.
In these instances, the previously existing static equilibrium between the two states is disrupted without being replaced by a new
equilibrium reflecting their relative competitive efforts in the race.
Instead, rapid shifts take place or appear about to take place in
the distribution of power which enhance the willingness of one
state or the other to precipitate a conflict. At least one and some-

times two danger points occur at the beginning of every arms race. The first point arises with the response of the challenged state to the initial increases in armaments by the challenging state. The second danger point is the reaction of the challenger who has been successful in initially achieving his goal to the frantic belated efforts of the challenged state to retrieve its former position.

The formal beginning of an arms race is the first increase in armaments by one state — the challenger — caused by a desire to alter the existing balance of power between it and another state. Prior to this initial action, a pre-arms race static equilibrium may be said to exist. This equilibrium does not necessarily mean an equality of power. It simply reflects the satisfaction of each state with the existing distribution of power in the light of its grievances and antagonisms with the other state. Some of the most stable equilibriums in history have also been ones which embodied an unbalance of power. From the middle of the eighteenth century down to the 1840s, a static equilibrium existed between the French and British navies in which the former was kept roughly two-thirds as strong as the latter. After the naval race of 1841–1865 when this ratio was challenged, the two powers returned to it for another twenty year period. From 1865 to 1884 both British and French naval expenditures were amazingly constant, England's expenditures varying between 9.5 and 10.5 million pounds (with the exception of the crisis years of 1876–77 when they reached 11 and 12 million pounds) and France's expenditures varying from 6.5 to 7.5 million pounds.[8] In some instances the equilibrium may receive the formal sanction of a treaty such as the Washington arms agreement of 1922 or the treaty of Versailles. In each of these cases, the equilibrium lasted until 1934 when the two powers — Germany and Japan — who had been relegated to a lower level of armaments decided that continued inferiority was incompatible with their national goals and ambitions. In both cases, however, it was not the disparity of power in itself which caused the destruction of the equilibrium, but rather the fact that this disparity was unacceptable to the particular groups which assumed control of those countries in the early 1930s. In other instances, the static equilibrium may last for only a passing moment, as when France began reconstructing its army almost immediately after its defeat by Germany in 1871.

For the purposes of analysis it is necessary to specify a particular

[8] See Richard Cobden, "Three Panics: An Historical Episode," *Political Writings* (London, 2 vols., 1867), II, p. 308; The Cobden Club, *The Burden of Armaments* (London, 1905), pp. 66–68.

increase in armaments by one state as marking the formal beginning of the arms race. This is done not to pass judgment on the
desirability or wisdom of the increase, but simply to identify the
start of the action and reaction which constitute the race. In most
instances, this initial challenge is not hard to locate. It normally
involves a major change in the policy of the challenging state, and
more likely than not it is formally announced to the world. The
reasons for the challenging state's discontent with the status quo
may stem from a variety of causes. It may feel that the growth of
its economy, commerce, and population should be reflected in
changes in the military balance of power (Germany, 1898; United
States, 1916; Soviet Union, 1946). Nationalistic, bellicose, or mili-
taristic individuals or parties may come to power who are unwilling
to accept an equilibrium which other groups in their society had
been willing to live with or negotiate about (Germany and Japan,
1934). New political issues may arise which cause a deterioration
in the relationships of the state with another power and which consequently lead it to change its estimate of the arms balance necessary for its security (France, 1841, 1875; England, 1884).

Normally the challenging state sets a goal for itself which derives from the relation between the military strengths of the two
countries prior to the race. If the relation was one of disparity, the
initial challenge usually comes from the weaker power which as-
pires to parity or better. Conceivably a stronger power could initiate
an arms race by deciding that it required an even higher ratio of
superiority over the weaker power. But in actual practice this is
seldom the case: the gain in security achieved in upping a $2:1$
ratio to $3:1$, for instance, rarely is worth the increased economic
costs and political tensions. If parity of military power existed between the two countries, the arms race begins when one state determines that it requires military force superior to that of the other
country.

In nine out of ten races the slogan of the challenging state is
either "parity" or "superiority." Only in rare cases does the challenger aim for less than this, for unless equality or superiority is
achieved, the arms race is hardly likely to be worthwhile. The most
prominent exception to the "parity or superiority" rule is the Anglo-
German naval race of 1898–1912. In its initial phase, German policy was directed not to the construction of a navy equal to England's
but rather to something between that and the very minor navy
which she possessed prior to the race. The rationale for building
such a force was provided by Tirpitz's "risk theory": Germany
should have a navy large enough so that Britain could not fight her
without risking damage to the British navy to such an extent that

it would fall prey to the naval forces of third powers (i.e., France and Russia). The fallacies in this policy became obvious in the following decade. On the one hand, for technical reasons it was unlikely that an inferior German navy could do serious damage to a superior British fleet, and, on the other hand, instead of making Britain wary of France and Russia the expansion of the German navy tended to drive her into their arms and consequently to remove the hostile third powers who were supposed to pounce upon a Britain weakened by Germany.[9] One can only conclude that it is seldom worthwhile either for a superior power to attempt significantly to increase its superiority or for a weaker power to attempt only to reduce its degree of inferiority. The rational goals in an arms race are parity or superiority.

In many respects the most critical aspect of a race is the initial response which the challenged state makes to the new goals posited by the challenger. In general, these responses can be divided into four categories, two of which preserve the possibility of peace, two of which make war virtually inevitable. The challenged state may, first, attempt to counterbalance the increased armaments of its rival through diplomatic means or it may, secondly, immediately increase its own armaments in an effort to maintain or directly to restore the previously existing balance of military power. While neither of these responses guarantees the maintenance of peace, they at least do not precipitate war. The diplomatic avenue of action, if it exists, is generally the preferred one. It may be necessary, however, for the state to enhance its own armaments as well as attempting to secure reliable allies. Or, if alliances are impossible or undesirable for reasons of state policy, the challenged state must rely upon its own increases in armaments as the way of achieving its goal. In this case a sustained arms race is likely to result. During her period of splendid isolation, for instance, England met the French naval challenge of the 1840s by increasing the size and effectiveness of her own navy. At the end of the century when confronted by the Russo-French challenge, she both increased her navy and made tentative unsuccessful efforts to form an alliance with Germany. In response to the German challenge a decade later, she again increased her navy and also arrived at a rapprochement with France and Russia.

If new alliances or increased armaments appear impossible or

[9] For the risk theory, see Alfred von Tirpitz, *My Memoirs* (New York, 2 vols., 1919), I, pp. 79, 84, 121, 159–160, and for a trenchant criticism, E. L. Woodward, *Great Britain and the German Navy* (Oxford, 1935), pp. 31–39.

undesirable, a state which sees its superiority or equality in military power menaced by the actions of another state may initiate preventive action while still strong enough to forestall the change in the balance of power. The factors which enter into the decision to wage preventive war are complex and intangible, but, conceivably, if the state had no diplomatic opportunities and if it was dubious of its ability to hold its own in an arms race, this might well be a rational course of behavior.[10] Tirpitz explicitly recognized this in his concept of a "danger zone" through which the German navy would pass and during which a strong likelihood would exist that the British would take preventive action to destroy the German fleet. Such an attack might be avoided, he felt, by a German diplomatic "peace offensive" designed to calm British fears and to assure them of the harmless character of German intentions. Throughout the decade after 1898 the Germans suffered periodic scares of an imminent British attack. Although preventive action was never seriously considered by the British government, enough talk went on in high British circles of "Copenhagening" the German fleet to give the Germans some cause for alarm. In the "war in sight" crisis of 1875, the initial success of French rearmament efforts aimed at restoring an equality of military power with Germany stimulated German statesmen and military leaders carefully to consider the desirability of preventive war. Similarly, the actions of the Nazis in overthrowing the restrictions of the Treaty of Versailles in the early 1930s and starting the European arms build-up produced arguments in Poland and France favoring preventive war. After World War II at the beginning of the arms race between the United States and the Soviet Union a small but articulate segment of opinion urged the United States to take preventive action before the Soviet Union developed nuclear weapons.[11] To a certain extent, the Japanese attack on the United States in 1941 can be considered a preventive action designed to forestall the inevitable loss of Japanese naval superiority in the western Pacific which would have resulted from the two-ocean navy program begun by the United States in 1939. In 1956 the Egyptians began to rebuild their armaments from Soviet sources and thus to disturb the equilibrium which had existed with Israel since 1949. This development was undoubtedly one factor leading Israel to attack Egypt and thereby attempt to resolve at least some of the outstanding issues between them before the increase in Egyptian military power.

[10] On the considerations going into the waging of preventive war, see my "To Choose Peace or War," *United States Naval Institute Proceedings*, LXXXIII (April, 1957), pp. 360–62.

[11] *Ibid.*, pp. 363–66.

At the other extreme from preventive action, a challenged state simply may not make any immediate response to the upset of the existing balance of power. The challenger may then actually achieve or come close to achieving the new balance of military force which it considers necessary. In this event, roles are reversed, the challenged suddenly awakens to its weakened position and becomes the challenger, engaging in frantic and strenuous last-ditch efforts to restore the previously existing military ratio. In general, the likelihood of war increases just prior to a change in military superiority from one side to the other. If the challenged state averts this change by alliances or increased armaments, war is avoidable. On the other hand, the challenged state may precipitate war in order to prevent the change, or it may provoke war by allowing the change to take place and then attempting to undo it. In the latter case, the original challenger, having achieved parity or superiority, is in no mood or position to back down; the anxious efforts of its opponent to regain its military strength appear to be obvious war preparation; and consequently the original challenger normally will not hesitate to risk or provoke a war while it may still benefit from its recent gains.

Belated responses resulting in last-gasp arms races are most clearly seen in the French and British reactions to German rearmament in the 1930s. The coming-to-power of the Nazis and their subsequent rearmament efforts initially provoked little military response in France. In part, this reflected confidence in the qualitative superiority of the French army and the defensive strength of the Maginot Line. In part, too, it reflected the French political situation in which those groups most fearful of Nazi Germany were generally those most opposed to large armies and militarism, while the usual right-wing supporters of the French army were those to whom Hitler appeared least dangerous. As a result, the French army and the War Ministry budget remained fairly constant between 1933 and 1936. Significant increases in French armaments were not made until 1937 and 1938, and the real French rearmament effort got under way in 1939. France proposed to spend more on armaments in that single year than the total of her expenditures during the preceding five years. By then, however, the five-to-one superiority in military effectives which she had possessed over Germany in 1933 had turned into a four-to-three inferiority.[12]

[12] N. M. Sloutzski, *World Armaments Race, 1919–1939* (Geneva Studies, Vol. XII, No. 1, July 1941), pp. 45–46, 99–101. In 1933 the French army numbered approximately 508,000 men, the German army roughly 100,000. In 1939 the French army numbered 629,000 men, the German army 800–900,000.

Roughly the same process was going on with respect to the ratio between the British and German air forces. At the beginning of the 1930s the Royal Air Force, although a relatively small force, was undoubtedly much stronger than anything which the Germans had managed to create surreptitiously. During the period from 1934 to 1938, however, the strength of the RAF in comparison to the Luftwaffe steadily declined. In July 1934, Churchill warned Parliament that the German air force had then reached two-thirds the strength of the British Home Defense Air Force, and that if present and proposed programs were continued, the Germans would achieve parity by December 1935. Baldwin assured the Commons that Britain would maintain a fifty per cent superiority over Germany. Subsequently, however, Churchill's estimates proved to be more correct than those of the Government, and the air program had to be drastically increased in 1936 and 1937. By then, however, two years had been lost. In 1936 Germany achieved parity with Britain. In the spring of 1937 the Luftwaffe exceeded the RAF in first-line strength and reserves. By September 1938 it was almost twice as large as the RAF, and the production of aircraft in Germany was double that in England. The British vigorously pushed their efforts to make up for lost time: British aviation expenditures which had amounted to 16.8 million pounds in 1934–35 rose to 131.4 millions in 1937–38, and were budgeted at 242.7 millions for 1939–40. The Germans were now on top and the British the challengers moving to close the gap. The readiness of the Germans to go to war consequently was not unnatural. As far back as 1936, the British Joint Planning Staff had picked September 1939 as the most likely date for the beginning of a war because in the fall of 1939 Germany's armed strength would reach its peak in comparison with that of the allies. This forecast proved true on both points, and it was not until after the start of the war that the British began seriously to catch up with the head start of the Luftwaffe. British aircraft production first equalled that of the Germans in the spring of 1940.

A slightly different example of a belated, last minute arms race is found in the German-French and German-Russian competitions of 1911–1914. In this instance, deteriorating relations between the two countries led both to make strenuous efforts to increase their forces in a short time and enhanced the willingness of each to go to war. For a decade or more prior to 1911, German and French armaments had been relatively stable, and during the years 1908–1911 relations between the two countries had generally improved. The Agadir crisis of 1911 and the Balkan War of the following year stimulated the Germans to reconsider their armaments position. Fear of a Franco-Russian surprise attack and concern over the quantitative superiority of the French army led the Germans to make a moderate increase in their forces in 1912. In the spring of 1913 a much larger increase of 117,000 men was voted. Simultaneously, the French extended their term of military service from two to three years, thereby increasing their peacetime army by some 200,000 men. The Russians also had an extensive program of military reorganization under way. During the three year period 1911–14 the French army increased from 638,500 men to 846,000, and the German army from 626,732 to 806,026 men. If war had not broken out in 1914, the French would have been faced with an acute problem in maintaining a military balance with Germany. The population of France was about 39,000,000, that of Germany 65,000,000. During the twenty years prior to 1914 the French trained 82 per cent of their men liable for military service, the Germans 55 per cent of theirs. As a result, the two armies were approximately equal in size. If the Germans had continued to expand their army, the French inevitably would have fallen behind in the race: the extension of service in 1913 was a sign that they were reaching the limit of their manpower resources. Their alternatives would have been either to have provoked a war before Germany gained a decisive superiority, to have surrendered their goal of parity with Germany and with it any hope of retrieving Alsace-Lorraine, or to have stimulated further improvement of the military forces of their Russian ally and further expansion of the military forces of their British ally — perhaps putting pressure on Great Britain to institute universal military service. The Germans, on the other hand, felt themselves menaced by the reorganization of the Russian army. Already significantly outnumbered by the combined Franco-Russian armies, the Germans could hardly view with equanimity a significant increase in the efficiency of the Tsarist forces. Thus each side tended to see itself losing out in the arms race in the future and hence each side was more willing to risk a test of arms when the opportunity presented itself in 1914.

The danger of war is highest in the opening phases of an arms race, at which time the greatest elements of instability and uncertainty are present. If the challenged state neither resorts to preventive war nor fails to make an immediate response to the challenger's activities, a sustained arms race is likely to result with the probability of war decreasing as the initial action and counteraction fade into the past. Once the initial disturbances to the pre-arms race static equilibrium are surmounted, the reciprocal increases of the two states tend to produce a new, dynamic equilibrium reflecting their relative strength and participation in the race. In all probability, the relative military power of the two states in this dynamic equilibrium will fall somewhere between the previous status quo and the ratio-goal of the challenger. The sustained regularity of the increases in itself becomes an accepted and anticipated stabilizing factor in the relations between the two countries. A sustained quantitative race still may produce a war, but a greater likelihood exists that either the two states will arrive at a mutual accommodation reducing the political tensions which started the race or that one state over the long haul will gradually but substantially achieve its objective while the other will accept defeat in the race if this does not damage its vital interests. Thus, a twenty-five year sporadic naval race between France and England ended in the middle 1860s when France gave up any serious effort to challenge the 3:2 ratio which England had demonstrated the will and the capacity to maintain. Similarly, the Anglo-German naval race slackened after 1912 when, despite failure to reach formal agreement, relations improved between the two countries and even Tirpitz acquiesced in the British 16:10 ratio in capital ships.[13] Britain also successfully maintained her two-power standard against France and Russia for twenty years until changes in the international scene ended her arms competition with those two powers. Germany and France successively increased their armies from the middle 1870s to the middle 1890s when tensions eased and the arms build-up in each country slackened. The

---

[13] Some question might be raised as to whether the Anglo-German naval race ended before World War I or in World War I. It would appear, however, that the race was substantially over before the war began. The race went through two phases. During the first phase, 1898–1905, German policy was directed toward the construction of a "risk" navy. During the second phase, 1906–1912, the Anglo-French entente had removed the basis for a risk navy, and the introduction of the Dreadnought opened to the Germans the possibility of naval parity with Britain. By 1912, however, it was apparent to all that Britain had the will and the determination to maintain the 60 per cent superiority which she desired over Germany, and to lay "two keels for one" if this should be necessary. In addition, increased tension with France and Russia over Morocco and the Balkans turned German attention to her army. In 1912 Bethmann-Hollweg accepted as the basis for negotiation a British memorandum the first point of which was: "Fundamental. Naval superiority recognized as essential to Great Britain." Relations between the two countries generally improved between 1912 and 1914: they cooperated in their efforts to limit the Balkan wars of 1912–13 and in the spring of 1914 arrived an agreement concerning the Baghdad railway and the Portuguese colonies. By June 1914 rivalry had abated to such an extent that the visit of a squadron of British battleships to Kiel became the occasion for warm expressions of friendship. "In a sense," as Bernadotte Schmitt says, "potential foes had become potential friends." *The Coming of the War: 1914*, I, pp. 72–73; Sidney B. Fay, *The Origins of the World War* (New York, 2 vols., 1928), I, pp. 299ff.; Tirpitz, *Memoirs*, I, pp. 271–72.

incipient naval races among the United States, Britain, and Japan growing out of World War I were restricted by the Washington naval agreement; the ten-year cruiser competition between the United States and England ended in the London Treaty of 1930; and eventually the rise of more dangerous threats in the mid-1930s removed any remaining vestiges of Anglo-American naval rivalry. The twelve-year arms race between Chile and Argentina ended in 1902 with a comprehensive agreement between the two countries settling their boundary disputes and restricting their armaments. While generalizations are both difficult and dangerous, it would appear that a sustained arms race is much more likely to have a peaceful ending than a bloody one.

QUANTITATIVE AND QUALITATIVE ARMS RACES

A state may increase its military power quantitatively, by expanding the numerical strength of its existing military forces, or qualitatively, by replacing its existing forms of military force (normally weapons systems) with new and more effective forms of force. Expansion and innovation are thus possible characteristics of any arms race, and to some extent both are present in most races. Initially and fundamentally every arms race is quantitative in nature. The race begins when two states develop conflicting goals as to what should be the distribution of military power between them and give these goals explicit statement in quantitative ratios of the relative strengths which each hopes to achieve in the decisive form of military force. The formal start of the race is the decision of the challenger to upset the existing balance and to expand its forces quantitatively. If at some point in the race a qualitative change produces a new decisive form of military force, the quantitative goals of the two states still remain roughly the same. The relative balance of power which each state desires to achieve is independent of the specific weapons and forces which enter into the balance. Despite the underlying adherence of both states to their original ratio-goals, however, a complex qualitative race produced by rapid technological innovation is a very different phenomenon from a race which remains simply quantitative.

Probably the best examples of races which were primarily quantitative in nature are those between Germany and France between 1871 and 1914. The decisive element was the number of effectives each power maintained in its peacetime army and the number of reserves it could call to the colors in an emergency. Quantitative increases by one state invariably produced comparable increases by the other. The German army bill of 1880, for instance, added 25,000 men to the army and declared in its preamble that "far-reaching military reforms had been carried out outside of Germany which cannot remain without influence upon the military power of the neighboring countries." These increases it was alleged would produce "too considerable a numerical superiority of the enemy's forces."[14] Again in 1887 Bismarck used Boulanger's agitation for an increase in the French army as a means of putting through an expansion of the German one. After the French reorganized their army in 1889 and drastically increased the proportion of young men liable to military service, the Germans added 20,000 men to their force in 1890. Three years later a still larger increase was made in the German army and justified by reference to recent French and Russian expansions. Similarly, the naval race of 1884–1905 between England, on the one hand, and France and Russia, on the other, was primarily quantitative in nature. Naval budgets and numerical strengths of the two sides tended to fluctuate in direct relation with each other.

A qualitative arms race is more complex than a quantitative one because at some point it involves the decision by one side to introduce a new weapons system or form of military force. Where the capacity for technological innovation exists, the natural tendency is for the arms race to become qualitative. The introduction of a new weapons system obviously is normally desirable from the viewpoint of the state which is behind in the quantitative race. The English-French naval rivalry of 1841–1865 grew out of the deteriorating relations between the two countries over Syria, Tahiti and Spain. Its first manifestation was quantitative: in 1841 the number of seamen in the French navy which for nearly a century had been about two-thirds the number in the British navy was suddenly increased so as to almost equal the British strength. Subsequently the large expansions which the French proposed to make in their dockyards, especially at Toulon, caused even Cobden to observe that "a serious effort seemed really to be made to rival us at sea."[15] The Anglo-French quantitative rivalry subsided with the departure of Louis Philippe in 1848, but shortly thereafter it resumed on a new qualitative level with the determination of Napoleon III to push the construction of steam warships. The *Napoléon*, a screw propelled ship of the line of 92 guns, launched by the French in 1850 was significantly superior to anything the British could bring against it, until the *Agamemnon* was launched two years later. The alliance of the two countries in the Crimean War only temporarily suspended the

[14] Kovacs, "Nation in Arms," p. 36.
[15] Cobden, "Three Panics," p. 224.

naval race, and by 1858 the French had achieved parity with the British in fast screw ships of the line. In that year the French had 114 fewer sailing vessels in their navy than they had in 1852, while the number of British sailing ships had declined only from 299 to 296. On the other hand, the British in 1852 had a superiority of 73 sailing ships of the line to 45 for the French. By 1858, however, both England and France had 29 steam ships of the line while England had an enhanced superiority of 35 to 10 in sailing ships. A head start in steam construction and conversion plus the concentration of effort on this program had enabled the French, who had been hopelessly outnumbered in the previously decisive form of naval power, to establish a rough parity in the new form. In view of the British determination to restore their quantitative superiority and the superior industrial resources at their disposal, however, parity could only be temporary. In 1861 the British had 53 screw battleships afloat and 14 building while the French had only 35 afloat and two building.[16]

By the time that the British had reestablished their superiority in steam warships, their opponents had brought forward another innovation which again threatened British control of the seas. The French laid down four ironclads in 1858 and two in 1859. The first was launched in November 1859 and the next in March 1860. The British launched their first ironclad in December 1860. The British program, however, was hampered by the Admiralty's insistence upon continuing to build wooden warships. The French stopped laying down wooden line of battleships in 1856, yet the British, despite warnings that wooden walls were obsolete, continued building wooden ships down through 1860, and in 1861 the Admiralty brought in the largest request in its history for the purchase of timber.[17] Meanwhile, in the fall of 1860 the French started a new construction program for ten more ironclads to supplement the six they already had underway. The British learned of these projects in February 1861 and responded with a program to add nine new ironclads to their fleet. In May 1861, the French had a total of fifteen ironclads built or building, the British only seven. From 1860 until 1865 the French possessed superiority or parity with the British in ironclad warships. In February 1863, for instance, the French had four ironclads mounting 146 guns ready for action, the British four ironclads mounting 116 guns. Thanks to the genius and initiative

---

[16] *Ibid.*, pp. 304–08, 392–93.

[17] *Ibid.*, pp. 343, 403; Robert G. Albion, *Forests and Sea Power* (Cambridge, 1926), p. 408.

of the director of French naval construction, Dupuy de Lôme, and the support of Napoleon III, there had occurred, as one British military historian put it,

> an astonishing change in the balance of power which might have been epoch-making had it not been so brief, or if France and Britain had gone to war, a reversal which finds no place in any but technical histories and which is almost entirely unknown in either country today. In a word, supremacy at sea passed from Britain to France.[18]

This was not a supremacy, however, which France could long maintain. By 1866, Britannia had retrieved the trident. In that year England possessed nineteen ironclads, France thirteen, and the English superiority was enhanced by heavier guns. Thereafter the naval strengths of the two powers resumed the 3:2 ratio which had existed prior to 1841.

In general, as this sequence of events indicates, technological innovation favors, at least temporarily, the numerically weaker power. Its long-run effects, however, depend upon factors other than the currently prevailing balance of military strength. It was indeed paradoxical that France should make the innovations which she did make in her naval race with England. In the 1850s and 1860s France normally had twice as much timber on hand in her dockyards as had the British, and she was, of course, inferior to England in her coal and iron resources. Nonetheless she led the way in the introduction of steam and iron, while the Royal Navy, which was acutely hampered by a timber shortage clung to the wooden ships.[19] In this instance, on both sides, immediate needs and the prospects of immediate success prevailed over a careful consideration of long-term benefits.

The problem which technological innovation presents to the quantitatively superior power is somewhat more complex. The natural tendencies for such a state are toward conservatism: any significant innovation will undermine the usefulness of the current type of weapons system in which it possesses a superiority. What, however, should be the policy of a superior power with respect to making a technological change which its inferior rivals are likely to make in the near future? The British navy had a traditional answer to this problem: never introduce any development which will render existing ships obsolete but be prepared if any other state does make an innovation to push ahead an emergency construction program which will restore the previously existing ratio. While this policy

---

[18] Cyril Falls, *A Hundred Years of War* (London, 1953), p. 102.
[19] Albion, *Forests and Sea Power*, pp. 406–07; Brodie, *Sea Power in the Machine Age*, p. 441.

resulted, as we have seen above, in some close shaves, by the beginning of the twentieth century it had become a fundamental maxim of British naval doctrine. Consequently, Sir John Fisher's proposal in 1904 to revolutionize naval construction by introducing the "all big gun ship" which would render existing capital ships obsolete was also a revolution in British policy. In terms of its impact upon the Anglo-German naval balance, Fisher's decision was welcomed by many Germans and condemned by many British. Although the construction of Dreadnoughts would force Germany to enlarge the Kiel Canal, the Germans seized the opportunity to start the naval race afresh in a class of vessels in which the British did not have an overwhelming numerical superiority. For the first few years the British by virtue of their headstart would have a larger number of Dreadnoughts, but then the German yards would start producing and the gap which had to be closed would be much smaller in the Dreadnoughts than in the pre-Dreadnought battleships. The introduction of the Dreadnought permitted the Germans to raise their sights from a "risk" navy (which had become meaningless since the Anglo-French entente in any event) to the possibility of parity with Britain. To many Britishers, on the other hand, construction of the Dreadnought seemed to be tantamount to sinking voluntarily a large portion of the British navy. The tremendous number of pre-Dreadnought capital ships which the Royal Navy possessed suddenly decreased in value. Great Britain, one British naval expert subsequently argued, had to write off seventy-five warships, the Germans only twenty-eight. British naval superiority fell by 40 or 50 per cent: in 1908 England had authorized twelve Dreadnoughts and the Germans nine; in pre-Dreadnought battleships the British had 63 and the Germans 26.[20]

Fisher's policy, however, was undoubtedly the correct one. Plans for an all-big-gun ship had been under consideration by various navies since 1903. The Russo-Japanese War underwrote the desirability of heavy armaments. The United States authorized the construction of two comparable vessels in March, 1905, and the Germans themselves were moving in that direction. The all-big-gun ship was inevitable, and this consideration led Fisher to insist that Britain must take the lead. While the superiority of the Royal Navy over the German fleet was significantly reduced, nonetheless at no time in the eight years after 1905 did the Germans approach the British in terms of numerical equality. Their highest point was in 1911 when their Dreadnought battleship and battle-cruiser strength

[20] Hector C. Bywater, *Navies and Nations* (London, 1927), pp. 27–28; Fay, *Origins of the World War*, I, p. 236.

amounted to 64 per cent of the British strength.[21] Thus, by reversing the nineteenth century policy of the British navy, Fisher avoided the British experience of the 1850s and 1860s when technological innovations by an inferior power temporarily suspended Britain's supremacy on the seas.

The very incentive which an inferior power has to make a technological innovation is reason for the superior power to take the lead, if it can, in bringing in the innovation itself. The British Dreadnought debate of 1904–1905 had its parallels in the problem confronting the American government in 1949–1950 concerning the construction of a hydrogen bomb. Like the British, the Americans possessed a superiority in the existing decisive type of weapons system. As in the British government, opinion was divided, and the arguments pro and con of the technicians and military experts had to be weighed against budgetary considerations. As with the Dreadnought, the new weapons system was pushed by a small group of zealots convinced of the inevitability and necessity of its development. In both cases, humanitarian statesmen and conservative experts wished to go slow. In each case, the government eventually decided to proceed with the innovation, and, in each case, the wisdom of its policy was demonstrated by the subsequent actions of its rival. In an arms race, what is technically possible tends to become politically necessary.

Whether an arms race is primarily quantitative or primarily qualitative in nature has a determining influence upon its outcome. This influence is manifested in the different impacts which the two types of races have on the balance of military power between the two states and on the relative demands which they make on state resources.

Qualitative and quantitative races and the balance of power. In a simple quantitative race one state is very likely to develop a definite superiority in the long run. The issue is simply who has the greater determination and the greater resources. Once a state falls significantly behind, it is most unlikely that it will ever be able to overcome the lead of its rival. A qualitative race, on the other hand, in which there is a series of major technological innovations in reality consists of a number of distinct races. Each time a new weapons system is introduced a new race takes place in the development and accumulation of that weapon. As the rate of technological innova-

---

[21] I am indebted to a paper by Mr. Peter E. Weil on "The Dreadnought and the Anglo-German Naval Race, 1905–1909" for statistics on British and German naval strengths.

tion increases each separate component race decreases in time and extent. The simple quantitative race is like a marathon of undetermined distance which can only end with the exhaustion of one state or both, or with the state which is about to fall behind in the race pulling out its firearms and attempting to despatch its rival. The qualitative race, on the other hand, resembles a series of hundred yard dashes, each beginning from a fresh starting line. Consequently, in a qualitative race hope springs anew with each phase. Quantitative superiority is the product of effort, energy, resources, and time. Once achieved it is rarely lost. Qualitative superiority is the product of discovery, luck, and circumstance. Once achieved it is always lost. Safety exists only in numbers. While a quantitative race tends to produce inequality between the two competing powers, a qualitative race tends toward equality irrespective of what may be the ratio-goals of the two rival states. Each new weapon instead of increasing the distance between the two states reduces it. The more rapid the rate of innovation the more pronounced is the tendency toward equality. Prior to 1905, for instance, Great Britain possessed a superiority in pre-Dreadnought battleships. By 1912 she had also established a clear and unassailable superiority in Dreadnoughts over Germany. But if Germany had introduced a super-Dreadnought in 1909, Great Britain could never have established its clear superiority in Dreadnoughts. She would have had to start over again in the new race. A rapid rate of innovation means that arms races are always beginning, never ending. In so far as the likelihood of war is decreased by the existence of an equality of power between rival states, a qualitative arms race tends to have this result. A quantitative arms race, on the other hand, tends to have the opposite effect. If in a qualitative race one power stopped technological innovation and instead shifted its resources to the multiplication of existing weapons systems, this would be a fairly clear sign that it was intending to go to war in the immediate future.

Undoubtedly many will question the proposition that rapid technological innovation tends to produce an equality of power. In an arms race each state lives in constant fear that its opponent will score a "technological breakthrough" and achieve a decisive qualitative superiority. This anxiety is a continuing feature of arms races but it is one which has virtually no basis in recent experience. The tendency toward simultaneity of innovation is overwhelming. Prior to World War I simultaneity was primarily the result of the common pool of knowledge among the advanced nations with respect to weapons technology. The development of weapons was largely the province of private firms who made their wares available to any state which was interested. As a result at any given time the armaments of the major powers all strikingly resembled one another.[22] During and after World War I military research and development became more and more a governmental activity, and, as a result, more and more enshrouded in secrecy. Nonetheless relative equality in technological innovation continued among the major powers. The reason for this was now not so much access to common knowledge as an equal ability and opportunity to develop that knowledge. The logic of scientific development is such that separate groups of men working in separate laboratories on the same problem are likely to arrive at the same answer to the problem at about the same time. Even if this were not the case, the greatly increased ratio of production time to use time in recent years has tended to diminish the opportunity of the power which has pioneered an innovation to produce it in sufficient quantity in sufficient time to be militarily decisive. When it takes several years to move a weapons system from original design to quantity operation, knowledge of it is bound to leak out, and the second power in the arms race will be able to get its own program under way before the first state can capitalize on its lead. The *Merrimac* reigned supreme for a day, but it was only for a day and it could be only for a day.

The fact that for four years from 1945 to 1949 the United States possessed a marked qualitative superiority over the Soviet Union has tended to obscure how rare this event normally is. American superiority, however, was fundamentally the result of carrying over into a new competitive rivalry a weapons system which had been developed in a previous conflict. In the latter rivalry the tendency toward simultaneity of development soon manifested itself. The Soviet Union developed an atomic bomb four years after the United States had done so. Soviet explosion of a hydrogen weapon lagged only ten months behind that of the United States. At a still later date in the arms race, both powers in 1957 were neck and neck in their efforts to develop long-range ballistic missiles.

---

[22] See Victor Lefebure, "The Decisive Aggressive Value of the New Agencies of War," in The Inter-Parliamentary Union, *What Would Be the Character of a New War?* (New York, 1933), pp. 97–101. See also Marion W. Boggs, *Attempts to Define and Limit "Aggressive" Armament in Diplomacy and Strategy* (Columbia, Mo., 1941), p. 76: ". . . the history of war inventions tends to emphasize the slowness and distinctively international character of peacetime improvements; no weapon has been perfected with secrecy and rapidity as the exclusive national property of any one state. At an early stage all nations secure access to the information, and develop not only the armament, but measures against it."

The ending of an arms race in a distinct quantitative victory for one side is perhaps best exemplified in the success of the British in maintaining their supremacy on the seas. Three times within the course of a hundred years the British were challenged by continental rivals, and three times the British outbuilt their competitors. In each case, also, implicitly or explicitly, the bested rivals recognized their defeat and abandoned their efforts to challenge the resources, skill and determination of the British. At this point in a quantitative race when it appears that one power is establishing its superiority over the other, proposals are frequently brought forward for some sort of "disarmament" agreement. These are as likely to come from the superior side as from the inferior one. The stronger power desires to clothe its *de facto* supremacy in *de jure* acceptance and legitimacy so that it may slacken its own arms efforts. From 1905 to 1912, for instance, virtually all the initiatives for Anglo-German naval agreement came from the British. Quite properly, the Germans regarded those advances as British efforts to compel "naval competition to cease at the moment of its own greatest preponderance." Such proposals only heightened German suspicion and bitterness. Similarly, after World War II the Soviet Union naturally described the American nuclear disarmament proposal as a device to prevent the Soviet Union from developing its own nuclear capability. A decade later a greater common interest existed between the Soviet Union and the United States in reaching an arms agreement which would permanently exclude "fourth powers" from the exclusive nuclear club. In disarmament discussions the superior power commonly attempts to persuade the inferior one to accept as permanent the existing ratio of strength, or, failing in this effort, the superior power proposes a temporary suspension of the race, a "holiday" during which period neither power will increase its armaments. In 1899 the Russians, with the largest army in Europe, proposed that for five years no increases be made in military budgets. In 1912–14 Churchill repeatedly suggested the desirability of a naval building holiday to the Germans who were quite unable to perceive its advantages. In 1936 the United States could easily agree to a six year holiday in 10,000 ton cruisers since it had already underway all the cruisers it was permitted by the London Treaty of 1930. Similarly, in its 1957 negotiations with the Soviet Union the United States could also safely propose an end to the production of nuclear weapons. The inferior participant in disarmament negotiations, on the other hand, inevitably supports measures based not upon the existing situation but either upon the abstract principle of "parity" or upon the inherent evil of large armaments as such and the desirability of reducing all arms down to a common low level. Thus, in most instances, a disarmament proposal is simply a maneuver in the arms race: the attempt by a state to achieve the ratio-goal it desires by means other than an increase in its armaments.

The domestic burden of quantitative and qualitative races. Quantitative and qualitative arms races have markedly different effects upon the countries participating in them. In a quantitative race the decisive ratio is between the resources which a nation devotes to military purposes and those which it devotes to civilian ones. A quantitative race of any intensity requires a steady shift of resources from the latter to the former. As the forms of military force are multiplied a larger and larger proportion of the national product is devoted to the purposes of the race, and, if it is a race in military manpower, an increasing proportion of the population serves a longer and longer time in the armed forces. A quantitative race of any duration thus imposes ever increasing burdens upon the countries involved in it. As a result, it becomes necessary for governments to resort to various means of stimulating popular support and eliciting a willingness to sacrifice other goods and values. Enthusiasm is mobilized, hostility aroused and directed against the potential enemy. Suspicion and fear multiply with the armaments. Such was the result of the quantitative races between the Triple Alliance and the Triple Entente between 1907 and 1914:

> In both groups of powers there was a rapid increase of military and naval armaments. This caused increasing suspicions, fears, and newspaper recriminations in the opposite camp. This in turn led to more armaments; and so to the vicious circle of ever growing war preparations and mutual fears and suspicions.[23]

Eventually a time is reached when the increasing costs and tensions of a continued arms race seem worse than the costs and the risks of war. Public opinion once aroused cannot be quieted. The economic, military and psychological pressures previously generated permit only further expansion or conflict. The extent to which an arms race is likely to lead to war thus varies with the burdens it imposes on the peoples and the extent to which it involves them psychologically and emotionally in the race. Prolonged sufficiently, a quantitative race must necessarily reach a point where opinion in one country or the other will demand that it be ended, if not by negotiation, then by war. The logical result of a quantitative arms race is a "nation in arms," and a nation in arms for any length of time must be a nation at war.

[23] Fay, *Origins of the World War,* I, p. 226.

A qualitative arms race, however, does not have this effect. In such a race the essential relationship is not between the military and the civilian, but rather between the old and the new forms of military force. In a quantitative race the principal policy issue is the extent to which resources and manpower should be diverted from civilian to military use. In a qualitative race, the principal issue is the extent to which the new weapons systems should replace the old "conventional" ones. In a quantitative race the key question is "How much?" In a qualitative race, it is "How soon?" A quantitative race requires continuous expansion of military resources, a qualitative race continuous redeployment of them. A qualitative race does not normally increase arms budgets, even when, as usually happens, the new forms of military force are more expensive than the old ones. The costs of a qualitative race only increase significantly when an effort is made to maintain both old and new forms of military force: steam and sail; ironclads and wooden walls; nuclear and nonnuclear weapons. Transitions from old to new weapons systems have not normally been accompanied by marked increases in military expenditures. During the decade in which the ironclad replaced the wooden ship of the line British naval expenditures declined from £12,779,000 in 1859 to less than eleven million pounds in 1867.[24] Similarly, the five years after the introduction of the Dreadnought saw British naval expenditures drop from £35,476,000 in 1903–04 to £32,188,000 in 1908–09. During the same period estimates for shipbuilding and repairs dropped from £17,350,000 to £14,313,-900. The years 1953–1956 saw the progressive adoption of nuclear weapons in the American armed forces, yet military budgets during this period at first dropped considerably and then recovered only slightly, as the increased expenditures for the new weapons were more than compensated for by reductions in expenditures for nonnuclear forces.

Quantitative and qualitative arms races differ also in the interests they mobilize and the leadership they stimulate. In the long run, a quantitative race makes extensive demands on a broad segment of the population. A qualitative race, however, tends to be a competition of elites rather than masses. No need exists for the bulk of the population to become directly involved. In a quantitative arms race, the users of the weapons — the military leaders — assume the key role. In a qualitative race, the creators of the weapons — the scientists — rival them for preeminence. Similarly, the most important private interests in a quantitative race are the large mass production

[24] James Phinney Baxter, 3rd, *The Introduction of the Ironclad Warship* (Cambridge, 1933), p. 321.

industrial corporations, while in a qualitative race they tend to be the smaller firms specializing in the innovation and development of weapons systems rather than in their mass output.

While the rising costs of a quantitative race may increase the likelihood of war, they may also enhance efforts to end the race by means of an arms agreement. Undoubtedly the most powerful motive (prior to the feasibility of utter annihilation) leading states to arms limitations has been the economic one. The desire for economy was an important factor leading Louis Philippe to propose a general reduction in European armaments in 1831. In the 1860s similar motives stimulated Napoleon III to push disarmament plans. They also prompted various British governments to be receptive to arms limitation proposals, provided, of course, that they did not endanger Britain's supremacy on the seas: the advent of the Liberal government in 1905, for instance, resulted in renewed efforts to reach accommodation with the Germans. In 1898 the troubled state of Russian finances was largely responsible for the Tsar's surprise move in sponsoring the first Hague Conference. Eight years later it was the British who, for economic reasons, wished to include the question of arms limitation on the agenda of the second Hague Conference.

The success of rising economic costs in bringing about the negotiated end of an arms race depends upon their incidence being relatively equal on each participant. A state which is well able to bear the economic burden normally spurns the efforts of weaker powers to call off the race. Thus, the Kaiser was scornful of the Russian economic debility which led to the proposal for the first Hague Conference, and a German delegate to that conference, in explaining German opposition to limitation, took pains to assure the participants that:

> The German people are not crushed beneath the weight of expenditures and taxes; they are not hanging on the edge of the precipice; they are not hastening towards exhaustion and ruin. Quite the contrary; public and private wealth is increasing, the general welfare, and standard of life, are rising from year to year.[25]

On the other hand, the relatively equal burdens of their arms race in the last decade of the nineteenth century eventually forced Argentina and Chile to call the race off in 1902. The victory of Chile in the War of the Pacific had brought her into conflict with an "expanding and prosperous Argentina" in the 1880s, and a whole series of boundary disputes exacerbated the rivalry which developed between the two powers for hegemony on the South American conti-

[25] Quoted in Tate, *Disarmament Illusion*, p. 281. See also pp. 193–94, 251–52.

nent. As a result, after 1892 both countries consistently expanded their military and naval forces, and relations between them staggered from one war crisis to another. Despite efforts made to arbitrate the boundary disputes,

> an uneasy feeling still prevailed that hostilities might break out, and neither State made any pretence of stopping military and naval preparations. Orders for arms, ammunition, and warships were not countermanded, and men on both sides of the Andes began to declaim strongly against the heavy expenditure thus entailed. The reply to such remonstrances invariably was that until the question of the boundary was settled, it was necessary to maintain both powers on a war footing. Thus the resources of Argentina and Chile were strained to the utmost, and public works neglected in order that funds might be forthcoming to pay for guns and ships bought in Europe.[26]

These economic burdens led the presidents of the two countries to arrive at an agreement in 1899 restricting additional expenditures on armaments. Two years later, however, the boundary issue again flared up, and both sides recommenced preparations for war. But again the resources of the countries were taxed beyond their limit. In August 1901 the Chilean president declared to the United States minister "that the burden which Chile is carrying . . . is abnormal and beyond her capacity and that the hour has come to either make use of her armaments or reduce them to the lowest level compatible with the dignity and safety of the country."[27] Argentina was also suffering from severe economic strain, and as a result, the two countries concluded their famous *Pactos de Mayo* in 1902 which limited their naval armaments and provided for the arbitration of the remaining boundary issues.

In summary, two general conclusions emerge as to the relations between arms races and war:

(1) War is more likely to develop in the early phases of an arms race than in its later phases.

(2) A quantitative race is more likely than a qualitative one to come to a definite end in war, arms agreement, or victory for one side.

ARMS RACES, DISARMAMENT, AND PEACE

In discussions of disarmament, a distinction has frequently been drawn between the presumably technical problem of arms limitation, on the one hand, and political problems, on the other. Consid-

---

[26] Charles E. Akers, *A History of South America* (New York, new ed., 1930), p. 112.

[27] Quoted in Robert N. Burr, "The Balance of Power in Nineteenth-Century South America: An Exploratory Essay," *Hispanic American Historical Review*, XXXV (February, 1955), 58n.

erable energy has been devoted to arguments as to whether it is necessary to settle political issues before disarming or whether disarmament is a prerequisite to the settlement of political issues. The distinction between arms limitation and politics, however, is a fallacious one. The achievement of an arms agreement cannot be made an end in itself. Arms limitation is the essence of politics and inseparable from other political issues. What, indeed, is more political than the relative balance of power between two distinct entities? Whether they be political parties competing for votes, lobbyists lining up legislative blocs, or states piling up armaments, the power ratio between the units is a decisive factor in their relationship. Virtually every effort (such as the Hague Conferences and the League of Nations) to reach agreement on arms apart from the resolution of other diplomatic and political issues has failed. Inevitably attempts to arrive at arms agreements have tended to broaden into discussions of all the significant political issues between the competing powers. On the other hand, it cannot be assumed that arms negotiations are hopeless, and that they only add another issue to those already disrupting the relations between the two countries and stimulating passion and suspicion. Just as the problem of armaments cannot be settled without reference to other political issues, so is it also impossible to resolve these issues without facing up to the relative balance of military power. The most notable successes in arms limitation agreements have been combined, implicitly or explicitly, with a resolution of other controversies. The Rush-Bagot Agreement, for instance, simply confirmed the settlement which had been reached in the Treaty of Paris. The *Pactos de Mayo* dealt with both armaments and boundaries and implicitly recognized that Argentina would not intervene in west coast politics and that Chile would not become involved in the disputes of the Plata region. The Washington naval agreements necessarily were part and parcel of a general Far Eastern settlement involving the end of the Anglo-Japanese alliance and at least a temporary resolution of the diplomatic issues concerning China. As has been suggested previously, in one sense armaments are to the twentieth century what territory was to the eighteenth. Just as divisions of territory were then the essence of general diplomatic agreements, so today are arrangements on armaments. If both sides are to give up their conflicting ratio-goals and compromise the difference, this arrangement must coincide with a settlement of the other issues which stimulated them to develop the conflicting ratio-goals in the first place. If one state is to retreat further from its ratio-goal than the other, it will have to receive compensations with respect to other points in dispute.

While arms limitation is seldom possible except as part of a broader political settlement, it is also seldom possible if the scope of the arms limitation is itself too broad. One of the corollaries of the belief that arms races produce wars is the assumption that disarmament agreements are necessary to peace. Too frequently it has been made to appear that failure to reach a disarmament agreement leaves war as the only recourse between the powers. In particular, it is false and dangerous to assume that any disarmament to be effective must be total disarmament. The latter is an impossible goal. Military force is inherent in national power and national power is inherent in the existence of independent states. In one way or another all the resources of a state contribute to its military strength. The discussions in the 1920s under the auspices of the League conclusively demonstrated that what are armaments for one state are the pacific instruments of domestic well-being and tranquility for another. The history of general disarmament conferences persuasively suggests the difficulties involved in deciding what elements of power should be weighed in the balance even before the issue is faced as to what the relative weight of the two sides should be. At the first Hague Conference, for instance, the Germans were quick to point out that the Russian proposal for a five year holiday in military budget increases was fine for Russia who had all the men in her army that she needed, but that such a restriction would not prevent Russia from building strategic railways to her western border which would constitute a greater menace to Germany than additional Russian soldiers. The demand for total disarmament frequently reflects an unwillingness to live with the problems of power. A feasible arms limitation must be part of the process of politics, not of the abolition of politics.

The narrower the scope of a proposed arms limitation agreement, the more likely it is to be successful. Disarmament agreements seldom actually disarm states. What they do is to exclude certain specified areas from the competition and thereby direct that competition into other channels. The likelihood of reaching such an agreement is greater if the states can have a clear vision of the impact of the agreement on the balance of power. The more restricted the range of armaments covered by the agreement, the easier it is for them to foresee its likely effects. In general, also, the less important the area in the balance of power between the two states, the easier it is to secure agreement on that area. Part of the success of the Washington agreements was that they were limited to capital ships, and, at that time, particularly in the United States the feeling existed that existing battleships were obsolete and that in any event the battleship had passed its peak as the supreme weapon of naval power. Similarly, in 1935 Germany and England were able to arrive at an agreement (which lasted until April 1939) fixing the relative size of their navies — something which had been beyond the capability of sincere and well-meaning diplomats of both powers before World War I — because air power had replaced sea power as the decisive factor in the arms balance between Germany and England. Restrictions on land armaments have generally been harder to arrive at than naval agreements because the continental European nations usually felt that their large armies were directly essential to their national existence and might have to be used at a moment's notice.

Successful disarmament agreements (and a disarmament agreement is successful if it remains in force for a half decade or more) generally establish quantitative restrictions on armaments. The quantitative ratio is the crucial one between the powers, and the quantitative element is much more subject to the control of governments than is the course of scientific development. Furthermore, a quantitative agreement tends to channel competition into qualitative areas, while an agreement on innovation tends to do just the reverse. Consequently, quantitative agreement tends to reduce the likelihood of war, qualitative agreement to enhance it. In the current arms race, for instance, some sort of quantitative agreement might be both feasible, since the race is primarily qualitative in nature, and desirable, since such an agreement would formally prohibit the more dangerous type of arms race. On the other hand, a qualitative agreement between the two countries prohibiting, say, the construction and testing of intercontinental ballistic missiles, might well be disastrous if it should stimulate a quantitative race in aircraft production, the construction of bases, and the multiplication of other forms of military force. In addition, the next phase in the arms race, for instance, may well be the development of defenses against ballistic missiles. A qualitative answer to this problem, such as an effective anti-missile missile, would, in the long run, be much less expensive and much less disturbing to peace than a quantitative answer, such as a mammoth shelter construction program, which would tax public resources, infringe on many established interests, and arouse popular concern and fear. Continued technological innovation could well be essential to the avoidance of war. Peace, in short, may depend less upon the ingenuity of the rival statesmen than upon the ingenuity of the rival scientists.

The balancing of power in any bipolar situation is inherently difficult due to the absence of a "balancer." In such a situation, however, a qualitative arms race may be the most effective means of achieving and maintaining parity of power over a long period of time. The inherent tendency toward parity of such a race may to some extent provide a substitute for the missing balancer. In particular, a qualitative race tends to equalize the differences which might otherwise exist between the ability and willingness of a democracy to compete with a totalitarian dictatorship. The great problem of international politics now is to develop forms of international competition to replace the total wars of the first half of the twentieth century. One such alternative is limited war. Another is the qualitative arms race. The emerging pattern of rivalry between the West and the Soviet bloc suggests that these may well be the primary forms of military activity which the two coalitions will employ. As wars become more frightening and less frequent, arms races may become longer and less disastrous. The substitution of the one for the other is certainly no mean step forward in the restriction of violence. In this respect the arms race may serve the same function which war served: "the intensely sharp competitive *preparation* for war by the nations," could become, as William James suggested, "*the real war*, permanent, unceasing. . . ."[28] A qualitative race regularizes this preparation and introduces an element of stability into the relations between the two powers. Even if it were true, as Sir Edward Grey argued, that arms races inevitably foster suspicion and insecurity, these would be small prices to pay for the avoidance of destruction. Until fundamental changes take place in the structure of world politics, a qualitative arms race may well be a most desirable form of competition between the Soviet Union and the United States.

[28] *Memories and Studies* (New York, 1912), p. 273.

On Stability
in Deterrent Races

MALCOLM W. HOAG

I

In modern strategy no distinction has been labored more than that between deterrence and defense. Everyone now knows that to avert war is not the same as to protect the nation or win if war occurs. But what everyone knows vaguely, few may know well, and what the distinction implies for the mixture of military forces the nation should buy, still fewer may perceive. For deterrence and defense as military objectives overlap as well as diverge, complement each other as well as compete, so that a simple distinction can become complicated. Of special contemporary relevance, moreover, what is alleged to strengthen deterrence in the short run may jeopardize it in the long. About our military preparations, few queries are more important than "How will they influence the nature and intensity of the arms race, and therefore the prospects for arms control?"

The simplest way to illustrate these points is to move indirectly from the pure concepts to their policy implications via hypothetical situations or models. By doing so the clutter of secondarily relevant detail is avoided. This overriding merit of abstraction is shared by neither of the customary alternatives — careful examination of historical instances, or a direct comparison of the probable performance of alternative modern military postures — for all their other virtues.

Given the freedom to generate the most convenient hypothetical situations, we choose an initial one circa 1900. That, among other

From Morton A. Kaplan, ed., *The Revolution in World Politics* (John Wiley and Sons, 1962), pp. 388–410. Originally published by The Rand Corporation. Reprinted by permission. Some footnotes have been omitted.

I am indebted to many colleagues at the National War College in 1959–1960. That persons so senior, informed, and intelligent about these matters could nonetheless profit from a reexamination of fundamentals motivated this article. My own understanding owes so much to current associates that acknowledgment in detail is unfortunately impossible.

things, gets rid of airpower but not deterrence. To eliminate sea-power, consider the situation of a landlocked country — say, Ruri-tania. For doctrines of airpower, landpower, or seapower tend to confuse the central issues more than they clarify them, not to men-tion the passions they arouse. Finally, to make our situation as sim-ple as possible, let us suppose that there is only one potential enemy on the land frontier, and that this enemy has roughly comparable resources. In short, we contrive initially to make military planning as easy as possible.

Let us assume that Ruritania's Defense Minister gets the follow-ing instructions as political guidelines: "We want to deter our threatening neighbor from attacking us, and to protect our country from invasion if he does attack." A realistic response from a de-fense planner, grateful for such comparative succinctness, modera-tion, and clarity, would stop at "Yes, sir." Any bureaucrat would dismiss as a hopelessly niggling philosopher a Defense Minister who, in so ideal a situation, would query: "But what comparative values do you assign to the objectives of deterrence and defense?" It would, in principle, be a legitimate question, but it would be un-necessarily disruptive. It would be very difficult to answer and, whatever the answer, it would have little effect on policy.

It would not be the similarity of the two goals, but the near-identity of military preparations directed toward either of them, that would render the distinction academic. An army is required. If one good enough and big enough is provided, Ruritania will be confident that any attack by her neighbor can be stopped. The same prospect should be evident to the neighbor, whose low confidence in the suc-cess of any attack should roughly mirror Ruritania's high confidence in successful defense. Therefore, the neighbor should be deterred. How strongly he is deterred by any given balance of opposed armies depends also, of course, upon his bellicosity and recklessness. De-terrence in the final analysis always rests upon a state of mind, which raises the age-old issue of whether defense planning should be based upon enemy capabilities or intent.

We assume in this case that a Ruritanian planner, following the classically conservative precept, places primary emphasis upon esti-mated enemy capabilities. About enemy intent he assumes not the worst, for that would be to assume an enemy so bent upon aggres-sion that he is unmoved by any rational calculations of excessive risk. But he assumes almost the worst: specifically, an enemy who will attack if his military prospects, soberly calculated, are promis-ing. By assuming a malevolent if rational foe, he will generate military requirements that will perhaps provide excessive protection against a neighbor more peaceably inclined. Any excess protection, however, will insure against any precarious misreading of future enemy intent as peaceable.

It will be possible to provide defense here, moreover, in a way that should not make a hitherto peaceable enemy suspiciously hostile. Ruritanian defense measures to strengthen deterrence need not incite an arms race and so, in part, negate themselves. This conclusion follows if we add a special assumption, in this case the empirically founded one that attacking armies require, other things being equal, a considerable numerical superiority to prevail over defending armies.[1] Then Ruritania can meet its stated military goals with lesser forces than its neighbor, and, provided both sides share this assumption of defense advantage, pose no aggressive threat. Passing over all the complex details of the area to be defended, terrain, equipment, and so forth, suppose that Ruritanian army planners conclude that the old rule of thumb is applicable and that a minimum of 10 divisions can hold against the 30 divisions that the enemy is expected to have. Suppose further that they prudently multiply this minimum estimate by two, and that a resultant force goal of 20 divisions is accepted by the government over the protests of a reluctant Finance Ministry. To its neighbor, this force will still fall far short of the numbers required if Ruritania is to be a successful aggressor. Why should it be troubled unless, indeed, it had contemplated attack? How could such explicitly defensive measures provoke enemy attack unless their announcement prior to implementation crystallized previously existing aggressive intentions, i.e., moved the enemy to seize an opportunity before it vanished? Barring either of these possibilities, Ruritania's defense measures are consistent with international tranquillity; and, barring only the second, they increase the probability of peace. In short, they lead not merely to deterrence, but to stable deterrence in the dual sense that neither an attack nor an explosive arms race is triggered.

That no such arms race need result follows from the assumption that Ruritania can meet her defense goals with forces numerically inferior to her neighbor's. Any further increase in enemy forces can then be countered by a lesser Ruritanian increase within the range of one-third to two-thirds as much, leaving the enemy to bear higher costs for greater force increases without any gain in prospective performance as an aggressor. This penalty of higher costs for the enemy just to stay even can be expected to damp his ardor for the

---

[1] See B. H. Liddell Hart, *Deterrent or Defense*, New York, 1960, esp. ch. 10. That both sides would have recognized the superiority of prepared defenses in 1900, when most nations were ignoring rather than profiting from the lessons of the U.S. Civil War, is unlikely, but we presume them unusually enlightened.

race, and to do so automatically. This damping effect makes for stability, rather than instability, in an arms competition. That is, if we look not merely at the first reaction of one side to a change, however caused, in the strength of the other, but at the entire sequence of actions, reactions, counter-reactions, etc., we get a series of increases of progressively diminishing size. Suppose that an initial increase of a division by the enemy is motivated by prestige, fear of a different neighbor, or whatever, but that it will respond only defensively by simply matching any subsequent increase in Ruritanian strength. Then if Ruritania responds initially, say, by increasing its army by one-half of a division and the enemy matches this increase, with Ruritania in turn then offsetting by half of that or an additional one-fourth, and so on, we get an especially simple progression which leads to a total of only one added division for Ruritania. No arms race ever progresses so mechanically or simply, but the illustrated point of whether a non-self-aggravating, or damped, competition occurs, remains crucial.

Because this aspect of arms races is of crucial importance, we shall refer often to military "exchange rates," which measure the effort that would be required by one side to restore any stipulated balance of forces after a given effort by the opposition. Where effort can be illustrated in kind, e.g., two equivalent divisions for one, the rate of exchange will be so expressed, although invariably in practice more complex measures of national cost or effort are required. The policy application is direct. It is not enough to find a military preparation efficacious against a fixed estimate of the enemy. It should be appraised also in terms of his likely reactions: Does it impose adverse rates of exchange upon him as he responds, or even, ideally, impossible ones? Some things may be worth doing even when they do not impose such rates, but they must be so valuable for special reasons that they can bear the onus of participating in and possibly provoking a losing arms race.

To recapitulate, Ruritania poses two goals — deterrence and defense — which can be met by the same military measures. Therefore any conflicts in goals can be overlooked. Military planning, simple both in itself and in terms of broader foreign policy, can legitimately proceed on the basis of "military considerations only." The first-order questions that are always posed by deterrence are easily answered: (1) From what is the enemy to be deterred? (2) By fear of what consequences? (3) How are these consequences to be inflicted? (4) How is the threat of these consequences to be made credible?

In this case, it is invasion by the enemy that is deterred through his fear of failure, with a Ruritanian army the means to promise failure. That the army would be used if deterrence failed is inherently credible, for its use to frustrate the enemy would be synonymous with protection of the homeland. In this case, deterrence, which typically rests upon threatening dire consequences to an opponent unless he is deterred, does not conflict with defense, which seeks to alleviate the consequences to one's self if the enemy is not deterred. By virtue of the happy coincidence of frustration for the enemy and protection for Ruritania if deterrence fails, an army fulfills all requirements. It could be provided, moreover, at favorable rates of exchange, even when planned conservatively on the basis of enemy capabilities rather than intent. To complete the idyllic picture, military planning could proceed with little risk of any troubling foreign policy by-products. Except for the special case of an enemy already so close to aggressive decision that announcements of strengthened future defenses would trigger attack. Ruritanian defense measures would not be provocative. Nor would an explosive arms race be generated.

II

A situation like this enables broad military issues to be put at their simplest, and so more easily viewed as a whole. To do so is relevant because fundamentally the military questions have not changed, just their answers; nor have the issues, just their complexity. But the complexities have grown so formidable that the fundamentals can easily be obscured. More particularly, old lessons are remembered more easily than their rationale. Precepts can be drilled into all — e.g., assess enemy capability, not intent; or, more broadly, to defend is to deter and not to provoke — and at their grandest can be elevated into principles of war. What we need, however, is not a group of precepts, but their rationale; not which precept, but which combination, and why.

In short, we must discriminate, for circumstances do alter cases. The hypothetical circumstances in our example were rigged to generate convenient and comforting simplifications. The nuclear revolution, naturally, is mainly responsible for changing typical military circumstances markedly from those in our contrived case, but it is by no means solely responsible. Without moving our example forward into the nuclear age, the picture can be changed by altering our assumptions about the military means, objectives, or both.

This can be vividly illustrated if we convert our example momentarily from land to old naval warfare. Suppose Ruritania to be an island, concentrating upon seapower. The principal effect upon our example would be to invalidate the assumption that a defender enjoys great numerical advantages by virtue of his role. The open seas provide no opportunity for a defender to benefit from dug-in positions on terrain mainly of his own choosing. The fleets of aggressor and defender start virtually even, with superior position in battle dependent upon tactics rather than nature. Moreover, because the firepower of numerically superior fleets may all be brought to bear simultaneously, while the inferior opposition is forced to divide its fire among too many targets, any advantage in numbers should be multiplied in battle effectiveness. The expected relative losses mount not merely in proportion to the relative numbers engaged, but, qualifications aside, to their square.[2] For example, if Ruritania faced five enemy ships with five of equal quality, the outcome would be a fifty-fifty proposition, dependent upon luck and superior seamanship. But if the enemy fleet were increased to seven ships, Ruritania's expected losses in an engagement relative to the enemy would mount in proportion to $(7)^2:(5)^2$, or nearly twice those of the enemy. Against firepower so disadvantageous, a tremendous load would be placed on good fortune and possible superior performance per ship. Consequently, a great penalty is attached to falling behind in such an arms race, and a correspondingly great premium to being ahead.

The arms race in dreadnoughts before World War I is a case in point. This kind of competition, unlike that in our army illustration, is not inherently self-damping. At best, precarious equilibrium results when each side is content with matching and a balance is somehow obtained. Then and only then no self-exacerbating series of retaliatory increases is generated. It takes only one side to generate such a series by seeking superiority, even if the other is content with matching. If Ruritania insists upon being one or more battleships ahead, while her opponent is firmly resolved not to fall behind, there is no natural limit. Either the race explodes into war or one side is priced out of the competition. The arithmetic of such an arms race is distressing, which places a much greater burden upon political accommodation.

Our earlier statement of Ruritanian defense objectives was restricted to deterrence and defense. If we add, "and *win* if the enemy does attack," we move beyond the acceptability of stalemate and get the more familiar trio of deterrence, defense, and victory. Then the arms race issues, or more generally the issues of provocation, are posed more sharply. These more ambitious aims, when coupled with our switch to a naval setting, obviously contain the seeds of an explosive international competition of the sort illustrated above. With

[2] The classic development of this finding is in F. W. Lanchester, *Aircraft in Warfare*, London, 1916.

a great premium upon concentration in battle to secure the "fire-power-squared" advantages, massed fleets might well meet in one decisive engagement. When the outcome might thus be settled overnight early in the war, little reliance could be placed upon wartime production of such long lead-time items as battleships. The arms race would therefore focus upon fleets-in-being. In these vital respects, if not in technology, the situation would anticipate modern aerospace competition.

If we revert to Ruritania as a land power, the addition of victory as an objective would also heighten international tension, but less so. Those who fear her always retain the option of adequate defensive counters that fall short of matching her force increases. Self-damping still characterizes the mechanics of the arms race. The race, moreover, would not depend as sensitively upon forces-in-being, because apprehensions about the possibility of overnight defeat would be lessened. Blitzes are still possible, but much less likely. Greater reliance can be placed by both sides upon mobilization potentials, especially of reserve forces. If, at best, one side knows that the other is not mobilizing, it is reassured; at worst, massive mobilization gives it warning. A defender must take care, of course, that it can neither be greatly overwhelmed in ultimate amount nor outpaced in speed by enemy mobilization. As with armies in being, however, these requirements need not call for matching man for man, and accordingly are less disruptive.

Our digression into naval aspects, to sum up, illustrates how unstable, trigger-happy, arms competition can arise, and the lessons are especially pertinent in a nuclear age. The naval example serves especially to emphasize the adverse impact upon international stability of adding victory as a military goal. But whether the naval or land warfare example be used, with their somewhat different impact upon stability, the direct impact upon military planning is only quantitative. In the hypothetical situation the same kind of forces meet the goals either of deterrence, defense, or victory. This crucial simplification, having served its purpose, must now be removed.

III

The conflict among kinds of military preparations can be put at its starkest if we leap to a missile age. Suppose that Ruritania can buy thermonuclear-tipped ballistic missiles as well as army divisions, that the missiles can be guided fairly accurately to any point in her neighbor's territory, and that they are, by any previous standard, phenomenally cheap per unit of promised destruction, although very expensive per complete installation. If we further assume a Ruritanian monopoly on this option, we get a different kind of classic simplicity in military planning. A missile force by itself can fulfill all military requirements if Ruritania is willing to gamble in one respect; and it can fulfill most requirements even if Ruritania is not willing.

The gamble in question is whether to rely solely upon the influence of an awesome missile threat upon enemy intent. Ruritania can choose to rely completely on nuclear intimidation before and also during any war. To deter, she can threaten to destroy one or many enemy cities if she is attacked; to defend, she can threaten to destroy other cities in order to compel the enemy to withdraw or even disarm; to win, she can perhaps use similar threats even to compel surrender. Given such a policy, which would dispense with an army, the enemy retains a capability to invade. Therefore, Ruritania must not plan to spend all her missiles at one blow if she is to defend after war starts as well as deter. What she needs is some combination of residual striking power linked to valuable remaining enemy targets in their vital role as hostages. The policy, in short, is dependent upon intra-war as well as prewar threats, and amounts to pure nuclear intimidation.

Alternative policies would mix missile and army capabilities in various proportions. One possibility would be a defensive army shield much as before, but with a sizably diminished mobilization potential because missile strikes were counted upon to reduce enemy potential. This policy, with its virtually complete insurance against enemy capability, deserves special mention as a natural outgrowth of old plans and doctrine. Incidentally, it would also be consistent with an all-out, single-strike philosophy for missile employment, however imprudent though conveniently simple such a philosophy might be.

The nuclear monopoly case is nostalgically interesting, but too easy. The interactions among military goals become lively only when both sides have nuclear striking (missile) opportunities. To examine the implications, it is convenient to suppose that both sides have the same technological options, and these we restrict, unrealistically, to a very few in order to avoid complicated calculations. Suppose the missiles are to be based in clusters of, say, 10 missiles apiece, in order to share common facilities and so greatly reduce costs per missile. However, the missiles can be separated enough within a cluster so that, if placed in hardened shelters underground, each becomes a separate target. To complete the list of drastic simplifications, suppose that future progress in technology is expected to lead to superior hardening so in step with increases in missile performance (yield, accuracy, and reliability) that the vulnerability of a missile remains constant. Specifically, we assume that the single-shot kill probability of a missile is one-half against either a single hardened missile or an unhardened cluster of 10 missiles, and that in the latter case it applies to air-burst tactics.

Now we can generate simple arms races again, of which the most horrendous arises if both sides seek soft missiles systems — say, 10 clusters or 100 missiles apiece as a beginning. In this situation the balance of terror is obviously precarious. If there is a missile war, whoever strikes first is decisively ahead. If the attacker reserves 50 missiles for intra-war threats and fires 50 (five at each enemy cluster), the probability of any particular cluster surviving is reduced to 3 per cent. The probability that at least one cluster out of the 10 will survive is, of course, higher, but it is only about one chance in four. The attacker, moreover, can hedge against the unfavorable outcome that the one chance in four occurs by threats of city attacks that may induce the defender not to retaliate. The attacker has a much greater residual missile force than the defender but, especially given air-burst tactics which minimize fallout, still retains most of the defender's population and industry as hostages. In terms of hostages, the bargaining power of the two sides is virtually even; but in terms of remaining striking power, greatly and perhaps decisively uneven. Nothing can assure the attacker that he will get off scot-free and victorious, but his chances are very good.

Lack of certainty of a favorable outcome may be enough to deter an attack, but that it will be enough requires more stringent conditions than believers in near-automatic nuclear deterrence sometimes realize. Our model incorporates not merely meager retaliatory power, but the disruptive feature of "the reciprocal fear of surprise attack."[3] A high probability of peace requires more than that each side prefers peace even to victory, when victory implies the risk of one chance in four of small but appreciable retaliatory power that might be used. The choices open to each are only two — attack or do not attack; but the possible results are three — attack, peace, or be attacked. If the third occurs, it is much worse than the first. Yet this worst result can be eliminated only by attacking, which rules out also the second result.

So it is not enough that each side prefers peace to war. Each must so much prefer peace to war even on advantageous terms, and be somehow so sure that its opponent will continue to do likewise, that

[3] See T. C. Schelling, *The Strategy of Conflict*, Cambridge, Mass., 1960, esp. ch. 9.

it is willing to live with the risk of catastrophe.[4] To do so may be easy when international tensions are minor, but difficult otherwise. Mutual deterrence here does not rest upon a solid foundation in objective conditions that promise to make victorious war nearly as disastrous to the attacker as losing war. It rests mainly instead upon subjective confidence in mutual benign intent, which international conflicts serve precisely to undermine. Wherever such conflicts generate a brinkman's cycle of bluff and counterbluff, originating perhaps in very minor and implicit threats but spiraling to an uncertain outcome, the incentive is strong to forestall the worst outcome by attacking. Each side is so driven, not least becauses it realizes that its enemy is equally tempted by fear of pre-emptive attack. This interacting sequence of reciprocating fears breeds war. Mutual deterrence that rests upon this shaky base can easily be converted to mutual incitement of the very event that one hopes to avoid.

Nobody finds such a situation tolerable, and hence the quest for stable deterrence firmly rooted in greatly reduced vulnerability of retaliatory power. A much more stable situation results if Ruritania and its neighbor harden their missiles. Then if one side fires 50 missiles at the other's, it can expect, given our assumptions, to kill only 25 of them. In purely military terms, the attacker loses in the ex-

---

[4] To illustrate the principle, once again we can calculate oversimply and precisely where policy-makers never can calculate precisely, even when they can face the calculation psychologically. Suppose a country estimates that its feared enemy is unlikely to attack, but may, with the probability in any single year only one in twenty. If it expects this probability to remain the same per year, and decides that it will never attack, the cumulative probability of peace over a decade is, barring accidents, about three chances in five. Assuming arbitrary value weights, we can get this situation:

State	Probability of occurrence	Utility score if it occurs	Expected value
Attack	0	5	0
Peace	.6	6	3.6
Defend	.4	1	0.4
Total			4.0

Here our country prefers peace to overwhelmingly victorious war 6 to 5, but victorious war over disastrous war 5 to 1, so that it can improve its expected "score" from 4 to 5 by rejecting deterrence in favor of "preventive" war.

Yet this illustration merely sets the stage for a compounding of reciprocal fears of attack. If the enemy estimates that you will estimate as above, clearly his incentive to pre-empt soars. This means that your original estimate of the probability of his attack was wildly optimistic, as his must have been of your intent, and so on in an explosively interacting sequence.

change. He is here trading missiles at the adverse rate of two for one, in contrast to the "soft" basing situation in which he could exchange missiles at rates up to nearly five to one in his favor. Such a trade is catastrophically foolish for the attacker unless he enjoys such overwhelming initial superiority that he can override an adverse rate of exchange by brute force of numbers. Such a superiority can be prevented by an opponent who stays in the arms race, but at less cost than matching missile for missile. A defender who buys one additional protected missile for every two bought by the enemy will not fall behind in terms of absolute retaliatory power, but will gain as the race proceeds.[5] Our new hypothetical arms race thus permits a damped competition like the army case discussed earlier, not the unstable naval case. Those who seek stable mutual nuclear deterrence find the key in retaliatory forces so well protected that they impose insufficiently rewarding or even adverse exchange rates upon any attacker.

Our example can also illustrate other aspects of comparative stability as a function of kind as well as amount of protection. Suppose the same degree of protection against unambiguous all-out attack could have been provided by warning measures rather than hardening. This alternative would not have implied the same security. Reliance upon warning for protection of soft missiles sites requires speedy launch, and the resultant trigger-happy system becomes more accident prone. It is also an all-or-nothing system in operation. Any missile war becomes total war because missiles cannot be withheld to back intra-war threats or, more generally, to permit a chaotic situation to be clarified, without inordinate risk that they will be destroyed on the ground. In contrast, missiles so hardened or otherwise protected that they can ride out attacks permit these options. They not only protect against surprise attack, but survive it, and are therefore consistent with wartime policies either of massive or limited strategic retaliation.

Given a securely hardened missile force equal to her enemy, need Ruritania add other arms? Should it instead try to deter the enemy from invasion as well as missile attack by threats of missile retaliation, forgoing defense in favor of pure deterrence? To do so involves no direct defense against enemy armies, but an indirect defense that, far from making punishment of the enemy in war

---

[5] The same percentage survival rate applied to a larger force will yield a greater absolute survival. In addition, as the attacker moves from initial parity to pre-attack superiority, he may go beyond the tactic of only one missile aimed at one missile, with resultant lower kills per missile. Higher absolute-force levels, moreover, will make defensive calculations less sensitive to errors in intelligence about enemy capabilities.

synonymous with protection of the homeland, implies the worst sort of reciprocal damage. The worst for him does not equal the best for you, but the worst.

Pure nuclear deterrence will accordingly be sharply questioned, but may nonetheless be sensible. In its favor will be powerful budgetary considerations, plus the paradox that has been elevated into a prime principle of deterrent strategy — "the rationality of irrationality." Viewed in isolation from other events, missile exchanges against an enemy whose retaliatory power is secure are "irrational." Shooting at enemy missiles, given our assumptions, costs you more than the enemy, and is militarily self-defeating. The alternative tactic is to attack civil rather than military targets. Yet, in trading cities with the enemy, surely the loss of one's own far outweighs any gain from enemy losses of comparable size. So it, too, is "irrational." Yet a policy of which city-trading is but one late element in a related sequence may nonetheless make sense, for commitment to the sequence as a whole may be the best means of reducing the probability of the "irrational" act to very low, and hopefully near-zero, proportions. Or, to put this central point the other way around, failure to commit yourself to the entire sequence may increase the probability of the feared act or other disastrous consequences. An alternative policy which leads to different sequential decisions, each of which is rational when judged separately, may generate a probability distribution of sequences that is worse.

The obvious case is massive retaliation in kind for attacks upon one's self. To retaliate after being hit may, in a cold-blooded calculation, be worse than to seek to minimize further damage by bargaining from residual strength that is not dissipated in retaliation. To announce beforehand, however, that one will assuredly not retaliate is madness, for it invites attack. The middle course of assuring the enemy that one will retaliate massively whatever the cost, while reserving with all possible secrecy the likely option of non-retaliation, is tempting but is feasible to only a limited extent. Any such policy invites corrosion of the morale as well as the capability of retaliatory forces, and yet evidence of the corrosion must not become apparent. Consequently, the generals emphasize advance commitment to retaliate, with resolve and fortitude as necessary to deterrence as appropriate weapons. They are right, although their good points can be driven too far. When the means to deter differ sharply from the means to mitigate damage if deterrence fails, difficult choices between them cannot validly be avoided simply by neglecting one goal in favor of the other. If a change in military preparations detracts only slightly from deterrence but promises to alleviate damage greatly in war, surely it should be made. The evident sense of such a change illustrates that a nation rarely, if ever, seeks singlemindedly to maximize deterrence, but seeks rather to maximize some complicated goal that, as a minimum, combines deterrence and defense.

But how are deterrence and defense to be weighted in this combination? We can rephrase the now-relevant question posed by military planners to political leaders: "How should we value increments to deterrence relative to increments to defense?" Answers now become unnecessary only if military resources are made so plentiful that competing claimants for different kinds of preparations are all satisfied, e.g., Ruritania gets all the hardened missiles and divisions she could want, which is hardly a realistic or interesting case. Suppose instead, to look at hard and therefore interesting choices, that Ruritania imposes budget constraints that permit only these alternatives: (1) hardened missiles cut from 100 to 25, plus army divisions cut from two-thirds of enemy divisions to one-half; (2) no army but the full force of 100 missiles. Now controversy will be rife, not least because intra-service lines will be sharply drawn.

Suppose the first, mixed-force alternative be adopted, in part because policy-makers find persuasive the argument that only 20 missiles delivered on city targets would be "adequate" and that 25 protected ones should therefore be more than enough. Critics of the policy will counter with at least two arguments. First, even granting that 20 delivered missiles would be enough, a pre-attack force of but 25 gives very little likelihood that enough could survive to meet this test of adequacy. Given the assumptions of our model, an enemy with 100 missiles could reserve 25, fire three at each one of Ruritania's, and reduce expected force survival to only three missiles. The numbers, of course, are arbitrary, but our model is realistic in speaking of degrees of vulnerability rather than of approachable but unattainable invulnerability, and so it serves to warn against the excesses of naive proponents of "minimum" deterrence. Second, would not the missile deterrent to invasion be so weakened as to offset the deterrent value of armies? Would not the very fact of providing an army as an alternative diminish the credibility in enemy eyes of missile response? Would not the credibility be further degraded by superior enemy missile bargaining-power, either pre-attack (100:25) or post-attack (25:3)? In short, with missiles so few, would not too great a load have been placed upon resolve to substitute for, rather than necessarily complement, inadequate strategic forces?

Answers are by no means self-evident. But these are proper questions, as are those that will be asked in return. Even if an army as an alternative diminishes the credibility of missile retaliation and diverts resources from retaliatory power, does it not compensate by providing local deterrents to invasion? As for reinforcing the credibility of missile retaliation, is not city-trading an inherently incredible response even to enemy occupation? In the final analysis, arms policies have always rested upon the willingness of some fighting men to put honor and the integrity of their country above considerations of personal safety. Now the issue is cruelly changed, for massive strategic retaliation may imply sacrificing one's country. We seek here to explain arms dilemmas, not solve them, and the most personal dilemma is surely that the path of military duty and honor is no longer clear.

IV

Having manipulated models to illustrate some arms fundamentals, we must ask what they have to do with the real world. Far-reaching simplifications have been made. Neglected, for example, are missile impacts upon tactical (army) operations via industrial and other damage in the classic view of the land battle as the pay-off. Yet to trace these impacts would be misleading, as well as tedious. Massive thermonuclear exchanges, if backed by implementable threats of more, will almost certainly dominate and shortly terminate any war in which they occur. Therefore we should emphasize nuclear intimidation during as well as before war, and can neglect "broken-back" tactical war. Any current fixation upon one great thermonuclear strike can only be deplored. This holds true whether it be derived as an outmoded legacy from "smash war-industry" philosophies, or from wishful thinking that all enemy capabilities would be completely crushed at a blow.

Other simplifications in the models may mislead. The retaliatory systems as a whole were either soft or hard, whereas in the real world they will always be a mixture. The system with no vulnerable places anywhere in the entire complex of retaliation, with respect to all its components, is but an ideal. Some less hard places will always be present, and there may even be an Achilles' heel in the system. Accordingly, there will always be some scope for militarily rewarding counterforce as well as countercity operations. How much scope cannot be answered without looking at particular situations, but that there will be some is itself a useful reminder to those who unrealistically view counterforce strategies as a flat go, no-go proposition (total disarming of the enemy at a blow, or not) and so convert a question of degree into one of kind. We have emphasized threat power during as well as before war, and that power, crudely put, is measured by destroyed enemy weapons as well as by preserved enemy hostages and unspent weapons of our own. Counterforce strategies must continually be reappraised, but they are certainly not outmoded.

Perhaps the most serious shortcoming of our model is its restriction to but two possible enemy provocations, with each of them necessarily a clear and massive challenge to an interest traditionally accepted as vital. We have considered only invasion of, or missile attack against, one's own country. Accordingly, we have stacked the cards in favor of those who stress massive retaliation, and have ruled out most limited-war questions by assumption. To consider the case for limited-war preparations fairly, one has to go into far murkier and subtler political issues, precisely those that our model neglects. Central issues there turn upon challenges to allies or neutrals where the nature of our interest — let alone how vital it is — is sometimes unclear; where much besides boundary disputes may be an open issue, with who provoked whom a pertinent question; and where challenges need not begin at all in overt or massive form. Accordingly, the appropriate role of force is very different.

How biased our models are against any advocacy of limited war preparations can be shown more concretely by concentrating upon one possible road to general war. Will control of the limits in any local war be maintained? The probability of general war by loss of such control is a product of two linked probabilities, that of getting into the limited war in the first place, and of escalation all the way upward in the second. Would-be massive retaliators stress reducing the first probability by awesome threats which, however, increase the second. Would-be limited warriors stress reducing the second probability by observing whatever limits may be mutually apparent and beneficial, the notable example being non-use of nuclear weapons. But they run the risk of emboldening local aggressors and so increasing the first probability. What compounded probabilities of general war will then arise from the alternative policies? No general answer is possible, but our restricted hypothetical situation suggests that a near-zero probability might be reached by Ruritanian concentration upon massive retaliation, i.e., upon reduction of the first of the linked probabilities. But other combinations of circumstances might suggest the opposite, although even in our models the merit of exclusive concentration upon missiles is not evident.

Rigged though it is to favor a policy of pure deterrence, the model nonetheless illustrates that there are conflicting choices between deterrence and defense. The first requisite for realism in military discussion is to perceive these conflicts; the second, to recognize that they cannot in practice be resolved by budgets so high that both of these military goals are met in full. Neither 100 per cent deterrence nor 100 per cent protection against the contingency when deterrence fails is now procurable, if they ever were. And even if they could be achieved, for that matter, conflict between them would be sharpened. For who would pay expensive insurance premiums to cover a contingency that could not happen? Or, if 100 per cent defense were the goal instead, who would pay to lessen the likelihood of events against which he was fully protected?

The military professional yearns for a position comparable to that of a physician, whose prescriptions supposedly are governed by considerations of health rather than the patient's income, and he frequently employs the analogy. But the doctor is constrained by knowledge that good medicine and nutrients must not be taken in excess, and is comforted because nature will not react malevolently against him in ways that exacerbate the original complaint. Typically, moreover, his prescriptions cost the patient only small parts of his income. When they do not, budgetary constraints may be nonetheless pervasive for being tacitly rather than openly taken into account. Not all of us who could profit from a three months' cruise find one prescribed. And, for that matter, the nation's deplorable lack of good $5 per hour psychoanalysts is reflected in tight rationing of existing services by the purse. The soldier's desire to rise above sordid politics and economics finds little support in the favorite medical analogy or in any other.

We harp on the point for an old but vital reason: Realistic expectations of budget constraints and choices among imperfect military alternatives should influence what one tries to buy, not merely how much. Starting out for "full requirements" in one military area and then cutting back under budgetary pressure may leave us not with one-half of the right sort of capability but with one-half of the wrong. We can illustrate such a development by another modification of our model.

Suppose Ruritania and her enemy can buy anti-missile missiles to defend their cities, but that the unit cost of these missiles matches that of an offensive hardened missile. Then substituting a defensive for an offensive missile changes, among other things, the type of defense. Direct defense replaces indirect, for a protected offensive weapon defends cities indirectly in two ways: it reduces the likelihood of enemy attack, and it draws enemy fire to itself and away from other targets if there is an attack. This second indirect defense may itself dominate the argument if we assume (1) that anti-missile defenses fall considerably short of the ideal of a kill probability of unity against an incoming missile — say, to a kill probability of 0.3; and (2) that Ruritania is seriously threatened by an enemy who has outpaced her quantitatively in missiles either through higher total budgets or greater concentration of military resources.

Suppose, specifically, that the enemy can fire two missiles at each of Ruritania's, can still withhold one missile as a threat against each Ruritanian city, and can expect an .8 kill probability against an undefended city. Then if Ruritania replaces one of its protected offensive missiles with an anti-missile defense of one city, its loss in indirect defense is measured by the two enemy missiles that are freed for city threats. This loss overwhelms the gain in direct defense, for two extra missiles reduce the survival probability of a city more than the anti-missile defense increases it.[6] Such a shift of Ruritanian defense from indirect to direct would therefore be a mistake from all points of view, for it would lessen defense as well as deterrence measured by survivable retaliatory power. Protected offensive missiles, on the other hand, would not so dominate over defensive missiles if Ruritanian total military resources rose markedly, relative to those of her enemy. Then the enemy would not have two missiles to be freed by every removal of a counterforce target, and anti-missile defenses would not confront so dismaying a prospect. The issue of anti-missile defenses would then be open. But an ambitious anti-missile or other program that is based on the premise that tolerable balance in other arms would be maintained as a prerequisite can be a disaster if that premise is falsified. To repeat, what one sensibly buys, as well as how much, depends upon the total resources to be made available relative to the enemy.[7]

V

The extreme case of no direct defense, which outrages military doctrine of happier days when defense conflicted much less with deterrence, is the most provocative aspect of a general military pol-

[6] With the kill probability of defense set at .3, 70 per cent of arriving missiles should survive. The kill probability of an undefended city was set at .8 to allow for unreliability and inaccuracy. Against a defended city only 70 per cent survival of the 80 per cent that arrive would be expected, yielding a .56 single-shot kill probability. The city survival probability would then be $1 - .56$, or .44, but if two extra missiles were shot at it, this probability would be cubed, falling to .085, or appreciably less than the assumed .20 single-shot survival probability of an undefended city.

In the interests of simplicity, we here and elsewhere overlook all sophisticated consideration of the added elements of uncertainty in Ruritanian and enemy calculations that would be induced. Our use of expected values makes discussion too simple, but introduces no significant errors for our restricted purposes.

[7] The military reader will recognize the old sound point that some guide to priorities is better than no guide to allocations at all. I have elsewhere tried to move in turn beyond the inadequacies of blunt military priorities to what, in economists' jargon, are income elasticities. See "Some Complexities in Military Planning," World Politics, XI, No. 4 (July 1959), pp. 553–77.

icy to which most of our remarks especially apply. That policy, sometimes labeled "finite" or "passive deterrence," is directed, above all, toward stable deterrence of thermonuclear war. It seeks stability, first, in terms of the balance of opposed forces at any moment of time, and, second, by tempering and damping the thermonuclear arms race over time. Hence it implies a kind of arms control policy. It tries, in essence, to institutionalize a less precarious balance of terror rather than to supplant it. The goal is stable mutual deterrence, which in practice amounts to playing for a stalemate rather than a win in the grimmest of games should deterrence fail, and so affronts an even deeper military preconception about proper objectives.

The radical version of this policy would be implemented and announced to our enemy something like this:

"We shall maintain a retaliatory capability so big, mixed in composition, and securely protected in all ways that we are confident that we could, at the least, smash most of the cities of any nation or coalition of nations that tried to cripple our retaliatory power by any conceivable attack. We expect, in short, to hold most of your industry and people in perpetual hostage, and to this end shall effectively counter by increased offensive power your defensive measures to remove our hostages. We expect that you will do the same. As a joint result, any rational grounds for surprise or pre-emptive mass thermonuclear strikes by either of us should disappear.

"The open question is the strategic budgetary scale, and consequent public image of arms intensity and political tension, on which we shall attain this condition. We propose that it be low in our mutual interest. Confident of our ability to protect our retaliatory power against even superior numbers and surprise, we are willing to tolerate rough parity in offensive power; pessimistic about the cost of further reductions in civilian vulnerability (after some first-order measures, perhaps rudimentary fall-out shelters)[8] relative to the costs of offensive improvements that negate them, we are prepared, if you are, to settle for cities whose direct defenses are inadequate. If you agree, we must both, of course, be assured that the implied measures of disarmament are taken reciprocally. If they are, we shall by joint action have pledged the safety of our

[8] The first-order civil defense measures cannot be detailed here. They might be constrained, however, by these criteria: (1) favorable exchange rates against enemy offensive counters; (2) catching up with, rather than outpacing, enemy civil defenses; (3) consistency with strike-second protection of people when the enemy tries to preserve them as hostages, e.g., shelters in cities that protect against the fall-out from an enemy first-strike against military targets. Each of these constraints limits our program markedly, and surely no resultant civil defenses could be provocative in any major sense.

obviously vulnerable peoples to the elimination of general thermonuclear war."

A stable deterrent policy like this is seductive in its very simplicity, not least because it is consistent with past sins of omission.
Its advocacy comforts those critics whose analyses have unpardon-
ably overlooked the vulnerability of delivery forces and the consequent genuine grounds for concern about reciprocal fears of
surprise attack, and who therefore, at best prematurely, have presumed a stability in the balance of terror that is far from automatic. Such a policy also rationalizes past neglect in preparations,
notably in paltry appropriations for civil defense that were so much
at variance with a declaratory policy of massive retaliation against
threats to our overseas interests. But these are suspect, if politically potent, reasons for adoption of any such policy. They should
not obscure the real promise of reduced probabilities of surprise attack and a visible slowing down in the arms race that so rightly
concerns an anxious world.

Any road to effective arms control looks long and uncertain to
all but the soft in heart and head. Yet some roads are surely far
less dismaying in prospect than others. While we may have little
choice about being in an arms race, we may and do exercise great
influence over the kind of race it will be. A policy aimed at stable
mutual deterrence, for example, can focus initially upon inspection
where it is easiest rather than hardest. Rigorous control of nuclear
weapons is probably impossible because they are so easily hidden,
and control of delivery vehicles is not much more promising when
any nominally civilian means of delivery (civilian airliners) may
do. But anti-missile defenses of cities should be highly specialized, prominent, and necessarily located near much-traveled places.
So they are much easier to detect. Elaborate civil defenses, e.g.,
shelters in cities designed to protect against high blast overpres-
sures, should be still more observable. Protecting 50 or 100 million
people can hardly be as discreet an activity as hiding a few hundred weapons. Satisfactory inspection of hostages, in short, can be
an easy if incomplete substitute for inspection of arms.

Another inducement for taking this road to arms control is that
the fundamental agreements can be tacit. One implements the policy by doing and proclaiming rather than by agreeing explicitly,
and therefore very slowly and cautiously, to terms that will be binding. What one does unilaterally is clear: First, remove or greatly
reduce vulnerabilities in the system of thermonuclear retaliation so
that the system can not only survive the worst of enemy attacks,
but will impose adverse rather than rewarding military rates of
exchange upon the enemy in his attack. Convert any extensive en-

emy counterforce operations, in short, from a winning to a losing game. Second, be prepared to resume, if necessary, the dangerous arms race that seeks to remove one's people but not the enemy's from hostage status. Because nobody can be sure that the enemy will reciprocate in control, such preparedness is a hedge. It is also a means of bargaining pressure to induce reciprocity, which raises the old dilemma that arms measures may either coerce desired arms control or explode into the race one seeks to avoid. Should one "arm to parley," or the reverse? Some compromise answers may hedge this question acceptably. For example, thorough research and development programs for anti-missile and civil defenses — programs that are required in order to reduce lead-times later if the worst arms race is forced upon us — need not provoke this race unless they move into production and implementation phases. So the dilemma may be resolved.

Appealing as such a policy is, it must face several searching questions, of which perhaps the greatest arises when we move from overly simple two-power to many-power considerations. What happens to deterrence of provocations in third areas if the residual fear of general war — otherwise so powerful a control upon whether local aggressions occur and what limits are observed — is deliberately reduced by a policy of stable mutual deterrence? One popular answer is that third-area deterrence will be bolstered by improved limited-war capabilities. This answer is good and very important as far as it goes, but no tactical limited-war capabilities, in themselves, answer threatened or actual nuclear attacks upon an ally's cities, to take the extreme case. Something more is required. It may be the deliberate proliferation of strategic deterrent forces in third areas, as many advocates of "finite deterrence" have suggested, but such a course hardly serves the global cause of arms control.[9]

A third possibility is a policy of limited strategic retaliation — the destruction of a city in the main enemy's homeland as a strategic reprisal for extreme provocations that cannot be met by limited war capabilities.[10] Such a policy suffers from the political defect, but analytic virtue, of explicit bizarreness. Unless one is

[9] An alliance-wide collective retaliatory force, notably for NATO, may be a good compromise, depending upon its design and control.

[10] The first systematic account of this policy, to my knowledge, was that of Morton A. Kaplan, *The Strategy of Limited Retaliation,* Policy Memorandum No. 19, Center of International Studies, Princeton University, 1959. See . . . Leo Szilard, "How to Live with the Bomb and Survive," *Bulletin of the Atomic Scientists,* xvi, No. 2 (February 1960), pp. 59–73.

confident that the prerequisites have been met for stable mutual deterrence, a strike limited to one city is madness. If the prerequisite of secure forces has not been met on the striking side, serious risk of national massive retaliation is incurred. If that prerequisite has not been met by the enemy, it is foolish to forgo the great military advantage of a sizable counterforce strike instead, for such a strike can also be made consistent with limited civilian damage if that be desired for bargaining purposes. If the prerequisites are met on both sides, however, a one-city strike, despite expectations of retaliation in kind, may be the best among the poor alternatives that range from appeasement to self-defeating massive retaliation. In any case, a situation of stable mutual deterrence does not rule out all strategic strikes, but only those so sweeping that they destroy the bargaining power of the striker by dissipation of relative military power or valuable hostages. Some residual strategic backing for limited-war capabilities in third areas is still possible.

If we move toward stable mutual deterrence, the choice will be open between controlled counterforce and limited city attacks as the last resort of international bargaining. The choice must be determined, of course, by empirical matters beyond the limited scope of our discussion. It is a merit of our primitive models that they show how relative numbers can still matter. But what the numbers are and will be are the decisive issues. How many and how soft, for example, will be the inevitable vulnerabilities in the opposing retaliatory systems? Other equally crucial issues will depend on more political considerations. If, say, a particular controlled counterforce operation promises to kill no more of the enemy than a one-city strike, but to improve the military balance significantly, although not decisively, will it strengthen the chances of a favorable outcome? Or will it weaken it because a mass strike runs much greater risk of triggering the kind of massive retaliation that is in nobody's interest, because it floods the alarmed enemy with confused intelligence in a fast-moving and catastrophic situation? Questions like these are pertinent, and their answers should determine the blend between controlled counterforce and limited city attacks.

Many will contend that we should not settle in any case for so modest a goal as mutual stability, or, more subtly, they fear that to try to do so will include lethargy that yields defeat rather than stalemate. They do not predict or espouse strategic symmetry, but project a favorable asymmetry if we are but resolute enough to exploit it, risks and all. Their classic aim, in contrast, is to win, or, its modern euphemism, to prevail. Again our hypothetical illustrations cannot resolve so fundamental a divergence; they can only illustrate aspects of it. Here we merely remind the reader that when our illustrations in Section II added victory as a third major goal to deterrence and defense, the impact was only quantitative. The prescription then became more of the same, with destabilizing repercussions or not upon the arms race dependent upon the type of arms in question. Those who now seek strategic dominance may argue that it will be destabilizing, and therefore risky but promising; or that it will not be destabilizing, and so not risky but militarily less rewarding. This issue will turn, once more, on the scale and rates of exchange that may be expected in strategic counterforce operations. Or they may argue for both reasonable stability and dominance, fundamentally because we outspend or outwit the enemy. Whichever variant is put forward, adding "to prevail" as an objective in thermonuclear war implies much more than quantitative changes. It implies adding different kinds of capabilities, more dramatically and obviously on the defensive side, that limit damage to us so appreciably that striking first and massively, under dire provocation, becomes a credible policy for us when no longer so for our enemy.[11]

The popular compromise between this ambitious goal and stable mutual deterrence is easy to define as an aspiration; namely, strategic capabilities that promise to lessen damage to us in general thermonuclear war, but not so much so that they need alarm the enemy about our willingness to strike and thus weaken deterrence. The compromisers want to insure against the catastrophe if it occurs, even though their main hopes are pinned upon its avoidance. And what could be more natural? Yet significant insurance can only be purchased at some cost in strengthening reciprocal fears of surprise attack, for it does make resort to thermonuclear war less costly and therefore less incredible. As always, an offsetting effect can be sought by budgetary increases rather than decreases — more protected striking power to strengthen deterrence, while the damage-alleviating measures weaken it. This expedient moves any possibly destabilizing impacts upon strategic equilibrium to the different plane of the arms race, and to a more complex assessment.

[11] I should not like the country to adopt as full-fledged and belligerent-appearing a central war preparedness as that advocated by Herman Kahn in *On Thermonuclear War* (Princeton, N.J., 1960), mainly because to go that far toward a "credible first strike" posture jeopardizes the longer-term prospects for arms control. My policy dissent, however, is coupled with great admiration for the book, which is enthusiastically recommended for, among other things, a much fuller treatment of many of the issues discussed in this article.

If the enemy matches us, mutual fears of pre-emptive attack may be calmed, but, with his greater striking power, what happens now to our prospects for alleviating damage? At what rate of exchange and to what extent has his increased power negated the increment to our protection?

We do well to leave these questions open, for again their answers require quantitative specification. To recognize that deterrence, defense, and victory as goals imply very different military prescriptions is not to supply them, although it is an indispensable first step toward good prescriptions. If we buy retaliatory power plus a wide range of capabilities that limit damage in thermonuclear war, the interactions among defense and deterrence will be many and important. Sensible policy will require that they be given fundamental and explicit consideration. On the other hand, if we opt for stable mutual deterrence, and explicitly rationalize the exchange of hostages as the main means of arms control, direct defense against thermonuclear war will be subordinated.

Having begun our discussion by reference to an old situation when the conflict between deterrence and defense did not matter, since achieving one automatically provided the other, we end by noting the possibility of a conflict among these objectives that matters so much that it must be radically settled. For general thermonuclear war, will deterrence definitely prevail over defense, with counterthreats posed to nullify enemy intent rather than capability, and victory forsworn? By turning classic military precepts upside down, do we come full circle to new simplicity, contrived rather than natural, in arms objectives? Finally, if we have not reached this radical situation yet, will we come to it later, more expensively?

VI*

Those who answer these questions with a ringing affirmative proclaim that there has been a revolution in strategy. Consistent with our earlier approach, this asserted revolution can best be illustrated in the extreme case. There its implications for politics are clearest. What national military capabilities would a radical "finite deterrer" aim for, and what would be the associated arms-control and foreign policies?

The quest for stability in the balance of opposed military forces is the key to the radical's prescription. To avoid disruptive and possibly explosive arms races, he would moderate national military objectives and give enhanced weight to some preparations at the

*This section was written a year after the preceding ones.

expense of others. For the contingency of nuclear war, he would give overwhelming weight to deterrence at the expense of direct defense and, still more, of victory. For the contingency of non-nuclear war, presumably at any one of several overseas locations, he would give priority to defense over victory. If these be the objectives, the main means to attain them in the two contingencies will be, respectively, extraordinarily well-protected retaliatory missiles and modern armies. In both cases the hope is that the technical characteristics of the means will combine with the modesty of chosen objectives to deter the enemy from not just one, but two vital things: (1) He will not attack; and (2) he will not try to offset our capabilities in the course of time by greater strength in kind, for he will perceive the folly of accelerating an arms race in which he must spend more than we without gaining a decisive advantage. The radical prescription, thus, is to cultivate those capabilities that promise to create the kind of objective relationship between future opposed forces that was illustrated by our hypothetical Ruritanian army example and to avoid that typified by the old navy example.

Such an approach relies heavily upon tacit mutual avoidance of grim competitions that promise mutual loss. This reliance is both its main political strength and weakness — strength because it translates shared interests among enemies, and deep but otherwise vague yearnings for a less threatening world, into a tangible prescription; weakness because it is dependent upon a degree of cooperation with a hostile enemy who may be fascinated with the temptations of brinkmanship. The weakness must not be overstated, for the approach is not dependent upon enemy benevolence. Deep-seated enmity need not rule out prudence. Still, what will make enemy acquiescence in this sweeping kind of tacit arms control sufficiently prudent for him?

Clearly the enemy must not be stupid, so that he fails to deduce simple implications; he must not be psychopathic, or so blinded by fanaticism that it comes to the same thing; and he must value human life and his civilian accomplishments highly, although not necessarily as highly as we. These are not stringent conditions, and yet . . . who is perfectly confident that they are and will continue to be met? And by how much would our confidence be further shaken if Red China had Russian military capabilities?

There remains, moreover, another requirement. Our enemies must not be too tempted to incur the risks of brinkmanship because, on our side, we fail to meet likewise indispensable conditions. First, of course, we must meet our modest military objectives with unremitting efforts of very high quality. Such efforts must pervade our military establishment, above all in Research and

Development and, disagreeable though it may sound, in Intelligence. Everyone's worst nightmare is the magical new weapon that is possessed by the enemy in sufficient quantity before we can counter it, whether it be a near perfect defense instrument that negates the ability of our retaliatory missiles to reach their targets, or some offensive device that destroys our missiles and planes before launch. We must take adequate safeguards against the possibility that this nightmare arises; the moral for our efforts should be obvious.

Second, and no less obvious: Resolve must continue to complement our capabilities. It is not enough that the enemy sees that we are capable of the promised response to a provocation, and that such a response promises an adverse outcome for him. He must also calculate that such a response is not too improbable, despite its cost to us. To the extent that the enemy has reason to expect that we will recoil before the brink much more readily than he, the temptation for him to initiate risky provocations is increased. The main penalty attached to a radical tacit arms-control policy arises here. This policy places, of necessity, a great reliance upon what was earlier called "the rationality of irrationality." Alternative policies, although they seek much less bleak consequences if deterrence fails, may nonetheless involve costs that greatly outweigh immediate gains in war. But the vital political difference may be that they do so far less explicitly. If a democracy adopts a radical tacit arms-control policy, the debate about it, especially about the last-resort threat of Limited Strategic Retaliation, will sharpen public awareness of the "irrational" component in the rational sequence of strategy. And if the public is made more aware, it may become more apprehensive. Can a democracy, still more a coalition composed mainly of democracies, nonetheless be so evidently ready to stand up to a test of nerves that enemies will desist from putting us to repeated tests?

One can pile gloom upon gloom by forecasting that the enemy will perceive such temptingly shaky nerves in the West that he will, riskily, make them shakier. His strategic prescription, in the worst case for us, would be compounded as follows: (1) continue the Pavlovian tactics that alternate local scares with soothing reassurances; (2) assert that the underlying strategic equilibrium, far from being stable, is and is becoming more asymmetrically unbalanced in his favor; and (3) act so that his assertions about nuclear war advantages are not palpably absurd. For example, he could intensify secrecy while undertaking vast programs to install anti-ICBM missile defenses and extend civil defenses in and around his cities. So he would hope to sow doubt in the West that his population remained hostage to us. His moves would demand appropriate counters in the West (in, hopefully, whatever offense/defense blend seemed most efficient), and so the arms race would take another spiral upward. Where arresting the race now looks more promising, because inspection of hostages seems so much easier than of weapons, it could be made unpromising. And, perhaps the most fearful prospect of all, these terror tactics could be amplified by a forthright Soviet supply of advanced offensive missiles and warheads to belligerent satellites.

If all these things were done, cruel pressure would be put upon the West, especially upon the allies of the United States. Certainly we would have to reassure them that our countering military moves were adequate, puncture exaggerated Soviet claims about Soviet capabilities, and continue to demonstrate a responsible but determined commitment to the defense of allies. But would these necessary reassurances be enough? Would incentives of allies to possess nuclear retaliatory capabilities not be strengthened?

We cannot cover the "Nth Country" problem here, but one aspect must be mentioned. The very moves by the enemy that might maximize incentives on the part of our allies to acquire independent deterrents are the moves that would maximize the technical difficulties in satisfying them. In a world where Russia and America settled for stable mutual deterrence at low strategic-budget levels and near-naked cities, a small power might be able to achieve, at moderate cost, a sizable retaliatory capability even against one of the giants. A force of small and unsophisticated missiles, if well protected and controlled, might promise to do the job. But against a future super-power armed with elaborate and ever-changing anti-missile defenses, plus big civil defense, how could a small power guarantee sufficient retaliation? Then we should be back to technical demands for retaliatory capabilities that promise to counter tough defenses with some intricate mixture of varied threats, brute force of numbers, big warheads that can accommodate super-bombs or shielding, etc. The cruel dilemma for our friends is clear. Only in a world where the arms race looked least threatening, and independent retaliatory capabilities accordingly least needed by them, do such capabilities look reasonably cheap and, therefore, feasible.

What, then, are they to do, and what are we to do? Surely the most general and satisfying answer is that we must cultivate ever-greater solidarity. To move increasingly from the gnawing doubt, "Will they stand up for us under pressure?" to the still agonizing but lesser imperative, "Will we stand up for us," is to attack the problem at its source. To meet a common threat, we must become increasingly united. Such a course alone meets our deepest shared values, and it coincides with military expediency. Neither a splintering of alliances in an effort to get independent capabilities, despite the noble slogan of "nuclear sharing," nor an attempt to make "tactical" nuclear war attractive to the countries where it might be fought, looks promising.[12]

For policy, we have now sketched the optimist's hopes for a damped nuclear-arms race and contrasted it with the worst possibilities for enemy non-cooperation. If forced to predict, most of us would share an intermediate outlook. In speculations about stabilizing the arms race, we must emphasize that it is not stabilized yet. Still, most of the current rearming is consistent with such a goal. In particular, the main aims of the American rearmament program have been to decrease the vulnerability of our retaliatory system, to control it still better and so reduce any chance of accidental war, and to increase our conventional capabilities so that the "threshold" would be raised beyond which we are driven to use nuclear weapons. Programs to achieve these ends not only enhance our security in virtually all respects, but also lower world risks. Even the decision to initiate significant civil-defense programs, which might appear inconsistent with the goal of stabilized mutual deterrence, will not actually be so unless pushed much farther than has thus far been indicated. In civil defense there are a lot of first-order things to do that should be possible at costs that compare favorably with enemy military counters and that merely try to catch up with the Soviets rather than precipitate an arms race by getting far ahead. We can defer worries about de-stabilizing repercussions for the contingency of much bigger and different second-order programs. Above all, our current rearmament program has not initiated programs to put nuclear warheads and modern delivery systems under the unilateral control of other nations. For those who hope for stable mutual deterrence, in short, we can say that we may have made the right signals to the enemy. Whether he reads them correctly and finds the prospects for tacit reciprocity rewarding enough, we shall see in terms of his militancy, programs, and secrecy.

[12] For argument, see my "What Interdependence for NATO?" *World Politics*, Vol. 12 (April 1960), pp. 369–90. For an incisive analysis of independent nuclear prospects, see Albert Wohlstetter, "Nuclear Sharing: NATO and the N + 1 Country," *Foreign Affairs* (April 1961), pp. 355–87.

**PART V
Successes
and Failures
in the Control
of Force**

The selections in Part IV set forth the general principles of arms races and the general problems of arms control. The selections in Part V are more concrete. Warner R. Schilling examines the reasons why the Americans failed to establish a "no merchant ships" doctrine at the Paris Peace Conference in 1919. The other selections focus on the two major bilateral arms races of the twentieth century. Kenneth L. Moll discusses why the British were seized by fears of a "dreadnought gap" in 1909. The authors whose selections are gathered under "The ABM and MIRV Deployments" analyze American-Russian interactions in the most recent round of the nuclear arms race.

Politics, Power, and Panic:
Britain's 1909 Dreadnought "Gap"

KENNETH L. MOLL

"You English are mad, mad, mad as March hares," blustered the Kaiser in a 1908 London *Daily Telegraph* interview. The statement was unprecedented even for the diplomatically illiterate Wilhelm II, yet it contained more than a grain of truth and sprang from a certain justifiable provocation. For the British were madly building dreadnoughts and battle cruisers while accusing Germany of starting a naval race.

For two centuries Britain had maintained almost undisputed control of the seas. In the latter nineteenth century the British public was so sure of its navy that "splendid isolation" became a way of life. Around the turn of the century, though, the British government and (to a degree) the public began to worry about the growing American and German industrial strength and Britain's own economic difficulties. They even began to worry about their Navy. The books of America's A. T. Mahan as well as several scares had aroused public interest in the navy after a century of negligible naval competition.

Yet by 1902 the Royal Navy still lingered lethargically in what Admiral Fisher called "the bow-and-arrow epoch."[1] There was concern about Britain's capability versus the growing naval power of Germany, France, and Russia. "It is a great comedown to have to confess that we have lost our superiority and are distinctly dropping to the rear," concluded Brassey's 1902 Naval Annual.[2]

Though the 1903 French Entente and the 1905 Russian defeat by the Japanese removed two bogeys from under Britain's bed, the German menace was looming larger. "If we possessed a navy," Wil-

From *Military Affairs*, Fall 1965, pp. 133–144. Reprinted by permission of the American Military Institute and the author. Some footnotes have been omitted.

[1] Arthur J. Marder, *From the Dreadnought to Scapa Flow, The Royal Navy in the Fisher Era, 1904–19*, Vol. I, *The Road to War, 1904–14* (London: Oxford Univ. Press, 1961), 8.

[2] John R. Spears, "A Transition in Naval Efficiency," *World's Work*, V (November, 1902), 2772.

helm II had grumbled to Count von Bülow at the turn of the century, "Chamberlain would never have dared to act in this way [in South Africa]."[3] The Kaiser was determined to make Germany a great power on the seas as well as on the land. So in 1898 Germany passed a Navy Law calling for a build-up to a nineteen-battleship fleet, and this goal was doubled by the 1900 Navy Law.[4]

Thus Germany started to build, and England watched. What should be done? There was talk by the Conservatives of the need for a bigger navy and complaints by the Liberals of Britain's already "bloated armaments" — the Navy's cost had tripled between 1889 and 1904. Two circumstances influenced the decision. The first, on Trafalgar Day 1904, was the appointment of Admiral Sir John Fisher as First Sea Lord, and the second was the momentous Conservative defeat by the Liberals in December, 1905.

Pugnacious as a Pekingese and bearing a slight resemblance, Fisher was one of the most courageous, magnetic, exuberant and controversial personalities to rise to eminence in the twentieth century. Though fifty at the time, he had retained a youthful enthusiasm and a questioning mind throughout a thirty-five year naval career in what has since been called "a drowsy, inefficient, moth-eaten organization."[5] Prior to his appointment Fisher had demonstrated his creative mind and administrative ability as Third and Second Sea Lord, and had impressed leaders in both parties as well as the King himself. His real appeal to politicians was that he was never blinded by naval loyalties. Fisher was uneasy about the growth in armament costs. "He put country first and looked on the Navy as a servant of the nation," Admiral Bacon remarked. "Like Napoleon, he was that very rare bird, a fighting man who considers the taxpayer," says Arthur J. Marder, the definitive authority on Fisher and his era.[6]

Fisher had already started applying his reform ideas under the Conservatives, bragging in a letter.

> The country will acclaim it [the Reform scheme]! the income-tax payer will worship it! the Navy will growl at first (they always do growl at first!) BUT WE SHALL BE THIRTY PERCENT MORE FIT TO FIGHT AND WE SHALL BE READY FOR INSTANT WAR![7]

[3] Elie Halévy, *Imperialism and the Rise of Labor (1895–1905)*, trans. E. I. Watkin (New York: Barnes and Noble Inc., 1961), pp. 112, 405.

[4] E. L. Woodward, *Great Britain and the German Navy* (Oxford: The Clarendon Press, 1935), pp. 25–29.

[5] Marder, *From the Dreadnought* . . ., I, 6.

[6] *Ibid.*, I, 12, 18.

[7] Arthur J. Marder, *The Anatomy of British Sea Power* (New York: Alfred A. Knopf, 1940), p. 487.

This policy aroused no argument from the Liberals who had come to office in 1906. They were committed to social benefits and reduced armament costs. Their "little navy" Radical wing was delighted to give "Jacky" Fisher a free hand in his attempt to obtain naval efficiency and economy, especially economy. Strange bedfellows indeed, yet Radical and Fisher interests were to run parallel for almost three years until Fisher was forced to fight for his belief that "economy must never be allowed to clash with fighting efficiency."[8]

Fisher is remembered for five major reforms, all initiated between 1902 and 1906. The first, a new education plan for student officers, was adopted in 1902 when he was Second Sea Lord and it was already a complete success by 1906. The next three "efficiency" reforms were the ones which were responsible for his great economies. The nucleus-crew system, scrapping of obsolete warships, and redistribution of the fleets formed a complex but unified policy. These three reforms were consciously but quietly aimed at one goal: a capability for rapid concentration against the German fleet. By the scrapping of 154 obsolete ships ("Napoleonic in its audacity and Cromwellian in its thoroughness," Fisher modestly claimed),[9] enough crews were obtained to man the modern reserve vessels with a three-fifths nucleus crew. This allowed for rapid mobilization and an effective reserve fleet in being. Redistribution of the fleet in Home waters allowed England to match Germany's North Sea strength at any time.

The Conservative press cries of anguish at these reforms were heartrending. Fisher had "betrayed the nation" to save a penny, and the Government was "sacrificing the security of the Empire to the exigencies of party politics." Fisher's old friend, Lord Knollys, the King's Secretary, was provoked to protest, "He is clever as a monkey and has persuaded the King that his nucleus fleet will be as efficient in every way as if it were afloat!"[10]

Yet this opposition was puny compared to the reception of Fisher's fifth reform, *H.M.S. Dreadnought*. Only an innovator of Fisher's daring and imagination could have launched it in 1906, as he did with the help of King Edward who contributed a champagne bottle and a strong right arm.

In some respects the *Dreadnought* — 490 feet long and 17,900 tons — was only an evolutionary development of the ever larger and

---

[8] Marder, *Fear God and Dread Nought,* Vol. II, *Years of Power, 1904–1914* (London: Oxford Univ. Press, 1959), 95.
[9] Marder, *The Anatomy . . .*, p. 491.
[10] Marder, *From the Dreadnought . . .*, I, 71–2.

more powerful capital ships which had begun to appear in 1899
with the launching of the 14,150 ton *Royal Sovereign* and by 1904
had reached 16,500 tons in the *Lord Nelson*. The Japanese had
laid down an even bigger ship five months earlier, but the *Dreadnought* was revolutionary in its technological advances. The Japanese had received a lesson of the value of long-range firing in
Tshushima Strait, yet they did not apply it to their ship designs; the
Americans rejected the idea of an all-big-gun ship in 1903; other
nations had accepted Mahan's pooh-poohing of speed's importance;
only a few engineers seriously considered the turbine engine to be
suitable for a warship. Fisher stole each of these unaccepted ideas,
and, as concluded by Marder, "it was the boldness with which he
resolved to combine them (in the *Dreadnought*) that constitutes his
chief contribution."[11]

A breakthrough in speed, staying power, hitting distance, and
gunpower, the *Dreadnought* caused a tremendous sensation amongst
the naval powers and paralyzed foreign admiralties for upwards of
two years after 1905.

It also caused some domestic agitation. The Radical Liberals
didn't like it. Lloyd George called it "this piece of wanton and profligate ostentation,"[12] and by 1908 could still howl:

> We said, let there be Dreadnoughts. What for? We did not require
> them. Nobody was building them, and if any one had started build-
> ing them, we, with our greater shipbuilding resources, could have
> built them faster than any other country in the world.[13]

And there was what Fisher later called the "unanimous naval
feeling against the *Dreadnought* when it first appeared."[14] The Old
Navy liked "bull at the gate, hammer and tongs action at short
ranges,"[15] not cowardly long-range guns. Naval writers protested
against putting "all one's naval eggs into one or two vast costly,
majestic, but vulnerable baskets."[16] Even the Conservatives were
unsure. Before the launching, Balfour hedged:

> While at first sight you might be inclined to say that . . . [British
> initiative] gives us an advantage in one sense, I am afraid it may en-
> tail upon us an expenditure which otherwise you might have avoided
> . . . we shall have to build this new type at a rate equal to any two
> Powers.[17]

[11] Marder, *The Anatomy* . . ., p. 516.
[12] Marder, *From the Dreadnought* . . ., I, 56.
[13] Woodward, *Great Britain* . . ., p. 105.
[14] Marder, *From the Dreadnought* . . ., I, 56.
[15] Marder, *The Anatomy* . . ., p. 519.
[16] *Ibid.*, p. 536.
[17] Woodward, *Great Britain* . . ., p. 110.

Fisher's persuasiveness carried the Admiralty and the Government with him, however, and by February, 1907, seven dreadnoughts and battle cruisers (a faster but more lightly armored version of the *Dreadnought*, equally revolutionary) were built or building.[18]

Fisher had also saved the happy Liberals £5,000,000 in the previous two years, but not without opposition. Lord Cawdor, the last Conservative First Lord of the Admiralty, had established a program of four ironclads per year. While accepting this for the first year "without prejudice," the Liberals cut back to two dreadnoughts for the 1907–08, estimates to lessen the "ruinous waste" of money. Not surprisingly, the Conservatives and big-navy advocates then accused the Sea Lords of being "tools of the little Englanders" and the Government of using the Admiralty "as a cloak for its cowardice." The *Daily Mail* decided, "The time has come to remind the Admiralty and the Government that the nation gave no mandate to weaken its Navy for the sole purpose of providing funds for doles to its Socialists."[19]

The Liberals blithely ignored such attacks and Fisher said, "It's simply stupid to talk of the loss of our naval supremacy. . . . We are not going to be frightened by foreign 'paper programmes' (the bogey of agitators!)."[20] Sir John, supremely confident of his reform program, was resistant to all criticism. He furnished a large segment of the friendly press with often secret "ammunition" to use against his opponents, believing that "the British public required . . . (repetition) continuously and persistently put before them . . . till they got impregnated with it and felt it as their own, with the consequent result called 'Public Opinion'!"[21]

Actually, England needed little urging to be interested in her Navy. There was no question that public opinion and both Parties basically supported a policy of naval supremacy: even to the workers the Navy was "one of the fixed points of the universe, admitting of no question or discussion."[22] Only the Radical Liberals, led by Prime Minister Campbell-Bannerman and after 1908, by Lloyd George and Winston Churchill, thought naval expenditures were too large.

In the summer of 1907 the Liberal stand was rudely undermined,

[18] "Century of Dreadnoughts," *Scientific American*, III (August 29, 1914), 146.

[19] Marder, *From the Dreadnought . . .*, I, 126–9.

[20] Marder, *Fear God . . .*, II, 92.

[21] *Ibid.*, p. 51.

[22] T. R. Threlfall, "Labour and the Navy," *The Nineteenth Century and After*, LXXV (March, 1914), 688.

not by the Conservatives or Fisher, but by their own idealism and by the Germans. The Second Hague Conference in 1907 (which followed the unsuccessful First Hague Conference in 1899) had been proposed by Russia to discuss various questions of international law. The pacifistic Liberals decided to introduce the subject of disarmament to insure world peace or at least to maintain the status quo (after all, no one else had dreadnoughts yet). It was a subject that was anathema to Europe's royalty including King Edward ("humbug," he said), and the Germans would have none of it. However sincere in their arguments that Britain's Navy was "defensive," the Liberals bungled their case at the Conference and aroused German suspicions. As Lord Reay said, the Conference did not result in "a greater sense of security, but rather the reverse." As a result of German intransigence the Liberals were forced to increase the 1907–08 program to three dreadnoughts while simultaneously arousing Conservative distrust of Liberal sanity.

Then a new increase in the German program was announced in November, 1907. Thus by early 1908 Britain had already begun to feel the pinch of staying ahead in the dreadnought race. Predictably, the pinch worried the Conservatives more than the Liberals. All the papers had an opinion. "Is Britain going to surrender her maritime supremacy to provide old age pensions?" asked the *Daily Mail*. The *Nation* reminded the Government of the "absolutely overwhelming" election promise for reduced armaments. Beyond mere partisan squabbles, the important thing was that "all sorts of sober-minded people in England began to be profoundly disquieted," as Churchill admitted later.[23]

The Admiralty did not panic but did demand that the 1908–09 estimates be increased to four dreadnoughts. The Liberals were unmoved. Lloyd George (Chancellor of the Exchequer) and Harcourt (First Commissioner of Works) threatened to resign from the Cabinet if the 1908 Naval Estimates were increased over 1907. It became a serious Cabinet crisis for a short while, resolved only after Fisher convinced Campbell-Bannerman that four dreadnoughts were absolutely necessary. The decision was announced by Asquith (the new Prime Minister following Campbell-Bannerman's resignation). Asquith made it "quite explicit" that the Government would increase the building program further "if we find that there is a probability or a reasonable probability of (German acceleration)."[24] With the exception of a couple of Radical papers crying "bloated

[23] Winston S. Churchill, *The World Crisis, 1911–14* (New York: Charles Scribner's Sons, 1928), p. 34.
[24] Woodward, *Great Britain* . . ., p. 165.

armaments" again, most of the press accepted the estimates. Lloyd George and Harcourt did not resign.

The race continued to intensify. Germany's Ambassador Metternich long had been convinced of Britain's peaceful intentions and particularly of the Liberal's sincere wish for disarmament. Time and again he repeated English arguments that without an army, Britain could not afford to lose naval supremacy whereas Germany, with the strongest army in the world, did not need a big navy for defense (Lloyd George reminded Metternich of Bismarck's jest that if England sent an invasion force to Germany, he would ask the police to arrest them). But the Kaiser was unshakeable in his determination to have a navy. Metternich's obvious lack of influence with Wilhelm cast another shadow on Anglo-German relations. So did Britain's massive naval maneuvers in the summer and the Bosnian crisis at the end of 1908.

Still, the most serious aspect was the increasing uneasiness and frustration of the British public. There remained a sizeable sentiment for reducing armaments, as evidenced by petitions signed by 136 Liberal M.P.'s in 1907 and by 144 in 1908.[25] This sentiment was consistently frustrated by the German shock tactics. In 1905 Britain had built four ships to Germany's two. When Britain decreased her program in 1906, Germany increased. In 1907 Britain further decreased her program while Germany increased once again. It took some British a little longer, but eventually most began to get the message. Optimistic naval writer Archibald Hurd had exulted of Britain's "cheerful" 1905 naval outlook and in 1907 said "the British people need not be alarmed." By 1908 he was worried that "the situation may become critical."[26] The events of 1908, including the frustrated hopes from King Edward's fruitless visit to the Kaiser in August, did nothing to allow a relaxation. By December, 1908, a contemporary writer stated "Public interest in the programme of shipbuilding for the Royal Navy is greater than . . . since . . . 1889."[27] Foreign Secretary Sir Edward Grey thought "Never since I have been in office has opinion been so thoroughly wide awake with regard to Germany, and on its guard as it is now."[28]

The Admiralty too was concerned. Fisher (THE Admiralty, some said) had held out against the Radicals for bigger 1908–09 Estimates and won. He was determined to try again for 1909–10, and

[25] *Ibid.*, p. 220.

[26] Hurd, *The Nineteenth Century and After,* LVII (February, 1905), 230; LXI (March, 1907), 384; LXIII (March, 1908), 485.

[27] W. H. White, "The Two Power Standard for the Navy," *The Nineteenth Century and After,* LXIV (December, 1908), 885.

[28] Marder, *From the Dreadnought . . .,* I, 145.

on May 5, 1908, wrote Lord Esher, "Yesterday with all the Sea Lords present McKenna [the new First Lord of the Admiralty] formally agreed to FOUR Dreadnoughts, AND IF NECESSARY SIX Dreadnoughts, next year (perhaps the greatest triumph ever known!)."[29] After a stormy secret meeting later that month, the Cabinet approved most of this tentative plan. McKenna and Grey had threatened to resign if the 4–6 program was not approved, but finally gave in at the urging of Lloyd George and Churchill who said four was ample. On cue, Harcourt said such naval scare-mongering was the "diseased imagination of inferior minds."[30]

Seemingly the battle of next year's budget had already been won. But Fisher knew better. In July, 1908, he wrote McKenna,

> I have an increasing fear of great trouble and a crisis. I am quite confident that the figure you have named to Lloyd George is inadequate, while he . . . [says he will cut] much further. . . . I write all this, as you might properly say to me in November: "You should have pressed all this on me in July, before I committed myself to Lloyd George." I have given the strongest proofs of being an economist . . . but . . . prudence would lay down SIX Dreadnoughts next year, *not four*.[31]

In view of their social program costing millions of pounds, it was extraordinarily difficult for the Government to agree to a big addition to naval estimates. Yet public opinion and the German menace made it even more difficult not to agree. The Germans had published their new annual program in November, 1908: it promised no respite. Therefore, that same month Asquith clarified Britain's long-nebulous shipbuilding policy: The Royal Navy would maintain a strength in capital ships 10 per cent over that of the next two strongest powers combined. Both sides of the House of Commons cheered. The navalists were delighted except for the fact that no increase in ships had been authorized yet, and the Government was keeping its 1909–10 budget plans secret until March.

Thus the year ended, but before it did the spectre of German acceleration had begun to materialize — a spectre which was to culminate in the great Panic of 1909. In answer to questions earlier in 1908, the Government had found it necessary to announce that Germany would take three years to build a dreadnought, and although this could be lowered the Government thought that Germany would hold to her published schedules. A decrease of building time hinged not upon keels, but upon the equipment — turrets,

[29] Marder, *Fear God . . .*, II, 175.
[30] *Marder, From the Dreadnought . . .*, I, 142.
[31] Marder, *Fear God . . .*, II, 185.

guns, turbines, etc. — which had to be made individually for each ship. Rumors of German stockpiling of such equipment and accounts of additional shipbuilding contracts began to be heard.

These rumors were so strong that on December 8th McKenna, still uncommitted thanks to Fisher's warning, asked the Cabinet to increase the estimates to six dreadnoughts instead of four. McKenna had concluded that Germany could build dreadnoughts as fast as Britain. He wrote Asquith that his conclusion was "most alarming, and if justified would give the public a rude awakening should it become known."[32] Fisher wrote to King Edward early in 1909:

> The outlook is very ominous. Herculean efforts, of which we know secretly and certainly, are being made by Germany . . . McKenna, who was when he came here an extreme "Little Navy" man, is now an ultra "Big Navy" man. . . .[33]

On January 15th the four Sea Lords, worried about the new evidence, recommended to McKenna that the 1909–10 estimates provide for *eight* dreadnoughts. The fat was in the fire. A few days later at an unofficial cabinet and naval meeting to discuss German accelerations, Churchill and Lloyd George held out for four. Lloyd George said,

> I think it shows extraordinary neglect on the part of the Admiralty that all this should not have been found out before. I don't think much of any of you admirals, and I should like to see Sir Charles Beresford [an admiral who was Fisher's mortal enemy] at the Admiralty and the sooner the better.

McKenna answered, "You know perfectly well that these facts were communicated to the Cabinet at the time we knew of them, and your remark was 'It's all contractor's gossip' — or words to that effect."[34] McKenna and many others violently distrusted both Lloyd George and Churchill. Viscount Knollys asked,

> What are Winston's reasons for acting as he does in this matter? Of course it cannot be from conviction or principle. The very idea of his having either is enough to make anyone laugh.

Lord Esher thought Churchill ambitious whereas Lloyd George was pro-Navy but "is just now hampered by the fact that he is a representative radical."[35]

The Admiralty was also distrusted — for not doing *enough* —

[32] Marder, *From the Dreadnought . . .*, I, 154.
[33] Marder, *Fear God . . .*, II, 220.
[34] Adm. Sir Frederick C. Dreyer, *The Sea Heritage, a Study of Maritime Warfare* (London: Museum Press Ltd., 1955), pp. 68–9.
[35] Marder, *From the Dreadnought . . .*, I, 160–61.

and in this case it helped their cause. The nation had heard the rumors of German acceleration despite Government secrecy. The Liberal press bewailed the assumed increase in naval expenditures, but most of public opinion was, according to *The Observer,* "in a mood of intense suspicion and even of painful anxiety."[36] *Blackwood's* bitterly recalled Fisher's 1907 statement, "I say, sleep quiet in your beds and do not be disturbed by those bogies, of invasion or otherwise, which are being periodically resuscitated."[37]

The intra-Government intrigues were violent. Lloyd George wrote Asquith in early February 1909,

> I will not dwell upon the emphatic pledges given by all of us before and at the last general election to reduce the gigantic expenditures on armaments built up by the recklessness of our predecessors. Scores of your most loyal supporters in the House of Commons take these pledges seriously and even a £3,000,000 increase will chill their zeal for the Gov't and an assured increase of £56,000,000 for the next year will stagger them. . . . [They] will hardly think it worth while to make any effort to keep in office a Liberal Ministry.[38]

A few days later Fisher wrote his assessment of the political climate to Knollys:

> Grey spent 1½ hours with me alone yesterday at my house, and no doubt about his being all right. . . . *The Prime Minister is as weak as water!* When McKenna last August would only go in for four *dreadnoughts,* Asquith pressed him that six were essential, and now when McKenna has . . . [agreed], Asquith deserts him.[39]

That Asquith was not as weak as Fisher thought is shown by a February 20th letter to his wife:

> The economists are in a state of wild alarm and Winston and Ll.G. by their combined machinations have got the bulk of the Liberal press into the same camp. . . . [They] go about darkly hinting at resignation (which is a bluff) . . . but there are moments when I am disposed summarily to cashier them both.[40]

Churchill soon broached a compromise through Grey to McKenna, who rejected it. McKenna himself toyed with a gesture that would allow the Radicals to save face. He proposed that the six-dreadnought estimates should authorize a reduction to four if the

[36] *Ibid.,* I, 146.
[37] "Musings Without Method," *Blackwood's Edinburgh Magazine,* CLXXXV (April, 1909), 590.
[38] Marder, *From the Dreadnought . . .,* I, 161.
[39] Marder, *Fear God . . .,* II, 222.
[40] Marder, *From the Dreadnought . . .,* I, 161.

Cabinet should so decide in November. Fisher distrusted the reservation, and wrote McKenna, "I don't feel as if I personally could acquiesce in any reservation whatever accompanying the *six* which we know in our hearts is too few . . . *we ought to build eight!*"[41]

It was up to Asquith to decide the final Government position, and this he did with grace on February 24th, 1909. The estimates would call for four dreadnoughts to be started immediately and four more (if necessary) on April 1, 1910. The latter was the first day of fiscal year 1910–11 but the program would require sizeable 1909–10 preliminary expenditures. The Admiralty obtained official sanction to make these preliminary expenditures. Lloyd George and Churchill now saw that they had been outmaneuvered and tried to change the plan back to McKenna's original proposal — six dreadnoughts. The Admiralty would have none of it. Thus, as Churchill himself reflected.

> In the end a curious and characteristic solution was reached. The Admiralty had demanded six ships: the economists offered four: and we finally compromised on eight.[42]

Even after Asquith's decision, Churchill continued to try to influence Fisher by letter. They had been and continued to be great friends (King Edward called them "the chatterers").[43] Churchill had expressed a great fellow-feeling for Fisher since they both painted with a big brush, and Fisher thought him "quite the nicest fellow I ever met."[44] But Churchill did not succeed. "I confess I never expected you to turn against the Navy after all you had said in public and in private ('Et tu, Brute!')," Fisher answered. Fisher, who could afford to be magnanimous, proposed to Churchill that the four extra dreadnoughts be called "Winston," "Churchill," "Lloyd," and "George." "How they would fight! Uncircumventable! Read this out to the Cabinet!"[45]

Finally came the day, March 16, 1909, when the whole country was to be let in on the estimates, and the House of Commons was overflowing. In the gallery the Prince of Wales watched as McKenna and Asquith painted a solemn picture. "We do not know, as we thought we did, the rate at which German construction is taking

[41] Dreyer, *The Sea Heritage* . . ., p. 70.
[42] Churchill, *The World Crisis,* p. 33.
[43] Sidney Lee, *King Edward VII,* Vol. II, *The Reign* (London: Macmillan & Co., Ltd., 1927), 604.
[44] Marder, *Fear God* . . ., II, 114.
[45] *Ibid.,* II, 226–7.

place," McKenna announced.[46] It was thought that by April, 1912, Germany would have seventeen dreadnoughts and England twenty (counting the extra four being proposed). Even Churchill was loud in his "hear hears" during the speech. When they were seated, there were several minutes of shocked silence. Then Balfour, speaking for the Opposition, said that Germany would have twenty-one dreadnoughts, not seventeen. The naval estimates passed their first vote 322–83, though the Conservatives felt that the Government was not doing enough. The few Radical protests quickly faded amidst the general national concern.

The Times and all the Conservative papers supported the eight dreadnoughts. Though "filled with despair," Liberal papers such as the *Liverpool Daily Post* had to admit "the force of Mr. McKenna's plea."[47] Mr. Frederic Harrison, a noted positivist philosopher and anti-militarist, immediately wrote *The Times* a panicky letter which predicted "England's national existence may be in peril within less than a generation from . . . [Germany's] navy."[48] Lord Rosebery, former Prime Minister and rarely inclined to rash actions, wrote a similar letter. "Panic, always infectious, is spreading like the plague," declared the *Daily News*.

The Government had miscalculated. They had argued against an ephemeral Radical opposition, only to inflame the long-growing public uneasiness and strengthen their real opposition which wanted to go much further.

"We want eight and we won't wait," the Conservatives began to shout. *The Observer* told voters to "insist on 'the Eight, the whole Eight, and nothing but the Eight,' with more to follow and buck any man or faction that now stands in the way." Lord Esher suggested hanging the Admiralty if they did not order eight ships at once.[49] Balfour introduced a vote of censure on March 19th which stated that the Government Policy "does not sufficiently secure the safety of the Empire." *The Daily Telegram* fumed, "Since Nero fiddled there has never been a spectacle more strange, more lamentable than the imperilling of . . . [our heritage] to balance a party Budget."[50]

There also happened to be a severe shipbuilding depression at the time: thousands of men were being let off. "If the Government is not composed of stoney-hearted pedants," the *Daily Mail* argued, "the

[46] Woodward, *Great Britain . . .*, p. 223.
[47] Woodward, *Great Britain . . .*, pp. 227–8.
[48] "The British Naval Scare," *The Independent*, LXVI (March, 1909), 607–8.
[49] Marder, *From the Dreadnought . . .*, I, 156.
[50] *Ibid.*, I, 168.

shipbuilding vote should be given out now ... 80 per cent of the cost ... goes ... to the British worker." Conservative leaflets lamented, "Our Navy and our unemployed may both be starved together."[51]

The Government's position was difficult, but Asquith struck back hard. "Unscrupulous, unpatriotic, and manipulated party agitation," he labeled Conservative efforts.[52] Fisher, for once, felt that "silence is patriotic. Don't check this wave of public opinion that will give us eight Dreadnoughts a year!" he wrote a friend. Yet Asquith, who was determined to wait until July before deciding on the extra four, won out. On March 29th the Government defeated the vote of censure by 353 to 135. Agitation continued throughout April and May of 1909, but the great Panic was nearly spent except for a final spasm in April from Italian and Austrian shipbuilding increases which finally convinced Asquith that the four extra ships should be ordered.

Once passions quieted, people began to wonder what it all had meant. An American magazine thought "All this would seem a sort of spring madness if one did not *read* the English press, which bristles with fear or with bravado — certainly with apprehension."[53] English commentators observed that "the nation has had Dreadnoughts on the brain"[54] and that it had awakened "like Rip Van Winkle."[55] "Surely the extent to which this expenditure has grown really becomes a satire, and a reflection on civilization," Sir Edward Grey said. "If it goes on at the [increasing] rate, ... it will submerge that civilization.[56] Balfour stated, "I do not believe that the country realizes the danger of the situation." Lord Rosebery observed,

> There is a hush in Europe ... there never was ... so threatening and so overpowering a preparation for war. ... I do begin to feel uneasy at the outcome of it all, and wonder where it will stop.[57]

In retrospect, it is obvious that Lord Rosebery's concern was justified. The "preparation for war," of which the Panic of 1909 was neither the cause nor the final episode did not stop until 1914.

[51] *Ibid.*, I, 156.

[52] *Ibid.*, I, 168.

[53] "The English War Excitement," *The World's Work*, XVIII (May, 1909), 11532.

[54] Hurd, "The Balance of Naval Power and the Triple Alliance," *The Nineteenth Century and After*, LXV (June, 1909), 1069.

[55] Erroll, "A Rude Awakening," *The Nineteenth Century and After*, LXV (April, 1909), 565.

[56] Woodward, *Great Britain ...*, p. 230.

[57] H. R. Chamberlain, "The Ominous Hush in Europe," *McClure's Magazine*, XXXIII (October, 1909), 598–600.

For Britain, the race had started with her decision to build the *Dreadnought*. Was this decision, as Marder says, Fisher's great "stroke of genius"?[58] Or did England lose a "moral advantage" by deserting her policy "never to take the initiative in inventing engines of war," as maintained by historian Elie Halévy?[59] E. L. Woodward, second-ranking authority next to Marder, dodged the issue by writing, "it is impossible to give an answer."[60]

There is no doubt that the *Dreadnought* quickly outdated all previous warships, of which Britain had by far the largest number. All sea-power nations began to build dreadnoughts, and German naval ambitions seemed to take on a new breath of life. But it did give the British a long technological lead on her competitors, especially since Germany needed £11,000,000 and eight years to broaden the Kiel Canal before her dreadnoughts were useful.[61] A review of contemporary opinions shows surprisingly little awareness of the ultimate effects of the dreadnought policy. For instance, the Admiralty considered the dreadnought inevitable (which it was). Yet they presented it as a revoluntary development (which it also was in 1905) and later tried to deny this when the implications for the Royal Navy came under public criticism. Opponents wanted to wait for other nations to begin, with Britain to "follow with something better, taking advantage of speed in building."[62]

Apparently neither side realized until 1909 that Britain's reputation for superior shipbuilding speed rested on shaky ground. Considering what was known in 1905, the *Dreadnought* was a grave mistake for Britain; yet with historical hindsight it is clear that technological lead-time was the real issue. As a British admiral wrote recently, "Fisher gained for us time — priceless time — the equivalent of, say, five years."[63] In the *Dreadnought* issue, Fisher was utterly right but for the wrong reasons.

And what of the Panic of 1909? The poor Liberals, impractical by constitution and divisive by nature, had been unable by 1909 to develop a viable strategic policy of their own or to abandon the one they inherited. The Liberals did not start the naval race: the Germans did in 1898. Neither did they start the first dreadnought: the

[58] Marder, *From the Dreadnought* . . ., I, 69.

[59] Elie Halévy, *The Rule of Democracy (1905–1914),* Trans. E. I. Watkin (New York: Barnes and Noble, Inc., 1961), p. 207.

[60] Woodward, *Great Britain* . . ., p. 114.

[61] Capt. Donald Macintyre, *Jutland* (New York: W. W. Norton & Co., 1958), p. 27.

[62] Marder, *The Anatomy* . . ., p. 536.

[63] Dreyer, *The Sea Heritage* . . ., p. 35.

Conservatives did in 1905. Stymied in their earnest desires for disarmament by their 1907 failure at The Hague, in 1909 the Liberals made their last meaningful attempt to moderate the madness that was enveloping Europe. They failed because of the Panic. This failure, together with the *Dreadnought* concept and the 1907–08 events, put the finishing touches on the World War I naval race which thenceforth was self-generating and irresistable.

Despite the clear causation from German aggressiveness, there was a certain inevitability of the Panic as a result of Liberal policies. Realizing the benefits from eye-catching headlines, Lloyd George and Churchill had captured the innocent minds of the little-navy pacifist group. They had also so frightened the Conservatives and the Admiralty by their ambitious but unpredictable radical policies that the Panic of 1909 was bound to happen — Germans or no Germans.

Whether or not there ever was any secret German acceleration is still uncertain. Years later McKenna maintained that Germany had actually begun the preparations but had discontinued them after the British discoveries. The German Ministry of Marine Archives, published after the War, indicates there was no planned or actual acceleration.[64] Woodward believes that the acceleration plan existed but was not followed because, after the British publicity and the formal denial by Germany, "it would have been more than foolish to make another attempt."[65]

Even before the Panic was over the British had found their fears were groundless. That the Admiralty was less than anxious to quell the excitement is shown by a letter Fisher wrote in March, 1909:

> Most reliable information arrived last night at the Admiralty which dissipates the alarm that the Germans were ahead of us.
> We certainly should not have got eight Dreadnoughts apart from all that has happened. Indeed it is now being freely said that the Admiralty engineered the scare!... The fact is we must have a large margin against lying [by the Germans]![66]

So the eight dreadnoughts of 1909–10 were started, and by 1910 Fisher bragged,

> We shall have twenty-two Dreadnoughts in March 1912, and the Germans will have only eleven! THIS ALL ABSOLUTE FACT! But ... 'the truth is we don't want anyone to know the truth,' for suppose I said all this! Why, Lloyd George & Co. would irresistably cut

[64] Marder, *From the Dreadnought...*, I, 177.
[65] Woodward, *Great Britain...*, pp. 240–41.
[66] Marder, *Fear God...*, II, 236.

down the Navy Estimates. Moreover, I am a real asset with the Little Navy Party! They look on me as a heavenly cheese-parer! *I am content to be vilified if my country wins by it!*[67]

Actually the British had fifteen dreadnoughts in commission by April, 1912, and the Germans nine. This was a superiority of six instead of only three as predicted by Asquith in 1909. Balfour had stated that the Germans would be superior. Therefore the Panic of 1909, based on overly pessimistic predictions, seems to have been unnecessary. Fisher had started it with his secret evidence and kept it alive even after he privately admitted the falsity of this evidence. He caused an unprecedented naval budget and nearly split asunder the Liberal party. What did these questionable tactics achieve?

According to Marder, "it was the contingent four capital ships of 1909 that gave the Navy its rather bare margin of security [twenty-five available dreadnoughts to Germany's twenty] in the critical early months of the war."[68] Churchill, Fisher's nemesis in 1909 and First Lord of the Admiralty himself after 1911, wrote in 1928:

> I was still a sceptic [in 1909] about the danger of the European situation, and not convinced by the Admiralty case. . . . [With Lloyd George I proceeded] to examine the reasons by which it was supported. The conclusions which we both reached were that a programme of four ships would sufficiently meet our needs. . . . I found the Admiralty figures on this subject were exaggerated. . . .
>
> Looking back on the voluminous papers of this controversy in the light of what actually happened, there can be no doubt whatever that, so far as facts and figures were concerned, we were strictly right. The gloomy Admiralty anticipations were in no respect fulfilled in the year 1912.
>
> But although the Chancellor of the Exchequer and I were right in the narrow sense, we were absolutely wrong in relation to the deep tides of destiny. . . . Little did I think, as this dispute proceeded, that when the next Cabinet crisis about the Navy arose our [McKenna's and Churchill's] roles would be reversed; and little did he think that the ships for which he contended so stoutly would eventually, when they arrived, be welcomed with open arms by me.[69]

In the end, Britain was saved by the "bare margin of security" which kept the Kaiser's dreadnought fleet bottled up throughout the war. Effective as the submarine turned out to be for Germany, she had made herself "dreadnought-poor." The few submarines she did have were countered eventually by small craft which could have operated only under the umbrella of the British dreadnoughts' power.

[67] *Ibid.*, II, 290–91.
[68] Marder, *From the Dreadnought . . .*, I, 179.
[69] Churchill, *The World Crisis*, pp. 32–33.

Thus the Panic of 1909 had a major if not decisive influence on Britain's ultimate victory. For that reason it was, though meaningless in itself, perhaps the most significant British political-strategic event in the twentieth century prior to Neville Chamberlain's Munich. Yet the real lesson, like all lessons from history, hinges upon the actions of men rather than upon events alone. Who were the heroes responsible for the "umbrella" of dreadnoughts?

McKenna was one, and so was Churchill for his valiant Admiralty work in the three pre-war years. Another hero is the stolid British public which never lost sight of its real security needs. The Conservatives, too, were usually alert. The press, neither hero nor villain, showing occasional courage and wisdom together with occasional self-interest and stupidity, usually could be counted upon only to support a particular party line. And the Liberals, who in general vacillated between unrealistic idealism and crass politics, did not qualify.

But the greatest hero of all was Sir John Fisher. Creator of the dreadnought for reasons that are questionable, instigator of the Panic of 1909 by means which scarcely justified the immediate end, never appreciating the danger of his position or the full implications of his actions, he was nevertheless far in advance of his contemporaries on both sides of the North Sea. As a doer he was unparalleled. As a prophet he was lucky. As a thinker he intuitively saw what others, more profound, lost in their philosophical dabblings.

Sensing the Kaiser's true aims as early as 1900, Fisher kept the British prepared and the Germans off balance. He did it once by building the "dreadnought," and he did it again in 1909. Despite the many fallacies of his decisions, "in relation to the deep tides of destiny" he was right all along. His actions were controversial and inconsistent when viewed in the murky light of contemporary politics, power, and panic: today they appear to have been guided by a single-minded and unshakeable awareness of danger. He recognized the danger from an aggressor and, even more, the danger from those who did *not* recognize it.

Weapons, Doctrine, and Arms Control:
A Case from the Good Old Days

WARNER R. SCHILLING

Instruments of warfare should be such as do not inflict unnecessary injury or damage. The principle of humanity condemns all instruments and methods of warfare that involve wanton cruelty, savagery or treachery. It condemns the ill-treatment of the helpless and the disarmed, including wounded and prisoners, the aged and feeble, women and children. When, however, one of the belligerents disregards the principle and usages of war, the other is entitled to adopt measures of reprisal. There is grave danger here that counter-reprisals will be resorted to and war quickly degenerate into savagery.[1]

The U.S. Naval Advisory Staff
Paris, March, 1919

I

World War I was a preview of many things to come. Among them was the accelerating development in this century of military doctrine and military weapons which by choice and design have proved incapable of keeping to former discriminations between the uniformed and the nonuniformed personnel of the enemy. Aircraft, bombs, and the doctrine of strategic bombardment were, to be sure, in their infancy. But they had their harbingers in kind, if not in degree, in the components of the Anglo-German naval war: the submarine and the strategic blockade. The submarine was a weapon whose technical characteristics made it incapable of effective use without departing from discriminations previously feasible between merchantman and warship, passenger and crew, cargo and life. The strategic blockade was guided by a doctrine which projected the success of its ultimate objective — the flow of food and munitions to combat troops — upon the indirect method of stopping the flow of food and goods to a whole nation. It was not the practice of blockade which was novel (or in the British case even

From *The Journal of Conflict Resolution* (1963), pp. 193–214. Reprinted by permission. Some footnotes have been omitted.
[1] See Naval Advisory Staff, Memorandum 23, March 5, 1919, House Collection, Yale University.

the military instruments); it was rather the departure from previous discriminations regarding what was proper to be blockaded. In a war in which civilian economies were responsible for the staying power of armies, civilians and their economy seemed as legitimate and necessary subjects for siege and attrition as the armies themselves.

Americans old enough to have gasped at the horror of the *Lusitania* (with its 35 suffocated babies) had yet to live through the war in which their nation would inflict more casualties on Japanese civilians than on Japanese military personnel, or to reach the comfortable age where they could retire in the shadow of war plans which anticipated the death of several hundred million Europeans — friend or foe — depending on which way the wind blew. Indeed, so far have the theories and mechanics of war developed in the space of a single life-span, that is now difficult to appreciate that in November, 1918, many Americans thought they stood on the threshold of a totally different era — one in which the world would be free at last from the ravages of war.

Nowhere was this expectation more manifest than in the policies of the President of the United States, Woodrow Wilson. Following the sinking of the *Lusitania*, Wilson's alter ego, Colonel House, had written him that America "must determine whether she stands for civilized or uncivilized warfare," and the President had more than answered the challenge.[2] He not only went to war because of the way Germany employed the submarine, but in his famous Fourteen Points address in January, 1918, he pledged himself to bring about a new order in world politics. In the most important of these Points, the Fourteenth, he proposed to establish a league of nations which, by virtue of its commitment to mobilize overwhelming power against a potential aggressor, would constitute an effective deterrent to war in the future.[3]

Although Wilson was primarily intent on measures which would

[2] Charles Seymour, ed., *The Intimate Papers of Colonel House* (4 vols.; Boston, 1926–1928), Vol. 1, p. 434.

[3] It is worth noting that in his analysis of the military requirements for such a league, Wilson was among the first to appreciate that arms control was not synonymous with disarmament. Although the Fourth of his Fourteen Points had called for the reduction of armaments "to the lowest point consistent with domestic safety," Wilson also believed that the stability of the postwar world would depend on the league's ability to coerce its strongest members (and among them the strongest naval Power, Great Britain). Accordingly, when he applied his "disarmament point" to the United States, he ended up asking Congress in December, 1918, to triple the size of the battle fleet the Navy had afloat in November when the shooting stopped.

prevent war in the first place, he had not neglected to deal in his Fourteen Points with the question of how war, if it were to be fought, could be fought in a civilized manner. His second Point — the Freedom of the Seas — met the issue of submarine warfare by proposing to abolish the practice of strategic blockade by any weapon. The merchant shipping of neutrals and belligerents alike was to be as free in time of war as it was in time of peace. Warships would be used only against other warships, even by a dominant naval Power.

This proposal would limit drastically the character of naval war in the future. House, who had originated the plan, had started with nothing more in mind than the traditional American concern for the protection of neutral trade during time of European war, but in the course of conversations with the British and Germans in the winter of 1915, his concern had broadened to include limiting the impact of war on belligerents as well. He was, he told the British Foreign Minister, intent on "rules of warfare that would take away much of the horror of war." In January, 1918, when Wilson and House drafted the Fourteen Points, they had added still a third idea: that nations might use their navies to restrict the merchant shipping of other states if it were done with the consent of an international organization for the purpose of enforcing international covenants.[4]

Wilson and House had developed these far-reaching ideas without any consultation with the officers of the American Navy, and the end of the war found the Navy without any plans of its own regarding the Freedom of the Seas. Once peace was upon it, the Navy made an earnest and energetic effort to come to grips with the problem of eliminating strategic blockade and to develop, in addition, plans for the abolition of the submarine itself. But the delay in the Navy's own planning, coupled with Wilson's customary disinterest in the free exchange of ideas with the ranking officers of his Navy, proved fatal for the goal of coordinated policy. There resulted, instead, two divergent sets of plans for producing a new turn in the character of war, and at the Peace Conference the President and his Chief of Naval Operations were to meet in intellectual isolation problems whose magnitude might well have exhausted their combined talents.[5]

[4] The text of the Point was: "Absolute freedom of navigation upon the seas, outside territorial waters, alike in peace and war, except as the seas may be closed in whole or in part by international action for the enforcement of international covenants." . . .

[5] Warner Schilling, "Civil-Naval Politics in World War I," *World Politics*, vol. 7 (July, 1955), pp. 572–591.

The purpose of this paper is to present an account of what happened during the peace negotiations to the American proposals to abolish strategic blockade and the submarine. The reader interested in more recent issues of arms control will find much that is familiar — in the problems involved and in the perspectives and interests the participants brought to bear on those problems. But this history will provide no direct prescriptions for the future. The interests which Americans believed would make possible a "no merchant ships" doctrine are not readily comparable to those which might today be expected to lead to a "no cities" doctrine, and the issues associated with the abolition of the submarine are not in all respects reliable analogues for those connected with the elimination of nuclear weapons or their carriers. Still, an account of the past may have some value, especially for those who tend to believe that it has no relevance at all. This history may be conceived, then, as a "cautionary tale," and like all good cautionary tales, its utility will vary with the prior perspectives of the reader.

II

Wilson's Fourteen Points, advanced in part to meet Bolshevik charges about the imperialist character of the war, represented his own statement of the principles which would govern the peace. They were not binding on his allies, and when Germany, in October, 1918, accepted the Points as the basis for an armistice, the first order of business was to see if the Allies would do the same. To this end, Wilson sent House to Paris, where he was in time to secure agreement to all except the Second. On the question of eliminating strategic blockade, British opposition was immediate and firm.

To further his negotiations, House had two members of his delegation (Frank Cobb and Walter Lippmann) draft an explanatory statement of the Fourteen Points. This statement was approved by Wilson, and with regard to the Freedom of the Seas it advanced a distinction between the conditions that would prevail in the event of a "general war" (one involving the League) and those in the event of a "limited war" (one in which the League was neutral). The first instance was simple: the League Powers would close the seas to the "outlaw nation." In the second case, it was the intention of the Point that the "rights of neutrals shall be maintained against the belligerents, the rights of both to be clearly and precisely defined in the law of nations."[6]

If the Cobb-Lippmann statement is considered in terms of the three ideas Wilson and House had originally entertained (the limi-

[6] Seymour, *op. cit.*, vol. 4, pp. 153, 193.

tation of belligerent action on neutrals, the limitation of the action of belligerents against each other, and the right of the League to close the seas), it is apparent that the statement contained two important shifts in emphasis. First, the idea that only the League *could* practice strategic blockade had now the form of a declaration that the only naval doctrine the League *would* follow would be that of strategic blockade. Secondly, although the statement indicated that in the event of non-League war, belligerent action against neutrals would be severely restricted, it was by no means evident what limitations were to be imposed on the actions of belligerents against each other.

These nuances had no effect on the British position. When the statement was presented at a meeting of Lloyd George, House, and Clemenceau, the Prime Minister declared that Britain would not accept the Freedom of the Seas "under any conditions." House warned the British to look to the future. In the next war, American sympathies might be with the blockaded Power. The British should also look to the present. If the Fourteen Points were not accepted, America might make a separate peace with Germany. Lloyd George remained adamant. Britain was being asked to hand over to the League of Nations the power to impose a blockade. "To give up the right of using its fleet was a thing which no one in England would consent to." Nor was the representative of France moved by the American proposal. Clemenceau could "not understand the meaning of the doctrine. War would not be war if there was freedom of the seas."[7]

Considering what the British thought they had at stake in the issue, one must wonder what gave the Americans hope that there was a basis for agreement. As the American Ambassador to Britain described it, the British held that

. . . no new doctrine can be acceptable which in any way diminishes [Britain's] control over transportation to and from the possible enemy. It is pointed out that the science of warfare has changed to such an extent that nations now fight almost en masse and that practically every commodity imported and exported has a direct bearing on the prosecution of hostilities. The British view is that . . . a blockade should be permissible [and] as effective as any large navy can make it.[8]

[7] See British Notes, Supreme War Council, October 29, 1918, House Collection.

[8] See Davis to Secstate, December 19, 1918, Department of State, *Papers Relating to the Foreign Relations of the United States, The Paris Peace Conference, Washington* (1942–47), vol. 1, p. 414.

Actually, it was this same changing "science of warfare" that had led House to believe that Britain might agree to refrain from the practice of strategic blockade. In 1915 the British Foreign Minister had expressed the fear that "the development of the submarine will a few years hence make it impossible for us ever again to close the sea to an enemy and keep it free ourselves." House had been quick to capitalize on this concern. Britain's best interests lay in accepting the Freedom of the Seas, he had argued. Otherwise, she would face in the future "the dangers of the submarine, aircraft, and other means of warfare against which no navy was a protection." Since House also believed that it would be to the advantage of Germany (and certainly America) to see strategic blockade abolished, the proposal had been an integral part of the unsuccessful effort he and Wilson made in 1915–16 to mediate an end to the war.[9]

The basis for House's expectation of agreement was, then, the presumption that as a result of the new naval technology all the maritime Powers, whether enemy or neutral, now shared a common interest in restricting the scope of naval war to the action of warship against warship. It is probable that he had been encouraged to believe in the validity of this expectation by the fact that, during the years of American neutrality, British statesmen had always been most circumspect in their treatment of the issue. In January, 1916, when House had discussed the concept with Lloyd George in London, the Colonel found it "laughable to hear him declare that militarism must go and in the same breath say that Great Britain must retain the supremacy of the seas. . . . He had looked upon the Freedom of the Seas as a German proposal. When he found it was mine and in accord with the President's views he seemed to think better of it."[10]

There was neither laughter nor circumspection at Paris. House assaulted the British position, not with further appeals to their self-interest, but with a battery of threats. He reminded them of the War of 1812 and declared that the United States was no more willing to submit to British domination of the seas than she was to German domination of the land, and that the sooner the British recognized this "the better it would be for them." If necessary, America would build both a bigger army and a bigger navy than Britain's. "We had more money, we had more men, and our natural resources were greater." If Britain persisted in her course, it could only point Anglo-

[9] Edward H. Buehrig, *Woodrow Wilson and the Balance of Power* (Bloomington: Indiana University Press, 1955), p. 196; Seymour, *op. cit.*, vol. 1, p. 370; *House Diary*, April 30, 1915, House Collection, Yale University.

[10] *House Diary*, January 14, 1916.

American relations in the same direction Anglo-German relations had gone, with the great difference that in a contest with the United States "Britain would lose." On his part, Wilson cabled from Washington that the British be told that the United States was "pledged to fight not only Prussian militarism but militarism everywhere," and that he was quite prepared to place the issue before Congress and thereby before world opinion, and that Congress would "have no sympathy whatever with spending American lives for British naval control."[11]

The only result was continued acrimony. House thought the British were demonstrating "the most extraordinary attitude I have ever known." He had thrown the whole book at them. He had charged that their position was equivalent to German militarism; he had warned that the President would take the dispute before world opinion; he had threatened to make a separate peace; he had declared that the United States would drive Britain to the wall in an armaments race; he had predicted that American sympathies would be with England's enemies in the next war; and he had even confronted the British with the probability of an Anglo-American war. Yet, after all this, he was as far away from securing Lloyd George's agreement to the principle of the Freedom of the Seas as ever. Indeed, he confessed to his diary, "I cannot get them to the point of even admitting that the matter is one for discussion at the Peace Conference."[12]

Despite the formidable character of their threats, Wilson and House had essentially the inferior bargaining position. House had set particular store by the threat of Wilson's publicizing the issue before Congress and world opinion. So far as Lloyd George was concerned this was an "unloaded blunderbuss." The public to which he was most responsive was the British, and here the danger "came from exactly the opposite direction" — i.e., in agreeing to the Second Point.[13] Lloyd George does not mention House's other threats in his memoirs, but it is not likely that the discussion of an Anglo-American war gave him much pause. It was not possible for America to go to war against Great Britain over the practice of strategic blockade until Britain *first* went to war with someone else. The proper time for Britain to ascertain her best interests, then, was when such a war in fact occurred. As for the threat of a separate peace, this was credible only to the extent that Wilson appeared

---

[11] *House Diary*, October 28, November 4, 1918.
[12] *House Diary*, November 2, 1918.
[13] George, David Lloyd, *The Truth About the Peace Treaties* (2 vols.; London: Victor Gallancz, Ltd., 1938), vol. 1, pp. 82–83.

willing to renounce an opportunity to secure the rest of his peace program simply because he could not have this part of it. Even House's promise to outbuild the British Navy had its difficulties, for of what use was naval superiority if Britain had to refrain from using it. Still, this was the most consequential of the American threats, and later in the Peace Conference the British were to turn it on the Americans by threatening to withhold agreement on the League Covenant unless Wilson cut back the American building program.

Finally, on November 3, House decided to throw in his hand. Along with the other details of the armistice, the matter had been under continuous negotiation since October 26, when House arrived in Paris, and he concluded that the best course was to postpone further discussion until Wilson himself reached France. "All he wanted," House told Lloyd George, "was the principle that the question could be discussed," and to this the Prime Minister agreed. Although he had secured only an agreement to the principle that the principle could be discussed, House's diary reveals that, like other diplomats caught up in the heat of negotiation, he had mistaken shadow for substance. "This has been a red letter day. I brought Lloyd George to terms concerning the Freedom of the Seas."[14]

The Prime Minister's verdict on the negotiations was quite different: "Gradually President Wilson was made to realize that he was up against a tradition that could not be overthrown by the blast of a single speech delivered from across the Atlantic." In Washington, to judge from Secretary of the Navy Josephus Daniels' account of a conference at the White House, the mood was one of a battle lost but a war to go on.

> WW had cabled House if E took course in opposition [to Freedom of the Seas] we would use our facilities to build the greatest navy. Decided to accept inasmuch G.B. agreed to all other 13 points and did not actually dissent from that in order to have unity. But he is resolved in later conference to win over the other countries to our point of view and secure it from League of Nations. Great disappointment to us.[15]

III

Admiral William S. Benson, the Chief of Naval Operations, had accompanied House to Paris, but he had played only a peripheral

[14] . . . British Notes, Supreme War Council, November 3, 1918, House Collection; *House Diary*, November 3, 1918.

[15] See Lloyd George (1938, vol. 1, p. 83); *Daniels Diary*, November 4, 1918, *Daniels Papers*, Library of Congress.

part in the Battle of the Second Point. He had been preoccupied with the drafting of the naval armistice terms. But Benson was aware of the intensity of the conflict that had taken place, and on the basis of statements he had received from House he was convinced that the Freedom of the Seas was going to be one of the main problems to engage the attention of the Peace Conference.[16]

The Navy's first formal analysis of Wilson's Second Point was a memorandum prepared for Benson on November 7, 1918 by the London Planning Section — a group of officers who had been detached from the War Plans Section of the Office of Naval Operations in the fall of 1917 to serve under the Commander of the American Naval Forces in Europe and whom Benson was shortly to reorganize into his own Naval Advisory Staff in Paris.[17]

The Section's memorandum identified four different conceptions of the Freedom of the Seas. First, there was the traditional American conception: that neutral trade should suffer the minimum possible restriction from belligerents. In contrast, there was the traditional British conception: that belligerents be free to adjust their actions to suit the necessities of their military and naval situations, a conception Britain favored in order to receive the maximum advantage from her "great naval supremacy." A third conception was the League of Nations interpretation: that the League could deny all maritime rights to a Power which refused peaceful settlement of its disputes. Finally, there was "complete Freedom of the Seas," the right of belligerent and neutral merchant ships alike to travel the high seas "without molestation by the naval vessels of the belligerents."

This last conception was, of course, an integral part of what Wilson and House had in mind. The memorandum held little hope for it. If this condition were to prevail, the need for navies would "disappear," except as a means for aiding or preventing land attacks, since the present objective of naval strategy — the control of sea communications — would be "illegal." The memorandum pointed out that this would be an end "distinctly in the special interests of land powers" and predicted that no international agreement would ever be able to rearrange "the life of nations to such a revolution in their relations."

The Planning Section therefore advised Benson to reject the idea of abolishing strategic blockade as impracticable. The Section took

[16]*House Diary*, November 8, 1918; Benson to Daniels, November 10, 1918, *Daniels Papers*.

[17] London Planning Section, Memorandum 70, November 7, 1918, Navy Department, Office of Naval Intelligence, *The American Naval Planning Section, London* (Washington, 1923), pp. 481–88.

quite seriously, however, the possibility of introducing *limitations* into the practice of strategic blockade. The most striking of its recommendations dealt with the treatment belligerents were to be permitted vis-à-vis each other's merchant ships. Since modern war gave belligerent merchant ships a "semimilitary status," it would be an "absurdity" not to make them liable to capture. But the *sinking* of such ships should be made illegal.

> Every merchant vessel built to meet a commercial need is a distinct acquisition to civilization. Every merchant vessel destroyed is a distinct economic loss to the world. Injury to the enemy does not require the destruction of his property but the sequestration of it. The world is too vitally concerned in the preservation of seaborne commerce to permit the sinking of merchant ships as an act of war.

The idea of prohibiting the sinking of merchant ships, instead of their capture, constituted an interesting and somewhat more realistic variation of Wilson's proposal for limiting the impact of naval war. The officers who advanced it said nothing in their memorandum about how international agreement to this restriction could be initially secured and afterwards enforced, but some insight into their thinking can be gained from a consideration of the content of their strategic planning at this time.

The officers who wrote the memorandum and who later became Benson's official advisers at the Peace Conference were convinced (as was Benson himself) that trade rivalry was the major cause of war and that America was destined to surpass England as the world's greatest commercial Power. Since they also believed that England had always gone to war against her leading trade rival, they assigned a high probability to the prospect of an Anglo-American war, and they were engaged in the fall of 1918 in developing plans for its fighting. In their strategic estimate, neither Britain nor the United States would be able to undertake a strategic blockade of the other's home waters, although each would deny its side of the Atlantic to the shipping of the other.[18] Accordingly, they could have reasoned that the proposed limitation would affect each side about equally and work to the special advantage of neither.

Admiral Benson gave a copy of the Section's memorandum to House, and at House's suggestion he discussed the Section's proposal with David Hunter Miller, soon to become Wilson's chief legal adviser at the Peace Conference. Miller was impressed by the character of the limitations Benson had in mind, and the two agreed to draft a detailed program for the Freedom of the Seas which would

[18] London Planning Section, Memorandum 67, November 21, 1918, Naval War Records, Record Group 45, S-file, National Archives.

be ready by the time Wilson reached Paris. But the more Miller thought about it, the less meaningful the President's Second Point became to him. On December 13, the day Wilson landed in France, Miller gathered his doubts together in a memorandum for House and Benson. Miller noted that both Wilson's Point and the Cobb-Lippmann statement seemed to assume that if the League were involved in a war it would exercise "unlimited use of sea power." It was Miller's thesis that once the League of Nations was established there would either be no war at all, or a war between two groups of Powers each claiming the rights of the League and each, therefore, practicing unlimited sea war. This being the case, he concluded that "any revision of the rules of capture, contraband, blockade, etc., is a matter of only academic interest."[19]

Neither House nor Benson was persuaded by Miller's argument, but it did put Benson on his own in drafting a program for the President, and the only recommendations prepared for Wilson's use in Paris with regard to the Second Point were those submitted to him by Benson's Naval Advisory Staff in January, 1919. The Staff's recommendations were essentially an elaboration of the ideas advanced in the Section's memorandum. Thus, the provision against the destruction of belligerent merhcant ships was justified on the grounds that "the society of nations can ill afford to countenance a practice so contrary to the interests of humanity." The most important new point related to the kind of goods that belligerents would be permitted to blockade, and here again the restrictions recommended by the Staff testify to the interests of the naval planners in limiting the effect of war on belligerents, as well as on neutrals.

> Food and clothing will undoubtedly remain on the free list, so that war in the future will be less apt to include among its horrors attempts at the starvation of peoples. We believe that starvation is not a sound measure of war since it, more than any other measure, breaks down social organization and thereby retards the progress of civilization in the world.[20]

The Navy's recommendation to prohibit starvation as a measure of war suffered from the same defect as its recommendation to prohibit the sinking of merchant ships. In neither case did the Advisory Staff's memorandum contain any serious discussion of the enforcement problem. Even more consequential was the failure

[19] See Miller (1928a, vol. 1, pp. 13–14; vol. 2, pp. 262–64); Miller to Frazier, December 13, 1918, House Collection.

[20] Naval Advisory Staff, Memorandum 11, January 10, 1919, House Collection.

of the memorandum to confront Miller's thesis: that the League would practice unlimited naval war; that once the League was established there would be either no war or a war in which each side claimed the rights of the League; and that, therefore, it was impossible to limit *any* naval war. Unknowingly, the Staff thereby lost an opportunity to influence Wilson's thinking at a critical juncture. For while the Naval Staff had been busy preparing for the great debate at the Peace Conference, the President's line of reasoning had gone off in another direction, and the idea that the League would render the whole issue meaningless was the rock on which his own conception of the Freedom of the Seas was to flounder.

IV

The British had awaited the President's arrival with grim determination. Lloyd George was determined to give Wilson "a thorough cross-examination" on what he meant by the Freedom of the Seas. On the public front, such sources as Winston Churchill and the London *Times* resolutely affirmed Britain's unshaken opposition to the concept, arguing, as Churchill phrased it, "a League of Nations is no substitute for the British Fleet."[21]

Wilson met with Lloyd George in London in late December, 1918. The personal confrontation of the two protagonists on the issue qualifies as one of diplomacy's more anticlimactic events. Lloyd George was pleased, and no doubt somewhat surprised, to report to his Cabinet that,

> . . . as regards the Freedom of the Seas, the President was very vague. He did not oppose his suggestion that the matter could be left for further discussion *after* the League of Nations had been established and *proved* its capacity in actual working.[22]

What led Wilson to give away in London the little that House had bargained so hard to get at Paris? House had advised him "to listen sympathetically," when Lloyd George brought up the Freedom of the Seas, "but not to commit himself and not to antagonize them. The main thing is to get the League of Nations. With that accomplished, everything else follows or becomes a minor consideration." But Wilson had been more than noncommittal. He had agreed to take the discussion of his Second Point off the agenda of the Peace Conference. The answer is that after House failed to secure Britain's agreement to the Point during the armistice negotiations, Wilson had apparently decided to postpone the whole matter until after the League was established. Thus in November he

---

[21] Cobb to House, November 19, 1919, House Collection.
[22] Lloyd George, *op. cit.*, vol. 1, p. 186, italics added.

had told Daniels in Washington (but not House or Benson in Paris) that "He looked for the League of Nations to settle freedom of the seas."[23]

The denouement is simply told. The first draft of the League Covenant Wilson wrote in Paris in January, 1919, did not even contain a clause to place the Freedom of the Seas on the League's agenda. "There is not a word in the paper regarding freedom of the seas," Miller exclaimed to House. Wilson remedied this by inserting an enabling clause in his next draft, but the British objected to the clause, and it was omitted from the draft which served as the working paper for the Commission on the League of Nations. The Commission did not once discuss the concept, and Wilson never tried again to put his enabling clause back into the League Covenant.

With this, Wilson's retreat on his Second Point was complete. The explanation lies in the fact that sometime in early February he decided that it did not make any sense. The circumstances of this conclusion are not a matter of record, but Wilson's reasoning emerges clearly in a speech he made in September, 1919.

> One of the principles I went to Paris most insisting on was freedom of the seas. Now, the freedom of the seas means the definition of the rights of neutrals to use the seas when other nations are at war, but under the League of Nations there are no neutrals, and, therefore, what I have called the practical joke on myself was that by the very thing that I was advocating it became unnecessary to define freedom of the seas.[24]

V

The Freedom of the Seas was no joke to the Naval Advisory Staff. They considered Wilson's new position completely unsound, but had no immediate opportunity to protest it. Wilson had presented a completed League Covenant to the Peace Conference on February 14 and promptly sailed for home. When he returned in March, the Staff's objections were waiting for him. Their memorandum advanced two arguments. The first was addressed to Wilson's idea that there would be no neutrals under the League. It was almost certain, the Staff maintained, that some states would decide to stay out of the League and might, therefore, be neutral in a League war. Since "justice" would require that the neutral rights of such states be respected, the League would need to exercise some restraint in its practice of strategic blockade. It was also pos-

---

[23] *House Diary*, December 27, 1918; *Daniels Diary*, November 6, 1918.
[24] Buehrig, *op. cit.*, pp. 262–263.

sible that a war might develop without any violation of League principles, and in this event the League Powers themselves might be neutral.

The Staff's second argument, and its major one, was that the presence or absence of neutrals was really an irrelevant consideration. It would be necessary to limit the practice of strategic blockade even if the war were one between the League and an outlaw Power. It was all well and good to speak of measures against the recalcitrant nation, but it was essential to remember that "*in any war there must always be two sides.*" If the League waged war without restraint, the outlaw Power would retaliate, and the war would then degenerate into a "conflict of savagery." This was a prospect which the Staff thought it most important to prevent. War might be an "abnormal condition" among states, but it was not "for that reason" to be an occasion for "unrestricted lawlessness and license." The instruments of warfare should be such as not to do violence to "the principles of humanity."[25]

The main contribution of this memorandum was to clarify the question of whether the restrictions the Naval Staff had earlier proposed were to hold in the event of a League war. The answer was now clear: they were. Wilson's original concept of the Freedom of the Seas had had three facets: the protection of neutral rights; the limitation of the action of belligerents against each other; and the closing of the seas by the League. Once he got the idea that the League would do away with neutrals, he saw clearly that the first and third facets canceled each other out. But what of the second? Had he never really accepted this aspect of House's plan? Was he that sure that the League would prevent war? Or did a "conflict of savagery" correspond to the form which he thought the League's struggle against an outlaw power would or should take?

One must guess at the President's thinking, but it is not necessary to do so for that of the Naval Advisory Staff. As it had developed in their minds, the Freedom of the Seas involved something more than the protection of neutral rights or the idea that national navies could only be used at the discretion of the League. The Staff saw the concept as addressed to a more basic problem: the need to exercise voluntary restraints in the conduct of war at sea, even if the war should be between League and outlaw.

The March memorandum found the Staff closer to, but still not at full grips with, the problem of enforcement. In the case where the League was neutral, the Staff expected enforcement to come

[25] Naval Advisory Staff, Memorandum 23, March 5, 1919, House Collection.

from the traditional source: the possibility that neutral Powers would intervene in the war if their rights were violated. The difficulty was that the Staff had gone far beyond the "traditional" restrictions. What incentive would neutral Powers have to intervene in the event the belligerents began to destroy *each other's* merchant ships? Here, and in the case of war between the League and an outlaw Power, the Staff seems to have expected the "principle of humanity" backed up by the fear of retaliation to provide the necessary mutual restraint.

The Staff's memorandum may have clarified its own position, but its impact on that of Wilson was nil. Nor did Benson's effort to rescue the Freedom of the Seas find any support among the other members of the American Peace Commission. "What has happened to 'The Freedom of the Seas,'" Secretary of State Lansing wondered in April. "Personally, I never did understand what the phrase meant or how it was to be applied."[26] The one man who thought he did was strangely silent. Colonel House did not share the President's joke either, but it was not until July, 1919, by which time both he and Wilson had left Paris, that he took note of the President's conclusion that there would be no neutrals under the League and wrote Wilson: "I do not agree with this position."

> It is quite conceivable that war might come between say France and England in which no other nations would be involved. However, the lack of sea laws would almost inevitably bring us into the conflict. If, on the other hand, we had a charter which all nations had accepted, then any two belligerents would of necessity have to conform to it or bring the world in arms upon themselves.[27]

In this letter House, like Wilson, appears to have gone back to a very pristine conception of the Freedom of the Seas: the protection of American neutrality during time of European war. There is nothing in his phraseology, at least, to remind one of his 1915 interest in outlawing the sinking of belligerent merchant ships in order to "take away much of the horror of war." So far as the Freedom of the Seas is concerned, one may choose between Wilson's epitaph in September and that penned by House in July. "This question," he wrote, ". . . is the one thing above all others that brought us into the war, and yet it is no nearer solution today than it was before Germany collapsed."

VI

It was not belligerent naval practice in general that had brought the United States into the war. It was the specific use made of a

---

[26] Memorandum, April 6, 1919, *Lansing Papers*, Library of Congress.
[27] Seymour, *op. cit.*, vol. 4, p. 497.

particular naval weapon: the German submarine. In recognition of this distinction, Admiral Benson excluded the question of submarine warfare from his recommendations regarding the limitation of strategic blockade in order to give the matter separate and special consideration.

Naval planning on this issue began, as in the case of the Freedom of the Seas, with a memorandum written for Benson by the London Planning Section in November, 1918. The memorandum argued at length that the efficiency of the submarine as a weapon against sea communications was dependent upon its illegitimate use (i.e., attacking without warning belligerent and neutral ships alike with no effort to take aboard survivors). German submarine operations were therefore typical of what could be expected in future wars. Even if belligerents should start a war with the intention of restricting the use of submarines, the "temptation" to use the weapon in its most efficacious manner would prove "too strong" for the side threatened with defeat, and the limitations would be abandoned.

This being the case, the Section concluded that the "moral and material interests of humanity" could be served only by the outright abolition of the submarine as an instrument of warfare. All extant submarines should be destroyed, and the Powers should pledge themselves to build none in the future. How was this radical solution to be achieved? It was the Section's contention that the agreement was feasible because the interests of the Great Powers coincided with those of humanity.

Great Britain, Japan, and Italy, who were dependent on sea communications, had "much to lose and little to gain by submarine warfare." They could be "confidently expected" to favor abolition. France would benefit from submarine warfare only if her enemy were Britain; otherwise she had nothing to gain from the weapon. This left only the United States to consider. (The Section excluded Germany because of the conditions of her defeat and did not mention Russia.) In general, the Section thought there was little the United States could do with submarines that could not be done with "a surface fleet second to none." The American interest in abolition was compounded, however, by a very special consideration.

> The chief reason why the United States should not build submarines is that public opinion would never permit their use in the same manner as that of our adversaries. Their chief use would be in the destruction of enemy merchant shipping. *This the national conscience would not permit*, certainly not after the German manner, while our probable adversaries would likely not be controlled by any such restrictions.[28]

[28] LPS, Memorandum 68, November 7, 1918, Navy Department, *op. cit.*, pp. 466–75, 522, italics added.

The argument that mutual self-interest would lead the Powers
to agree to abolish the submarine and to keep such an agreement
was a decided improvement over the Section's treatment of the limitations it had proposed for strategic blockade — which had largely
ignored the problem of enforcement. Nevertheless, the Section's
analysis was not without its flaws. How were Powers — which if
they *had* submarines would be unable to resist the temptation to
use them without restriction when threatened with defeat — to
be expected to resist the temptation to *build* submarines for just
such a contingency? Perhaps this was the thought in the mind of
the Commander of the American Naval Forces in Europe when he
forwarded the memorandum to Benson and Washington with the
comment that the arguments advanced did not "support the conclusions reached."

The feasibility of abolishing the submarine was also questioned
in Washington by the Navy's senior planning body, the General
Board. In a statement presented to Wilson before he left for France,
the Board (which had not yet received the Section's analysis) predicted that Britain would propose the abolition of the submarine
because it was to her advantage: she was critically dependent on
merchant shipping and had, after all, the strongest surface navy.
But the Board thought it most unlikely that submarines would
"ever be definitely proscribed by a conference composed of both
strong and weak nations, so long as there is the possibility of their
use to prevent international injustice, to preserve independence, or
for any of the other vital matters for which nations go to war."
The Board therefore concluded that the Peace Conference would do
better to work toward such rules "as will mitigate the unavoidable
horrors of war, rather than to seek to interdict the use of weapons
which have proved their efficacy."[29]

Admiral Benson's reaction to the idea of abolition was more enthusiastic. Once again, under his leadership, the conclusions of the
Paris Advisory Staff followed the earlier lead of the Planning Section. This was no accident; the personnel was largely the same in
the two groups, and the dominant thinker on both, Captain Frank
H. Schofield, was a protégé of Benson's (Interview with Commodore D. W. Knox, December 17, 1953). On Christmas Eve, 1918,
the Advisory Staff formally recommended to Wilson that the

[29] General Board to Secnav, December 2, 1918, Naval War Records,
R. G. 45, D-file; Daniels to Wilson, December 3, 1918, *Wilson Papers,*
Library of Congress. Composed of senior admirals and a few selected
captains, the Board had been the Navy's only planning body until the
establishment of the Office of Naval Operations in 1915.

United States propose to the Peace Conference the destruction of all submarines in existence and the prohibition of their future construction.

The argument to the President made no reference to the "chief reason" cited by the London Section: that the American national conscience would not permit the Navy to use submarines in the only way they could be effective. Instead, the main advantage stressed was that of "placing the plane of naval warfare on a higher level." American naval power, the Staff explained, would not be "greatly affected." The result would be "about a stand-off" in the case of Japan, and while there would be some loss of relative power with regard to Great Britain, this could be canceled by increasing the surface strength of the Navy. Happily, then, "no possible disadvantage to the United States need outweigh the higher ideal of warfare that the abolition of submarine warfare undoubtedly serves."[30]

VII

The Chief of Naval Operations and his Paris advisers were living in a world of their own. Far from having identified a proposal that the other Great Powers would recognize as being in their interest as well, the Staff soon found itself assaulted from all sides: by the British, by the French, and most of all by their own colleagues back in Washington.

In order to explain the dispute that developed between the officers in Washington and those in Paris, it is necessary to note that, after the defeat of Germany, the naval planners in the Office of Naval Operations were divided on the question of whether Japan or England was now the nation's more probable foe. Admiral Benson had assigned about half of his total staff to duty in Europe (first for the London Planning Section and then for his own Naval Advisory Staff), and he selected for this duty, by design or accident, those officers who, like himself, cast England in the role of the major enemy. As a result, the planners remaining in Washington (hereafter identified as the Washington Planning Section) were largely those who considered Japan the more probable enemy. The planning groups in Washington and Paris had, therefore, quite divergent strategic orientations, and it was this difference which underlay many of the issues that developed between them with regard to the abolition of the submarine.

[30] Naval Advisory Staff, Memorandum 8, December 24, 1918, House Collection.

The Washington Planning Section did not receive a copy of the London Section's November recommendation until January, 1919. The reaction of Captain Thomas C. Hart, the member of the Section responsible for submarine plans and operations, was electric. Until this memorandum came along, Hart protested, "it was supposed that our Naval Officers nearly unanimously appreciated the suitability of submarines for our national defense." Unlike the London Section, Hart was not worried about the Navy's use of submarines being inhibited by the American "national conscience." He doubted "if public opinion would influence our submarine operations more than it would those of certain other nations." Hart also questioned the alleged inhumanity of the weapon. Paralleling the argument advanced by the German Admiralty in 1916 (and anticipating that which Americans were to use a world war later when they felt obliged to introduce a novel and destructive weapon), Hart contrasted the 15,000 lives the Germans took with the submarine with the millions lost in the theatre of operations they had hoped to bypass: the Western Front.[31]

Spurred by Hart's arguments, the Washington Planning Section concluded that "we would make a great mistake in agreeing to give up the Submarines," and Hart and two other members were assigned the task of preparing a case to this effect. They completed their memorandum on January 17, mailed it to Paris, and alerted Benson to its coming with a cable "strongly" advising him that the "abolition of submarines should not be advocated or agreed to by our representative at the Peace Conference." By this time, of course, Benson had already asked Wilson to take the initiative in abolishing the submarine.[32]

[31]Capt. Thomas C. Hart to Acting CNO, January 6, 1919, Naval War Records, R. G. 80, C: 169–71. The German Admiralty had argued that the moral justification for the resumption of unrestricted submarine war lay in the fact that the U-boat war would produce a quick victory, whereas without it the "frightful loss of life" on the Western Front would continue. It would be "far more inhumane to sacrifice additional hundreds of thousands" than to spare an infinitesimal number of seamen who, in spite of all warnings, hasten on to their doom." The Germans, however, missed one touch the Americans were later to add. In enumerating their "hundreds of thousands," they listed only German nationals. See Chief of the Admiralty Staff to Hindenburg, December 22, 1916, Carnegie Endowment for International Peace, *Official German Documents Relating to the World War* (2 vols., New York, Oxford University Press, 1923), 2:1266–68.

[32] See Minutes, Opnav Plans Division, January 7, 1919, Naval War Records, R. G. 80, C: 100; Opnav to Benson, January 17, 1919, *ibid.*, Cable Collection; and Washington Planning Section to Benson, n.d., *ibid.*, R. G. 45, D-file.

The Washington Section's memorandum reached Benson early in February. Their case for the submarine was simple and direct.

> The United States being a self-contained nation, as far as food and war material are concerned, the destruction of our sea commerce will not compel us to make peace.
>
> On the other hand, sea commerce is vitally necessary to most European countries and to Japan.
>
> It is dangerous to evade the fact that Japan is our most probable enemy at the present time.
>
> In a war between the United States and Japan, the submarine will be an extremely valuable weapon for (1) defense of the Philippines (2) operations against Japanese commerce. There is no quicker or more effective method of defeating Japan than the cutting of her sea communication.

Captain Hart decided to buttress this statement with an independent memorandum of his own which Benson received a few weeks later. Hart described Japan as the same kind of nation Germany had been five years ago and predicted that her "predatory instinct" would soon be directed against China. It was possible that Americans might conclude that this was "no concern of ours." But it was also possible that the United States would decide to resist "such aggression," either as a "matter of justice" or in order "to forestall the world domination that might be possible if the hundreds of millions of orientals became organized and trained for war." In this event a force of submarines would be most useful, for they "would put Japan in the same position that the German submarines did the British Islands."[33]

There were some curious omissions in the arguments advanced by the Washington Section and Hart's supplementary statement, if they are viewed as an effort at rebuttal. One of the London Section's major reasons for abolition was the contention that limitation would be infeasible. Yet, while both documents from Washington made general reference to the possibility of using the submarine in a humane manner, they did not state what restrictions they thought should or could be placed on future submarine operations. Similarly, neither attempted to refute the London Section's assertion that American submarines would be restricted by public opinion while those of foreign states would not. Hart did not include either the arguments he had advanced in Washington on this point or his doubts about the alleged inhumanity of the submarine in the memorandum he sent to Benson.

---

[33] Hart to Benson, February 4, 1919, *Benson Papers,* courtesy Commodore H. H. J. Benson.

Of the two documents from Washington, only Hart's independent statement endeavored to put the case negatively, by arguing the infeasibility of abolition. The points he advanced have occurred to others in similar circumstances, but they are no less telling by virtue of being obvious. The abolition of a useful weapon, he reminded Benson, "has never occurred in history." Second, while a simple agreement to do so might be all that would be required "for *us*," others could not be relied upon to live up to it. Finally, if the United States should enter into an agreement to ban the submarine, it should only be on the condition that the agreement was tied in with a general disarmament treaty "that would at least retain all the advantages we now possess, and that we do not agree if outlawing submarines should come to stand alone."

Benson wrote Hart that he had read his paper with interest. But interest was not the same as approval, and at the end of February, the Paris Staff reaffirmed its original position with a second memorandum to Wilson. This document was in the form of a rebuttal to the memorandum of the Washington Section, and to permit the President to follow the debate, Benson enclosed both the Washington memorandum and the London Section's November statement.[34]

Why did Benson decide to air the dispute? Most probably it was because Wilson was then back in Washington, and Benson feared that the Washington Section would get his ear. And so they did through the Secretary of the Navy. Daniels told Wilson that there was "much sentiment" in the Navy for keeping submarines, and he advised the President that, while in his opinion all submarines "should be sunk and no more should be built," abolition should be postponed until "the League of Nations becomes a fact."[35]

The Paris Staff's main critique of the Washington memorandum was that it advocated, for all practical purposes, the very "policy of unrestricted submarine warfare, which drew our country into war with Germany." It was unrealistic to imply, as the Washington officers did, that submarine operations could ever be guided by any other policy. What nations, "fighting for their existence," would hesitate to choose "between effective and illegal use of submarines or national defeat"? Even officials in the British Admiralty had admitted that "under similar conditions" any other power would have done the same as Germany. There was simply no escaping the fact that "*the efficiency of the submarine as an instrument of warfare is in direct proportion to the illegality of its use.*" It was all well

[34] Benson to Hart, February 24, 1919, *Benson Papers;* Naval Advisory Staff, Memorandum 21, February 28, 1919, House Collection.
[35] Daniels to Wilson, March 4, 1919, *Daniels Papers.*

and good to talk of using submarines to cut off Japan's sea communications, but it should be recognized that this was something "which it is almost impossible for the United States to do with either legality or humanity."

The Washington Section had made its major case for the submarine by reference to the strategic contribution it could make in the event of a war with Japan, which the Washington officers had identified as "our most probable foe." On their part, the Paris officers were convinced that Britain was by far the more probable enemy. But this was a judgment which the Paris Staff had yet to reveal to Wilson, and they did not choose to do so in this memorandum. Instead, they dismissed the assertion that Japan was the most probable enemy as "a matter of judgment" and went on to argue that it was, anyway, irrelevant. American policy with regard to "principles of just warfare" should have a "stronger foundation than fear of some other nation." The moral tone of this statement was somewhat leavened by the assertion that the United States was powerful enough to defeat Japan without submarines, and the prediction that the United States would not be able to use submarines if it had them. Advancing, this time, the "chief reason" for the London Section's recommendation, the Staff declared: "Public opinion in the United States would never permit the illegal use of submarines against Japanese merchant ships, and no other use would be effective."

The argument between Washington and Paris was imperfectly joined. The Washington officers ignored the contention in Paris that the Powers would never limit their use of the submarine once war began, and the Paris officers never answered the contention in Washington that the Powers could not be trusted to keep an agreement to ban the weapon. In the case of the Washington officers, it would appear that they were simply less bothered than those in Paris by the prospect of unrestricted submarine warfare and were, therefore, inclined to view the problem of limitation with relative indifference. The content of the statement Hart had circulated in Washington (but not Paris) would support this impression, and it was obviously a suspicion that occurred to those in Paris.

Why the Paris officers, on their part, continued to ignore the problem of how to enforce a ban on the submarine — especially after Hart presented the questions that he did — is harder to explain. It is possible that the Paris Staff, since it believed public opinion would prevent the United States from using submarines effectively in any event, reasoned that the nation had little to lose from an attempt to abolish the weapon and that it should therefore accept the risk that others might evade the agreement. But if these were the Staff's thoughts, they were closely guarded. Certainly, the quality of its analysis in connection with strategic blockade, where limitations had been proposed without any rigorous reference to the question of what was to keep nations from violating them, would suggest that, whatever the Staff's views about the problem of enforcing the ban on the submarines, they were not likely to have been thought through with great care.

In understanding the Staff's approach to the problem of evasion, which appears surprisingly casual by contemporary standards, there are two points that should be borne in mind. The first is that in 1919 there seemed far less need for the kind of special inspection measures that have become customary in recent disarmament planning. No special measures were planned for Germany, although all parties at the Peace Conference agreed that she was to be prohibited from building submarines. The intelligence experience of the prewar years had been such that Lloyd George, for example, declared himself perfectly willing to rely on "the ordinary means which Governments possess of checking on the doings of other countries." Thus, the Paris Staff was not likely to have been too concerned about the problem of detecting an evasion.

The second point to note about the Staff's approach to the evasion problem is that it was, in one respect, quite modern. Both the Washington and the Paris officers expected Great Britain to take the lead in the effort to abolish the submarine, and Britain was "the most probable foe" so far as the Paris Staff was concerned. The Paris officers had, therefore, a sense of mutual interest with "the enemy" that was not shared by the Japanese-oriented strategists in Washington, and this undoubtedly contributed greatly to the difference in the sensitivity of the two groups to the problem of enforcement.

VIII

British policy on the submarine followed closely, at first, the expectations of the Americans. In November, 1918, when the War Cabinet agreed to try the Kaiser for war crimes, it planned to make the practice of unrestricted submarine warfare one of the major counts in the indictment. It was "vital," the British Attorney-General declared on that occasion, that in any future war, those responsible for its conduct realize that unrestricted submarine warfare had "definitely passed into the category of international crime. . . . The commission of such crimes, and their possible future development, menace us more directly than any other nation in the world." Pursuant to this conviction, the draft naval terms circulated by the

Admiralty late in January, 1919, called for a "universal prohibition against building submarines, together with the general destruction of existing submarines, under the effective guarantee of a League of Nations."[36]

Knowledge of the Admiralty's terms undoubtedly helped to sustain the Paris Staff when its position came under attack from Washington in February. The weight given to British support is, for example, very much evident in a comment by Captain Schofield, Benson's chief adviser, on the Washington Section's memorandum.

> For your private information [he wrote to an officer in London] I can say that the [memorandum] has been carefully placed on file and will not influence the attitude of the Naval Advisory Staff in Paris on the subject. The British agree with us completely and we are hoping that the programme will go through.

But even as he wrote his words, British policy began to change. The British draft circulated on February 17 contained merely a clause stating that Germany should accept whatever decisions the Peace Conference reached "regarding the use of submarines," and even this reference disappeared in the draft of February 25.[37]

Benson had been warned that a shift in British policy might be forthcoming. In January, he had received a report about two British Admiralty memoranda. The first, prepared by the Admiralty's Department of Naval Construction, argued that it would be "impracticable" to prohibit the submarine. In the event of war at least one enterprising nation could be counted upon to build submarines, and in order to be prepared for this contingency, all the other nations would be obliged to make plans and preparations to do the same. The Construction Department further argued that it would be most difficult to detect the building of small submarines. The memorandum concluded that it would be better to concentrate on an effort to develop rules for restricting the use of the submarine than to try to prohibit it and that, since the submarine made war more risky, there was something to be said for encouraging the development of the weapon.

At the time this memorandum was circulated, Benson was told, the majority of the department heads in the Admiralty still favored the abolition of the submarine. Since then a second memorandum

<hr>

[36] Lloyd George, *op. cit.*, vol. 1, p. 111; Naval Advisory Staff, Memorandum 17, January 28, 1919.

[37] Schofield to Knox, February 11, 1919, Naval War Records, R. G. 45, D-file; Naval Advisory Staff, Memorandum, 18, 20; February 20, 25, 1919, House Collection.

had been circulated. This paper strongly endorsed the reasoning of the Construction Department and argued that it was an "impracticable proposition to prohibit the construction of any recognized efficient instrument of war." The allies might make a "Gentleman's Agreement" to abolish the submarine, but it would break down as soon as a "serious disagreement" arose among them. The report to Benson concluded with the information that, following the circulation of the second memorandum, the opinion of the majority of the Admiralty department heads had turned against an effort to ban the submarine.[38]

It is difficult to judge if these considerations led the British government to reverse its position on the submarine, since there was still another reason why the references to abolition should have disappeared from the Admiralty's draft terms. The London Section's November analysis had been able to posit a French interest in abolition only by making the assumption that France did not plan on the possibility of a war with England. Perhaps the analysis was right and the assumption false. In any event, it became clear in February that France did not share the Anglo-American enthusiasm for abolishing the submarine. The Admiralty may, therefore, have concluded that there was no point in carrying such a provision any further in its drafts.

French opposition centered on the British proposal (which Benson heartily seconded) that all submarines taken from Germany should be destroyed. The French Naval Representative, Admiral de Bon, wished to keep France's share. When this issue was argued in the Council of Four on April 25, Lloyd George "demurred to the idea that any nation should add to its submarines." Clemenceau observed that "France had very few, whereas Great Britain had very many."

The matter was referred back to the Admirals, who delivered a split report on May 7. All except de Bon were agreed that:

> Whatever be the future as regards submarine warfare, they see no necessity for increasing submarine armaments by distributing the German submarines at a moment when the menace of the German fleet has been removed and a general reduction of armaments is desired.

De Bon's argument was that "the two questions, *viz.*, the destruction of the submarines and the future of submarine warfare cannot be separated." This language somewhat masked his real thought, which is more clearly seen in an earlier draft of the report. In this,

---

[38] Land to Sims, January 6, 1919, *Benson Papers*.

de Bon announced that he was firmly opposed to the abolition of submarines.

> To speak frankly, the suppression is especially desired because it is considered especially advantageous for certain Maritime Powers sufficiently rich to construct and maintain enormous fleets of men-of-war. The submarine is the weapon of the weak. If they employ it loyally, why should they not have the right to defend themselves?[39]

Between French opposition and British indecision, there was no chance that the Peace Conference would abolish the submarine. But if this were not enough, Benson also faced the fact that he had been unable to persuade Wilson to back the proposal. Although Germany's use of the weapon had served as the *casus belli* for his entry into the war, Wilson had made no specific plans for the future control of the submarine. The issue had, of course, been covered by his proposal for the Freedom of the Seas, but in February the President had abandoned his Second Point. Did this mean that he saw his opposition to unrestricted submarine warfare as still another "practical joke" he had played on himself and the nation? Apparently not, for during the exchange between Lloyd George and Clemenceau on April 25, Wilson interjected that he himself was opposed to submarines altogether, and hoped the time would come when they would be contrary to international law. In his view they should be regarded as outlaws.

Despite this opinion, Wilson made no effort to get the Conference to outlaw the weapon. He had ignored the Naval Advisory Staff's initial recommendation for abolition in December, 1918. Neither did he respond to a suggestion made in January by Miller that he add a clause abolishing submarines and submarine warfare to his draft of the League Covenant. (Both Miller's previous contact with Benson and the text of the suggested clause point to Benson as the inspiration for this proposal.) Silence had also greeted the Naval Staff's reaffirmation of the case for abolition in February. Doggedly, Benson persisted. On May 16 he delivered a third memorandum on the subject. This recapitulated all the Staff's earlier arguments and once more recommended abolition. The submarine would be "an anachronism under the League of Nations." Abolition was essential to "place the plane of naval warfare on a higher level."[40]

[39] Naval Advisory Staff, Memorandum 20; *United States Foreign Relations, Peace Conference* (vol. 5, pp. 240–41, vol. 7, pp. 365–66); Preliminary Draft of Admiral's Report, May 7, 1919, *Benson Papers.*

[40] Naval Advisory Staff, Memorandum 28, May 16, 1919, House Collection.

By this time Benson could not have had much hope left. Later in May, House asked him to list the naval items which he thought would remain to be acted upon after the end of the Peace Conference. In his reply Benson noted that the question of abolishing submarines might be left to the League, but that he would like to invite attention to it now. House included the item in his own list to Wilson along with a paraphrase of Benson's comment. On the text, where House had invited his attention to the question of abolition, Wilson wrote: "Not for the Conference I think."[41]

The President had ample cause to move cautiously on the recommendation of his Naval Advisory Staff. He had received contrary advice from the General Board in December, from the Washington Planning Section in February, and from Daniels in March. There is no evidence, however, that Wilson followed the debate among his naval experts with close attention or that he felt inhibited by the conflict in their judgments. It is possible that the Washington officers exercised some influence through Daniels. The Secretary's advice — that the submarine be put beyond the pale but that it be left to the League to do it — did correspond with the President's eventual position. Nevertheless, Wilson had decided before he reached Paris to leave the Freedom of the Seas to the League, and he probably needed no encouragement to do the same with the issue of submarine warfare. The President's guiding perspective continued to be that expressed by House in December: "The main thing is to get the League of Nations. With that accomplished, everything else follows or becomes a minor consideration."

The naval officers back in Washington had less opportunity than Benson to grasp the President's approach to peace-making, and the fears of the Washington Section did not fully subside until mid-July. By then Benson had returned from Paris, and the Section had received a copy of a memorandum sent to Benson by a member of the British naval delegation explaining the shift in the Admiralty's position. The British memorandum expressed its agreement with the idea that it was "in the interests of humanity" to have a universal prohibition against submarines. But unless the ban could be made "absolutely effective," a treacherous Power might secretly build submarines and have all others at its mercy. In case of doubt, it would be better to avoid abolition and try, instead, to reach an agreement regarding rules to limit the use of the weapon.

Hart's comment on this paper was caustic. Submarines, he wrote the other members of the Section, were no worse than mines or

41 Benson to House, May 21, 1919; House to Wilson, May 22, 1919, House Collection.

aerial bombing. In the Royal Navy as in our own, "abolition senti-ment is due to natural big ship conservatism and reluctance to deal with a thing that may upset the old order. We need to be on our guard that such a sentiment does not mislead us and leave us at a disadvantage with some enemy who progresses and develops along other lines." In a second statement, probably concurrent, he expressed his doubt that Benson planned "any further steps" in the direction of abolition, and since discussion of the possibility was having an "adverse effect on morale," he suggested the "advisability of intimating that our representatives in Europe should lay off of it." This proved the last word from the Navy on the matter at the Peace Conference.[42]

IX

The Naval Advisory Staff had a vision of the future. This vision was not so sharp that it saw from the doctrine of strategic blockade — designed to deprive a nation's economy of food and raw ma-terials — all the way to the doctrine of strategic bombing — de-signed to destroy the human and material components of the economy itself. Nor did the Staff see from a weapons system built around the submarine and torpedo, which could not discriminate between the adults and children on a ship, to an H-bomb-missile system that cannot discriminate between the adults and children in a whole city. But as the Staff's repeated references to the pros-pect of war degenerating into "savagery" indicate, they did sense the direction in which man's weapons and the ideas which governed their use were taking him. It was this vision, this sense of direction, that spurred their recommendations.

> Acts which before the war were held illegal [the Staff wrote in its March memorandum on the Freedom of the Seas], have been justified by interested nations on the grounds they were necessary for the suc-cessful prosecution of the war. If these acts are permitted to stand as precedents and are not hereafter formally forbidden, there will not exist in the future even such regulation of maritime warfare as was possible before the present war.

The precedents were permitted to stand. Wilson, whose differ-ences with one belligerent turned on the application of naval doc-trine and who fought another because of the use made of a naval weapon, turned out to be singularly indifferent at the Peace Con-ference to the future development of that doctrine and to the

[42] Fuller to McNamee, June 17, 1919; Hart to WPS, July 16, 1919; Hart to Evans, n.d., Naval War Records, R. G. 80, C-169–71.

prospects for the limitation and control of the weapon. Yet Wilson's insight into the military future was in some respects even sharper than that of his Naval Staff.

> ... we must take [he told the Peace Conference in January], so far as we can, a picture of the world into our minds. Is it not a startling circumstance for one thing that the great discoveries of science, that the quiet study of men in laboratories, that the thoughtful developments which have taken place in quiet lecture rooms, have now been turned to the destruction of civilization? ... The enemy whom we have just overcome had at its seats of learning some of the principal centres of scientific study and discovery, and used them in order to make destruction sudden and complete; and only the watchful, continuous co-operation of men can see to it that science, as well as armed men, is kept within the harness of civilization.[43]

In the League of Nations Wilson believed he had found a watchdog for civilization. Indeed, the establishment of a league to keep the peace so captured his attention that he showed little concern for measures to limit the destructiveness of such wars as might arise in spite of it. In this, Wilson was a classic exemplification of the American interest in measures to do away with war altogether (through *the* disarmament treaty or *the* international organization, or by means of one *final* war) to the exclusion of less spectacular and less total policy adjustments to man's most consuming outdoor social activity.

Aside from the contribution he expected the League to make to the problem, Wilson had still another reason for optimism regarding the future products of science and armed men. Unlike his Naval Staff, he believed that the precedents of the recent war spoke for themselves, that man had learned his lesson and that there was no need to italicize it through political action. In June, 1919, House recorded a conversation which explains much of the President's indifference to Benson's concern.

> The other day when the President was here, [General] Bliss and I suggested, as an argument in favor of the League of Nations, that war in future would become so atrocious that it might lead to the death of civilization. We thought the ingenuity of man would be directed toward every form of destruction. The President took the contrary view. He believed this war had been so terrible that it would restrain such efforts in future wars. Bliss and I argued with him that if two nations went to war and the balance of the world remained neutral, this might be true, but if all the world became involved, there would be no

[43] *United States Foreign Relations, Peace Conference*, vol. 3, p. 179.

bystanders to see fair play, therefore warfare would be unrestrained in every sense and would be terrible in its consequences. We could not get him to see it as we did.... The President has some peculiar quirks. This is one of them.... He has not many, but occasionally he astonishes one.[44]

House, unfortunately, had the better sense for the direction man's ingenuity would take. He also saw a problem where the President did not. The League, if it did away with neutrals, would remove one of the few restraints on the conduct of belligerents that had been, on occasion, historically effective. (The influence the United States had exercised on German submarine policy, 1915–17, was obviously fresh in his mind.) What did the League offer in return? House never thought his way through this question. His last words on the Freedom of the Seas, for example, had avoided the issue by discussing only the case in which the League was neutral. In the end, like Wilson, House fell back on the idea that the League must prevent war in the first place.

The contribution of the Naval Advisory Staff was to cut to the heart of this problem. What kind of war would *the League* fight? The ability of the Staff to raise this question can be attributed to their theory of international politics. The Staff had little hope that the League would end wars and was, accordingly, more sensitive to the question of whether and how they could be limited. The manner in which the Staff answered this question can be attributed to their theory of war. As illustrated by the quotation introducing this paper, the Staff held to a military doctrine that had begun to seem old-fashioned even in 1919. It is easy to find the flaws in this doctrine, but hard to poke fun at the considerations which moved it.

In perspective, the members of the Staff seem as futile figures as Wilson. Their diagnosis was clearer but their remedies equally faulty. The Staff never confronted the difficulties involved in securing compliance with the limitations they proposed for the practice of strategic blockade, and their assumptions about the multilateral interest in abolishing submarines were contradicted in three capitals, including their own. In one respect only was the Staff's advice borne out. An agreement to restrict submarine operations in time of war, signed in 1936 by the United States, Britain, Japan, Germany, France, and Italy, proved as fruitless as the Staff had predicted. The two most successful practitioners of unrestricted submarine warfare in World War II were the United States and Germany. The Germans abandoned the treaty restrictions piece-

[44] *House Diary*, June 23, 1919.

meal between September, 1939, and August, 1940, and American operations commenced promptly on December 7, 1941.[45]

How to judge the peacemakers of 1919? In one sense it is possible to be quite critical. They saw an edge of the future, but failed to change it. They were not so far into the box that twentieth-century western man has been building for himself with his foreign policy, military doctrine, technology, and moral ethos. They had, therefore, more freedom of innovation, of choice. In a way, what was really at stake in the abolition of the submarine was the later opportunity to abolish nuclear weapons. History has not moved in a straight line from 1919 to the present, but if the men of that year had been able to turn the development of weapons and doctrine in a different direction, they could have contributed toward the shaping of a different present. Certainly, much of the necessary political raw stuff for effective arms control — attitudes, values, perspectives — present then has since disappeared. Where are the politicians with Lloyd George's approach to inspection, the military with Benson's theories for waging war, or the publics with the American response to the *Lusitania*? We are today, and not without cause, more suspicious, more hardheaded, and less sensitive.

On the other hand, judgment should not be too critical. The dimensions of the box have since become more terrifying, but its geometry remains the same. Most of the discussion between Washington and Paris with regard to the abolition of the submarine needs only to have the terms of reference changed to make it contemporary. House was not the last diplomat to find that even the most impressive barrage of argument may be insufficient to produce a change in foreign military policy; the French were not the last "third party" to upset a possible arms control negotiation; nor was the Advisory Staff the last to have made an erroneous identification of the interest of other Powers in an arms control possibility. And if the disappearance of a multiplicity of possible enemies has eased the problem the Washington and Paris officers confronted in identifying their own strategic interest, the more recent multiplication in the number of possible strategies for dealing with one enemy has complicated it. It might be best, then, if one wishes the peacemakers of 1919 had been wiser, to wish them wiser than ourselves.

[45] Neither British nor German prewar doctrine took the agreement seriously, and the plans and preparations of each were made in the expectation it would be violated. (German policy until August, 1940, reflected Hitler's hopes for an early peace with France and Britain.) In contrast, American and Japanese prewar doctrine stressed the use of the submarine as a "counterforce" weapon, and Japanese practice, curiously, continued to be largely counterforce during the war. . . .

Finally, it might be noted that if the peacemakers of 1919 had more opportunity to achieve limitations in weapons and warfare, they also had, in a way, less incentive. It was not only that they saw what appeared to be a promising alternative in the League to enforce peace, it is also true that they stood on the edge of the future, not in it. With all due allowance for the difficulty of intercomparisons of value, it seems fair to state that there is a qualitative difference between the incentives in 1919 to abolish submarines and spare merchantmen and those of today to spare cities and abolish missiles.

On the face of it, this would appear an encouraging thought. It has, however, a discouraging side. As the Naval Staff learned to its sorrow, the recognition that one can share an interest in limiting war and weapons even with one's enemy offers no insurance that those interests can be translated into policy. In the political world there are many problems which have no answers, even with the best of incentives to find one. The problems to which the Naval Advisory Staff addressed itself provide a good example; even from hindsight, it is not possible to see how they could have achieved their ends. One might add, then, to the wish that the men of 1919 had been wiser, the hope that we will be luckier.

The ABM and MIRV Deployments

During the 1960s, the superpowers made two significant changes in their strategic nuclear forces: each built a large number of long range missiles, and each improved the accuracy of its guidance systems. By the end of the decade, the United States and the Soviet Union came close to parity in deliverable megatonnage, if not in numbers of warheads. Such parity in megatonnage might have persuaded the superpowers to slacken their efforts to improve their nuclear forces were it not for the second change. The tremendous increases in the accuracy of guidance systems threatened to make land-based missiles in hardened, underground silos vulnerable to a first strike. Facing the possible obsolescence of their land-based missiles, the two superpowers began to deploy anti-ballistic missile (ABM) systems. The deployment of such systems in turn accelerated each country's efforts to pene-

trate the other's defenses. The development of
multiple, independently-targeted, reentry vehicles
(MIRVs) was one such attempt. George W. Rathjens
discusses the effects of ABM and MIRV development
on the arms race. Both superpowers invoked the
Chinese nuclear threat to justify their ABM systems.
Robert S. McNamara presents the Chinese (or area
defense) rationale for the American ABM system;
Richard Nixon, the protection-of-the-deterrent (or
hard-point defense) rationale. Donald G. Brennan
argues that population defense is both feasible and
desirable.

The Dynamics of the Arms Race

GEORGE W. RATHJENS

The world stands at a critical juncture in the history of the strategic arms race. Within the past two years both the U.S. and the
U.S.S.R. have decided to deploy new generations of offensive and defensive nuclear weapons systems. These developments, stimulated
in part by the emergence of China as a nuclear power, threaten
to upset the qualitatively stable "balance of terror" that has prevailed between the two superpowers during most of the 1960's.
The new weapons programs portend for the 1970's a decade of
greatly increased military budgets, with all the concomitant social
and political costs these entail for both countries. Moreover, it appears virtually certain that at the end of all this effort and all this
spending neither nation will have significantly advanced its own
security. On the contrary, it seems likely that another upward
spiral in the arms race would simply make a nuclear exchange
more probable, more damaging or both.

As an alternative to this prospect, the expectation of serious arms-limitation talks between the U.S. and the U.S.S.R. holds forth the possibility of at least preventing an acceleration of the arms race. In the circumstances it seems worthwhile to inquire into the nature of the forces that impel an arms race. In doing so we may determine how best to damp this newest cycle of military competition, either by mutual agreement or by unilateral restraint, before it is beyond control.

There are a number of new weapons systems under development in both the U.S. and the U.S.S.R., but the possibilities that are likely to be at the center of discussion not only in the forthcoming negotiations but also in the current Congressional debate are the anti-ballistic-missile (ABM) concept and the multiple-independently-targeted-reentry-vehicle (MIRV) concept. These systems, one defensive and the other offensive, can usefully be discussed together because of the way they interact. In fact, the intrinsic dynamics of the arms race can be effectively illustrated by concentrating on these two developments.

It is now 18 months since former Secretary of Defense McNamara announced the decision of the Johnson Administration to proceed with the deployment of the Sentinel system: a "thin" ABM system originally described as being intended to cope with a hypothetical Chinese missile attack during the 1970's. The technology of the Sentinel system and some of the means a determined adversary might employ to defeat it were discussed in some detail a year ago in this magazine [see "Anti-Ballistic-Missile Systems," by Richard L. Garwin and Hans A. Bethe; *Scientific American,* March, 1968]. At this point I should like to review some of the background of the ABM problem.

Before the Sentinel decision most of the interest in a ballistic-missile defense for the U.S. was focused on the Nike-X program. This concept involved the use of two kinds of interceptor to protect the population and industry of the country against a hypothetical Russian missile attack. Interception would first be attempted outside the earth's atmosphere with Spartans, long-range missiles with nuclear warheads in the megaton range. The effectiveness of the defense, however, would depend primarily on the use of Sprints, short-range missiles with kiloton-yield warheads designed to intercept incoming missiles after they have reentered the atmosphere. The system also envisaged suitable radars and computers to control the engagement.

The Spartans could in principle defend large areas; indeed, about a dozen sites could defend the entire country. A defense based solely on them could be rendered ineffective, however, by fairly simple countermeasures, in particular by large numbers of lightweight decoys (which would be indistinguishable to a radar from an actual reentry vehicle containing a warhead) or by measures that would make the radar ineffective, for example the use of nuclear explosions, electronic jammers or light, widely dispersed metal "chaff."

The effectiveness of a Sprint defense would be less degraded by such counter-measures. Light decoys could be distinguished from actual reentry vehicles because they would be disproportionately slowed by the atmosphere and possibly because their wake in the atmosphere would be different. Radar blackout would also be much less of a problem. Because of their short range, however, Sprints could defend only those targets in their immediate vicinity. Thus an adversary could choose to attack some cities with enough weapons to overwhelm the defense while leaving others untargeted. Heavy radioactive fallout could also be produced over large parts of the country by an adversary's delivering large-yield weapons outside the areas covered by Sprint defenses. A nationwide defense of the Sprint type would therefore require a nationwide fallout-shelter program.

Although combining Sprints and Spartans in a single system, as was proposed for the Nike-X system, would complicate an adversary's penetration problem, in a competition with a determined and resourceful adversary the advantage in an offense-defense duel would still lie with the offense. As a result, in spite of strong advocacy by the Army and support from the other branches of the military and from members of Congress, the decision to deploy the Nike-X system was never made.

At the heart of the debate about whether or not to deploy the Nike-X system was the question of what the Russian reaction to such a decision would be. It was generally conceded that the system might well save large numbers of lives in the event of war, if the U.S.S.R. were simply to employ the forces projected in the available intelligence estimates. On that basis proponents argued in favor of deployment in spite of the high costs, variously estimated as being from $13 billion to $50 billion. Such deployment was opposed, particularly by Secretary McNamara, because of the belief that the U.S.S.R. could and would improve its offensive capabilities in order to negate whatever effectiveness the system might 'have had. Indeed, because the deployment of a U.S. ABM system would introduce large uncertainties into the calculus of the strategic balance, there were occasional expressions of concern that the U.S.S.R. might overreact. Hence the damage inflicted on us in the event of war might even be greater than it would be if the Nike-X system were not deployed.

The Sentinel system announced in 1967 would have far less capability than the Nike-X system. It would include some Sprint missiles to defend key radars (five or six perimeter acquisition radars, or PARs, to be deployed across the northern part of the country), but the main defense would be provided by Spartan missiles located to provide a "thin" or "light" defense for the entire country [see illustration]. Spokesmen for the Johnson Administration argued that such a deployment would be almost completely effective in dealing

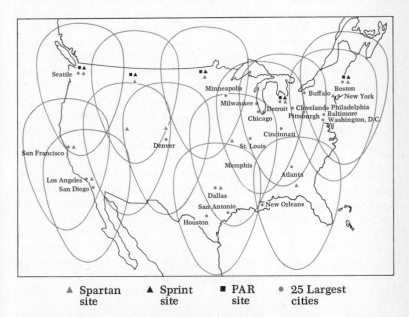

| ▲ Spartan site | ▲ Sprint site | ■ PAR site | ● 25 Largest cities |

Sentinel system, a "thin" anti-ballistic-missile (ABM) system described by the Johnson Administration as being intended to defend the U.S. against a hypothetical Chinese missile attack in the 1970's, is depicted on this map in its original form. The main defense would be provided by Spartan missiles, long-range ABM missiles with nuclear warheads in the megaton range, designed to intercept incoming missiles outside the earth's atmosphere. The Spartans would be deployed at about 14 locations in order to provide a "thin" or "light" area defense of the whole country. The range of each "farm" of Spartans is indicated by the egg-shaped area around it; for missiles attacking over the northern horizon, the intercept range of the Spartan is elongated somewhat to the south. The Sentinel system would also include some Sprint missiles, short-range ABM missiles with much smaller warheads, designed to intercept incoming missiles after they have reentered the atmosphere. The Sprints were originally to be deployed to defend only the five or six perimeter acquisition radars, or PAR's, which were to be deployed across the northern part of the country. In President Nixon's proposed modification of the Sentinel scheme Spartans, Sprints and PAR sites would be deployed in a somewhat different array to provide additional protection for our land-based retaliatory forces against a hypothetical surprise attack by the Russians.

with a possible Chinese missile attack during the 1970's, but that it would be so ineffective against a possible Russian attack that the U.S.S.R. would not feel obliged to improve its strategic offensive forces as a response to the decision. Both arguments were seriously questioned.

Garwin and Bethe, for example, contended that even the first-generation Chinese missiles might well be equipped with penetration aids that would defeat the Sentinel system. Other experts pointed out that the system, like the Nike-X system, could never be tested adequately short of actual war, and that in view of its complexity there would be a high probability of a catastrophic failure.

The contention that the U.S.S.R. would not react to the Sentinel decision seemed at least as questionable as the assertions of great effectiveness against the Chinese. Whatever the initial capability of the Sentinel system, it seemed clear that the Sentinel decision would at least shorten the lead time for the deployment of a system of the Nike-X type. Moreover, the fact that Sentinel was strongly and publicly supported as a first step toward an "anti-Soviet" system could hardly escape the attention of Russian decision-makers.

Since the announcement of the Sentinel decision, and particularly since the change in the Administration, the arguments in favor of the decision have become confused. It has been variously suggested by Administration spokesmen that the primary purpose would be (1) to defend the American population and industry against a possible Chinese attack, (2) to provide at least some protection for population and industry against a possible Russian attack, (3) to defend Minuteman missile sites against a possible Russian attack and (4) to serve as a bargaining counter in strategic-arms-limitation talks with the U.S.S.R. It might be noted that no one in recent months has seriously suggested that a Russian reaction to the decision is unlikely. In fact, all but the first of the arguments cited above imply the likelihood of a Russian response.

President Nixon's reaffirmation, albeit with some modification, of the Sentinel decision was presumably made on the basis of his judgment that the first and third of the aforementioned arguments justify the costs of such a system, not only the direct dollar cost but also the cost in terms of the impact on Russian decision-making and any other costs that may be imputed to the system. Whether or not his decision is correct depends strongly on how serious the possibility of a Russian reaction is. Before dealing further with that question it will be useful to bring MIRV's into the picture.

The problem of simulating an actual warhead reentry vehicle is a comparatively easy one, provided that the attacker need not be

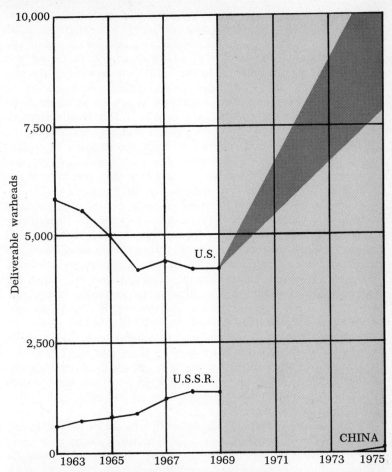

Strategic offensive forces of the U.S., the U.S.S.R., and China are compared here in terms of the number of megaton-range nuclear warheads the U.S. could deliver against either of the two other powers as of a given date, and vice versa. The U.S. missile force grew rapidly during the 1960's, offsetting a partial phasing-out of intercontinental bombers. The Russian bomber force, meanwhile, has remained at a constant level, while their missile force has grown steadily and shows no sign of leveling off. Thus at present the U.S. maintains a superiority over the U.S.S.R. of about four to one in numbers of deliverable warheads. The hypothetical Chinese strategic force was recently estimated by Secretary of Defense Laird to be 20 to 30 deliverable warheads by the mid-1970's. The effect of the present U.S. program to equip its Minuteman III and its Poseidon missiles with multiple independently targeted reentry vehicles (MIRV's) would be to increase greatly the number of U.S. deliverable warheads by 1975 (*dark gray area*). It is not known what compensating actions, if any, will be taken by the other powers in response to this development. It has been estimated by former Secretary of Defense McNamara that 400 one-megaton warheads would suffice to destroy 75 percent of the industry and 33 percent of the population of the U.S.S.R.

concerned with differences in the interaction of decoys and warheads with the atmosphere during reentry. If one wishes to build decoys and warheads that will be indistinguishable down to low altitudes, however, the problem is a formidable one, particularly if one demands high confidence in the indistinguishability of the two types of object. Improved radar resolution and increased traffic-handling and data-processing capability make the problem of effective decoy design increasingly difficult. The development of interceptors capable of high acceleration will also complicate the offense's problem. With such interceptors the decision to engage reentering objects can be deferred until they are well down into the atmosphere; the longer the defense can wait, the more stringent are the demands of decoy simulation on the offense.

As the problem becomes more difficult, the ratio of decoy weight to warhead weight increases. There comes a point at which, if one wants really high confidence of penetration, one might just as well use several warheads on each missile rather than a single warhead and several decoys, each of which may be as heavy, or nearly as heavy, as a warhead. Hence multiple warheads are in a sense the ultimate in high-confidence penetration aids (assuming that one relies on exhaustion or saturation of defense capabilities as the preferred tactic for defeating the defense). To be effective, however, multiple warheads must be sufficiently separated so that a single interceptor burst will not destroy more than one incoming warhead. Moreover, the utility of multiple warheads for destroying targets, particularly small ones that would not justify attack by more than one or two small warheads, will be greatly enhanced if they can be individually guided.

In principle each reentry vehicle could have its own "post-boost" guidance and propulsion system. That, however, is not the concept of the MIRV's in our Poseidon and Minuteman III missile systems, which are now under development. Rather, a single guidance and propulsion system will control the orientation and velocity of a "bus" from which reentry vehicles will be released sequentially [see illustration]. After each release there will be a further adjustment in the velocity and direction of the bus. Thus each reentry vehicle can be directed to a separate target. The targets can be rather widely separated, the actual separation depending on how much energy (and therefore weight) one is willing to expend in the post-boost maneuvers of the bus. It is an ingenious — and demanding — concept.

Two rationales have been advanced for the decision to proceed with the U.S. MIRV programs. One is that with MIRV's the U.S. can have a high confidence of being able to penetrate an adversary's ABM defenses. The apparent deployment of a limited Russian ABM system in the vicinity of Moscow and U.S. concern about a possibly more widespread Russian ABM-system deployment have been important considerations in the decision to go ahead with the U.S. MIRV programs.

The second rationale is that a MIRV system enables one to strike more targets with a given number of boosters than would be the case if one were using one warhead per missile. This rationale has been important for two reasons.

First, it enabled spokesmen for the Johnson Administration to argue against expanding the size of our strategic missile force during a period when Russian forces were growing rapidly. They were able to contend in the face of political opposition on both flanks that, whereas we did not contemplate expanding the number of our offensive missiles, the number of warheads we could deliver would increase rapidly.

Second, it raised the prospect of a missile force that could be used as a very effective "counterforce" weapon. This means that with MIRV's a limited number of missiles might be capable of destroying a larger intercontinental-ballistic-missile (ICBM) force in a preemptive attack. To achieve this performance, however, particularly against hardened offensive missile sites, would require a substantial improvement in accuracy and a high post-boost reliability — no mean feats with a device as complicated as the MIRV bus.

What bearing will the deployment of the ABM and the MIRV systems have on the future of the arms race? In attempting to answer this difficult question it is instructive to consider the extent to which the choices of each of the superpowers regarding strategic weapons have been influenced by the other's decisions.

The actual role of this action-reaction phenomenon is a matter of considerable debate in American defense circles. Indeed, the differences in views on this question account for most of the dispute of the past few years regarding the objectives to be served by strategic forces and their desired size and qualities. Thus whether the U.S. should be content with an adequate retaliatory, or "assured destruction," capability or go further and try to build a capability that would permit us to reduce damage to ourselves in the event of war must clearly depend on a judgment on whether Russian defense decisions could be influenced significantly by our decision. Those who have felt that Russian defense planning would be responsive to our actions have held that for the most part any attempt by us to develop such "damage-limiting" capabilities with respect to the U.S.S.R. would be an effort doomed to failure. The U.S.S.R. would simply improve its offensive capabilities to offset the effects of any

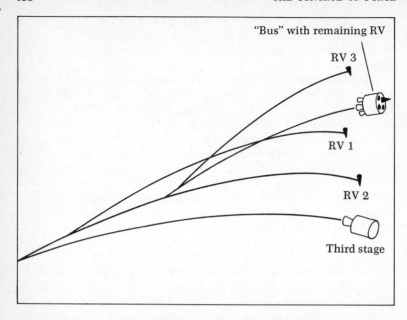

MIRV concept on which the current U.S. Minuteman III and Poseidon programs are based is illustrated by the idealized drawings on these two pages. Each offensive missile will carry aloft a "bus," containing a number of individual reentry vehicles, or RV's (in this example four are shown). A single guidance and propulsion system will control the orientation and velocity of the bus, from which the reentry vehicles will be released sequentially (*left*). After each release there will

measures we might take. This was the basis for the rejection by the American leadership of the requests by the Army for large-scale ABM-system deployment and for the rejection of requests by the Air Force for much larger ICBM forces.

Although there is considerable evidence to support the claim that the action-reaction phenomenon does apply to defense decision-making, to explain all the major decisions of the superpowers in terms of an action-reaction hypothesis is an obvious oversimplification. The American MIRV deployment has been rationalized as a logical response to a possible Russian ABM-system deployment, but there were also other motivations that were important: the desire to keep our total missile force constant while increasing the number of warheads we could deploy, the long-term possibility of MIRV's giving us an effective counterforce capability, and finally the simple desire to bring to fruition an interesting and elegant technological concept.

Nevertheless, the action-reaction phenomenon, with the reaction often premature and/or exaggerated, has clearly been a major stimulant of the strategic arms race. Examples from the past can

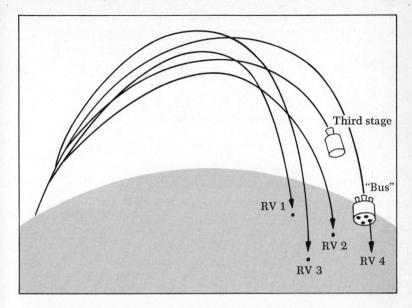

Third stage

"Bus"

RV 1

RV 2

RV 3

RV 4

be a further adjustment in the velocity and the direction of the bus. Thus each reentry vehicle can be directed to a separate target (*right*). The actual separation of the targets depends on how much energy (and therefore weight) one is willing to expend in the post-boost maneuvers of the bus. Besides being a potentially attractive means of penetrating an adversary's ABM defenses, MIRV's could conceivably be effective some day as a "counterforce" weapon, that is, a system capable of destroying the adversary's strategic offensive forces in a preemptive attack.

be cited to support this point: (1) the American reaction, indeed overreaction, to uncertainty at the time of the "missile gap," which played a central role in the 1960 Presidential election but was soon afterward shown by improved intelligence to be, if anything, in favor of the U.S.; (2) the Russian decision to deploy the "Tallinn" air-defense system, possibly made in the mistaken expectation that the U.S. would go ahead with the deployment of B-70 bombers or SR-71 strike-reconnaissance aircraft; (3) the U.S. response to the Tallinn system (which until recently was thought to be an ABM system) and to the possible extension of the Moscow ABM system into a countrywide system. It was in order to have high assurance of its ability to get through these possible Russian ABM defenses that the U.S. embarked on the development of various penetration aids and even of new missiles: Minuteman III and Poseidon.

These examples have in common the fact that if doubt exists about the capabilities or intentions of an adversary, prudence normally requires that one respond not on the basis of what one expects but on a considerably more pessimistic projection. The U.S. gener-

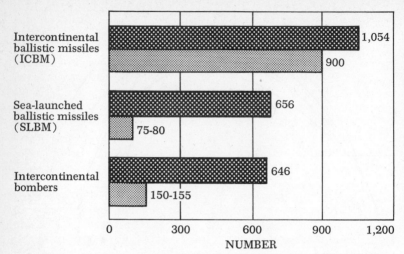

Inventory of the intercontinental delivery vehicles possessed by the U.S. (*dark gray*) and the U.S.S.R. (*light gray*) as of October, 1968, shows that in this category also the U.S. continues to hold a clear superiority over the U.S.S.R. This measure is not entirely satisfactory, however, in that it does not take into account qualitative differences in the various systems, the expected interactions during a nuclear exchange or the match of the weapons with the targets. When such factors are taken into account, the differences between the U.S. and the U.S.S.R. are not significant. In his final "posture" statement for fiscal 1969, for example, former Secretary McNamara estimated that, barring drastic changes in the strategic balance, in an all-out nuclear exchange in the mid-1970's each country could inflict a minimum of 120 million fatalities on the other — regardless of which country struck first.

ally bases its plans — and makes much of the fact — on what has become known as the "greater-than-expected threat." In so doing, the Americans (and presumably the Russians) have often overreacted. The extent of the overreaction is directly dependent on the degree of uncertainty about any adversary's intentions and capabilities.

The problem is compounded by lead-time requirements for response. According to the Johnson Administration, the decisions to go ahead with Minuteman III, Poseidon and Sentinel had to be made when they were because of the possibility that in the mid-1970's the Russians might have a reasonably effective ABM system and the Chinese an ICBM capability. The Russians had to make a decision to develop the Tallinn system (if the decision was made because of the B-70 program) long before we ourselves knew whether or not we would deploy an operational B-70 force.

Once the decisions to respond to ambiguous indications of adversary activity were made it often proved impossible to modify the response, even when new intelligence became available. For example, between the time the Sentinel decision was announced and the first Congressional debate on the appropriation took place during the summer of 1968, evidence became available that the Chinese threat was not developing as rapidly as had been feared. Yet in spite of this information those in Congress who attempted at that time to defer the appropriation for Sentinel failed. Similarly, at this writing, as the Poseidon and Minuteman III programs begin to gain momentum, it seems much less likely than it did at the time of their conception that the U.S.S.R. will deploy the kind of ABM system that was the Johnson Administration's main rationale for these programs. On the Russian side, the Tallinn deployment continued long after it became clear that no operational B-70 force would ever be built.

Of the kinds of weapons development that can stimulate over-response on the part of one's adversary, it is hard to imagine one more troublesome than ABM defenses. In addition to uncertainty about adversary intentions and the need (because of lead-time requirements) for early response to what the adversary might do, there is the added fact that the uncertainties about how well an ABM system might perform are far larger than they are for strategic offensive systems. The conservative defense planner will design his ABM system on the assumption that it may not work as well as he hopes, that is, he will overdesign it to take into account as fully as he can all imaginable modes of failure and enemy offensive threats. The offensive planner, on the other hand, will assume that the defense might perform much better than he expects and will overdesign his response. Thus there is overreaction on both sides. These uncertainties result in a divergent process: an arms race with no apparent limits other than economic ones, each round being more expensive than the last. Moreover, because of over-reaction on the part of the offense there may be an increase in the ability of each side to inflict damage on the other.

All one needs to make this possibility a reality is a triggering mechanism. The Russian ABM program, by stimulating the Minuteman III and Poseidon programs, may have served that purpose. The Chinese nuclear program may also have triggered an action-reaction chain, of which the Sentinel response is the second link [*See illustration on page 500*].

It can be assumed that there will be considerable pressure and effort to make Sentinel highly effective against a "greater than expected" Chinese threat. Such a system will undoubtedly have some capability against Russian ICBM's. Russian decision-makers, who must assume that Sentinel might perform better than they expect, will at least have to consider this possibility as they plan their offensive capabilities. More important, they will have to respond on the assumption that the Sentinel decision may foreshadow a decision to build an anti-Russian ABM system. Hence it is probably not a question of whether the U.S.S.R. will respond to Sentinel but rather of whether the U.S.S.R. will limit its response to one that does not require a U.S. counterresponse, and of whether it is too late to stop the Sentinel deployment.

It is apparent that reduction in uncertainty about adversary intentions and capabilities is a *sine qua non* to curtailing the strategic arms race. There are a number of ways to accomplish this (in addition to the gathering of intelligence, which obviously makes a great contribution).

First, there is unilateral disclosure. In the case of the U.S. there has been a conscious effort to inform both the American public and the Russian leadership of the rationale for many American decisions regarding strategic systems and, to the extent consistent with security, of U.S. capabilities. This has been done particularly through the release by the Secretary of Defense of an annual "posture" statement, a practice that, it is hoped, will be continued by the U.S. and will be emulated someday by the U.S.S.R. This would be in the interest of both countries. Because there has been no corresponding effort by the Russians the U.S. probably overreacts to Russian decisions more than the U.S.S.R. does to American decisions. (At least it is easier to trace a casual relationship between Russian decisions and U.S. reactions than it is between U.S. decisions and Russian reactions.)

Second, negotiations to curtail the arms race (even if abortive) or any other dialogue may be very useful if such efforts result in a reduction of uncertainty about the policies, capabilities or intentions of the parties.

Third, some weapons systems may be less productive of uncertainty than others that might be chosen instead. For example, it is likely to be less difficult to measure the size of a force of submarine-launched or fixed missiles than it is to measure the size of a mobile land force. Similarly, it would be easier to persuade an adversary that a small missile carried only a single warhead than would be the case with a large vehicle. Such considerations must be borne in mind in evaluating alternative weapons systems.

In short, although uncertainty about adversary capabilities and intentions may not always be bad (in some instances the existence of uncertainty has contributed to deterrence), the U.S. and the U.S.S.R. would seem well advised to make great efforts to avoid giving each other cause for overreacting to decisions because of inadequate understanding of their meaning.

The importance of somehow breaking the action-reaction chains that seem to drive the arms race is obvious when one considers the enormous resources involved that could otherwise be used to meet pressing social needs. In addition, there is particular importance in doing so at present because the concurrent deployment of MIRV's and ABM systems is likely to have drastic destabilizing consequences. It is conceivable that one of the superpowers with an ABM system might develop MIRV's to the point where it could use them to destroy the bulk of its adversary's ICBM force in a preemptive attack. Its air and ABM defenses would then have to deal with a much degraded retaliatory blow, consisting of the sea-launched forces and any ICBM's and aircraft that might have survived the preemptive attack. The problems of defense in such a contingency would remain formidable. They would be significantly less difficult, however, than if the adversary's ICBM force had not been seriously depleted. In fact, the defense problem would be relatively simple if a large fraction of the adversary's retaliatory capability were, as is true for the U.S. and to a far greater degree for the U.S.S.R., in its land-based ICBM's, most of which would presumably have been destroyed.

It may seem unlikely that either superpower would initiate such a preemptive attack, in view of the great uncertainties in effectiveness (particularly with respect to defense) and the disastrous consequences if even a comparatively small fraction of the adversary's retaliatory force should get through. With both MIRV's and an ABM system, however, such a preemptive attack would not seem as unlikely as it does now. It might not appear irrational to some, for example, if an uncontrollable nuclear exchange seemed almost certain, and if by striking first one could limit damage to a significantly lower level than if the adversary were to strike the first blow. In short, if one or both of the two superpowers had such capabilities, the world would be a much more unstable place than it is now.

Obviously neither superpower would permit its adversary to develop such capabilities without responding, if it could, by strengthening its retaliatory forces. The response problem becomes more difficult, however, if the adversary develops both MIRV's and an ABM system than if only one is developed.

Against a MIRV threat alone there are such obvious responses as defense of ICBM sites or greater reliance on sea-launched or other mobile systems. Such responses are likely to be acceptable because, whereas the costs of highly invulnerable systems are large (perhaps several times larger than the costs of simple undefended ICBM's), only relatively small numbers of such secure retaliatory weapons would be required to provide an adequate "assured destruction" capability. Indeed, a force the size of the present Polaris sub-

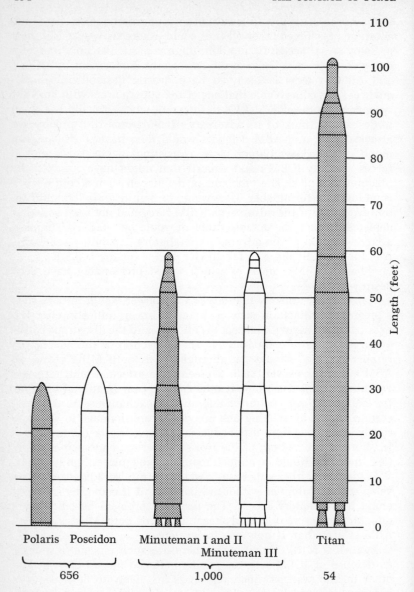

U.S. offensive missiles currently deployed or under development are drawn here to scale. The sea-based Polaris and Poseidon and the land-based Minuteman are capable of carrying warheads with a total explosive yield of about one megaton each. The land-based Titan II can carry a warhead of more than five megatons. Poseidon and Minuteman III, which are under development, are designed to carry MIRV warheads. The total number of missiles scheduled for deployment in each category is indicated at the bottom.

marine fleet would seem to be more than adequate. The response to an ABM system alone might also be kept within acceptable limits because the expenditures required to offset the effects of defense are likely to be small compared with the costs of the defense.

If it is necessary to acquire retaliatory capabilities that are comparatively invulnerable to MIRV attack in numbers sufficient to saturate or exhaust ABM defenses, however, the total cost could be very great. In fact, if one continued to rely heavily on exhaustion of defenses as the preferred technique for penetration, the offense might no longer have a significant cost-effectiveness advantage over the defense. Thus the concurrent development of MIRV's and ABM systems raises the specter of a more precarious balance of terror a few years hence, a rapidly escalating arms race in the attempt to prevent the instabilities from getting out of hand, or quite possibly both.

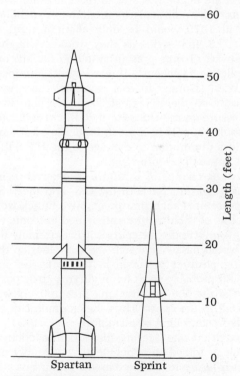

U.S. defensive missiles currently being deployed as part of the modified Sentinel system are drawn here to scale. The Spartan and Sprint carry warheads in the megaton range and kiloton range respectively.

With this background about the roles of uncertainty and the action-reaction phenomenon in stimulating the arms race, one can draw some general conclusions about the functions and qualities of future strategic forces. We must first recognize that two kinds of instability must be considered: crisis instability (the possibility that when war seems imminent, one side or the other will be motivated to attack preemptively in the hope of limiting damage to itself) and arms-race instability (the possibility that the development or deployment decisions of one country, or even the possibility of such decisions, may trigger new development or deployment decisions by another country).

The first kind of instability is illustrated in the chart on the opposite page, which is based on former Secretary McNamara's posture statement for fiscal 1967. This shows that — assuming two possible expanded Russian threats, various damage-limiting efforts by the U.S. and failure of the U.S.S.R. to react to extensive U.S. damage-limiting efforts by improving its retaliatory capability — American fatalities in 1975 would be only about a third as great in the event of a U.S. first strike as they would be in the case of a Russian first strike. (In the present situation the advantage of the attacker is negligible.) Obviously if war seemed imminent, with the strategic balances assumed in this example, there would be tremendous pressure on the U.S. to strike first. There would be corresponding pressure on the U.S.S.R. to do likewise if a Russian first strike could result not only in a much higher level of damage to the U.S. but also in a diminution in damage to the U.S.S.R. The incentives would be mutually reinforcing.

To minimize the chance of a failure of deterrence in a time of crisis, it seems important for both the U.S. and the U.S.S.R. to develop strategic postures such that preemptive attack would have as small an effect as possible on the anticipated outcome of a thermonuclear exchange. Actually, of course, it is extremely unlikely that the Russians would passively watch the U.S. develop the extensive damage-limiting postures assumed in the foregoing example. Instead they would probably react by modifying their posture so that the advantage to the U.S. of attacking preemptively would be less than is indicated in the chart. Thus the example can also be used to illustrate the second kind of instability.

To the extent that one accepts the action-reaction view of the arms race, one is forced to conclude that virtually anything we might attempt in order to reduce damage to ourselves in the event of war is likely to provoke an escalation in the race. Moreover, many of the choices we might make with damage limitation in mind are likely to make preemptive attack more attractive and war therefore more probable. The concurrent development of MIRV's and ABM systems is a particularly good example of this.

One is struck by the fact that there is an inherent inconsonance in the objectives spelled out in our basic military policy, namely "to deter aggression at any level and, should deterrence fail, to terminate hostilities in concert with our allies under conditions of relative advantage while limiting damage to the U.S. and allied interests." Hard choices must be made between attempting to minimize the chance of war's occurring in a time of crisis and attempting to minimize the consequences if it does occur.

The decisions made by U.S. planners in recent years with respect to new weapons development and deployment reflect a somewhat inconsistent philosophy on this point. The U.S. has generally avoided actions whose primary rationale was to limit damage that the U.S.S.R. might inflict on it, actions to which the Russians would probably respond. Accordingly the U.S. has not deployed an anti-Russian ABM system and has given air defense a low priority.

On the other hand, where there were reasons other than a desire to improve American damage-limiting capability with respect to the U.S.S.R., the U.S. has proceeded with programs in spite of their probably escalating effect on the arms race or their effect on first-strike incentives. This was true in the case of the MIRV's and Sentinel.

The U.S. will face more such decisions. For example it may appear necessary to change the U.S. strategic offensive posture in order to make American forces less vulnerable to possible Russian MIRV attack. The nature of these decisions will depend on the importance attached to the action-reaction phenomenon and to the effect of improved counterforce capabilities on the probability of war. Emphasis on these two factors implies discounting options that would increase U.S. counterforce capability against Russian strategic forces, which in turn might provoke an expansion of Russian offensive forces. Options requiring long lead times would also be discounted, since decisions regarding them might have to be made while there was still uncertainty about whether the U.S.S.R. was developing MIRV's.

Should more weight be given in the future to developing damage-limiting capabilities? Or should more weight be given to minimizing the probability of a thermonuclear exchange and curtailing the strategic arms race? It is hard to see how one can have it both ways.

In spite of some changes in technology, there is little to indicate that the U.S. could get very far with damage-limiting efforts, con-

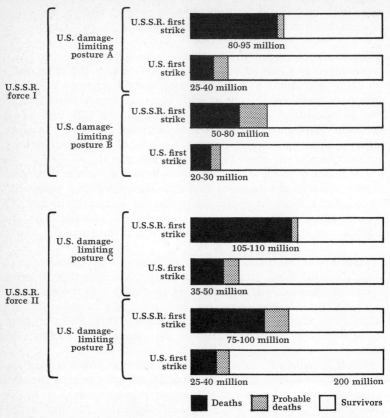

U.S. fatalities in a variety of hypothetical nuclear exchanges in the mid-1970's are rounded off to the nearest five million in this bar chart. U.S.S.R. force *I* is basically an extrapolation of current Russian forces reflecting some future growth in both offensive and defensive capability; force *II* assumes a major Russian response to our deployment of an ABM system. Two of the four U.S. damage-limiting programs, postures *A* and *B*, are tailored against U.S.S.R. force *I*; the other two, postures *C* and *D*, are tailored against U.S.S.R. force *II*. The chart illustrates the basic incompatibility between a policy of attempting to minimize the consequences of nuclear war and a policy of attempting to minimize the probability of nuclear war. If war seemed imminent, with the strategic balances as hypothesized in this chart, there would be tremendous pressure on both sides to strike first, and as a result of this added incentive the chances of escalation would be enhanced. The chart is based on information contained in former Secretary McNamara's posture statement for fiscal 1967.

sidering the determination of the Russians and the options available to them for denying the attainment of such U.S. capabilities. The emergence of new nuclear powers, the rapid pace of technological advance and the other important demands on American resources suggest that a clear first priority should be assigned to moderating the action-reaction cycle. Moving toward greater emphasis on damage-limitation would seem justified only if the U.S. can persuade itself that the Russians will not react to American moves as the U.S. would to theirs, and if means can be chosen that will not increase the probability of war.

No treatment of the dynamics of the strategic arms race would be complete without some discussion of the possibility of ending it, or at least curtailing it, through negotiations. Both the urgency and the opportunity are great, but the latter may be waning. This opportunity is in part a consequence of the present military balance, as well as of somewhat changed views in both the U.S. and the U.S.S.R. about strategic capabilities and objectives.

With the rapid growth in its strategic offensive forces during the past few years, the U.S.S.R. can at long last enter negotiations without conceding inferiority or (which is worse from the Russian point of view) exposing itself to the possibility of being frozen in such a position. Moreover, the U.S.S.R. may at long last be prepared to accept the prevailing American view about the action-reaction phenomenon, and about the intrinsic advantage of the offense and the futility of defense. The apparent decision of the Russians not to proceed with a nation-wide ABM system at present, and their professed willingness to enter into negotiations to control both offensive and defensive systems, may be evidence of this convergence of viewpoints.

On the American side there is at long last a quite general, if not yet universal, acceptance of the concept of nuclear "sufficiency": the idea that beyond a certain point increased nuclear force cannot be translated into useful political power. Acceptance of this concept is an almost necessary condition to termination of the arms race.

In considering negotiations with the U.S.S.R. on the strategic arms problem, the first factor to be kept in mind is the objectives to be sought. It would be a mistake to expect too much or to aspire to too little. One obvious aim is to reduce strategic armaments in order to lessen significantly the damage that would be sustained by the U.S. (and the U.S.S.R.) in the event of a nuclear exchange. Regrettably this goal is not likely to be realized in the near future. In the first place, any initial understandings will probably not involve reductions in strategic forces. Even if they did, the reductions would be limited. One cannot expect potential damage levels to be lowered by more than a few percent, even with fairly substantial cuts in strategic forces, because the capabilities of the superpowers are already so great.

Other objectives have been considered: reducing the incentives to strike preemptively in time of crisis, reducing the probability of

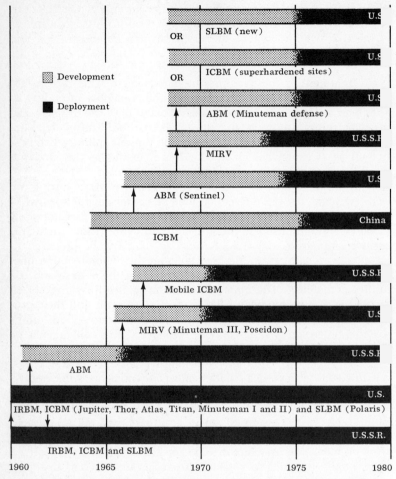

Action-reaction phenomenon, stimulated in most cases by uncertainty about an adversary's intentions and capabilities, characterizes the dynamics of the arms race. Starting at bottom left, American overreaction to uncertainty at the time of the erroneous "missile gap" in 1960 led to the massive growth of U.S. missile forces during the 1960's. The scale of this deployment may have led in turn to the recent large Russian buildup in strategic offensive forces and also to the deployment of a limited ABM system around Moscow. The U.S. response to the possible extension of the Moscow ABM system into a countrywide system (and to the deployment of a Russian anti-aircraft system, which until recently was thought to be a countrywide ABM system) was to equip its Minuteman III and Poseidon missiles with MIRV warheads. A likely Russian reaction to the potential counterforce threat posed by the MIRV's is the development of land-mobile ICBM's. Another action-reaction chain may have been triggered by the emergence of China as a nuclear power. The resulting deployment of the U.S. Sentinel system, particularly in its expanded versions, seems certain to have an effect on Russian planners, who may push for the development of their own MIRV systems, provoking a variety of American counterresponses. In the author's view, breaking the action-reaction cycle by limiting ABM defenses should be given first priority in any forthcoming arms-control talks.

accident or miscalculation, and increasing the time available for decision-making in the hope that the increased opportunity for communication might prevent a nuclear exchange from running its full course. Last but not least, one might also hope to change the international political climate so as to lessen tension, to reduce the incentive for powers that currently do not have nuclear weapons to acquire them and to increase the possibility for agreement by the superpowers on other meaningful arms-control measures.

It is reasonable to expect that successful negotiations might to some degree achieve all these objectives except the first: the reduction of potential damage. To focus on any one objective, or combination of objectives, however, is to obscure the immediate problem. In spite of the restraint of the U.S. in its choices regarding strategic weapons development and deployment during the first two-thirds of this decade, it now appears that in the absence of some understanding between the U.S. and the U.S.S.R. the action-reaction sequence that impels the arms race will not be broken. Therefore the immediate objective of any negotiations must be simply to bring that sequence to a halt, or to moderate its pace so that there will be a better chance of ending the arms race than is offered by continuing the policies of the past two decades.

In retrospect, controlling or reversing the growth of strategic capabilities could have been accomplished more easily a few years ago, when the possibility of ABM-system deployment seemed to be the main factor that would trigger another round in the arms race. Now the prospect of ABM systems is more troublesome because of technological advances. In addition, there are the two other stimuli already discussed: the possibility of effective conterforce capabilities as a result of the development of MIRV's, and the possibility that the Chinese nuclear capability may serve as a catalyst to the Russian-American action-reaction phenomenon.

Obviously, short of destroying China by nuclear attack, there is little the U.S. can do about Chinese capabilities except to make sure that it does not give them more weight in its thinking than they deserve. This leaves the option of trying to break the ABM-MIRV chain by focusing on the control of MIRV's or ABM defenses.

Whereas one might hope to limit both, if a choice must be made the focus should clearly be on the control of ABM defenses. Verification of compliance would be relatively simple and could probably be accomplished without intrusive inspection. In addition, the incentive to acquire MIRV's for penetrating defenses would be eliminated, although the incentive to acquire them for counterforce purposes would remain.

The problems of verifying compliance with an agreement to control MIRV's would be much more difficult. Moreover if an ABM system were deployed, there would be great pressure to abrogate or violate any agreement prohibiting MIRV deployment because MIRV's offer high assurance for penetrating defenses. Although reversing the MIRV decision would be difficult, reversing the Sentinel one would present less of a problem.

To be attractive to the U.S.S.R. any proposal to limit defenses would almost certainly have to be coupled with an agreement to limit, if not reduce, inventories of deployed strategic offensive forces. In principle this should not be difficult, since it need not involve serious verification problems.

Complicating any attempt to reach an understanding with the U.S.S.R. on the strategic balance, however, is the fact that the American and Russian positions are not symmetrical. The U.S. has allies and bases around the periphery of the U.S.S.R., whereas the latter has neither near the U.S., unless one counts Cuba. It is clear that a Pandora's box of complications could be opened by any attempt in the context of negotiations on the strategic balance to deal with the threat to America's allies posed by short-range Russian delivery systems, and with the potential threat to the U.S.S.R. of systems in Europe that could reach the U.S.S.R. even though they are primarily tactical in nature. One may hope that initial understandings will not have to include specific agreements on such thorny issues as foreign bases and dual-purpose systems.

Virtually all the above is based on the premise that for the foreseeable future each side will probably insist on maintaining substantial deterrent capabilities. For some time to come there will unfortunately be little basis for expecting negotiations with the U.S.S.R. to result in a strategic balance with each side relying on a few dozen weapons as a deterrent. The difficulties and importance of verification of compliance at such low levels, the problem of China, the existence of large numbers of tactical nuclear weapons on both sides and the general political climate all militate against this. At the other extreme, negotiations would almost necessarily fail if either party based its negotiating position on the expectation that it might achieve a significant damage-limiting capability with respect to the other.

Thus the range of possible agreement is quite narrow. There is a basis for hope, if both sides can accept the fact that for some time the most they can expect to achieve is a strategic balance at quite high, but less rapidly escalating, force levels, and if both recognize that breaking the action-reaction cycle should be given first priority in any negotiations, and also in unilateral decisions.

There will be risks in negotiating arms limitation. These must be weighed not against the risks that might characterize the peaceful world in which everyone would like to live, or even against the risks of the present. Rather, the risks implicit in any agreement must be weighed against the risks and costs that in the absence of agreement one will probably have to confront in the 1970's.

Whether the superpowers strive to curtail the strategic arms race through mutual agreement or through a combination of unilateral restraint and improved dialogue, they should not do so in the mistaken belief that the bases for the Russian-American confrontation of the past two decades will soon be eliminated. Many of the sources of tension have their origins deep in the social structures and political institutions of the two countries. Resolution of these differences will not be accomplished overnight. Restraining the arms race, however, may shorten the time required for resolution of the more basic conflicts between the two superpowers, it may increase the chances of survival during that period, and it may enable the U.S.S.R. and the U.S. to work more effectively on the other large problems that confront the two societies.

The Chinese Threat

ROBERT S. MC NAMARA

. . . The cornerstone of our strategic policy continues to be to deter deliberate nuclear attack upon the United States, or its allies, by maintaining a highly reliable ability to inflict an unacceptable degree of damage upon any single aggressor, or combination of aggressors, at any time during the course of a strategic nuclear exchange — even after our absorbing a surprise first strike.

This can be defined as our "assured destruction capability."

Excerpts from a speech delivered before the editors of United Press International, San Francisco, California, September 18, 1967.

Now it is imperative to understand that assured destruction is the very essence of the whole deterrence concept.

We must possess an actual assured destruction capability. And that actual assured destruction capability must also be credible. Conceivably, our assured destruction capability could be actual, without being credible — in which case, it might fail to deter an aggressor.

The point is that a potential aggressor must himself believe that our assured destruction capability is in fact actual, and that our will to use it in retaliation to an attack is in fact unwavering.

The conclusion, then, is clear: If the United Staes is to deter a nuclear attack on itself or on our allies, it must possess an actual and a credible assured destruction capability.

When calculating the force we require, we must be "conservative" in all our estimates of both a potential aggressor's capabilities, and his intentions. Security depends upon taking a "worst plausible case" — and having the ability to cope with that eventuality.

In that eventuality, we must be able to absorb the total weight of nuclear attack on our country — on our strike-back forces; on our command and control apparatus; on our industrial capacity; on our cities; and on our population — and still be fully capable of destroying the aggressor to the point that his society is simply no longer viable in any meaningful, twentieth century sense.

That is what deterrence to nuclear aggression means. It means the certainty of suicide to the aggressor — not merely to his military forces, but to his society as a whole.

Now let us consider another term: "First-strike capability." This, in itself, is an ambiguous term, since it could mean simply the ability of one nation to attack another nation with nuclear forces first. But as it is normally used, it connotes much more: The substantial elimination of the attacked nation's retaliatory second-strike forces.

This is the sense in which "first-strike capability" should be understood.

Now, clearly, such a first-strike capability is an important strategic concept. The United States cannot — and will not — ever permit itself to get into the position in which another nation, or combination of nations, would possess such a first-strike capability, which could be effectively used against it.

To get into such a position vis-à-vis any other nation or nations would not only constitute an intolerable threat to our security, but it would obviously remove our ability to deter nuclear aggression — both against ourselves and against our allies.

Now, we are not in that position today — and there is no foreseeable danger of our ever getting into that position. . . .

Now what about the Soviet Union?

Does it today possess a powerful nuclear arsenal?

The answer is that it does.

Does it possess a first-strike capability against the United States?

The answer is that it does not.

Can the Soviet Union, in the foreseeable future, acquire such a first-strike capability against the United States?

The answer is that it cannot.

It cannot because we are determined to remain fully alert, and we will never permit our own assured destruction capability to be at a point where a Soviet first-strike capability is even remotely feasible.

Is the Soviet Union seriously attempting to acquire a first-strike capability against the United States?

Although this is a question we cannot answer with absolute certainty, we believe the answer is no. In any event, the question itself, is — in a sense — irrelevant. It is irrelevant since the United States will so continue to maintain — and where necessary strengthen — our retaliatory forces, that whatever the Soviet Union's intentions or actions, we will continue to have an assured destruction capability vis-à-vis their society in which we are completely confident.

But there is another question that is most relevant.

And that is, do we — the United States — possess a first-strike capability against the Soviet Union?

The answer is that we do not.

And we do not, not because we have neglected our nuclear strength. On the contrary, we have increased it to the point that we posses a clear superiority over the Soviet Union.

We do not possess first-strike capability against the Soviet Union for precisely the same reason that they do not possess it against us.

And that is that we have both built up our "second-strike capability" to the point that a first-strike capability on either side has become unattainable. (A "second-strike capability" is the capability to absorb a surprise nuclear attack and survive with sufficient power to inflict unacceptable damage on the aggressor.)

There is, of course, no way in which the United States could have prevented the Soviet Union from acquiring its present second-strike capability — short of a massive pre-emptive first-strike on the Soviet Union in the 1950s.

The blunt fact is, then, that neither the Soviet Union nor the United States can attack the other without being destroyed in retaliation; nor can either of us attain a first-strike capability in the foreseeable future.

The further fact is that both the Soviet Union and the United States presently possess an actual and credible second-strike capa-

bility against one another — and it is precisely this mutual capability that provides us both with the strongest possible motive to avoid
a nuclear war.

The more frequent question that arises in this connection is
whether or not the United States possesses nuclear superiority over
the Soviet Union.

The answer is that we do.

But the answer is — like everything else in this matter — technically complex.

The complexity arises in part out of what measurement of superiority is most meaningful and realistic.

Many commentators on the matter tend to define nuclear superiority in terms of gross megatonnage, or in terms of the number of
missile launchers available.

Now, by both these two standards of measurement, the United
States does have a substantial superiority over the Soviet Union in
the weapons targeted against each other.

But it is precisely these two standards of measurement that are
themselves misleading.

For the most meaningful and realistic measurement of nuclear
capability is neither gross megatonnage, nor the number of
available missile launchers; but rather the number of separate warheads that are capable of being *delivered* with accuracy on individual high-priority targets with sufficient power to destroy them.

Gross megatonnage in itself is an inadequate indicator of assured
destruction capability, since it is unrelated to surviveability, accuracy, or penetrability, and poorly related to effective elimination of
multiple high-priority targets. There is manifestly no advantage in
over-destroying one target, at the expense of leaving undamaged
other targets of equal importance.

Further, the number of missile launchers available is also an
inadequate indicator of assured destruction capability, since the
fact is that many of our launchers will carry multiple warheads.

But by using the realistic measurement of the number of warheads available, capable of being reliably delivered with accuracy
and effectiveness on the appropriate targets in the United States or
Soviet Union, I can tell you that the United States currently possesses a superiority over the Soviet Union of at least three or four
to one.

Furthermore, we will maintain a superiority — by these same
realistic criteria — over the Soviet Union for as far ahead in the
future as we can realistically plan.

I want, however, to make one point patently clear: our current
numerical superiority over the Soviet Union in reliable, accurate,

and effective warheads is both greater than we had originally planned, and is in fact more than we require.

Moreover, in the larger equation of security, our "superiority" is of limited significance — since even with our current superiority, or indeed with any numerical superiority realistically attainable, the blunt, inescapable fact remains that the Soviet Union could still — with its present forces — effectively destroy the United States even after absorbing the full weight of an American first strike.

I have noted that our present superiority is greater than we had planned. Let me explain to you how this came about, for I think it is a significant illustration of the intrinsic dynamics of the nuclear arms race.

In 1961, when I became Secretary of Defense, the Soviet Union possessed a very small operational arsenal of intercontinental missiles. However, they did possess the technological and industrial capacity to enlarge that arsenal very substantially over the succeeding several years.

Now, we had no evidence that the Soviets did in fact plan to fully use that capability.

But as I have pointed out, a strategic planner must be "conservative" in his calculations; that is, he must prepare for the worst plausible case and not be content to hope and prepare merely for the most probable.

Since we could not be certain of Soviet intentions — since we could not be sure that they would not undertake a massive build-up — we had to insure against such an eventuality by undertaking ourselves a major buildup of the Minuteman and Polaris forces.

Thus, in the course of hedging against what was then only a theoretically possible Soviet buildup, we took decisions which have resulted in our current superiority in numbers of warheads and deliverable megatons.

But the blunt fact remains that if we had had more accurate information about planned Soviet strategic forces, we simply would not have needed to build as large a nuclear arsenal as we have today.

Now let me be absolutely clear. I am not saying that our decision in 1961 was unjustified. I am simply saying that it was necessitated by a lack of accurate information.

Furthermore, that decision in itself — as justified as it was — in the end, could not possibly have left unaffected the Soviet Union's future nuclear plans.

What is essential to understand here is that the Soviet Union and the United States mutually influence one another's strategic plans.

Whatever be their intentions, whatever be our intentions, actions — or even realistically potential actions — on either side relating to the buildup of nuclear forces, be they either offensive or defensive weapons, necessarily trigger reactions on the other side.

It is precisely this action-reaction phenomenon that fuels an arms race. . . .

In recent years the Soviets have substantially increased their offensive forces. We have, of course, been watching and evaluating this very carefully.

Clearly, the Soviet buildup is in part a reaction to our own buildup since the beginning of this decade.

Soviet strategic planners undoubtedly reasoned that if our buildup were to continue at its accelerated pace, we might conceivably reach, in time, a credible first-strike capability against the Soviet Union.

That was not in fact our intention. Our intention was to assure that they — with their theoretical capacity to reach such a first-strike capability — would not in fact outdistance us.

But they could not read our intentions with any greater accuracy than we could read theirs. And thus the result has been that we have both built up our forces to a point that far exceeds a credible second-strike capability against the forces we each started with.

In doing so, neither of us has reached a first-strike capability. And the realities of the situation being what they are — whatever we believe their intentions to be, and whatever they believe our intentions to be — each of us can deny the other a first-strike capability in the foreseeable future.

Now, how can we be so confident that this is the case?

How can we be so certain that the Soviets cannot gradually outdistance us — either by some dramatic technology breakthrough, or simply through our imperceptively lagging behind, for whatever reason: reluctance to spend the requisite funds; distraction with military problems elsewhere; faulty intelligence; or simple negligence and naivete?

All of these reasons — and others — have been suggested by some commentators in this country, who fear that we are in fact falling behind to a dangerous degree.

The answer to all of this is simple and straightforward.

We are not going to permit the Soviets to outdistance us, because to do so would be to jeopardize our very viability as a nation.

No President, no Secretary of Defense, no Congress of the United States — of whatever political party and of whatever political persuasion is going to permit this nation to take that risk.

We do not want a nuclear arms race with the Soviet Union —

primarily because the action-reaction phenomenon makes it foolish and futile. But if the only way to prevent the Soviet Union from obtaining first-strike capability over us is to engage in such a race, the United States possesses in ample abundance the resources, the technology, and the will to run faster in that race for whatever distance is required.

But what we would much prefer to do is to come to a realistic and reasonably riskless agreement with the Soviet Union, which would effectively prevent such an arms race. We both have strategic nuclear arsenals greatly in excess of a credible assured destruction capability. These arsenals have reached that point of excess in each case for precisely the same reason: we each have reacted to the other's buildup with very conservative calculations. We have, that is, each built a greater arsenal than either of us needed for a second-strike capability, simply because we each wanted to be able to cope with the "worst plausible case."

But since we now each possess a deterrent in excess of our individual needs, both of our nations would benefit from a properly safeguarded agreement first to limit, and later to reduce, both our offensive and defensive strategic nuclear forces.

We may, or we may not, be able to achieve such an agreement. We hope we can. And we believe such an agreement is fully feasible, since it is clearly in both our nations' interests.

But reach the formal agreement or not, we can be sure that neither the Soviets nor we are going to risk the other's obtaining a first-strike capability.

On the contrary, we can be sure that we are both going to maintain a maximum effort to preserve an assured destruction capability.

It would not be sensible for either side to launch a maximum effort to achieve a first-strike capability. It would not be sensible because the intelligence-gathering capability of each side being what it is, and the realities of lead-time from technological breakthrough to operational readiness being what they are, neither of us would be able to acquire a first-strike capability in secret.

Now, let me take a specific case in point.

The Soviets are now deploying an antiballistic missile system. If we react to this deployment intelligently, we have no reason for alarm.

The system does not impose any threat to our ability to penetrate and inflict massive and unacceptable damage on the Soviet Union. In other words, it does not presently affect in any significant manner our assured destruction capability.

It does not impose such a threat because we have already taken the steps necessary to assure that our land-based Minuteman missiles, our nuclear submarine-launched new Poseidon missiles, and our strategic bomber forces have the requisite penetration aids — and in the sum, constitute a force of such magnitude, that they guarantee us a force strong enough to survive a Soviet attack and penetrate the Soviet A.B.M. deployment.

Now let me come to the issue that has received so much attention recently: The question of whether or not we should deploy an A.B.M. system against the Soviet nuclear threat.

To begin with, this is not in any sense a new issue. We have had both the technical possibility and the strategic desirability of an American A.B.M. deployment under constant review since the late 1950s.

While we have substantially improved our technology in the field, it is important to understand that none of the systems at the present or foreseeable state of the art would provide an impenetrable shield over the United States. Were such a shield possible, we would certainly want it — and we would certainly build it.

And at this point, let me dispose of an objection that is totally irrelevant to this issue.

It has been alleged that we are opposed to deploying a large-scale A.B.M. system because it would carry the heavy price tag of $40-billion.

Let me make very clear that the $40-billion is not the issue.

If we could build and deploy a genuinely impenetrable shield over the United States, we would be willing to spend not $40-billion, but any reasonable multiple of that amount that was necessary.

The money in itself is not the problem: The penetrability of the proposed shield is the problem.

There is clearly no point, however, in spending $40-billion if it is not going to buy us a significant improvement in our security. If it is not, then we should use the substantial resources it represents on something that will.

Every A.B.M. system that is now feasible involves firing defensive missiles at incoming offensive warheads in an effort to destroy them.

But what many commentators on this issue overlook is that any such system can rather obviously be defeated by an enemy simply sending more offensive warheads, or dummy warheads, than there are defensive missiles capable of disposing of them.

And this is the whole crux of the nuclear action-reaction phenomenon.

Were we to deploy a heavy A.B.M. system throughout the United States, the Soviets would clearly be strongly motivated to so increase their offensive capability as to cancel out our defensive advantage.

It is futile for each of us to spend $4-billion, $40-billion, or $400-billion — and at the end of all the spending, and at the end of all the deployment, and at the end of all the effort, to be relatively at the same point of balance on the security scale that we are now.

In point of fact, we have already initiated offensive weapons programs costing several billions in order to offset the small present Soviet A.B.M. deployment, and the possibly more extensive future Soviet A.B.M. deployments.

That is money well spent; and it is necessary.

But we should bear in mind that it is money spent because of the action-reaction phenomenon.

If we in turn opt for heavy A.B.M. deployment — at whatever price — we can be certain that the Soviets will react to offset the advantage we would hope to gain.

It is precisely because of this certainty of a corresponding Soviet reaction that the four prominent scientists — men who have served with distinction as the science advisers to Presidents Eisenhower, Kennedy and Johnson, and the three outstanding men who have served as directors of research and engineering to three Secretaries of Defense — have unanimously recommended against the deployment of an A.B.M. system designed to protect our population against a Soviet attack.

These men are Doctors Killian, Kistiakowsky, Wiesner, Hornig, York, Brown and Foster.

The plain fact of the matter is that we are now facing a situation analogous to the one we faced in 1961; we are uncertain of the Soviets' intentions.

At that time we were concerned about their potential offensive capabilities; now we are concerned about their potential defensive capabilities.

But the dynamics of the concern are the same.

We must continue to be cautious and conservative in our estimates — leaving no room in our calculations for unnecessary talk. And at the same time, we must measure our own response in such a manner that it does not trigger a senseless spiral upward of nuclear arms.

Now, as I have emphasized, we have already taken the necessary steps to guarantee that our offensive strategic weapons will be able to penetrate future, more advanced, Soviet defenses.

Keeping in mind the careful clockwork of lead-time, we will be forced to continue that effort over the next few years if the evidence is that the Soviets intend to turn what is now a light and modest A.B.M. deployment into a massive one.

Should they elect to do so, we have both the lead-time and the technology available to so increase both the quality and quantity of our offensive strategic forces — with particular attention to highly reliable penetration aids — that their expensive defensive efforts will give them no edge in the nuclear balance whatever.

But we would prefer not to have to do that. For it is a profitless waste of resources, provided we and the Soviets can come to a realistic strategic arms-limitation agreement.

As you know, we have proposed U.S.-Soviet talks on this matter. Should these talks fail, we are fully prepared to take the appropriate measures that such a failure would make necessary.

The point for us to keep in mind is that should the talks fail — and the Soviets decide to expand their present modest A.B.M. deployment into a massive one — our response must be realistic. There is no point whatever in our responding by going to a massive A.B.M. deployment to protect our population, when such a system would be ineffective against a sophisticated Soviet offense.

Instead, realism dictates that if the Soviets elect to deploy a heavy A.B.M. system, we must further expand our sophisticated offensive forces, and thus preserve our overwhelming assured destruction capability.

But the intractable fact is that should the talks fail, both the Soviets and ourselves would be forced to continue on a foolish and reckless course.

It would be foolish and reckless because — in the end — it would provide neither the Soviets nor us with any greater relative nuclear capability.

The time has come for us both to realize that, and to act reasonably. It is clearly in our own mutual interest to do so.

Having said that, it is important to distinguish between an A.B.M. system designed to protect against a Soviet attack on our cities, and A.B.M. systems which have other objectives.

One of the other uses of an A.B.M. system which we should seriously consider is the greater protection of our strategic offensive forces.

Another is in relation to the emerging nuclear capability of Communist China.

There is evidence that the Chinese are devoting very substantial resources to the development of both nuclear warheads and missile delivery systems. As I stated last January, indications are that they will have medium-range ballistic missiles within a year or so, an initial intercontinental ballistic missile capability in the early 1970s, and a modest force in the mid-70s.

Up to now, the lead-time factor has allowed us to postpone a decision on whether or not a light A.B.M. deployment might be advantageous as a countermeasure to Communist China's nuclear development.

But the time will shortly be right for us to initiate production if we desire such a system.

China at the moment is caught up in internal strife, but it seems likely that her basic motivation in developing a strategic nuclear capability is an attempt to provide a basis for threatening her neighbors, and to clothe herself with the dubious prestige that the world pays to nuclear weaponry.

We deplore her development of these weapons, just as we deplore it in other countries. We oppose nuclear proliferation because we believe that in the end it only increases the risk of a common and cataclysmic holocaust.

President Johnson has made it clear that the United States will oppose any efforts of China to employ nuclear blackmail against her neighbors.

We possess now, and will continue to possess or as far ahead as we can foresee, an overwhelming first-strike capability with respect to China. And despite the shrill and raucous propaganda directed at her own people that "the atomic bomb is a paper tiger," there is ample evidence that China well appreciates the destructive power of nuclear weapons.

China has been cautious to avoid any action that might end in a nuclear clash with the United States — however wild her words — and understandably so. We have the power not only to destroy completely her entire nuclear offensive forces, but to devastate her society as well.

Is there any possibility, then, that by the mid-1970s China might become so incautious as to attempt a nuclear attack on the United States or our allies?

It would be insane and suicidal for her to do so, but one can conceive conditions under which China might miscalculate. We wish to reduce such possibilities to a minimum.

And since, as I have noted, our strategic planning must always be conservative, and take into consideration even the possible irrational behavior of potential adversaries, there are marginal grounds for concluding that a light deployment of U.S. A.B.M.s against this possibility is prudent.

The system would be relatively inexpensive — preliminary estimates place the cost at about $5-billion — and would have a much higher degree of reliability against a Chinese attack than the much more massive and complicated system that some have recommended against a possible Soviet attack.

Moreover, such an A.B.M. deployment designed against a possible Chinese attack would have a number of other advantages. It would provide an additional indication to Asians that we intend to deter China from nuclear blackmail, and thus would contribute toward our goal of discouraging nuclear weapon proliferation among the present non-nuclear countries.

Further, the Chinese-oriented A.B.M. deployment would enable us to add — as a concurrent benefit — a further defense of our Minuteman sites against Soviet attack, which means that at modest cost we would in fact be adding even greater effectiveness to our offensive missile force and avoiding a much more costly expansion of that force.

Finally, such a reasonably reliable A.B.M. system would add protection of our population against the improbable but possible accidental launch of an intercontinental missile by any of the nuclear powers.

After a detailed review of all these considerations, we have decided to go forward with this Chinese-oriented A.B.M. deployment, and we will begin actual production of such a system at the end of this year.

In reaching this decision, I want to emphasize that it contains two possible dangers — and we should guard carefully against each.

The first danger is that we may psychologically lapse into the old over-simplification about the adequacy of nuclear power. The simple truth is that nuclear weapons can serve to deter only a narrow range of threats. This A.B.M. deployment will strengthen our defensive posture — and will enhance the effectiveness of our land-based I.C.B.M. offensive forces. But the independent nations of Asia must realize that these benefits are no substitute for their maintaining and, where necessary, strengthening their own conventional forces in order to deal with more likely threats to the security of the region.

The second danger is also psychological. There is a kind of mad momentum intrinsic to the development of all new nuclear weaponry. If a weapon system works — and works well — there is strong pressure from many directions to produce and deploy the weapon out of all proportion to the prudent level required.

The danger in deploying this relatively light and reliable Chinese-oriented A.B.M. system is going to be that pressures will develop to expand it into a heavy Soviet-oriented A.B.M. system.

We must resist that temptation firmly — not because we can for a moment afford to relax our vigilance against a possible Soviet first strike — but precisely because our greatest deterrent against such a strike is not a massive, costly, but highly penetrable A.B.M. shield, but rather a fully credible offensive assured destruction capability.

The so-called heavy A.B.M. shield — at the present state of technology — would in effect be no adequate shield at all against a Soviet attack, but rather a strong inducement for the Soviets to vastly increase their own offensive forces. That, as I have pointed out, would make it necessary for us to respond in turn — and so the arms race would rush hopelessly on to no sensible purpose on either side.

Let me emphasize — and I cannot do so too strongly — that our decision to go ahead with *limited* A.B.M. deployment in no way indicates that we feel an agreement with the Soviet Union on the limitation of strategic nuclear offensive and defensive forces is any the less urgent or desirable.

The road leading from the stone ax to the I.C.B.M. — though it may have been more than a million years in the building — seems to have run in a single direction.

If one is inclined to be cynical, one might conclude that man's history seems to be characterized not so much by consistent periods of peace, occasionally punctuated by warfare; but rather by persistent outbreaks of warfare, wearily put aside from time to time by periods of exhaustion and recovery — that parade under the name of peace.

I do not view man's history with that degree of cynicism, but I do believe that man's wisdom in avoiding war is often surpassed by his folly in promoting it.

However foolish unlimited war may have been in the past, it is now no longer merely foolish, but suicidal as well.

It is said that nothing can prevent a man from suicide, if he is sufficiently determined to commit it.

The question is what is our determination in an era when unlimited war will mean the death of hundreds of millions — and the possible genetic impairment of a million generations to follow?

Man is clearly a compound of folly and wisdom — and history is clearly a consequence of the admixture of those two contradictory traits.

History has placed our particular lives in an area when the consequences of human folly are waxing more and more catastrophic in the matter of war and peace.

In the end, the root of man's security does not lie in his weaponry.

In the end, the root of man's security lies in his mind.

What the world requires in its 22nd Year of the Atomic Age is not a new race towards armament.

What the world requires in its 22nd Year of the Atomic Age is a new race towards reasonableness.

We had better all run that race.

Not merely we the administrators. But we the people.

Hard-Point Defense

RICHARD M. NIXON

Ladies and gentlemen, today I am announcing the decision which I believe is vital for the security and defense of the United States and also in the interests of peace throughout the world.

Last year a program, the Sentinel antiballistic missile program, was adopted and that program . . . has been the subject of very strong debate and controversy over the past few months. After a long study of all of the options available I have concluded that the Sentinel program previously adopted should be substantially modified.

The new program that I have recommended this morning to the leaders and that I announce today is one that perhaps best can be described as a safeguard program. It is a safeguard against any attack by the Chinese Communists that we can foresee over the next 10 years.

It is a safeguard of our deterrent system, which is increasingly vulnerable due to the advances that have been made by the Soviet Union since the year 1967, when the Sentinel program was first laid out.

From opening statement of the transcript of President's news conference, March 14, 1969, *The New York Times,* March 15, 1969.

It is a safeguard, also, against any irrational or accidental attack that might occur, of less than massive magnitude, which might be launched from the Soviet Union.

The program also does not do some things, which should be clearly understood. It does not provide defense for our cities and, for that reason, the sites have been moved away from our major cities.

I have made the decision with regard to this particular point because I found that there is no way, even if we were to expand the limited Sentinel system which was planned for some of our cities, to a so-called heavy or thick system, there is no way that we can adequately defend our cities without an unacceptable loss of life.

The only way that I have concluded that we can save lives — which is the primary purpose of our defense system — is to prevent war. And that is why the emphasis of this system is on protecting our deterrent, which is the best preventive for war.

The system differs from the previous Sentinel system in another major respect. The Sentinel system called for a fixed deployment schedule. I believe that because of a number of reasons that we should have a phase system. That is why, on an annual basis, the new safeguard will be reviewed. And the review may bring about the changes in the system based on our evaluation of three major points.

First, what our intelligence shows us with regard to the magnitude of the threat, whether from the Soviet Union or from the Chinese.

And, second, in terms of what our evaluation is of any talks that we are having by that time or may be having with regard to arms control.

And, finally, because we believe that since this is a new system, we should constantly examine what progress has been made in the development of the technique to see if changes in the system should be made.

I should admit at this point that this decision has not been an easy one. . . . But it is one that I have made after considering all of the options and I would indicate . . . two major options that I have overruled.

One is moving to a massive city defense. I've already indicated why I do not believe that is, first, feasible, and there is another reason. Moving to a massive city defense system, even starting with a thin system and then going to a heavy system, tends to be more provocative in terms of making credible a first strike capability against the Soviet Union. I want no provocation which might deter arms talks.

The other alternative at the other extreme was to do nothing or to delay for six months or 12 months, which would be the equivalent, really, of doing nothing, or for example, going the road only of research and development.

I have examined those options. I have ruled them out because I have concluded that the first deployment of this system which will not occur until 1973, that the first deployment is essential by that date if we are to meet the threat that our present intelligence indicates will exist by 1973.

In other words, we must begin now. If we delay a year, for example, it means that first deployment will be delayed until 1975. That might be too late. . . .

There are, of course, other possibilities that have been strongly urged by some of the leaders this morning. For example, that we could increase our offensive capabilities, our submarine force, or even our Minuteman force, or our bomber force.

That I would consider to be, however, the wrong road because it would be provocative to the Soviet Union and might escalate an arms race. This system is truly a safeguard system, a defensive system only. It safeguards our deterrent and under those circumstances, can in no way, in my opinion, delay the progress which I hope will continue to be made toward arms talks which will limit arms not only this kind of system, but particularly offensive systems. . . .

The Case for Missile Defense

DONALD G. BRENNAN

INTRODUCTION

The subject of defense against ballistic missiles occupies, in terms of the debate about it, a unique position among strategic issues of the nuclear era. Missile defenses have been more intensely debated in the U.S. than any other weapon system selected for deployment, such as the air defense system or the Polaris and Minuteman offensive missile systems, or any arms-control measure adopted to date, including the ban on nuclear tests. In fact, the decision to deploy defenses may well be more important than any other single decision made to date concerning our strategic nuclear forces.

But the published literature of this debate has been one-sided. With few exceptions, and those few mainly confined to journals not noted for their opposition to any weapon system whatever, most of the articles and editorials relating to ballistic missile defense (BMD for short — sometimes, but not here, denoted ABM) published before the spring of 1969 have opposed U.S. deployment of missile defense. For example, there have been three articles in *Foreign Affairs* prior to the April 1969 issue concerned in whole or part with BMD, and all three opposed U.S. deployment.[1] In view of the facts that the U.S. Administration clearly supports American deployment of BMD, and that most of the senior American academic strategists and many prominent students or advocates of arms con-

This paper appears as Chapter 5 in the volume *Why ABM? Policy Issues in the Missile Defense Controversy*, edited by Johan J. Holst and William Schneider, Jr., published by Pergamon Press in July 1969. It is based partly on the author's article "The Case for Missile Defense" in the April 1969 issue of *Foreign Affairs* and partly on "Post-Deployment Policy Issues in Ballistic Missile Defence" in D. G. Brennan and Johan J. Holst, *Ballistic Missile Defence: Two Views*, Adelphi Paper No. 43, The Institute for Strategic Studies, London, November 1967.

[1] J. I. Coffey, "The Anti-Ballistic Missile Debate," April 1967; Robert L. Rothstein, "The ABM, Proliferation and International Stability," April 1968; and Carl Kaysen, "Keeping the Strategic Balance," July 1968.

trol favor deployment at least under some conditions, it is odd that so much of the early published material was single-mindedly in opposition to BMD.[2] The present article is an attempt to clarify for a larger audience some of the reasons why many analysts think it entirely reasonable to favor American deployment.

Missile defenses can have either or both of two major applications: for the protection of people and resources, and for the protection of strategic offensive forces. The Safeguard program announced by President Nixon on March 14, 1969 has important elements of both kinds. The defense of strategic forces has been discussed elsewhere,[3] and I shall concentrate mainly on the protection of people and resources.

I shall discuss several considerations relating to a U.S. BMD system intended to have substantial effectiveness against major Soviet attacks, rather than discuss only a so-called "light" or "thin" system intended to be effective only against Chinese or other marginal attacks. Much of the support (both inside and outside the Government) for the original deployment decision for the former Sentinel system came from quarters that believed the system would eventually have significant capability against large Soviet attacks. It seems both possible and desirable that whatever system finally emerges will eventually have such a capability, and therefore it seems appropriate to provide some discussion here of the policy issues this prospect presents. However, I shall also mention a number of points that relate equally to a "light" defense of cities.

In the next section I shall take up the technical-effectiveness issues and state several positive reasons favoring BMD deployment. The section following provides an examination of certain fundamental problems of deterrence and attempts to show that some of the arguments about deterrence made by some critics of BMD are unsound. Arms-control issues are then taken up and it is argued that BMD deployment can contribute positively to traditional objectives of arms control and, in particular, need not lead to a new arms race.

[2] An important exception is in Charles M. Herzfeld, "Ballistic Missile Defense and National Security," *Annals of the N.Y. Academy of Sciences,* vol. 134, pp. 119–25, November 22, 1965. Beginning in the spring of 1969, a substantial amount of material favorable to deployment began appearing in various sources.

[3] See especially Albert Wohlstetter, "Statement before the Senate Armed Services Committee," April 23, 1969, and supplementary statements submitted by Wohlstetter for the record of those hearings, included as Chapter 6 of Johan J. Holst and William Schneider, Jr., *Why ABM? Policy Issues in the Missile Defense Controversy,* New York, Pergamon Press, 1969.

SOME TECHNICAL ESTIMATES

In an important sense, the key issues in the debate about BMD are not technical. The sense is as follows. There are certain estimates generally believed within the community of people who have carried out the U.S. BMD development to characterize the plausible range of technical and economic effectiveness of systems achievable in the near future. These estimates are subject to some controversy. The sense involved is that even if the uncertainty and controversy concerning the prevailing estimates were wholly removed, most of the articulate critics of BMD deployment would remain critical: their objections are rooted in other concerns, which I shall discuss below.

On the other hand, there is an important sense in which technical issues are vital to the debate, namely that most of the support for BMD deployment, at least within those quarters in which such opinion is subject to change, depends on the fact that the prevailing estimates indicate that a defense of substantial effectiveness is feasible. Indeed, I myself was shifted from being a mild opponent to something of a proponent of deployment in part by a substantial shift in the estimates of effectiveness prevailing in the 1963–65 era. (The other major reason for my own shift stemmed from an improved understanding of Soviet perceptions of these matters, which will be taken up below.)

With this perspective on their role in the debate, let us consider briefly some of the prevailing technical estimates. The main published sources of such information are the unclassified "posture statements" issued annually in recent years by the Secretary of Defense, especially those issued by McNamara in 1967 and 1968, although some supplementary information has been contained in Government hearings and speeches.

A useful way of characterizing the effect of a substantial BMD system is to estimate the number of lives it might save in various specified circumstances. In a table of such estimates given in McNamara's 1968 posture statement, it was indicated that there could be one hundred twenty million American fatalities in certain possible wars of the mid-1970's if no significant BMD were deployed in the U.S. Against the same Soviet forces and attacks, it was indicated that BMD systems costing from ten to twenty billion dollars could reduce expectable fatalities to between ten and forty million Americans, depending on the level of the defense and the details of the war. Damage to production and transportation resources would, of course, be similarly reduced, a result not achievable with economically feasible civil-defense shelter programs.

Thus, such a defense might change the postwar U.S. situation from one in which over half the population was gone and recovery in any time period would be problematical to one in which perhaps ninety per cent survived and economic recovery might be complete within five to ten years. This difference would be enormous.

It is this possible difference that constitutes the major motivation for deploying heavy defenses, at least in the minds of many analysts, myself included. In effect, procuring such defenses is like buying "insurance" that would limit the consequences of a war; the outcome would still be a disaster, but probably one of a very different order than the result of having the same offensive forces expended in a war with no defenses. The immediate survivors of the war would certainly notice this difference — indeed, it would probably make all the difference in their own long-term prospects for survival and economic recovery.

It is possible that a BMD system might perform in an actual war much less well than expected, because of some unforeseen technical failure; it is, however, about equally likely that the opposing offensive forces will perform against the defenses much less well than expected, which is to say that the defenses may perform much better than expected. (Critics of BMD are prone to emphasize the first of these points much more than the second.) And, as I shall indicate below, the deployment of defenses may result in saving many millions of lives in a war even if they fail altogether in the war itself.

Of course, the U.S. defense might have to face a Soviet offensive force larger than the one that would have existed if the U.S. defense did not exist. In other words, the Soviets could increase their offensive force so as to nullify, partly or wholly, the U.S. defense. I shall later discuss whether it seems likely that the Soviets would do this; let us here consider how difficult it would be for them to do it. This is one of the important technical characteristics of offense-defense interactions.

A useful way of characterizing the degree of difficulty is with a parameter called the "cost exchange ratio," defined as follows. The U.S. might deploy a particular defense system at a particular cost. It would generally be feasible for the Soviets to add an increment to their strategic offensive forces that would offset or nullify the opposing defense, and this increment of offense would also have a particular cost. The ratio (cost of the offsetting increment of offense)/(cost of the defense) is called the "cost exchange ratio." Thus, relatively ineffective defenses would have a relatively low cost exchange ratio, while a defense system that would be relatively difficult to penetrate would have a relatively high ratio.

Several years ago, it was widely believed that missile defenses were easy to penetrate, so easy that offensive increments costing only one or a few per cent of the opposing defense would serve to nullify it. In recent years, however, it has become apparent that cheap forms of decoys and other penetration aids cannot be relied upon to nullify modern defense techniques. A good defense can be overcome, but it is difficult. This is reflected in the fact that cost exchange ratios for a good defense are in region of 1:1, i.e., unity. Thus, *it is about as expensive to nullify a good defense as to build it.*

Some specific examples were provided in the 1967 posture statement. Two postulated defense systems were considered, one costing ten billion dollars and the other twenty billion dollars. Under the conditions of a hypothetical war in which the U.S. fatalities were estimated to be one hundred million without any missile defenses, these BMD systems reduced the fatalities to thirty million and twenty million, respectively, if the Soviets did not change their offensive forces in reaction to the defenses. If the Soviets added an increment to their offensive forces costing one-quarter as much as the BMD, they could raise American fatalities to forty million; if they spent one-half the cost of the defenses, they could raise the level to sixty million; and if they spent as much as the full cost of the defense, the fatalities would rise to ninety million. To raise the level of fatalities back up to the undefended level (one hundred million) — the usual criterion of offsetting a defense — would require an incremental Soviet expenditure on their offensive forces that would exceed the cost of the defense. These calculations assumed that the Soviets had advanced technology for their offensive forces and made effective use of it.

It is worth pointing out that these estimates were published by McNamara, who was an intense critic of missile defenses. It is therefore in no way to be expected that these estimates are biased in favor of missile defenses.

Although McNamara published information showing that exchange ratios were about unity as far back as January 1967, and although information to this effect was known in the Government for perhaps two or three years before that, many critics of missile defenses continue to assert that it is cheaper to offset defenses than to build them. For example, Kaysen, in his July 1968 article in *Foreign Affairs,* said: "Were we to deploy much stronger and more costly defenses [than the initial Sentinel program] it would remain within the Soviet capability to counter them by corresponding increases in the size of their offensive deployments — *which could probably be made at significantly less cost than that of our increased defenses.*" (Emphasis added.) If "counter" means "wholly or largely offset," as is usual and as Kaysen's context suggests, there is no objective basis for the italicized statement, and there has not been for some few years. As additional examples of peculiar reporting of this matter, an unambiguous misstatement of fact concerning exchange ratios was contained in a much-cited article by Garwin and Bethe,[4] and a very misleading statement was made by Wiesner.[5]

Some remarks on these estimates of effectiveness and cost are in order. To begin with the matter of cost, the two deployments considered above were estimated to cost ten and twenty billion dollars. McNamara, in speaking about the latter program, several times referred to the fact that many weapon systems proved to cost twice as much as originally estimated, as indeed they have, and suggested that this program would more likely cost forty billion dollars when completed.[6] Some journalists and others have in turn doubled McNamara's estimate once again, and one can find articles and newspaper editorials referring to BMD systems alleged to cost eighty to one hundred billion dollars. It is difficult to escape the feeling that these latter estimates are made purely for their political effect, and have no significant basis in reality. Missile defense systems had been much more extensively studied at the time these estimates were worked out than was true of many of the weapon systems whose early cost estimates proved much too low. Moreover, it is possible for the Secretary of Defense to decide to spend no more than a certain sum, say fifteen billion dollars, on investment cost in missile defense, and to instruct the services to produce the best possible defense within that budget, rather than to commit himself to a deployment specified in quantities and characteristics of equipment of possibly uncertain cost.

Obviously the relationship between cost and performance of a system as large and complex as those considered here cannot be

[4] "[McNamara] finds invariably (in the 1968 Posture Statement) that the offense, by spending considerably less money than the defense, can restore casualties and destruction to the original level before defenses were installed," Richard L. Garwin and Hans A. Bethe, "Anti-Ballistic Missile Systems," *Scientific American*, March 1968, pp. 21–31. (Quotation at p. 31.)

[5] "Secretary McNamara . . . concede[s] that an anti-Soviet ABM defense would not be worth the huge expense, because the Russians could nullify its effectiveness at considerably lower cost to themselves." Jerome B. Wiesner, "The Case Against an Antiballistic Missile System," *Look* Magazine, November 28, 1967, pp. 25–27. (Quotation at p. 26.) The Secretary had perhaps quoted such estimates in earlier years, but ten months preceding Wiesner's article he had published a posture statement including unity cost exchange ratios.

[6] The Polaris program, with a total hardware cost of about fourteen billion dollars through Fiscal Year 1969, is an example of a major program in which the actual costs were very close to the estimated costs.

specified in advance with anything like precision. This should not obscure the fact that the range receiving major consideration or advocacy is, say, eight to twenty billion dollars.

For some perspective on this range of costs, it is instructive to consider that the U.S. has spent perhaps fifty billion dollars on air defense since World War II.[7] We are currently still spending almost two billion dollars per year on air defense. And, while estimates of the impact of the air defense system on U.S. casualties from Soviet bomber attacks are not available, it is a good bet that the current air defense system is and has been less important as insurance for the country than the major proposed BMD systems would be.

It would be fair to ask how stable these estimates of effectiveness are likely to prove in the future. That is, while it now appears that a U.S. BMD system costing between ten and twenty billion dollars could reduce American fatalities from one hundred or one hundred twenty million to perhaps ten to forty million in possible wars of the mid-1970's if the Soviets do not substantially increase their offensive forces in reaction, and that the cost to the Soviets to substantially nullify the defense would be at least comparable to the cost of the defense, is it likely that these estimates will still seem reasonable when we get to the mid-1970's?

A question of this form does not admit an unequivocal answer; one cannot say with confidence whether inventions not yet made or developments not yet realized will more favor offense or defense, although there are some reasons for thinking the trend will continue to favor the defense. But a parallel may be useful. In the U.S., we have had fairly high confidence for over a decade that the Polaris submarine force is a reasonably secure component of our strategic offensive forces. The main reason for this confidence resides in the fact that we have conducted a major research and development program—on the order of one-half billion dollars per year—in anti-submarine warfare for many years, and no cheap and reliable way of attacking such submarines has been found. A similar statement is beginning to be true in relation to BMD: we have conducted a major research and development program — on the order of one-third billion dollars per year — in means of penetrating missile defenses for several years, and no cheap and reliable way of penetrating a good defense has been found. This does not guarantee that one cannot be found, and it does not say that expensive ways of penetrating are not known — as are expensive

---

[7] Herbert Roback, Staff Administrator of the Military Operations Subcommittee, U.S. House of Representatives, in E. P. Wigner (ed.) *Who Speaks for Civil Defense?* Scribner's, New York, 1968, p. 95.

ways of attacking Polaris submarines. But it does suggest that the technical prospects for missile offense-defense interactions, while not yet as stable as the submarine-antisubmarine situation, are likely to prove acceptably stable, and in particular should be a great deal better than the early estimates of air defense proved.

It is worth noting that a BMD system may possibly have important effects even if it later failed to perform as expected in a war. If the Soviets were to react to a U.S. defense by retrofitting their existing missile force with decoys and other penetration aids, without a major increase in the number of rockets, they would reduce the total payload available for warheads, and thereby reduce the potential damage the U.S. might incur in a war even if the defense failed utterly. This effect, which is known in the trade as "virtual attrition" and is often encountered in defensive systems of other kinds, is likely to be quite modest. A more important possibility could arise through re-targeting of the Soviet offensive force because of a U.S. defense; the Soviets might concentrate most or all of their offensive missiles (apart from those used for missile bases or other military targets) on the largest cities to be sure of destroying them, and leave unattacked many medium and small cities. Or they might attack only undefended areas, and leave aside most or all the largest (defended) cities. In either case, the mere presence of the defense could result in saving many millions of lives no matter whether it "worked" or not. Freeman Dyson has summarized this possibility with the amusing observation that BMD is very good at protecting cities that are not attacked; the real point, of course, is that it may sharply reduce the number of significant cities that are attacked.

Let us mention briefly here three other positive reasons favoring U.S. BMD deployment. First, the time may soon arrive, if it is not already here, when there will be some possibility of attacks of anonymous or disguised origin. Since these would not be subject to standard threats of deterrence, active defenses may be the primary protection against such attacks. Second, the possibility of a purely accidental launch of some part of the Soviet force is probably very remote, but the possibility of an unauthorized launch, especially during an intense crisis, may not be so remote and should be protected against. Even a modest defense might be very effective against such an attack; this has been one of the arguments used — rightly, I believe — in support of the current Safeguard program. Third, missile defenses (even light defenses) considerably complicate the planning of an attacker who would penetrate them; this phenomenon seems likely to serve as an additional "firebreak" to the initiation of a strategic nuclear war.

It may be useful to expand briefly upon one of these points, viz., the possibility of a disguised attack, or what is sometimes called a "catalytic" attack — an attempt by some third country to trigger a war between two countries by attacking one in such a way that it will be thought to have been done by the other. Some strategists have been skeptical of the possibility that such an attack could or would be carried out. While it does seem unlikely that disguised attacks would be a serious threat in periods of low international tension, the possibility could be very real — and correspondingly dangerous, in a period of acute crisis.

Consider, for example, the Cuban missile crisis. At the onset of that crisis, President Kennedy said: "It shall be the policy of this nation to regard any nuclear missile launched from Cuba against any nation in the Western hemisphere as an attack by the Soviet Union on the United States requiring a full retaliatory response upon the Soviet Union." If the Chinese had had a missile-launching submarine near Cuba at that time, they might well have been tempted by what would have appeared, as a consequence of that statement, to be a possibility of eliminating both of their major opponents with one stroke. And if they *had* been tempted, the stratagem might, as a consequence of the intense tension within the U.S. government at the time, possibly have worked.

It is not possible to protect against threats of this kind by ordinary deterrence; indeed, the major hazard of a catalytic attack arises out of, and is motivated and made possible by, an existing posture of deterrence. The potential role of active defense against such attacks is twofold. First, since such an attack would be relatively "small" (perhaps a few tens of missiles might be plausible in some circumstances), there is a good chance that even a light defense would completely or almost completely eliminate the damage the attack would have produced in the absence of any defense. Second, eliminating or greatly reducing the possible damage the attack might cause would greatly reduce the likelihood that the attack would trigger a near-reflex catastrophic, and catastrophically mistaken, response.

It should be noted that there are still other possibilities of undeterrable attacks, apart from the disguised variety, but construction of the relevant scenarios would take us too far from the main path.

PROBLEMS OF DETERRENCE

One of the main areas of concern to critics of missile defense has to do with the impact of missile defense on fundamentals of deterrence. While it is certainly natural that this concern should arise, I believe that any specific justification for the concern largely evaporates on examination. Let us consider this area.

The problem has often been related to what McNamara termed the "Assured Destruction" mission of the U.S. strategic forces, identified by him in his 1968 posture statement to mean "an ability to inflict at all times and under all foreseeable conditions an unacceptable degree of damage upon any single aggressor, or combination of aggressors — even after absorbing a surprise attack." (p. 47.) McNamara recognized that what constituted "an unacceptable degree of damage" was not subject to precise specification, and in spelling out this requirement, he said (*ibid.*, p. 50): "In the case of the Soviet Union, I would judge that a capability on our part to destroy, say one-fifth to one-fourth of her population [i.e., about fifty million Russians] and one-half of her industrial capacity would serve as an effective deterrent."[8]

Let us note here that in this and in every other context in which McNamara discussed this issue, he defined the "Assured Destruction" requirement *without any reference to the nature or scale of the Soviet threat*. I shall come back to this fact.[9]

Because McNamara came to regard the ability to destroy fifty million Russians as the keystone of Western security, he viewed Soviet deployment of BMD as a potential threat to that security, and intended to nullify any Soviet defenses with added U.S. offensive forces. He also appeared to believe, and frequently asserted, that the Soviets had a similar requirement for an "Assured Destruction" capacity, and that any U.S. interference with this requirement would in all likelihood only cause the Soviets to increase their offensive forces. It appears that this perception was at the core of McNamara's opposition to BMD deployment, as it was for many other opponents of missile defenses. The U.S. strategic posture that has evolved from this perception in recent years has been aptly dubbed a posture of "Assured Vulnerability" by Steuart Pittman.[10] I shall later discuss the evidence concerning Soviet views on this matter; let us first review the origin and nature of the alleged American requirement for a fixed large number of Russian hostages.

---

[8] However, in his table on p. 57 of Soviet population and industry destroyed at various levels of attack, McNamara underlined the entries for 74 million fatalities and 76 per cent industrial capacity destroyed.

[9] It will appear throughout that I am highly critical of McNamara's handling of BMD — as, indeed, I am. I should like to add that, in spite of this fact, I still believe he was the greatest Secretary of Defense the U.S. has had, at least until 1964 or 1965.

[10] *Government and Civil Defense*, Steuart Pittman, former Assistant Secretary of Defense for Civil Defense, in Wigner, *op. cit.*

The U.S. first became involved in the business of strategic nuclear deterrence in the very late 1940's and the early 1950's, say up through 1953. The Soviets had no major ability to attack the U.S. directly in this period and the primary perceived requirement of the American strategic forces was to deter a Soviet assault on Western Europe. This requirement (among others) was articulated by John Foster Dulles in his famous "massive retaliation" policy early in 1954. The U.S. offensive forces that were intended to provide the deterring threat were changing in this period, but the U.S. threat may be roughly summarized as a few hundred bombers armed with pure fission (not thermonuclear) bombs with a yield of a few tens of kilotons, for a total deliverable threat of a few tens of megatons. It is doubtful if the Soviet fatalities that this force would have produced were accurately estimated in that period, and they certainly were not publicized, but it is most unlikely that they would have exceeded a few million, at least until quite late in the period.

Now, there were many criticisms made of the "massive retaliation" policy when it was first publicized, but there were few if any criticisms to the effect that the U.S. threat was inadequately deterring. It is therefore instructive to recall the perceived Soviet threat of that period: It was the Soviet Union of Stalin, believed to have a six-million-man army, a Soviet Union which had only recently subjugated Eastern Europe, and which was believed to have instigated or at least approved the Korean war. Not even the recent Czech invasion makes the Soviet Union of today seem nearly as threatening. And this was the threat that was widely judged to be adequately deterred by a few tens of megatons.[11]

Beginning in about 1954, two important changes occurred. The first of these was what can fairly be called a technological accident, namely, it was found that thermonuclear bombs could be made to work. This made it possible to increase the explosive yield achievable in a given weight of bomb by factors such as twenty or fifty or one hundred. The other (and more important) change was that the advent of a Soviet long-range bomber force armed with substantial numbers of nuclear weapons presented the threat of a direct attack on the U.S.

In the period when the Soviets could not mount a major attack on the U.S., an implicit part of the U.S. threat to protect Europe

---

[11] As McNamara and others have rightly pointed out, the total yield in megatons does not adequately reflect the total effect of a force. We have, however, no better measure readily available with which to make these comparisons, and the comparisons in these terms will at least not be grossly misleading.

was the fact that, even if the Soviets overran Europe at a time when U.S. strategic forces could not have put an immediate full stop to the Soviet production and military establishments, the Soviets would have been unable to prevent the continuation of the U.S. as a fighting society and the continuation of U.S. attacks against Soviet facilities and forces. The Soviets could scarcely have counted on any net gain from an attack on Europe in this situation and could not have eliminated their principal opponent.

When major direct Soviet attacks on the U.S. became possible, the structure of the situation changed considerably. It might then have become possible for the Soviets to have eliminated the U.S. as a fighting society, and thereby to secure Europe and eliminate their principal opponent at one blow. Thus, many strategists judged that there were two reinforcing reasons why it was appropriate to react to this possibility with a large strategic threat to deter it: On the one hand, this possibility might in some crisis have loomed as extremely valuable to the Soviets, a possibility for which they might have been prepared to pay large costs, such as a few million fatalities; on the other hand, if such a possibility came to pass, it would have been essentially and promptly lethal for the whole of the West — in a political sense, in a literal physical sense for many millions, and in an economic sense for the survivors.

The Soviets might in some circumstance have badly wanted to do it, and we certainly wanted badly that they should not do it. Moreover, there appeared to be no technical defense in sight that would have substantially reduced the possible Soviet motivation to do it, or our motivation to deter it. This was the fundamental driving force behind the evolution in the late 1950's and early 1960's of a U.S. strategic threat measured in thousands of megatons — a deterrent threat for which "Assured Destruction" was indeed the correct phrase. It was the result of designing a force that would assure the Soviets that they could not mount a lethal attack against the West without encountering lethal retaliation.

It is clear from the origin of this perfectly reasonable logic that, to the extent the maximum possible Soviet motivation for such an attack might have been reduced, or to the extent the U.S. motivation to deter it might have been reduced, the scale of the retaliatory threat might have been reduced in some corresponding degree. It is this linkage that appears to have been wholly absent from McNamara's thinking about strategic forces in recent years. So far as can be seen from the record, at least when missile defense was under consideration, McNamara was determined to be able to kill fifty million Russians *no matter what* the maximum Soviet threat.

If a maximal Soviet strategic attack were capable of destroying, say, ten million Americans and fifteen per cent of our industry, they would no doubt be more deterred by the threat of losing fifty million Russians and fifty per cent of their industry than if our retaliatory threat were "only" fifteen million Russians and twenty per cent of their industry, other things being equal. There is therefore a certain attractiveness in trying to forget about any linkage between threat and retaliation, and fixing once and for all some intended level of "Assured Destruction" which is believed capable of deterring the Soviets from any actions whatever that might bring this force into play. Among other things, this would spare the necessity of thinking through some difficult issues (though it brings in some new ones of its own, notably the question of how much "Assured Destruction" is "enough"). But there are a number of problems resulting from such a posture, of which the most immediate for our purposes is that it tends to make it difficult for us to limit damage to *ourselves* — i.e., it tends to force *us* into a posture of "Assured Vulnerability."

In particular, a determination to maintain a large fixed level of "Assured Destruction" capability against the Soviets led McNamara to respond to incipient Soviet missile defenses by increasing U.S. offensive-force capabilities, and the theory that the Soviets would do likewise led McNamara to oppose the deployment by the U.S. of an anti-Soviet BMD system. In view of the effectiveness of modern defense, we might better have used the U.S. resources committed to increasing our offensive forces to increase our defenses instead. By thus reducing the Soviet threat, rather than increasing our own, we should have reduced both the extent to which the Soviets might gain by attacking us, and the extent to which we are intensely motivated to deter the attack.

It is easy to understand the effects involved here in a simplified case. Consider a situation in which Soviet and American offensive forces are fixed at similar unchanging levels on each side, and in which both the U.S. and the Soviet Union are building comparable levels of defenses. If the American and Soviet defenses are both "light," then our BMD would not much diminish Soviet ability to destroy us, but the Soviet BMD would not much reduce the effectiveness of our assured-destruction forces either; if both American and Soviet defenses are "heavy," then our assured-destruction forces would be significantly degraded, but so too would the capability of the Soviets to eliminate the U.S. as a fighting society.

This points to the following formulation of a reasonable requirement for a conservative American strategic posture:

Following any plausibly feasible strategic attack by the Soviet Union, the U.S. should have the capacity to inflict as much or more total damage (of similar kind) on the Soviet Union as the Soviets had inflicted and could still inflict on the U.S.[12]

In short, we should have a reliable capability to do at least as badly unto the Soviets as they had done or could do unto us. This would imply that, if the Soviets started a strategic war with us, they would be guaranteed to come out worse, a powerful deterrent to starting such a war. The Soviets could not achieve a significant military advantage by a strategic attack, and an irrational, coercive, or punitive attack — whether large or small — would risk bringing as much or more destruction on the Soviets as they could or did bring on us. This would make the initiation of nuclear blackmail unattractive to any reasonable decision-maker at any effective level of strategic forces.

Let us note explicitly that this posture does not imply that a U.S. capability to destroy fifty or seventy-four or one hundred million Russians is a fundamental requirement of nature, without regard to the circumstances. It indicates that both the U.S. and the Soviet Union might reasonably engage in some measures to limit the possible damage of a war without necessarily impairing U.S. security in the process. Such measures might include, for instance, direct reduction of strategic offensive forces by agreement, or deployment of defenses with or without explicit agreement.

It is interesting that the U.S. has, in fact, proposed direct reductions in strategic offensive forces. For several years, we have had a proposal before the Geneva disarmament negotiations to reduce such forces by cutting a substantial percentage from each side in each of two stages.[13] It is obvious that this proposal must have been evaluated with regard to some criterion for a strategic posture similar to the one discussed just above; one cannot carry out unlimited reductions in offensive forces and still be able to guarantee the capability to kill seventy-four million Russians, or whatever such number is selected. Now, if certain necessary requirements are met, as they can be, a symmetric increase in active defenses deployed by each of the superpowers would have approximately the same kind of potential impact on possible war outcomes that percentage cuts in offensive forces would have. It seems odd that McNamara (among others) never appeared willing even to consider possibilities of missile defense in the light of the strategic criteria he applied to percentage cuts in offensive forces.

One may ask: If BMD deployed in both superpowers would have roughly the same effect on possible war outcomes as direct reduc-

[12] This principle implies that the strategic offensive forces must be quite well protected, which appears to be feasible.
[13] U.S. Draft Treaty of April 29, 1965.

tions on both sides in offensive forces, why not simply reduce the latter, and save the money and trouble of the BMD? The answer is that in some circumstances one might, but the circumstances are not those now prevailing. To reduce U.S. and Soviet offensive forces to a level where the possible casualties on each side (without defenses) did not exceed, say, twenty million would likely be acceptable to the U.S. only with a degree of inspection that is most unlikely to be acceptable to the Soviets. In other words, there appears to be no current political feasibility of offensive-force cuts on such a scale, while there seems to be ample feasibility of suitable BMD deployment — which, rather than increasing U.S. needs for inspection of Soviet offensive forces, might actually *reduce* our sensitivity to such information. This effect, indeed, would facilitate later direct reductions in offensive forces. (There are other motives for BMD, such as protection against Chinese or anonymous attacks, that would not be affected by Soviet-American reductions. These motives, however, might be satisfied by a light defense.)

From the mid-1950's to the mid-1960's, the strategic postures of the superpowers were dominated by the logic that, since we could not defend, we had to deter. This position, for which there was originally ample justification, now seems to be interpreted in some minds, chiefly certain American ones, to mean that, since we must deter, we cannot defend. This should count as the *non sequitur* of the decade.

ARMS RACES AND ARMS CONTROLS

The final major area of concern to critics of missile defenses is that of arms races, and correlated arms-control problems. The kind of arms race involved here is what is called an offense-defense race. The usual image of this is that if, say, the U.S. procures some missile defenses, the Soviet Union will feel obliged to respond by increasing its offensive forces sufficiently to nullify the defense. This increase in Soviet offense capability might in turn motivate the U.S. to increase its defense capability still further, and so on. For example, McNamara said (in his 1967 posture statement, p. 53): *"It is the virtual certainty that the Soviets will act to maintain their deterrent which casts such grave doubts on the advisability of our deploying the Nike X system for the protection of our cities against the kind of heavy, sophisticated missile attack they could launch in the 1970s. In all probability, all we would accomplish would be to increase greatly both their defense expenditures and ours without any gain in real security to either side."* (The whole of this passage is underscored in the original.)

If arms-race responses of this kind occur, they will not be be-

cause of some fundamental law of nature, but will result from interactions of achievable technology with prevailing attitudes and
budgets. Each of these factors is of importance.

It is useful to discuss this problem in terms of the concept of
cost exchange ratios. If cost exchange ratios were as low as .01, or
one per cent, there would be little doubt that, within the present
political environment, a defense system deployed by one superpower would be nullified by the other. For example, if the Soviets
built, say, a twenty billion dollar system, and if it would cost the
U.S. only two hundred million dollars to neutralize it, there would
scarcely be any debate about the matter within the U.S. bureaucracy, the Congress, or the public: the Defense Department would
simply go ahead and neutralize the Soviet defense. In this world,
the technology (as linked to budgets) would surely dominate the attitudes, and deterrence would reign supreme; defense could have
at most a marginal role, at least as between the superpowers. There
would be very slight motivation in either country to build defenses against the other, and most likely they would not be built.

On the other hand, if cost exchange ratios were in the neighbor-
hood of one hundred or more, there would again be little debate,
but in this world, defense would reign supreme, and deterrence
would rest on very different threats and counter-threats than those
that loom as dominant today. In this case, to nullify a twenty billion
dollar Soviet defense would cost the U.S. $2,000 billion. The ex-
penditure of such a sum within foreseeable budgets is not, of
course, a realistic possibility, and the U.S. would instead be building its own defense — about which there would be little controversy, and which the Soviets could not offset either. Again, the
technology would dominate prevailing attitudes.[14]

In the actual world that is upon us of cost exchange ratios near
unity, perhaps one-half or three but not one-tenth or ten, the attitudes prevailing are not driven by the technology toward either deterrence or defense, but may (and do) go in either direction. It is
much more a matter of preference and conscious decision whether
we and the Soviets wish to spend our strategic-force budgets chiefly
to increase the level of "hostages" on the other side, or to decrease
our own. Thus, whether we are to have an offense-defense arms
race or not depends in the first instance on whether Soviet and
American attitudes are lined up the same way or not. If both
governments are willing to accept a high level of hostages on

[14] Experts may recognize that this discussion is simplified. The principle illustrated, however, remains valid when the complications are
taken into account.

each side, with modest or no defenses, there will be no great pressures for an offense-defense race; similarly if both are willing to live with substantial defenses and relatively low levels of hostages, with modest or no attempts on either side to offset the defense of the other. But if one side attempts to reduce its own hostages below the level demanded by the other, or attempts to increase the hostages of the other above a level the other considers acceptable in the circumstances, and especially if both happen together in any combination, the resulting pressures for an arms race might well be limited mainly by budgetary forces.

The fact that these issues are importantly influenced by attitudes is not always clearly recognized. There is, however, something of a "fashion" in some circles against interfering with the so-called requirements for "Assured Destruction" capabilities on either side especially when (almost only when) the interference comes from missile defense. But, as I have argued earlier, maintaining very high levels of possible Soviet damage does not seem to be a requirement of U.S. security in circumstances where we can correspondingly limit damage to ourselves, and indeed it is in some degree antithetical to the objective of limiting our own possible damage. Still less, of course, is it a requirement of U.S. security to maintain high levels of U.S. hostages on behalf of the Soviets. Outside of the group who have been actively opposing defenses, I believe that these facts are generally recognized among people concerned with national defense. "Assured Vulnerability" has characterized the trend of our strategic posture in recent years because of the views of McNamara and a few others, not because of the defense community as a whole, most of which has opposed the trend. Therefore, while the kind of fashion mentioned above has and has had important adherents, it seems unlikely to prove dominant in the U.S. policy process in the future. American attitudes in this regard are mixed, but there is at least a fair chance that views favoring more emphasis on defense, views which are in fact rather widely held, will prove important in the evolution of the U.S. strategic posture.

Soviet attitudes concerning hostage levels seem much less mixed, so far as can be seen; they are much more friendly to the deployment of defenses. In particular, contrary to many statements made by American critics of U.S. BMD, it appears that the Soviets are not substantially antagonized by the prospect of U.S. BMD. I shall mention some of the evidence for this.

Let us begin with the passage of McNamara's quoted above, in which he implied that it was a "virtual certainty" that the Soviets "will act to maintain their deterrent," i.e., will act to nullify any

U.S. defense by increasing their offense. Now, if the Soviets were in fact committed to a response of the sort McNamara said they were, which would at least cost them substantial money, the first ones we should expect to hear making such statements would be, not McNamara, but the Soviets themselves. So far as can be seen, the Soviets have never been bashful about making political and diplomatic statements designed to deter publicly known U.S. programs they did not like, or to embarrass the U.S. over programs that at least were not advantageous to them. For example, they have repeatedly made public statements opposing the operation of U.S. Polaris submarines in the Mediterranean, and the operation of nuclear-armed air-alert bomber forces.

In the light of past Soviet political offensives against unwanted U.S. programs, it would be remarkable in the extreme if the Soviets had the attitudes attributed to them by McNamara and yet did absolutely nothing to discourage U.S. defenses. The fact is, however, that there seems to be no reliable report of any Soviet attempts to deter our BMD by such statements, either public or private, official or unofficial.

There is a great deal of additional evidence, beyond this negative but persuasive fact, indicating that Soviet attitudes have not been at all in McNamara's direction. There have, for instance, been many statements by individual Russians at both official and unofficial levels, both impromptu and carefully considered. In a press conference in London on 9 February 1967, Premier Kosygin was asked: "Do you believe it is possible to agree on the moratorium on the [deployment] of an anti-missile defense system [a then-current American proposal] and if possible on what conditions?" He replied in part: "I believe that defensive systems, which prevent attack, are not the cause of the arms race, but constitute a factor preventing the death of people. Some argue like this: What is cheaper, to have offensive weapons which can destroy towns and whole states or to have defensive weapons which can prevent this destruction? At present the theory is current somewhere that the system which is cheaper should be developed. Such so-called theoreticians argue as to the cost of killing a man — $500,000 or $100,000. Maybe an anti-missile system is more expensive than an offensive system, but it is designed not to kill people but to preserve human lives. I understand that I do not reply to the question I was asked, but you can draw yourselves the appropriate conclusions." Indeed, one can.

A detailed rebuttal to the standard arguments against BMD was given by the late Soviet military publicist Major General N. I. Talensky in the quasi-official Soviet journal *International Affairs* in October 1964. It may be interesting to note that the Talensky article, though not so identified, was at least partly a response to a paper presented to Talensky and other Russians earlier in 1964 by a group of Americans that included the present writer, a paper opposing defenses written by Jeremy Stone but which I had a good deal to do with. I have, of course, since changed my views, although Stone has not.[15] Many other contacts with Russians at official and unofficial levels, including several meetings I personally have had the chance to observe, illustrate that the attitude exemplified by the Kosygin quotation above is very widely held in the Soviet Union, while the attitude held by American critics of BMD, such as McNamara or Kaysen, toward the alleged importance of maintaining high hostage levels seems not to be held at all. Soviet strategic literature also does not reflect a McNamara-like view. So far as can be seen, the Soviets simply do not adhere to such a model of deterrence.

The main criticisms of BMD that have been expressed by any Russians, so far as I am aware, have come from a few scientists who have been skeptical of the effectiveness of defenses and therefore regarded them as wasteful of resources. It is probably significant that these scientists seem not closely associated with current Soviet weapon programs; I believe it likely that they are following the lead of some of their Western friends and counterparts, except that even these Russian critics seem not to share in the theoretical opposition to BMD. One major Russian scientist who *is* closely associated with the Soviet missile program has said (to Americans) that effective missile defense is on the whole probably realizable. Other Soviet criticisms, arising out of the March 1969 "Safeguard" decision, have been political (rather than strategic) in character.[16]

One additional bit of evidence is worth mentioning. After McNamara announced the decision to deploy the Sentinel BMD system in September 1967, the U.S. came under attack from several of our allies and neutral friends, especially from several countries participating in the Eighteen-Nation Disarmament Committee then meeting in Geneva, who complained that the American deployment decision would be bad for the incipient non-proliferation treaty and would only heighten the arms race. There was one country that came to our assistance in that context, holding that the deci-

[15] Stone's paper was later published, with modifications, in his book. See J. J. Stone, *Containing the Arms Race,* The M.I.T. Press, Cambridge, Mass., 1966, especially Chapter One, "Antiballistic Missiles and Arms Control."

[16] See Johan J. Holst, "Missile Defense, the Soviet Union, and the Arms Race," Chapter 7; Holst and Schneider, eds., *Why ABM?, op. cit.*

sion would not harm the prospects for the non-proliferation treaty: that country was the Soviet Union.[17] So far as I am aware, this is the only case on record in which the Soviet Union has defended us diplomatically against our friends and allies. This is all the more remarkable in view of the fact that the Soviets did not, then or since, believe that the Sentinel system was intended only for Chinese attacks. (In some sense, as will be evident from this article, their skepticism was well placed.)

The fact that the Soviets apparently do not share the view of McNamara and some of his associates toward deterrence and "Assured Destruction" requirements does not, of course, mean that they are disinterested in military matters. It appears that Soviet strategists generally emphasize the importance of maintaining a good position in relation to the U.S., but seem not to understand this to mean that they must maintain some large fixed number of American hostages without regard to the circumstances. The sharp increase in Soviet offensive forces that has taken place in the recent past is evidence that they did not wish to remain in a position inferior to the U.S. in such forces; it provides no evidence whatever that they have come to hold the "Assured Destruction" dogma that has held sway here.

Some American critics of BMD have described these Soviet attitudes as "unsophisticated," and argued that the Soviets will "get over it," and come to respond to an American defense as McNamara predicted even if they are not yet committed to it. It is true that strenuous efforts to "educate" the Soviets have been made by McNamara and others, and one cannot say with certainty that these efforts will fail; it would not be the first time that the Soviets lost their senses over some issue just as we were coming to ours. But their views in the past should not be denigrated; it seems to me, and to many other Western strategists, that the defense-oriented philosophy exhibited by the Soviets makes good sense. As to matters of fundamental approach to deterrence and defense, I should say that we in the U.S. might better acquire some "education" from the Soviets.

In view of the fact that Soviet attitudes already seem to favor defenses, and that American attitudes, while currently mixed, *ought* to favor defenses, the obvious way of trying to improve prevailing strategic postures through arms control arrangements is to limit offensive forces primarily, and to limit defenses only secon-

---

[17] See Thomas J. Hamilton, "U.S. Says Nike Net Will Spur Atom Pact," *The New York Times*, September 20, 1967.

darily, if at all. This is exactly the reverse of the order of priorities frequently suggested in the U.S. in the past few years. It is, however, more in keeping with the traditional aims of arms control. The primary objectives of arms control have often been stated to be reducing the likelihood of war or mitigating its consequences if it occurs.[18] In view of the arguments of the preceding sections, it seems to me highly probable that deployment of missile defenses will contribute to both of these objectives, while abstaining from defenses will likely contribute to neither. If the deployments are managed with at least modest intelligence in both the U.S. and the Soviet Union, there need not even be arms-race responses that would further add to prevailing arms expenditures.

This is not the place for detailed examination of technical issues, but I should remark that a suitable way of limiting offensive forces in such a context might well be to have an understanding between the U.S. and the Soviet Union, preferably an informal and flexible one, that the total weight of all offensive forces on each side, missiles, planes, and tankers, should be held within some ceiling. This ceiling should be the same for each side and set high enough, at least initially, to include forces on hand or already in procurement. In that case, it would impose no new inspection requirements, i.e., beyond those we already try to satisfy in the present world. My personal inclination would be to exempt defensive forces from controls altogether, except perhaps for interceptor missiles that were large enough to serve as offensive missiles, but if there were a suitable consensus that some mild limitation was desirable, such as limiting the rate of deployment to (say) one thousand interceptors per year, I should not oppose it.

Many opponents of BMD have agreed that an arms-control program of this form seemed fundamentally preferable to a posture of abstaining from defenses and leaving the offensive forces unconstrained; they argue that a program of the type suggested here will not prove feasible, because it will not prove acceptable to the U.S. military "establishment."[19] This assertion is subject to investigation, and considerable investigation suggests it is incorrect. Many senior military officers, in the U.S. Air Force as well as in other services, are favorably disposed to a suitable ceiling on offensive

[18] See my introductory chapter, "Setting and Goals of Arms Control," in D. G. Brennan, ed., *Arms Control, Disarmament, and National Security*, Braziller, N.Y., 1961. The definitions given there have been widely used.

[19] For instance, this seems to be the main point of difference between J. B. Wiesner and myself.

forces (at prevailing levels) providing it is possible to deploy defenses.

A more important objection to postures with a heavy component of defense that is sometimes encountered is the following. The Soviets might, it is argued, find some way of attacking our offensive forces with sufficient effectiveness so that their defenses could intercept most or all of our remaining offensive forces. By thus initiating the first strike, they might escape relatively unscathed — which, if true, could motivate the initiation of the strike in an intense crisis. It should be noted that the major studies of BMD performance do not show a dramatic dependence on who attacks first, so this concern has no current substantial basis; it is rather an apprehension about some future possible vulnerability that might occur.

Obviously, no one could give an absolute guarantee that such a weakness could not occur. It requires, however, a vulnerability in our offensive forces of the kind that people have been trying to prevent for years; only the degree of vulnerability that would be significant would be changed by a heavy Soviet defense. If the U.S. were to provide added protection of its offensive forces by BMD, there would seem to be no reason whatever for believing that postures with heavy defense in both the U.S. and the Soviet Union would leave us more vulnerable to this type of problem than we are at present.

In fact, such vulnerabilities might be reduced. It is important in considering problems of this type to evaluate the risks of proposed postures in comparison to realistic alternatives, which are not without some risks themselves. In particular, our offensive forces of the present and recent past may well have had important vulnerabilities, including the possibility of undetected ones. For example, Senator Henry Jackson, in a Senate speech of September 25, 1968, discussed electromagnetic-pulse phenomena from nuclear bursts in terms that suggest these phenomena are a continuing source of concern for the security of our offensive forces. A potential vulnerability of a different type might have threatened the fixed component of our offensive forces if the Soviets had developed multiple, independently guided reentry vehicles (MIRV) before we had understood the concept ourselves. There is nothing in the public record that suggests that these have been the only vulnerabilities of major or potentially major concern in our strategic postures of the past. In view of this, it is not at all obvious, to say the least, that a posture of pure deterrence, based wholly on offensive forces, would be more secure against unpleasant surprises (such as a suddenly-discovered extreme vulnerability to a first-strike) than postures with heavy emphasis on defense. Even if there were some added risk associated with the defensive posture, this would have to be weighed against the possibility that the defense might save fifty or eighty million Americans in the event of a major war, and make possible much more rapid economic recovery.

It will be clear that I believe an arms-control program giving first priority to constraints on offensive forces, and second priority to limitations on defensive forces, is in the national interest of the U.S.; in particular, it would sharply reduce any remaining pressures for an offense-defense arms race. It is no contradiction that I believe such a program would also be in the interest of the Soviet Union, and therefore in our common interest. Moreover, as recently as September 1968, I have heard senior Russians suggesting unofficially exactly this order of priorities. There is thus some reason to believe that U.S.-Soviet discussions about stabilizing strategic forces may prove fruitful.

This discussion has mainly concerned near-term limitations on strategic forces. In the longer term, it may prove possible to bring about major disarmament of the offensive forces. I mentioned before that suitable BMD deployment, by reducing our sensitivity to inspection information, would facilitate direct reductions in offensive forces. Indeed, I believe the only possible routes to major reductions in offensive forces — i.e., to a degree that would make a large difference in the scale of possible damage — that could prove feasible in the next decade or so all involve substantial defenses.

It may be useful to illustrate the effect involved with numerical examples. At 1969 levels of offensive forces, an uncertainty of, say, one hundred missiles in the number of Soviet missiles deployed would be of relatively little consequence for the United States. However, if it were decided to reduce offensive forces by agreement to a level that could not cause more than, say twenty million fatalities, then the allowed forces themselves would have to be limited to something like one hundred missiles on each side, if there were no defenses. At *this* level of offensive forces, a clandestine stock of one hundred missiles could be of great — indeed, literally overwhelming — significance, again if there were no defenses.

Now, an inspection system that would reliably detect as few as one hundred clandestine missiles does not seem likely to be politically feasible within the next decade or more. On the other hand, a BMD system that would reliably intercept all or almost all of one hundred or two hundred missiles is highly feasible, and, if deployed, would substantially reduce or wholly eliminate the threat a modest clandestine force could constitute. (A large clandestine force probably could be detected by inspection.) Thus, defenses would make possible major disarmament of the offensive forces, as well as reducing the possible impact of forces in being when the defenses were deployed.

In contrast, I do not believe that any of the critics of BMD have even the beginnings of a plausible program for achieving major disarmament of the offensive forces by, say, 1980. Many of them seem committed to support forever a strategic posture that appears to favor dead Russians over live Americans, I believe that this choice is just as bizarre as it appears; we should rather prefer live Americans to dead Russians, and we should not choose deliberately to live forever under a nuclear sword of Damocles.

Quite apart from offense-defense races, a different mechanism that might lead to an arms race — perhaps a defense-defense race, or simply a one-sided race of escalating requirements — is sometimes said to reside in the possibility of generalized public pressures for "more." This line of argument is sometimes summarized by saying that, in matters of defense, one cannot be "a little bit pregnant." Our experience in both air defense and civil defense is so much against this idea that it should be dismissed without further discussion. Similarly, it is sometimes said that the American public would not tolerate any inequalities in local defense effectiveness.[20] We have had a major air defense system with substantial inequalities in local defense effectiveness for perhaps fifteen years, and scarcely anyone other than experts associated with the system is even sure of whether his own home city even *has* a local defense, much less how it compares to other cities. The degree of awareness of these matters that has prevailed in the past in the general public is reflected in a public-opinion poll conducted in 1964, which found that two-thirds of the U.S. public believed we had a BMD system all deployed and ready for action!

CONCLUSION

Space has not permitted here a discussion of several other problem areas sometimes associated with missile defense, such as the implications of U.S. BMD for the Western Alliance, or the frequently-repeated assertion (which I believe is false) that BMD

[20] A good design objective for a BMD planner is to make all targets equally unattractive for the opposing offense. This requires that large cities be more heavily defended than smaller ones, but has the effect of protecting everyone equally in a suitable sense. Actual BMD deployments can approximate this objective, so the alleged problem is of limited relevance even in its own terms.

would require as a prerequisite a major expansion of civil-defense programs. Several scholars have, however, studied these problems, and I believe it is fair to say that, on examination, they seem even less likely to prove troublesome than the problems already considered.

It seems to me there is little doubt about which way the policy process in the U.S. ought to evolve in relation to BMD. The American body politic is unlikely to judge that pursuit of "Assured Vulnerability" is a proper objective of the Department of Defense.

Suggestions for Further Reading

The literature on the uses of force in international relations is extensive. This list of books is by no means comprehensive, but it should be useful to those who wish to pursue in more depth the subjects covered in this book.

Raymond Aron. *The Great Debate*. New York: Doubleday, 1965.

Leonard Beaton and John Maddox. *The Spread of Nuclear Weapons*. New York: Praeger, 1962.

André Beaufre. *Deterrence and Strategy*. New York: Praeger, 1966.

Donald G. Brennan, editor. *Arms Control, Disarmament, and National Security*. New York: George Braziller, 1961.

Bernard Brodie. *Sea Power in the Machine Age*. Princeton: Princeton University Press, 1944.

———. *Strategy in the Missile Age*. Princeton: Princeton University Press, 1959.

Abram Chayes and Jerome B. Wiesner, editors. *ABMs An Evaluation of the Decision to Deploy an Antiballistic Missile System*. New York: New American Library, 1969.

Edward Meade Earle, editor. *Makers of Modern Strategy*. New York: Atheneum, 1966 (first published in 1941).

J. F. C. Fuller. *Armaments and History*. New York: Scribner's, 1945.

Michael Howard. *The Franco-Prussian War*. London: Rupert Hart-Davis, 1968.

Herman Kahn. *On Thermonuclear War*. Princeton: Princeton University Press, 1961.

Robert A. Levine. *The Arms Debate*. Cambridge: Harvard University Press, 1963.

B. H. Liddell Hart. *Deterrent or Defense*. London: Stevens and Sons, 1960.

———. *Strategy*. New York: Praeger, 1962.

William W. Kaufmann. *The McNamara Strategy*. New York: Harper and Row, 1964.

Salvador de Madariaga. *Disarmament*. New York: Coward-McCann, 1929.

Arthur J. Marder. *The Anatomy of British Sea Power*. New York: Alfred A. Knopf, 1940.

Elting E. Morison. *Men, Machines and Modern Times.* Cambridge: Massachusetts Institute of Technology Press, 1968.

Lewis Mumford. *Technics and Civilization.* New York: Harcourt, Brace and World, 1963 (first published in 1934.)

Robert E. Osgood. *Limited War.* Chicago: The University of Chicago Press, 1957.

Anatol Rapoport. *Eights, Games, and Debates.* Ann Arbor: The University of Michigan Press, 1961.

Gerhard Ritter. *The Schlieffen Plan.* London: Oswald Wolff, 1958.

Theodore Ropp. *War in the Modern World.* New York: Collier Books, 1962.

Thomas C. Schelling. *The Strategy of Conflict.* Cambridge: Harvard University Press, 1960.

Jonathan Steinberg. *Yesterday's Deterrent.* New York: Macmillan, 1965.

J. W. Wheeler-Bennett. *The Pipe Dream of Peace.* New York: W. Morrow, 1935.

E. L. Woodward. *Great Britain and the German Navy.* London: Frank Cass and Company, 1964 (first published in 1935).

Quincy Wright. *A Study of War.* 2 vols. Chicago: University of Chicago Press, 1942.

Contributors

Donald G. Brennan is a staff member of the Hudson Institute.

Frederic J. Brown is a Lieutenant Colonel in the United States Army.

Hedley Bull is a Professor in the Department of International Relations, Research School of Pacific Studies, at the Australian National University.

Morton H. Halperin is a Senior Fellow at the Brookings Institution.

Malcolm W. Hoag is associated with the RAND Corporation.

Samuel P. Huntington is a Profesor of Government at Harvard University.

Edward L. Katzenbach, Jr., is Vice President of the University of Oklahoma.

Henry A. Kissinger, Professor of Government at Harvard University, is currently serving as the Special Assistant for National Security Affairs to President Nixon.

Ernest R. May is Dean of the College of Harvard University.

Kenneth L. Moll is a Lieutenant Colonel in the United States Air Force.

Hans J. Morgenthau is Professor of Political Science and Modern History at the University of Chicago.

Louis Morton is Professor of History at Dartmouth College.

Robert E. Osgood is Director of the Washington Center of Foreign Policy Research and a Professor of Political Science at the School of Advanced International Studies, Johns Hopkins University.

George H. Quester is an Associate Professor of Government at Cornell University.

George W. Rathjens is a Professor of Political Science at Massachusetts Institute of Technology.

Sir George Sansom was a writer and a British diplomat with extensive experience in the Far East.

Thomas C. Schelling is a Professor of Economics at Harvard University.

Warner R. Schilling is a Professor of Political Science at Columbia University.

Glenn H. Snyder is a Professor of Political Science at the State University of New York at Buffalo.

Jeremy J. Stone is director of the Federation of American Scientists.

Leonard Wainstein is associated with the Institute of Defense Analyses.

Albert Wohlstetter, formerly with the RAND Corporation, is a Professor of Political Science at the University of Chicago.

Roberta Wohlstetter is the author of *Pearl Harbor: Warning and Decision*.